THE HISTORY OF ROME

(BOOKS IX-XXVI)

BY TITUS LIVIUS

TRANSLATED BY
D. SPILLAN AND CYRUS EDMONDS

A Digireads.com Book
Digireads.com Publishing

The History of Rome (Books IX-XXVI)
By Titus Livius Livy
Translated by D. Spillan and Cyrus Edmonds
ISBN: 1-4209-3385-X

Please visit *www.digireads.com*

CONTENTS

4

BOOK IX.

B.C. 321-304

Titus Veturius and Spurius Postumius, with their army, surrounded by the Samnites at the Caudine forks; enter into a treaty, give six hundred hostages, and are sent under the yoke. The treaty declared invalid; the two generals and the other sureties sent back to the Samnites, but are not accepted. Not long after, Papirius Cursor obliterates this disgrace, by vanquishing the Samnites, sending them under the yoke, and recovering the hostages. Two tribes added. Appius Claudius, censor, constructs the Claudian aqueduct, and the Appian road; admits the sons of freedom into the senate. Successes against the Apulians, Etruscans, Umbrians, Marsians, Pelignians, Æquans, and Samnites. Mention made of Alexander the Great, who flourished at this time; a comparative estimate of his strength, and that of the Roman people, tending to show, that if he had carried his arms into Italy, he would not have been as successful there as he had been in the Eastern countries.

This year is followed by the convention of Caudium, so memorable on account of the misfortune of the Romans, the consuls being Titus Veturius Calvinus and Spurius Postumius. The Samnites had as their commander that year Caius Ponius, son to Herennius, born of a father most highly renowned for wisdom, and himself a consummate warrior and commander. When the ambassadors, who had been sent to make restitution, returned, without concluding a peace, he said, "That ye may not think that no purpose has been effected by this embassy, whatever degree of anger the deities of heaven had conceived against us, on account of the infraction of the treaty, has been hereby expiated. I am very confident, that whatever deities they were, whose will it was that you should be reduced to the necessity of making the restitution, which had been demanded according to the treaty, it was not agreeable to them, that our atonement for the breach of treason should be so haughtily spurned by the Romans. For what more could possibly be done towards appeasing the gods, and softening the anger of men, than we have done? The effects of the enemy, taken among the spoils, which appeared to be our own by the right of war, we restored: the authors of the war, as we could not deliver them up alive, we delivered them dead: their goods we carried to Rome, lest by retaining them, any degree of guilt should remain among us. What more, Roman, do I owe to thee? what to the treaty? what to the gods, the guarantees of the treaty? What arbitrator shall I call in to judge of your resentment, and of my punishment? I decline none; neither nation nor private person. But if nothing in human law is left to the weak against stronger, I will appeal to the gods, the avengers of intolerant arrogance, and will beseech them to turn their wrath against those for whom neither the restoration of their own effects nor additional heaps of other men's property, can suffice, whose cruelty is not satiated by the death of the guilty, by the surrender of their lifeless bodies, nor by their goods accompanying the surrender of the owner; who cannot be appeased otherwise than by giving them our blood to drink, and our entrails to be torn. Samnites, war is just to those for whom it is necessary, and arms are clear of impiety for those who have no hope left but in arms. Wherefore, as in every human undertaking, it is of the utmost importance what matter men may set about with the favour, what under the displeasure of the gods, be assured that the former wars ye waged in opposition to the gods more than to men; in this, which is now impending, ye will act under the immediate guidance of the gods themselves."

After uttering these predictions, not more cheering than true, he led out the troops, and placed his camp about Caudium as much out of view as possible. From thence he sent to Calatia, where he heard that the Roman consuls were encamped, ten soldiers, in the habit of shepherds, and ordered them to keep some cattle feeding in several different places, at a small distance from the Roman posts; and that, when they fell in with any of their foragers, they should all agree in the same story, that the legions of the Samnites were then in Apulia, that they were besieging Luceria with their whole force, and very near taking it by storm. Such a rumour had been industriously spread before, and had already reached the Romans; but these prisoners increased the credit of it, especially as they all concurred in the same report. There was no doubt but that the Romans would carry succour to the Lucerians, as being good and faithful allies; and for this further reason, lest all Apulia, through apprehension of the impending danger, might go over to the enemy. The only point of deliberation was, by what road they should go. There were two roads leading to Luceria, one along the coast of the upper sea, wide and open; but, as it was the safer, so it was proportionably longer: the other, which was shorter, through the Caudine forks. The nature of the place is this: there are two deep glens, narrow and covered with wood, connected together by mountains ranging on both sides from one to the other; between these lies a plain of considerable extent, enclosed in the middle, abounding in grass and water, and through the middle of which the passage runs: but before you can arrive at it, the first defile must be passed, while the only way back is through the road by which you entered it; or if in case of resolving to proceed forward, you must go by the other glen, which is still more narrow and difficult. Into this plain the Romans, having marched down their troops by one of those passes through the cleft of a rock, when they advanced onward to the other defile, found it blocked up by trees thrown across, and a mound of huge stones lying in their way. When the stratagem of the enemy now became apparent, there is seen at the same time a body of troops on the eminence over the glen. Hastening back, then, they proceed to retrace the road by which they had entered; they found that also shut up by such another fence, and men in arms. Then, without orders, they halted; amazement took possession of their minds, and a strange kind of numbness seized their limbs: they then remained a long time motionless and silent, each looking to the other, as if each thought the other more capable of judging and advising than himself. After some time, when they saw that the consul's pavilions were being erected, and that some were getting ready the implements for throwing up works, although they were sensible that it must appear ridiculous the attempt to raise a fortification in their present desperate condition, and when almost every hope was lost, would be an object of necessity, yet, not to add a fault to their misfortunes, they all, without being advised or ordered by any one, set earnestly to work, and enclosed a camp with a rampart, close to the water, while themselves, besides that the enemy heaped insolent taunts on them, seemed with melancholy to acknowledge the apparent fruitlessness of their toil and labour. The lieutenants-general and tribunes, without being summoned to consultation, (for there was no room for either consultation or remedy,) assembled round the dejected consul; while the soldiers, crowding to the general's quarters, demanded from their leaders that succour, which it was hardly in the power of the immortal gods themselves to afford them.

Night came on them while lamenting their situation rather than consulting, whilst they urged expedients, each according to his temper; one crying out, "Let us go over those fences of the roads;" others, "over the steeps; through the woods; any way, where arms can be carried. Let us be but permitted to come to the enemy, whom we have been used to conquer now near thirty years. All places will be level and plain to a Roman, fighting against the perfidious Samnite." Another would say, "Whither, or by what way can we go? Do we expect to remove the mountains from their foundations? While these cliffs hang over us, by what road will you reach the enemy? Whether armed or unarmed, brave or dastardly, we are all, without distinction, captured and vanquished. The enemy will not even show us a weapon by which we might die with honour. He will finish the war without moving from his seat." In such discourse, thinking of neither food nor rest, the night was passed. Nor could the Samnites, though in circumstances so joyous, instantly determine how to act: it was therefore universally agreed that Herennius Pontius, father of the general, should be consulted by letter. He was now grown feeble through age, and had withdrawn himself, not only from all military, but also from all civil occupations; yet, notwithstanding the decline of his bodily strength, his mind retained its full vigour. When he heard that the Roman armies were shut up at the Caudine forks between the two glens, being consulted by his son's messenger, he gave his opinion, that they should all be immediately dismissed from thence unhurt. On this counsel being rejected, and the same messenger returning a second time, he recommended that they should all, to a man, be put to death. When these answers, so opposite to each other, like those of an ambiguous oracle, were given, although his son in particular considered that the powers of his father's mind, together with those of his body, had been impaired by age, was yet prevailed on, by the general desire of all, to send for him to consult him. The old man, we are told, complied without reluctance, and was carried in a waggon to the camp, where, when summoned to give his advice, he spoke in such way as to make no alteration in his opinions; he only added the reasons for them. That "by his first plan, which he esteemed the best, he meant, by an act of extraordinary kindness, to establish perpetual peace and friendship with a most powerful nation: by the other, to put off the return of war to the distance of many ages, during which the Roman state, after the loss of those two armies, could not easily recover its strength." A third plan there was not. When his son, and the other chiefs, went on to ask him if "a plan of a middle kind might not be adopted; that they both should be dismissed unhurt, and, at the same time, by the right of war, terms imposed on them as vanquished?" "That, indeed," said he, "is a plan of such a nature, as neither procures friends or removes enemies. Only preserve those whom ye would irritate by ignominious treatment. The Romans are a race who know not how to sit down quiet under defeat; whatever that is which the present necessity shall brand will rankle in their breasts for ever, and will not suffer them to rest, until they have wreaked manifold vengeance on your heads." Neither of these plans was approved, and Herennius was carried home from the camp.

In the Roman camp also, when many fruitless efforts to force a passage had been made, and they were now destitute of every means of subsistence, forced by necessity, they send ambassadors, who were first to ask peace on equal terms; which, if they did not obtain, they were to challenge the enemy to battle. To this Pontius answered, that "the war was at an end; and since, even in their present vanquished and captive state, they were not willing to acknowledge their situation, he would send them under the yoke unarmed, each with a single garment; that the other conditions of peace should be such as were just between the conquerors and the conquered. If their troops would depart, and their colonies be withdrawn out of the territories of the Samnites; for the future, the Romans and Samnites, under a treaty of equality, shall live according to their own respective laws. On these terms he was ready to negotiate with the consuls: and if any of these should not be accepted, he forbade the ambassadors to come to him again." When the result of this embassy was made known, such general lamentation suddenly arose, and such melancholy took possession of them, that had they been told that all were to die on the spot, they could not have felt deeper affliction. After silence continued a long time, and the consuls were not able to utter a word, either in favour of a treaty so disgraceful, or against a treaty so necessary; at length, Lucius Lentulus, who was the first among the lieutenants-general, both in respect of bravery, and of the public honours which he had attained, addressed them thus: "Consuls, I have often heard my father say, that he was the only person in the Capitol who did not advise the senate to ransom the state from the Gauls with gold; and these he would not concur in, because they had not been enclosed with a trench and rampart by the enemy, (who were remarkably slothful with respect to works and raising fortifications,) and because they might sally forth, if not without great danger, yet without certain destruction. Now if, in like manner as they had it in their power to run down from the Capitol in arms against their foe, as men besieged have often sallied out on the besiegers, it were possible for us to come to blows with the enemy, either on equal or unequal ground, I would not be wanting in the high quality of my father's spirit in stating my advice. I acknowledge, indeed, that death, in defence of our country, is highly glorious; and I am ready, either to devote myself for the Roman people and the legions, or to plunge into the midst of the enemy. But in this spot I behold my country: in this spot, the whole of the Roman legions, and unless these choose to rush on death in defence of their own individual characters, what have they which can be preserved by their death? The houses of the city, some may say, and the walls of it, and the crowd who dwell in it, by which the city is inhabited. But in fact, in case of the destruction of this army, all these are betrayed, not preserved. For who will protect them? An unwarlike and unarmed multitude, shall I suppose? Yes, just as they defended them against the attack of the Gauls. Will they call to their succour an army from Veii, with Camillus at its head? Here on the spot, I repeat, are all our hopes and strength; by preserving which, we preserve our country; by delivering them up to death, we abandon and betray our country. But a surrender is shameful and ignominious. True: but such ought to be our affection for our country, that we should save it by our own disgrace, if necessity required, as freely as by our death. Let therefore that indignity be undergone, how great soever, and let us submit to that necessity which even the gods themselves do not overcome. Go, consuls, ransom the state for arms, which your ancestors ransomed with gold."

The consuls having gone to Pontius to confer with him, when he talked, in the strain of a conqueror, of a treaty, they declared that such could not be concluded without an order of the people, nor without the ministry of the heralds, and the other customary rites. Accordingly the Caudine peace was not ratified by settled treaty, as is commonly believed, and even asserted by Claudius, but by conventional sureties. For what occasion would these be either for sureties or hostages in the former case, where the ratification is performed by the imprecation, "that whichever nation shall give occasion to the said terms being violated, may Jupiter strike that nation in like manner as the swine is struck by the heralds." The consuls, lieutenants-general, quæstors, and military tribunes, became sureties; and the names of all these who became sureties are extant; where, had the business been transacted by treaty, none would have appeared but those of the two heralds. On account of the necessary delay of the treaty six hundred horsemen were demanded as hostages, who were to suffer death if the compact were not fulfilled; a time was then fixed for delivering up the hostages, and sending away the troops disarmed. The return of the consuls renewed the general grief in the camp, insomuch that the men hardly refrained from offering violence to them, "by whose rashness," they said, "they had been brought into such a situation; and through whose cowardice they were likely to depart with greater disgrace than they came. They had employed no guide through the country, nor scouts; but were sent out blindly, like beasts into a pitfall" They cast looks on each other, viewed earnestly the arms which they must presently surrender; while their persons would be subject to the whim of the enemy: figured to themselves the hostile yoke, the scoffs of the conquerors, their haughty looks, and finally, thus disarmed, their march through the midst of an armed foe. In a word, they saw with horror the miserable journey of their dishonoured band through the cities of the allies; and their return into their own country, to their parents, whither themselves, and their ancestors, had so often come in triumph. Observing, that "they alone had been conquered without a fight, without a weapon thrown, without a wound; that they had not been permitted to draw their swords, nor to engage the enemy. In vain had arms, in vain had strength, in vain had courage been given them." While they were giving vent to such grievous reflections, the fatal hour of their disgrace arrived, which was to render every circumstance still more shocking in fact, than they had preconceived it in their imaginations. First, they were ordered to go out, beyond the rampart, unarmed, and with single garments; then the hostages were surrendered, and carried into custody. The lictors were next commanded to depart from the consuls, and the robes of the latter were stripped off. This excited such a degree of commiseration in the breasts of those very men, who a little before, pouring execrations upon them, had proposed that they should be delivered up and torn to pieces, that every one, forgetting his own condition, turned away his eyes from that degradation of so high a dignity, as from a spectacle too horrid to behold.

First, the consuls, nearly half naked, were sent under the yoke; then each officer, according to his rank, was exposed to disgrace, and the legions successively. The enemy stood on each side under arms, reviling and mocking them; swords were pointed at most of them, several were wounded and some even slain, when their looks, rendered too fierce by the indignity to which they were subjected, gave offence to the conquerors. Thus were they led under the yoke; and what was still more intolerable, under the eyes of the enemy. When they had got clear of the defile, they seemed as if they had been drawn up from the infernal regions, and then for the first time beheld the light; yet, when they viewed the ignominious appearance of the army, the light itself was more painful to them than any kind of death could have been; so that although they might have arrived at Capua before night, yet, uncertain with respect to the fidelity of the allies, and because shame embarrassed them, in need of every thing, they threw themselves carelessly on the ground, on each side of the road: which being told at Capua, just compassion for their allies got the better of the arrogance natural to the Campanians. They immediately sent to the consuls their ensigns of office, the fasces and lictors; to the soldiers, arms, horses, clothes, and provisions in abundance: and, on their approach to Capua, the whole senate and people went out to meet them, and performed every proper office of hospitality, both public and private. But the courtesy, kind looks, and address of the allies, could not only not draw a word from them, but it could not even prevail on them to raise their eyes, or look their consoling friends in the face, so completely did shame, in addition to grief, oblige them to shun the conversation and society of these their friends. Next day, when some young nobles, who had been sent from Capua, to escort them on their road to the frontiers of Campania, returned, they were called into the senate-house, and, in answer to the inquiries of the elder members, said, that "to them they seemed deeply sunk in melancholy and dejection; that the whole body moved on in silence, almost as if dumb; the former genius of the Romans was prostrated, and that their spirit had been taken from them, together with their arms. Not one returned a salute, nor returned an answer to those who greeted them; as if, through fear, they were unable to utter a word; as if their necks still carried the yoke under which they had been sent. That the Samnites had obtained a victory, not only glorious, but lasting also; for they had subdued, not Rome merely, as the Gauls had formerly done, but what was a much wore warlike achievement, the Roman courage." When these remarks were made and attentively listened to, and the almost extinction of the Roman name was lamented in this assembly of faithful allies, Ofilius Calavius, son of Ovius, a man highly distinguished, both by his birth and conduct, and at this time further respectable on account of his age, is said to have declared that he entertained a very different opinion in the case. "This obstinate silence," said he, "those eyes fixed on the earth,—those ears deaf to all comfort,—with the shame of beholding the light,—are indications of a mind calling forth, from its inmost recesses, the utmost exertions of resentment. Either he was ignorant of the temper of the Romans, or that silence would shortly excite, among the Samnites, lamentable cries and groans; for that the remembrance of the Caudine peace would be much more sorrowful to the Samnites than to the Romans. Each side would have their own native spirit, wherever they should happen to engage, but the Samnites would not, every where, have the glens of Caudium."

Their disaster was, by this time, well known at Rome also. At first, they heard that the troops were shut up; afterwards the news of the ignominious peace caused greater affliction than had been felt for their danger. On the report of their being surrounded, a levy of men was begun; but when it was understood that the army had surrendered in so disgraceful a manner, the preparations were laid aside; and immediately, without any public directions, a general mourning took place, with all the various demonstrations of grief. The shops were shut; and all business ceased in the forum, spontaneously, before it was proclaimed. Laticlaves [1] and gold rings were laid aside: and the public were in greater tribulation, if possible, than the army itself; they were not only enraged against the commanders, the advisers and sureties of the peace, but detested even the unoffending soldiers, and asserted, that they ought not to be admitted into the city or its habitations. But these transports of passion were allayed by the arrival of the troops, which excited compassion even in the angry; for entering into the city, not like men returning into their country with unexpected safety, but in the habit and with the looks of captives, late in the evening; they hid themselves so closely in their houses, that, for the next, and several following days, not one of them could bear to come in sight of the forum, or of the public. The consuls, shut up in private, transacted no official business, except that which was wrung from them by a decree of the senate, to nominate a dictator to preside at the elections. They nominated Quintus Fabius Ambustus, and as master of the horse Publius Ælius Pætus. But they having been irregularly appointed, there were substituted in their room, Marcus Æmilius Papus dictator, and Lucius Valerius Flaccus master of the horse. But neither did these hold the elections: and the people being dissatisfied with all the magistrates of that year, an interregnum ensued. The interreges were, Quintus Fabius Maximus and Marcus Valerius Corvus, who elected consuls Quintus Publilius Philo, and Lucius Papirius Cursor a second time; a choice universally approved, for there were no commanders at that time of higher reputation.

They entered into office on the day they were elected, for so it had been determined by the fathers. When the customary decrees of the senate were passed, they proposed the consideration of the Caudine peace; and Publilius, who was in possession of the fasces, said, "Spurius Postumius, speak:" he arose with just the same countenance with which he had passed under the yoke, and delivered himself to this effect: "Consuls, I am well aware that I have been called up first with marked ignominy, not with honour; and that I am ordered to speak, not as being a senator, but as a person answerable as well for an unsuccessful war as for a disgraceful peace. However, since the question propounded by you is not concerning our guilt, or our punishment; waving a defence, which would not be very difficult, before men who are not unacquainted with human casualties or necessities, I shall briefly state my opinion on the matter in question; which opinion will testify, whether I meant to spare myself or your legions, when I engaged as surety to the convention, whether dishonourable or necessary: by which, however, the Roman people are not bound, inasmuch as it was concluded without their order; nor is any thing liable to be forfeited to the Samnites, in consequence of it, except our persons. Let us then be delivered up to them by the heralds, naked, and in chains. Let us free the people of the religious obligation, if we have bound them under any such; so that there may be no restriction, divine or human, to prevent your entering on the war anew, without violating either religion or justice. I am also of opinion, that the consuls, in the mean time, enlist, arm, and lead out an army; but that they should not enter the enemy's territories before every particular, respecting the surrender of us, be regularly executed. You, O immortal gods! I pray and beseech that, although it has not been your will that Spurius Postumius and Titus Veturius, as consuls, should wage war with success against the Samnites, ye may yet deem it sufficient to have seen us sent under the yoke; to have seen us bound under an infamous convention; to have seen us delivered into the hands of our foes naked and shackled, taking on our own heads the whole weight of the enemy's resentment. And grant, that the consuls and legions of Rome may wage war against the Samnites, with the same fortune with which every war has been waged before we became consuls." On his concluding this speech, men's minds were so impressed with both admiration and compassion, that now they could scarce believe him to be the same Spurius Postumius who had been the author of so shameful a peace; again lamenting, that such a man was likely to undergo, among the enemy, a punishment even beyond that of others, through resentment for annulling the peace. When all the members, extolling him with praises, expressed their approbation of his sentiments, a protest was attempted for a time by Lucius Livius and Quintus Mælius, tribunes of the commons, who said, that "the people could not be acquitted of the religious obligation by the consuls being given up, unless all things were restored to the Samnites in the same state in which they had been at Caudium; nor had they themselves deserved any punishment, for having, by becoming sureties to the peace, preserved the army of the Roman people; nor, finally, could they, being sacred and inviolable, be surrendered to the enemy or treated with violence."

To this Postumius replied, "In the mean time surrender us as unsanctified persons, which ye may do, without offence to religion; those sacred and inviolable personages, the tribunes, ye will afterwards deliver up as soon as they go out of office: but, if ye listen to me, they will be first scourged with rods, here in the Comitium, that they may pay this as interest for their punishment being delayed. For, as to their denying that the people are acquitted of the religious obligation, by our being given up, who is there so ignorant of the laws of the heralds, as not to know, that those men speak in that manner, that they themselves may not be surrendered, rather than because the case is really so? Still I do not deny, conscript fathers, that compacts, on sureties given, are as sacred as treaties, in the eyes of all who regard faith between men, with the same reverence which is paid to duties respecting the gods: but I insist, that without the order of the people, nothing can be ratified that is to bind the people. Suppose that, out of the same arrogance with which the Samnites wrung from us the convention in question, they had compelled us to repeat the established form of words for the surrendering of cities, would ye, tribunes, say, that the Roman people was surrendered? and, that this city, these temples, and consecrated grounds, these lands and waters, were become the property of the Samnites? I say no more of the surrender, because our having become sureties is the point insisted on. Now, suppose we had become sureties that the Roman people should quit this city; that they should set it on fire; that they should have no magistrates, no senate, no laws; that they should, in future, be ruled by kings: the gods forbid, you say. But, the enormity of the articles lessens not the obligation of a compact. If there is any thing in which the people can be bound, it can in all. Nor is there any importance in another circumstance, which weighs, perhaps, with some: whether a consul, a dictator, or a prætor, be the surety. And this, indeed, was what even the Samnites themselves proved, who were not satisfied with the security of the consuls, but compelled the lieutenants-general, quæstors, and military tribunes to join them. Let no one, then, demand of me, why I entered into such a compact, when neither such power was vested in a consul, and when I could not either to them, insure a peace, of which I could not command the ratification; or in behalf of you, who had given me no powers. Conscript fathers, none of the transactions at Caudium were directed by human wisdom. The immortal gods deprived of understanding both your generals and those of the enemy. On the one side we acted not with sufficient caution in the war; on the other, they threw away a victory, which through our folly they had obtained, while they hardly confided in the places, by means of which they had conquered; but were in haste, on any terms, to take arms out of the hands of men who were born to arms. Had their reason been sound, would it have been difficult, during the time which they spent in sending for old men from home to give them advice, to send ambassadors to Rome, and to negotiate a peace and treaty with the senate, and with the people? It would have been a journey of only three days to expeditious travellers. In the interim, matters might have rested under a truce, that is, until their ambassadors should have brought from Rome, either certain victory or peace. That would have been really a compact, on the faith of sureties, for we should have become sureties by order of the people. But, neither would ye have passed such an order, nor should we have pledged our faith; nor was it right that the affair should have any other issue, than, that they should be vainly mocked with a dream, as it were, of greater prosperity than their minds were capable of comprehending, and that the same fortune, which had entangled our army, should extricate it; that an ineffectual victory should be frustrated by a more ineffectual peace; and that a convention, on the faith of a surety, should be introduced, which bound no other person beside the surety. For what part had ye, conscript fathers; what part had the people, in this affair? Who can call upon you? Who can say, that he has been deceived by you? Can the enemy? Can a citizen? To the enemy ye engaged nothing. Ye ordered no citizen to engage on your behalf. Ye are therefore no way concerned either with us, to whom ye gave no commission; nor with the Samnites, with whom ye transacted no business. We are sureties to the Samnites; debtors, sufficiently wealthy in that which is our own, in that which we can offer—our bodies and our minds. On these, let them exercise their cruelty; against these, let them whet their resentment and their swords. As to what relates to the tribunes, consider whether the delivering them up can be effected at the present time, or if it must be deferred to another day. Meanwhile let us, Titus Veturius, and the rest concerned, offer our worthless persons, as atonements for the breaking our engagements, and, by our sufferings liberate the Roman armies."

Both these arguments, and, still more, the author of them, powerfully affected the senators; as they did likewise every one, not excepting even the tribunes of the commons who declared, that they would be directed by the senate. They then instantly resigned their office, and were delivered, together with the rest, to the heralds, to be conducted to Caudium. On passing this decree of the senate, it seemed as if some new light had shone upon the state: Postumius was in every mouth: they extolled him to heaven; and pronounced his conduct as equal even to the devoting act of the consul Publius Decius, and to other illustrious acts. "Through his counsel, and exertions," they said, "the state had raised up its head from an ignominious peace. He now offered himself to the enemy's rage, and to torments; and was suffering, in atonement for the Roman people." All turned their thoughts towards arms and war, [and the general cry was,] "When shall we be permitted with arms in our hands to meet the Samnites?" While the state glowed with resentment and rancour, the levies were composed almost entirely of volunteers. New legions, composed of the former soldiers, were quickly formed, and an army marched to Caudium. The heralds, who went before, on coming to the gate, ordered the sureties of the peace to be stripped of their clothes, and their hands to be tied behind their backs. As the apparitor, out of respect to his dignity, was binding Postumius in a loose manner, "Why do you not," said he, "draw the cord tight, that the surrender may be regularly performed?" Then, when they came into the assembly of the Samnites, and to the tribunal of Pontius, Aulus Cornelius Arvina, a herald, pronounced these words: "Forasmuch as these men, here present, without orders from the Roman people, the Quirites, entered into surety, that a treaty should be made, and have thereby rendered themselves criminal; now, in order that the Roman people may be freed from the crime of impiety, I here surrender these men into your hands." On the herald saying thus, Postumius gave him a stroke on the thigh with his knee, as forcibly as he could, and said with a loud voice, that "he was now a citizen of Samnium, the other a Roman ambassador; that the herald had been, by him, violently ill-treated, contrary to the law of nations; and that his people would therefore have the more justice on their side, in waging war."

Pontius then said, "Neither will I accept such a surrender, nor will the Samnites deem it valid. Spurius Postumius, if you believe that there are gods, why do you not undo all that has been done, or fulfil your agreement? The Samnite nation is entitled, either to all the men whom it had in its power, or, instead of them, to a peace. But why do I call on you, who, with as much regard to faith as you are able to show, return yourself a prisoner into the hands of the conqueror? I call on the Roman people. If they are dissatisfied with the convention made at the Caudine forks, let them replace the legions within the defile where they were pent up. Let there be no deception on either side. Let all that has been done pass as nothing. Let them receive again the army which they surrendered by the convention; let them return into their camp. Whatever they were in possession of, the day before the conference, let them possess again. Then let war and resolute counsels be adopted. Then let the convention, and peace, be rejected. Let us carry on the war in the same circumstances, and situations, in which we were before peace was mentioned. Let neither the Roman people blame the convention of the consuls, nor us the faith of the Roman people. Will ye never want an excuse for not standing to the compacts which ye make on being defeated? Ye gave hostages to Porsena: ye clandestinely withdrew them. Ye ransomed your state from the Gauls, for gold: while they were receiving the gold, they were put to the sword. Ye concluded a peace with us, on condition of our restoring your captured legions: that peace ye now annul; in fine, ye always spread over your fraudulent conduct some show of right. Do the Roman people disapprove of their legions being saved by an ignominious peace? Let them have their peace, and return the captured legions to the conqueror. This would be conduct consistent with faith, with treaties, and with the laws of the heralds. But that you should, in consequence of the convention, obtain what you desired, the safety of so many of your countrymen, while I obtain not, what I stipulated for on sending you back those men, a peace; is this the law which you, Aulus Cornelius, which ye, heralds, prescribe to nations? But for my part, I neither accept those men whom ye pretend to surrender, nor consider them as surrendered; nor do I hinder them from returning into their own country, which stands bound under an actual convention, formally entered into carrying with them the wrath of all the gods, whose authority is thus baffled. Wage war, since Spurius Postumius has just now struck with his knee the herald, in character of ambassador. The gods are to believe that Postumius is a citizen of Samnium, not of Rome; and that a Roman ambassador has been violated by a Samnite; and that therefore a just war has been waged against us by you. That men of years, and of consular dignity, should not be ashamed to exhibit such mockery of religion in the face of day! And should have recourse to such shallow artifices to palliate their breach of faith, unworthy even of children! Go, lictor, take off the bonds from those Romans. Let no one delay them from departing when they think proper." Accordingly they returned unhurt from Caudium to the Roman camp, having acquitted, certainly, their own faith, and perhaps that of the public.

The Samnites finding that instead of a peace which flattered their pride, the war was revived, and with the utmost inveteracy, not only felt, in their minds, a foreboding of all the consequences which ensued, but saw them, in a manner, before their eyes. They now, too late and in vain, applauded the plans of old Pontius, by blundering between which, they had exchanged the possession of victory for an uncertain peace; and having lost the opportunity of doing a kindness or an injury, were now to fight against men, whom they might have either put out of the way, for ever, as enemies; or engaged, for ever, as friends. And such was the change which had taken place in men's minds, since the Caudine peace, even before any trial of strength had shown an advantage on either side, that Postumius, by surrendering himself, had acquired greater renown among the Romans, than Pontius among the Samnites, by his bloodless victory. The Romans considered their being at liberty to make war, a certain victory; while the Samnites supposed the Romans victorious, the moment they resumed their arms. Meanwhile, the Satricans revolted to the Samnites, who attacked the colony of Fregellæ, by a sudden surprise in the night, accompanied, as it appears, by the Satricans. From that time until day, their mutual fears kept both parties quiet: the daylight was the signal for battle, which the Fregellans contrived to maintain, for a considerable time, without loss of ground; both because they fought for their religion and liberty; and the multitude, who were unfit to bear arms, assisted them from the tops of the houses. At length a stratagem gave the advantage to the assailants; for they suffered the voice of a crier to be heard proclaiming, that "whoever laid down his arms might retire in safety." This relaxed their eagerness in the fight, and they began almost every where to throw away their arms. A part, more determined, however, retaining their arms, rushed out by the opposite gate, and their boldness brought greater safety to them, than their fear, which inclined them to credulity, did to the others: for the Samnites, having surrounded the latter with fires, burned them all to death, while they made vain appeals to the faith of gods and men. The consuls having settled the province between them, Papirius proceeded into Apulia to Luceria where the Roman horsemen, given as hostages at Caudium were kept in custody:

Publilius remained in Samnium, to oppose the Caudine legions. This proceeding perplexed the minds of the Samnites: they could not safely determine either to go to Luceria, lest the enemy should press on their rear or to remain where they were, lest in the mean time Luceria should be lost. They concluded, therefore, that it would be most advisable to trust to the decision of fortune, and to take the issue of a battle with Publilius: accordingly they drew out their forces into the field.

When Publilius was about to engage, considering it proper to address his soldiers first, he ordered an assembly be summoned. But though they ran together to the general's quarters with the greatest alacrity, yet so loud were the clamours, demanding the fight, that none of the general's exhortations were heard: each man's own reflections on the late disgrace served as an exhortation. They advanced therefore to battle, urging the standard-bearers to hasten; at rest, in beginning the conflict, there should be any delay, in wielding their javelins and then drawing their swords, they threw away the former, as if a signal to that purpose had been given, and, drawing the latter, rushed in full speed upon the foe. Nothing of a general's skill was displayed in forming ranks or reserves; the resentment of the troops performed all, with a degree of fury little inferior to madness. The enemy, therefore, were not only completely routed, not even daring to embarrass their flight by retreating to their camp but dispersing, made towards Apulia in scattered parties: afterwards, however, collecting their forces into one body, they reached Luceria. The same exasperation, which had carried the Romans through the midst of the enemy's line, carried them forward also into their camp, where greater carnage was made, and more blood spilt, than even in the field, while the greater part of the spoil was destroyed in their rage. The other army, with the consul Papirius, had now arrived at Arpi, on the sea-coast, having passed without molestation through all the countries in their way; which was owing to the ill-treatment received by those people from the Samnites, and their hatred towards them, rather than to any favour received from the Roman people. For such of the Samnites as dwelt on the mountains in separate villages, used to ravage the low lands, and the places on the coast; and being mountaineers, and savage themselves, despised the husbandmen who were of a gentler kind, and, as generally happens, resembled the district they inhabited. Now if this tract had been favourably affected towards the Samnites, either the Roman army could have been prevented from reaching Arpi, or, as it lay between Rome and Arpi, it might have intercepted the convoys of provisions, and utterly destroyed them by the consequent scarcity of all necessaries. Even as it was, when they went from thence to Luceria, both the besiegers and the besieged were distressed equally by want. Every kind of supplies was brought to the Romans from Arpi; but in so very scanty proportion, that the horsemen had to carry corn from thence to the camp, in little bags, for the foot, who were employed in the outposts, watches, and works; and sometimes falling in with the enemy, they were obliged to throw the corn from off their horses, in order to fight. Before the arrival of the other consul and his victorious army, both provisions had been brought in to the Samnites, and reinforcements conveyed in to them from the mountains; but the coming of Publilius contracted all their resources; for, committing the siege to the care of his colleague, and keeping himself disengaged, he threw every difficulty in the way of the enemy's convoys. There being therefore little hope for the besieged, or that they would be able much longer to endure want, the Samnites, encamped at Luceria, were obliged to collect their forces from every side, and come to an engagement with Papirius.

At this juncture, while both parties were preparing for an action, ambassadors from the Tarentines interposed, requiring both Samnites and Romans to desist from war; with menaces, that "if either refused to agree to a cessation of hostilities, they would join their arms with the other party against them." Papirius, on hearing the purport of their embassy, as if influenced by their words, answered, that he would consult his colleague: he then sent for him, employing the intermediate time in the necessary preparations; and when he had conferred with him on a matter, about which no doubt was entertained, he made the signal for battle. While the consuls were employed in performing the religious rites and the other usual business preparatory to an engagement the Tarentine ambassadors put themselves in their way, expecting an answer: to whom Papirius said, "Tarentines, the priest reports that the auspices are favourable, and that our sacrifices have been attended with excellent omens: under the direction of the gods, we are proceeding, as you see, to action." He then ordered the standards to move, and led out the troops; thus rebuking the exorbitant arrogance of that nation, which at a time when, through intestine discord and sedition, it was unequal to the management of its own affairs, yet presumed to prescribe the bounds of peace and war to others. On the other side, the Samnites, who had neglected every preparation for fighting, either because they were really desirous of peace, or it seemed their interest to pretend to be so, in order to conciliate the favour of the Tarentines, when they saw, on a sudden, the Romans drawn up for battle, cried out, that "they would continue to be directed by the Tarentines, and would neither march out, nor carry their arms beyond the rampart. That if deceived, they would rather endure any consequence which chance may bring, than show contempt to the Tarentines, the advisers of peace." The consuls said that "they embraced the omen, and prayed that the enemy might continue in the resolution of not even defending their rampart." Then, dividing the forces between them, they advanced to the works; and, making an assault on every side at once, while some filled up the trenches, others tore down the rampart, and tumbled it into the trench. All were stimulated, not only by their native courage, but by the resentment which, since their disgrace, had been festering in their breasts. They made their way into the camp; where, every one repeating, that here was not Caudium, nor the forks, nor the impassable glens, where cunning haughtily triumphed over error; but Roman valour, which no rampart nor trench could ward off;— they slew, without distinction, those who resisted and those who fled, the armed and unarmed, freemen and slaves, young and old, men and cattle. Nor would a single animal have escaped, had not the consuls given the signal for retreat; and, by commands and threats, forced out of the camp the soldiers, greedy of slaughter. As they were highly incensed at being thus interrupted in the gratification of their vengeance, a speech was immediately addressed to them, assuring the soldiers, that "the consuls neither did nor would fall short of any one of the soldiers, in hatred toward the enemy; on the contrary, as they led the way in battle, so would they have done the same in executing unbounded vengeance, had not the consideration of the six hundred horsemen, who were confined as hostages in Luceria, restrained their inclinations; lest total despair of pardon might drive on the enemy blindly to take vengeance on them, eager to destroy them before they themselves should perish." The soldiers highly applauded this conduct, and rejoiced that their resentment had been checked, and acknowledged that every thing ought to be endured, rather than that the safety of so many Roman youths of the first distinction should be brought into danger.

The assembly being then dismissed, a consultation was held, whether they should press forward the siege of Luceria, with all their forces; or, whether with one of the commanders, and his army, trial should be made of the Apulians, a nation in the neighbourhood still doubtful. The consul Publilius set out to make a circuit through

Apulia, and in the one expedition either reduced by force, or received into alliance on conditions, a considerable number of the states. Papirius likewise, who had remained to prosecute the siege of Luceria, soon found the event agreeable to his hopes: for all the roads being blocked up through which provisions used to be conveyed from Samnium, the Samnites, who were in garrison, were reduced so low by famine, that they sent ambassadors to the Roman consul, proposing that he should raise the siege, on receiving the horsemen who were the cause of the war, to whom Papirius returned this answer, that "they ought to have consulted Pontius, son of Herennius, by whose advice they had sent the Romans under the yoke, what treatment he thought fitting for the conquered to undergo. But since, instead of offering fair terms themselves, they chose rather that they should be imposed on them by their enemies, he desired them to carry back orders to the troops in Luceria, that they should leave within the walls their arms, baggage, beasts of burthen, and all persons unfit for war. The soldiers he would send under the yoke with single garments, retaliating the disgrace formerly inflicted, not inflicting a new one." The terms were not rejected. Seven thousand soldiers were sent under the yoke, and an immense booty was seized in Luceria, all the standards and arms which they had lost at Caudium being recovered; and, what greatly surpassed all their joy, recovered the horsemen whom the Samnites had sent to Luceria to be kept as pledges of the peace. Hardly ever did the Romans gain a victory more distinguished for the sudden reverse produced in the state of their affairs; especially if it be true, as I find in some annals, that Pontius, son of Herennius, the Samnite general, was sent under the yoke along with the rest, to atone for the disgrace of the consuls. I think it indeed more strange that there should exist any doubt whether it was Lucius Cornelius, in quality of dictator, Lucius Papirius Cursor being master of the horse, who performed these achievements at Caudium, and afterwards at Luceria, as the single avenger of the disgrace of the Romans, enjoying the best deserved triumph, perhaps, next to that of Furius Camillus, which had ever yet been obtained; or whether that honour belongs to the consuls, and particularly to Papirius. This uncertainty is followed by another, whether, at the next election, Papirius Cursor was chosen consul a third time, with Quintus Aulus Ceretanus a second time, being re-elected in requital of his services at Luceria; or whether it was Lucius Papirius Mugillanus, the surname being mistaken.

From henceforth, the accounts are clear, that the other wars were conducted to a conclusion by the consuls. Aulius by one successful battle, entirely conquered the Forentans. The city, to which their army had retreated after its defeat, surrendered on terms, hostages having been demanded. With similar success the other consul conducted his operations against the Satricans; who, though Roman citizens, had, after the misfortune at Caudium, revolted to the Samnites, and received a garrison into their city. The Satricans, however, when the Roman army approached their walls, sent deputies to sue for peace, with humble entreaties; to whom the consul answered harshly, that "they must not come again to him, unless they either put to death, or delivered up, the Samnite garrison:" by which terms greater terror was struck into the colonists than by the arms with which they were threatened. The deputies, accordingly, several times asking the consul, how he thought that they, who were few and weak, could attempt to use force against a garrison so strong and well-armed: he desired them to "seek counsel from those, by whose advice they had received that garrison into the city." They then departed, and returned to their countrymen, having obtained from the consul, with much difficulty, permission to consult their senate on the matter, and bring back their answer to him. Two factions divided the senate; one that whose leaders had been the authors of the defection from the Roman people, the other consisted of the citizens who retained their loyalty; both, however, showed an earnest desire, that every means should be used towards effecting an accommodation with the consul for the restoration of peace. As the Samnite garrison, being in no respect prepared for holding out a siege, intended to retire the next night out of the town, one party thought it sufficient to discover to the consul, at what hour, through what gate, and by what road, his enemy was to march out. The other, against whose wishes defection to the Samnites had occurred, even opened one of the gates for the consul in the night, secretly admitting the armed enemy into the town. In consequence of this twofold treachery, the Samnite garrison was surprised and overpowered by an ambush, placed in the woody places, near the road; and, at the same time, a shout was raised in the city, which was now filled with the enemy. Thus, in the short space of one hour, the Samnites were put to the sword, the Satricans made prisoners, and all things reduced under the power of the consul; who, having instituted an inquiry by whose means the revolt had taken place, scourged with rods and beheaded such as he found to be guilty; and then, disarming the Satricans, he placed a strong garrison in the place. On this those writers state, that Papirius Cursor proceeded to Rome to celebrate his triumph, who say, that it was under his guidance Luceria was retaken, and the Samnites sent under the yoke. Undoubtedly, as a warrior, he was deserving of every military praise, excelling not only in vigour of mind, but likewise in strength of body. He possessed extraordinary swiftness of foot, surpassing every one of his age in running, from whence came the surname into his family; and he is said, either from the robustness of his frame, or from much practice, to have been able to digest a very large quantity of food and wine. Never did either the foot-soldier or horseman feel military service more laborious, under any general, because he was of a constitution not to be overcome by fatigue. The cavalry, on some occasion, venturing to request that, in consideration of their good behaviour, he would excuse them some part of their business, he told them, "Ye should not say that no indulgence has been granted you,—I excuse you from rubbing your horses' backs when ye dismount." He supported also the authority of command, in all its vigour, both among the allies and his countrymen. The prætor of Præneste, through fear, had been tardy in bringing forward his men from the reserve to the front: he, walking before his tent, ordered him to be called, and then bade the lictor to make ready his axe, on which, the Prænestine standing frightened almost to death, he said, "Here, lictor, cut away this stump, it is troublesome to people as they walk;" and, after thus alarming him with the dread of the severest punishment, he imposed a fine and dismissed him. It is beyond doubt, that during that age, than which none was ever more productive of virtuous characters, there was no man in whom the Roman affairs found a more effectual support; nay, people even marked him out, in their minds, as a match for Alexander the Great, in case that, having completed the conquest of Asia, he should have turned his arms on Europe.

Nothing can be found farther from my intention, since the commencement of this history, than to digress, more than necessity required, from the course of narration; and, by embellishing my work with variety, to seek pleasing resting-places, as it were, for my readers, and relaxation for my own mind: nevertheless, the mention of so great a king and commander, now calls forth to public view those silent reflections, whom Alexander must have fought. Manlius Torquatus, had he met him in the field, might, perhaps, have yielded to Alexander in discharging military duties in battle (for these also render him no less illustrious); and so might Valerius Corvus; men who were distinguished soldiers, before they became commanders. The same, too, might have been the case with the

Decii, who, after devoting their persons, rushed upon the enemy; or of Papirius Cursor, though possessed of such powers, both of body and mind. By the counsels of one youth, it is possible the wisdom of a whole senate, not to mention individuals, might have been baffled, [consisting of such members,] that he alone, who declared that "it consisted of kings," conceived a correct idea of a Roman senate. But then the danger was, that with more judgment than any one of those whom I have named he might choose ground for an encampment, provide supplies, guard against stratagems, distinguish the season for fighting, form his line of battle, or strengthen it properly with reserves. He would have owned that he was not dealing with Darius, who drew after him a train of women and eunuchs; saw nothing about him but gold and purple; was encumbered with the trappings of his state, and should be called his prey, rather than his antagonist; whom therefore he vanquished without loss of blood and had no other merit, on the occasion, than that of showing a proper spirit in despising empty show. The aspect of Italy would have appeared to him of a quite different nature from that of India, which he traversed in the guise of a traveller, at the head of a crew of drunkards, if he had seen the forests of Apulia, and the mountains of Lucania, with the vestiges of the disasters of his house, and where his uncle Alexander, king of Epirus, had been lately cut off.

We are now speaking of Alexander not yet intoxicated by prosperity, the seductions of which no man was less capable of withstanding. But, if he is to be judged from the tenor of his conduct in the new state of his fortune, and from the new disposition, as I may say, which he put on after his successes, he would have entered Italy more like Darius than Alexander; and would have brought thither an army that had forgotten Macedonia, and were degenerating into the manners of the Persians. It is painful, in speaking of so great a king, to recite his ostentatious change of dress; of requiring that people should address him with adulation, prostrating themselves on the ground, a practice insupportable to the Macedonians, had they even been conquered, much more so when they were victorious; the shocking cruelty of his punishments; his murdering his friends in the midst of feasting and wine; with the folly of his fiction respecting his birth. What must have been the consequence, if his love of wine had daily become more intense? if his fierce and uncontrollable anger? And as I mention not any one circumstance of which there is a doubt among writers, do we consider these as no disparagements to the qualifications of a commander? But then, as is frequently repeated by the silliest of the Greeks, who are fond of exalting the reputation, even of the Parthians, at the expense of the Roman name, the danger was that the Roman people would not have had resolution to bear up against the splendour of Alexander's name, who, however, in my opinion, was not known to them even by common fame; and while, in Athens, a state reduced to weakness by the Macedonian arms, which at the very time saw the ruins of Thebes smoking in its neighbourhood, men had spirit enough to declaim with freedom against him, as is manifest from the copies of their speeches, which have been preserved; [we are to be told] that out of such a number of Roman chiefs, no one would have freely uttered his sentiments. How great soever our idea of this man's greatness may be, still it is the greatness of an individual, constituted by the successes of a little more than ten years; and those who give it pre-eminence on account that the Roman people have been defeated, though not in any entire war, yet in several battles, whereas Alexander was never once unsuccessful in a single fight, do not consider that they are comparing the actions of one man, and that a young man, with the exploits of a nation waging wars now eight hundred years. Can we wonder if, when on the one side more ages are numbered than years on the other, fortune varied more in so long a lapse of time than in the short term of thirteen years? [2] But why not compare the success of one general with that of another? How many Roman commanders might I name who never lost a battle? In the annals of the magistrates, and the records, we may run over whole pages of consuls and dictators, with whose bravery, and successes also, the Roman people never once had reason to be dissatisfied. And what renders them more deserving of admiration than Alexander, or any king, is, that some of these acted in the office of dictator, which lasted only ten, or it might be twenty days, none, in a charge of longer duration than the consulship of a year; their levies obstructed by plebeian tribunes; often late in taking the field; recalled, before the time, on account of elections; amidst the very busiest efforts of the campaign, their year of office expired; sometimes the rashness, sometimes the perverseness of a colleague, proving an impediment or detriment; and finally succeeding to the unfortunate administration of a predecessor, with an army of raw or ill-disciplined men. But, on the other hand, kings, being not only free from every kind of impediment, but masters of circumstances and seasons, control all things in subserviency to their designs, themselves uncontrolled by any. So that Alexander, unconquered, would have encountered unconquered commanders; and would have had stakes of equal consequence pledged on the issue. Nay, the hazard had been greater on his side; because the Macedonians would have had but one Alexander, who was not only liable, but fond of exposing himself to casualties; the Romans would have had many equal to Alexander, both in renown, and in the greatness of their exploits; any one of whom might live or die according to his destiny, without any material consequence to the public.

It remains that the forces be compared together, with respect to their numbers, the quality of the men, and the supplies of auxiliaries. Now, in the general surveys of the age, there were rated two hundred and fifty thousand men, so that, on every revolt of the Latin confederates, ten legions were enlisted almost entirely in the city levy. It often happened during those years, that four or five armies were employed at a time, in Etruria, in Umbria, the Gauls too being at war, in Samnium, in Lucania. Then as to all Latium, with the Sabines, and Volscians, the Æquans, and all Campania; half of Umbria, Etruria, and the Picentians, Marsians, Pelignians, Vestinians, and Apulians; to whom may add, the whole coast of the lower sea, possessed by the Greeks, from Thurii to Neapolis and Cumæ; and the Samnites from thence as far as Antium and Ostia: all these he would have found either powerful allies to the Romans or deprived of power by their arms. He would have crossed the sea with his veteran Macedonians, amounting to no more than thirty thousand infantry and four thousand horse, these mostly Thessalians. This was the whole of his strength. Had he brought with him Persians and Indians, and those other nations, it would be dragging after him an encumbrance other than a support. Add to this, that the Romans, being at home, would have had recruits at hand: Alexander, waging war in a foreign country, would have found his army worn out with long service, as happened afterwards to Hannibal. As to arms, theirs were a buckler and long spears; those of the Romans, a shield, which covered the body more effectually, and a javelin, a much more forcible weapon than the spear, either in throwing or striking. The soldiers, on both sides, were used to steady combat, and to preserve their ranks. But the Macedonian phalanx was unapt for motion, and composed of similar parts throughout: the Roman line less compact, consisting of several various parts, was easily divided as occasion required, and as easily conjoined. Then what soldier is comparable to the Roman in the throwing up of works? who better calculated to endure fatigue? Alexander, if overcome in one battle, would have been overcome in war. The Roman, whom Claudium, whom Cannæ, did not crush, what line of battle could crush? In truth, even should events have been favourable to him at first, he would have often wished for the Persians, the Indians, and the effeminate tribes of Asia, as opponents; and would have acknowledged, that his wars had been waged with women, as we are told was said by Alexander, king of Epirus, after receiving his mortal wound, when comparing the wars waged in Asia by this very youth, with those in which himself had been engaged. Indeed, when I reflect that, in the first Punic war, a contest was maintained by the Romans with the Carthaginians, at sea, for twenty-four years, I can scarcely suppose that the life of Alexander would have been long enough for the finishing of one war [with either of those nations]. And perhaps, as both the Punic state was united to the Roman by ancient treaties, and as similar apprehensions might arm against a common foe those two nations the most potent of the time in arms and in men, he might have been overwhelmed in a Punic and a Roman war at once. The Romans have had experience of the boasted prowess of the Macedonians in arms, not indeed under Alexander as their general, or when their power was at the height, but in the wars against Antiochus, Philip, and Perses; and not only not with any losses, but not even with any danger to themselves. Let not my assertion give offence, nor our civil wars be brought into mention; never were we worsted by an enemy's cavalry, never by their infantry, never in open fight, never on equal ground, much less when the ground was favourable. Our soldiers, heavy laden with arms, may reasonably fear a body of cavalry, or arrows; defiles of difficult passage, and places impassable to convoys. But they have defeated, and will defeat a thousand armies, more formidable than those of Alexander and the Macedonians, provided that the same love of peace and solicitude about domestic harmony, in which we now live, continue permanent.

Marcus Foslius Flaccinator and Lucius Plautius Venno were the next raised to the consulship. In this year ambassadors came from most of the states of the Samnites to procure a renewal of the treaty; and, after they had moved the compassion of the senate, by prostrating themselves before them, on being referred to the people, they found not their prayers so efficacious. The treaty therefore, being refused, after they had importuned them individually for several days, was obtained. The Teaneans likewise, and Canusians of Apulia, worn out by the devastations of their country, surrendered themselves to the consul, Lucius Plautius, and gave hostages. This year præfects first began to be created for Capua, and a code of laws was given to that nation, by Lucius Furius the prætor; both in compliance with their own request, as a remedy for the disorder of their affairs, occasioned by intestine dissensions. At Rome, two additional tribes were constituted, the Ufentine and Falerine. On the affairs of Apulia falling into decline, the Teatians of that country came to the new consuls, Caius Junius Bubulcus, and Quintus Æmilius Barbula, suing for an alliance; and engaging, that peace should be observed towards the Romans through every part of Apulia. By pledging themselves boldly for this, they obtained the grant of an alliance, not however on terms of equality, but of their submitting to the dominion of the Roman people. Apulia being entirely reduced, (for Junius had also gained possession of Forentum, a town of great strength,) the consuls advanced into Lucania; there Nerulum was surprised and stormed by the sudden advance of the consul Æmilius. When fame had spread abroad among the allies, how firmly the affairs of Capua were settled by [the introduction of] the Roman institutions, the Antians, imitating the example, presented a complaint of their being without laws, and without magistrates; on which the patrons of the colony itself were appointed by the senate to form a body of laws for it. Thus not only the arms, but the laws, of Rome became extensively prevalent.

The consuls, Caius Junius Bubulcus and Quintus Æmilius Barbula, at the conclusion of the year, delivered over the legions, not to the consuls elected by themselves, who were Spurius Nautius and Marcus Popillius, but to a dictator, Lucius Æmilius. He, with Lucius Fulvius, master of the horse, having commenced to lay siege to Saticula, gave occasion to the Samnites of reviving hostilities. Hence a twofold alarm was occasioned to the Roman army. On one side, the Samnites having collected a numerous force to relieve their allies from the siege, pitched their camp at a small distance from that of the Romans: on the other side, the Saticulans, opening suddenly their gates, ran up with violent tumult to the posts of the enemy. Afterwards, each party, relying on support from the other, more than on its own strength, formed a regular attack, and pressed on the Romans. The dictator, on his part, though obliged to oppose two enemies at once, yet had his line secure on both sides; for he both chose a position not easily surrounded, and also formed two different fronts. However, he directed his greater efforts against those who had sallied from the town, and, without much resistance, drove them back within the walls. He then turned his whole force against the Samnites: there he found greater difficulty. But the victory, though long delayed, was neither doubtful nor alloyed by losses. The Samnites, being forced to fly into their camp, extinguished their fires at night, and marched away in silence; and renouncing all hopes of relieving Saticula, sat themselves down before Plistia, which was in alliance with the Romans, that they might, if possible, retort equal vexation on their enemy.

The year coming to a conclusion, the war was thenceforward conducted by a dictator, Quintius Fabius. The new consuls, Lucius Papirius Cursor and Quintus Publilius Philo, both a fourth time, as the former had done, remained at Rome. Fabius came with a reinforcement to Saticula, to receive the army from Æmilius. For the Samnites had not continued before Plistia; but having sent for a new supply of men from home, and relying on their numbers, had encamped in the same spot as before; and, by provoking the Romans to battle, endeavoured to divert them from the siege. The dictator, so much the more intently, pushed forward his operations against the fortifications of the enemy; considering that only as war which was directed against the city, and showing an indifference with respect to the Samnites, except that he placed guards in proper places, to prevent any attempt on his camp. The more furiously did the Samnites ride up to the rampart, and allowed him no quiet. When the enemy were now come up close to the gates of the camp, Quintus Aulius Cerretanus, master of the horse, without consulting the dictator, sallied out furiously at the head of all the troops of cavalry, and drove back the enemy. In this desultory kind of fight, fortune worked up the strength of the combatants in such a manner, as to occasion an extraordinary loss on both sides, and the remarkable deaths of the commanders themselves. First, the general of the Samnites, indignant at being repulsed, and compelled to fly from a place to which he had advanced so confidently, by entreating and exhorting his horsemen, renewed the battle. As he was easily distinguished among the horsemen, while he urged on the fight, the Roman master of the horse galloped up against him, with his spear directed, so furiously, that, with one stroke, he tumbled him lifeless from his horse. The multitude, however, were not, as is generally the case, dismayed by the fall of their leader, but rather raised to fury. All who were within reach darted their weapons at Aulius, who incautiously pushed forward among the enemy's troops; but the chief share of the honour of revenging the death of the Samnite general they assigned to his brother; he, urged by rage and grief, dragged down the victorious master of the horse from his seat, and slew him. Nor were the Samnites far from obtaining his body also, as he had fallen among the enemies' troops: but the Romans instantly dismounted, and the Samnites were obliged to do the same; and lines being thus formed suddenly but, at the same time, untenable through scarcity of necessaries: "for all the country round, from which provisions could be supplied, has revolted; and besides, even were the inhabitants disposed to aid us, the ground is unfavourable. I will not therefore mislead you by leaving a camp here, into which ye may retreat, as on a former day, without completing the victory. Works ought to be secured by arms, not arms by works. Let those keep a camp, and repair to it, whose interest it is to protract the war; but let us cut off from ourselves every other prospect but that of conquering. Advance the standards against the enemy; as soon as the troops shall have marched beyond the rampart, let those who have it in orders burn the camp. Your losses, soldiers, shall be compensated with the spoil of all the nations round who have revolted." The soldiers advanced against the enemy with spirit inflamed by the dictator's discourse, which seemed indication of an extreme necessity; and, at the same time, the very sight of the camp burning behind them, though the nearest part only was set on fire, (for so the dictator had ordered,) was small incitement: rushing on therefore like madmen, they disordered the enemy's battalions at the very first onset; and the master of the horse, when he saw at a distance the fire in the camp, which was a signal agreed on, made a seasonable attack on their rear. The Samnites, thus surrounded on either side, fled different ways. A vast number, who had gathered into a body through fear, yet from confusion incapable of fleeing, were surrounded and cut to pieces. The enemy's camp was taken and plundered; and the soldiers being laden with spoil, the dictator led them back to the Roman camp, highly rejoiced at the success, but by no means so much as at finding, contrary to their expectation, every thing there safe, except a small part only, which was injured or destroyed by the fire.

They then marched back to Sora; and the new consuls, Marcus Pœtelius and Caius Sulpicius, receive the army from the dictator Fabius, discharging a great part of the veteran soldiers, having brought with them new cohorts to supply their place. Now while, on account of the dire situation of the city, no certain mode of attack could be devised, and success must either be distant in time, or at desperate risk; a deserter from Sora came out of the town privately by night, and when he had got as far as the Roman watches, desired to be conducted instantly to the consuls: which being complied with, he made them an offer of delivering the place into their hands. When he answered their questions, respecting the means by which he intended to make good his promise, appearing to state a project by no means idle, he persuaded them to remove the Roman camp, which was almost close to the walls, to the distance of six miles; that the consequence would be that this would render the guards by day, and the watches by night, the less vigilant. He then desired that some cohorts should post themselves the following night in the woody places under the town, and took with himself ten chosen soldiers, through steep and almost impassable ways, into the citadel, where a quantity of missive weapons had been collected, larger than bore proportion to the number of men. There were stones besides, some lying at random, as in all craggy places, and others heaped up designedly by the townsmen, to add to the security of the place. Having posted the Romans here, and shown them a steep and narrow path leading up from the town to the citadel—"From this ascent," said he, "even three armed men would keep off any multitude whatever. Now ye are ten in number; and, what is more, Romans, and the bravest among the Romans. The night is in your favour, which, from the uncertainty it occasions, magnifies every object to people once alarmed. I will immediately fill every place with terror: be ye alert in defending the citadel." He then ran down in haste, crying aloud, "To arms, citizens, we are undone, the citadel is taken by the enemy; run, defend it." This he repeated, as he passed the doors of the principal men, the same to all whom he met, and also to those who ran out in a fright into the streets. The alarm, communicated first by one, was soon spread by numbers through all the city. The magistrates, dismayed on hearing from scouts that the citadel was full of arms and armed men, whose number they multiplied, laid aside all hopes of recovering it. All places are filled with terror: the gates are broken open by persons half asleep, and for the most part unarmed, through one of which the body of Roman troops, roused by the noise, burst in, and slew the terrified inhabitants, who attempted to skirmish in the streets. Sora was now taken, when, at the first light, the consuls arrived, and accepted the surrender of those whom fortune had left remaining after the flight and slaughter of the night. Of these, they conveyed in chains to Rome two hundred and twenty-five, whom all men agreed in pointing out as the authors, both of the revolt, and also of the horrid massacre of the colonists. The rest they left in safety at Sora, a garrison being placed there. All those who were brought to Rome were beaten with rods in the forum, and beheaded, to the great joy of the commons, whose interest it most highly concerned, that the multitudes, sent to various places in colonies should be in safety.

The consuls, leaving Sora, turned their warlike operations against the lands and cities of the Ausonians; for all places had been set in commotion by the coming of the Samnites, when the battle was fought at Lautulæ: conspiracies likewise had been formed in several parts of Campania; nor was Capua itself clear of the charge: nay, the business spread even to Rome, and inquiries came to be instituted respecting some of the principal men there. However, the Ausonian nation fell into the Roman power, in the same manner as Sora, by their cities being betrayed: these were Ausona Minturnæ, and Vescia. Certain young men, of the principal families, twelve in number, having conspired to betray their respective cities, came to the consuls; they informed them that their countrymen, who had for a long time before honestly wished for the coming of the Samnites, on hearing of the battle at Lautulæ, had looked on the Romans as defeated, and had assisted the Samnites with supplies of young men and arms; but that, since the Samnites had been beaten out of the country, they were wavering between peace and war, not shutting their gates against the Romans, lest they should thereby invite an attack; yet determined to shut them if an army should approach; that in that fluctuating state they might easily be overpowered by surprise. By these men's advice the camp was moved nearer; and soldiers were sent, at the same time, to each of the three towns; some armed, who were to lie concealed in places near the walls; others, in the garb of peace, with swords hidden under their clothes, when, on the opening of the gates at the approach of day, were to enter into the cities. These latter began with killing the guards; at the same time, a signal was made to the men with arms, to hasten up from the ambuscades. Thus the gates were seized, and the three towns taken in the same hour and by the same device. But as the attacks were made in the absence of the generals, there were no bounds to the carnage which ensued; and the nation of the Ausonians, when there was scarcely any clear proof of the charge of its having revolted, was utterly destroyed, as if it had supported a contest through a deadly war.

During this year, Luceria fell into the hands of the Samnites, the Roman garrison being betrayed to the enemy. This matter did not long go unpunished with the traitors: the Roman army was not far off, by whom the city, which lay in a plain, was taken at the first onset. The Lucerians and Samnites were to a man put to the sword; and to such a length was resentment carried, that at Rome, on the senate being consulted about sending a colony to Luceria, many voted for the demolition of it. Besides, their hatred was of the bitterest kind, against a people whom they had been obliged twice to subdue by arms; the great distance, also, made them averse from sending away their citizens among nations so ill-affected towards them. However the resolution was carried, that the colonists should be sent; and accordingly two thousand five hundred were transported thither. This year, when all places were becoming disaffected to the Romans, secret conspiracies were formed among the leading men at Capua, as well as at other places; a motion concerning which being laid before the senate, the matter was by no means neglected. Inquiries were decreed, and it was resolved that a dictator should be appointed to enforce these inquiries. Caius Mænius was accordingly nominated, and he appointed Marcus Foslius master of the horse. People's dread of that office was very great, insomuch that the Calavii, Ovius and Novius, who were the heads of the conspiracy, either through fear of the dictator's power, or the consciousness of guilt, previous to the charge against them being laid in form before him, avoided, as appeared beyond doubt, trial by a voluntary death. As the subject of the inquiry in Campania was thus removed, the proceedings were then directed towards Rome: by construing the order of the senate to have meant, that inquiry should be made, not specially who at Capua, but generally who at any place had caballed or conspired against the state; for that cabals, for the attaining of honours, were contrary to the edicts of the state. The inquiry was extended to a greater latitude, with respect both to the matter, and to the kind of persons concerned, the dictator scrupling not to avow, that his power of research was unlimited: in consequence, some of the nobility were called to account; and though they applied to the tribunes for protection, no one interposed in their behalf, or to prevent the charges from being received. On this the nobles, not those only against whom the charge was levelled, but the whole body jointly insisted that such an imputation lay not against the nobles, to whom the way to honours lay open if not obstructed by fraud, but against the new men: so that even the dictator and master of the horse, with respect to that question, would appear more properly as culprits than suitable inquisitors; and this they should know as soon as they went out of office. Then indeed Mænius, who was more solicitous about his character than his office, advanced into the assembly and spoke to this effect, "Romans, both of my past life ye are all witnesses; and this honourable office, which ye conferred on me, is in itself a testimony of my innocence. For the dictator, proper to be chosen for holding these inquiries, was not, as on many other occasions, where the exigencies of the state so required, the man who was most renowned in war; but him whose counsel of life was most remote from such cabals. But certain of the nobility (for what reason it is more proper that ye should judge than that I, as a magistrate, should, without proof, insinuate) have laboured to stifle entirely the inquiries; and then, finding their strength unequal to it, rather than stand a trial have fled for refuge to the stronghold of their adversaries, an appeal and the support of the tribunes; and on being there also repulsed, (so fully were they persuaded that every other measure was safer than the attempt to clear themselves,) have made an attack upon us; and, though in private characters have not been ashamed of instituting a criminal process against a dictator. Now, that gods and men may perceive that they to avoid a scrutiny as to their own conduct, attempt even things which are impossible, and that I willingly meet the charge, and face the accusations of my enemies, I divest myself of the dictatorship. And, consuls, I beseech you, that if this business is put into your hands by the senate, ye make me and Marcus Foslius the first objects of our your examinations; that it may be manifested that we are safe from such imputations by our own innocence, not by the dignity of office." He then abdicated the dictatorship, as did Marcus Foslius, immediately after, his office of master of the horse; and being the first brought to trial before the consuls, for to them the senate had committed the business, they were most honourably acquitted of all the charges brought by the nobles. Even Publilius Philo, who had so often been invested with the highest honours, and had performed so many eminent services, both at home and abroad, being disagreeable to the nobility, was brought to trial, and acquitted. Nor did the inquiry continue respectable on account of the illustrious names of the accused, longer than while it was new, which is usually the case; it then began to descend to persons of inferior rank; and, at length, was suppressed, by means of those factions and cabals against which it had been instituted.

The accounts received of these matters, but more especially the hope of a revolt in Campania, for which a conspiracy had been formed, recalled the Samnites, who were turning towards Apulia, back to Caudium; so that from thence, being near, they might, if any commotion should open them an opportunity, snatch Capua out of the hands of the Romans. To the same place the consuls repaired with a powerful army. They both held back for some time, on the different sides of the defiles, the roads being dangerous to either party. Then the Samnites, making a short circuit through an open tract, marched down their troops into level ground in the Campanian plains, and there the hostile camps first came within view of each other. Trial of their strength in slight skirmishes was made on both sides, more frequently between the horse than the foot; and the Romans were no way dissatisfied either at the issue of these, or at the delay by which they protracted the war. The Samnite generals, on the contrary, considered that their battalions were becoming weakened daily by small losses, and the general vigour abated by prolonging the war. They therefore marched into the field, disposing their cavalry on both wings, with orders to give more heedful attention to the camp behind than to the battle; for that the line of infantry would be able to provide for their own safety. The consuls took post, Sulpicius on the right wing, Pœtelius on the left. The right wing was stretched out wider than usual, where the Samnites also stood formed in thin ranks, either with design of turning the flank of the enemy, or to avoid being themselves surrounded. On the left, besides that they were formed in more compact order, an addition was made to their strength, by a sudden act of the consul Pœtelius; for the subsidiary cohorts, which were usually reserved for the exigencies of a tedious fight, he brought up immediately to the front, and, in the first onset, pushed the enemy with the whole of his force. The Samnite line of infantry giving way, their cavalry advanced to support them; and as they were charging in an oblique direction between the two lines, the Roman horse, coming up at full speed, disordered their battalions and ranks of infantry and cavalry, so as to oblige the whole line on that side to give ground. The left wing had not only the presence of Pœtelius to animate them, but that of Sulpicius likewise; who, on the shout being first raised in that quarter, rode thither from his own division, which had not yet engaged. When he saw victory no longer doubtful there, he returned to his own post with twelve hundred men, but found the state of things there very different; the Romans driven from their ground, and the victorious enemy pressing on them thus dismayed. However, the arrival of the consul effected a speedy change in every particular; for, on the sight of their leader, the spirit of the soldiers was revived, and the bravery of the men who came with him rendered them more powerful aid than even their number; while the news of success in the other wing, which was heard, and after seen, restored the fight. From this time, the Romans became victorious through the whole extent of the line, and the Samnites, giving up the contest, were slain or taken prisoners, except such as made their escape to Maleventum, the town which is now called Beneventum. It is recorded that thirty thousand of the Samnites were slain or taken.

The consuls, after this important victory, led forward the legions to lay siege to Bovianum; and there they passed the winter quarters, until Caius Pœtelius, being nominated dictator, with Marcus Foslius, master of the horse, received the command of the army from the new consuls, Lucius Papirius Cursor a fifth, and Caius Junius Bubulcus a second time. On hearing that the citadel of Fregellæ was taken by the Samnites, he left Bovianum, and proceeded to Fregellæ, whence, having recovered possession of it without any contest, the Samnites abandoning it in the night, and having placed a strong garrison there, he returned to Campania, directing his operations principally to the recovery of Nola. Within the walls of this place, the whole multitude of the Samnites, and the inhabitants of the country about Nola, betook themselves on the approach of the dictator. Having taken a view of the situation of the city, in order that the approach to the fortifications may be the more open, he set fire to all the buildings which stood round the walls, which were very numerous; and, in a short time after, Nola was taken, either by the dictator Pœtelius, or the consul Caius Junius, for both accounts are given. Those who attribute to the consul the honour of taking Nola, add, that Atina and Calatia were also taken by him, and that Pœtelius was created dictator in consequence of a pestilence breaking out, merely for the purpose of driving the nail. The colonies of Suessa and Pontiæ were established in this year. Suessa had belonged to the Auruncians: the Volscians had occupied Pontiæ, an island lying within sight of their shore. A decree of the senate was also passed for conducting colonies to Interamna and Cassinum. But commissioners were appointed, and colonists, to the number of four thousand, were sent by the succeeding consuls, Marcus Valerius and Publius Decius.

The war with the Samnites being now nearly put an end to, before the Roman senate was freed from all concern on that side, a report arose of an Etrurian war; and there was not, in those times, any nation, excepting the Gauls, whose arms were more dreaded, by reason both of the vicinity of their country, and of the multitude of their men. While therefore one of the consuls prosecuted the remains of the war in Samnium, Publius Decius, who, being attacked by a severe illness, remained at Rome, by direction of the senate, nominated Caius Junius Bubulcus dictator. He, as the magnitude of the affair demanded, compelled all the younger citizens to enlist, and with the utmost diligence prepared arms, and the other matters which the occasion required. Yet he was not so elated by the power he had collected, as to think of commencing offensive operations, but prudently determined to remain quiet, unless the Etrurians should become aggressors. The plans of the Etrurians were exactly similar with respect to preparing for, and abstaining from, war: neither party went beyond their own frontiers. The censorship of Appius Claudius and Caius Plautius, for this year, was remarkable; but the name of Appius has been handed down with more celebrity to posterity, on account of his having made the road, [called after him, the Appian,] and for having conveyed water into the city. These works he performed alone; for his colleague, overwhelmed with shame by reason of the infamous and unworthy choice made of senators, had abdicated his office. Appius possessing that inflexibility Of temper, which, from the earliest times, had been the characteristic of his family, held on the censorship by himself. By direction of the same Appius, the Potitian family, in which the office of priests attendant on the great altar of Hercules was hereditary, instructed some of the public servants in the rites of that solemnity, with the intention to delegate the same to them. A circumstance is recorded, wonderful to be told, and one which should make people scrupulous of disturbing the established modes of religious solemnities: for though there were, at that time, twelve branches of the Potitian family, all grown-up persons, to the number of thirty, yet they were every one, together with their offspring, cut off within the year; so that the name of the Potitii became extinct, while the censor Appius also was, by the unrelenting wrath of the gods, some years after, deprived of sight.

The consuls of the succeeding year were, Caius Junius Bubulcus a third time, and Quintus Æmilius Barbula a second. In the commencement of their office, they complained before the people, that, by the improper choice of members of the senate, that body had been disgraced, several having been passed over who were preferable to the persons chosen in; and they declared, that they would pay no regard to such election, which had been made without distinction of right or wrong, merely to gratify interest or humour: they then immediately called over the list of the senate, in the same order which had existed before the censorship of Appius Claudius and Caius Plautius. Two public employments, both relating to military affairs, came this year into the disposal of the people; one being an order, that sixteen of the tribunes, for four legions, should be appointed by the people; whereas hitherto they had been generally in the gift of the dictators and consuls, very few of the places being left to suffrage. This order was proposed by Lucius Atilius and Caius Marcius, plebeian tribunes. Another was, that the people likewise should constitute two naval commissioners, for the equipping and refitting of the fleet. The person who introduced this order of the people, was Marcus Decius, plebeian tribune. Another transaction of this year I should pass over as trifling, did it not seem to bear some relation to religion. The flute-players, taking offence because they had been prohibited by the last censors from holding their repasts in the temple of Jupiter, which had been customary from very early times, went off in a body to Tibur; so that there was not one left in the city to play at the sacrifices. The religious tendency of this affair gave uneasiness to the senate; and they sent envoys to Tibur to endeavour that these men might be sent back to Rome. The Tiburtines readily promised compliance, and first, calling them into the senate-house, warmly recommended to them to return to Rome; and then, when they could not be prevailed on, practised on them an artifice not ill adapted to the dispositions of that description of people: on a festival day, they invited them separately to their several houses, apparently with the intention of heightening the pleasure of their feasts with music, and there plied them with wine, of which such people are always fond, until they laid them asleep. In this state of insensibility they threw them into waggons, and carried them away to Rome: nor did they know any thing of the matter, until, the waggons having been left in the forum, the light surprised them, still heavily sick from the debauch. The people then crowded about them, and, on their consenting at length to stay, privilege was granted them to ramble about the city in full dress, with music, and the licence which is now practised every year during three days. And that licence, which we see practised at present, and the right of being fed in the temple, was restored to those who played at the sacrifices. These incidents occurred while the public attention was deeply engaged by two most important wars.

The consuls adjusting the provinces between them, the Samnites fell by lot to Junius, the new war of Etruria to Æmilius. In Samnium the Samnites had blockaded and reduced by famine Cluvia, a Roman garrison, because they had been unable to take it by storm; and, after torturing with stripes, in a shocking manner, the townsmen who surrendered, they had put them to death. Enraged at this cruelty, Junius determined to postpone every thing else to the attacking of Cluvia; and, on the first day that he assaulted the walls, took it by storm, and slew all who were grown to man's estate. The victorious troops were led from thence to Bovianum; this was the capital of the Pentrian Samnites, by far the most opulent of their cities, and the most powerful both in men and arms. The soldiers, stimulated by the hope of plunder, for their resentment was not so violent, soon made themselves masters of the town: where there was less severity exercised on the enemy; but a quantity of spoil was carried off, greater almost than had ever been collected out of all Samnium, and the whole was liberally bestowed on the assailants. And when neither armies, camps, or cities could now withstand the vast superiority of the Romans in arms; the attention of all the leading men in Samnium became intent on this, that an opportunity should be sought for some stratagem, if by any chance the army, proceeding with incautious eagerness for plunder, could be caught in a snare and overpowered. Peasants who deserted and some prisoners (some thrown in their way by accident, some purposely) reporting to the consul a statement in which they concurred, and one which was at the same time true, that a vast quantity of cattle had been driven together into a defile of difficult access, prevailed on them to lead thither the legions lightly accoutred for plunder. Here a very numerous army of the enemy had posted themselves, secretly, at all the passes; and, as soon as they saw that the Romans had got into the defile, they rose up suddenly, with great clamour and tumult, and attacked them unawares. At first an event so unexpected caused some confusion, while they were taking their arms, and throwing the baggage into the centre; but, as fast as each had freed himself from his burden and fitted himself with arms, they assembled about the standards, from every side; and all, from the long course of their service, knowing their particular ranks, the line was formed of its own accord without any directions. The consul, riding up to the place where the fight was most warm, leaped from his horse, and called "Jupiter, Mars, and the other gods to witness, that he had come into that place, not in pursuit of any glory to himself, but of booty for his soldiers; nor could any other fault be charged on him, than too great a solicitude to enrich his soldiers at the expense of the enemy. From that disgrace nothing could extricate him but the valour of the troops: let them only join unanimously in a vigorous attack against a foe, already vanquished in the field, beaten out of their camps, and stripped of their towns, and now trying their last hope by the contrivance of an ambuscade, placing their reliance on the ground they occupied, not on their arms. But what ground was now unsurmountable to Roman valour?" The citadel of Fregellæ, and that of Sora, were called to their remembrance, with many other places where difficulties from situation had been surmounted. Animated by these exhortations, the soldiers, regardless of all difficulties, advanced against the line of the enemy, posted above them; and here there was some fatigue whilst the army was climbing the steep. But as soon as the first battalions got footing in the plain, on the summit, and the troops perceived that they now stood on equal ground, the dismay was instantly turned on the plotters; who, dispersing and casting away their arms, attempted, by flight, to recover the same lurking-places in which they had lately concealed themselves. But the difficulties of the ground, which had been intended for the enemy, now entangled them in the snares of their own contrivance. Accordingly very few found means to escape; twenty thousand men were slain, and the victorious Romans hastened in several parties to secure the booty of cattle, spontaneously thrown in their way by the enemy.

While such was the situation of affairs in Samnium, all the states of Etruria, except the Arretians, had taken arms, and vigorously commenced hostilities, by laying siege to Sutrium; which city, being in alliance with the Romans, served as a barrier against Etruria. Thither the other consul, Æmilius, came with an army to deliver the allies from the siege. On the arrival of the Romans, the Sutrians conveyed a plentiful supply of provisions into their camp, which was pitched before the city. The Etrurians spent the first day in deliberating whether they should expedite or protract the war. On the day following, when the speedier plan pleased the leaders in preference to the safer, as soon as the sun rose the for battle was displayed, and the troops marched out to the field; which being reported to the consul, he instantly commanded notice to be given, that they should dine, and after taking refreshment, then appear under arms. The order was obeyed; and the consul, seeing them armed and in readiness, ordered the standards to be carried forth beyond the rampart, and drew up his men at a small distance from the enemy. Both parties stood a long time with fixed attention, each waiting for the shout and fight to begin on the opposite side; and the sun had passed the meridian before a weapon was thrown by either side. Then, rather than leave the place without something being done, the shout was given by the Etrurians, the trumpets sounded, and the battalions advanced. With no less alertness do the Romans commence the fight: both rushed to the fight with violent animosity; the enemy were superior in numbers, the Romans in valour. The battle being doubtful, carries off great numbers on both sides, particularly the men of greatest courage; nor did victory declare itself, until the second line of the Romans came up fresh to the front, in the place of the first, who were much fatigued. The Etrurians, because their front line was not supported by any fresh reserves, fell all before and round the standards, and in no battle whatever would there have been seen less disposition to run, or a greater effusion of human blood, had not the night sheltered the Etrurians, who were resolutely determined on death; so that the victors, not the vanquished, were the first who desisted from fighting. After sunset the signal for retreat was given, and both parties retired in the night to their camps. During the remainder of the year, nothing memorable was effected at Sutrium; for, of the enemy's army, the whole first line had been cut off in one battle, the reserves only being left, who were scarce sufficient to guard the camp; and, among the Romans, so numerous were the wounds, that more wounded men died after the battle than had fallen in the field.

Quintus Fabius, consul for the ensuing year, succeeded to the command of the army at Sutrium; the colleague given to him was Caius Marcius Rutilus. On the one side, Fabius brought with him a reinforcement from Rome, and on the other, a new army had been sent for, and came from home, to the Etrurians. Many years had now passed without any disputes between the patrician magistrates and plebeian tribunes, when a contest took its rise from that family, which seemed raised by fate as antagonists to the tribunes and commons of those times; Appius Claudius, being censor, when the eighteen months had expired, which was the time limited by the Æmilian law for the duration of the censorship, although his colleague Caius Plautius had already resigned his office, could not be prevailed on, by any means, to give up his. There was a tribune of the commons, Publius Sempronius; he undertook to enforce a legal process for terminating the censorship within the lawful time, which was not more popular than just, nor more pleasing to the people generally than to every man of character in the city. After he frequently appealed to the Æmilian law, and bestowed commendations on Mamercus Æmilius, who, in his dictatorship, had been the author of it, for having contracted, within the space of a year and six months, the censorship, which formerly had lasted five years, and was a power which, in consequence of its long continuance, often became tyrannical, he proceeded thus: "Tell me, Appius Claudius, in what manner you would have acted, had you been censor, at the time when Caius Furius and Marcus Geganius were censors?" Appius insisted, that "the tribune's question was irrelevant to his case. For, although the Æmilian law might bind those censors, during whose magistracy it was passed,—because the people made that law after they had become censors; and whatever order is the last passed by the people, that is held to be the law, and valid:—yet neither he, nor any of those who had been created censors subsequent to the passing of that law, could be bound by it."

While Appius urged such frivolous arguments as these, which carried no conviction whatever, the other said, "Behold, Romans, the offspring of that Appius, who being created decemvir for one year, created himself for a second; and who, during a third, without being created even by himself or by any other, held on the fasces and the government though a private individual; nor ceased to continue in office, until the government itself, ill acquired, ill administered, and ill retained, overwhelmed him in ruin. This is the same family, Romans, by whose violence and injustice ye were compelled to banish yourselves from your native city, and seize on the Sacred mount; the same, against which ye provided for yourselves the protection of tribunes; the same, on account of which two armies of you took post on the Aventine; the same, which violently opposed the laws against usury, and always the agrarian laws; the same, which broke through the right of intermarriage between the patricians and the commons; the same, which shut up the road to curule offices against the commons: this is a name, more hostile to your liberty by far, than that of the Tarquins. I pray you, Appius Claudius, though this is now the hundredth year since the dictatorship of Mamercus Æmilius, though there have been so many men of the highest characters and abilities censors, did none of these ever read the twelve tables? none of them know, that, whatever was the last order of the people, that was law? Nay, certainly they all knew it; and they therefore obeyed the Æmilian law, rather than the old one, under which the censors had been at first created; because it was the last order; and because, when two laws are contradictory, the new always repeals the old. Do you mean to say, Appius, that the people are not bound by the Æmilian law? Or, that the people are bound, and you alone exempted? The Æmilian law bound those violent censors, Caius Furius and Marcus Geganius, who showed what mischief that office might do in the state; when, out of resentment for the limitation of their power, they disfranchised Mamercus Æmilius, the first man of the age, either in war or peace. It bound all the censors thenceforward, during the space of a hundred years. It binds Caius Plautius your colleague, created under the same auspices, with the same privileges. Did not the people create him with the fullest privileges with which any censor ever was created? Or is yours an excepted case, in which this peculiarity and singularity takes place? Shall the person, whom you create king of the sacrifices, laying hold of the style of sovereignty, say, that he was created with the fullest privileges with which any king was ever created at Rome? Who then, do you think, would be content with a dictatorship of six months? who, with the office of interrex for five days? Whom would you, with confidence, create dictator, for the purpose of driving the nail, or of exhibiting games? How foolish, how stupid, do ye think, those must appear in this man's eyes, who, after performing most important services, abdicated the dictatorship within the twentieth day; or who, being irregularly created, resigned their office? Why should I bring instances from antiquity? Lately, within these last ten years, Caius Mænius, dictator, having enforced inquiries, with more strictness than consisted with the safety of some powerful men, a charge was thrown out by his enemies, that he himself was infected with the very crime against which his inquiries were directed;—now Mænius, I say, in order that he might, in a private capacity, meet the imputation, abdicated the dictatorship. I expect not such moderation in you; you will not degenerate from your family, of all others the most imperious and assuming; nor resign your office a day, nor even an hour, before you are forced to it. Be it so: but then let no one exceed the time limited. It is enough to add a day, or a month, to the censorship. But Appius says, I will hold the censorship, and hold it alone, three years and six months longer than is allowed by the Æmilian law. Surely this is like kingly power. Or will you fill up the vacancy with another colleague, a proceeding not allowable, even in the case of the death of a censor? You are not satisfied that, as if a religious censor, you have degraded a most ancient solemnity, and the only one instituted by the very deity to whom it is performed, from priests of that rite who were of the highest rank to the ministry of mere servants. [You are not satisfied that] a family, more ancient than the origin of this city, and sanctified by an intercourse of hospitality with the immortal gods, has, by means of you and your censorship, been utterly extirpated, with all its branches, within the space of a year, unless you involve the whole commonwealth in horrid guilt, which my mind feels a horror even to contemplate. This city was taken in that lustrum in which Lucius Papirius Cursor, on the death of his colleague Julius, the censor, rather than resign his office, substituted Marcus Cornelius Maluginensis. Yet how much more moderate was his ambition, Appius, than yours! Lucius Papirius neither held the censorship alone, nor beyond the time prescribed by law. But still he found no one who would follow his example; all succeeding censors, in case of the death of a colleague, abdicated the office. As for you, neither the expiration of the time of your censorship, nor the resignation of your colleague, nor law, nor shame restrains you. You make fortitude to consist in arrogance, in boldness, in a contempt of gods and men. Appius Claudius, in consideration of the dignity and respect due to that office which you have borne, I should be sorry, not only to offer you personal violence, but even to address you in language too severe. With respect to what I have hitherto said, your pride and obstinacy forced me to speak. And now, unless you pay obedience to the Æmilian law, I shall order you to be led to prison. Nor, since a rule has been established by our ancestors, that in the election of censors unless two shall obtain the legal number of suffrages, neither shall be returned, but the election deferred,—will I suffer you, who could not singly be created censor, to hold the censorship without a colleague." Having spoken to this effect he ordered the censor to be seized, and borne to prison. But although six of the tribunes approved of the proceeding of their colleague, three gave their support to Appius, on his appealing to them, and he held the censorship alone, to the great disgust of all ranks of men.

While such was the state of affairs at Rome, the Etrurians had laid siege to Sutrium, and the consul Fabius, as he was marching along the foot of the mountains, with a design to succour the allies, and attempt the enemy's works, if it were by any means practicable, was met by their army prepared for battle. As the wide-extended plain below showed the greatness of their force, the consul, in order to remedy his deficiency in point of number, by advantage of the ground, changed the direction of his route a little towards the hills, where the way was rugged and covered with stones, and then formed his troops, facing the enemy. The Etrurians, thinking of nothing but their numbers, on which alone they depended, commence the fight with such haste and eagerness, that, in order to come the sooner to a close engagement, they threw away their javelins, drew their swords, rushing against the enemy. On the other side, the Romans poured down on them, sometimes javelins, and sometimes stones which the place abundantly supplied; so that whilst the blows on their shields and helmets confused even those whom they did not wound, (it was neither an easy matter to come to close quarters, nor had they missive weapons with which to fight at a distance,) when there was nothing now to protect them whilst standing and exposed to the blows, some even giving way, and the whole line wavering and unsteady the spearmen and the first rank, renewing the shout, rush on them with drawn swords. This attack the Etrurians could not withstand, but, facing about, fled precipitately towards their camp; when the Roman cavalry, getting before them by galloping obliquely across the plain, threw themselves in the way of their flight, on which they quitted the road, and bent their course to the mountains. From thence, in a body, almost without arms, and debilitated with wounds, they made their way into the Ciminian forest. The Romans, having slain in many thousands of the Etrurians, and taken thirty-eight military standards, took also possession of their camp, together with a vast quantity of spoil. They then began to consider of pursuing the enemy.

The Ciminian forest was in those days deemed as impassable and frightful as the German forests have been in latter times; not even any trader having ever attempted to pass it. Hardly any, besides the general himself, showed boldness enough to enter it; the others had not the remembrance of the disaster at Caudium effaced from their mind. On this, of those who were present, Marcus Fabius, the consul's brother, (some say Cæso, others Caius Claudius, born of the same mother with the consul,) undertook to go and explore the country, and to bring them in a short time an account of every particular. Being educated at Cære, where he had friends, he was perfectly acquainted with the Etrurian language. I have seen it affirmed, that, in those times, the Roman youth were commonly instructed in the Etrurian learning, as they are now in the Greek: but it is more probable, that there was something very extraordinary in the person who acted so daringly a counterfeit part, and mixed among the enemy. It is said, that his only attendant was a slave, who had been bred up with him, and who was therefore not ignorant of the same language. They received no further instructions at their departure, than a summary description of the country through which they were to pass; to this was added the names of the principal men in the several states, to prevent their being at a loss in conversation, and from being discovered by making some mistake. They set out in the dress of shepherds, armed with rustic weapons, bills, and two short javelins each. But neither their speaking the language of the country, nor the fashion of their dress and arms, concealed them so effectually, as the incredible circumstance of a stranger's passing the Ciminian forest. They are said to have penetrated as far as the Camertian district of the Umbrians: there the Romans ventured to own who they were, and being introduced to the senate, treated with them, in the name of the consul, about an alliance and friendship; and after being entertained with courteous hospitality, were desired to acquaint the Romans, that if they came into those countries, there should be provisions in readiness for the troops sufficient for thirty days, and that they should find the youth of the Camertian Umbrians prepared in arms to obey their commands. When this information was brought to the consul, he sent forward the baggage at the first watch, ordering the legions to march in the rear of it. He himself staid behind with the cavalry, and the next day, as soon as light appeared, rode up to the posts of the enemy, which had been stationed on the outside of the forest; and, when he had detained them there for a sufficient length of time, he retired to his camp, and marching out by the opposite gate, overtook the main body of the army before night. At the first light, on the following day, he had gained the summit of Mount Ciminius, from whence having a view of the opulent plains of Etruria, he let loose his soldiers upon them. When a vast booty had been driven off, some tumultuary cohorts of Etrurian peasants, hastily collected by the principal inhabitants of the district, met the Romans; but in such disorderly array, that these rescuers of the prey were near becoming wholly a prey themselves. These being slain or put to flight, and the country laid waste to a great extent, the Romans returned to their camp victorious, and enriched with plenty of every kind. It happened that, in the mean time, five deputies, with two plebeian tribunes, had come hither, to charge Fabius, in the name of the senate, not to attempt to pass the Ciminian forest. These, rejoicing that they had arrived too late to prevent the expedition, returned to Rome with the news of its success.

By this expedition of the consul, the war, instead of being brought nearer to a conclusion, was only spread to a wider extent: for all the tract adjacent to the foot of Mount Ciminius had felt his devastations; and, out of the indignation conceived thereat, had roused to arms, not only the states of Etruria, but the neighbouring parts of Umbria. They came therefore to Sutrium, with such a numerous army as they had never before brought into the field; and not only ventured to encamp on the outside of the wood, but through their earnest desire of coming to an engagement as soon as possible, marched down the plains to offer battle. The troops, being marshalled, stood at first, for some time, on their own ground, having left a space sufficient for the Romans to draw up, opposite to them; but perceiving that the enemy declined fighting, they advanced to the rampart; where, when they observed that even the advanced guards had retired within the works, a shout at once was raised around their generals, that they should order provisions for that day to be brought down to them: "for they were resolved to remain there under arms; and either in the night, or, at all events, at the dawn of day, to attack the enemy's camp." The Roman troops, though not less eager for action, were restrained by the commands of the general. About the tenth hour, the consul ordered his men a repast; and gave directions that they should be ready in arms, at whatever time of the day or night he should give the signal. He then addressed a few words to them; spoke in high terms of the wars of the Samnites, and disparagingly of the Etrurians, who "were not," he said, "as an enemy to be compared with other enemies, nor as a numerous force, with others in point of numbers. Besides, he had an engine at work, as they should find in due time; at present it was of importance to keep it secret." By these hints he intimated that the enemy was circumvented in order to raise the courage of his men, damped by the superiority of the enemy's force; and, from their not having fortified the post where they lay, the insinuation of a stratagem formed against them seemed the more credible. After refreshing themselves, they consigned themselves to rest, and being roused without noise, about the fourth watch, took arms. Axes are distributed among the servants following the army, to tear down the rampart and fill up the trench. The line was formed within the works, and some chosen cohorts posted close to the gates. Then, a little before day, which in summer nights is the time of the profoundest sleep, the signal being given, the rampart was levelled, and the troops rushing forth, fell upon the enemy, who were every where stretched at their length. Some were put to death before they could stir; others half asleep, in their beds; the greatest part, while they ran in confusion to arms; few, in short, had time afforded them to arm themselves; and these, who followed no particular leader, nor orders, were quickly routed by the Romans and pursued by the Roman horse. They fled different ways; to the camp and to the woods. The latter afforded the safer refuge; for the former, being situated in a plain, was taken the same day. The gold and silver was ordered to be brought to the consul; the rest of the spoil was given to the soldiers. On that day, sixty thousand of the enemy were slain or taken. Some affirm, that this famous battle was fought on the farther side of the Ciminian forest, at Perusia; and that the public had been under great dread, lest the army might be enclosed in such a dangerous pass, and overpowered by a general combination of the Etrurians and Umbrians. But on whatever spot it was fought, it is certain that the Roman power prevailed; and, in consequence thereof, ambassadors from Perusia, Cortona, and Arretium, which were then among the principal states of Etruria, soliciting a peace and alliance with the Romans, obtained a truce for thirty years.

During these transactions in Etruria, the other consul, Caius Marcius Rutilus, took Allifæ by storm from the Samnites; and many of their forts, and smaller towns, were either destroyed by his arms, or surrendered without being injured. About the same time also, the Roman fleet, having sailed to Campania, under Publius Cornelius, to whom the senate had given the command on the sea-coast, put into Pompeii. Immediately on landing, the soldiers of the fleet set out to ravage the country about Nuceria: and after they had quickly laid waste the parts which lay nearest, and whence they could have returned to the ships with safety, they were allured by the temptation of plunder, as it often happens, to advance too far, and thereby roused the enemy against them. While they rambled about the country, they met no opposition, though they might have been cut off to a man; but as they were returning, in a careless manner, the peasants overtook them, not far from the ships, stripped them of the booty, and even slew a great part of them. Those who escaped were driven in confusion to the ships. As Fabius' having marched through the Ciminian forest had occasioned violent apprehensions at Rome, so it had excited joy in proportion among the enemy in Samnium: they talked of the Roman army being pent up, and surrounded; and of the Caudine forks, as a model of their defeat. "Those people," they said, "ever greedy after further acquisitions, were now brought into inextricable difficulties, hemmed in, not more effectually by the arms of their enemy, than by the disadvantage of the ground." Their joy was even mingled with a degree of envy, because fortune, as they thought, had transferred the glory of finishing the Roman war, from the Samnites to the Etrurians: they hastened, therefore, with their whole collected force, to crush the consul Caius Marcius; resolving, if he did not give them an opportunity of fighting, to proceed, through the territories of the Marsians and Sabines, into Etruria. The consul met them, and a battle was fought with great fury on both sides, but without a decisive issue. Although both parties suffered severely, yet the discredit of defeat fell on the Romans, because several of equestrian rank, some military tribunes, with one lieutenant-general, had fallen; and, what was more remarkable than all, the consul himself was wounded. On account of this event, exaggerated by report as is usual, the senate became greatly alarmed, so that they resolved on having a dictator nominated. No one entertained a doubt that the nomination would light on Papirius Cursor, who was then universally deemed to possess the greatest abilities as a commander: but they could not be certain, either that a message might be conveyed with safety into Samnium, where all was in a state of hostility, or that the consul Marcius was alive. The other consul, Fabius, was at enmity with Papirius, on his own account; and lest this resentment might prove an obstacle to the public good, the senate voted that deputies of consular rank should be sent to him, who, uniting their own influence to that of government, might prevail on him to drop, for the sake of his country, all remembrance of private animosities. When the deputies, having come to Fabius, delivered to him the decree of the senate, adding such arguments as were suitable to their instructions, the consul, casting his eyes towards the ground, retired in silence, leaving them in uncertainty what part he intended to act. Then, in the silent time of the night, according to the established custom, he nominated Lucius Papirius dictator. When the deputies returned him thanks, for so very meritoriously subduing his passion, he still persevered in obstinate silence, and dismissed them without any answer, or mention of what he had done: a proof that he felt an extraordinary degree of resentment, which had been suppressed within his breast. Papirius appointed Caius Junius Bubulcus master of the horse; and, as he was proceeding in an assembly of the Curiae [3] to get an order passed respecting the command of the army, an unlucky omen obliged him to adjourn it; for the Curia which was to vote first, happened to be the Faucian, remarkably distinguished by two disasters, the taking of the city, and the Caudine peace; the same Curia having voted first in those years in which the said events are found. Licinius Macer supposes this Curia ominous, also, on account of a third misfortune, that which was experienced at the Cremera.

Next day the dictator, taking the auspices anew, obtained the order, and, marching out at the head of the legions, lately raised on the alarm occasioned by the army passing the Ciminian forest, came to Longula; where having received the old troops of the consul Marcius, he led on his forces to battle; nor did the enemy seem to decline the combat. However, they stood drawn up for battle and under arms, until night came on; neither side choosing to begin the fray. After this, they continued a considerable time encamped near each other, without coming to action; neither diffident of their own strength, nor despising the adversary. Meanwhile matters went on actively in Etruria; for a decisive battle was fought with the Umbrians, in which the enemy was routed, but lost not many men, for they did not maintain the fight with the vigour with which they began it. Besides this the Etrurians, having raised an army under the sanctions of the devoting law, each man choosing another, came to an engagement at the Cape of Vadimon, with more numerous forces, and, at the same time, with greater spirit than they had ever shown before. The battle was fought with such animosity that no javelins were thrown by either party: swords alone were made use of; and the fury of the combatants was still higher inflamed by the long-continued contest; so that it appeared to the Romans as if they were disputing, not with Etrurians, whom they had so often conquered, but with a new race. Not the semblance of giving ground appeared in any part; the first lines fell; and lest the standards should be exposed, without defence, the second lines were formed in their place. At length, even the men forming the last reserves were called into action; and to such an extremity of difficulty and danger had they come, that the Roman cavalry dismounted, and pressed forward, through heaps of arms and bodies, to the front ranks of the infantry. These starting up a new army, as it were, among men now exhausted, disordered the battalions of the Etrurians; and the rest, weak as their condition was, seconding their assault, broke at last through the enemy's ranks. Their obstinacy then began to give way: some companies quitted their posts, and, as soon as they once turned their backs, betook themselves to more decided flight. That day first broke the strength of the Etrurians, now grown exuberant through a long course of prosperity; all the flower of their men were cut off in the field, and in the same assault their camp was seized and sacked.

Equal danger, and an issue equally glorious, soon after attended the war with the Samnites; who, besides their many preparations for the field, made their army to glitter with new decorations of their armour. Their troops were in two divisions, one of which had their shields embossed with gold, the other with silver. The shape of the shield was this; broad at the middle to cover the breast and shoulders, the summit being flat, sloping off gradually so as to become pointed below, that it might be wielded with ease; a loose coat of mail also served as a protection for the breast, and the left leg was covered with a greave; their helmets were adorned with plumes, to add to the appearance of their stature. The golden-armed soldiers wore tunics of various colours; the silver-armed, of white linen. To the latter the right wing was assigned; the former took post on the left. The Romans had been apprized of these splendid accoutrements, and had been taught by their commanders, that "a soldier ought to be rough; not decorated with gold and silver, but placing his confidence in his sword. That matters of this kind were in reality spoil rather than armour; glittering before action, but soon becoming disfigured amid blood and wounds. That the brightest ornament of a soldier was valour; that all those trinkets would follow victory, and that those rich enemies would be valuable prizes to the conquerors, however poor." Cursor, having animated his men with these observations, led them on to battle. He took post himself on the right wing, he gave the command of the left to the master of the horse. As soon as they engaged, the struggle between the two armies became desperate, while it was no less so between the dictator and the master of the horse, on which wing victory should first show itself. It happened that Junius first, with the left wing, made the right of the enemy give way; this consisted of men devoted after the custom of Samnites, and on that account distinguished by white garments and armour of equal whiteness. Junius, saying "he would sacrifice these to Pluto," pressed forward, disordered their ranks, and made an evident impression on their line: which being perceived by the dictator, he exclaimed, "Shall the victory begin on the left wing, and shall the right, the dictator's own troops, only second the arms of others, and not claim the greatest share of the victory?" This spurred on the soldiers: nor did the cavalry yield to the infantry in bravery, nor the ardour of lieutenants-general to that of the commanders. Marcius Valerius from the right wing, and Publius Decius from the left, both men of consular rank, rode off to the cavalry, posted on the extremities of the line, and, exhorting them to join in putting in for a share of the honour, charged the enemy on the flanks. When the addition of this new alarm assailed the enemies' troops on both sides, and the Roman legions, having renewed the shout to confound the enemy, rushed on, they began to fly. And now the plains were quickly filled with heaps of bodies and splendid armour. At first, their camp received the dismayed Samnites; but they did not long retain even the possession of that: before night it was taken, plundered, and burnt. The dictator triumphed, in pursuance of a decree of the senate; and the most splendid spectacle by far, of any in his procession, was the captured arms: so magnificent were they deemed, that the shields, adorned with gold, were distributed among the owners of the silver shops, to serve as embellishments to the forum. Hence, it is said, arose the custom of the forum being decorated by the ædiles, when the grand processions are made on occasion of the great games. The Romans, indeed, converted these extraordinary arms to the honour of the gods: but the Campanians, out of pride, and in hatred of the Samnites, gave them as ornaments to their gladiators, who used to be exhibited as a show at their feasts, and whom they distinguished by the name of Samnites. During this year, the consul Fabius fought with the remnants of the Etrurians at Perusia, which city also had violated the truce, and gained an easy and decisive victory. He would have taken the town itself (for he marched up to the walls,) had not deputies come out and capitulated. Having placed a garrison at Perusia, and sent on before him to the Roman senate the embassies of Etruria, who solicited friendship, the consul rode into the city in triumph, for successes more important than those of the dictator. Besides, a great share of the honour of reducing the Samnites was attributed to the lieutenants-general, Publius Decius and Marcius Valerius: whom, at the next election, the people, with universal consent, declared the one consul, the other prætor.

To Fabius, in consideration of his extraordinary merit in the conquest of Etruria, the consulship was continued. Decius was appointed his colleague. Valerius was created prætor a fourth time. The consuls divided the provinces between them. Etruria fell to Decius, Samnium to Fabius. The latter, having marched to Nuceria, rejected the application of the people of Alfaterna, who then sued for peace, because they had not accepted it when offered, and by force of arms compelled them to surrender. A battle was fought with the Samnites; the enemy were overcome without much difficulty: nor would the memory of that engagement have been preserved, except that in it the Marsians first appeared in arms against the Romans. The Pelignians, imitating the defection of the Marsians, met the same fate. The other consul, Decius, was likewise very successful in his operations: through terror he compelled the Tarquinians to supply his army with corn, and to sue for a truce for forty years. He took several forts from the Volsinians by assault, some of which he demolished, that they might not serve as receptacles to the enemy, and by extending his operations through every quarter, diffused such a dread of his arms, that the whole Etrurian nation sued to the consul for an alliance: this they did not obtain; but a truce for a year was granted them. The pay of the Roman army for that year was furnished by the enemy; and two tunics for each soldier were exacted from them: this was the purchase of the truce. The tranquillity now established in Etruria was interrupted by a sudden insurrection of the Umbrians, a nation which had suffered no injury from the war, except what inconvenience the country had felt in the passing of the army. These, by calling into the field all their own young men, and forcing a great part of the Etrurians to resume their arms, made up such a numerous force, that speaking of themselves with ostentatious vanity and of the Romans with contempt, they boasted that they would leave Decius behind in Etruria, and march away to besiege Rome; which design of theirs being reported to the consul Decius, he removed by long marches from Etruria towards their city, and sat down in the district of Pupinia, in readiness to act according to the intelligence received of the enemy. Nor was the insurrection of the Umbrians slighted at Rome: their very threats excited tears among the people, who had experienced, in the calamities suffered from the Gauls, how insecure a city they inhabited. Deputies were therefore despatched to the consul Fabius with directions, that, if he had any respite from the war of the Samnites, he should with all haste lead his army into Umbria. The consul obeyed the order, and by forced marches proceeded to Mevania, where the forces of the Umbrians then lay. The unexpected arrival of the consul, whom they had believed to be sufficiently employed in Samnium, far distant from their country, so thoroughly affrighted the Umbrians, that several advised retiring to their fortified towns; others, the discontinuing the war. However, one district, called by themselves Materina, prevailed on the rest not only to retain their arms, but to come to an immediate engagement. They fell upon Fabius while he was fortifying his camp. When the consul saw them rushing impetuously towards his rampart, he called off his men from the work, and drew them up in the best manner which the nature of the place and the time allowed; encouraging them by displaying, in honourable and just terms, the glory which they had acquired, as well in Etruria as in Samnium, he bade them finish this insignificant appendage to the Etrurian war, and take vengeance for the impious expressions in which these people had threatened to attack the city of Rome. Such was the alacrity of the soldiers on hearing this, that, raising the shout spontaneously, they interrupted the general's discourse, and, without waiting for orders, advanced, with the sound of all the trumpets and cornets, in full speed against the enemy. They made their attack not as on men, or at least men in arms, but, what must appear wonderful in the relation, began by snatching the standards out of the hands which held them; and then, the standard-bearers themselves were dragged to the consul, and the armed soldiers transferred from the one line to the other; and wherever resistance was any where made, the business was performed, not so much with swords, as with their shields, with the bosses of which, and thrusts of their elbows, they bore down the foe. The prisoners were more numerous than the slain, and through the whole line the Umbrians called on each other, with one voice, to lay down their arms.

Thus a surrender was made in the midst of action, by the first promoters of the war; and on the next and following days, the other states of the Umbrians also surrendered. The Ocriculans were admitted to a treaty of friendship on giving security.

Fabius, successful in a war allotted to another, led back his army into his own province. And as, in the preceding year, the people had, in consideration of his services so successfully performed, re-elected him to the consulship, so now the senate, from the same motive, notwithstanding a warm opposition made by Appius, prolonged his command for the year following, in which Appius Claudius and Lucius Volumnius were consuls. In some annals I find, that Appius, still holding the office of censor, declared himself a candidate for the consulship, and that his election was stopped by a protest of Lucius Furius, plebeian tribune, until he resigned the censorship. After his election to the consulship, the new war with the Sallentine enemies being decreed to his colleague, he remained at Rome, with design to increase his interest by city intrigues, since the means of procuring honour in war were placed in the hands of others. Volumnius had no reason to be dissatisfied with his province: he fought many battles with good success, and took several cities by assault. He was liberal in his donations of the spoil; and this munificence, engaging in itself, he enhanced by his courteous demeanour, by which conduct he inspired his soldiers with ardour to meet both toil and danger. Quintus Fabius, proconsul, fought a pitched battle with the armies of the Samnites, near the city of Allifæ. The victory was complete. The enemy were driven from the field, and pursued to their camp; nor would they have kept possession of that, had not the day been almost spent. It was invested, however, before night, and guarded until day, lest any should slip away. Next morning, while it was scarcely clear day, they proposed to capitulate, and it was agreed, that such as were natives of Samnium should be dismissed with single garments. All these were sent under the yoke. No precaution was taken in favour of the allies of the Samnites: they were sold by auction, to the number of seven thousand. Those who declared themselves subjects of the Hernicians, were kept by themselves under a guard. All these Fabius sent to Rome to the senate; and, after being examined, whether it was in consequence of a public order, or as volunteers, that they had carried arms on the side of the Samnites against the Romans, they were distributed among the states of the Latins to be held in custody; and it was ordered, that the new consuls, Publius Cornelius Arvina and Quintus Marcius Tremulus, who by this time had been elected, should lay that affair entire before the senate: this gave such offence to the Hernicians, that, at a meeting of all the states, assembled by the Anagnians, in the circus called the Maritime, the whole nation of the Hernicians, excepting the Alatrians, Ferentines, and Verulans, declared war against the Roman people.

In Samnium also, in consequence of the departure of Fabius, new commotions arose. Calatia and Sora, and the Roman garrisons stationed there, were taken, and extreme cruelty was exercised towards the captive soldiers: Publius Cornelius was therefore sent thither with an army. The command against the new enemy (for by this time an order had passed for declaring war against the Anagnians, and the rest of the Hernicians) was decreed to Marcius. These, in the beginning, secured all the passes between the camps of the consuls, in such a manner, that no messenger, however expert, could make his way from one to the other; and each consul spent several days in absolute uncertainty regarding every matter and in anxious suspense concerning the state of the other. Apprehensions for their safety spread even to Rome; so that all the younger citizens were compelled to enlist and two regular armies were raised, to answer sudden emergencies. The conduct of the Hernicians during the progress of the war afterwards, showed nothing suitable to the present alarm, or to the ancient renown of that nation. Without ever venturing any effort worth mentioning, being stripped of three different camps within a few days, they stipulated for a truce of thirty days, during which they might send to Rome, to the senate, on the terms of furnishing two months' pay, and corn, and a tunic to every soldier. They were referred back to Marcius by the senate, whom by a decree they empowered to determine regarding the Hernicians, and he accepted their submission. Meanwhile, in Samnium, the other consul, though superior in strength, was very much embarrassed by the nature of his situation; the enemy had blocked up all the roads, and seized on the passable defiles, so that no provisions could be conveyed; nor could the consul, though he daily drew out his troops and offered battle, allure them to an engagement. It was evident, that neither could the Samnites support an immediate contest, nor the Romans a delay of action. The approach of Marcius, who, after he had subdued the Hernicians, hastened to the succour of his colleague, put it out of the enemy's power any longer to avoid fighting: for they, who had not deemed themselves a match in the field, even for one of the armies, could not surely suppose that if they should allow the two consular armies to unite, they could have any hope remaining: they made an attack therefore on Marcius, as he was approaching in the irregular order of march. The baggage was hastily thrown together in the centre, and the line formed as well as the time permitted. First the shout which reached the standing camp of Cornelius, then the dust observed at a distance, excited a bustle in the camp of the other consul. Ordering his men instantly to take arms, and leading them out to the field with the utmost haste, he charged the flank of the enemy's line, which had enough to do in the other dispute, at the same time exclaiming, that "it would be the height of infamy if they suffered Marcius's army to monopolize the honour of both victories, and did not assert their claim to the glory of their own war." He bore down all before him, and pushed forward, through the midst of the enemy's line, to their camp, which, being left without a guard, he took and set on fire; which when the soldiers of Marcius saw in flames, and the enemy observed it on looking about, a general flight immediately took place among the Samnites. But they could not effect an escape in any direction; in every quarter they met death. After a slaughter of thirty thousand men, the consuls had now given the signal for retreat; and were collecting, into one body, their several forces, who were employed in mutual congratulations, when some new cohorts of the enemy, which had been levied for a reinforcement, being seen at a distance, occasioned a renewal of the carnage. On these the conquerors rushed, without any order of the consuls, or signal received, crying out, that they would make these Samnites pay dearly for their introduction to service. The consuls indulged the ardour of the legions, well knowing that the raw troops of the enemy, mixed with veterans dispirited by defeat, would be incapable even of attempting a contest. Nor were they wrong in their judgment: all the forces of the Samnites, old and new, fled to the nearest mountains. These the Roman army also ascended, so that no situation afforded safety to the vanquished; they were beaten off, even from the summits which they had seized. And now they all, with on voice, supplicated for a suspension of arms. On which, being ordered to furnish corn for three months, pay for a year, and a tunic to each of the soldiers, they sent deputies to the senate to sue for peace. Cornelius was left in Samnium. Marcius returned into the city, in triumph over the Hernicians; and a decree was passed for erecting to him, in the forum, an equestrian statue, which was placed before the temple of Castor. To three states of the Hernicians, (the Alatrians, Verulans, and Ferentines,) their own laws were restored, because they preferred these to the being made citizens of Rome; and they were permitted to intermarry with each other, a privilege which they alone of the Hernicians, for a long time after, enjoyed. To the Anagnians, and the others, who had made war on the Romans, was granted the freedom of the state, without the right of voting; public assemblies, and intermarriages, were not allowed them, and their magistrates were prohibited from acting except in the ministration of public worship. During this year, Caius Junius Bubulcus, censor, contracted for the building of a temple to Health, which he had vowed during his consulate in the war with the Samnites. By the same person, and his colleague, Marcus Valerius Maximus, roads were made through the fields at the public expense. During the same year the treaty with the Carthaginians was renewed a third time, and ample presents made to their ambassadors who came on that business.

This year had a dictator in office, Publius Cornelius Scipio, with Publius Decius Mus, master of the horse. By these the election of consuls was held, being the purpose for which they had been created, because neither of the consuls could be absent from the armies. The consuls elected were Lucius Postumius and Titus Minucius; whom Piso places next after Quintus Fabius and Publius Decius, omitting the two years in which I have set down Claudius with Volumnius, and Cornelius with Marcius, as consuls. Whether this happened through a lapse of memory in digesting his annals, or whether he purposely passed over those two consulates as deeming the accounts of them false, cannot be ascertained. During this year the Samnites made incursions into the district of Stellæ in the Campanian territory. Both the consuls were therefore sent into Samnium, and proceeded to different regions, Postumius to Tifernum, Minucius to Bovianum. The first engagement happened at Tifernum, under the command of Postumius. Some say, that the Samnites were completely defeated, and twenty thousand of them made prisoners. Others, that the army separated without victory on either side; and that Postumius, counterfeiting fear, withdrew his forces privately by night, and marched away to the mountains; whither the enemy also followed, and took possession of a stronghold two miles distant. The consul, having created a belief that he had come thither for the sake of a safe post, and a fruitful spot, (and such it really was,) secured his camp with strong works. Furnishing it with magazines of every thing useful, he left a strong guard to defend it; and at the third watch, led away the legions lightly accoutred, by the shortest road which he could take, to join his colleague, who lay opposite to his foe. There, by advice of Postumius, Minucius came to an engagement with the enemy; and when the fight had continued doubtful through a great part of the day, Postumius, with his fresh legions, made an unexpected attack on the enemy's line, spent by this time with fatigue: thus, weariness and wounds having rendered them incapable even of flying, they were cut off to a man, and twenty-one standards taken. The Romans then proceeded to Postumius's station, where the two victorious armies falling upon the enemy, already dismayed by the news of what had passed, routed and dispersed them: twenty-six military standards were taken here, and the Samnite general, Statius Gellius, with a great number of other prisoners, and both the camps were taken. Next day Bovianum was besieged, and soon after taken. Both the consuls were honoured with a triumph, with high applause of their excellent conduct. Some writers say, that the consul Minucius was brought back to the camp grievously wounded, and that he died there; that Marcus Fulvius was substituted consul in his place, and that it was he who, being sent to command Minucius's army, took Bovianum. During the same year, Sora, Arpinum, and Censennia were recovered from the Samnites. The great statue of Hercules was erected in the Capitol, and dedicated.

In the succeeding consulate of Publius Sulpicius Saverrio and Publius Sempronius Sophus, the Samnites, desirous either of a termination or a suspension of hostilities, sent ambassadors to Rome to treat of peace; to whose submissive solicitations this answer was returned, that, "had not the Samnites frequently solicited peace, at times when they were actually preparing for war, their present application might, perhaps, in the course of negotiating, have produced the desired effect. But now, since words had hitherto proved vain, people's conduct must be guided by facts: that Publius Sempronius the consul would shortly be in Samnium with an army: that he could not be deceived in judging whether their dispositions inclined to peace or war. He would bring the senate certain information respecting every particular, and their ambassadors might follow the consul on his return from Samnium." When the Roman army accordingly marched through all parts of Samnium, which was in a state of peace, provisions being liberally supplied, a renewal of the old treaty was, this year, granted to the Samnites. The Roman arms were then turned against the Æquans, their old enemies, but who had, for many years past, remained quiet, under the guise of a treacherous peace, because, while the Hernicians were in a state of prosperity, these had, in conjunction with them, frequently sent aid to the Samnites; and after the Hernicians were subdued, almost the whole nation, without dissembling that they acted by public authority, had revolted to the enemy; and when, after the conclusion of the treaty with the Samnites at Rome, ambassadors were sent to demand satisfaction, they said, that "this was only a trial made of them, on the expectation that they would through fear suffer themselves to be made Roman citizens. But how much that condition was to be wished for, they had been taught by the Hernicians; who, when they had the option, preferred their own laws to the freedom of the Roman state. To people who wished for liberty to choose what they judged preferable, the necessity of becoming Roman citizens would have the nature of a punishment." In resentment of these declarations, uttered publicly in their assemblies, the Roman people ordered war to be made on the Æquans; and, in prosecution of this new undertaking, both the consuls marched from the city, and sat down at the distance of four miles from the camp of the enemy. The troops of the Æquans, like tumultuary recruits, in consequence of their having passed such a number of years without waging war on their own account, were all in disorder and confusion, without established officers and without command. Some advised to give battle, others to defend the camp; the greater part were influenced by concern for the devastation of their lands, likely to take place, and the consequent destruction of their cities, left with weak garrisons. Among a variety of propositions, one, however, was heard which, abandoning all concern for the public interest, tended to transfer every man's attention to the care of his private concerns. It recommended that, at the first watch, they should depart from the camp by different roads, so as to carry all their effects into the cities, and to secure them by the strength of the fortifications; this they all approved with universal assent. When the enemy were now dispersed through the country, the Romans, at the first dawn, marched out to the field, and drew up in order of battle; but no one coming to oppose them, they advanced in a brisk pace to the enemy's camp. But when they perceived neither guards before the gates, nor soldiers on the ramparts, nor the usual bustle of a camp,—surprised at the extraordinary silence, they halted in apprehension of some stratagem. At length, passing over the rampart, and finding the whole deserted, they proceeded to search out the tracks of the enemy. But these, as they scattered themselves to every quarter, occasioned perplexity at first. Afterwards discovering their design by means of scouts, they attacked their cities, one after another, and within the space of fifty days took, entirely by force, forty-one towns, most of which were razed and burnt, and the race of the Æquans almost extirpated. A triumph was granted over the Æquans. The Marrucinians, Marsians,

Pelignians, and Ferentans, warned by the example of their disasters, sent deputies to Rome to solicit peace and friendship; and these states, on their submissive applications, were admitted into alliance.

In the same year, Cneius Flavius, son of Cneius, grandson of a freed man, a notary, in low circumstances originally, but artful and eloquent, was appointed curule ædile. I find in some annals, that, being in attendance on the ædiles, and seeing that he was voted ædile by the prerogative tribe, but that his name would not be received, because he acted as a notary, he threw down his tablet, and took an oath, that he would not, for the future, follow that business. But Licinius Macer contends, that he had dropped the employment of notary a considerable time before, having already been a tribune, and twice a triumvir, once for regulating the nightly watch, and another time for conducting a colony. However, of this there is no dispute, that against the nobles, who threw contempt on the meanness of his condition, he contended with much firmness. He made public the rules of proceeding in judicial causes, hitherto shut up in the closets of the pontiffs; and hung up to public view, round the forum, the calendar on white tablets, that all might know when business could be transacted in the courts. To the great displeasure of the nobles, he performed the dedication of the temple of Concord, in the area of Vulcan's temple; and the chief pontiff, Cornelius Barbatus, was compelled by the united instances of the people, to dictate to him the form of words, although he affirmed, that, consistently with the practice of antiquity, no other than a consul, or commander-in-chief, could dedicate a temple. This occasioned a law to be proposed to the people, by direction of the senate, that no person should dedicate a temple, or an altar, without an order from the senate, or from a majority of the plebeian tribunes. The incident which I am about to mention would be trivial in itself, were it not an instance of the freedom assumed by plebeians in opposition to the pride of the nobles. When Flavius had come to make a visit to his colleague, who was sick, and when, by an arrangement between some young nobles who were sitting there, they did not rise on his entrance, he ordered his curule chair to be brought thither, and from his honourable seat of office enjoyed the sight of his enemies tortured with envy. However, a low faction, which had gathered strength during the censorship of Appius Claudius, had made Flavius an ædile; for he was the first who degraded the senate, by electing into it the immediate descendants of freed men; and when no one allowed that election as valid, and when he had not acquired in the senate-house that influence in the city which he had been aiming at, by distributing men of the meanest order among all the several tribes, he thus corrupted the assemblies both of the forum and of the field of Mars; and so much indignation did the election of Flavius excite, that most of the nobles laid aside their gold rings and bracelets in consequence of it. From that time the state was split into two parties. The uncorrupted part of the people, who favoured and supported the good, held one side; the faction of the rabble, the other; until Quintus Fabius and Publius Decius were made censors; and Fabius, both for the sake of concord, and at the same time to prevent the elections remaining in the hands of the lowest of the people, purged the rest of the tribes of all the rabble of the forum, and threw it into four, and called them city tribes. And this procedure, we are told, gave such universal satisfaction, that, by this regulation in the orders of the state, he obtained the surname of Maximus, which he had not obtained by his many victories. The annual review of the knights, on the ides of July, is also said to have been instituted by him.

BOOK X.

Submission of the Marcians accepted. The college of Augurs augmented from four to nine. The law of appeal to the people carried by Valerius the consul. Two more tribes added. War declared against the Samnites. Several successful actions. In an engagement against the combined forces of the Etruscans, Umbrians, Samnites, and Gauls, Publius Decius, after the example of his father, devotes himself for the army. Dies, and, by his death, procures the victory to the Romans. Defeat of the Samnites by Papirius Cursor. The census held. The lustrum closed. The number of the citizens two hundred and sixty-two thousand three hundred and twenty-two.

During the consulate of Lucius Genucius and Servius Cornelius, the state enjoyed almost uninterrupted rest from foreign wars. Colonies were led out to Sora and Alba. For the latter, situated in the country of the Æquans, six thousand colonists were enrolled. Sora had formerly belonged to the Volscian territory, but had fallen into the possession of the Samnites: thither were sent four thousand settlers. This year the freedom of the state was granted to the Arpinians and Trebulans. The Frusinonians were fined a third part of their lands, because it was discovered that the Hernicians had been tampered with by them; and the heads of that conspiracy, after a trial before the consuls, held in pursuance of a decree of the senate, were beaten with rods and beheaded. However, that the Romans might not pass the year entirely exempt from war, a little expedition was made into Umbria; intelligence being received from thence, that excursions of men, in arms, had been made, from a certain cave, into the adjacent country. Into this cave the troops penetrated with their standards, and, the place being dark, they received many wounds, chiefly from stones thrown. At length the other mouth of the cave being found, for it was pervious, both the openings were filled up with wood, which being set on fire, there perished by means of the smoke and heat, no less than two thousand men; many of whom, at the last, in attempting to make their way out, rushed into the very flames. The two Marci, Livius Denter and Æmilius, succeeding to the consulship, war was renewed with the Æquans; who, being highly displeased at the colony established within their territory, as if it were a fortress, having made an attempt, with their whole force, to seize it, were repulsed by the colonists themselves. They caused, however, such an alarm at Rome, that, to quell this insurrection, Caius Junius Bubulcus was nominated dictator: for it was scarcely credible that the Æquans, after being reduced to such a degree of weakness, should by themselves alone have ventured to engage in a war. The dictator, taking the field, with Marcus Titinius, master of the horse, in the first engagement reduced the Æquans to submission; and returning into the city in triumph, on the eighth day, dedicated, in the character of dictator, the temple of Health, which he had vowed when consul, and contracted for when censor.

During this year a fleet of Grecians, under the command of Cleonymus, a Lacedæmonian, arrived on the coast of Italy, and took Thuriæ, a city in the territory of the Sallentines. Against this enemy the consul Æmilius was sent, who, in one battle, completely defeated them, and drove them on board their ships. Thuriæ was then restored to its old inhabitants, and peace re-established in the country of the Sallentines. In some annals, I find that Junius Bubulcus was sent dictator into that country, and that Cleonymus, without hazarding an engagement with the Romans, retired out of Italy. He then sailed round the promontory of Brundusium, and, steering down the middle of the

Adriatic gulf, because he dreaded, on the left hand, the coasts of Italy destitute of harbours, and, on the right, the Illyrians, Liburnians, and Istrians, nations of savages, and noted in general for piracy, he passed on to the coasts of the Venetians. Here, having landed a small party to explore the country, and being informed that a narrow beach stretched along the shore, beyond which were marshes, overflowed by the tides; that dry land was seen at no great distance, level in the nearest part, and rising behind into hills, beyond which was the mouth of a very deep river, into which they had seen ships brought round and moored in safety, (this was the river Meduacus,) he ordered his fleet to sail into it and go up against the stream. As the channel would not admit the heavy ships, the troops, removing into the lighter vessels, arrived at a part of the country occupied by three maritime cantons of the Patavians, settled on that coast. Here they made a descent, leaving a small guard with the ships, made themselves masters of these cantons, set fire to the houses, drove off a considerable booty of men and cattle, and, allured by the sweets of plunder, proceeded still further from the shore. When news of this was brought to Patavium, where the contiguity of the Gauls kept the inhabitants constantly in arms, they divided their young men into two bands, one of which was led towards the quarter where the marauders were said to be busy; the other by a different route, to avoid meeting any of the pirates, towards the station of the ships, fifteen miles distant from the town. An attack was made on the small craft, and the guards being killed, the affrighted mariners were obliged to remove their ships to the other bank of the river. By land, also, the attack on the dispersed plunderers was equally successful; and the Grecians, flying back towards their ships, were opposed in their way by the Venetians. Thus they were enclosed on both sides, and cut to pieces; and some, who were made prisoners, gave information that the fleet, with their king, Cleonymus, was but three miles distant. Sending the captives into the nearest canton, to be kept under a guard, some soldiers got on board the flat-bottomed vessels, so constructed for the purpose of passing the shoals with ease; others embarked in those which had been lately taken from the enemy, and proceeding down the river, surrounded their unwieldy ships, which dreaded the unknown sands and flats more than they did the Romans, and which showed a greater eagerness to escape into the deep than to make resistance. The soldiers pursued them as far as the mouth of the river; and having taken and burned a part of the fleet, which in the hurry and confusion had been stranded, returned victorious. Cleonymus, having met success in no part of the Adriatic sea, departed with scarce a fifth part of his navy remaining. Many, now alive, have seen the beaks of his ships, and the spoils of the Lacedæmonians, hanging in the old temple of Juno. In commemoration of this event, there is exhibited at Patavium, every year, on its anniversary day, a naval combat on the river in the middle of the town.

A treaty was this year concluded at Rome with the Vestinians, who solicited friendship. Various causes of apprehension afterwards sprung up. News arrived, that Etruria was in rebellion; the insurrection having arisen from the dissensions of the Arretians; for the Cilnian family having grown exorbitantly powerful, a party, out of envy of their wealth, had attempted to expel them by force of arms. [Accounts were also received] that the Marsians held forcible possession of the lands to which the colony of Carseoli, consisting of four thousand men, had been sent. By reason, therefore, of these commotions, Marcus Valerius Maximus was nominated dictator, and chose for his master of the horse Marcus Æmilius Paullus. This I am inclined to believe, rather than that Quintus Fabius, at such an age as he then was, and after enjoying many honours, was placed in a station subordinate to Valerius: but I think it not unlikely that the mistake arose from the surname Maximus. The dictator, having set out at the head of an army, in one battle utterly defeated the Marsians, drove them into their fortified towns, and afterwards, in the course of a few days, took Milionia, Plestina, and Fresilia; and then finding Marsians in a part of their lands, granted them a renewal of the treaty. The war was then directed against the Etrurians; and when the dictator had gone to Rome, for the purpose of renewing the auspices, the master of the horse, going out to forage, was surrounded by an ambuscade, and obliged to fly shamefully into his camp, after losing several standards and many of his men. The occurrence of which discomfiture to Fabius is exceedingly improbable; not only because, if in any particular, certainly, above all, in the qualifications of a commander, he fully merited his surname; but besides, mindful of Papirius's severity, he never could have been tempted to fight, without the dictator's orders.

The news of this disaster excited at Rome an alarm greater than suited the importance of the affair; for, as if the army had been destroyed, a justitium was proclaimed, guards mounted at the gates, and watches set in every street: and armour and weapons were heaped on the walls. All the younger citizens being compelled to enlist, the dictator was ordered to join the army. There he found every thing in a more tranquil state than he expected, and regularity established through the care of the master of the horse, the camp removed to a place of greater safety, the cohorts, which had lost their standards, left without tents on the outside of the ramparts and the troops ardently impatient for battle, that their disgrace might be the sooner obliterated. He therefore immediately advanced his camp into the territory of Rusella. Thither the enemy also followed, and although, since their late success, they entertained the most sanguine hopes from an open trial of strength, yet they endeavoured to circumvent the enemy by a stratagem which they had before practised with success. There were, at a small distance from the Roman camp, the half-ruined houses of a town which had been burnt in the devastation of the country. A body of troops being concealed there, some cattle was driven on, within view of a Roman post, commanded by a lieutenant-general, Cneius Fulvius. When no one was induced by this temptation to stir from his post, one of the herdsmen, advancing close to the works, called out, that others were driving out those cattle at their leisure from the ruins of the town, why did they remain idle, when they might safely drive them through the middle of the Roman camp? When this was interpreted to the lieutenant-general, by some natives of Cære, and great impatience prevailed through every company of the soldiers, who, nevertheless, dared not to move without orders, he commanded some who were skilled in the language to observe attentively, whether the dialect of the herdsmen resembled that of rustics or of citizens. When these reported, that their accent in speaking, their manner and appearance, were all of a more polished cast than suited shepherds, "Go then," said he, "tell them that they may uncover the ambush which they vainly conceal, that the Romans understand all their devices, and can now be no more taken by stratagem than they can be conquered by arms." When these words were heard, and carried to those who lay in ambush, they immediately arose from their lurking place, and marched out in order into the plain which was open to view on every side The lieutenant-general thought their force too powerful for his small band to cope with. He therefore sent in haste to Valerius for support, and in the mean time, by himself, sustained the enemy's onset.

On receiving his message, the dictator ordered the standards to move, and the troops to follow in arms. But every thing was executed more quickly, almost, than ordered. The standards and arms were instantly snatched up, and they were with difficulty restrained from running impetuously on, both indignation at their late defeat stimulated them, as well as the shouts striking their ears with increasing vehemence, as the contest grew hotter They therefore urged each other, and pressed the standard-bearers to quicken their pace. The dictator, the more eagerly he saw them push forward, took the more pains to repress their haste, and ordered them to march at a slower rate. On the other side, the Etrurians, putting themselves in motion, on the first beginning of the fray had come up with their whole force, and several expresses came to the dictator, one after another, that all the regions of the Etrurians had joined in the fight, and that his men could not any longer withstand them: at the same time, he himself saw, from the higher ground, in how perilous a situation the party was. Confident, however, that the lieutenant-general was able, even yet, to support the contest, and considering that he himself was at hand to rescue him from defeat, he wished to let the enemy be fatigued, as much as might be, in order that, when in that state, he might fall on them with his fresh troops. Slowly as these marched, the distance was now just sufficient for the cavalry to begin their career for a charge. The battalions of the legions marched in front, lest the enemy might suspect any secret or sudden movement, but intervals had been left in the ranks of the infantry, affording room for the horses to gallop through. At the same instant the line raised the shout, and the cavalry, charging at full speed, poured on the enemy, and spread at once a general panic. After this, as succour had arrived, almost too late, to the party surrounded, so now they were allowed entire rest, the fresh troops taking on themselves the whole business of the fight. Nor was that either long or dubious. The enemy, now routed, fled to their camp, and the Romans advancing to attack it, they gave way, and are crowded all together in the remotest part of it. In their flight they are obstructed by the narrowness of the gates, the greater number climbed up on the mounds and ramparts, to try if they could either defend themselves with the aid of the advantageous ground, or get over, by any means, and escape. One part of the rampart, happening to be badly compacted sunk under the weight of the multitude who stood on it, and fell into the trench. On which, crying out that the gods had opened that pass to give them safety, they made their way out, most of them leaving their arms behind. By this battle the power of the Etrurians was, a second time, effectually crushed, so that, engaging to furnish a year's pay, and corn for two months, with the dictator's permission, they sent ambassadors to Rome to treat of peace. This was refused, but a truce for two years was granted to them. The dictator returned into the city in triumph. I have seen it asserted, that tranquillity was restored in Etruria by the dictator, without any memorable battle, only by composing the dissensions of the Arretians, and effecting a reconciliation between the Cilnian family and the commons. Marcus Valerius was elected consul, before the expiration of his dictatorship, many have believed, without his soliciting the office, and even while he was absent; and that the election was held by an interrex. In one point all agree, that he held the consulship with Quintus Appuleius Pansa.

During this consulate of Marcus Valerius and Quintus Appuleius, affairs abroad wore a very peaceable aspect. Their losses sustained in war, together with the truce, kept the Etrurians quiet. The Samnites, depressed by the misfortunes of many years, had not yet become dissatisfied with their new alliance. At Rome, also, the carrying away of such multitudes to colonies, rendered the commons tranquil, and lightened their burthens. But, that things might not be tranquil on all sides, a contention was excited between the principal persons in the commonwealth, patricians on one hand, and plebeians on the other, by the two Ogulnii, Quintus and Cneius, plebeian tribunes, who, seeking every where occasions of criminating the patricians in the hearing of the people, and having found other attempts fruitless, set on foot a proceeding by which they might inflame, not the lowest class of the commons, but their chief men, the plebeians of consular and triumphal rank, to the completion of whose honours nothing was now wanting but the offices of the priesthood, which were not yet laid open to them. They therefore published a proposal for a law, that, whereas there were then four augurs and four pontiffs, and it had been determined that the number of priests should be augmented, the four additional pontiffs and five augurs should all be chosen out of the commons. How the college of augurs could be reduced to the number of four, except by the death of two, I do not understand: for it is a rule among the augurs, that their number should be composed of threes, so that the three ancient tribes, the Ramnes, Titienses, and Luceres, should have each its own augur; or, in case there should be occasion for more, that each should increase its number of augurs, in equal proportion with the rest, in like manner as when, by the addition of five to four, they made up the number nine, so that there were three to each tribe. However, as it was proposed that they should be chosen out of the commons, the patricians were as highly offended at the proceeding, as when they saw the consulship made common; yet they pretended that the business concerned not them so much as it did the gods, who would "take care that their own worship should not be contaminated; that, for their parts, they only wished that no misfortune might ensue to the commonwealth." But they made a less vigorous opposition, as being now accustomed to suffer defeat in such kind of disputes; and they saw their adversaries, not, as formerly, grasping at that which they could scarcely hope to reach, the higher honours; but already in possession of all those advantages, on the uncertain prospect of which they had maintained the contest, manifold consulships, censorships, and triumphs.

The principal struggle, however, in supporting and opposing the bill, they say, was between Appius Claudius and Publius Decius Mus. After these had urged nearly the same topics, respecting the privileges of patricians and plebeians, which had been formerly employed for and against the Licinian law, when the proposition was brought forward of opening the consulship to plebeians, Decius is said to have drawn a lively description of his own father, such as many then present in the assembly had seen him, girt in the Gabine dress, standing on a spear, in the attitude in which he had devoted himself for the people and the legions, and to have added, that the consul Publius Decius was then deemed by the immortal gods an offering equally pure and pious, as if his colleague, Titus Manlius, had been devoted. And might not the same Publius Decius have been, with propriety, chosen to perform the public worship of the Roman people? Was there any danger that the gods would give less attention to his prayers than to those of Appius Claudius? Did the latter perform his private acts of adoration with a purer mind, or worship the gods more religiously than he? Who had any reason to complain of the vows offered in behalf of the commonwealth, by so many plebeian consuls and dictators, either when setting out to their armies, or in the heat of battle? Were the numbers of commanders reckoned, during those years since business began to be transacted under the conduct and auspices of plebeians, the same number of triumphs might be found. The commons had now no reason to be dissatisfied with their own nobility. On the contrary, they were fully convinced, that in case of a sudden war breaking out, the senate and people of Rome would not repose greater confidence in patrician than in plebeian commanders. "Which being the case," said he, "what god or man can deem it an impropriety, if those whom ye have honoured with curule chairs, with the purple bordered gown, with the palm-vest and embroidered robe, with the triumphal crown and laurel, whose houses ye have rendered conspicuous above others, by affixing to them the spoils of conquered enemies, should add to these the badges of augurs or pontiffs? If a person, who has rode through the city in a gilt chariot; and, decorated with the ensigns of Jupiter, supremely good and great, has mounted the Capitol, should be seen with a chalice and wand; what impropriety, I say, that he should, with his head veiled, slay a victim, or take an augury in the citadel? When, in the inscription on a person's statue, the consulship, censorship, and triumph shall be read with patience, will the eyes of readers be unable to endure the addition of the office of augur or pontiff? In truth (with deference to the gods I say it) I trust that we are, through the kindness of the Roman people, qualified in such a manner that we should, by the dignity of our characters, reflect back, on the priesthood, not less lustre than we should receive; and may demand, rather on behalf of the gods, than for our own sakes, that those whom we worship in our private we may also worship in a public capacity."

"But why do I argue thus, as if the cause of the patricians, respecting the priesthood, were untouched? and as if we were not already in possession of one sacerdotal office, of the highest class? We see plebeian decemvirs, for performing sacrifices, interpreters of the Sibylline prophecies, and of the fates of the nation; we also see them presidents of Apollo's festival, and of other religious performances. Neither was any injustice done to the patricians, when, to the two commissioners for performing sacrifices, an additional number was joined, in favour of the plebeians; nor is there now, when a tribune, a man of courage and activity, wishes to add five places of augurs, and four of pontiffs, to which plebeians may be nominated; not Appius, with intent to expel you from your places; but, that men of plebeian rank may assist you, in the management of divine affairs, with the same zeal with which they assist you in matters of human concernment. Blush not, Appius, at having a man your colleague in the priesthood, whom you might have a colleague in the censorship or consulship, whose master of the horse you yourself may be, when he is dictator, as well as dictator when he is master of the horse. A Sabine adventurer, the first origin of your nobility, either Attus Clausus, or Appius Claudius, which you will, the ancient patricians of those days admitted into their number: do not then, on your part, disdain to admit us into the number of priests. We bring with us numerous honours; all those honours, indeed, which have rendered your party so proud. Lucius Sextius was the first consul chosen out of the plebeians; Caius Licinius Stolo, the first master of the horse; Caius Marcius Rutilus, the first dictator, and likewise censor; Quintus Publilius Philo, the first prætor. On all occasions was heard a repetition of the same arguments; that the right of auspices was vested in you; that ye alone had the rights of ancestry; that ye alone were legally entitled to the supreme command, and the auspices both in peace and war. The supreme command has hitherto been, and will continue to be, equally prosperous in plebeian hands as in patrician. Have ye never heard it said, that the first created patricians were not men sent down from heaven, but such as could cite their fathers, that is, nothing more than free born. I can now cite my father, a consul; and my son will be able to cite a grandfather. Citizens, there is nothing else in it, than that we should never obtain any thing without a refusal. The patricians wish only for a dispute; nor do they care what issue their disputes may have. For my part, be it advantageous, happy, and prosperous to you and to the commonwealth, I am of opinion that this law should receive your sanction."

The people ordered that the tribes should be instantly called; and there was every appearance that the law would be accepted. It was deferred, however, for that day, by a protest, from which on the day following the tribunes were deterred; and it passed with the approbation of a vast majority. The pontiffs created were, Publius Decius Mus, the advocate for the law; Publius Sempronius Sophus, Caius Marcius Rutilus, and Marcus Livius Denter. The five augurs, who were also plebeians, were, Caius Genucius, Publius Ælius Pætus, Marcus Minucius Fessus, Caius Marcius, and Titus Publilius. Thus the number of the pontiffs was made eight; that of the augurs nine. In the same year Marcus Valerius, consul, procured a law to be passed concerning appeals; more carefully enforced by additional sanctions. This was the third time, since the expulsion of the kings, of this law being introduced, and always by the same family. The reason for renewing it so often was, I believe, no other, than that the influence of a few was apt to prove too powerful for the liberty of the commons. However, the Porcian law seems intended, solely, for the security of the persons of the citizens; as it visited with a severe penalty any one for beating with stripes or putting to death a Roman citizen. The Valerian law, after forbidding a person, who had appealed, to be beaten with rods and beheaded, added, in case of any one acting contrary thereto, that it shall yet be only deemed a wicked act. This, I suppose, was judged of sufficient strength to enforce obedience to the law in those days; so powerful was then men's sense of shame; at present one would scarcely make use of such a threat seriously. The Æquans rebelling, the same consul conducted the war against them; in which no memorable event occurred; for, except ferocity, they retained nothing of their ancient condition. The other consul, Appuleius, invested the town of Nequinum in Umbria. The ground, the same whereon Narnia now stands, was steep (on one side even perpendicular); this rendered the town impregnable either by assault or works. That business, therefore, came unfinished into the hands of the succeeding consuls, Marcus Fulvius Pætinus and Titus Manlius Torquatus. When all the centuries named Quintus Fabius consul for that year though not a candidate, Macer Licinius and Tubero state that he himself recommended them to postpone the conferring the consulship on him until a year wherein there might be more employment for their arms; adding, that, during the present year, he might be more useful to the state in the management of a city magistracy; and thus, neither dissembling what he preferred, nor yet making direct application for it, he was appointed curule ædile with Lucius Papirius Cursor. Piso, a more ancient writer of annals, prevents me from averring this as certain; he asserts that the curule ædiles of that year were Caius Domitius Calvinus, son of Cneius, and Spurius Carvilius Maximus, son of Caius. I am of opinion, that this latter surname caused a mistake concerning the ædiles; and that thence followed a story conformable to this mistake, patched up out of the two elections, of the ædiles, and of the consuls. The general survey was performed, this year, by Publius Sempronius Sophus and Publius Sulpicius Saverrio, censors; and two tribes were added, the Aniensian and Terentine. Such were the occurrences at Rome.

Meanwhile, after much time had been lost in the tedious siege of Nequinum, two of the townsmen, whose houses were contiguous to the wall, having formed a subterraneous passage, came by that private way to the Roman advanced guards; and being conducted thence to the consul, offered to give admittance to a body of armed men within the works and walls. The proposal was thought to be such as ought neither to be rejected, nor yet assented to without caution. With one of these men, the other being detained as an hostage, two spies were sent through the mine, and certain information being received from them, three hundred men in arms, guided by the deserter, entered the city, and seized by night the nearest gate, which being broken open, the Roman consul and his army took possession of the city without any opposition. In this manner came Nequinum under the dominion of the Roman people. A colony was sent thither as a barrier against the Umbrians, and called Narnia, from the river Nar. The troops returned to Rome with abundance of spoil. This year the Etrurians made preparations for war in violation of the truce. But a vast army of the Gauls, making an irruption into their territories, while their attention was directed to another quarter, suspended for a time the execution of their design. They then, relying on the abundance of money which they possessed, endeavour to make allies of the Gauls, instead of enemies; in order that, with their armies combined, they might attack the Romans. The barbarians made no objection to the alliance, and a negotiation was opened for settling the price; which being adjusted and paid, and every thing else being in readiness for commencing their operations, the Etrurians desired them to accompany them in their march. This they refused, alleging that "they had stipulated a price for making war against the Romans: that the payment already made, they had received in consideration of their not wasting the Etrurian territory, or using their arms against the inhabitants. That notwithstanding, if it was the wish of the Etrurians, they were still willing to engage in the war, but on no other condition than that of being allowed a share of their lands, and obtaining at length some permanent settlement." Many assemblies of the states of Etruria were held on this subject, and nothing could be settled; not so much by reason of their aversion from the dismemberment of their territory, as because every one felt a dread of fixing in so close vicinity to themselves people of such a savage race. The Gauls were therefore dismissed, and carried home an immense sum of money, acquired without toil or danger. The report of a Gallic tumult, in addition to an Etrurian war, had caused serious apprehensions at Rome; and, with the less hesitation on that account, an alliance was concluded with the state of the Picentians.

The province of Etruria fell by lot to the consul Titus Manlius; who, when he had but just entered the enemy's country, as he was exercising the cavalry, in wheeling about at full speed, was thrown from his horse, and almost killed on the spot; three days after the fall, he died. The Etrurians, embracing this omen, as it were, of the future progress of the war, and observing that the gods had commenced hostilities on their behalf, assumed new courage. At Rome the news caused great affliction, on account both of the loss of such a man and of the unseasonableness of the juncture; insomuch that an assembly, held for the purpose of substituting a new consul, having been conducted agreeably to the wishes of people of the first consequence, prevented the senate from ordering a dictator to be created. All the votes and centuries concurred unanimously in appointing Marcus Valerius consul, the same whom the senate would have ordered to be made dictator. They then commanded him to proceed immediately into Etruria, to the legions. His coming gave such a check to the Etrurians, that not one of them dared thenceforward to appear on the outside of their trenches; their own fears operating as a blockade. Nor could the new consul, by wasting their lands and burning their houses, draw them out to an engagement; for not only country-houses, but numbers of their towns, were seen smoking and in ashes, on every side. While this war proceeded more slowly than had been expected, an account was received of the breaking out of another; which was, not without reason, regarded as terrible, in consequence of the heavy losses formerly sustained by both parties, from information given by their new allies, the Picentians, that the Samnites were looking to arms and a renewal of hostilities, and that they themselves had been solicited to join therein. The Picentians received the thanks of the state; and a large share of the attention of the senate was turned from Etruria towards Samnium. The dearness of provisions also distressed the state very much, and they would have felt the extremity of want, according to the relation of those who make Fabius Maximus curule ædile that year, had not the vigilant activity of that man, such as he had on many occasions displayed in the field, been exerted then with equal zeal at home, in the management of the market, and in procuring and forming magazines of corn. An interregnum took place this year, the reason of which is not mentioned. Appius Claudius, and, after him, Publius Sulpicius, were interreges. The latter held an election of consuls, and chose Lucius Cornelius Scipio and Cneius Fulvius. In the beginning of this year, ambassadors came from the Lucanians to the new consuls to complain, that "the Samnites, finding that they could not, by any offers, tempt them to take part in the war, had marched an army in a hostile manner into their country, and were now laying it waste, and forcing them into a war; that the Lucanian people had on former occasions erred enough and more than enough; that their minds were so firmly fixed that they thought it more endurable to bear and suffer every hardship, rather than ever again to outrage the Roman name: they besought the senate to take the people of Lucania into their protection, and defend them from the injustice and outrage of the Samnites; that although fidelity on their part to the Romans would now become necessary, a war being undertaken against the Samnites, still they were ready to give hostages."

The deliberation of the senate was short. They all, to a man, concurred in opinion, that a compact should be entered into with the Lucanians, and satisfaction demanded from the Samnites: accordingly, a favourable answer was returned to the Lucanians, and the alliance concluded. Heralds were then sent, to require of the Samnites, that they should depart from the country of the allies, and withdraw their troops from the Lucanian territory. These were met by persons despatched for the purpose by the Samnites, who gave them warning, that "if they appeared at any assembly in Samnium, they must not expect to depart in safety." As soon as this was heard at Rome, the senate voted, and the people ordered, that war should be declared against the Samnites. The consuls, then, dividing the provinces between them, Etruria fell to Scipio, the Samnites to Fulvius; and they set out by different routes, each against the enemy allotted to him. Scipio, while he expected a tedious campaign, like that of the preceding year, was met near Volaterra by the Etrurians, in order of battle. The fight lasted through the greater part of the day, while very many fell on both sides, and night came on while it was uncertain to which side victory inclined. But the following dawn showed the conqueror and the vanquished; for the Etrurians had decamped in the dead of the night. The Romans, marching out with intent to renew the engagement, and seeing their superiority acknowledged by the departure of the enemy, advanced to their camp; and, finding even this fortified post deserted, took possession of it, evacuated as it was, together with a vast quantity of spoil. The consul then, leading back his forces into the Faliscian territory, and leaving his baggage with a small guard at Falerii, set out with his troops, lightly accoutred, to ravage the enemy's country. All places are destroyed with fire and sword; plunder driven from every side; and not only was the ground left a mere waste to the enemy, but their forts and small towns were set on fire; he refrained from attacking the cities into which fear had driven the Etrurians. The consul Cneius Fulvius fought a glorious battle in Samnium, near Bovianum, attended with success by no means equivocal. Then, having attacked Bovianum, and not long after Aufidena, he took them by storm. This year a colony was carried out to Carseoli, into the territory of the Æquicolæ. The consul Fulvius triumphed on his defeat of the Samnites.

When the consular elections were now at hand, a report prevailed, that the Etrurians and Samnites were raising vast armies; that the leaders of the Etrurians were, in all their assemblies, openly censured for not having procured the aid of the Gauls on any terms; and the magistrates of the Samnites arraigned, for having opposed to the Romans an army destined to act against the Lucanians. That, in consequence, the people were rising up in arms, with all their own strength and that of their allies combined; and that this affair seemed not likely to be terminated without a contest of much greater difficulty than the former. Although the candidates for the consulship were men of illustrious characters, yet this alarming intelligence turned the thoughts of all on Quintus Fabius Maximus, who sought not the employment at first, and afterwards, when he discovered their wishes, even declined it. "Why," said he, "should they impose such a difficult task on him, who was now in the decline of life, and had passed through a full course of labours, and of the rewards of labour? Neither the vigour of his body, nor of his mind, remained the same; and he dreaded fortune herself, lest to some god she should seem too bountiful to him, and more constant than the course of human affairs allowed. He had himself succeeded, in gradual succession, to the dignities of his seniors; and he beheld, with great satisfaction, others rising up to succeed to his glory. There was no scarcity at Rome, either of honours suited to men of the highest merit, or of men of eminent merit suited to the highest honours." This disinterested conduct, instead of repressing, increased, while in fact it justified their zeal. But thinking that this ought to be checked by respect for the laws, he ordered that clause to be read aloud by which it was not lawful that the same person shall be re-elected consul within ten years. The law was scarcely heard in consequence of the clamour; and the tribunes of the commons declared, that this "decree should be no impediment; for they would propose an order to the people, that he should be exempted from the obligation of the laws." Still he persisted in his opposition, asking, "To what purpose were laws enacted, if they eluded by the very persons who procured them? The laws now," he said, "instead of being rulers, were overruled." The people, nevertheless, proceeded to vote; and, according as each century was called in, it immediately named Fabius consul. Then at length, overcome by the universal wish of the state, he said, "Romans, may the gods approve your present, and all your future proceedings. But since, with respect to me, ye intend to act according to your own wills, let my interest find room with you, with respect to my colleague. I earnestly request, that ye will place in the consulship with me Publius Decius; a man with whom I have already experienced the utmost harmony in our joint administration of that office; a man worthy of you, worthy of his father." The recommendation was deemed well founded, and all the remaining centuries voted Quintus Fabius and Publius Decius consuls. This year, great numbers were prosecuted by the ædiles, for having in possession larger quantities of land than the state allowed; and hardly any were acquitted: by which means, a very great restraint was laid on exorbitant covetousness.

Whilst the new consuls, Quintus Fabius Maximus a fourth, and Publius Decius Mus a third time, were settling between themselves that one should command against the Samnites, and the other against the Etrurians; and what number of forces would be sufficient for this and for that province; and which would be the fitter commander in each war; ambassadors from Sutrium, Nepete, and Falerii, stating that the states of Etruria were holding assemblies on the subject of suing for peace, they directed the whole force of their arms against Samnium. The consuls, in order that the supply of provisions might be the more ready, and to leave the enemy in the greater uncertainty on what quarter the war would fall, Fabius led his legions towards Samnium through the territory of Sora, and Decius his through that of Sidicinum. As soon as they arrived at the frontiers of the enemy, both advanced briskly, spreading devastation wherever they came; but still they explore the country, to a distance beyond where the troops were employed in plundering. Accordingly the fact did not escape the notice of the Romans, that the enemy were drawn up in a retired valley, near Tifernum, which, when the Romans entered, they were preparing to attack them from the higher ground. Fabius, sending away his baggage to a place of safety, and setting a small guard over it, and having given notice to his soldiers that a battle was at hand, advanced in a square body to the hiding-place of the enemy already mentioned. The Samnites, disappointed in making an unexpected attack, determined on a regular engagement, as the matter was now likely to come to an open contest. They therefore marched out into the plain; and, with a greater share of spirit than of hopes, committed themselves to the disposal of fortune. However, whether in consequence of their having drawn together, from every state, the whole of the force which it possessed, or that the consideration of their all being at stake, heightened their courage, they occasioned, even in open fight, a considerable alarm. Fabius, when he saw that the enemy in no place gave way, ordered Marcus Fulvius and Marcus Valerius, military tribunes, with whom he hastened to the front, to go to the cavalry, and to exhort them, that, "if they remembered any instance wherein the public had received advantage from the service of the horsemen, they would, on that day, exert themselves to insure the invincible renown of that body; telling them that the enemy stood immovable against the efforts of the infantry, and the only hope remaining was in the charge of horse." He addressed particularly both these youths, and with the same cordiality, loading them with praises and promises. But considering that, in case that effort should also fail, it would be necessary to accomplish by stratagem what his strength could not effect; he ordered Scipio, one of his lieutenants-general, to draw off the spearmen of the first legion out of the line; to lead them round as secretly as possible to the nearest mountains; and, by an ascent concealed from view, to gain the heights, and show himself suddenly on the rear of the enemy. The cavalry, led on by the tribunes, rushing forward unexpectedly before the van, caused scarcely more confusion among the enemy than among their friends. The line of the Samnites stood firm against the furious onset of the squadrons; it neither could be driven from its ground, nor broken in any part. The cavalry, finding their attempts fruitless, withdrew from the fight, and retired behind the line of infantry. On this the enemies' courage increased, so that the Roman troops in the van would not have been able to support the contest, nor the force thus increasing by confidence in itself, had not the second line, by the consul's order, come up into the place of the first. These fresh troops checked the progress of the Samnites, who had now began to gain ground; and, at this seasonable juncture, their comrades appearing suddenly on the mountains, and raising a shout, occasioned in the Samnites a fear of greater danger than really threatened them; Fabius called out aloud that his colleague Decius was approaching; on which all the soldiers, elated with joy, repeated eagerly, that the other consul was come, the legions were arrived! This artifice, useful to the Romans, filled the Samnites with dismay and terror; terrified chiefly lest fatigued as they were, they should be overpowered by another army fresh and unhurt. As they dispersed themselves in their flight on every side, there was less effusion of blood than might have been expected, considering the completeness of the victory. There were three thousand four hundred slain, about eight hundred and thirty made prisoners, and twenty-three military standards taken.

The Apulians would have joined their forces to the Samnites before this battle, had not the consul, Publius Decius, encamped in their neighbourhood at Maleventum; and, finding means to bring them to an engagement, put them to the rout. Here, likewise, there was more of flight than of bloodshed. Two thousand of the Apulians were slain; but Decius, despising such an enemy, led his legions into Samnium. There the two consular armies, overrunning every part of the country during the space of five months, laid it entirely waste. There were in Samnium forty-five places where Decius, and eighty-six where the other consul, encamped. Nor did they leave traces only of having been there, as ramparts and trenches, but other dreadful mementos of it—general desolation and regions depopulated. Fabius also took the city of Cimetra, where he made prisoners two thousand four hundred soldiers; and there were slain in the assault about four hundred and thirty. Going thence to Rome to preside at the elections, he used all expedition in despatching that business. All the first-called centuries voted Quintus Fabius consul. Appius Claudius was a candidate, a man of consular rank, daring and ambitious; and as he wished not more ardently for the attainment of that honour for himself, than he did that the patricians might recover the possession of both places in the consulship, he laboured, with all his own power, supported by that of the whole body of the nobility, to prevail on them to appoint him consul along with Quintus Fabius. To this Fabius objected, giving, at first, the same reasons which he had advanced the year before. The nobles then all gathered round his seat, and besought him to raise up the consulship out of the plebeian mire, and to restore both to the office itself, and to the patrician rank, their original dignity. Fabius then, procuring silence, allayed their warmth by a qualifying speech, declaring, that "he would have so managed, as to have received the names of two patricians, if he had seen an intention of appointing any other than himself to the consulship. As things now stood, he would not set so bad a precedent as to admit his own name among the candidates; such a proceeding being contrary to the laws." Whereupon Appius Claudius, and Lucius Volumnius, a plebeian, who had likewise been colleagues in that office before, were elected consuls. The nobility reproached Fabius for declining to act in conjunction with Appius Claudius, because he evidently excelled him in eloquence and political abilities.

When the election was finished, the former consuls, their command being continued for six months, were ordered to prosecute the war in Samnium. Accordingly, during this next year also, in the consulate of Lucius Volumnius and Appius Claudius, Publius Decius, who had been left consul in Samnium by his colleague, in the character of proconsul, ceased not to spread devastation through all parts of that country; until, at last, he drove the army of the Samnites, which never dared to face him in the field, entirely out of the country. Thus expelled from home, they bent their route to Etruria; and, supposing that the business, which they had often in vain endeavoured to accomplish by embassies, might now be negotiated with more effect, when they were backed by such a powerful armed force, and could intermix terror with their entreaties, they demanded a meeting of the chiefs of Etruria: which being assembled, they set forth the great number of years during which they had waged war with the Romans, in the cause of liberty; "they had," they said, "tried to sustain, with their own strength, the weight of so great a war: they had also made trial of the support of the adjoining nations, which proved of little avail. When they were unable longer to maintain the conflict, they had sued the Roman people for peace; and had again taken up arms, because they felt peace was more grievous to those with servitude, than war to free men. That their one only hope remaining rested in the Etrurians. They knew that nation to be the most powerful in Italy, in respect of arms, men, and money; to have the Gauls their closest neighbours, born in the midst of war and arms, of furious courage, both from their natural temper, and particularly against the people of Rome, whom they boasted, without infringing the truth, of having made their prisoners, and of having ransomed for gold. If the Etrurians possessed the same spirit which formerly Porsena and their ancestors once had, there was nothing to prevent their obliging the Romans, driven from all the lands on this side of the Tiber, to fight for their own existence, and not for the intolerable dominion which they assumed over Italy. The Samnite army had come to them, in readiness for action, furnished with arms and pay, and were willing to follow that instant, even should they lead to the attack of the city of Rome itself."

While they were engaged in these representations, and intriguing at Etruria, the operations of the Romans in their own territories distressed them severely. For Publius Decius, when he ascertained through his scouts the departure of the Samnite army, called a council, and there said, "Why do we ramble through the country, carrying the war from village to village? Why not attack the cities and fortified places? No army now guards Samnium. They have fled their country; they are gone into voluntary exile." The proposal being universally approved, he marched to attack Murgantia, a city of considerable strength; and so great was the ardour of the soldiers, resulting from their affection to their commander, and from their hopes of richer treasure than could be found in pillaging the country places, that in one day they took it by assault. Here, two thousand one hundred of the Samnites, making resistance, were surrounded and taken prisoners; and abundance of other spoil was captured. Decius, not choosing that the troops should be encumbered in their march with heavy baggage, ordered them to be called together, and said to them, "Do ye intend to rest satisfied with this single victory, and this booty? or do ye choose to cherish hopes proportioned to your bravery? All the cities of the Samnites, and the property left in them, are your own; since, after so often defeating their legions, ye have finally driven them out of the country. Sell those effects in your hands; and allure traders, by a prospect of profit, to follow you on your march. I will, from time to time, supply you with goods for sale. Let us go hence to the city of Romulea, where no greater labour, but greater gain awaits you." Having sold off the spoil, and warmly adopting the general's plan, they proceeded to Romulea. There, also, without works or engines, as soon as the battalions approached, the soldiers, deterred from the walls by no resistance, hastily applying ladders wherever was most convenient to each, they mounted the fortifications. The town was taken and plundered. Two thousand three hundred men were slain, six thousand taken prisoners, and the soldiers obtained abundance of spoil. This they were obliged to sell in like manner as the former; and, though no rest was allowed them, they proceeded, nevertheless, with the utmost alacrity to Ferentinum. But here they met a greater share both of difficulty and danger: the fortifications were defended with the utmost vigour, and the place was strongly fortified both by nature and art. However, the soldiers, now inured to plunder, overcame every obstacle. Three thousand of the enemy were killed round the walls, and the spoil was given to the troops. In some annals, the principal share of the honour of taking these cities is attributed to Maximus. They say that Murgantia was taken by Decius; Romulea and Ferentinum by Fabius. Some ascribe this honour to the new consuls: others not to both, but to one of these, Lucius Volumnius: that to him the province of Samnium had fallen.

While things went on thus in Samnium, whoever it was that had the command and auspices, powerful combination, composed of many states, was formed in Etruria against the Romans, the chief promoter of which was Gellius Egnatius, a Samnite. Almost all the Etrurians had united in this war. The neighbouring states of Umbria were drawn in, as it were, by the contagion; and auxiliaries were procured from the Gauls for hire: all their several numbers assembled at the camp of the Samnites. When intelligence of this sudden commotion was received at Rome, after the consul, Lucius Volumnius, had already set out for Samnium, with the second and third legions, and fifteen thousand of the allies; it was, therefore, resolved, that Appius Claudius should, at the very earliest opportunity, go into Etruria. Two Roman legions followed him, the first and fourth, and twelve thousand allies; their camp was pitched at a small distance from the enemy. However, advantage was gained by his early arrival in this particular, that the awe of the Roman name kept in check some states of Etruria which were disposed to war, rather than from any judicious or successful enterprise achieved under the guidance of the consul. Several battles were fought, at times and places unfavourable, and increasing confidence rendered the enemy daily more formidable; so that matters came nearly to such a state, as that neither could the soldiers rely much on their leader, nor the leader on his soldiers. It appears in three several histories, that a letter was sent by the consul to call his colleague from Samnium. But I will not affirm what requires stronger proof, as that point was a matter of dispute between these two consuls of the Roman people, a second time associated in the same office; Appius denying that the letter was sent, and Volumnius affirming that he was called thither by a letter from Appius. Volumnius had, by this time, taken three forts in Samnium, in which three thousand of the enemy had been slain, and about half that number made prisoners; and, a sedition having been raised among the Lucanians by the plebeians and the more indigent of the people, he had, to the great satisfaction of the nobles, quelled it by sending thither Quintus Fabius, proconsul, with his own veteran army. He left to Decius the ravaging of the enemy's country; and proceeded with his troops into Etruria to his colleague; where, on his arrival, the whole army received him with joy. Appius, if he did not write the letter, being conscious of this, had, in my opinion, just ground of displeasure; but if he had actually stood in need of assistance, his disowning it, as he did, arose from an illiberal and ungrateful mind. For, on going out to receive him, when they had scarcely exchanged salutations, he said, "Is all well, Lucius Volumnius? How stand affairs in Samnium? What motive induced you to remove out of your province?" Volumnius answered, that "affairs in Samnium were in a prosperous state; and that he had come thither in compliance with the request in his letter. But, if that were a forged letter, and that there was no occasion for him in Etruria, he would instantly face about, and depart." "You may depart." replied the other; "no one detains you: for it is a perfect inconsistency, that when, perhaps, you are scarcely equal to the management of your own war, you should vaunt of coming hither to succour others." To this Volumnius rejoined, "May Hercules direct all for the best; for his part, he was better pleased that he had taken useless trouble, than that any conjuncture should have arisen which had made one consular army insufficient for Etruria."

As the consuls were parting, the lieutenants-general and tribunes of Appius's army gathered round them. Some entreated their own general that he would not reject the voluntary offer of his colleague's assistance, which ought to have been solicited in the first instance: the greater number used their endeavours to stop Volumnius, beseeching him "not, through a peevish dispute with his colleague, to abandon the interest of the commonwealth; and represented to him, that in case any misfortune should happen, the blame would fall on the person who forsook the other, not on the one forsaken; that the state of affairs was such, that the credit and discredit of every success and failure in Etruria would be attributed to Lucius Volumnius: for no one would inquire, what were the words of Appius, but what the situation of the army. Appius indeed had dismissed him, but the commonwealth, and the army, required his stay. Let him only make trial of the inclinations of the soldiers." By such admonitions and entreaties they, in a manner, dragged the consuls, who almost resisted, to an assembly. There, longer discourses were made to the same purport, as had passed before in the presence of a few. And when Volumnius, who had the advantage of the argument, showed himself not deficient in oratory, in despite of the extraordinary eloquence of his colleague; Appius observed with a sneer, that "they ought to acknowledge themselves indebted to him, in having a consul who possessed eloquence also, instead of being dumb and speechless, when in their former consulate, particularly during the first months, he was not able so much as to open his lips; but now, in his harangues, even aspired after popularity." Volumnius replied, "How much more earnestly do I wish, that you had learned from me to act with spirit, than I from you to speak with elegance: that now he made a final proposal, which would determine, not which is the better orator, for that is not what the public wants, but which is the better commander. The provinces are Etruria and Samnium: that he might select which he preferred; that he, with his own army, will undertake to manage the business either in Etruria or in Samnium." The soldiers then, with loud clamours, requested that they would, in conjunction, carry on the war in Etruria; when Volumnius perceiving that it was the general wish, said, "Since I have been mistaken in apprehending my colleague's meaning, I will take care that there shall be no room for mistake with respect to the purport of your wishes. Signify by a shout whether you choose that I should stay or depart." On this, a shout was raised, so loud, that it brought the enemy out of their camp: they snatched up their arms, and marched down in order of battle. Volumnius likewise ordered the signal to be sounded, and the standard to be advanced from the camp. It is said that Appius hesitated, perceiving that, whether he fought or remained inactive, his colleague would have the victory; and that, afterwards, dreading lest his own legions also should follow Volumnius, he also gave the signal, at the earnest desire of his men. On neither side were the forces drawn up to advantage; for, on the one, Gellius Egnatius, the Samnite general, had gone out to forage with a few cohorts, and his men entered on the fight as the violence of their passions prompted, rather than under any directions or orders. On the other, the Roman armies neither marched out together, nor had time sufficient to form: Volumnius began to engage before Appius came up to the enemy, consequently the engagement commenced, their front in the battle being uneven; and by some accidental interchange of their usual opponents, the Etrurians fought against Volumnius; and the Samnites, after delaying some time on account of the absence of their general, against Appius. We are told that Appius, during the heat of the fight, raising his hands toward heaven, so as to be seen in the foremost ranks, prayed thus, "Bellona, if thou grantest us the victory this day, I vow to thee a temple." And that after this vow, as if inspirited by the goddess, he displayed a degree of courage equal to that of his colleague and of the troops. The generals performed every duty, and each of their armies exerted, with emulation, its utmost vigour, lest victory should commence on the other side. They therefore routed and put to flight the enemy, who were ill able to withstand a force so much superior to any with which they had been accustomed to contend: then pressing them as they gave ground, and pursuing them closely as they fled, they drove them into their camp. There, by the interposition of Gellius and his Samnite cohorts, the fight was renewed for a little time. But these being likewise soon dispersed, the camp was now stormed by the conquerors; and whilst Volumnius, in person, led his troops against one of the gates, Appius, frequently invoking Bellona the victorious, inflamed the courage of his men, they broke in through the rampart and trenches. The camp was taken and plundered, and an abundance of spoil was found, and given up to the soldiers. Of the enemy seven thousand three hundred were slain; and two thousand one hundred and twenty taken.

While both the consuls, with the whole force of the Romans, pointed their exertions principally against the war in Etruria, a new army which arose in Samnium, with design to ravage the frontiers of the Roman empire, passed over through the country of the Vescians, into the Campanian and Falernian territories, and committed great depredations. Volumnius, as he was hastening back to Samnium, by forced marches, because the term for which Fabius and Decius had been continued in command was nearly expired, heard of this army of Samnites, and of the mischief which they had done in Campania; determining, therefore, to afford protection to the allies, he altered his route towards that quarter. When he arrived in the district of Gales, he found marks of their recent ravages; and the people of Gales informed him that the enemy carried with them such a quantity of spoil, that they could scarcely observe any order in their march: and that the commanders then directed publicly that the troops should go immediately to Samnium, and having deposited the booty there, that they should return to the business of the expedition, as they must not commit to the hazard of an engagement an army so heavily laden. Notwithstanding that this account carried every appearance of truth, he yet thought it necessary to obtain more certain information; accordingly he despatched some horsemen, to seize on some of the straggling marauders; from these he learned, on inquiry, that the enemy lay at the river Vulturnus; that they intended to remove thence at the third watch; and that their route was towards Samnium. On receiving this intelligence, which could be depended upon, he set out, and sat down at such a distance from the enemy, that his approach could not be discovered by his being too near them, and, at the same time, that he might surprise them, as they should be coming out of their camp. A long time before day, he drew nigh to their post, and sent persons, who understood the Oscan language, to discover how they were employed: these, mixing with the enemy, which they could easily do during the confusion in the night, found that the standards had gone out thinly attended; that the booty, and those appointed to guard it, were then setting out, a contemptible train; each busied about his own affairs, without any concert with the rest, or much regard to orders. This was judged the fittest time for the attack, and daylight was now approaching; he gave orders to sound the charge, and fell on the enemy as they were marching out. The Samnites being embarrassed with the spoil, and very few armed, some quickened their pace, and drove the prey before them; others halted, deliberating whether it would be safer to advance, or to return again to the camp; and while they hesitated, they were overtaken and cut off. The Romans had by this time passed over the rampart, and filled the camp with slaughter and confusion: the Samnite army, in addition to the disorder caused by the enemy, had their disorder increased by a sudden insurrection of their prisoners; some of whom, getting loose, set the rest at liberty, while others snatched the arms which were tied up among the baggage, and being intermixed with the troops, raised a tumult more terrible than the battle itself. They then performed a memorable exploit: for making an attack on Statius Minacius, the general, as he was passing between the ranks and encouraging his men; then, dispersing the horsemen who attended him, they gathered round himself, and dragged him, sitting on his horse, a prisoner to the Roman consul. By this movement the foremost battalions of the Samnites were brought back, and the battle, which seemed to have been already decided, was renewed: but they could not support it long. Six thousand of them were slain, and two thousand five hundred taken, among whom were four military tribunes, together with thirty standards, and, what gave the conquerors greater joy than all, seven thousand four hundred prisoners were recovered. The spoil which had been taken from the allies was immense, and the owners were summoned by a proclamation, to claim and receive then property. On the day appointed, all the effects, the owners of which did not appear, were given to the soldiers, who were obliged to sell them, in order that they might have nothing to think of but their duty.

The depredations, committed on the lands of Campania, had occasioned a violent alarm at Rome, and it happened, that about the same time intelligence was brought from Etruria, that, after the departure of Volumnius's army, all that country had risen up in arms, and that Gellius Egnatius, the leader of the Samnites, was causing the Umbrians to join in the insurrection, and tempting the Gauls with high offers. Terrified at this news, the senate ordered the courts of justice to be shut, and a levy to be made of men of every description. Accordingly not only free-born men and the younger sort were obliged to enlist, but cohorts were formed of the elder citizens, and the sons of freed-men were incorporated in the centuries. Plans were formed for the defence of the city, and the prætor, Publius Sempronius, was invested with the chief command. However, the senate was exonerated of one half of their anxiety, by a letter from the consul, Lucius Volumnius informing them that the army, which had ravaged Campania, had been defeated and dispersed whereupon, they decreed a public thanksgiving for this success, in the name of the consul. The courts were opened, after having been shut eighteen days, and the thanksgiving was performed with much joy. They then turned their thoughts to devising measures for the future security of the country depopulated by the Samnites, and, with this view, it was resolved, that two colonies should be settled on the frontiers of the Vescian and Falernian territories, one at the mouth of the river Liris, which has received the name of Minturnæ, the other in the Vescian forest, which borders on the Falernian territory, where, it is said, stood Sinope, a city of Grecians, called thenceforth by the Roman colonists Sinuessa. The plebeian tribunes were charged to procure an order of the commons, commanding Publius Sempronius, the prætor, to create triumphs for conducting the colonies to those places. But persons were not readily found to give in their names, because they considered that they were being sent into what was almost a perpetual advanced guard in a hostile country, not as a provision from concord between consuls, and the evils arising from their disagreement in the conduct of military affairs; at the same time remarking, "how near the extremity of danger matters had been brought, by the late dispute between his colleague and himself." He warmly recommended to Decius and Fabius to "live together with one mind and one spirit." Observed that "they were men qualified by nature for military command: great in action, but unpractised in the strife of words and eloquence; their talents were such as eminently became consuls. As to the artful and the ingenious lawyers and orators, such as Appius Claudius, they ought to be kept at home to preside in the city and the forum; and to be appointed prætors for the administration of justice." In these proceedings that day was spent, and, on the following, the elections both of consuls and prætor were held, and were guided by the recommendations suggested by the consul. Quintus Fabius and Publius Decius were chosen consuls; Appius Claudius, prætor; all of them absent; and, by a decree of the senate, followed by an order of the commons, Lucius Volumnius was continued in the command for another year.

During that year many prodigies happened. For the purpose of averting which, the senate decreed a supplication for two days: the wine and frankincense for the sacrifices were furnished at the expense of the public; and numerous crowds of men and women attended the performance. This supplication was rendered remarkable by a quarrel, which broke out among the matrons in the chapel of patrician chastity, which stands in the cattle market, near the round temple of Hercules. Virginia, daughter of Aulus, a patrician, but married to Volumnius the consul, a plebeian, was, because she had married out of the patricians, excluded by the matrons from sharing in the sacred rites: a short altercation ensued, which was afterwards, through the intemperance of passion incident to the sex, kindled into a flame of contention. Virginia boasted with truth that she had a right to enter the temple of patrician chastity, as being of patrician birth, and chaste in her character, and, besides, the wife of one husband, to whom she was betrothed a virgin, and had no reason to be dissatisfied either with her husband, or his exploits or honours: to her high-spirited words, she added importance by an extraordinary act. In the long street where she resided, she enclosed with a partition a part of the house, of a size sufficient for a small chapel, and there erected an altar. Then calling together the plebeian matrons, and complaining of the injurious behaviour of the patrician ladies, she said, "This altar I dedicate to plebeian chastity, and exhort you, that the same degree of emulation which prevails among the men of this state, on the point of valour, may be maintained by the women on the point of chastity; and that you contribute your best care, that this altar may have the credit of being attended with a greater degree of sanctity, and by chaster women, than the other, if possible." Solemn rites were performed at this altar under the same regulations, nearly, with those at the more ancient one; no person being allowed the privilege of taking part in the sacrifices, except a woman of approved chastity, and who was the wife of one husband. This institution, being afterwards debased by [the admission of] vicious characters, and not only by matrons, but women of every description, sunk at last into oblivion. During this year the Ogulnii, Cneius and Quintus, being curule ædiles, carried on prosecutions against several usurers; whose property being fined, out of the produce, which was deposited in the treasury, they ordered brazen thresholds for the Capitol, utensils of plate for three tables in the chapel of Jupiter, a statue of Jupiter in a chariot drawn by four horses placed on the roof, and images of the founders of the city in their infant state under the teats of the wolf, at the Ruminal fig-tree. They also paved with square stones the roads from the Capuan gate to the temple of Mars. By the plebeian ædiles likewise, Lucius Ælius Pætus and Caius Fulvius Corvus, out of money levied as fines on farmers of the public pastures, whom they had convicted of malpractices, games were exhibited, and golden bowls were placed in the temple of Ceres.

Then came into the consulship Quintus Fabius a fifth time, and Publius Decius a fourth. They had been colleagues from the censorship, and twice in the consulship, and were celebrated not more for their glorious achievements, splendid as these were, than for the unanimity which had ever subsisted between them. The continuance of this feeling I am inclined to think was interrupted by a jarring between the [opposite] orders rather than between themselves, the patricians endeavouring that Fabius should have Etruria for his province, without casting lots, and the plebeians insisting that Decius should bring the matter to the decision of lots. There was certainly a contention in the senate, and the interest of Fabius being superior there, the business was brought before the people. Here, between military men who laid greater stress on deeds than on words, the debate was short. Fabius said, "that it was unreasonable, after he had planted a tree, another should gather the fruit of it. He had opened the Ciminian forest, and made a way for the Roman arms, through passes until then impracticable. Why had they disturbed him, at that time of his life, if they intended to give the management of the war to another?" Then, in the way of a gentle reproof, he observed, that "instead of an associate in command, he had chosen an adversary; and that Decius thought it too much that their unanimity should last through three consulates." Declaring, in fine, that "he desired nothing further, than that, if they thought him qualified for the command in the province, they should send him thither. He had submitted to the judgment of the senate, and would now be governed by the authority of the people." Publius Decius complained of injustice in the senate; and asserted, that "the patricians had laboured, as long as possible, to exclude the plebeians from all access to the higher honours; and since merit, by its own intrinsic power, had prevailed so far, as that it should not, in any rank of men, be precluded from the attainment of honours, expedients were sought how not only the suffrages of the people, but even the decisions of fortune may be rendered ineffectual, and be converted to the aggrandizement of a few. All the consuls before him had disposed of the provinces by lots; now, the senate bestowed a province on Fabius without lots. If this was meant as a mark of honour, the merits of Fabius were so great towards the commonwealth, and towards himself in particular, that he would gladly second the advancement of his reputation, provided only its splendour could be increased without reflecting dishonour on himself. But who did not see, that, when a war of difficulty and danger, and out of the ordinary course, was committed to only that one consul, the other would be considered as useless and insignificant. Fabius gloried in his exploits performed in Etruria: Publius Decius wished for a like subject of glory, and perhaps would utterly extinguish that fire, which the other left smothered, in such a manner that it often broke out anew, in sudden conflagrations. In fine, honours and rewards he would concede to his colleague, out of respect to his age and dignified character: but when danger, when a vigorous struggle with an enemy was before them, he never did, nor ever would, willingly, give place. With respect to the present dispute, this much he would gain at all events, that a business, appertaining to the jurisdiction of the people, should be determined by an order of that people, and not complimented away by the senate. He prayed Jupiter, supremely good and great, and all the immortal gods, not to grant him an equal chance with his colleague, unless they intended to grant him equal ability and success, in the management of the war. It was certainly in its nature reasonable, in the example salutary, and concerned the reputation of the Roman people, that the consuls should be men of such abilities, that under either of them a war with Etruria could be well managed." Fabius, after requesting of the people nothing else than that, before the tribes were called in to give their votes, they would hear the letters of the prætor Appius Claudius, written from Etruria, withdrew from the Comitium, and with no less unanimity of the people than of the senate, the province of Etruria was decreed to him without having recourse to lots.

Immediately almost all the younger citizens flocked together to the consul, and readily gave in their names; so strong was their desire of serving under such a commander. Seeing so great a multitude collected round him, he said, "My intention is to enlist only four thousand foot and six hundred horse: such of you as give in your names to-day and to-morrow, I will carry with me. I am more solicitous to bring home all my soldiers rich, than to employ a great multitude." Accordingly, with a competent number of men, who possessed greater hopes and confidence because a numerous army had not been required, he marched to the town of Aharna, from which the enemy were not far distant, and proceeded to the camp of the prætor Appius. When within a few miles of it, he was met by some soldiers, sent to cut wood, attended by a guard. Observing the lictors preceding him, and learning that he was Fabius the consul, they were filled with joy and alacrity; they expressed their thanks to the gods, and to the Roman people, for having sent them such a commander. Then as they gathered round to pay their respects, Fabius inquired whither they were going, and on their answering they were going to provide wood, "What do you tell me," said he, "have you not a rampart, raised about your camp?" When to this they replied, "they had a double rampart, and a trench, and, notwithstanding, were in great apprehension." "Well then," said he, "you have abundance of wood, go back and level the rampart." They accordingly returned to the camp and there levelling the rampart threw the soldiers who had remained in it, and Appius himself, into the greatest fright, until with eager joy each called out to the rest, that, "they acted by order of the consul, Quintus Fabius." Next day the camp was moved from thence, and the prætor, Appius, was dismissed to Rome. From that time the Romans had no fixed post, the consul affirming, that it was prejudicial to an army to lie in one spot, and that by frequent marches, and changing places, it was rendered more healthy, and more capable of brisk exertions, and marches were made as long as the winter, which was not yet ended, permitted. Then, in the beginning of spring, leaving the second legion near Clusium, which they formerly called the Camertian, and giving the command of the camp to Lucius Scipio, as proprætor, he returned to Rome, in order to adjust measures for carrying on the war, either led thereto by his own judgment, because the war seemed to him more serious than he had believed, from report, or, being summoned by a decree of the senate, for writers give both accounts. Some choose to have it believed, that he was forced back by the prætor, Appius Claudius, who, both in the senate, and before the people, exaggerated, as he was wont in all his letters, the danger of the Etrurian war, contending, that "one general, or one army, would not be sufficient to oppose four nations. That whether these directed the whole of their combined force against him alone, or acted separately in different parts, there was reason to fear, that he would be unable to provide against every emergency. That he had left there but two Roman legions; and that the foot and horse, who came with Fabius, did not amount to five thousand. It was, therefore, his opinion, that the consul, Publius Decius should, without delay, set out to his colleague in Etruria, and that the province of Samnium should be given to Lucius Volumnius. But if the consul preferred going to his own province, that then Volumnius should march a full consular army into Etruria, to join the other consul." When the advice of the prætor influenced a great part of the members, they say that Publius Decius recommended that every thing should be kept undetermined, and open for Quintus Fabius; until he should either come to Rome, if he could do so without prejudice to the public, or send some of his lieutenants, from whom the senate might learn the real state of the war in Etruria; and with what number of troops, and by how many generals, it should be carried on.

Fabius, as soon as he returned to Rome, qualified his discourses, both in the senate and when brought before the people, in such a manner as to appear neither to exaggerate or lessen, any particular relating to the war; and to show, that, in agreeing to another general being joined with him, he rather indulged the apprehensions of others, than guarded against any danger to himself, or the public. "But if they chose," he said, "to give him an assistant in the war, and associate in command, how could he overlook Publius Decius the consul, whom he had tried during so many associations in office? There was no man living whom he would rather wish to be joined in commission with him: with Publius Decius he should have forces sufficient, and never too many enemies. If, however, his colleague preferred any other employment, let them then give him Lucius Volumnius as an assistant." The disposal of every particular was left entirely to Fabius by the people and the senate, and even by his colleague. And when Decius declared that he was ready to go either to Etruria or Samnium, such general congratulation and satisfaction took place, that victory was anticipated, and it seemed as if a triumph, not a war, had been decreed to the consuls. I find in some writers, that Fabius and Decius, immediately on their entering into office, set out together for Etruria, without any mention of the casting of lots for the provinces, or of the disputes which I have related. Others, not satisfied with relating those disputes, have added charges of misconduct, laid by Appius before the people against Fabius, when absent; and a stubborn opposition, maintained by the prætor against the consul, when present; and also another contention between the colleagues, Decius insisting that each consul should attend to the care of his own separate province. Certainty, however, begins to appear from the time when both consuls set out for the campaign. Now, before the consuls arrived in Etruria, the Senonian Gauls came in a vast body to Clusium, to attack the Roman legion and the camp. Scipio, who commanded the camp, wishing to remedy the deficiency of his numbers by an advantage in the ground, led his men up a hill, which stood between the camp and the city but having, in his haste, neglected to examine the place, he reached near the summit, which he found already possessed by the enemy, who had ascended on the other side. The legion was consequently attacked on the rear, and surrounded in the middle, when the enemy pressed it on all sides. Some writers say, that the whole were cut off, so that not one survived to give an account of it, and that no information of the misfortune reached the consuls, who were, at the time, not far from Clusium, until the Gallic horsemen came within sight, carrying the heads of the slain, some hanging before their horses' breasts, others on the points of their spears, and expressing their triumph in songs according to their custom. Others affirm, that the defeat was by Umbrians, not Gauls, and that the loss sustained was not so great. That a party of foragers, under Lucius Manlius Torquatus, lieutenant-general, being surrounded, Scipio, the proprætor, brought up relief from the camp, and the battle being renewed, that the Umbrians, lately victorious, were defeated, and the prisoners and spoil retaken. But it is more probable that this blow was suffered from a Gallic than an Umbrian enemy, because during that year, as was often the case at other times, the danger principally apprehended by the public, was that of a Gallic tumult, for which reason, notwithstanding that both the consuls had marched against the enemy, with four legions, and a large body of Roman cavalry, joined by a thousand chosen horsemen of Campania, supplied on the occasion, and a body of the allies and Latin confederates, superior in number to the Romans, two other armies were posted near the city, on the side facing Etruria, one in the Faliscian, the other in the Vatican territory. Cneius Fulvius and Lucius Postumius Megellus, both proprætors, were ordered to keep the troops stationed in those places.

The consuls, having crossed the Apennines, came up with the enemy in the territory of Sentinum, their camp was pitched there at the distance of about four miles. Several councils were then held by the enemy, and their plan of operations was thus settled: that they should not encamp together, nor go out together to battle; the Gauls were united to the Samnites, the Umbrians to the Etrurians. The day of battle was fixed. The part of maintaining the fight was committed to the Samnites and Gauls; and the Etrurians and Umbrians were ordered to attack the Roman camp during the heat of the engagement. This plan was frustrated by three Clusian deserters, who came over by night to Fabius, and after disclosing the above designs, were sent back with presents, in order that they might discover, and bring intelligence of, any new scheme which should be determined on. The consuls then wrote to Flavius and Postumius to move their armies, the one from the Faliscian, the other from the Vatican country, towards Clusium; and to ruin the enemy's territory by every means in their power. The news of these depredations drew the Etrurians from Sentinum to protect their own region. The consuls, in their absence, practised every means to bring on an engagement. For two days they endeavoured, by several attacks, to provoke the enemy to fight; in which time, however, nothing worth mention was performed. A few fell on each side, but still the minds [of the Romans] were irritated to wish for a general engagement; yet nothing decisive was hazarded. On the third day, both parties marched out their whole force to the field: here, while the armies stood in order of battle, a hind, chased by a wolf from the mountains, ran through the plain between the two lines: there the animals taking different directions, the hind bent its course towards the Gauls, the wolf towards the Romans: way was made between the ranks for the wolf, the Gauls slew the hind with their javelins; on which one of the Roman soldiers in the van said, "To that side, where you see an animal, sacred to Diana, lying prostrate, flight and slaughter are directed; on this side the victorious wolf of Mars, safe and untouched, reminds us of our founder, and of our descent from that deity." The Gauls were posted on the right wing, the Samnites on the left: against the latter, Fabius drew up, as his right wing, the first and third legions: against the Gauls, Decius formed the left wing of the fifth and sixth. The second and fourth were employed in the war in Samnium, under the proconsul, Lucius Volumnius. In the first encounter the action was supported with strength so equal on both sides, that had the Etrurians and Umbrians been present, either in the field or at the camp, in whichever place they might have employed their force, the Romans must have been defeated.

However, although the victory was still undecided, fortune not having declared in favour of either party, yet the course of the fight was by no means similar on both right and left wings. The Romans, under Fabius, rather repelled than offered assault, and the contest was protracted until very late in the day, for their general knew very well, that both Samnites and Gauls were furious in the first onset, so that, to withstand them would be sufficient. It was known, too, that in a protracted contest the spirits of the Samnites gradually flagged, and even the bodies of the Gauls, remarkably ill able to bear labour and heat, became quite relaxed, and although, in their first efforts, they were more than men, yet in their last they were less than women. He, therefore, reserved the strength of his men as unimpaired as possible, until the time when the enemy were the more likely to be worsted. Decius, more impetuous, as being in the prime of life and full flow of spirits, exerted whatever force he had to the utmost in the first encounter, and thinking the infantry not sufficiently energetic, brought up the cavalry to the fight. Putting himself at the head of a troop of young horsemen of distinguished bravery, he besought those youths, the flower of the army, to charge the enemy with him, [telling them] "they would reap a double share of glory, if the victory should commence on the left wing, and through their means." Twice they compelled the Gallic cavalry to give way. At the second charge, when they advanced farther and were briskly engaged in the midst of the enemy's squadrons, by a method of fighting new to them, they were thrown into dismay. A number of the enemy, mounted on chariots and cars, made towards them with such a prodigious clatter from the trampling of the cattle and rolling of wheels, as affrighted the horses of the Romans, unaccustomed to such tumultuous operations. By this means the victorious cavalry were dispersed, through a panic, and men and horses, in their headlong flight, were tumbled promiscuously on the ground. Hence also the battalions of the legions were thrown into disorder, through the impetuosity of the horses, and of the carriages which they dragged through the ranks, many of the soldiers in the van were trodden or bruised to death, while the Gallic line, as soon as they saw their enemy in confusion, pursued the advantage, nor allowed them time to take breath or recover themselves. Decius, calling aloud, "Whither were they flying, or what hope could they have in running away?" strove to stop them as they turned their backs, but finding that he could not, by any efforts, prevail on them to keep their posts, so thoroughly were they dismayed, he called on his father, Publius Decius, by name. He said, "Why do I any longer defer the fate entailed on my family? It is destined to our race, that we should serve as expiatory victims to avert the public danger. I will now offer the legions of the enemy, together with myself, to be immolated to Earth, and the infernal gods." Having thus said, he commanded Marcus Livius, a pontiff, whom, at his coming out to the field, he had charged not to stir from him, to dictate the form of words in which he was to devote himself, and the legions of the enemy, for the army of the Roman people, the Quirites. He was accordingly devoted with the same imprecations, and in the same habit, in which his father, Publius Decius, had ordered himself to be devoted at the Veseris in the Latin war. When, immediately after the solemn imprecation, he added, that "he drove before him dismay and flight, slaughter and blood, and the wrath of the gods celestial and infernal, that, with the contagious influence of the furies, the ministers of death, he would infect the standards, the weapons, and the armour of the enemy, and that the same spot should be that of his perdition, and that of the Gauls and Samnites." After uttering these execrations on himself and the foe, he spurred forward his horse, where he saw the line of the Gauls thickest, and, rushing upon the enemy's weapons, met his death.

Thenceforward the battle seemed to be fought with a degree of force scarcely human. The Romans, on the loss of their general, a circumstance which, on other occasions, is wont to inspire terror, stopped their flight, and were anxious to begin the combat afresh. The Gauls, and especially the multitude which encircled the consul's body, as if deprived of reason, cast their javelins at random without execution, some became so stupid as not to think of either fighting or flying, while on the other side, Livius, the pontiff, to whom Decius had transferred his lictors, with orders to act as proprætor, cried out aloud, that "the Romans were victorious, being saved by the death of their consul. That the Gauls and Samnites were now the victims of mother Earth and the infernal gods. That Decius was summoning and dragging to himself the army devoted along with him, and that, among the enemy, all was full of dismay, and the vengeance of all the furies." While the soldiers were busy in restoring the fight, Lucius Cornelius Scipio and Caius Marcius, with some reserved troops from the rear, who had been sent by Quintus Fabius, the consul, to the support of his colleague, came up. There the fate of Decius is ascertained, a powerful stimulus to brave every danger in the cause of the public. Wherefore, when the Gauls stood in close order, with their shields formed into a fence before them, and but little prospect of success appeared from a close fight, the javelins, which lay scattered between the two lines, were, therefore, by order of the lieutenants-general, gathered up from the ground, and thrown against the enemy's shields, and as most of them pierced the fence, the long pointed ones even into their bodies, their compact band was overthrown in such a manner, that a great many, who were unhurt, yet fell as if thunderstruck. Such were the changes of fortune on the left wing of the Romans; on the right, Fabius had at first protracted the time, as we mentioned above, in slow operations, then, as soon as he perceived that neither the shout, nor the efforts of the enemy, nor the weapons which they threw, retained their former force, having ordered the commanders of the cavalry to lead round their squadrons to the flank of the Samnites, so that, on receiving the signal, they should charge them in flank, with all possible violence, he commanded, at the same time, his infantry to advance leisurely, and drive the enemy from their ground. When he saw that they were unable to make resistance, and that their exhaustion was certain, drawing together all his reserves, whom he had kept fresh for that occasion, he made a brisk push with the legions, and gave the cavalry the signal to charge. The Samnites could not support the shock, but fled precipitately to their camp, passing by the line of the Gauls, and leaving their allies to fight by themselves. These stood in close order under cover of their shields. Fabius, therefore, having heard of the death of his colleague, ordered the squadron of Campanian cavalry, in number about five hundred, to fall back from the ranks, and riding round, to attack the rear of the Gallic line, then the chief strength of the third legion to follow, with directions that wherever they should see the enemy's troops disordered by the charge, to follow the blow, and cut them to pieces, when in a state of consternation. After vowing a temple and the spoils of the enemy to Jupiter the Victorious, he proceeded to the camp of the Samnites, whither all their forces were hurrying in confusion. The gates not affording entrance to such very great numbers, those who were necessarily excluded, attempted resistance just at the foot of the rampart, and here fell Gellius Egnatius, the Samnite general. These, however, were soon driven within the rampart; the camp was taken after a slight resistance; and at the same time the Gauls were attacked on the rear, and overpowered. There were slain of the enemy on that day twenty-five thousand: eight thousand were taken prisoners. Nor was the victory an unbloody one; for, of the army of Publius Decius, the killed amounted to seven thousand; of the army of Fabius, to one thousand two hundred. Fabius, after sending persons to search for the body of his colleague, had the spoils of the enemy collected into a heap, and burned them as an offering to Jupiter the Victorious. The consul's body could not be found that day, being hid under a heap of slaughtered Gauls: on the following, it was discovered and brought to the camp, amidst abundance of tears shed by the soldiers. Fabius, discarding all concern about any other business, solemnized the obsequies of his colleague in the most honourable manner, passing on him the high encomiums which he had justly merited.

During the same period, matters were managed successfully by Cneius Fulvius, proprætor, he having, besides the immense losses occasioned to the enemy by the devastation of their lands, fought a battle with extraordinary success, in which there were above three thousand of the Perusians and Clusians slain, and twenty military standards taken. The Samnites, in their flight, passing through the Pelignian territory, were attacked on all sides by the Pelignians; and, out of five thousand, one thousand were killed. The glory of the day on which they fought at Sentinum was great, even when truly estimated; but some have gone beyond credibility by their exaggerations, who assert in their writings, that there were in the army of the enemy forty thousand three hundred and thirty foot, six thousand horse, and one thousand chariots, that is, including the Etrurians and Umbrians, who [they affirm] were present in the engagement: and, to magnify likewise the number of Roman forces, they add to the consuls another general, Lucius Volumnius, proconsul, and his army to the legions of the consul. In the greater number of annals, that victory is ascribed entirely to the two consuls. Volumnius was employed in the mean time in Samnium; he drove the army of the Samnites to Mount Tifernus, and, not deterred by the difficulty of the ground, routed and dispersed them. Quintus Fabius, leaving Decius's army in Etruria, and leading off his own legions to the city, triumphed over the Gauls, Etrurians, and Samnites: the soldiers attended him in his triumph. The victory of Quintus Fabius was not more highly celebrated, in their coarse military verses, than the illustrious death of Publius Decius; and the memory of the father was recalled, whose fame had been equalled by the praiseworthy conduct of the son, in respect of the issue which resulted both to himself and to the public. Out of the spoil, donations were made to the soldiers of eighty-two *asses* [4] to each, with cloaks and vests; rewards for service, in that age, by no means contemptible.

Notwithstanding these successes, peace was not yet established, either among the Samnites or Etrurians: for the latter, at the instigation of the Perusians, resumed their arms, after his army had been withdrawn by the consul; and the Samnites made predatory incursions on the territories of Vescia and Formiæ; and also on the other side, on those of

Æsernia, and the parts adjacent to the river Vulturnus. Against these was sent the prætor Appius Claudius, with the army formerly commanded by Decius. In Etruria, Fabius, on the revival of hostilities, slew four thousand five hundred of the Perusians, and took prisoners one thousand seven hundred and forty, who were ransomed at the rate of three hundred and ten *asses* [5] each. All the rest of the spoil was bestowed on the soldiers. The legions of the Samnites, though pursued, some by the prætor Appius Claudius, the others by Lucius Volumnius, proconsul, formed a junction in the country of the Stellatians. Here sat down the whole body of the Samnites; and Appius and Volumnius, with their forces united in one camp. A battle was fought with the most rancorous animosity, one party being spurred on by rage against men who had so often renewed their attacks on them, and the other now fighting in support of their last remaining hope. Accordingly, there were slain, of the Samnites, sixteen thousand three hundred, and two thousand and seven hundred made prisoners: of the Roman army fell two thousand and seven hundred. This year, so successful in the operations of war, was filled with distress at home, arising from a pestilence, and with anxiety, occasioned by prodigies: for accounts were received that, in many places, showers of earth had fallen; and that very many persons, in the army of Appius Claudius, had been struck by lightning; in consequence of which, the books were consulted. At this time, Quintus Fabius Gurges, the consul's son, having prosecuted some matrons before the people on a charge of adultery, built, with the money accruing from the fines which they were condemned to pay, the temple of Venus, which stands near the circus. Still we have the wars of the Samnites on our hands, notwithstanding that the relation of them has already extended, in one continued course, through four volumes of our history, and through a period of forty-six years, from the consulate of Marcus Valerius and Aulus Cornelius, who first carried the Roman arms into Samnium. And, not to recite the long train of disasters sustained by both nations, and the toils which they underwent, by which, however, their stubborn breasts could not be subdued; even in the course of the last year, the Samnites, with their own forces separately, and also in conjunction with those of other nations, had been defeated by four several armies, and four generals of the Romans, in the territory of Sentinum, in that of the Pelignians, at Tifernum, and in the plains of the Stellatians; had lost the general of the highest character in their nation; and, now, saw their allies in the war, the Etrurians, the Umbrians, and the Gauls, in the same situation with themselves; but, although they could now no longer stand, either by their own or by foreign resources, yet did they not desist from the prosecution of hostilities. So far were they from being weary of defending liberty, even though unsuccessfully: and they preferred being defeated to not aspiring after victory. Who does not find his patience tired, either in writing, or reading, of wars of such continuance; and which yet exhausted not the resolution of the parties concerned?

Quintus Fabius and Publius Decius were succeeded in the consulship by Lucius Postumius Megellus and Marcus Atilius Regulus. The province of Samnium was decreed to both in conjunction; because intelligence had been received that the enemy had embodied three armies; with one that Etruria was to be recovered; with another the ravages in Campania were to be repeated; and the third was intended for the defence of their frontiers. Sickness detained Postumius at Rome, but Atilius set out immediately, with design to surprise the enemy in Samnium, before they should have advanced beyond their own borders; for such had been the directions of the senate. The Romans met the enemy, as if by mutual appointment, at a spot where, while they could be hindered, not only from ravaging, but even from entering the Samnite territory, they could likewise hinder the Samnites from continuing their progress into the countries which were quiet, and the lands of the allies of the Roman people. While their camps lay opposite to each other, the Samnites attempted an enterprise, which the Romans, so often their conquerors, would scarcely have ventured to undertake; such is the rashness inspired by extreme despair: this was to make an assault on the Roman camp. And although this attempt, so daring, succeeded not in its full extent, yet it was not without effect. There was a fog, which continued through a great part of the day, so thick as to exclude the light of the sun, and to prevent not only the view of any thing beyond the rampart, but scarcely the sight of each other, when they should meet. Depending on this, as a covering to the design, when the sun was scarcely yet risen, and the light which he did afford was obscured by the fog, the Samnites came up to an advanced guard of the Romans at one of the gates, who were standing carelessly on their post. In the sudden surprise, these had neither courage nor strength to make resistance: an assault was then made, through the Decuman gate, in the rear of the camp: the quæstor's quarters in consequence were taken, and the quæstor, Lucius Opimius Pansa, was there slain; on this a general alarm was given to take up arms.

The consul, being roused by the tumult, ordered two cohorts of the allies, a Lucanian and Suessanian, which happened to be nearest, to defend the head-quarters, and led the companies of the legions down the principal street. These ran into the ranks, scarcely taking time to furnish themselves with arms; and, as they distinguished the enemy by their shout rather than by sight, could form no judgment how great their number might be: thus, ignorant of the circumstances of their situation, they at first drew back, and admitted the enemy into the heart of the camp. Then when the consul cried out, asking them, whether they intended to let themselves be beaten out beyond the rampart, and then to return again to storm their own camp, they raised the shout, and uniting their efforts, stood their ground; then made advances, pushed closely on the enemy, and having forced them to give way, drove them back, without suffering their first terror to abate. They soon beat them out beyond the gate and the rampart, but not daring to pursue them, because the darkness of the weather made them apprehend an ambush, and content with having cleared the camp, they retired within the rampart, having killed about three hundred of the enemy. Of the Romans, including the first advanced guard and the watchmen, and those who were surprised at the quæstor's quarters, two hundred and thirty perished. This not unsuccessful piece of boldness raised the spirits of the Samnites so high, that they not only did not suffer the Romans to march forward into their country, but even to procure forage from their lands; and the foragers were obliged to go back into the quiet country of Sora. News of these events being conveyed to Rome, with circumstances of alarm magnified beyond the truth, obliged Lucius Postumius, the consul, though scarcely recovered from his illness, to set out for the army. However, before his departure, having issued a proclamation that his troops should assemble at Sora, he dedicated the temple of Victory, for the building of which he had provided, when curule ædile, out of the money arising from fines; and, joining the army, he advanced from Sora towards Samnium, to the camp of his colleague. The Samnites, despairing of being able to make head against the two armies, retreated from thence, on which the consuls, separating, proceeded by different routes to lay waste the enemy's lands and besiege their towns.

Postumius attempted to make himself master of Milionia, at first by storm and an assault; but these not succeeding, he carried his approaches to the walls, and thus gained an entrance into the place. The fight was continued in all parts of the city from the fourth hour until near the eighth, the result being a long time uncertain: the Romans at last gained possession of the town. Three thousand two hundred of the Samnites were killed, four thousand seven hundred taken, besides the other booty. From thence the legions were conducted to Ferentinum, out of which the inhabitants had, during the night, retired in silence through the opposite gate, with all their effects which could be either carried or driven. The consul, on his arrival, approached the walls with the same order and circumspection, as if he were to meet an opposition here equal to what he had experienced at Milionia. Then, perceiving a dead silence in the city, and neither arms nor men on the towers and ramparts, he restrains the soldiers, who were eager to mount the deserted fortifications, lest they might fall into a snare. He ordered two divisions of the confederate Latin horse to ride round the walls, and explore every particular. These horsemen observed one gate, and, at a little distance, another on the same side, standing wide open, and on the roads leading from these every mark of the enemy having fled by night. They then rode up leisurely to the gates, from whence, with perfect safety, they took a clear view through straight streets quite across the city. They report to the consul, that the city was abandoned by the enemy, as was plain from the solitude, the recent tracks on their retreat, and the things which, in the confusion of the night, they had left scattered up and down. On hearing this, the consul led round the army to that side of the city which had been examined, and making the troops halt at a little distance from the gate, gave orders that five horsemen should ride into the city; and when they should have advanced a good way into it, then, if they saw all things safe, three should remain there, and the other two return to him with intelligence. These returned and said, that they had proceeded to a part of the town from which they had a view on every side, and that nothing but silence and solitude reigned through the whole extent of it. The consul immediately led some light-armed cohorts into the city; ordering the rest to fortify a camp in the mean time. The soldiers who entered the town, breaking open the doors, found only a few persons, disabled by age or sickness; and such effects left behind as could not, without difficulty, be removed. These were seized as plunder: and it was discovered from the prisoners, that several cities in that quarter had, in pursuance of a concerted plan, resolved on flight; that their towns-people had gone off at the first watch, and they believed that the same solitude they should find in the other places. The accounts of the prisoners proved well-founded, and the consul took possession of the forsaken towns.

The war was by no means so easy with the other consul, Marcus Atilius. As he was marching his legions towards Luceria, to which he was informed that the Samnites had laid siege, the enemy met him on the border of the Lucerian territory. Rage supplied them, on this occasion, with strength to equal his: the battle was stubbornly contested, and the victory doubtful; in the issue, however, more calamitous on the side of the Romans, both because they were unaccustomed to defeat, and that, on leaving the field, they felt more sensibly, than during the heat of the action, how much more wounds and bloodshed had been on their side. In consequence of this, such dismay spread through the camp, as, had it seized them during the engagement, a signal defeat would have been the result. Even as the matter stood, they spent the night in great anxiety; expecting, every instant, that the Samnites would assault the camp; or that, at the first light, they should be obliged to stand a battle with a victorious enemy. On the side of the enemy, however, although there was less loss, yet there was not greater courage. As soon as day appeared, they wished to retire without any more fighting; but there was only one road, and that leading close by the post of their enemy; on their taking which, they seemed as if advancing directly to attack the camp. The consul, therefore, ordered his men to take arms, and to follow him outside the rampart, giving directions to the lieutenants-general, tribunes, and the præfects of the allies, in what manner he would have each of them act.

They all assured him that "they would do every thing in their power, but that the soldiers were quite dejected; that, from their own wounds, and the groans of the dying, they had passed the whole night without sleep; that if the enemy had approached the camp before day, so great were the fears of the troops, that they would certainly have deserted their standards." "Even at present they were restrained from flight merely by shame; and, in other respects, were little better than vanquished men." This account made the consul judge it necessary to go himself among the soldiers, and speak to them; and, as he came up to each, he rebuked them for their backwardness in taking arms, asking, "Why they loitered, and declined the fight? If they did not choose to go out of the camp, the enemy would come into it; and they must fight in defence of their tents, if they would not in defence of the rampart. Men who have arms in their hands, and contend with their foe, have always a chance for victory; but the man who waits naked and unarmed for his enemy, must suffer either death or slavery." To these reprimands and rebukes they answered, that "they were exhausted by the fatigue of the battle of yesterday; and had no strength, nor even blood remaining; and besides, the enemy appeared more numerous than they were the day before." The hostile army, in the mean time, drew near; so that, seeing every thing more distinctly as the distance grew less, they asserted that the Samnites carried with them pallisades for a rampart, and evidently intended to draw lines of circumvallation round the camp. On this the consul exclaimed, with great earnestness, against submitting to such an ignominious insult, and from so dastardly a foe. "Shall we even be blockaded," said he, "in our camp, and die, with ignominy, by famine, rather than bravely by the sword, if it must be so? May the gods be propitious! and let every one act in the manner which he thinks becomes him. The consul Marcus Atilius, should no other accompany him, will go out, even alone, to face the enemy; and will fall in the middle of the Samnite battalions, rather than see the Roman camp enclosed by their trenches." The lieutenants-general, tribunes, every troop of the cavalry, and the principal centurions, expressed their approbation of what the consul said; and the soldiers at length, overcome by shame, took up their arms, but in a spiritless manner; and in the same spiritless manner, marched out of the camp. In a long train, and that not every where connected, melancholy, and seemingly subdued, they proceeded towards the enemy, whose hopes and courage, were not more steady than theirs. As soon therefore as the Roman standards were beheld, a murmur spread from front to rear of the Samnites, that, as they had feared, "the Romans were coming out to oppose their march; that there was no road open, through which they could even fly thence; in that spot they must fall, or else cut down the enemy's ranks, and make their way over their bodies."

They then threw the baggage in a heap in the centre, and, with their arms prepared for battle, formed their line, each falling into his post. There was now but a small interval between the two armies, and both stood, waiting until the shout and onset should be begun by their adversary. Neither party had any inclination to fight, and they would have separated, and taken different roads, unhurt and untouched, but that each had a dread of being harassed, in retreat, by the other. Notwithstanding this shyness and reluctance, an engagement unavoidably began, but spiritless, and with a shout which discovered neither resolution nor steadiness; nor did any move a foot from his post. The Roman consul, then, in order to infuse life into the action, ordered a few troops of cavalry to advance out of the line and charge: most of whom being thrown from their horses and the rest put in disorder, several parties ran forward, both from the Samnite line, to cut off those who had fallen, and from the Roman, to protect their friends. In consequence the battle became a little more brisk, but the Samnites had come forward with more briskness, and also in greater numbers, and the disordered cavalry, with their affrighted horses, trod down their own party who came to their relief. Flight commencing in this quarter, caused the whole Roman line to turn their backs. And now the Samnites had no employment for their arms but against the rear of a flying enemy, when the consul, galloping on before his men to the gate of the camp, posted there a body of cavalry, with orders to treat as an enemy any person who should make towards the rampart, whether Roman or Samnite; and, placing himself in the way of his men, as they pressed in disorder towards the camp, denounced threats to the same purport: "Whither are you going, soldiers?" said he; "here also you will find both men and arms; nor, while your consul lives, shall you pass the rampart, unless victorious. Choose therefore which you will prefer, fighting against your own countrymen, or the enemy." While the consul was thus speaking the cavalry gathered round, with the points of their spears presented, and ordered the infantry to return to the fight. Not only his own brave spirit, but fortune likewise aided the consul, for the Samnites did not push their advantage; so that he had time to wheel round his battalions, and to change his front from the camp towards the enemy. The men then began to encourage each other to return to the battle, while the centurions snatched the ensigns from the standard-bearers and bore them forward, pointing out to the soldiers the enemy, coming on in a hurry, few in number, and with their ranks disordered. At the same time the consul, with his hands lifted up towards heaven, and raising his voice so as to be heard at a distance, vowed a temple to Jupiter Stator, if the Roman army should rally from flight, and, renewing the battle, cut down and defeat the Samnites. All divisions of the army, now, united their efforts to restore the fight; officers, soldiers, the whole force, both of cavalry and infantry; even the powers of heaven seemed to have looked, with favour, on the Roman cause; so speedily was a thorough change effected in the fortune of the day, the enemy being repulsed from the camp, and, in a short time, driven back to the spot where the battle had commenced. Here they stopped, being obstructed by the heap of baggage, lying in their way, where they had thrown it together; and then, to prevent the plundering of their effects, formed round them a circle of troops. On this, the infantry assailed them vigorously in front, while the cavalry, wheeling, fell on their rear: and, being thus enclosed between the two, they were all either slain, or taken prisoners. The number of the prisoners was seven thousand two hundred, who were all sent under the yoke; the killed amounted to four thousand eight hundred. The victory did not prove a joyous one, even on the side of the Romans: when the consul took an account of the loss sustained in the two days, the number returned, of soldiers lost, was seven thousand three hundred. During these transactions in Apulia, the Samnites with the other army having attempted to seize on Iteramna, a Roman colony situated on the Latin road, did not however obtain the town; whence, after ravaging the country, as they were driving off spoil, consisting of men and cattle, together with the colonists whom they had taken, they met the consul returning victorious from Luceria, and not only lost their booty, but marching in disorder, in a long train, and heavily encumbered, were themselves cut to pieces. The consul, by proclamation, summoned the owners to Interamna, to claim and receive again their property, and leaving his army there, went to Rome to hold the elections. On his applying for a triumph, that honour was refused him, because he had lost so many thousands of his soldiers; and also, because he had sent the prisoners under the yoke without imposing any conditions.

The other consul, Postumius, because there was no employment for his arms in Samnium, having led over his forces into Etruria, first laid waste the lands of the Volsinians; and afterwards, on their marching out to protect their country, gained a decisive victory over them, at a small distance from their own walls. Two thousand two hundred of the Etrurians were slain; the proximity of their city protected the rest. The army was then led into the territory of Rusella, and there, not only were the lands wasted, but the town itself taken. More than two thousand men were made prisoners, and somewhat less than that number killed on the walls. But a peace, effected that year in Etruria, was still more important and honourable than the war had been. Three very powerful cities, the chief ones of Etruria, (Volsinii, Perusia, and Arretium,) sued for peace; and having stipulated with the consul to furnish clothing and corn for his army, on condition of being permitted to send deputies to Rome, they obtained a truce for forty years, and a fine was imposed on each state of five hundred thousand *asses*, [6] to be immediately paid. When the consul demanded a triumph from the senate, in consideration of these services, rather to comply with the general practice, than in hope of succeeding; and when he saw that one party, his own personal enemies, another party, the friends of his colleague, refused him the triumph, the latter to console a similar refusal, some on the plea that he had been rather tardy in taking his departure from the city; others, that he had passed from Samnium into Etruria without orders from the senate; he said, "Conscript fathers, I shall not be so far mindful of your dignity, as to forget that I am consul. By the same right of office by which I conducted the war, I shall now have a triumph, when this war has been brought to a happy conclusion, Samnium and Etruria being subdued, and victory and peace procured. With these words he left the senate." On this arose a contention between the plebeian tribunes; some of them declaring that they would protest against his triumphing in a manner unprecedented; others, that they would support his pretensions, in opposition to their colleagues. The affair came at length to be discussed before the people, and the consul being summoned to attend, when he represented, that Marcus Horatius and Lucius Valerius, when consuls, and lately Caius Marcus Rutilus, father of the present censor, had triumphed, not by direction of the senate, but by that of the people; he then added that "he would in like manner have laid his request before the public, had he not known that some plebeian tribunes, the abject slaves of the nobles, would have obstructed the law. That the universal approbation and will of the people were and should be with him equivalent to any order whatsoever." Accordingly, on the day following, by the support of three plebeian tribunes, in opposition to the protest of the other seven, and the declared judgment of the senate, he triumphed; and the people paid every honour to the day. The historical accounts regarding this year are by no means consistent; Claudius asserts, that Postumius, after having taken several cities in Samnium, was defeated and put to flight in Apulia; and that, being wounded himself, he was driven, with a few attendants, into Luceria. That the war in Etruria was conducted by Atilius, and that it was he who triumphed. Fabius writes, that the two consuls acted in conjunction, both in Samnium and at Luceria; that an army was led over into Etruria, but by which of the consuls he has not mentioned; that at Luceria, great numbers were slain on both sides; and that in that battle, the temple of Jupiter Stator was vowed, the same vow having been formerly made by Romulus, but the fane only, that is, the area appropriated for the temple, had been yet consecrated. However, in this year, the state having been twice bound by the same vow, it became a matter of religious obligation that the senate should order the temple to be erected.

In the next year, we find a consul, distinguished by the united splendour of his own and his father's glory, Lucius Papirius Cursor, as also a war of vast importance, and a victory of such consequence, as no man, excepting Lucius Papirius, the consul's father, had ever before obtained over the Samnites. It happened too that these had, with the same care and pains as on the former occasion, decorated their soldiers with the richest suits of splendid armour; and they had, likewise, called in to their aid the power of the gods, having, as it were, initiated the soldiers, by administering the military oath, with the solemn ceremonies practised in ancient times, and levied troops in every part of Samnium, under an ordinance entirely new, that "if any of the younger inhabitants should not attend the meeting, according to the general's proclamation, or shall depart without permission, his head should be devoted to Jupiter." Orders being then issued, for all to assemble at Aquilonia, the whole strength of Samnium came together, amounting to forty thousand men. There a piece of ground, in the middle of the camp, was enclosed with hurdles and boards, and covered overhead with linen cloth, the sides being all of an equal length, about two hundred feet. In this place sacrifices were performed, according to directions read out of an old linen book, the priest being a very old man, called Ovius Paccius, who affirmed, that he took these ceremonials from the ancient ritual of the Samnites, being the same which their ancestors used, when they had formed the secret design of wresting Capua from the Etrurians. When the sacrifices were finished, the general ordered a beadle to summon every one of those who were most highly distinguished by their birth or conduct: these were introduced singly. Besides the other exhibitions of the solemnity, calculated to impress the mind with religious awe, there were, in the middle of the covered enclosure, altars erected, about which lay the victims slain, and the centurions stood around with their swords drawn. The soldier was led up to the altars, rather like a victim, than a performer in the ceremony, and was bound by an oath not to divulge what he should see and hear in that place. He was then compelled to swear, in a dreadful kind of form, containing execrations on his own person, on his family and race, if he did not go to battle, whithersoever the commanders should lead; and, if either he himself fled from the field, or, in case he should see any other flying, did not immediately kill him. At first some, refusing to take the oath, were put to death round the altars, and lying among the carcasses of the victims, served afterwards as a warning to others not to refuse it. When those of the first rank in the Samnite nation had been bound under these solemnities, the general nominated ten, whom he desired to choose each a man, and so to proceed until they should have called up the number of sixteen thousand. This body, from the covering of the enclosure wherein the nobility had been thus devoted, was called the linen legion. They were furnished with splendid armour and plumed helmets, to distinguish them above the rest. They had another body of forces, amounting to somewhat more than twenty thousand, not inferior to the linen legion, either in personal appearance, or renown in war, or their equipment. This number, composing the main strength of the nation, sat down at Aquilonia.

On the other side, the consuls set out from the city. First, Spurius Carvilius, to whom had been decreed the veteran legions, which Marcus Atilius, the consul of the preceding year, had left in the territory of Interamna, marched at their head into Samnium; and, while the enemy were busied in their superstitious rites, and holding their secret meeting, he took by storm the town of Amiternum. Here were slain about two thousand eight hundred men; and four thousand two hundred and seventy were made prisoners. Papirius, with a new army, which he raised in pursuance of a decree of the senate, made himself master of the city of Duronia. He took fewer prisoners than his colleague; but slew much greater numbers. Rich booty was acquired in both places. The consuls then, overrunning Samnium, and wasting the province of Atinum with particular severity, arrived, Carvilius at Cominium, and Papirius at Aquilonia, where the main force of the Samnites were posted. Here, for some time, there was neither a cessation of action, nor any vigorous effort. The day was generally spent in provoking the enemy when quiet, and retiring when they offered resistance; in menacing, rather than making an attack. By which practice of beginning, and then desisting, even those trifling skirmishes were continually left without a decision. The other Roman camp was twenty miles distant, and the advice of his absent colleague was appealed to on every thing which he undertook, while Carvilius, on his part, directed a greater share of his attention to Aquilonia, where the state of affairs was more critical and important, than to Cominium, which he himself was besieging. When Papirius had fully adjusted every measure, preparatory to an engagement, he despatched a message to his colleague, that "he intended, if the auspices permitted, to fight the enemy on the day following; and that it would be necessary that he (Carvilius) should at the same time make an assault on Cominium, with his utmost force, that the Samnites there might have no leisure to send any succour to Aquilonia." The messenger had the day for the performance of his journey, and he returned in the night, with an answer to the consul, that his colleague approved of the plan. Papirius, on sending off the messenger, had instantly called an assembly, where he descanted, at large, on the nature of the war in general, and on the present mode of equipment adopted by the enemy, which served for empty parade, rather than for any thing effectual towards insuring success; for "plumes," he said, "made no wounds; that a Roman javelin would make its way through shields, however painted and gilt; and that the army, refulgent from the whiteness of their tunics, would soon be besmeared with blood, when matters came to be managed with the sword. His father had formerly cut off, to a man, a gold and silver army of the Samnites; and such accoutrements had made a more respectable figure, as spoils, in the hands of the conquering foe, than as arms in those of the wearers. Perhaps it was allotted, by destiny, to his name and family, that they should be opposed in command against the most powerful efforts of the Samnites; and should bring home spoils, of such beauty, as to serve for ornaments to the public places. The immortal gods were certainly on his side, on account of the leagues so often solicited and so often broken. Besides, if a judgment might be formed of the sentiments of the deities, they never were more hostile to any army, than to that which, smeared with the blood of human beings mixed with that of cattle in their abominable sacrifice, doomed to the twofold resentment of the gods, dreading on the one hand the divinities, witnesses of the treaties concluded with the Romans, on the other hand the imprecations expressed in the oath sworn in contradiction to those treaties, swore with reluctance, abhorred the oath, and feared at once the gods, their countrymen, and their enemies."

When the consul had recounted these particulars, ascertained from the information of the deserters, to the soldiers already enraged of themselves, they then, filled with confidence in both divine and human aid, with one universal shout, demanded the battle; were dissatisfied at the action being deferred to the following day; they are impatient under the intended delay of a day and a night. Papirius, at the third watch, having received his colleague's letter, arose in silence, and sent the keeper of the chickens to take the auspices. There was no one description of men in the camp who felt not earnest wishes for the fight: the highest and the lowest were equally eager; the general watching the ardour of the soldiers, and the soldiers that of the general. This universal zeal spread even to those employed in taking the auspices; for the chickens having refused to feed, the auspex ventured to misrepresent the omen, and reported to the consul that they had fed voraciously. [7] The consul, highly pleased, and giving notice that the auspices were excellent, and that they were to act under the direction of the gods, displayed the signal for battle. Just as he was going out to the field, he happened to receive intelligence from a deserter, that twenty cohorts of Samnites, consisting of about four hundred each, had marched towards Cominium. Lest his colleague should be ignorant of this, he instantly despatched a messenger to him, and then ordered the troops to advance with speed, having already assigned to each division of the army its proper post, and appointed general officers to command them. The command of the right wing he gave to Lucius Volumnius, that of the left to Lucius Scipio, that of the cavalry to the other lieutenants-general, Caius Cædicius and Caius Trebonius. He ordered Spurius Nautius to take off the panniers from the mules, and to lead them round quickly, together with his auxiliary cohorts, to a rising ground in view; and there to show himself during the heat of the engagement, and to raise as much dust as possible. While the general was employed in making these dispositions, a dispute arose among the keepers of the chickens, about the auspices of the day, which was overheard by some Roman horsemen, who, deeming it a matter not to be slighted, informed Spurius Papirius, the consul's nephew, that there was a doubt about the auspices. The youth, born in an age when that sort of learning which inculcates contempt of the gods was yet unknown, examined into the affair, that he might not carry an uncertain report to the consul; and then acquainted him with it. His answer was, "I very much applaud your conduct and zeal. However, the person who officiates in taking the auspices, if he makes a false report, draws on his own head the evil portended; but to the Roman people and their army, the favourable omen reported to me is an excellent auspice." He then commanded the centurions to place the keepers of the chickens in the front of the line. The Samnites likewise brought forward their standards; their main body followed, armed and decorated in such a manner, that the enemy afforded a magnificent show. Before the shout was raised, or the battle begun, the auspex, wounded by a random cast of a javelin, fell before the standards; which being told to the consul, he said, "The gods are present in the battle; the guilty has met his punishment." While the consul uttered these words, a crow, in front of him, cawed with a clear voice; at which augury, the consul being rejoiced, and affirming, that never had the gods interposed in a more striking manner in human affairs, ordered the charge to be sounded and the shout to be raised.

A furious conflict now ensued, but with very unequal spirit [in the combatants]. Anger, hope, and ardour for conquest, hurried on the Romans to battle, thirsting for their enemy's blood; while the Samnites, for the most part reluctantly, as if compelled by necessity and religious dread, rather stood on their defence, than made an attack. Nor would they, familiarized as they were to defeats, through a course of so many years, have withstood the first shout and shock of the Romans, had not another fear, operating still more powerfully in their breasts, restrained them from flying. For they had before their eyes the whole scene exhibited at the secret sacrifice, the armed priests, the promiscuous carnage of men and cattle, the altars besmeared with the blood of victims and of their murdered countrymen, the dreadful curses, and the direful form of imprecation, drawn up for calling down perdition on their family and race. Prevented by these shackles from running away, they stood, more afraid of then countrymen than of the enemy. The Romans pushed on both the wings, and in the centre, and made great havoc among them, stupified as they were, through their fears of the gods and of men. A faint resistance is now made, as by men whom fear alone prevented from running away. The slaughter had now almost reached to their standards, when, on one side, appeared a cloud of dust, as if raised by the marching of a numerous army: it was Spurius Nautius, (some say Octavius Metius,) commander of the auxiliary cohorts: for these raised a greater quantity of dust than was proportioned to the number of men, the servants of the camp, mounted on the mules, trailing boughs of trees, full of leaves, along the ground. Through the light thus obscured, arms and standards were seen in front; behind, a higher and denser cloud of dust presented the appearance of horsemen bringing up the rear. This effectually deceived, not only the Samnites, but the Romans themselves: and the consul confirmed the mistake, by calling out among the foremost battalions, so that his voice reached also the enemy, that "Cominium was taken, and that his victorious colleague was approaching," bidding his men "now make haste to complete the defeat of the enemy, before the glory should fall to the share of the other army." This he said as he sat on horseback, and then ordered the tribunes and centurions to open passages for the horse. He had given previous directions to Trebonius and Cædicius, that, when they should see him waving the point of his spear aloft, they should incite the cavalry to charge the enemy with all possible violence. Every particular, as previously concerted, was executed with the utmost exactness. The passages were opened between the ranks, the cavalry darted through, and, with the points of their spears presented, rushed into the midst of the enemy's battalions, breaking down the ranks wherever they charged. Voluminius and Scipio seconded the blow, and taking advantage of the enemy's disorder, made a terrible slaughter. Thus attacked, the cohorts, called *linteatae*, regardless of all restraints from either gods or men, quitted their posts in confusion, the sworn and the unsworn all fled alike, no longer dreading aught but the enemies. The body of their infantry which survived the battle, were driven into the camp at Aquilonia. The nobility and cavalry directed their flight to Bovianum. The horse were pursued by the Roman horse, the infantry by their infantry, while the wings proceeded by different roads; the right, to the camp of the Samnites; the left to the city. Volumnius succeeded first in gaining possession of the camp. At the city, Scipio met a stouter resistance; not because the conquered troops there had gained courage, but because walls were a better defence against armed men than a rampart. From these they repelled the enemy with stones. Scipio, considering that unless the business were effected during their first panic, and before they could recover their spirits, the attack of so strong a town would be very tedious, asked his soldiers "if they could endure, without shame, that the other wing should already have taken the camp, and that they, after all their success, should be repulsed from the gates of the city?" Then, all of them loudly declaring their determination to the contrary, he himself advanced, the foremost, to the gate, with his shield raised over his head: the rest, following under the like cover of their shields conjoined, burst into the city, and dispersing the Samnites who were near the gate, took possession of the walls, but they ventured not to push forward into the interior of the city in consequence of the smallness of their number.

Of these transactions the consul was for some time ignorant; and was busily employed in calling home his troops, for the sun was now hastening to set, and the approach of night rendered every place suspicious and dangerous, even to victorious troops. Having rode forward a considerable way, he saw on the right the camp taken, and heard on the left a shouting in the city, with a confused noise of fighting, and cries of terror. This happened while the fight was going on at the gate. When, on riding up nearer, he saw his own men on the walls, and so much progress already made in the business, pleased at having gained, through the precipitate conduct of a few, an opportunity of striking an important blow, he ordered the troops, whom he had sent back to the camp, to be called out, and to march to the attack of the city: these, having made good their entrance on the nearest side, proceeded no farther, because night approached. Before morning, however, the town was abandoned by the enemy. There were slain of the

Samnites on that day, at Aquilonia, thirty thousand three hundred and forty; taken, three thousand eight hundred and seventy, with ninety-seven military standards. One circumstance, respecting Papirius, is particularly mentioned by historians: that, hardly ever was any general seen in the field with a more cheerful countenance; whether this was owing to his natural temper or to his confidence of success. From the same firmness of mind it proceeded, that he did not suffer himself to be diverted from the war by the dispute about the auspices; and that, in the heat of the battle, when it was customary to vow temples to the immortal gods, he vowed to Jupiter the victorious, that if he should defeat the legions of the enemy, he would, before he tasted of any generous liquor, make a libation to him of a cup of wine and honey. This kind of vow proved acceptable to the gods, and they conducted the auspices to a fortunate issue.

Matters were conducted with the same success by the other consul at Cominium: leading up his forces to the walls, at the first dawn, he invested the city on every side, and posted strong guards opposite to the gates to prevent any sally being made. Just as he was giving the signal, the alarming message from his colleague, touching the march of the twenty Samnite cohorts, not only caused him to delay the assault, but obliged him to call off a part of his troops, when they were formed and ready to begin the attack. He ordered Decius Brutus Scæva, a lieutenant-general, with the first legion, ten auxiliary cohorts, and the cavalry, to go and oppose the said detachment; and in whatever place he should meet the foe, there to stop and detain them, and even to engage in battle, should opportunity offer for it; at all events not to suffer those troops to approach Cominium. He then commanded the scaling ladders to be brought up to the walls, on every side of the city; and, under a fence of closed shields, advanced to the gates. Thus, at the same moment, the gates were broken open, and the assault made on every part of the walls. Though the Samnites, before they saw the assailants on the works, had possessed courage enough to oppose their approaches to the city, yet now, when the action was no longer carried on at a distance, nor with missile weapons, but in close fight; and when those, who had with difficulty gained the walls, having overcome the disadvantage of ground, which, they principally dreaded, fought with ease on equal ground, against an enemy inferior in strength, they all forsook the towers and walls, and being driven to the forum, they tried there for a short time, as a last effort, to retrieve the fortune of the fight; but soon throwing down their arms, surrendered to the consul, to the number of eleven thousand four hundred; four thousand three hundred and eighty were slain. Such was the course of events at Cominium, such at Aquilonia. In the middle space between the two cities, where a third battle had been expected, the enemy were not found; for, when they were within seven miles of Cominium, they were recalled by their countrymen, and had no part in either battle. At night-fall, when they were now within sight of their camp, and also of Aquilonia, shouts from both places reaching them with equal force induced them to halt; then, on the side of the camp, which had been set on fire by the Romans, the wide-spreading flames indicating with more certainty the disaster [which had happened], prevented their proceeding any farther. In that same spot, stretched on the ground at random under their arms, they passed the whole night in great inquietude, at one time wishing for, at another dreading the light. At the first dawn, while they were still undetermined to what quarter they should direct their march, they were obliged to betake themselves hastily to flight, being descried by the cavalry; who having gone in pursuit of the Samnites, that left the town in the night, saw the multitude unprotected either by a rampart or advanced guard. This party had likewise been perceived from the walls of Aquilonia, and the legionary cohorts now joined in the pursuit. The foot were unable to overtake them, but about two hundred and eighty of their rear guard were cut off by the cavalry. In their consternation they left behind them a great quantity of arms and eighteen military standards: they reached Bovianum with the rest of their party in safety, as far as could be expected after so disorderly a rout.

The joy of both Roman armies was enhanced by the success achieved on the other side. Each consul, with the approbation of his colleague, gave to his soldiers the plunder of the town which he had taken; and, when the houses were cleared, set them on fire. Thus, on the same day, Aquilonia and Cominium were both reduced to ashes. The consuls then united their camps, where mutual congratulations took place between them and between their soldiers. Here, in the view of the two armies, Carvilius bestowed on his men commendations and presents according to the desert of each; and Papirius likewise, whose troops had been engaged in a variety of actions, in the field, in the assault of the camp, and in that of the city, presented Spurius Nautius, Spurius Papirius, his nephew, four centurions, and a company of the spearmen, with bracelets and crowns of gold:—to Nautius, on account of his behaviour at the head of his detachment, when he had terrified the enemy with the appearance as of a numerous army; to young Papirius, on account of his zealous exertions with the cavalry, both in the battle and in harassing the Samnites in their flight by night, when they withdrew privately from Aquilonia; and to the centurions and company of soldiers, because they were the first who gained possession of the gate and wall of that town. All the horsemen he presented with gorgets and bracelets of silver, on account of their distinguished conduct on many occasions. As the time was now come for withdrawing the army out of Samnium, the expediency was considered, as to whether they should withdraw both, or at least one. It was concluded, that the lower the strength of the Samnites was reduced, the greater perseverance and vigour ought to be used in prosecuting the war, so that Samnium might be given up to the succeeding consuls perfectly subjected. As there was now no army of the enemy which could be supposed capable of disputing the field, there remained one mode of operations, the besieging of the cities; by the destruction of which, they might be enabled to enrich their soldiers with the spoil; and, at the same time, utterly to destroy the enemy, reduced to the necessity of fighting, their all being at stake. The consuls, therefore, after despatching letters to the senate and people of Rome, containing accounts of the services which they had performed, led away their legions to different quarters; Papirius going to attack Sæpioura, Carvilius to Volana.

The letters of the consuls were heard with extraordinary exultation, both in the senate-house and in the assembly of the people; and, in a thanksgiving of four days' continuance, the public rejoicings were celebrated with zeal by individuals. These successes were not only important in themselves to the Roman people, but peculiarly seasonable; for it happened, that at the same time intelligence was brought that the Etrurians were again in arms. The reflection naturally occurred to people's minds, how it would have been possible, in case any misfortune had happened in Samnium, to have withstood the power of Etruria; which, being encouraged by the conspiracy of the Samnites, and seeing both the consuls, and the whole force of the Romans, employed against them, had made use of that juncture, in which the Romans had so much business on their hands, for reviving hostilities. Ambassadors from the allies, being introduced to the senate by the prætor Marcus Atilius, complained that their countries were wasted with fire and sword by the neighbouring Etrurians, because they had refused to revolt from the Romans; and they besought the conscript fathers to protect them from the violence and injustice of their common enemy. The ambassadors were answered, that "the senate would take care that the allies should not repent their fidelity." That the "Etrurians should shortly be in the same situation with the Samnites." Notwithstanding which, the business respecting Etruria would have been prosecuted with less vigour, had not information been received, that the Faliscians likewise, who had for many years lived in friendship with Rome, had united their arms with those of the Etrurians. The consideration of the near vicinity of that nation quickened the attention of the senate; insomuch that they passed a decree that heralds should be sent to demand satisfaction: which being refused, war was declared against the Faliscians by direction of the senate, and order of the people; and the consuls were desired to determine, by lots, which of them should lead an army from Samnium into Etruria. Carvilius had, in the mean time, taken from the Samnites Volana, Palumbinum, and Herculaneum; Volana after a siege of a few days, Palumbinum the same day on which he approached the walls. At Herculaneum, it is true, the consul had two regular engagements without any decisive advantage on either side, and with greater loss on his side than on that of the enemy; but afterwards, encamping on the spot, he shut them up within their works. The town was besieged and taken. In these three towns were taken or slain ten thousand men, of whom the prisoners composed somewhat the greater part. On the consuls casting lots for the provinces, Etruria fell to Carvilius, to the great satisfaction of the soldiers, who could no longer bear the intensity of the cold in Samnium. Papirius was opposed at Sæpinum with a more powerful force: he had to fight often in pitched battles, often on a march, and often under the walls of the city, against the eruptions of the enemy; and could neither besiege, nor engage them on equal terms; for the Samnites not only protected themselves by walls, but likewise protected their walls with numbers of men and arms. At length, after a great deal of fighting, he forced them to submit to a regular siege. This he carried on with vigour, and made himself master of the city by means of his works, and by storm. The rage of the soldiers on this occasion caused the greatest slaughter in the taking of the town; seven thousand four hundred fell by the sword; the number of the prisoners did not amount to three thousand. The spoil, of which the quantity was very great, the whole substance of the Samnites being collected in a few cities, was given up to the soldiers.

The snow had now entirely covered the face of the country, and they could no longer dispense with the shelter of houses: the consul therefore led home his troops from Samnium. While he was on his way to Rome, a triumph was decreed him with universal consent; and accordingly he triumphed while in office, and with extraordinary splendour, considering the circumstances of those times. The cavalry and infantry marched in the procession, adorned with presents. Great numbers of civic, vallar, and mural crowns were seen. [8] The spoils of the Samnites were inspected with much curiosity, and compared, in respect of magnificence and beauty, with those taken by his father, which were well known, from being frequently exhibited as ornaments of the public places. Several prisoners of distinction, renowned for their own exploits and those of their ancestors, were led in the cavalcade. There were carried in the train two millions and thirty-three thousand *asses* in weight. [9] This money was said to be produced by the sale of the prisoners. Of silver, taken in the cities, one thousand three hundred and thirty pounds. All the silver and brass were lodged in the treasury, no share of this part of the spoil being given to the soldiers. The ill humour in the commons was further exasperated, because the tax for the payment of the army was collected by contribution; whereas, said they, if the vain parade of conveying the produce of the spoil to the treasury had been disregarded, donations might have been made to the soldiers out of the spoil, and the pay of the army also supplied out of that fund. The temple of Quirinus, vowed by his father when dictator, (for that he himself had vowed it in the heat of battle, I do not find in any ancient writer, nor indeed could he in so short a time have finished the building of it,) the son, in the office of consul, dedicated and adorned with military spoils. And of these, so great was the abundance, that not only that temple and the forum were decorated with them, but some were also distributed among the allies and colonies in the neighbourhood, to serve as ornaments to their temples and public places. Immediately after his triumph, he led his army into winter quarters in the territory of Vescia; because that country was harassed by the Samnites. Meanwhile, in Etruria, the consul Carvilius having set about laying siege to Troilium, suffered four hundred and seventy of the richest inhabitants to depart; they had paid a large sum of money for permission to leave the place: the town, with the remaining multitude, he took by storm. He afterwards reduced, by force, five forts strongly situated, wherein were slain two thousand four hundred of the enemy, and not quite two thousand made prisoners. To the Faliscians, who sued for peace, he granted a truce for a year, on condition of their furnishing a hundred thousand *asses* in weight, [10] and that year's pay for his army. This business completed, he returned home to a triumph, which, though it was less illustrious than that of his colleague, in respect of his share in the defeat of the Samnites, was yet raised to an equality with it, by his having put a termination to the war in Etruria. He carried into the treasury three hundred and ninety thousand *asses* in weight. [11] Out of the remainder of the money accruing to the public from the spoils, he contracted for the building of a temple to Fors Fortuna, near to that dedicated to the same goddess by king Servius Tullius; and gave to the soldiers, out of the spoil, one hundred and two asses each, and double that sum to the centurions and horsemen, who received this donative the more gratefully, on account of the parsimony of his colleague.

The favour of the consul saved from a trial, before the people, Postumius; who, on a prosecution being commenced against him by Marcus Scantius, plebeian tribune, evaded, as was said, the jurisdiction of the people, by procuring the commission of lieutenant-general, so the indictment against him could only be held out as a threat, and not put in force. The year having now elapsed, new plebeian tribunes had come unto office; and for these, in consequence of some irregularity on their appointments, others had been, within five days after, substituted in their room. The lustrum was closed this year by the censors Publius Cornelius Arvina and Caius Marcius Rutilus. The number of citizens rated was two hundred and sixty-two thousand three hundred and twenty-two. These were the twenty-sixth pair of censors since the first institution of that office; and this the nineteenth lustrum. In this year, persons who had been presented with crowns, in consideration of meritorious behaviour in war, first began to wear them at the exhibition of the Roman games. Then, for the first time, palms were conferred on the victors according to a custom introduced from Greece. In the same year the paving of the road from the temple of Mars to Bovillæ was completed by the curule ædiles, who exhibited those games out of fines levied on the farmers of the pastures. Lucius Papirius presided at the consular election, and returned consuls Quintus Fabius Gurges, son of Maximus, and Decius Junius Brutus Scæva. Papirius himself was made prætor. This year, prosperous in many particulars, was scarcely sufficient to afford consolation for one calamity, a pestilence, which afflicted both the city and country: the mortality was prodigious. To discover what end, or what remedy, was appointed by the gods for that calamity, the books were consulted: in the books it was found that Æsculapius must be brought to Rome from Epidaurus. Nor were any steps taken that year in that matter, because the consuls were fully occupied in the war, except that a supplication was performed to

Æsculapius for one day.

[*Here ten books of the original are lost, making a chasm of seventy-five years. The translator's object being to publish the work of Livy only, he has not thought it his duty to attempt to supply this deficiency, either by a compilation of his own, or by transcribing or translating those of others. The leader, however, who may be desirous of knowing the events which took place during this interval, will find as complete a detail of them as can now be given, in Hooke's or Rollin's Roman History. The contents of the lost books have been preserved, and are as follows—*]

BOOK XI.

[Y.R. 460. B.C. 292.] Fabius Gurges, consul, having fought an unsuccessful battle with the Samnites, the senate deliberate about dismissing him from the command of the army; are prevailed upon not to inflict that disgrace upon him, principally by the entreaties of his father, Fabius Maximus, and by his promising to join the army, and serve, in quality of lieutenant-general, under his son: which promise he performs, and the consul, aided by his counsel and co-operation, obtains a victory over the Samnites, and a triumph in consequence. C. Pontius, the general of the Samnites, led in triumph before the victor's carriage, and afterwards beheaded. A plague at Rome. [Y.R. 461. B.C. 291.] Ambassadors sent to Epidaurus, to bring from thence to Rome the statue of Æsculapius: a serpent, of itself, goes on board their ship; supposing it to be the abode of the deity, they bring it with them; and, upon its quitting their vessel, and swimming to the island in the Tiber, they consecrate there a temple to Æsculapius. L. Postumius, a man of consular rank, condemned for employing the soldiers under his command in working upon his farm. [Y.R. 462. B.C. 290] Curius Dentatus, consul, having subdued the Samnites, and the rebellious Sabines, triumphs twice during his year of office. [Y.R. 463. B.C. 289.] The colonies of Castrum, Sena, and Adria, established. Three judges of capital crimes now first appointed. A census and lustrum: the number of citizens found to be two hundred and seventy-three thousand. After a long-continued sedition, on account of debts, the commons secede to the Janiculum: [Y.R. 466. B.C. 286.] are brought back by Hortensius, dictator, who dies in office. Successful operations against the Volsinians and Lucanians, [Y.R. 468. B.C. 284.] against whom it was thought expedient to send succour to the Thuringians.

BOOK XII.

[Y.R. 469. B.C. 283.] The Senonian Gauls having slain the Roman ambassadors, war is declared against them: they cut off L. Cæcilius, prætor, with the legions under his command, [Y.R. 470. B.C. 282.] The Roman fleet plundered by the Tarentines, and the commander slain: ambassadors, sent to complain of this outrage, are ill-treated and sent back; whereupon war is declared against them. The Samnites revolt; against whom, together with the Lucanians, Bruttians, and Etruscans, several unsuccessful battles are fought by different generals. [Y.R. 471. B.C. 281.] Pyrrhus, king of Epirus, comes into Italy, to succour the Tarentines. A Campanian legion, sent, under the command of Decius Jubellius, to garrison Rhegium, murder the inhabitants, and seize the city.

BOOK XIII.

[Y.R. 472. B.C. 280.] Valerius Lævinus, consul, engages with Pyrrhus, and is beaten, his soldiers being terrified at the unusual appearance of elephants. After the battle, Pyrrhus, viewing the bodies of the Romans who were slain, remarks, that they all of them lay with their faces turned towards their enemy. He proceeds towards Rome, ravaging the country as he goes along. C. Fabricius is sent by the senate to treat for the redemption of the prisoners: the king, in vain, attempts to bribe him to desert his country. The prisoners restored without ransom. Cineas, ambassador from Pyrrhus to the senate, demands, as a condition of peace, that the king be admitted into the city of Rome: the consideration of which being deferred to a fuller meeting, Appius Claudius, who, on account of a disorder in his eyes, had not, for a long time, attended in the senate, comes there; moves, and carries his motion, that the demand of the king be refused. Cneius Domitius, the first plebeian censor, holds a lustrum; the number of the citizens found to be two hundred and seventy-eight thousand two hundred and twenty-two. A second, but undecided battle with Pyrrhus. [Y.R. 473. B.C. 279.] The treaty with the Carthaginians renewed a fourth time. An offer made to Fabricius, the consul, by a traitor, to poison Pyrrhus; [Y. R. 474. B. C. 278.] he sends him to the king, and discovers to him the treasonable offer. Successful operations against the Etruscans, Lucanians, Bruttians, and Samnites.

BOOK XIV.

Pyrrhus crosses over into Sicily. [Y. R. 475. B. C. 277.] Many prodigies, among which, the statue of Jupiter in the Capitol is struck by lightning, and thrown down. [Y. R. 476. B. C. 276.] The head of it afterwards found by the priests. Curius Dentatus, holding a levy, puts up to sale the goods of a person who refuses to answer to his name when called upon. [Y. R. 477. B. C. 275.] Pyrrhus, after his return from Sicily, is defeated, and compelled to quit Italy. The censors hold a lustrum, and find the number of the citizens to be two hundred and seventy-one thousand two hundred and twenty-four. [Y. R. 479. B. c. 273.] A treaty of alliance formed with Ptolemy, king of Egypt. Sextilia, a vestal, found guilty of incest, and buried alive. Two colonies sent forth, to Posidonium and Cossa. [Y. R. 480. B. C. 272.] A Carthaginian fleet sails, in aid of the Tarentines, by which act the treaty is violated. Successful operations against the Lucanians, Samnites, and Bruttians. Death of king Pyrrhus.

BOOK XV.

The Tarentines overcome: peace and freedom granted to them. [Y. R. 481. B. C. 271.] The Campanian legion, which had forcibly taken possession of Rhegium, besieged there; lay down their arms, and are punished with death. Some young men, who had ill-treated the ambassadors from the Apollonians to the senate of Rome, are delivered up to them. Peace granted to the Picentians. [Y. R. 484. B. C. 268.] Two colonies established; one at Ariminum in Picenum, another at Beneventum in Samnium. Silver coin now, for the first time, used by the Roman people. [Y. R. 485. B. C. 267.] The Umbrians and Sallentines subdued. The number of quæstors increased to eight.

BOOK XVI.

[Y. R. 488. B. C. 264.] Origin and progress of the Carthaginian state. After much debate, the senate resolves to succour the Mammertines against the Carthaginians, and against Hiero, king of Syracuse. Roman cavalry, then, for the first time, cross the sea, and engage successfully, in battle with Hiero; who solicits and obtains peace. [Y.R. 489. B.C. 263.] A lustrum: the number of the citizens amounts to two hundred and ninety-two thousand two hundred and twenty-four. D. Junius Brutus exhibits the first show of gladiators, in honour of his deceased father. [Y.R. 490. B.C. 262.] The Æsernian colony established. Successful operations against the Carthaginians and Vulsinians. [Y.R. 491. B.C. 261.]

BOOK XVII.

[Y.R. 492. B.C. 260.] Cneius Cornelius, consul, surrounded by the Carthaginian fleet; and, being drawn into a conference by a stratagem, is taken. [Y.R. 493. B.C. 259.] C. Duilius, consul, engages with and vanquishes the Carthaginian fleet; is the first commander to whom a triumph was decreed for a naval victory; in honour of which, he is allowed, when returning to his habitation at night, to be attended with torches and music. L. Cornelius, consul, fights and subdues the Sardinians and Corsicans, together with Hanno, the Carthaginian general, in the island of Sardinia. [Y.R. 494. B.C. 258.] Atilius Calatinus, consul, drawn into an ambuscade by the Carthaginians, is rescued by the skill and valour of M. Calpurnius, a military tribune, who making a sudden attack upon the enemy, with a body of only three hundred men, turns their whole force against himself. [Y.R. 495. B.C. 257.] Hannibal, the commander of the Carthaginian fleet which was beaten, is put to death by his soldiers.

BOOK XVIII.

[Y.R. 496. B.C. 256.] Attilius Regulus, consul, having overcome the Carthaginians in a sea-fight, passes over into Africa: kills a serpent of prodigious magnitude, with great loss of his own men. [Y.R. 497. B.C. 255.] The senate, on account of his successful conduct of the war, not appointing him a successor, he writes to them, complaining; and, among other reasons for desiring to be recalled, alleges, that his little farm, being all his subsistence, was going to ruin, owing to the mismanagement of hired stewards. [Y.R. 498. B.C. 254.] A memorable instance of the instability of fortune exhibited in the person of Regulus, who is overcome in battle, and taken prisoner by Xanthippus, a Lacedæmonian general. [Y. R. 499. B. C. 253.] The Roman fleet shipwrecked; which disaster entirely reverses the good fortune which had hitherto attended their affairs. Titus Corucanius, the first high priest chosen from among the commons. [Y. R. 500. B. C. 252.] P. Sempronius Sophus and M. Valerius Maximus, censors, examine into the state of the senate, and expel thirteen of the members of that body. [Y. R. 501. B. C. 251.] They hold a lustrum, and find the number of citizens to be two hundred and ninety-seven thousand seven hundred and ninety-seven. [Y. R. 502. B. C. 250.] Regulus being sent by the Carthaginians to Rome to treat for peace, and an exchange of prisoners, binds himself by oath to return if these objects be not attained; dissuades the senate from agreeing to the propositions: and then, in observance of his oath, returning to Carthage, is put to death by torture.

BOOK XIX.

[Y. R. 502. B. C. 250.] C. Cæcilius Metellus, having been successful in several engagements with the Carthaginians, triumphs with more splendour than had ever yet been seen; thirteen generals of the enemy, and one hundred and twenty elephants, being exhibited in the procession, [Y. R. 503. B. C. 249.] Claudius Pulcher, consul, obstinately persisting, notwithstanding the omens were inauspicious, engages the enemy's fleet, and is beaten; drowns the sacred chickens which would not feed: recalled by the senate, and ordered to nominate a dictator; he appoints Claudius Glicia, one of the lowest of the people, who, notwithstanding his being ordered to abdicate the office, yet attends the celebration of the public games in his dictator's robe. [Y. R. 504. B. C. 248.] Atilius Calatinus, the first dictator who marches with an army out of Italy. An exchange of prisoners with the Carthaginians. Two colonies established at Fregenæ and Brundusium in the Sallentine territories. [Y. R. 505. B. C. 247.] A lustrum; the citizens numbered amount to two hundred and fifty-one thousand two hundred and twenty-two. [Y. R. 506. B. C. 246.] Claudia, the sister of Claudius, who had fought unsuccessfully, in contempt of the auspices, being pressed by the crowd, as she was returning from the game, cries out, *I wish my brother were alive and had again the command of the fleet*: for which offence she is tried and fined. [Y. R. 507. B. C. 245.] Two prætors now first created. Aulus Postumius, consul, being priest of Mars, forcibly detained in the city by Cæcilius Metellus, the high priest, and not suffered to go forth to war, being obliged by law to attend to the sacred duties of his office. [Y.R. 508. B.C. 244.] After several successful engagements with the Carthaginians, Caius Lutatius, consul, puts an end to the war, [Y.R. 509. B.C. 243.] by gaining a complete victory over their fleet, at the island of Ægate. The Carthaginians sue for peace, which is granted to them. [Y.R. 510. B.C. 242.] The temple of Vesta being on fire, the high priest, Cæcilius Metellus, saves the sacred utensils from the flames. [Y.R. 511. B.C. 241.] Two new tribes added, the Veline and Quirine. The Falisci rebel; are subdued in six days.

BOOK XX.

A colony settled at Spoletum. [Y.R. 512. B.C. 240.] An army sent against the Ligurians; being the first war with that state. The Sardinians and Corsicans rebel, and are subdued. [Y.R. 514. B.C. 238.] Tuccia, a vestal, found guilty of incest. War declared against the Illyrians, who had slain an ambassador; they are subdued and brought to submission. [Y.R. 515. B.C. 237.] The number of prætors increased to four. The Transalpine Gauls make an irruption into Italy: are conquered and put to the sword. [Y.R. 516. B.C. 236.] The Roman army, in conjunction with the Latins, is said to have amounted to no less than three hundred thousand men. [Y.R. 517. B.C. 235.] The Roman army for the first time crosses the Po; fights with and subdues the Insubrian Gauls. [Y.R. 530. B.C. 222.] Claudius Marcellus, consul, having slain Viridomarus, the general of the Insubrian Gauls, carries off the *spolia opima*. [Y.R. 531. B.C. 221.] The Istrians subdued; also the Illyrians, who had rebelled. [Y.R. 532. B.C. 220.] The censors hold a lustrum, in which the number of the citizens is found to be two hundred and seventy thousand two hundred and thirteen. The sons of freed-men formed into four tribes; the Esquiline, Palatine, Suburran, and Colline. [Y.R. 533. B.C. 219.] Caius Flaminius, censor, constructs the Flaminian road, and builds the Flaminian circus.

BOOK XXI.

Origin of the second Punic war. Hannibal's character. In violation of a treaty, he passes the Iberus. Besieges Saguntum, and at length takes it. The Romans send ambassadors to Carthage; declare war. Hannibal crosses the Pyrenees: makes his way through Gaul; then crosses the Alps; defeats the Romans at the Ticinus. The Romans again defeated at the Trebia. Cneius Cornelius Scipio defeats the Carthaginians in Spain, and takes Hanno, their general, prisoner.

I may be permitted to premise at this division of my work, what most historians [12] have professed at the beginning of their whole undertaking; that I am about to relate the most memorable of all wars that were ever waged: the war which the Carthaginians, under the conduct of Hannibal, maintained with the Roman people. For never did any states and nations more efficient in their resources engage in contest; nor had they themselves at any other period so great a degree of power and energy. They brought into action too no arts of war unknown to each other, but those which had been tried in the first Punic war; and so various was the fortune of the conflict, and so doubtful the victory, that they who conquered were more exposed to danger. The hatred with which they fought also was almost greater than their resources; the Romans being indignant that the conquered aggressively took up arms against their victors; the Carthaginians, because they considered that in their subjection it had been lorded over them with haughtiness and avarice. There is besides a story, that Hannibal, when about nine years old, while he boyishly coaxed his father Hamilcar that he might be taken to Spain, (at the time when the African war was completed, and he was employed in sacrificing previously to transporting his army thither,) was conducted to the altar; and, having laid his hand on the offerings, was bound by an oath to prove himself, as soon as he could, an enemy to the Roman people. The loss of Sicily and Sardinia grieved the high spirit of Hamilcar: for he deemed that Sicily had been given up through a premature despair of their affairs; and that Sardinia, during the disturbances in Africa, had been treacherously taken by the Romans, while, in addition, the payment of a tribute had been imposed.

Being disturbed with these anxieties, he so conducted himself for five years in the African war, which commenced shortly after the peace with Rome, and then through nine years employed in augmenting the Carthaginian empire in Spain, that it was obvious that he was revolving in his mind a greater war than he was then engaged in; and that if he had lived longer, the Carthaginians under Hamilcar would have carried the war into Italy, which, under the command of Hannibal, they afterwards did. The timely death of Hamilcar and the youth of Hannibal occasioned its delay. Hasdrubal, intervening between the father and the son, held the command for about eight years. He was first endeared to Hamilcar, as they say, on account of his youthful beauty, and then adopted by him, when advanced in age, as his son-in-law, on account of his eminent abilities; and, because he was his son-in-law, he obtained the supreme authority, against the wishes of the nobles, by the influence of the Barcine faction, [13] which was very powerful with the military and the populace. Prosecuting his designs rather by stratagem than force, by entertaining the princes, and by means of the friendship of their leaders, gaining the favour of unknown nations, he aggrandized the Carthaginian power, more than by arms and battles. Yet peace proved no greater security to himself. A barbarian, in resentment of his master's having been put to death by him, publicly murdered him; and, having been seized by the bystanders, he exhibited the same countenance as if he had escaped; nay, even when he was lacerated by tortures, he preserved such an expression of face, that he presented the appearance of one who smiled, his joy getting the better of his pains. With this Hasdrubal, because he possessed such wonderful skill in gaining over the nations and adding them to his empire, the Roman people had renewed the treaty, [14] on the terms, that the river Iberus should be the boundary of both empires; and that to the Saguntines, who lay between the territories of the two states, their liberty should be preserved.

There was no doubt that in appointing a successor to Hasdrubal, the approbation of the commons would follow the military prerogative, by which the young Hannibal had been immediately carried to the prætorium, and hailed as general, amid the loud shouts and acquiescence of all. Hasdrubal had sent for him by letter, when scarce yet arrived at manhood; and the matter had even been discussed in the senate, the Barcine faction using all their efforts, that Hannibal might be trained to military service and succeed to his father's command. Hanno, the leader of the opposite faction, said, "Hasdrubal seems indeed to ask what is reasonable, but I, nevertheless, do not think his request ought to be granted." When he had attracted to himself the attention of all, through surprise at this ambiguous opinion, he proceeded: "Hasdrubal thinks that the flower of youth which he gave to the enjoyment of Hannibal's father, may justly be expected by himself in return from the son: but it would little become us to accustom our youth, in place of a military education, to the lustful ambition of the generals. Are we afraid that the son of Hamilcar should be too late in seeing the immoderate power and splendour of his father's sovereignty? or that we shall not soon enough become slaves to the son of him, to whose son-in-law our armies were bequeathed as an hereditary right? I am of opinion, that this youth should be kept at home, and taught, under the restraint of the laws and the authority of magistrates, to live on an equal footing with the rest of the citizens, lest at some time or other this small fire should kindle a vast conflagration."

A few, and nearly every one of the highest merit, concurred with Hanno; but, as usually happens, the more numerous party prevailed over the better. Hannibal, having been sent into Spain, from his very first arrival drew the eyes of the whole army upon him. The veteran soldiers imagined that Hamilcar, in his youth, was restored to them; they remarked the same vigour in his looks and animation in his eye the same features and expression of countenance; and then, in a short time, he took care that his father should be of the least powerful consideration in conciliating their esteem. There never was a genius more fitted for the two most opposite duties of obeying and commanding; so that you could not easily decide whether he were dearer to the general or the army: and neither did Hasdrubal prefer giving the command to any other, when any thing was to be done with courage and activity; nor did the soldiers feel more confidence and boldness under any other leader. His fearlessness in encountering dangers, and his prudence when in the midst of them, were extreme. His body could not be exhausted, nor his mind subdued, by any toil. He could alike endure either heat or cold. The quantity of his food and drink was determined by the wants of nature, and not by pleasure. The seasons of his sleeping and waking were distinguished neither by day nor night. The time that remained after the transaction of business was given to repose; but that repose was neither invited by a soft bed nor by quiet. Many have seen him wrapped in a military cloak, lying on the ground amid the watches and outposts of the soldiers. His dress was not at all superior to that of his equals: his arms and his horses were conspicuous. He was at once by far the first of the cavalry and infantry; and, foremost to advance to the charge, was last to leave the engagement. Excessive vices counterbalanced these high virtues of the hero; inhuman cruelty, more than Punic perfidy, no truth, no reverence for things sacred, no fear of the gods, no respect for oaths, no sense of religion. With a character thus made up of virtue and vices, he served for three years under the command of Hasdrubal, without neglecting any thing which ought to be done or seen by one who was to become a great general.

But from the day on which he was declared general, as if Italy had been decreed to him as his province, and the war with Rome committed to him, thinking there should be no delay, lest, while he procrastinated, some unexpected accident might defeat him, as had happened to his father, Hamilcar, and afterwards to Hasdrubal, he resolved to make war the Saguntines. As there could be no doubt that by attacking them the Romans would be excited to arms, he first led his army into the territory of the Olcades, a people beyond the Iberus, rather within the boundaries than under the dominion of the Carthaginians, so that he might not seem to have had the Saguntines for his object, but to have been drawn on to the war by the course of events; after the adjoining nations had been subdued, and by the progressive annexation of conquered territory. He storms and plunders Carteia, a wealthy city, the capital of that nation; at which the smaller states being dismayed, submitted to his command and to the imposition of a tribute. His army, triumphant and enriched with booty, was led into winter-quarters to New Carthage. Having there confirmed the attachment of all his countrymen and allies by a liberal division of the plunder, and by faithfully discharging the arrears of pay, the war was extended, in the beginning of spring, to the Vaccæi. The cities Hermandica and Arbocala were taken by storm. Arbocala was defended for a long time by the valour and number of its inhabitants. Those who escaped from Hermandica joining themselves to the exiles of the Olcades, a nation subdued the preceding summer, excite the Carpetani to arms; and having attacked Hannibal near the river Tagus, on his return from the Vaccæi, they threw into disorder his army encumbered with spoil. Hannibal avoided an engagement, and having pitched his camp on the bank, as soon as quiet and silence prevailed among the enemy, forded the river; and having removed his rampart so far that the enemy might have room to pass over, resolved to attack them in their passage. He commanded the cavalry to charge as soon as they should see them advanced into the water. He drew up the line of his infantry on the bank with forty elephants in front. The Carpetani, with the addition of the Olcades and Vaccæi amounted to a hundred thousand, an invincible army, were the fight to take place in the open plain. Being therefore both naturally ferocious and confiding in their numbers; and since they believed that the enemy had retired through fear thinking that victory was only delayed by the intervention of the river, they raise a shout, and in every direction, without the command of any one, dash into the stream, each where it nearest to him. At the same time, a heavy force of cavalry poured into the river from its opposite bank, and the engagement commenced in the middle of the channel on very unequal terms; for there the foot-soldier, having no secure footing, and scarcely trusting to the ford, could be borne down even by an unarmed horseman, by the mere shock of his horse urged at random; while the horseman, with the command of his body and his weapons, his horse moving steadily even through the middle of the eddies, could maintain the fight either at close quarters or at a distance. A great number were swallowed up by the current; some being carried by the whirlpools of the stream to the side of the enemy, were trodden down by the elephants; and whilst the last, for whom it was more safe to retreat to their own bank, were collecting together after their various alarms, Hannibal, before they could regain courage after such excessive consternation, having entered the river with his army in a close square, forced them to fly from the bank.

Having then laid waste their territory, he received the submission of the Carpetani also within a few days. And now all the country beyond the Iberus, excepting that of the Saguntines, was under the power of the Carthaginians.

As yet there was no war with the Saguntines, but already, in order to a war, the seeds of dissension were sown between them and their neighbours, particularly the Turdetani, with whom when the same person sided who had originated the quarrel, and it was evident, not that a trial of the question of right, but violence, was his object, ambassadors were sent by the Saguntines to Rome to implore assistance in the war which now evidently threatened them. The consuls then at Rome were Publius Cornelius Scipio and Tiberius Sempronius Longus, who, after the ambassadors were introduced into the senate, having made a motion on the state of public affairs, it was resolved that envoys should be sent into Spain to inspect the circumstances of the allies; and if they saw good reason, both to warn Hannibal that he should refrain from the Saguntines, the allies of the Roman people, and to pass over into Africa to Carthage, and report the complaints of the allies of the Roman people. This embassy having been decreed but not yet despatched, the news arrived, more quickly than any one expected, that Saguntum was besieged. The business was then referred anew to the senate. And some, decreeing Spain and Africa as provinces for the consuls, thought the war should be maintained both by sea and land, while others wished to direct the whole hostilities against Spain and Hannibal. There were others again who thought that an affair of such importance should not be entered on rashly; and that the return of the ambassadors from Spain ought to be awaited. This opinion, which seemed the safest, prevailed; and Publius Valerius Flaccus, and Quintus Bæbius Tamphilus, were, on that account, the more quickly despatched as ambassadors to Hannibal at Saguntum, and from thence to Carthage, if he did not desist from the war, to demand the general himself in atonement for the violation of the treaty.

While the Romans thus prepare and deliberate, Saguntum was already besieged with the utmost vigour. That city, situated about a mile from the sea, was by far the most opulent beyond the Iberus. Its inhabitants are said to have been sprung from the island Zacynthus, and some of the Rutulian race from Ardea to have been also mixed with them; but they had risen in a short time to great wealth, either by their gains from the sea or the land, or by the increase of their numbers, or the integrity of their principles, by which they maintained their faith with their allies, even to their own destruction. Hannibal having entered their territory with a hostile army, and laid waste the country in every direction, attacks the city in three different quarters. There was an angle of the wall sloping down into a more level and open valley than the other space around; against this he resolved to move the vineæ, by means of which the battering-ram might be brought up to the wall. But though the ground at a distance from the wall was sufficiently level for working the vineæ, yet their undertakings by no means favourably succeeded, when they came to effect their object. Both a huge tower overlooked it, and the wall, as in a suspected place, was raised higher than in any other part; and a chosen band of youths presented a more vigorous resistance, where the greatest danger and labour were indicated. At first they repelled the enemy with missile weapons, and suffered no place to be sufficiently secure for those engaged in the works; afterwards, not only did they brandish their weapons in defence of the walls and tower, but they had courage to make sallies on the posts and works of the enemy; in which tumultuary engagements, scarcely more Saguntines than Carthaginians were slain. But when Hannibal himself, while he too incautiously approached the wall, fell severely wounded in the thigh by a javelin, such flight and dismay spread around, that the works and vineæ had nearly been abandoned.

For a few days after, while the general's wound was being cured, there was rather a blockade than a siege: during which time, though there was a respite from fighting, yet there was no intermission in the preparation of works and fortifications. Hostilities, therefore, broke out afresh with greater fury, and in more places, in some even where the ground scarcely admitted of the works, the vineæ began to be moved forward, and the battering-ram to be advanced to the walls. The Carthaginian abounded in the numbers of his troops; for there is sufficient reason to believe that he had as many as a hundred and fifty thousand in arms. The townsmen began to be embarrassed, by having their attention multifariously divided, in order to maintain their several defences, and look to every thing; nor were they equal to the task, for the walls were now battered by the rams, and many parts of them were shattered. One part by continuous ruins left the city exposed; three successive towers and all the wall between them had fallen down with an immense crash, and the Carthaginians believed the town taken by that breach; through which, as if the wall had alike protected both, there was a rush from each side to the battle. There was nothing resembling the disorderly fighting which, in the storming of towns, is wont to be engaged in, on the opportunities of either party; but regular lines, as in an open plain, stood arrayed between the ruins of the walls and the buildings of the city, which lay but a slight distance from the walls. On the one side hope, on the other despair, inflamed their courage; the Carthaginian believing that, if a little additional effort were used, the city was his; the Saguntines opposing their bodies in defence of their native city deprived of its walls, and not a man retiring a step, lest he might admit the enemy into the place he deserted. The more keenly and closely, therefore, they fought on both sides, the more, on that account, were wounded, no weapon falling without effect amidst their arms and persons. There was used by the Saguntines a missile weapon, called falarica, with the shaft of fir, and round in other parts except towards the point, whence the iron projected: this part, which was square, as in the pilum, they bound around with tow, and besmeared with pitch. It had an iron head three feet in length, so that it could pierce through the body with the armour. But what caused the greatest fear was, that this weapon, even though it stuck in the shield and did not penetrate into the body, when it was discharged with the middle part on fire, and bore along a much greater flame, produced by the mere motion, obliged the armour to be thrown down, and exposed the soldier to succeeding blows.

When the contest had for a long time continued doubtful, and the courage of the Saguntines had increased, because they had succeeded in their resistance beyond their hopes, while the Carthaginian, because he had not conquered, felt as vanquished, the townsmen suddenly set up a shout, and drive their enemies to the ruins of the wall; thence they force them, while embarrassed and disordered; and lastly, drove them back, routed and put to flight, to their camp. In the mean time it was announced that ambassadors had arrived from Rome; to meet whom messengers were sent to the sea-side by Hannibal, to tell them that they could not safely come to him through so many armed bands of savage tribes, and that Hannibal at such an important conjuncture had not leisure to listen to embassies. It was obvious that, if not admitted, they would immediately repair to Carthage: he therefore sends letters and messengers beforehand to the leaders of the Barcine faction, to prepare the minds of their partisans, so that the other party might not be able in any thing to give an advantage to the Romans.

That embassy, therefore, excepting that the ambassadors were admitted and heard, proved likewise vain and fruitless. Hanno alone, in opposition to the rest of the senate, pleaded the cause of the treaty, amidst deep silence on account of his authority, and not from the approbation of the audience. He said: that he had admonished and forewarned them by the gods, the arbiters and witnesses of treaties, that they should not send the son of Hamilcar to the army; that the manes, that the offspring of that man could not rest in peace, nor ever, while any one of the Barcine name and blood survived, would the Roman treaties continue undisturbed. "You, supplying as it were fuel to the flame, have sent to your armies a youth burning with the desire of sovereign power, and seeing but one road to his object, if by exciting war after war, he may live surrounded by arms and legions. You have therefore fostered this fire, in which you now burn. Your armies invest Saguntum, whence they are forbidden by the treaty: ere long the Roman legions will invest Carthage, under the guidance of those gods through whose aid they revenged in the former war the infraction of the treaty. Are you unacquainted with the enemy, or with yourselves, or with the fortune of either nation? Your good general refused to admit into his camp ambassadors coming from allies and in behalf of allies, and set at nought the law of nations. They, however, after being there repulsed, where not even the ambassadors of enemies are prohibited admittance, come to you: they require restitution according to the treaty: let not guilt attach to the state, they demand to have delivered up to them the author of the transgression, the person who is chargeable with this offence. The more gently they proceed,—the slower they are to begin, the more unrelentingly, I fear, when they have once commenced, will they indulge resentment. Set before your eyes the islands Ægates and Eryx, all that for twenty-four years ye have suffered by land and sea. Nor was this boy the leader, but his father Hamilcar himself, a second Mars, as these people would have it: but we had not refrained from Tarentum, that is, from Italy, according to the treaty; as now we do not refrain from Saguntum. The gods and men have, therefore, prevailed over us; and as to that about which there was a dispute in words, whether of the two nations had infringed the treaty, the issue of the war, like an equitable judge, hath awarded the victory to the party on whose side justice stood. It is against Carthage that Hannibal is now moving his vineæ and towers: it is the wall of Carthage that he is shaking with his battering-ram. The ruins of Saguntum (oh that I may prove a false prophet!) will fall on our heads; and the war commenced against the Saguntines must be continued against the Romans. Shall we, therefore, some one will say, deliver up Hannibal? In what relates to him I am aware that my authority is of little weight, on account of my enmity with his father. But I both rejoice that Hamilcar perished, for this reason, that, had he lived we should have now been engaged in a war with the Romans; and this youth, as the fury and firebrand of this war, I hate and detest. Nor ought he only to be given up in atonement for the violated treaty; but even though no one demanded him, he ought to be transported to the extremest shores of earth or sea, and banished to a distance, whence neither his name nor any tidings of him can reach us, and he be unable to disturb the peace of a tranquil state. I therefore give my opinion, that ambassadors be sent immediately to Rome to satisfy the senate; others to tell Hannibal to lead away his army from Saguntum, and to deliver up Hannibal himself, according to the treaty to the Romans; and I propose a third embassy to make restitution to the Saguntines."

When Hanno had concluded, there was no occasion for any one to contend with him in debate, to such a decree were almost all the senators devoted to Hannibal; and they accused Hanno of having spoken with more malignity than Flaccus Valerius, the Roman ambassador. It was then said in answer to the Roman ambassadors, "that the war had been commenced by the Saguntines, not by Hannibal; and that the Roman people acted unjustly if they preferred the Saguntines to the most ancient [15] alliance of the Carthaginians." Whilst the Romans waste time in sending embassies, Hannibal, because his soldiers were fatigued with the battles and the works, allowed them rest for a few days, parties being stationed to guard the vineæ and other works. In the mean time he inflames their minds, now by inciting their anger against the enemy, now with the hope of reward. But when he declared before the assembled army, that the plunder of the captured city should be given to the soldiers, to such a degree were they all excited, that if the signal had been immediately given, it appeared that they could not have been resisted by any force. The Saguntines, as they had a respite from fighting, neither for some days attacking nor attacked, so they had not, by night or day, ever ceased from toiling, that they might repair anew the wall in the quarter where the town had been exposed by the breach. A still more desperate storming than the former then assailed them; nor whilst all quarters resounded with various clamours, could they satisfactorily know where first or principally they should lend assistance. Hannibal, as an encouragement, was present in person, where a movable tower, exceeding in height all the fortifications of the city, was urged forward. When being brought up it had cleared the walls of their defenders by means of the catapultæ and ballistæ ranged through all its stories, then Hannibal, thinking it a favourable opportunity, sends about five hundred Africans with pickaxes to undermine the wall: nor was the work difficult, since the unhewn stones were not fastened with lime, but filled in their interstices with clay, after the manner of ancient building. It fell, therefore, more extensively than it was struck, and through the open spaces of the ruins troops of armed men rushed into the city. They also obtain possession of a rising ground; and having collected thither catapultæ and ballistæ, so that they might have a fort in the city itself, commanding it like a citadel, they surround it with a wall: and the Saguntines raise an inner wall before the part of the city which was not yet taken. On both sides they exert the utmost vigour in fortifying and fighting: but the Saguntines, by erecting these inner defences, diminish daily the size of their city. At the same time, the want of all supplies increased through the length of the siege, and the expectation of foreign aid diminished, since the Romans, their only hope, were at such a distance, and all the country round was in the power of the enemy. The sudden departure of Hannibal against the Oretani and Carpetani [16] revived for a little their drooping spirits; which two nations, though, exasperated by the severity of the levy, they had occasioned, by detaining the commissaries, the fear of a revolt, having been suddenly checked by the quickness of Hannibal, laid down the arms they had taken up.

Nor was the siege of Saguntum, in the mean time, less vigorously maintained; Maharbal, the son of Himilco, whom Hannibal had set over the army, carrying on operations so actively that neither the townsmen nor their enemies perceived that the general was away. He both engaged in several successful battles, and with three battering-rams overthrew a portion of the wall; and showed to Hannibal, on his arrival the ground all covered with fresh ruins. The army was therefore immediately led against the citadel itself, and a desperate combat was commenced with much slaughter on both sides, and part of the citadel was taken. The slight chance of a peace was then tried by two persons; Alcon a Saguntine, and Alorcus a Spaniard. Alcon, thinking he could effect something by entreaties, having passed over, without the knowledge of the Saguntines, to Hannibal by night, when his tears produced no effect, and harsh conditions were offered as from an exasperated conqueror, becoming a deserter instead of an advocate, remained with the enemy; affirming that the man would be put to death who should treat for peace on such terms. For it was required that they should make restitution to the Turdetani; and after delivering up all their gold and silver, departing from the city each with a single garment, should take up their dwelling where the Carthaginian should direct. Alcon having denied that the Saguntines would accept such terms of peace, Alorcus, asserting that when all else is subdued, the mind becomes subdued, offers himself as the proposer of that peace. Now at that time he was a soldier of Hannibal's, but publicly the friend and host of the Saguntines. Having openly delivered his weapon to the guards of the enemy and passed the fortifications, he was conducted, as he had himself requested, to the Saguntine prætor; whither when there was immediately a general rush of every description of people, the rest of the multitude being removed, an audience of the senate is given to Alorcus; whose speech was to the following effect:

"If your citizen Alcon, as he came to implore a peace from Hannibal, had in like manner brought back to you the terms of peace proposed by Hannibal, this journey of mine would have been unnecessary; by which circumstance I should not have had to come to you as the legate of Hannibal, nor as a deserter. Since he has remained with your enemies, either through your fault or his own, (through his own, if he counterfeited fear; through yours, if among you there be danger to those who tell the truth,) that you may not be ignorant that there are some terms of safety and peace for you, I have come to you in consideration of the ancient ties of hospitality which subsist between us. But that I speak what I address to you for your sake and that of no other, let even this be the proof: that neither while you resisted with your own strength, nor while you expected assistance from the Romans, did I ever make any mention of peace to you. But now, after you have neither any hope from the Romans, nor your own arms nor walls sufficiently defend you, I bring to you a peace rather necessary than just: of effecting which there is thus some hope, if, as Hannibal offers it in the spirit of a conqueror, you listen to it as vanquished; if you will consider not what is taken from you as loss, (since all belongs to the conqueror,) but whatever is left as a gift. He takes away from you your city, which, already for the greater part in ruins, he has almost wholly in his possession; he leaves you your territory, intending to mark out a place in which you may build a new town; he commands that all the gold and silver, both public and private, shall be brought to him; he preserves inviolate your persons and those of your wives and children, provided you are willing to depart from Saguntum, unarmed, each with two garments. These terms a victorious enemy dictates. These, though harsh and grievous, your condition commends to you. Indeed I do not despair, when the power of every thing is given him, that he will remit something from these terms. But even these I think you ought rather to endure, than suffer, by the rights of war, yourselves to be slaughtered, your wives and children to be ravished and dragged into captivity before your faces."

When an assembly of the people, by the gradual crowding round of the multitude, had mingled with the senate to hear these proposals, the chief men suddenly withdrawing before an answer was returned, and throwing all the gold and silver collected, both from public and private stores, into a fire hastily kindled for that purpose, the greater part flung themselves also into it. When the dismay and agitation produced by this deed had pervaded the whole city, another noise was heard in addition from the citadel. A tower, long battered, had fallen down; and when a Carthaginian cohort, rushing through the breach, had made a signal to the general that the city was destitute of the usual outposts and guards, Hannibal, thinking that there ought to be no delay at such an opportunity, having attacked the city with his whole forces, took it in a moment, command being given that all the adults should be put to death; which command, though cruel, was proved in the issue to have been almost necessary. For to whom of those men could mercy have been shown, who, either shut up with their wives and children, burned their houses over their own heads, or abroad in arms made no end of fighting, except in death.

The town was taken, with immense spoil. Though the greater part of the goods had been purposely damaged by their owners, and resentment had made scarce any distinction of age in the massacre, and the captives were the booty of the soldiers; still it appears that some money was raised from the price of the effects that were sold, and that much costly furniture and garments were sent to Carthage. Some have written that Saguntum was taken in the eighth month after it began to be besieged; that Hannibal then retired to New Carthage, into winter quarters; and that in the fifth month after he had set out from Carthage he arrived in Italy. If this be so, it was impossible that Publius Cornelius and Tiberius Sempronius could have been consuls, to whom both at the beginning of the siege the Saguntine ambassadors were despatched, and who, during their office, fought with Hannibal; the one at the river Ticinus, and both some time after at the Trebia. Either all these events took place in a somewhat shorter period, or Saguntum was not begun to be besieged, but taken at the beginning of the year in which Publius Cornelius and Tiberius Sempronius were consuls. For the battle at Trebia could not have been so late as the year of Cneius Servilius and Caius Flaminius, since Flaminius entered on the office at Ariminum, having been created by the consul Tiberius Sempronius; who, having repaired to Rome after the battle at Trebia for the purpose of creating consuls, returned when the election was finished to the army into winter quarters.

Nearly about the same time, both the ambassadors who had returned from Carthage brought intelligence to Rome that all appearances were hostile, and the destruction of Saguntum was announced. Then such grief, and pity for allies so undeservingly destroyed, and shame that aid was withheld, and rage against the Carthaginians, and fear for the issue of events, as if the enemy were already at the gates, took at once possession of the senators, that their minds, disturbed by so many simultaneous emotions, trembled with fear rather than deliberated. For they considered that neither had a more spirited or warlike enemy ever encountered them nor had the Roman state been ever so sunk in sloth, and unfit for war: that the Sardinians, the Corsicans, the Istrians, and the Illyrians, had rather kept in a state of excitement than exercised the Roman arms; and with the Gauls it had been more properly a tumult than a war. That the Carthaginian, a veteran enemy, ever victorious during the hardest service for twenty-three years among the tribes of Spain, first trained to war under Hamilcar, then Hasdrubal, now Hannibal, a most active leader, and fresh from the destruction of a most opulent city, was passing the Iberus; that along with them he was bringing the numerous tribes of Spain, already aroused, and was about to excite the nations of Gaul, ever desirous of war; and that a war against the world was to be maintained in Italy and before the walls of Rome.

The provinces had already been previously named for the consuls; and having been now ordered to cast lots for them, Spain fell to Cornelius, and Africa with Sicily to Sempronius. Six legions were decreed for that year, and as many of the allies as should seem good to the consuls, and as great a fleet as could be equipped. Twenty-four thousand Roman infantry were levied, and one thousand eight hundred horse: forty thousand infantry of the allies, and four thousand four hundred horse: two hundred and twenty ships of three banks of oars, and twenty light galleys, were launched. It was then proposed to the people, "whether they willed and commanded that war should be declared against the people of Carthage;" and for the sake of that war a supplication was made through the city, and the gods were implored that the war which the Roman people had decreed might have a prosperous and fortunate issue. The forces were thus divided between the consuls. To Sempronius two legions were given, (each of these consisted of four thousand infantry and three hundred horse,) and sixteen thousand of the infantry of the allies, and one thousand eight hundred horse: one hundred and sixty ships of war, and twelve light galleys. With these land and sea forces Tiberius Sempronius was despatched to Sicily, in order to transport his army to Africa if the other consul should be able to prevent the Carthaginian from invading Italy. Fewer troops were given to Cornelius, because Lucius Manlius, the prætor, also had been sent with no weak force into Gaul. The number of ships in particular was reduced to Cornelius. Sixty of five banks of oars were assigned to him, (for they did not believe that the enemy would come by sea, or would fight after that mode of warfare,) and two Roman legions with their regular cavalry, and fourteen thousand of the infantry of the allies, with one thousand six hundred horse. The province of Gaul being not as yet exposed to the Carthaginian invasion, had, in the same year, two Roman legions, ten thousand allied infantry, one thousand allied cavalry, and six hundred Roman.

These preparations having been thus made, in order that every thing that was proper might be done before they commenced war, they send Quintus Fabius, Marcus Livius, Lucius Æmilius, Caius Licinius, and Quintus Bæbius, men of advanced years, as ambassadors into Africa, to inquire of the Carthaginians if Hannibal had laid siege to Saguntum by public authority; and if they should confess it, as it seemed probable they would, and defend it as done by public authority, to declare war against the people of Carthage. After the Romans arrived at Carthage, when an audience of the senate was given them, and Quintus Fabius had addressed no further inquiry than the one with which they had been charged, then one of the Carthaginians replied: "Even your former embassy, O Romans, was precipitate, when you demanded Hannibal to be given up, as attacking Saguntum on his own authority: but your present embassy, though so far milder in words, is in fact more severe. For then Hannibal was both accused, and required to be delivered up: now both a confession of wrong is exacted from us, and, as though we had confessed, restitution is immediately demanded. But I think that the question is not, whether Saguntum was attacked by private or public authority, but whether it was with right or wrong. For in the case of our citizen, the right of inquiry, whether he has acted by his own pleasure or ours, and the punishment also, belongs to us. The only dispute with you is, whether it was allowed to be done by the treaty. Since, therefore, it pleases you that a distinction should be made between what commanders do by public authority, and what on their own suggestion, there was a treaty between us made by the consul Lutatius; in which, though provision was made for the allies of both, there is no provision made for the Saguntines, for they were not as yet your allies. But in that treaty which was made with Hasdrubal, the Saguntines are excepted; against which I am going to say nothing but what I have learned from you. For you denied that you were bound by the treaty which Caius Lutatius the consul first made with us, because that it had neither been made by the authority of the senate nor the command of the people; and another treaty was therefore concluded anew by public authority. If your treaties do not bind you unless they are made by your authority and your commands, neither can the treaty of Hasdrubal, which he made without our knowledge, be binding on us. Cease, therefore, to make mention of Saguntum and the Iberus, and let your mind at length bring forth that with which it has long been in labour." Then the Roman, having formed a fold in his robe, said, "Here we bring to you peace and war; take which you please." On this speech they exclaimed no less fiercely in reply: "he might give which he chose;" and when he again, unfolding his robe, said "he gave war," they all answered that "they accepted it, and would maintain it with the same spirit with which they accepted it."

This direct inquiry and denunciation of war seemed more consistent with the dignity of the Roman people, both before and now, especially when Saguntum was destroyed, than to cavil in words about the obligation of treaties. For if it was a subject for a controversy of words, in what was the treaty of Hasdrubal to be compared with the former treaty of Lutatius, which was altered? Since in the treaty of Lutatius, was expressly added, "that it should only be held good if the people sanctioned it;" but in the treaty of Hasdrubal, neither was there any such exception; and that treaty during its life had been so established by the silence of so many years, that not even after the death of its author was any change made in it. Although even were they to abide by the former treaty, there had been sufficient provision made for the Saguntines by excepting the allies of both states; for neither was it added, "those who then were," nor "those who should afterwards be admitted." and since it is allowable to admit new allies, who could think it proper, either that no people should be received for any services into friendship? or that, being received under protection, they should not be defended? It was only stipulated, that the allies of the Carthaginians should not be excited to revolt, nor, revolting of their own accord, be received. The Roman ambassadors, according as they had been commanded at Rome, passed over from Carthage into Spain, in order to visit the nations, and either to allure them into an alliance, or dissuade them from joining the Carthaginians. They came first to the Bargusii, by whom having been received with welcome, because they were weary of the Carthaginian government, they excited many of the states beyond the Iberus to the desire of a revolution. Thence they came to the Volciani, whose reply being celebrated through Spain, dissuaded the other states from an alliance with the Romans; for thus the oldest member in their council made answer: "What sense of shame have ye, Romans, to ask of us that we should prefer your friendship to that of the Carthaginians, when you, their allies, betrayed the Saguntines with greater cruelty than that with which the Carthaginians, their enemies, destroyed them? There, methinks, you should look for allies, where the massacre of Saguntum is unknown. The ruins of Saguntum will remain a warning as melancholy as memorable to the states of Spain, that no one should confide in the faith or alliance of Rome." Having been then commanded to depart immediately from the territory of the Volciani, they afterwards received no kinder words from any of the councils of Spain: they therefore pass into Gaul, after having gone about through Spain to no purpose.

Among the Gauls a new and alarming spectacle was seen, by reason of their coming (such is the custom of the nation) in arms to the assembly. When, extolling in their discourse the renown and valour of the Roman people, and the wide extent of their empire, they had requested that they would refuse a passage through their territory and cities to the Carthaginian invading Italy; such laughter and yelling is said to have arisen, that the youths were with difficulty composed to order by the magistrates and old men. So absurd and shameless did the request seem, to propose that the Gauls, rather than suffer the war to pass on to Italy, should turn it upon themselves and expose their own lands to be laid waste instead of those of others. When the tumult was at length allayed, answer was returned to the ambassadors, "that they had neither experienced good from the Romans, nor wrong from the Carthaginians, on account of which they should either take up arms in behalf of the Romans, or against the Cathaginians. On the contrary, they had heard that men of their nation had been driven from the lands and confines of Italy by the Roman people, that they had to pay a tribute, and suffered other indignities." Nearly the same was said and heard in the other assemblies of Gaul; nor did they hear any thing friendly or pacific before they came to Marseilles. There, every thing found out by the care and fidelity of the allies was made known to them—"that the minds of the Gauls had been already prepossessed by Hannibal, but that not even by him would that nation be found very tractable, (so fierce and untameable are their dispositions,) unless the affections of the chiefs should every now and then be conciliated with gold, of which that people are most covetous." Having thus gone round through the tribes of Spain and Gaul, the ambassadors return to Rome not long after the consuls had set out for their provinces. They found the whole city on tiptoe in expectation of war, the report being sufficiently confirmed, that the Carthaginians had already passed the Iberus.

Hannibal, after the taking of Saguntum, had retired to New Carthage into winter quarters; and there, having heard what had been done and decreed at Rome and Carthage, and that he was not only the leader, but also the cause of the war, after having divided and sold the remains of the plunder, thinking there ought to be no longer delay, he calls together and thus addresses his soldiers of the Spanish race: "I believe, tribes, that even you yourselves perceive that, all the tribes of Spain having been reduced to peace, we must either conclude our campaigns and disband our armies, or transfer the war into other regions: for thus these nations will flourish amid the blessings not only of peace, but also of victory, if we seek from other countries spoils and renown. Since, therefore, a campaign far from home soon awaits you, and it is uncertain when you shall again see your homes, and all that is there dear to you, if any one of you wishes to visit his friends, I grant him leave of absence. I give you orders to be here at the beginning of spring, that, with the good assistance of the gods, we may enter on a war which will prove one of great glory and spoil." This power of visiting their homes, voluntarily offered, was acceptable to almost all, already longing to see their friends, and foreseeing in future a still longer absence Repose through the whole season of winter, between toils already undergone and those that were soon to be endured, repaired the vigour of their bodies and minds to encounter all difficulties afresh. At the beginning of spring they assembled according to command. Hannibal, when he had reviewed the auxiliaries of all the nations, having gone to Gades, performs his vows to Hercules; and binds himself by new vows, provided his other projects should have a prosperous issue. Then dividing his care at the same time between the offensive and defensive operations of the war, lest while he was advancing on Italy by a land journey through Spain and Gaul, Africa should be unprotected and exposed to the Romans from Sicily, he resolved to strengthen it with a powerful force. For this purpose he requested a reinforcement from Africa, chiefly of light-armed spearmen, in order that the Africans might serve in Spain, and the Spaniards in Africa, each likely to be a better soldier at a distance from home, as if bound by mutual pledges. He sent into Africa thirteen thousand eight hundred and fifty targetteers, eight hundred and seventy Balearic slingers, and one thousand two hundred horsemen, composed of various nations. He orders these forces partly to be used as a garrison for Carthage and partly to be distributed through Africa: at the same time having sent commissaries into the different states, he orders four thousand chosen youth whom they had levied to be conducted to Carthage, both as a garrison and as hostages.

Thinking also that Spain ought not to be neglected (and the less because he was aware that it had been traversed by the Roman ambassadors, to influence the minds of the chiefs,) he assigns that province to his brother Hasdrubal, a man of active spirit, and strengthens him chiefly with African troops: eleven thousand eight hundred and fifty African infantry, three hundred Ligurians, and five hundred Balearians. To these forces of infantry were added four hundred horsemen of the Libyphœnicians, a mixed race of Carthaginians and Africans; of the Numidians and Moors, who border on the ocean, to the number of one thousand eight hundred, and a small band of Ilergetes from Spain, amounting to two hundred horse: and, that no description of land force might be wanting, fourteen elephants. A fleet was given him besides to defend the sea-coast, (because it might be supposed that the Romans would then fight in the same mode of warfare by which they had formerly prevailed,) fifty quinqueremes, two quadriremes, five triremes: but only thirty-two quinqueremes and five triremes were properly fitted out and manned with rowers. From Gades he returned to the winter quarters of the army at Carthage; and thence setting out, he led his forces by the city Etovissa to the Iberus and the sea-coast. There, it is reported, a youth of divine aspect was seen by him in his sleep, who said, "that he was sent by Jupiter as the guide of Hannibal into Italy, and that he should, therefore, follow him, nor in any direction turn his eyes away from him." At first he followed in terror, looking no where, either around or behind: afterwards, through the curiosity of the human mind, when he revolved in his mind what that could be on which he was forbidden to look back, he could not restrain his eyes; then he beheld behind him a serpent of wonderful size moving along with an immense destruction of trees and bushes, and after it a cloud following with thunderings from the skies; and that then inquiring "what was that great commotion, and what the cause of the prodigy," he heard in reply: "That it was the devastation of Italy: that he should continue to advance forward, nor inquire further, but suffer the fates to remain in obscurity."

Cheered by this vision, he transported his forces in three divisions across the Iberus, having sent emissaries before him to conciliate by gifts the minds of the Gauls, in the quarter through which his army was to be led, and to examine the passes of the Alps. He led ninety thousand infantry and twelve thousand cavalry across the Iberus. He then subdued the Ilergetes, the Bargusii, the Ausetani, and that part of Lacetania which lies at the foot of the Pyrenæan mountains; and he placed Hanno in command over all this district, that the narrow gorges which connect Spain with Gaul might be under his power. Ten thousand infantry, and a thousand cavalry, were given to Hanno for the defence of the country he was to occupy. After the army began to march through the passes of the Pyrenees, and a more certain rumour of the Roman war spread through the barbarians, three thousand of the Carpetanian infantry turned back: it clearly appeared that they were not so much swayed by the prospect of the war as by the length of the journey and the insuperable passage of the Alps. Hannibal, because it was hazardous to recall or detain them by force, lest the fierce minds of the rest might also be irritated, sent home above seven thousand men, whom also he had observed to be annoyed with the service, pretending that the Carpetani had also been dismissed by him.

Then, lest delay and ease might unsettle their minds, he crosses the Pyrenees with the rest of his forces, and pitches his camp at the town Illiberis. The Gauls, though they had heard that the war was directed against Italy, yet because there was a report that the Spaniards on the other side of the Pyrenees had been reduced by force, and that strong forces had been imposed on them, being roused to arms through the fear of slavery, assembled certain tribes at Ruscino. When this was announced to Hannibal, he, having more fear of the delay than of the war, sent envoys to say to their princes, "that he wished to confer with them; and that they should either come nearer to Illiberis, or that he would proceed to Ruscino, that their meeting might be facilitated by vicinity: for that he would either be happy to receive them into his camp, or would himself without hesitation come to them: since he had entered Gaul as a friend, and not as an enemy, and would not draw the sword, if the Gauls did not force him, before he came to Italy." These proposals, indeed, were made by his messengers. But when the princes of the Gauls, having immediately moved their camp to Illiberis, came without reluctance to the Carthaginian, being won by his presents, they suffered his army to pass through their territories, by the town of Ruscino, without any molestation.

In the mean time no further intelligence had been brought into Italy to Rome by the ambassadors of Marseilles than that Hannibal had passed the Iberus; when the Boii asked if he had already passed the Alps, revolted after instigating the Insubrians; not so much through their ancient resentment towards the Roman people, as on account of their having felt aggrieved that the colonies of Placentia and Cremona had been lately planted in the Gallic territory about the Po. Having therefore, suddenly taken up arms, and made an attack on that very territory, they created so much of terror and tumult, that not only the rustic population, but even the Roman triumvirs, Caius Lutatius, Caius Servilius, and Titus Annius, who had come to assign the lands, distrusting the walls of Placentia, fled to Mutina. About the name of Luttius there is no doubt: in place of Caius Servilius and Titus Annius, some annals have Quintus Acilius and Caius Herenrius; others, Publius Cornelius Asina and Caius Papirius Maso. This point is also uncertain, whether the ambassadors went to expostulate to the Boii suffered violence, or whether an attack was made on the triumvirs while measuring out the lands. While they were shut up in Mutina, and a people unskilled in the arts of besieging towns, and, at the same time, most sluggish at military operations, lay inactive before the walls, which they had not touched, pretended proposals for a peace were set on foot; and the ambassadors, being invited out to a conference by the chiefs of the Gauls, are seized, not only contrary to the law of nations, but in violation of the faith which was pledged on that very occasion; the Gauls denying that they would set them free unless their hostages were restored to them. When this intelligence respecting the ambassadors was announced, and that Mutina and its garrison were in danger, Lucius Manlius, the prætor, inflamed with rage, led his army in haste to Mutina. There were then woods on both sides of the road, most of the country being uncultivated. There, having advanced without previously exploring his route, he fell suddenly into an ambuscade; and after much slaughter of his men, with difficulty made his way into the open plains. Here a camp was fortified, and because confidence was wanting to the Gauls to attack it, the spirit of the soldiers revived, although it was sufficiently evident that their strength was much clipped. The journey was then commenced anew; nor while the army was led in march through open tracts did the enemy appear: but, when the woods were again entered, then attacking the rear, amid great confusion and alarm of all, they slew eight hundred soldiers, and took six standards. There was an end to the Gauls of creating, and to the Romans of experiencing terror, when they escaped from the pathless and entangled thicket; then easily defending their march through the open ground, the Romans directed their course to Tanetum, a village near the Po; where, by a temporary fortification, and the supplies conveyed by the river, and also by the aid of the Brixian Gauls, they defended themselves against the daily increasing multitude of their enemies.

When the account of this sudden disturbance was brought to Rome, and the senators heard that the Punic had also been increased by a Gallic war, they order Caius Atilius, the prætor, to carry assistance to Manlius with one Roman legion and five thousand of the allies, enrolled in the late levy by the consul: who, without any contest, for the enemy had retired through fear, arrived at Tanetum. At the same time Publius Cornelius, a new legion having been levied in the room of that which was sent with the prætor, setting out from the city with sixty ships of war, by the coast of Etruria and Liguria, and then the mountains of the Salyes, arrived at Marseilles, and pitched his camp at the nearest mouth of the Rhone, (for the stream flows down to the sea divided into several channels,) scarcely as yet well believing that Hannibal had crossed the Pyrenæan mountains; whom when he ascertained to be also meditating the passage of the Rhone, uncertain in what place he might meet him, his soldiers not yet being sufficiently recovered from the tossing of the sea, he sends forward, in the mean time, three hundred chosen horses, with Massilian guides and Gallic auxiliaries, to explore all the country, and observe the enemy from a safe distance. Hannibal, the other states being pacified by fear or bribes, had now come into the territory of the Volcæ, a powerful nation. They, indeed, dwell on both sides of the Rhone: but doubting that the Carthaginian could be driven from the hither bank, in order that they might have the river as a defence, having transported almost all their effects across the Rhone, occupied in arms the farther bank of the river. Hannibal, by means of presents, persuades the other inhabitants of the river-side, and some even of the Volcæ themselves, whom their homes had detained, to collect from every quarter and build ships; and they at the same time themselves desired that the army should be transported, and their country relieved, as soon as possible, from the vast multitude of men that burthened it. A great number, therefore, of ships and boats rudely formed for the neighbouring passages, were collected together; and the Gauls, first beginning the plan, hollowed out some new ones from single trees; and then the soldiers themselves, at once induced by the plenty of materials and the easiness of the work, hastily formed shapeless hulks, in which they could transport themselves and their baggage, caring about nothing else, provided they could float and contain their burthen.

And now, when all things were sufficiently prepared for crossing, the enemy over against them occupying the whole bank, horse and foot, deterred them. In order to dislodge them, Hannibal orders Hanno, the son of Bomilcar, at the first watch of the night, to proceed with a part of the forces, principally Spanish, one day's journey up the river; and having crossed it where he might first be able, as secretly as possible, to lead round his forces, that when the occasion required he might attack the enemy in the rear. The Gauls, given him as guides for the purpose, inform him that about twenty-five miles from thence, the river spreading round a small island, broader where it was divided, and therefore with a shallower channel, presented a passage. At this place timber was quickly cut down and rafts formed, on which men, horses, and other burthens might be conveyed over. The Spaniards, without making any difficulty, having put their clothes in bags of leather, and themselves leaning on their bucklers placed beneath them, swam across the river. And the rest of the army, after passing on the rafts joined together, and pitching their camp near the river, being fatigued by the journey of the night and the labour of the work, are refreshed by the rest of one day, their leader being anxious to execute his design at a proper season. Setting out next day from this place, they signify by raising a smoke that they had crossed, and were not far distant; which when Hannibal understood, that he might not be wanting on the opportunity, he gives the signal for passing. The infantry already had the boats prepared and fitted; a line of ships higher up transporting the horsemen for the most part near their horses swimming beside them, in order to break the force of the current, rendered the water smooth to the boats crossing below. A great part of the horses were led across swimming, held by bridles from the stern, except those which they put on board saddled and bridled, in order that they might be ready to be used by the rider the moment he disembarked on the strand.

The Gauls run down to the bank to meet them with various whoopings and songs, according to their custom, shaking their shields above their heads, and brandishing their weapons in their right hands, although such a multitude of ships in front of them alarmed them, together with the loud roaring of the river, and the mingled clamours of the sailors and soldiers, both those who were striving to break through the force of the current, and those who from the other bank were encouraging their comrades on their passage. While sufficiently dismayed by this tumult in front, more terrifying shouts from behind assailed them, their camp having been taken by Hanno; presently he himself came up, and a twofold terror encompassed them, both such a multitude of armed men landing from the ships, and this unexpected army pressing on their rear. When the Gauls, having made a prompt and bold effort to force the enemy, were themselves repulsed, they break through where a way seemed most open, and fly in consternation to their villages around. Hannibal, now despising these tumultuary onsets of the Gauls, having transported the rest of his forces at leisure, pitches his camp. I believe that there were various plans for transporting the elephants; at least there are various accounts of the way in which it was done. Some relate, that after the elephants were assembled together on the bank, the fiercest of them being provoked by his keeper, pursued him as he swam across the water, to which he had run for refuge, and drew after him the rest of the herd; the mere force of the stream hurrying them to the other bank, when the bottom had failed each, fearful of the depth. But there is more reason to believe that they were conveyed across on rafts; which plan, as it must have appeared the safer before execution, is after it the more entitled to credit. They extended from the bank into the river one raft two hundred feet long and fifty broad, which, fastened higher up by several strong cables to the bank, that it might not be carried down by the stream they covered, like a bridge, with earth thrown upon it, so that the beasts might tread upon it without fear, as over solid ground. Another raft equally broad and a hundred feet long, fit for crossing the river, was joined to this first; and when the elephants, driven along the stationary raft as along a road had passed, the females leading the way, on to the smaller raft which was joined to it, the lashings, by which it was slightly fastened, being immediately let go, it was drawn by some light boats to the opposite side. The first having been thus landed, the rest were then returned for and carried across. They gave no signs of alarm whatever while they were driven along as it were on a continuous bridge. The first fear was, when, the raft being loosed from the rest, they were hurried into the deep. Then pressing together, as those at the edges drew back from the water, they produced some disorder, till mere terror, when they saw water all around, produced quiet. Some, indeed, becoming infuriated, fell into the river; but, steadied by their own weight, having thrown off their riders, and seeking step by step the shallows, they escaped to the shore.

Whilst the elephants were conveyed over, Hannibal, in the mean time, had sent five hundred Numidian horsemen towards the camp of the Romans, to observe where and how numerous their forces were, and what they were designing. The three hundred Roman horsemen sent, as was before said, from the mouth of the Rhone, meet this band of cavalry; and a more furious engagement than could be expected from the number of the combatants takes place. For, besides many wounds, the loss on both sides was also nearly equal: and the flight and dismay of the Numidians gave victory to the Romans, now exceedingly fatigued. There fell of the conquerors one hundred and sixty, not all Romans, but partly Gauls: of the vanquished more than two hundred. This commencement, and at the same time omen of the war, as it portended to the Romans a prosperous issue of the whole, so did it also the success of a doubtful and by no means bloodless contest. When, after the action had thus occurred, his own men returned to each general, Scipio could adopt no fixed plan of proceeding, except that he should form his measures from the plans and undertakings of the enemy: and Hannibal, uncertain whether he should pursue the march he had commenced into Italy, or fight with the Roman army which had first presented itself, the arrival of ambassadors from the Boii, and of a petty prince called Magalus, diverted from an immediate engagement; who, declaring that they would be the guides of his journey and the companions of his dangers, gave it as their opinion, that Italy ought to be attacked with the entire force of the war, his strength having been no where previously impaired. The troops indeed feared the enemy, the remembrance of the former war not being yet obliterated; but much more did they dread the immense journey and the Alps, a thing formidable by report, particularly to the inexperienced.

Hannibal, therefore, when his own resolution was fixed to proceed in his course and advance on Italy, having summoned an assembly, works upon the minds of the soldiers in various ways, by reproof and exhortation. He said, that "he wondered what sudden fear had seized breasts ever before undismayed: that through so many years they had made their campaigns with conquest; nor had departed from Spain before all the nations and countries which two opposite seas embrace, were subjected to the Carthaginians. That then, indignant that the Romans demanded those, whosoever had besieged Saguntum, to be delivered up to them, as on account of a crime, they had passed the Iberus to blot out the name of the Romans, and to emancipate the world. That then the way seemed long to no one, though they were pursuing it from the setting to the rising of the sun. That now, when they saw by far the greater part of their journey accomplished, the passes of the Pyrenees surmounted, amid the most ferocious nations, the Rhone, that mighty river, crossed, in spite of the opposition of so many thousand Gauls, the fury of the river itself having been overcome, when they had the Alps in sight, the other side of which was Italy, should they halt through weariness at the very gates of the enemy, imagining the Alps to be—what else than lofty mountains? That supposing them to be higher than the summits of the Pyrenees, assuredly no part of the earth reached the sky, nor was insurmountable by mankind. The Alps in fact were inhabited and cultivated;—produced and supported living beings. Were they passable by a few men and impassable to armies? That those very ambassadors whom they saw before them had not crossed the Alps borne aloft through the air on wings; neither were their ancestors indeed natives of the soil, but settling in Italy from foreign countries, had often as emigrants safely crossed these very Alps in immense bodies, with their wives and children. To the armed soldier, carrying nothing with him but the instruments of war, what in reality was impervious or insurmountable? That Saguntum might be taken, what dangers, what toils were for eight months undergone! Now, when their aim was Rome, the capital of the world, could any thing appear so dangerous or difficult as to delay their undertaking? That the Gauls had formerly gained possession of that very country which the Carthaginian despairs of being able to approach. That they must, therefore, either yield in spirit and valour to that nation which they had so often during those times overcome; or look forward, as the end of their journey, to the plain which spreads between the Tiber and the walls of Rome."

He orders them, roused by these exhortations, to refresh themselves and prepare for the journey. Next day, proceeding upward along the bank of the Rhone, he makes for the inland part of Gaul: not because it was the more direct route to the Alps, but believing that the farther he retired from the sea, the Romans would be less in his way; with whom, before he arrived in Italy, he had no intention of engaging. After four days' march he came to the Island: there the streams of the Arar and the Rhone, flowing down from different branches of the Alps, after embracing a pretty large tract of country, flow into one. The name of the Island is given to the plains that lie between them. The Allobroges dwell near, a nation even in those days inferior to none in Gaul in power and fame. They were at that time at variance. Two brothers were contending for the sovereignty. The elder, named Brancus, who had before been king, was driven out by his younger brother and a party of the younger men, who, inferior in right, had more of power. When the decision of this quarrel was most opportunely referred to Hannibal, being appointed arbitrator of the kingdom, he restored the sovereignty to the elder, because such had been the opinion of the senate and the chief men. In return for this service, he was assisted with a supply of provisions, and plenty of all necessaries, particularly clothing, which the Alps, notorious for extreme cold, rendered necessary to be prepared. After composing the dissensions of the Allobroges, when he now was proceeding to the Alps, he directed his course thither, not by the straight road, but turned to the left into the country of the Tricastini, thence by the extreme boundary of the territory of the Vocontii he proceeded to the Tricorii; his way not being any where obstructed till he came to the river Druentia. This stream, also arising amid the Alps, is by far the most difficult to pass of all the rivers in Gaul; for though it rolls down an immense body of water, yet it does not admit of ships; because, being restrained by no banks, and flowing in several and not always the same channels, and continually forming new shallows and new whirlpools, (on which account the passage is also uncertain to a person on foot,) and rolling down besides gravelly stones, it affords no firm or safe passage to those who enter it; and having been at that time swollen by showers, it created great disorder among the soldiers as they crossed, when, in addition to other difficulties, they were of themselves confused by their own hurry and uncertain shouts.

Publius Cornelius the consul, about three days after Hannibal moved from the bank of the Rhone, had come to the camp of the enemy, with his army drawn up in square, intending to make no delay in fighting: but when he saw the fortifications deserted, and that he could not easily come up with them so far in advance before him, he returned to the sea and his fleet, in order more easily and safely to encounter Hannibal when descending from the Alps. But that Spain, the province which he had obtained by lot, might not be destitute of Roman auxiliaries, he sent his brother Cneius Scipio with the principal part of his forces against Hasdrubal, not only to defend the old allies and conciliate new, but also to drive Hasdrubal out of Spain. He himself, with a very small force, returned to Genoa, intending to defend Italy with the army which was around the Po. From the Druentia, by a road that lay principally through plains, Hannibal arrived at the Alps without molestation from the Gauls that inhabit those regions. Then, though the scene had been previously anticipated from report, (by which uncertainties are wont to be exaggerated,) yet the height of the mountains when viewed so near, and the snows almost mingling with the sky, the shapeless huts situated on the cliffs, the cattle and beasts of burden withered by the cold, the men unshorn and wildly dressed, all things, animate and inanimate, stiffened with frost, and other objects more terrible to be seen than described, renewed their alarm. To them, marching up the first acclivities, the mountaineers appeared occupying the heights over head; who, if they had occupied the more concealed valleys, might, by rushing out suddenly to the attack, have occasioned great flight and havoc. Hannibal orders them to halt, and having sent forward Gauls to view the ground, when he found there was no passage that way, he pitches his camp in the widest valley he could find, among places all rugged and precipitous. Then, having learned from the same Gauls, when they had mixed in conversation with the mountaineers, from whom they differed little in language and manners, that the pass was only beset during the day, and that at night each withdrew to his own dwelling, he advanced at the dawn to the heights, as if designing openly and by day to force his way through the defile. The day then being passed in feigning a different attempt from that which was in preparation, when they had fortified the camp in the same place where they had halted, as soon as he perceived that the mountaineers had descended from the heights, and that the guards were withdrawn, having lighted for show a greater number of fires than was proportioned to the number that remained, and having left the baggage in the camp, with the cavalry and the principal part of the infantry, he himself with a party of light-armed, consisting of all the most courageous of his troops, rapidly cleared the defile, and took post on those very heights which the enemy had occupied.

At dawn of light the next day the camp broke up, and the rest of the army began to move forward. The mountaineers, on a signal being given, were now assembling from their forts to their usual station, when they suddenly behold part of the enemy overhanging them from above, in possession of their former position, and the others passing along the road. Both these objects, presented at the same time to the eye and the mind, made them stand motionless for a little while; but when they afterwards saw the confusion in the pass, and that the marching body was thrown into disorder by the tumult which itself created, principally from the horses being terrified, thinking that whatever terror they added would suffice for the destruction of the enemy, they scramble along the dangerous rocks, as being accustomed alike to pathless and circuitous ways. Then indeed the Carthaginians were opposed at once by the enemy and by the difficulties of the ground; and each striving to escape first from the danger, there was more fighting among themselves than with their opponents. The horses in particular created danger in the lines, which, being terrified by the discordant clamours which the groves and re-echoing valleys augmented, fell into confusion; and if by chance struck or wounded, they were so dismayed that they occasioned a great loss both of men and baggage of every description: and as the pass on both sides was broken and precipitous, this tumult threw many down to an immense depth, some even of the armed men; but the beasts of burden, with their loads, were rolled down like the fall of some vast fabric. Though these disasters were shocking to view, Hannibal however kept his place for a little, and kept his men together, lest he might augment the tumult and disorder; but afterwards, when he saw the line broken, and that there was danger that he should bring over his army, preserved to no purpose if deprived of their baggage, he hastened down from the higher ground; and though he had routed the enemy by the first onset alone, he at the same time increased the disorder in his own army: but that tumult was composed in a moment, after the roads were cleared by the flight of the mountaineers; and presently the whole army was conducted through, not only without being disturbed, but almost in silence. He then took a fortified place, which was the capital of that district, and the little villages that lay around it, and fed his army for three days with the corn and cattle he had taken; and during these three days, as the soldiers were neither obstructed by the mountaineers, who had been daunted by the first engagement, nor yet much by the ground, he made considerable way.

He then came to another state, abounding, for a mountainous country, with inhabitants; where he was nearly overcome, not by open war, but by his own arts of treachery and ambuscade. Some old men, governors of forts, came as deputies to the Carthaginian, professing, "that having been warned by the useful example of the calamities of others, they wished rather to experience the friendship than the hostilities of the Carthaginians: they would, therefore, obediently execute his commands, and begged that he would accept of a supply of provisions, guides of his march, and hostages for the sincerity of their promises." Hannibal, when he had answered them in a friendly manner, thinking that they should neither be rashly trusted nor yet rejected, lest if repulsed they might openly become enemies, having received the hostages whom they proffered, and made use of the provisions which they of their own accord brought down to the road, follows their guides, by no means as among a people with whom he was at peace, but with his line of march in close order. The elephants and cavalry formed the van of the marching body; he himself, examining every thing around, and intent on every circumstance, followed with the choicest of the infantry. When they came into a narrower pass, lying on one side beneath an overhanging eminence, the barbarians, rising at once on all sides from their ambush, assail them in front and rear, both at close quarters and from a distance, and roll down huge stones on the army. The most numerous body of men pressed on the rear; against whom the infantry, facing about and directing their attack, made it very obvious, that had not the rear of the army been well supported, a great loss must have been sustained in that pass. Even as it was they came to the extremity of danger, and almost to destruction: for while Hannibal hesitates to lead down his division into the defile, because, though he himself was a protection to the cavalry, lie had not in the same way left any aid to the infantry in the rear; the mountaineers, charging obliquely, and on having broken through the middle of the army, took possession of the road; and one night was spent by Hannibal without his cavalry and baggage.

Next day, the barbarians running in to the attack between (the two divisions) less vigorously, the forces were re-united, and the defile passed, not without loss, but yet with a greater destruction of beasts of burden than of men. From that time the mountaineers fell upon them in smaller parties, more like an attack of robbers than war, sometimes on the van, sometimes on the rear, according as the ground afforded them advantage, or stragglers advancing or loitering gave them an opportunity. Though the elephants were driven through steep and narrow roads with great loss of time, yet wherever they went they rendered the army safe from the enemy, because men unacquainted with such animals were afraid of approaching too nearly. On the ninth day they came to a summit of the Alps, chiefly through places trackless; and after many mistakes of their way, which were caused either by the treachery of the guides, or, when they were not trusted, by entering valleys at random, on their own conjectures of the route. For two days they remained encamped on the summit; and rest was given to the soldiers, exhausted with toil and fighting: and several beasts of burden, which had fallen down among the rocks, by following the track of the army arrived at the camp. A fall of snow, it being now the season of the setting of the constellation of the Pleiades, caused great fear to the soldiers, already worn out with weariness of so many hardships. On the standards being moved forward at daybreak, when the army proceeded slowly over all places entirely blocked up with snow, and languor and despair strongly appeared in the countenances of all, Hannibal, having advanced before the standards, and ordered the soldiers to halt on a certain eminence, whence there was a prospect far and wide, points out to them Italy and the plains of the Po, extending themselves beneath the Alpine mountains; and said "that they were now surmounting not only the ramparts of Italy, but also of the city of Rome; that the rest of the journey would be smooth and down-hill; that after one, or, at most, a second battle, they would have the citadel and capital of Italy in their power and possession." The army then began to advance, the enemy now making no attempts beyond petty thefts, as opportunity offered. But the journey proved much more difficult than it had been in the ascent, as the declivity of the Alps being generally shorter on the side of Italy is consequently steeper; for nearly all the road was precipitous, narrow, and slippery, so that neither those who made the least stumble could prevent themselves from falling, nor, when fallen, remain in the same place, but rolled, both men and beasts of burden, one upon another.

They then came to a rock much more narrow, and formed of such perpendicular ledges, that a light-armed soldier, carefully making the attempt, and clinging with his hands to the bushes and roots around, could with difficulty lower himself down. The ground, even before very steep by nature, had been broken by a recent falling away of the earth into a precipice of nearly a thousand feet in depth. Here when the cavalry had halted, as if at the end of their journey, it is announced to Hannibal, wondering what obstructed the march that the rock was impassable. Having then gone himself to view the place, it seemed clear to him that he must lead his army round it, by however great a circuit, through the pathless and untrodden regions around. But this route also proved impracticable; for while the new snow of a moderate depth remained on the old, which had not been removed, their footsteps were planted with ease as they walked upon the new snow, which was soft and not too deep; but when it was dissolved by the trampling of so many men and beasts of burden, they then walked on the bare ice below, and through the dirty fluid formed by the melting snow. Here there was a wretched struggle, both on account of the slippery ice not affording any hold to the step, and giving way beneath the foot more readily by reason of the slope; and whether they assisted themselves in rising by their hands or their knees, their supports themselves giving way, they would stumble again; nor were there any stumps or roots near; by pressing against which, one might with hand or foot support himself; so that they only floundered on the smooth ice and amid the melted snow. The beasts of burden sometimes also went into this lower ice by merely treading upon it, at others they broke it completely through, by the violence with which they struck in their hoofs in their struggling, so that most of them, as if taken in a trap, stuck in the hardened and deeply frozen ice.

At length, after the men and beasts of burden had been fatigued to no purpose, the camp was pitched on the summit, the ground being cleared for that purpose with great difficulty, so much snow was there to be dug out and carried away. The soldiers being then set to make a way down the cliff by which alone a passage could be effected, and it being necessary that they should cut through the rocks, having felled and lopped a number of large trees which grew around, they make a huge pile of timber; and as soon as a strong wind fit for exciting the flames arose, they set fire to it, and, pouring vinegar on the heated stones, they render them soft and crumbling. They then open a way with iron instruments through the rock thus heated by the fire, and soften its declivities by gentle windings, so that not only the beasts of burden, but also the elephants could be led down it. Four days were spent about this rock, the beasts nearly perishing through hunger: for the summits of the mountains are for the most part bare, and if there is any pasture the snows bury it. The lower parts contain valleys, and some sunny hills, and rivulets flowing beside woods, and scenes more worthy of the abode of man. There the beasts of burden were sent out to pasture, and rest given for three days to the men, fatigued with forming the passage: they then descended into the plains, the country and the dispositions of the inhabitants being now less rugged.

In this manner chiefly they came to Italy in the fifth month (as some authors relate) after leaving New Carthage, having crossed the Alps in fifteen days. What number of forces Hannibal had when he had passed into Italy is by no means agreed upon by authors. Those who state them at the highest, make mention of a hundred thousand foot and twenty thousand horse; those who state them at the lowest, of twenty thousand foot and six thousand horse. Lucius Cincius Alimentus, who relates that he was made prisoner by Hannibal, would influence me most as an authority, did he not confound the number by adding the Gauls and Ligurians. Including these, (who, it is more probable, flocked to him afterwards, and so some authors assert,) he says, that eighty thousand foot and ten thousand horse were brought into Italy; and that he had heard from Hannibal himself, that after crossing the Rhone he had lost thirty-six thousand men, and an immense number of horses, and other beasts of burden, among the Taurini, the next nation to the Gauls, as he descended into Italy. As this circumstance is agreed on by all, I am the more surprised that it should be doubtful by what road he crossed the Alps; and that it should commonly be believed that he passed over the Pennine mountain, and that thence [17] the name was given to that ridge of the Alps. Cœlius says, that he passed over the top of Mount Cremo; both which passes would have brought him, not to the Taurini, but through the Salasian mountaineers to the Libuan Gauls. Neither is it probable that these roads into Gaul were then open, especially once those which, lead to the Pennine mountain would have been unlocked up by nations half German; nor by Hercules (if this argument has weight with any one) do the Veragri, the inhabitants of this ridge, know of the name being given to these mountains from the passage of the Carthaginians, but from the divinity, whom the mountaineers style Penninus, worshipped on the highest summit.

Very opportunely for the commencement of his operations, a war had broken out with the Taurini, the nearest nation, against the Insubrians; but Hannibal could not put his troops under arms to assist either party, as they very chiefly felt the disorders they had before contracted, in remedying them; for ease after toil, plenty after want, and attention to their persons after dirt and filth, had variously affected their squalid and almost savage-looking bodies. This was the reason that Publius Cornelius, the consul, when he had arrived at Pisa with his fleet, hastened to the Po, though the troops he received from Manlius and Atilius were raw and disheartened by their late disgraces, in order that he might engage the enemy when not yet recruited. But when the consul came to Placentia, Hannibal had already moved from his quarters, and had taken by storm one city of the Taurini, the capital of the nation, because they did not come willingly into his alliance; and he would have gained over to him, not only from fear, but also from inclination, the Gauls who dwell beside the Po, had not the arrival of the consul suddenly checked them while watching for an opportunity of revolt. Hannibal at the same time moved from the Taurini, thinking that the Gauls, uncertain which side to choose, would follow him if present among them. The armies were now almost in sight of each other, and their leaders, though not at present sufficiently acquainted, yet met each other with a certain feeling of mutual admiration. For the name of Hannibal, even before the destruction of Saguntum, was very celebrated among the Romans; and Hannibal believed Scipio to be a superior man, from the very circumstance of his having been specially chosen to act as commander against himself. They had increased too their estimation of each other; Scipio, because, being left behind in Gaul, he had met Hannibal when he had crossed into Italy; Hannibal, by his daring attempt of crossing the Alps and by its accomplishment. Scipio, however, was the first to cross the Po, and having pitched his camp at the river Ticinus, he delivered the following oration for the sake of encouraging his soldiers before he led them out to form for battle:

"If, soldiers, I were leading out that army to battle which I had with me in Gaul, I should have thought it superfluous to address you; for of what use would it be to exhort either those horsemen who so gloriously vanquished the cavalry of the enemy at the river Rhone, or those legions with whom, pursuing this very enemy flying before us, I obtained in lieu of victory, a confession of superiority, shown by his retreat and refusal to fight?

Now because that army, levied for the province of Spain, maintains the war under my auspices [18] and the command of my brother Cneius Scipio, in the country where the senate and people of Rome wished him to serve, and since I, that you might have a consul for your leader against Hannibal and the Carthaginians, have offered myself voluntarily for this contest, few words are required to be addressed from a new commander to soldiers unacquainted with him. That you may not be ignorant of the nature of the war nor of the enemy, you have to fight, soldiers, with those whom in the former war you conquered both by land and sea; from whom you have exacted tribute for twenty years; from whom you hold Sicily and Sardinia, taken as the prizes of victory. In the present contest, therefore, you and they will have those feelings which are wont to belong to the victors and the vanquished. Nor are they now about to fight because they are daring, but because it is unavoidable; except you can believe that they who declined the engagement when their forces were entire, should have now gained more confidence when two-thirds of their infantry and cavalry have been lost in the passage of the Alps, and when almost greater numbers have perished than survive. Yes, they are few indeed, (some may say,) but they are vigorous in mind and body; men whose strength and power scarce any force may withstand. On the contrary, they are but the resemblances, nay, are rather the shadows of men; being worn out with hunger, cold, dirt, and filth, and bruised and enfeebled among stones and rocks. Besides all this, their joints are frost-bitten, their sinews stiffened with the snow, their limbs withered up by the frost, their armour battered and shivered, their horses lame and powerless. With such cavalry, with such infantry, you have to fight: you will not have enemies in reality, but rather their last remains. And I fear nothing more than that when you have fought Hannibal, the Alps may appear to have conquered him. But perhaps it was fitting that the gods themselves should, without any human aid, commence and carry forward a war with a leader and a people that violate the faith of treaties; and that we, who next to the gods have been injured, should finish the contest thus commenced and nearly completed."

"I do not fear lest any one should think that I say this ostentatiously for the sake of encouraging you, while in my own mind I am differently affected. I was at liberty to go with my army into Spain, my own province, whither I had already set out; where I should have had a brother as the bearer of my councils and my dangers, and Hasdrubal, instead of Hannibal, for my antagonist, and without question a less laborious war: nevertheless, as I sailed along the coast of Gaul, having landed on hearing of this enemy, and having sent forward the cavalry, I moved my camp to the Rhone. In a battle of cavalry, with which part of my forces the opportunity of engaging was afforded, I routed the enemy; and because I could not overtake by land his army of infantry, which was rapidly hurried away, as if in flight, having returned to the ships with all the speed I could, after compassing such an extent of sea and land, I have met him at the foot of the Alps. Whether do I appear, while declining the contest, to have fallen in unexpectedly with this dreaded foe, or encounter him in his track? to challenge him and drag him out to decide the contest? I am anxious to try whether the earth has suddenly, in these twenty years, sent forth a new race of Carthaginians, or whether these are the same who fought at the islands Ægates, and whom you permitted to defeat from Eryx, valued at eighteen denarii a head; and whether this Hannibal be, as he himself gives out, the rival of the expeditions of Hercules, or one left by his father the tributary and taxed subject and slave of the Roman people; who, did not his guilt at Saguntum drive him to frenzy, would certainly reflect, if not upon his conquered country, at least on his family, and his father, and the treaties written by the hand of Hamilcar; who, at the command of our consul, withdrew the garrison from Eryx; who, indignant and grieving, submitted to the harsh conditions imposed on the conquered Carthaginians; who agreed to depart from Sicily, and pay tribute to the Roman people. I would, therefore, have you fight, soldiers, not only with that spirit with which you are wont to encounter other enemies, but with a certain indignation and resentment, as if you saw your slaves suddenly taking up arms against you. We might have killed them when shut up in Eryx by hunger, the most dreadful of human tortures; we might have carried over our victorious fleet to Africa, and in a few days have destroyed Carthage without any opposition. We granted pardon to their prayers; we released them from the blockade; we made peace with them when conquered; and we afterwards considered them under our protection when they were oppressed by the African war. In return for these benefits, they come under the conduct of a furious youth to attack our country. And I wish that the contest on your side was for glory, and not for safety: it is not about the possession of Sicily and Sardinia, concerning which the dispute was formerly, but for Italy, that you must fight: nor is there another army behind, which, if we should not conquer, can resist the enemy; nor are there other Alps, during the passage of which fresh forces may be procured: here, soldiers, we must make our stand, as if we fought before the walls of Rome. Let every one consider that he defends with his arms not only his own person, but his wife and young children: nor let him only entertain domestic cares and anxieties, but at the same time let him revolve in his mind, that the senate and people of Rome now anxiously regard our efforts; and that according as our strength and valour shall be, such henceforward will be the fortune of that city and of the Roman empire."

Thus the consul addressed the Romans. Hannibal, thinking that his soldiers ought to be roused by deeds rather than by words, having drawn his army around for the spectacle, placed in their midst the captive mountaineers in fetters; and after Gallic arms had been thrown at their feet, he ordered the interpreter to ask, "whether any among them, on condition of being released from chains, and receiving, if victorious, armour and a horse, was willing to combat with the sword?" When they all, to a man, demanded the combat and the sword, and lots were cast into the urn for that purpose, each wished himself the person whom fortune might select for the contest. As the lot of each man came out, eager and exulting with joy amidst the congratulations of his comrades, and dancing after the national custom, he hastily snatched up the arms: but when they fought, such was the state of feeling, not only among their companions in the same circumstances, but among the spectators in general, that the fortune of those who conquered was not praised more than that of those who died bravely.

When he had dismissed the soldiers, thus affected after viewing several pairs of combatants, having then summoned an assembly, he is said to have addressed them in these terms: "If, soldiers, you shall by and by, in judging of your own fortune, preserve the same feelings which you experienced a little before in the example of the fate of others, we have already conquered; for neither was that merely a spectacle, but as it were a certain representation of your condition. And I know not whether fortune has not thrown around you still stronger chains and more urgent necessities than around your captives. On the right and left two seas enclose you, without your possessing a single ship even for escape. The river Po around you, the Po larger and more impetuous than the Rhone, the Alps behind, scarcely passed by you when fresh and vigorous, hem you in. Here, soldiers, where you have first met the enemy, you must conquer or die; and the same fortune which has imposed the necessity of fighting, holds out to you, if victorious, rewards, than which men are not wont to desire greater, even from the immortal gods. If we were only about to recover by our valour Sicily and Sardinia, wrested from our fathers, the recompence would be sufficiently ample; but whatever, acquired and amassed by so many triumphs, the Romans possess, all, with its masters themselves, will become yours. To gain this rich reward, hasten, then, and seize your arms with the favour of the gods. Long enough in pursuing cattle among the desert mountains of Lusitania [19] and Celtiberia, you have seen no emolument from so many toils and dangers: it is time to make rich and profitable campaigns, and to gain the great reward of your labours, after having accomplished such a length of journey over so many mountains and rivers, and so many nations in arms. Here fortune has granted you the termination of your labours; here she will bestow a reward worthy of the service you have undergone. Nor, in proportion as the war is great in name, ought you to consider that the victory will be difficult. A despised enemy has often maintained a sanguinary contest, and renowned states and kings been conquered by a very slight effort. For, setting aside only the splendour of the Roman name, what remains in which they can be compared to you? To pass over in silence your service for twenty years, distinguished by such valour and success you have made your way to this place from the pillars of Hercules, [20] from the ocean, and the remotest limits of the world advancing victorious through so many of the fiercest nations of Gaul and Spain: you will fight with a raw army, which this very summer was beaten, conquered, and surrounded by the Gauls, as yet unknown to its general, and ignorant of him. Shall I compare myself, almost born, and certainly bred in the tent of my father, that most illustrious commander, myself the subjugator of Spain and Gaul, the conqueror too not only of the Alpine nations, but what is much more, of the Alps themselves, with this six months' general, the deserter of his army? To whom, if any one, having taken away their standards, should show to-day the Carthaginians and Romans, I am sure that he would not know of which army he was consul. I do not regard it, soldiers, as of small account, that there is not a man among you before whose eyes I have not often achieved some military exploit; and to whom, in like manner, I the spectator and witness of his valour, could not recount his own gallant deeds, particularized by time and place. With soldiers who have a thousand times received my praises and gifts, I, who was the pupil of you all before I became your commander, will march out in battle-array against those who are unknown to and ignorant of each other."

"On whatever side I turn my eyes I see nothing but what is full of courage and energy; a veteran infantry; calvary, both those with and those without the bridle, composed of the most gallant nations, you our most faithful and valiant allies, you Carthaginians, who are about to fight as well for the sake of your country as from the justest resentment. We are the assailants in the war, and descend into Italy with hostile standards, about to engage so much more boldly and bravely than the foe, as the confidence and courage of the assailant are greater than those of him who is defensive. Besides suffering, injury and indignity inflame and excite our minds: they first demanded me your leader for punishment, and then all of you who had laid siege to Saguntum; and had we been given up they would have visited us with the severest tortures. That most cruel and haughty nation considers every thing its own, and at its own disposal; it thinks it right that it should regulate with whom we are to have war, with whom peace: it circumscribes and shuts us up by the boundaries of mountains and rivers, which we must not pass; and then does not adhere to those boundaries which it appointed. Pass not the Iberus; have nothing to do with the Saguntines. Saguntum is on the Iberus; you must not move a step in any direction. Is it a small thing that you take away my most ancient provinces Sicily and Sardinia? will you take Spain also? and should I withdraw thence, you will cross over into Africa—will cross, did I say? they have sent the two consuls of this year one to Africa, the other to Spain: there is nothing left to us in any quarter, except what we can assert to ourselves by arms. Those may be cowards and dastards who have something to look back upon; whom, flying through safe and unmolested roads, their own lands and their own country will receive: there is a necessity for you to be brave; and since all between victory and death is broken off from you by inevitable despair, either to conquer, or, if fortune should waver, to meet death rather in battle than flight. If this be well fixed and determined in the minds of you all, I will repeat, you have already conquered: no stronger incentive to victory has been given to man by the immortal gods."

When the minds of the soldiers on both sides had been animated to the contest by these exhortations, the Romans throw a bridge over the Ticinus, and, for the sake of defending the bridge, erect a fort on it. The Carthaginian, while the Romans were engaged in this work, sends Maharbal with a squadron of five hundred Numidian horse, to lay waste the territories of the allies of the Roman people. He orders that the Gauls should be spared as much as possible, and the minds of their chiefs be instigated to a revolt. When the bridge was finished, the Roman army being led across into the territory of the Insubrians, took up its station five miles from Victumviæ. At this place Hannibal lay encamped; and having quickly recalled Maharbal and the cavalry, when he perceived that a battle was approaching, thinking that in exhorting the soldiers enough could never be spoken or addressed by way of admonition, he announces to them, when summoned to an assembly, stated rewards, in expectation of which they might fight. He promised, "that he would give them land in Italy, Africa, Spain, where each man might choose, exempt from all burdens to the person who received it, and to his children: if any one preferred money to land, he would satisfy him in silver; if any of the allies wished to become citizens of Carthage, he would grant them permission; if others chose rather to return home, he would lend his endeavours that they should not wish the situation of any one of their countrymen exchanged for their own." To the slaves also who followed their masters he promised freedom, and that he would give two slaves in place of each of them to their masters. And that they might know that these promises were certain, holding in his left hand a lamb, and in his right a flint, having prayed to Jupiter and the other gods, that, if he was false to his word, they would thus slay him as he slew the lamb; after the prayer he broke the skull of the sheep with the stone. Then in truth all, receiving as it were the gods as sureties, each for the fulfilment of his own hopes, and thinking that the only delay in obtaining the object of their wishes arose from their not yet being engaged, with one mind and one voice demanded the battle.

By no means so great an alacrity prevailed among the Romans, who, in addition to other causes, were also alarmed by recent prodigies; for both a wolf had entered the camp, and having torn those who met him, had escaped unhurt; and a swarm of bees had settled on a tree overhanging the general's tent. After these prodigies were expiated, Scipio having set out with his cavalry and light-armed spearmen towards the camp of the enemy, to observe from a near point their forces, how numerous, and of what description they were, falls in with Hannibal, who had himself also advanced with his cavalry to explore the circumjacent country: neither at first perceived the other, but the dust arising from the trampling of so many men and horses soon gave the signal of approaching enemies. Both armies halted, and were preparing themselves for battle. Scipio places his spearmen and Gallic cavalry in front; the Romans and what force of allies he had with him, in reserve. Hannibal receives the horsemen who rode with the rein in the centre, and strengthens his wings with Numidians. When the shout was scarcely raised, the spearmen fled among the reserve to the second line: there was then a contest of the cavalry, for some time doubtful; but afterwards, on account of the foot soldiers, who were intermingled, causing confusion among the horses, many of the riders falling off from their horses, or leaping down where they saw their friends surrounded and hard pressed, the battle for the most part came to be fought on foot; until the Numidians, who were in the wings, having made a small circuit, showed themselves on the rear. That alarm dismayed the Romans, and the wound of the consul, and the danger to his life, warded off by the interposition of his son, then just arriving at the age of puberty, augmented their fears. This youth will be found to be the same to whom the glory of finishing this war belongs, and to whom the name of Africanus was given, on account of his splendid victory over Hannibal and the Carthaginians. The flight, however, of the spearmen, whom the Numidians attacked first, was the most disorderly. The rest of the cavalry, in a close body, protecting, not only with their arms, but also with their bodies, the consul, whom they had received into the midst of them, brought him back to the camp without any where giving way in disorder or precipitation. Cœlius attributes the honour of saving the consul to a slave, by nation a Ligurian. I indeed should rather wish that the account about the son was true, which also most authors have transmitted, and the report of which has generally obtained credit.

This was the first battle with Hannibal; from which it clearly appeared that the Carthaginian was superior in cavalry; and on that account, that open plains, such as lie between the Po and the Alps, were not suited to the Romans for carrying on the war. On the following night, therefore, the soldiers being ordered to prepare their baggage in silence, the camp broke up from the Ticinus, and they hastened to the Po, in order that the rafts by which the consul had formed a bridge over the river, being not yet loosened, he might lead his forces across without disturbance or pursuit of the enemy. They arrived at Placentia before Hannibal had ascertained that they had set out from the Ticinus. He took, however, six hundred of those who loitered on the farther bank, who were slowly unfastening the raft; but he was not able to pass the bridge, as the whole raft floated down the stream as soon as the ends were unfastened. Cœlius relates that Mago, with the cavalry and Spanish infantry, immediately swam the river; and that Hannibal himself led the army across by fords higher up the Po, the elephants being opposed to the stream in a line to break the force of the current. These accounts can scarcely gain credit with those who are acquainted with that river; for it is neither probable that the cavalry could bear up against the great violence of the stream, without losing their arms or horses, even supposing that inflated bags of leather had transported all the Spaniards; and the fords of the Po, by which an army encumbered with baggage could pass, must have been sought by a circuit of many days' march. Those authors are more credited by me, who relate that in the course of two days a place was with difficulty found fit for forming a bridge of rafts across the river, and that by this way the light-armed Spanish cavalry was sent forward with Mago. Whilst Hannibal, delaying beside the river to give audience to the embassies of the Gauls, conveys over the heavy-armed forces of infantry, in the mean time Mago and the cavalry proceed towards the enemy at Placentia one day's journey after crossing the river. Hannibal, a few days after, fortified his camp six miles from Placentia, and on the following day, having drawn up his line of battle in sight of the enemy, gave them an opportunity of fighting.

On the following night a slaughter was made in the Roman camp by the auxiliary Gauls, which appeared greater from the tumult than it proved in reality. Two thousand infantry and two hundred horse, having killed the guards at the gates, desert to Hannibal;

whom the Carthaginians having addressed kindly, and excited by the hope of great rewards, sent each to several states to gain over the minds of their countrymen. Scipio, thinking that that slaughter was a signal for the revolt of all the Gauls, and that, contaminated with the guilt of that affair, they would rush to arms as if a frenzy had been sent among them, though he was still suffering severely from his wound, yet setting out for the river Trebia at the fourth watch of the following night with his army in silence, he removes his camp to higher ground and hills more embarrassing to the cavalry. He escaped observation less than at the Ticinus: and Hannibal, having despatched first the Numidians and then all the cavalry, would have thrown the rear at least into great confusion, had not the Numidians, through anxiety for booty, turned aside into the deserted Roman camp. There whilst, closely examining every part of the camp, they waste time, with no sufficient reward for the delay, the enemy escaped out of their hands; and when they saw the Romans already across the Trebia, and measuring out their camp, they kill a few of the loiterers intercepted on that side of the river. Scipio being unable to endure any longer the irritation of his wound, caused by the roughness of the road, and thinking that he ought to wait for his colleague, (for he had now heard that he was recalled from Sicily,) fortified a space of chosen ground, which, adjoining the river, seemed safest for a stationary camp. When Hannibal had encamped not far from thence, being as much elated with the victory of his cavalry, as anxious on account of the scarcity which every day assailed him more severely, marching as he did through the territory of the enemy, and supplies being no where provided, he sends to the village of Clastidium, where the Romans had collected a great stock of corn. There, whilst they were preparing for an assault, a hope of the town being betrayed to them was held out: Dasius, a Brundusian, the governor of the garrison, having been corrupted for four hundred pieces of gold, (no great bribe truly,) Clastidium is surrendered to Hannibal. It served as a granary for the Carthaginians while they lay at the Trebia. No cruelty was used towards the prisoners of the surrendered garrison, in order that a character for clemency might be acquired at the commencement of his proceedings.

While the war by land was at a stand beside the Trebia, in the mean time operations went on by land and sea around Sicily and the islands adjacent to Italy, both under Sempronius the consul, and before his arrival. Twenty quinqueremes, with a thousand armed men, having been sent by the Carthaginians to lay waste the coast of Italy, nine reached the Liparæ, eight the island of Vulcan, and three the tide drove into the strait. On these being seen from Messana, twelve ships sent out by Hiero king of Syracuse, who then happened to be at Messana, waiting for the Roman consul, brought back into the port of Messana the ships taken without any resistance. It was discovered from the prisoners that, besides the twenty ships, to which fleet they belonged, and which had been despatched against Italy, thirty-five other quinqueremes were directing their course to Sicily, in order to gain over their ancient allies: that their main object was to gain possession of Lilybæum, and they believed that that fleet had been driven to the islands Ægates by the same storm by which they themselves had been dispersed. The king writes these tidings, according as they had been received, to Marcus Æmilius the prætor, whose province Sicily was, and advises him to occupy Lilybæum with a strong garrison. Immediately the lieutenants, generals, and tribunes, with the prætor, were despatched to the different states, in order that they might keep their men on vigilant guard; above all things it was commanded, that Lilybæum should be secured: an edict having been put forth that, in addition to such warlike preparations, the crews should carry down to their ships dressed provisions for ten days, so that no one when the signal was given might delay in embarking; and that those who were stationed along the whole coast should look out from their watch-towers for the approaching fleet of the enemy. The Carthaginians, therefore, though they had purposely slackened the course of their ships, so that they might reach Lilybæum just before daybreak, were descried before their arrival, because both the moon shone all night, and they came with their sails set up. Immediately the signal was given from the watch-towers, and the summons to arms was shouted through the town, and they embarked in the ships: part of the soldiers were left on the walls and at the stations of the gates, and part went on board the fleet. The Carthaginians, because they perceived that they would not have to do with an unprepared enemy, kept back from the harbour till daylight, that interval being spent in taking down their rigging and getting ready the fleet for action. When the light appeared, they withdrew their fleet into the open sea, that there might be room for the battle, and that the ships of the enemy might have a free egress from the harbour. Nor did the Romans decline the conflict, being emboldened both by the recollection of the exploits they had performed near that very spot, and by the numbers and valour of their soldiers.

When they had advanced into the open sea, the Romans wished to come to close fight, and to make a trial of strength hand to hand. The Carthaginians, on the contrary, eluded them, and sought to maintain the fight by art, not by force, and to make it a battle of ships rather than of men and arms: for though they had their fleet abundantly supplied with mariners, yet it was deficient in soldiers; and when a ship was grappled, a very unequal number of armed men fought on board of it. When this was observed, their numbers increased the courage of the Romans, and their inferiority of force diminished that of the others. Seven Carthaginian ships were immediately surrounded; the rest took to flight: one thousand seven hundred soldiers and mariners were captured in the ships, and among them were three noble Carthaginians. The Roman fleet returned without loss to the harbour, only one ship being pierced, and even that also brought back into port. After this engagement, before those at Messana were aware of its occurrence, Titus Sempronius the consul arrived at Messana. As he entered the strait, king Hiero led out a fleet fully equipped to meet him; and having passed from the royal ship into that of the general, he congratulated him on having arrived safe with his army and fleet, and prayed that his expedition to Sicily might be prosperous and successful. He then laid before him the state of the island and the designs of the Carthaginians, and promised that with the same spirit with which he had in his youth assisted the Romans during the former war, he would now assist them in his old age; that he would gratuitously furnish supplies of corn and clothing to the legions and naval crews of the consul; adding, that great danger threatened Lilybæum and the maritime states, and that a change of affairs would be acceptable to some of them. For these reasons it appeared to the consul that he ought to make no delay, but to repair to Lilybæum with his fleet. The king and the royal squadron set out along with him, and on their passage they heard that a battle had been fought at Lilybæum, and that the enemy's ships had been scattered and taken.

The consul having dismissed Hiero with the royal fleet, and left the prætor to defend the coast of Sicily, passed over himself from Lilybæum to the island Melita, which was held in possession by the Carthaginians. On his arrival, Hamilcar, the son of Gisgo, the commander of the garrison, with little less than two thousand soldiers, together with the town and the island, are delivered up to him: thence, after a few days, he returned to Lilybæum, and the prisoners taken, both by the consul and the prætor, excepting those illustrious for their rank, were publicly sold. When the consul considered that Sicily was sufficiently safe on that side, he crossed over to the islands of Vulcan, because there was a report that the Carthaginian fleet was stationed there: but not one of the enemy was discovered about those islands. They had already, as it happened, passed over to ravage the coast of Italy, and having laid waste the territory of Vibo, were also threatening the city. The descent made by the enemy on the Vibonensian territory is announced to the consul as he was returning to Sicily: and letters were delivered to him which had been sent by the senate, about the passage of Hannibal into Italy, commanding him as soon as possible to bring assistance to his colleague. Perplexed with having so many anxieties at once, he immediately sent his army, embarked in the fleet, by the upper sea to Ariminum; he assigned the defence of the territory of Vibo, and the sea-coast of Italy, to Sextus Pomponius, his lieutenant-general, with twenty-five ships of war: he made up a fleet of fifty ships for Marcus Æmilius the prætor; and he himself, after the affairs of Sicily were settled, sailing close along the coast of Italy with ten ships, arrived at Ariminum, whence, setting out with his army for the river Trebia, he joined his colleague.

Both the consuls and all the strength of Rome being now opposed to Hannibal, made it sufficiently obvious that the Roman empire could either be defended by those forces, or that there was no other hope left. Yet the one consul being dispirited by the battle of the cavalry and his own wound, wished operations to be deferred: the other having his spirits unsubdued, and being therefore the more impetuous, admitted no delay. The tract of country between the Trebia and the Po was then inhabited by the Gauls, who, in this contest of two very powerful states, by a doubtful neutrality, were evidently looking forward to the favour of the conqueror. The Romans submitted to this conduct of the Gauls with tolerable satisfaction, provided they did not take any active part at all; but the Carthaginian bore it with great discontent, giving out that he had come invited by the Gauls to set them at liberty. On account of that resentment, and in order that he might at the same time maintain his troops from the plunder, he ordered two thousand foot and a thousand horse, chiefly Numidians, with some Gauls intermixed, to lay waste all the country straightforward as far as the banks of the Po. The Gauls, being in want of assistance, though they had up to this time kept their inclinations doubtful, are forced by the authors of the injury to turn to some who would be their supporters; and having sent ambassadors to the consul, they implore the aid of the Romans in behalf of a country which was suffering for the too great fidelity of its inhabitants to the Romans. Neither the cause nor the time of pleading it was satisfactory to Cornelius; and the nation was suspected by him, both on account of many treacherous actions, and though others might have been forgotten through length of time, on account of the recent perfidy of the Boii. Sempronius, on the contrary, thought that it would be the strongest tie upon the fidelity of the allies, if those were defended who first required support. Then, while his colleague hesitated, he sends his own cavalry, with about a thousand spearmen on foot in their company, to protect the Gallic territory beyond the Trebia. These, when they had unexpectedly attacked the enemy while scattered and disordered, and for the most part encumbered with booty, caused great terror, slaughter, and flight, even as far as the camp and outposts of the enemy; whence being repulsed by the numbers that poured out, they again renewed the fight with the assistance of their own party. Then pursuing and retreating in doubtful battle, though they left it at last equal, yet the fame of the victory was more with the Romans than the enemy.

But to no one did it appear more important and just than to the consul himself. He was transported with joy "that he had conquered with that part of the forces with which the other consul had been defeated; that the spirits of the soldiers were restored and revived; that there was no one, except his colleague, who would wish an engagement delayed; and that he, suffering more from disease of mind than body, shuddered, through recollection of his wound, at arms and battle. But others ought not to sink into decrepitude together with a sick man. For why should there be any longer protraction or waste of time? What third consul, what other army did they wait for? The camp of the Carthaginians was in Italy, and almost in sight of the city. It was not Sicily and Sardinia, which had been taken from them when vanquished, nor Spain on this side of the Iberus, that was their object, but that the Romans should be driven from the land of their fathers, and the soil in which they were born. How deeply," he continued, "would our fathers groan, who were wont to wage war around the walls of Carthage, if they should see us their offspring, two consuls and two consular armies, trembling within our camps in the heart of Italy, while a Carthaginian had made himself master of all the country between the Alps and the Apennine!" Such discourses did he hold while sitting beside his sick colleague, and also at the head-quarters, almost in the manner of an harangue. The approaching period of the elections also stimulated him, lest the war should be protracted till the new consuls were chosen, and the opportunity of turning all the glory to himself, while his colleague lay sick. He orders the soldiers, therefore, Cornelius in vain attempting to dissuade him, to get ready for an immediate engagement. Hannibal, as he saw what conduct would be best for the enemy, had scarce at first any hope that the consuls would do any thing rashly or imprudently, but when he discovered that the disposition of the one, first known from report, and afterwards from experience, was ardent and impetuous, and believed that it had been rendered still more impetuous by the successful engagement with his predatory troops, he did not doubt that an opportunity of action was near at hand. He was anxious and watchful not to omit this opportunity, while the troops of the enemy were raw, while his wound rendered the better of the two commanders useless, and while the spirits of the Gauls were fresh; of whom he knew that a great number would follow him with the greater reluctance the farther they were drawn away from home. When, for these and similar reasons, he hoped that an engagement was near and desired to make the attack himself, if there should be any delay; and when the Gauls, who were the safer spies to ascertain what he wished, as they served in both camps, had brought intelligence that the Romans were prepared for battle, the Carthaginian began to look about for a place for an ambuscade.

Between the armies was a rivulet, bordered on each side with very high banks, and covered around with marshy plants, and with the brushwood and brambles with which uncultivated places are generally overspread; and when, riding around it, he had, with his own eyes, thoroughly reconnoitred a place which was sufficient to afford a covert even for cavalry, he said to Mago his brother: "This will be the place which you must occupy. Choose out of all the infantry and cavalry a hundred men of each, with whom come to me at the first watch. Now is the time to refresh their bodies." The council was thus dismissed, and in a little time Mago came forward with his chosen men. "I see," said Hannibal, "the strength of the men; but that you may be strong not only in resolution, but also in number, pick out each from the troops and companies nine men like yourselves: Mago will show you the place where you are to lie in ambush. You will have an enemy who is blind to these arts of war." A thousand horse and a thousand foot, under the command of Mago, having been thus sent off, Hannibal orders the Numidian cavalry to ride up, after crossing the river Trebia by break of day, to the gates of the enemy, and to draw them out to a battle by discharging their javelins at the guards; and then, when the fight was commenced, by retiring slowly to decoy them across the river. These instructions were given to the Numidians: to the other leaders of the infantry and cavalry it was commanded that they should order all their men to dine; and then, under arms and with their horses equipped, to await the signal. Sempronius, eager for the contest, led out, on the first tumult raised by the Numidians, all the cavalry, being full of confidence in that part of the forces; then six thousand infantry, and lastly all his army, to the place already determined in his plan. It happened to be the winter season and a snowy day, in the region which lies between the Alps and the Apennine, and excessively cold by the proximity of rivers and marshes: besides, there was no heat in the bodies of the men and horses thus hastily led out without having first taken food, or employed any means to keep off the cold; and the nearer they approached to the blasts from the river, a keener degree of cold blew upon them. But when, in pursuit of the flying Numidians, they entered the water, (and it was swollen by rain in the night as high as their breasts,) then in truth the bodies of all, on landing, were so benumbed, that they were scarcely able to hold their arms; and as the day advanced they began to grow faint, both from fatigue and hunger.

In the mean time the soldiers of Hannibal, fires having been kindled before the tents, and oil sent through the companies to soften their limbs, and their food having been taken at leisure, as soon as it was announced that the enemy had passed the river, seized their arms with vigour of mind and body, and advanced to the battle. Hannibal placed before the standards the Baliares and the light-armed troops, to the amount of nearly eight thousand men; then the heavier-armed infantry, the chief of his power and strength: on the wings he posted ten thousand horse, and on their extremities stationed the elephants divided into two parts. The consul placed on the flanks of his infantry the cavalry, recalled by the signal for retreat, as in their irregular pursuit of the enemy they were checked, while unprepared, by the Numidians suddenly turning upon them. There were of infantry eighteen thousand Romans, twenty thousand allies of the Latin name, besides the auxiliary forces of the Cenomani, the only Gallic nation that had remained faithful: with these forces they engaged the enemy. The battle was commenced by the Baliares; whom when the legions resisted with superior force, the light-armed troops were hastily drawn off to the wings; which movement caused the Roman cavalry to be immediately overpowered: for when their four thousand already with difficulty withstood by themselves ten thousand of the enemy, the wearied, against men for the most part fresh, they were overwhelmed in addition by a cloud as it were of javelins, discharged by the Baliares; and the elephants besides, which held a prominent position at the extremities of the wings, (the horses being greatly terrified not only at their appearance, but their unusual smell,) occasioned flight to a wide extent. The battle between the infantry was equal rather in courage than strength; for the Carthaginian brought the latter entire to the action, having a little before refreshed themselves, while, on the contrary, the bodies of the Romans, suffering from fasting and fatigue, and stiff with cold, were quite benumbed. They would have made a stand, however, by dint of courage, if they had only had to fight with the infantry. But both the Baliares, having beaten off the cavalry, poured darts on their flanks, and the elephants had already penetrated to the centre of the line of the infantry; while Mago and the Numidians, as soon as the army had passed their place of ambush without observing them, starting up on their rear, occasioned great disorder and alarm. Nevertheless, amid so many surrounding dangers, the line for some time remained unbroken, and, most contrary to the expectation of all, against the elephants. These the light infantry, posted for the purpose, turned back by throwing their spears; and following them up when turned, pierced them under the tail, where they received the wounds in the softest skin.

Hannibal ordered the elephants, thus thrown into disorder, and almost driven by their terror against their own party, to be led away from the centre of the line to its extremity against the auxiliary Gauls on the left wing. In an instant they occasioned unequivocal flight; and a new alarm was added to the Romans when they saw their auxiliaries routed. About ten thousand men, therefore, as they now were fighting in a circle, the others being unable to escape, broke through the middle of the line of the Africans, which was supported by the Gallic auxiliaries, with immense slaughter of the enemy: and since they neither could return to the camp, being shut out by the river, nor, on account of the heavy rain, satisfactorily determine in what part they should assist their friends, they proceeded by the direct road to Placentia. After this several irruptions were made in all directions; and those who sought the river were either swallowed up in its eddies, or whilst they hesitated to enter it were cut off by the enemy. Some, who had been scattered abroad through the country in their flight, by following the traces of the retreating army, arrived at Placentia; others, the fear of the enemy inspired with boldness to enter the river, having crossed it, reached the camp. The rain mixed with snow, and the intolerable severity of the cold, destroyed many men and beasts of burden, and almost all the elephants. The river Trebia was the termination of the Carthaginians' pursuit of the enemy; and they returned to the camp so benumbed with cold, that they could scarcely feel joy for the victory. On the following night, therefore, though the guard of the camp and the principal part of the soldiers that remained passed the Trebia on rafts, they either did not perceive it, on account of the beating of the rain, or being unable to bestir themselves, through their fatigue and wounds, pretended that they did not perceive it; and the Carthaginians remaining quiet, the army was silently led by the consul Scipio to Placentia, thence transported across the Po to Cremona, lest one colony should be too much burdened by the winter quarters of two armies.

Such terror on account of this disaster was carried to Rome, that they believed that the enemy was already approaching the city with hostile standards, and that they had neither hope nor aid by which they might repel his attack from the gates and walls. One consul having been defeated at the Ticinus, the other having been recalled from Sicily, and now both consuls and their two consular armies having been vanquished, what other commanders, what other legions were there to be sent for? The consul Sempronius came to them whilst thus dismayed, having passed at great risk through the cavalry of the enemy, scattered in every direction in search of plunder, with courage, rather than with any plan or hope of escaping, or of making resistance if he should not escape it. Having held the assembly for the election of the consuls, the only thing which was particularly wanting at present, he returned to the winter quarters. Cneius Servilius and Caius Flaminius were elected consuls. But not even the winter quarters of the Romans were undisturbed, the Numidian horse ranging at large, and where the ground was impracticable for these, the Celtiberians and Lusitanians. All supplies, therefore, from every quarter, were cut off, except such as the ships conveyed by the Po. There was a magazine near Placentia, both fortified with great care and secured by a strong garrison. In the hope of taking this fort, Hannibal having set out with the cavalry and the light-armed horse, and having attacked it by night, as he rested his main hope of effecting his enterprise on keeping it concealed, did not escape the notice of the guards. Such a clamour was immediately raised, that it was heard even at Placentia. The consul; therefore, came up with the cavalry about daybreak, having commanded the legions to follow in a square band. In the mean time an engagement of cavalry commenced, in which the enemy being dismayed because Hannibal retired wounded from the fight, the fortress was admirably defended. After this, having taken rest for a few days, and before his wound was hardly as yet sufficiently healed, he sets out to lay siege to Victumviæ. This magazine had been fortified by the Romans in the Gallic war; afterwards a mixture of inhabitants from the neighbouring states around had made the place populous; and at this time the terror created by the devastation of the enemy had driven together to it numbers from the country. A multitude of this description, excited by the report of the brave defence of the fortress near Placentia, having snatched up their arms, went out to meet Hannibal. They engaged on the road rather like armies in order of march than in line of battle; and since on the one side there was nothing but a disorderly crowd, and on the other a general confident in his soldiers, and soldiers in their general, as many as thirty-five thousand men were routed by a few. On the following day, a surrender having been made, they received a garrison within their walls; and being ordered to deliver up their arms, as soon as they had obeyed the command, a signal is suddenly given to the victors to pillage the city, as if it had been taken by storm; nor was any outrage, which in such cases is wont to appear to writers worthy of relation, left unperpetrated; such a specimen of every kind of lust, barbarity, and inhuman insolence was exhibited towards that unhappy people. Such were the expeditions of Hannibal during the winter.

For a short time after, while the cold continued intolerable, rest was given to the soldiers; and having set out from his winter quarters on the first and uncertain indications of spring, he leads them into Etruria, intending to gain that nation to his side, like the Gauls and Ligurians, either by force or favour. As he was crossing the Apennines, so furious a storm attacked him, that it almost surpassed the horrors of the Alps. When the rain and wind together were driven directly against their faces, they at first halted, because their arms must either be cast away, or striving to advance against the storm they were whirled round by the hurricane, and dashed to the ground: afterwards, when it now stopped their breath, nor suffered them to respire, they sat down for a little, with their backs to the wind. Then indeed the sky resounded with loud thunder, and the lightnings flashed between its terrific peals; all, bereft of sight and hearing, stood torpid with fear. At length, when the rain had spent itself, and the fury of the wind was on that account the more increased, it seemed necessary to pitch the camp in that very place where they had been overtaken by the storm. But this was the beginning of their labours, as it were, afresh; for neither could they spread out nor fix any tent, nor did that which perchance had been put up remain, the wind tearing through and sweeping every thing away: and soon after, when the water raised aloft by the wind had been frozen above the cold summits of the mountains, it poured down such a torrent of snowy hail, that the men, casting away every thing, fell down upon their faces, rather buried under than sheltered by their coverings; and so extreme an intensity of cold succeeded, that when each wished to raise and lift himself from that wretched heap of men and beasts of burden, he was for a long time unable, because their sinews being stiffened by the cold, they had great difficulty in bending their joints. Afterwards, when, by continually moving themselves to and fro, they succeeded in recovering the power of motion, and regained their spirits, and fires began to be kindled in a few places, every helpless man had recourse to the aid of others. They remained as if blockaded for two days in that place. Many men and beasts of burden, and also seven elephants, of those which had remained from the battle fought at the Trebia, were destroyed.

Having descended from the Apennines, he moved his camp back towards Placentia, and having proceeded as far as ten miles, took up his station. On the following day he leads out twelve thousand infantry and five thousand cavalry against the enemy. Nor did

Sempronius the consul (for he had now returned from Rome) decline the engagement; and during that day three miles intervened between the two camps. On the following day they fought with amazing courage and various success. At the first onset the Roman power was so superior, that they not only conquered the enemy in the regular battle, but pursued them when driven back quite into their camp, and soon after also assaulted it. Hannibal, having stationed a few to defend the rampart and the gates, and having admitted the rest in close array into the middle of the camp orders them to watch attentively the signal for sallying out. It was now about the ninth hour of the day when the Roman, having fatigued his soldiers to no purpose, after there was no hope of gaining possession of the camp, gave the signal for retreat; which when Hannibal heard, and saw that the attack was slackened, and that they were retreating from the camp, instantly having sent out the cavalry on the right and left against the enemy, he himself in the middle with the main force of the infantry rushed out from the camp. Seldom has there been a combat more furious, and few would have been more remarkable for the loss on both sides, if the day had suffered it to continue for a longer time. Night broke off the battle when raging most from the determined spirit of the combatants. The conflict therefore was more severe than the slaughter: and as it was pretty much a drawn battle, they separated with equal loss. On neither side fell more than six hundred infantry, and half that number of cavalry. But the loss of the Romans was more severe than proportionate to the number that fell, because several of equestrian rank, and five tribunes of the soldiers, and three prefects of the allies were slain. After this battle Hannibal retired to the territory of the Ligurians, and Sempronius to Luca. Two Roman quæstors, Caius Fulvius and Lucius Lucretius, who had been treacherously intercepted, with two military tribunes and five of the equestrian order, mostly sons of senators, are delivered up to Hannibal when coming among the Ligurians, in order that he might feel more convinced that the peace and alliance with them would be binding.

While these things are transacting in Italy, Cneius Cornelius Scipio having been sent into Spain with a fleet and army, when, setting out from the mouth of the Rhone, and sailing past the Pyrenæan mountains, he had moored his fleet at Emporiæ, having there landed his army, and beginning with the Lacetani, he brought the whole coast, as far as the river Iberus, under the Roman dominion, partly by renewing the old, and partly by forming new alliances. The reputation for clemency, acquired by these means, had influence not only with the maritime states, but now also with the more savage tribes in the inland and mountainous districts; nor was peace only effected with them, but also an alliance of arms, and several fine cohorts of auxiliaries were levied from their numbers. The country on this side of the Iberus was the province of Hanno, whom Hannibal had left to defend that region. He, therefore, judging that he ought to make opposition, before every thing was alienated from him, having pitched his camp in sight of the enemy, led out his forces in battle-array; nor did it appear to the Roman, that the engagement ought to be deferred, as he knew that he must fight with Hanno and Hasdrubal, and wished rather to contend against each of them separately, than against both together. The conflict did not prove one of great difficulty; six thousand of the enemy were slain, and two thousand made prisoners, together with the guard of the camp; for both the camp was stormed, and the general himself, with several of the chief officers, taken; and Scissis, a town near the camp, was also carried by assault. But the spoil of this town consisted of things of small value, such as the household furniture used by barbarians and slaves that were worth little. The camp enriched the soldiers; almost all the valuable effects, not only of that army which was conquered, but of that which was serving with Hannibal in Italy, having been left on this side the Pyrenees, that the baggage might not be cumbrous to those who conveyed it.

Before any certain news of this disaster arrived, Hasdrubal, having passed the Iberus with eight thousand foot and a thousand horse, intending to meet the Romans on their first approach, after he heard of the ruin of their affairs at Scissis, and the loss of the camp, turned his route towards the sea. Not far from Tarraco, having despatched his cavalry in various directions, he drove to their ships, with great slaughter, and greater route, the soldiers belonging to the fleet and the mariners, while scattered and wandering through the fields (for it is usually the case that success produces negligence), but not daring to remain longer in that quarter, lest he should be surprised by Scipio, he withdrew to the other side of the Iberus. And Scipio, having quickly brought up his army on the report of fresh enemies, after punishing a few captains of ships and leaving a moderate garrison at Tarraco, returned with his fleet to Emporiæ. He had scarcely departed, when Hasdrubal came up, and having instigated to a revolt the state of the Ilergetes, which had given hostages to Scipio, he lays waste, with the youth of that very people, the lands of the faithful allies of the Romans. Scipio being thereupon roused from his winter quarters, Hasdrubal again retires from in all the country on this side the Iberus. Scipio, when with a hostile army he had invaded the state of the Ilergetes, forsaken by the author of their revolt, and having driven them all into Athanagia, which was the capital of that nation laid siege to the city; and within a few days, having imposed the delivery of more hostages than before, and also fined the Ilergetes in a sum of money, he received them back into his authority and dominion. He then proceeded against the Ausetani near the Iberus, who were also the allies of the Carthaginians; and having laid siege to their city, he cut off by an ambuscade the Lacetani, while bringing assistance by night to their neighbours, having attacked them at a small distance from the city, as they were designing to enter it. As many as twelve thousand were slain; the rest, nearly all without their arms, escaped home, by dispersing through the country in every direction. Nor did any thing else but the winter, which was unfavourable to the besiegers, secure the besieged. The blockade continued for thirty days, during which the snow scarce ever lay less deep than four feet; and it had covered to such a degree the sheds and mantelets of the Romans, that it alone served as a defence when fire was frequently thrown on them by the enemy. At last, when Amusitus, their leader, had fled to Hasdrubal, they are surrendered, on condition of paying twenty talents of silver. They then returned into winter quarters at Tarraco.

At Rome during this winter many prodigies either occurred about the city, or, as usually happens when the minds of men are once inclined to superstition, many were reported and readily believed; among which it was said that an infant of good family, only six months old, had called out "Io triumphe" in the herb market: that in the cattle market an ox had of his own accord ascended to the third story, and that thence, being frightened by the noise of the inhabitants, had flung himself down; that the appearance of ships had been brightly visible in the sky, and that the temple of Hope in the herb market had been struck by lightning; that the spear at Lanuvium had shaken itself; that a crow had flown down into the temple of Juno and alighted on the very couch; that in the territory of Amiternum figures resembling men dressed in white raiment had been seen in several places at a distance, but had not come close to any one; that in Picenum it had rained stones; that at Cære the tablets for divination had been lessened in size; and that in Gaul a wolf had snatched out the sword from the scabbard of a soldier on guard, and carried it off. On account of the other prodigies the decemvirs were ordered to consult the books; but on account of its having rained stones in Picenum the festival of nine days was proclaimed, and almost all the state was occupied in expiating the rest, from time to time. First of all the city was purified, and victims of the greater kind were sacrificed to those gods to whom they were directed to be offered; and a gift of forty pounds' weight of gold was carried to the temple of Juno at Lanuvium; and the matrons dedicated a brazen statue to Juno on the Aventine; and a lectisternium was ordered at Cære, where the tablets for divination had diminished; and a supplication to Fortune at Algidum; at Rome also a lectisternium was ordered to Youth, and a supplication at the temple of Hercules, first by individuals named and afterwards by the whole people at all the shrines; five greater victims were offered to Genius; and Caius Atilius Serranus the prætor was ordered to make certain vows if the republic should remain in the same state for ten years. These things, thus expiated and vowed according to the Sibylline books, relieved, in a great degree, the public mind from superstitious fears.

Flaminius, one of the consuls elect, to whom the legions which were wintering at Placentia had fallen by lot, sent an edict and letter to the consul, desiring that those forces should be ready in camp at Ariminum on the ides of March. He had a design to enter on the consulship in his province, recollecting his old contests with the fathers, which he had waged with them when tribune of the people, and afterwards when consul, first about his election to the office, which was annulled, and then about a triumph. He was also odious to the fathers on account of a new law which Quintus Claudius, tribune of the people, had carried against the senate, Caius Flaminius alone of that body assisting him, that no senator, or he who had been father of a senator, should possess a ship fit for sea service, containing more than three hundred amphorae. This size was considered sufficient for conveying the produce of their lands: all traffic appeared unbecoming a senator. This contest, maintained with the warmest opposition, procured the hatred of the nobility to Flaminius, the advocate of the law; but the favour of the people, and afterwards a second consulship. For these reasons, thinking that they would detain him in the city by falsifying the auspices, by the delay of the Latin festival, and other hinderances to which a consul was liable, he pretended a journey, and, while yet in a private capacity, departed secretly to his province. This proceeding, when it was made public, excited new and additional anger in the senators, who were before irritated against him. They said, "That Caius Flaminius waged war not only with the senate, but now with the immortal gods; that having been formerly made consul without the proper auspices, he had disobeyed both gods and men recalling him from the very field of battle; and now, through consciousness of their having been dishonoured, had shunned the Capitol and the customary offering of vows, that he might not on the day of entering his office approach the temple of Jupiter, the best and greatest of gods; he might not see and consult the senate, himself hated by it, as it was hateful to him alone; that he might not proclaim the Latin festival, or perform on the Alban mount the customary rights to Jupiter Latiaris; that he might not, under the direction of the auspices, go up to the Capitol to recite his vows, and thence, attended by the lictors, proceed to his province in the garb of a general; but that he had set off, like some camp boy, without his insignia, without the lictors, in secrecy and stealth, just as if he had been quitting his country to go into banishment; as if forsooth he would enter his office more consistently with the dignity of the consul at Ariminum than Rome, and assume the robe of office in a public inn better than before his own household gods."—it was unanimously resolved that he, should be recalled and brought back, and be constrained to perform in person every duty to gods and men before he went to the army and the province. Quintus Terentius and Marcus Antistius having set out on this embassy, (for it was decreed that ambassadors should be sent,) prevailed with him in no degree more than the letter sent by the senate in his former consulship. A few days after he entered on his office, and as he was sacrificing a calf, after being struck, having broken away from the hands of the ministers, sprinkled several of the bystanders with its blood. Flight and disorder ensued, to a still greater degree at a distance among those who were ignorant what was the cause of the alarm. This circumstance was regarded by most persons as an omen of great terror. Having then received two legions from Sempronius, the consul of the former year, and two from Caius Atilius, the prætor, the army began to be led into Etruria, through the passes of the Apennines.

BOOK XXII.

Hannibal, after an uninterrupted march of four days and three nights, arrives in Etruria, through the marshes, in which he lost an eye. Caius Flaminius, the consul, an inconsiderate man, having gone forth in opposition to the omens, dug up the standards which could not otherwise be raised, and been thrown from his horse immediately after he had mounted, is insnared by Hannibal, and cut off by his army near the Thrasimene lake. Three thousand who had escaped are placed in chains by Hannibal, in violation of pledges given. Distress occasioned in Rome by the intelligence. The Sibylline books consulted, and a sacred spring decreed. Fabius Maximus sent as dictator against Hannibal, whom he frustrates by caution and delay. Marcus Minucius, the master of the horse, a rash and impetuous man, inveighs against the caution of Fabius, and obtains an equality of command with him. The army is divided between them, and Minucius engaging Hannibal in an unfavourable position, is reduced to the extremity of danger, and is rescued by the dictator, and places himself under his authority. Hannibal, after ravaging Campania, is shut up by Fabius in a valley near the town of Casilinum, but escapes by night, putting to flight the Romans on guard by oxen with lighted faggots attached to their horns. Hannibal attempts to excite a suspicion of the fidelity of Fabius by sparing his farm while ravaging with fire the whole country around it. Æmilius Paulus and Terentius Varro are routed at Cannæ, and forty thousand men slain, among whom were Paulus the consul, eighty senators, and thirty who had served the office of consul, prætor, or edile. A design projected by some noble youths of quitting Italy in despair after this calamity, is intrepidly quashed by Publius Cornelius Scipio, a military tribune, afterwards surnamed Africanus. Successes in Spain, eight thousand slaves are enlisted by the Romans, they refuse to ransom the captives, they go out in a body to meet Varro, and thank him for not having despaired of the commonwealth.

Spring was now at hand, when Hannibal quitted his winter quarters, having both attempted in vain to cross the Apennines, from the intolerable cold, and having remained with great danger and alarm. The Gauls, whom the hope of plunder and spoil had collected, when, instead of being themselves engaged in carrying and driving away booty from the lands of others, they saw their own lands made the seat of war and burdened by the wintering of the armies of both forces, turned their hatred back again from the Romans to Hannibal; and though plots were frequently concerted against him by their chieftains, he was preserved by the treachery they manifested towards each other; disclosing their conspiracy with the same inconstancy with which they had conspired; and by changing sometimes his dress, at other times the fashion of his hair, he protected himself from treachery by deception. However, this fear was the cause of his more speedily quitting his winter quarters. Meanwhile Cneius Servilius, the consul, entered upon his office at Rome, on the ides of March. There, when he had consulted the senate on the state of the republic in general, the indignation against Flaminius was rekindled. They said "that they had created indeed two consuls, that they had but one; for what regular authority had the other, or what auspices? That their magistrates took these with them from home, from the tutelar deities of themselves and the state, after the celebration of the Latin holidays; the sacrifice upon the mountain being completed, and the vows duly offered up in the Capitol: that neither could an unofficial individual take the auspices, nor could one who had gone from home without them, take them new, and for the first time, in a foreign soil." Prodigies announced from many places at the same time, augmented the terror: in Sicily, that several darts belonging to the soldiers had taken fire; and in Sardinia, that the staff of a horseman, who was going his rounds upon a wall, took fire as he held it in his hand; that the shores had blazed with frequent fires; that two shields had sweated blood at Præneste; that redhot stones had fallen from the heavens at Arpi; that shields were seen in the heavens, and the sun fighting with the moon, at Capena; that two moons rose in the day-time; that the waters of Cære had flowed mixed with blood; and that even the fountain of Hercules had flowed sprinkled with spots of blood. In the territory of Antium, that bloody ears of corn had fallen into the basket as they were reaping. At Falerii, that the heavens appeared cleft as if with a great chasm; and, that where it had opened, a vast light had shone forth; that the prophetic tablets had spontaneously become less; and that one had fallen out thus inscribed, "Mars shakes his spear." During the same time, that the statue of Mars at Rome, on the Appian way, had sweated at the sight of images of wolves. At Capua that there had been the appearance of the heavens being on fire, and of the moon as falling amidst rain. After these, credence was given to prodigies of less magnitude: that the goats of certain persons had borne wool; that a hen had changed herself into a cock; and a cock into a hen: these things having been laid before the senate as reported, the authors being conducted into the senate-house, the consul took the sense of the fathers on religious affairs. It was decreed that those prodigies should be expiated, partly with full-grown, partly with sucking victims; and that a supplication should be made at every shrine for the space of three days; that the other things should be done accordingly as the gods should declare in their oracles to be agreeable to their will when the decemviri had examined the books. By the advice of the decemviri it was decreed, first, that a golden thunderbolt of fifty pounds' weight should be made as an offering to Jupiter; that offerings of silver should be presented to Juno and Minerva; that sacrifices of full-grown victims should be offered to Juno Regina on the Aventine; and to Juno Sospita at Lanuvium; that the matrons, contributing as much money as might be convenient to each, should carry it to the Aventine, as a present to Juno Regina; and that a lectisternium should be celebrated. Moreover, that the very freed-women should, according to their means, contribute money from which a present might be made to Feronia. When these things were done, the decemviri sacrificed with the larger victims in the forum at Ardea. Lastly, it being now the month of December, a sacrifice was made at the temple of Saturn at Rome, and a lectisternium ordered, in which senators prepared the couch and a public banquet. Proclamation was made through the city, that the Saturnalia should be kept for a day and a night; and the people were commanded to account that day as a holiday, and observe it for ever.

While the consul employs himself at Rome in appeasing the gods and holding the levy, Hannibal, setting out from his winter quarters, because it was reported that the consul Flaminius had now arrived at Arretium, although a longer but more commodious route was pointed out to him, takes the nearer road through a marsh where the Arno had, more than usual, overflowed its banks. He ordered the Spaniards and Africans (in these lay the strength of his veteran army) to lead, their own baggage being intermixed with them, lest, being compelled to halt any where, they should want what might be necessary for their use: the Gauls he ordered to go next, that they might form the middle of the marching body; the cavalry to march in the rear: next, Mago with the light-armed Numidians to keep the army together, particularly coercing the Gauls, if, fatigued with exertion and the length of the march, as that nation is wanting in vigour for such exertions, they should fall away or halt. The van still followed the standards wherever the guides did but lead them, through the exceeding deep and almost fathomless eddies of the river, nearly swallowed up in mud, and plunging themselves in. The Gauls could neither support themselves when fallen, nor raise themselves from the eddies. Nor did they sustain their bodies with spirit, nor their minds with hope; some scarce dragging on their wearied limbs; others dying where they had once fallen, their spirits being subdued with fatigue, among the beasts which themselves also lay prostrate in every place. But chiefly watching wore them out, endured now for four days and three nights. When, the water covering every place, not a dry spot could be found where they might stretch their weary bodies, they laid themselves down upon their baggage, thrown in heaps into the waters. Piles of beasts, which lay every where through the whole route, afforded a necessary bed for temporary repose to those seeking any place which was not under water. Hannibal himself, riding on the only remaining elephant, to be the higher from the water, contracted a disorder in his eyes, at first from the unwholesomeness of the vernal air, which is attended with transitions from heat to cold; and at length from watching, nocturnal damps, the marshy atmosphere disordering his head, and because he had neither opportunity nor leisure for remedies, loses one of them.

Many men and cattle having been lost thus wretchedly, when at length he had emerged from the marshes, he pitched his camp as soon as he could on dry ground. And here he received information, through the scouts sent in advance, that the Roman army was round the walls of Arretium. Next the plans and temper of the consul, the situation of the country, the roads, the sources from which provisions might be obtained, and whatever else it was useful to know; all these things he ascertained by the most diligent inquiry. The country was among the most fertile of Italy, the plain of Etruria, between Fæsulæ and Arretium, abundant in its supply of corn, cattle, and every other requisite. The consul was haughty from his former consulship, and felt no proper degree of reverence not only for the laws and the majesty of the fathers, but even for the gods. This temerity, inherent in his nature, fortune had fostered by a career of prosperity and success in civil and military affairs. Thus it was sufficiently evident that, heedless of gods and men, he would act in all cases with presumption and precipitation; and, that he might fall the more readily into the errors natural to him, the Carthaginian begins to fret and irritate him; and leaving the enemy on his left, he takes the road to Fæsulæ, and marching through the centre of Etruria, with intent to plunder, he exhibits to the consul, in the distance, the greatest devastation he could with fires and slaughters. Flaminius, who would not have rested even if the enemy had remained quiet; then, indeed, when he saw the property of the allies driven and carried away almost before his eyes, considering that it reflected disgrace upon him that the Carthaginian now roaming at large through the heart of Italy, and marching without resistance to storm the very walls of Rome, though every other person in the council advised safe rather than showy measures, urging that he should wait for his colleague, in order that, joining their armies, they might carry on the war with united courage and counsels; and that, meanwhile, the enemy should be prevented from his unrestrained freedom in plundering by the cavalry and the light-armed auxiliaries; in a fury hurried out of the council, and at once gave out the signal for marching and for battle. "Nay, rather," says he, "let him be before the walls of Arretium, for here is our country, here our household gods. Let Hannibal, slipping through our fingers, waste Italy through and through; and, ravaging and burning every thing, let him arrive at the walls of Rome; let us move hence till the fathers shall have summoned Flaminius from Arretium, as they did Camillus of old from Veii." While reproaching them thus, and in the act of ordering the standards to be speedily pulled up, when he had mounted upon his horse, the animal fell suddenly, and threw the unseated consul over his head. All the bystanders being alarmed at this as an unhappy omen in the commencement of the affair, in addition word is brought, that the standard could not be pulled up, though, the standard-bearer strove with all his force. Flaminius, turning to the messenger, says, "Do you bring, too, letters from the senate, forbidding me to act. Go, tell them to dig up the standard, if, through fear, their hands are so benumbed that they cannot pluck it up." Then the army began to march; the chief officers, besides that they dissented from the plan, being terrified by the twofold prodigy; while the soldiery in general were elated by the confidence of their leader, since they regarded merely the hope he entertained, and not the reasons of the hope.

Hannibal lays waste the country between the city Cortona and the lake Trasimenus, with all the devastation of war, the more to exasperate the enemy to revenge the injuries inflicted on his allies. They had now reached a place formed by nature for an ambuscade, where the Trasimenus comes nearest to the mountains of Cortona. A very narrow passage only intervenes, as though room enough just for that purpose had been left designedly; after that a somewhat wider plain opens itself, and then some hills rise up. On these he pitches his camp, in full view, where he himself with his Spaniards and Africans only might be posted. The Baliares and his other light troops he leads round the mountains; his cavalry he posts at the very entrance of the defile, some eminences conveniently concealing them; in order that when the Romans had entered, the cavalry advancing, every place might be enclosed by the lake and the mountains. Flaminius, passing the defiles before it was quite daylight, without reconnoitering, though he had arrived at the lake the preceding day at sunset, when the troops began to be spread into the wider plain, saw that part only of the enemy which was opposite to him; the ambuscade in his rear and overhead escaped his notice. And when the Carthaginian had his enemy enclosed by the lake and mountains, and surrounded by his troops, he gives the signal to all to make a simultaneous charge; and each running down the nearest way, the suddenness and unexpectedness of the event was increased to the Romans by a mist rising from the lake, which had settled thicker on the plain than on the mountains; and thus the troops of the enemy ran down from the various eminences, sufficiently well discerning each other, and therefore with the greater regularity. A shout being raised on all sides, the Roman found himself surrounded before he could well see the enemy; and the attack on the front and flank had commenced ere his line could be well formed, his arms prepared for action, or his swords unsheathed.

The consul, while all were panic-struck, himself sufficiently undaunted though in so perilous a case, marshals, as well as the time and place permitted, the lines which were thrown into confusion by each man's turning himself towards the various shouts; and wherever he could approach or be heard exhorts them, and bids them stand and fight: for that they could not escape thence by vows and prayers to the gods but by exertion and valour; that a way was sometimes opened by the sword through the midst of marshalled armies, and that generally the less the fear the less the danger. However, from the noise and tumult, neither his advice nor command could be caught; and so far were the soldiers from knowing their own standards, and ranks, and position, that they had scarce sufficient courage to take up arms and make them ready for battle; and certain of them were surprised before they could prepare them, being burdened rather than protected by them; while in so great darkness there was more use of ears than of eyes. They turned their faces and eyes in every direction towards the groans of the wounded, the sounds of blows upon the body or arms, and the mingled clamours of the menacing and the affrighted. Some, as they were making their escape, were stopped, having encountered a body of men engaged in fight; and bands of fugitives returning to the battle, diverted others. After charges had been attempted unsuccessfully in every direction, and on their flanks the mountains and the lake, on the front and rear the lines of the enemy enclosed them, when it was evident that there was no hope of safety but in the right hand and the sword; then each man became to himself a leader, and encourager to action; and an entirely new contest arose, not a regular line, with principes, hastati, and triarii; nor of such a sort as that the vanguard should fight before the standards, and the rest of the troops behind them; nor such that each soldier should be in his own legion, cohort, or company: chance collects them into bands; and each man's own will assigned to him his post, whether to fight in front or rear; and so great was the ardour of the conflict, so intent were their minds upon the battle, that not one of the combatants felt an earthquake which threw down large portions of many of the cities of Italy, turned rivers from their rapid courses, carried the sea up into rivers, and levelled mountains with a tremendous crash.

The battle was continued near three hours, and in every quarter with fierceness; around the consul, however, it was still hotter and more determined. Both the strongest of the troops, and himself too, promptly brought assistance wherever he perceived his men hard pressed and distressed. But, distinguished by his armour, the enemy attacked him with the utmost vigour, while his countrymen defended him; until an Insubrian horseman, named Ducarius, knowing him also by his face, says to his countrymen, "Lo, this is the consul who slew our legions and laid waste our fields and city. Now will I offer this victim to the shades of my countrymen, miserably slain;" and putting spurs to his horse, he rushes through a very dense body of the enemy; and first slaying his armour-bearer, who had opposed himself to his attack as he approached, ran the consul through with his lance; the triarii, opposing their shields, kept him off when seeking to despoil him. Then first the flight of a great number began; and now neither the lake nor the mountains obstructed their hurried retreat; they run through all places, confined and precipitous, as though they were blind; and arms and men are tumbled one upon another. A great many, when there remained no more space to run, advancing into the water through the first shallows of the lake, plunge in, as far as they could stand above it with their heads and shoulders. Some there were whom inconsiderate fear induced to try to escape even by swimming; but as that attempt was inordinate and hopeless, they were either overwhelmed in the deep water, their courage failing, or, wearied to no purpose, made their way back, with extreme difficulty, to the shallows; and there were cut up on all hands by the cavalry of the enemy, which had entered the water. Near upon six thousand of the foremost body having gallantly forced their way through the opposing enemy, entirely unacquainted with what was occurring in their rear, escaped from the defile; and having halted on a certain rising ground, and hearing only the shouting and clashing of arms, they could not know nor discern, by reason of the mist, what was the fortune of the battle. At length, the affair being decided, when the mist, dispelled by the increasing heat of the sun, had cleared the atmosphere, then, in the clear light, the mountains and plains showed their ruin and the Roman army miserably destroyed; and thus, lest, being descried at a distance, the cavalry should be sent against them, hastily snatching up their standards, they hurried away with all possible expedition. On the following day, when in addition to their extreme sufferings in other respects, famine also was at hand, Maharbal, who had followed them during the night with the whole body of cavalry, pledging his honour that he would let them depart with single garments, if they would deliver up their arms, they surrendered themselves; which promise was kept by Hannibal with Punic fidelity, and he threw them all into chains.

This is the celebrated battle at the Trasimenus, and recorded among the few disasters of the Roman people. Fifteen thousand Romans were slain in the battle. Ten thousand, who had been scattered in the flight through all Etruria, returned to the city by different roads. One thousand five hundred of the enemy perished in the battle; many on both sides died afterwards of their wounds. The carnage on both sides is related, by some authors, to have been many times greater. I, besides that I would relate nothing drawn from a worthless source, to which the minds of historians generally incline too much, have as my chief authority Fabius, who was contemporary with the events of this war. Such of the captives as belonged to the Latin confederacy being dismissed without ransom, and the Romans thrown into chains, Hannibal ordered the bodies of his own men to be gathered from the heaps of the enemy, and buried: the body of Flaminius too, which was searched for with great diligence for burial, he could not find. On the first intelligence of this defeat at Rome, a concourse of the people, dismayed and terrified, took place in the forum. The matrons, wandering through the streets, ask all they meet, what sudden disaster was reported? what was the fate of the army? And when the multitude, like a full assembly, having directed their course to the comitium and senate-house, were calling upon the magistrates, at length, a little before sunset, Marcus Pomponius, the prætor, declares, "We have been defeated in a great battle;" and though nothing more definite was heard from him, yet, full of the rumours which they had caught one from another, they carry back to their homes intelligence, that the consul, with a great part of his troops, was slain; that a few only survived, and these either widely dispersed in flight through Etruria, or else captured by the enemy. As many as had been the calamities of the vanquished army, into so many anxieties were the minds of those distracted whose relations had served under Flaminius, and who were uninformed of what had been the fate of their friends, nor does any one know certainly what he should either hope or fear. During the next and several successive days, a greater number of women almost than men stood at the gates, waiting either for some one of their friends or for intelligence of them, surrounding and earnestly interrogating those they met: nor could they be torn away from those they knew especially, until they had regularly inquired into every thing. Then as they retired from the informants you might discern their various expressions of countenance according as intelligence, pleasing or sad, was announced to each; and those who congratulated or condoled on their return home. The joy and grief of the women were especially manifested. They report that one, suddenly meeting her son, who had returned safe, expired at the very door before his face—that another, who sat grieving at her house at the falsely reported death of her son, became a corpse, from excessive joy, at the first sight of him on his return. The prætors detained the senators in the house for several days from sunrise to sunset, deliberating under whose conduct and by what forces, the victorious Carthaginians could be opposed.

Before their plans were sufficiently determined another unexpected defeat is reported: four thousand horse, sent under the conduct of C. Centenius, propraetor, by Servilius to his colleague, were cut off by Hannibal in Umbria, to which place, on hearing of the battle at Trasimenus, they had turned their course. The report of this event variously affected the people. Some, having their minds preoccupied with heavier grief, considered the recent loss of cavalry trifling, in comparison with their former losses; others did not estimate what had occurred by itself, but considered that, as in a body already labouring under disease, a slight cause would be felt more violently than a more powerful one in a robust constitution, so whatever adverse event befell the state in its then sickly and impaired condition, ought to be estimated, not by the magnitude of the event itself, but with reference to its exhausted strength, which could endure nothing that could oppress it. The state therefore took refuge in a remedy for a long time before neither wanted nor employed, the appointment of a dictator, and because the consul was absent, by whom alone it appeared he could be nominated, and because neither message nor letter could easily be sent to him through the country occupied by Punic troops, and because the people could not appoint a dictator, which had never been done to that day, the people created Quintus Fabius Maximus pro dictator, and Marcus Minucius Rufus master of the horse. To them the senate assigned the task of strengthening the walls and towers of the city, of placing guards in such quarters as seemed good, and breaking down the bridges of the river, considering that they must now fight at home in defence of their city, since they were unable to protect Italy.

Hannibal, marching directly through Umbria, arrived at Spoletum, thence, having completely devastated the adjoining country, and commenced an assault upon the city, having been repulsed with great loss and conjecturing from the strength of this one colony, which had been not very successfully attacked, what was the size of the city of Rome, turned aside into the territory of Picenum, which abounded not only with every species of grain, but was stored with booty, which his rapacious and needy troops eagerly seized. There he continued encamped for several days, and his soldiers were refreshed, who had been enfeebled by winter marches and marshy ground, and with a battle more successful in its result than light or easy. When sufficient time for rest had been granted for soldiers delighting more in plunder and devastation than ease and repose, setting out, he lays waste the territories of Pretutia and Hadria, then of the Marsi, the Marrucini, and the Peligni, and the contiguous region of Apulia around Arpi and Luceria. Cneius Servilius, the consul, having fought some slight battles with the Gauls, and taken one inconsiderable town, when he heard of the defeat of his colleague and the army, alarmed now for the walls of the capital, marched towards the city, that he might not be absent at so extreme a crisis. Quintus Fabius Maximus, a second time dictator, assembled the senate the very day he entered on his office; and commencing with what related to the gods, after he had distinctly proved to the fathers, that Caius Flaminius had erred more from neglect of the ceremonies and auspices than from temerity and want of judgment, and that the gods themselves should be consulted as to what were the expiations of their anger, he obtained a resolution that the decemviri should be ordered to inspect the Sibylline books, which is rarely decreed, except when some horrid prodigies were announced. Having inspected the prophetic books, they reported, that the vow which was made to Mars on account of this war, not having been regularly fulfilled, must be performed afresh and more fully; that the great games must be vowed to Jupiter, temples to Venus Erycina and Mens; that a supplication and lectisternium must be made, and a sacred spring vowed, if the war should proceed favourably and the state continue the condition it was in before the war. Since the management of the war would occupy Fabius, the senate orders Marcus Æmilius, the prætor, to see that all these things are done in good time, according to the directions of the college of pontiffs.

These decrees of the senate having been passed, Lucius Cornelius Lentulus, pontifex maximus, the college of prætors consulting with him, gives his opinion that, first of all, the people should be consulted respecting a sacred spring: that it could not be without the order of the people. The people having been asked according to this form: Do ye will and order that this thing should be performed in this manner? If the republic of the Roman people, the Quirites, shall be safe and preserved as I wish it may, from these wars for the next five years, (the war which is between the Roman people and the Carthaginian, and the wars which are with the Cisalpine Gauls), the Roman people, the Quirites, shall present whatsoever the spring shall produce from herds of swine, sheep, goats, oxen and which shall not have been consecrated, to be sacrificed to Jupiter, from the day which the senate and people shall appoint. Let him who shall make an offering do it when he please, and in what manner he please; in whatsoever manner he does it, let it be considered duly done. If that which ought to be sacrificed die, let it be unconsecrated, and let no guilt attach; if any one unwittingly wound or kill it, let it be no injury to him; if any one shall steal it, let no guilt attach to the people or to him from whom it was stolen; if any one shall unwittingly offer it on a forbidden day, let it be esteemed duly offered; also whether by night or day, whether slave or free-man perform it. If the senate and people shall order it to be offered sooner than any person shall offer it, let the people being acquitted of it be free. On the same account great games were vowed, at an expense of three hundred and thirty-three thousand three hundred and thirty-three *asses* and a third; moreover, it was decreed that sacrifice should be done to Jupiter with three hundred oxen, to many other deities with white oxen and the other victims. The vows being duly made, a supplication was proclaimed; and not only the inhabitants of the city went with their wives and children, but such of the rustics also as, possessing any property themselves, were interested in the welfare of the state. Then a lectisternium was celebrated for three days, the decemviri for sacred things superintending. Six couches were seen, for Jupiter and Juno one, for Neptune and Minerva another, for Mars and Venus a third, for Apollo and Diana a fourth, for Vulcan and Vesta a fifth, for Mercury and Ceres a sixth. Then temples were vowed. To Venus Erycina, Quintus Fabius Maximus vowed a temple; for so it was delivered from the prophetic books, that he should vow it who held the highest authority in the state. Titus Otacilius, the prætor vowed a temple to Mens.

Divine things having been thus performed, the dictator then put the question of the war and the state; with what, and how many legions the fathers were of opinion that the victorious enemy should be opposed. It was decreed that he should receive the army from Cneius Servilius, the consul: that he should levy, moreover, from the citizens and allies as many horse and foot as seemed good; that he should transact and perform every thing else as he considered for the good of the state. Fabius said he would add two legions to the army of Servilius. These were levied by the master of the horse, and were appointed by Fabius to meet him at Tibur on a certain day. And then having issued proclamation that those whose towns or castles were unfortified should quit them and assemble in places of security; that all the inhabitants of that tract through which Hannibal was about to march, should remove from the country, having first burnt their buildings and spoiled their fruits, that there might not be a supply of any thing; he himself set out on the Flaminian road to meet the consul and his army; and when he saw in the distance the marching body on the Tiber, near Ocriculum, and the consul with the cavalry advancing to him, he sent a beadle to acquaint the consul that he must meet the dictator without the lictors. When he had obeyed his command, and their meeting had exhibited a striking display of the majesty of the dictatorship before the citizens and allies, who, from its antiquity, had now almost forgotten that authority; a letter arrived from the city, stating that the ships of burden, conveying provisions from Ostia into Spain to the army, had been captured by the Carthaginian fleet off the port of Cossa. The consul, therefore, was immediately ordered to proceed to Ostia, and, having manned the ships at Rome or Ostia with soldiers and sailors, to pursue the enemy, and protect the coasts of Italy. Great numbers of men were levied at Rome, sons of freed-men even, who had children, and were of the military age, had taken the oath. Of these troops levied in the city, such as were under thirty-five were put on board ships, the rest were left to protect the city.

The dictator, having received the troops of the consul from Fulvius Flaccus, his lieutenant-general, marching through the Sabine territory, arrived at Tibur on the day which he had appointed the new-raised troops to assemble. Thence he went to Præneste, and cutting across the country, came out in the Latin way, whence he led his troops towards the enemy, reconnoitering the road with the utmost diligence; not intending to expose himself to hazard any where, except as far as necessity compelled him. The day he first pitched his camp in sight of the enemy, not far from Arpi, the Carthaginian, without delay, led out his troops, and forming his line gave an opportunity of fighting: but when he found all still with the enemy, and his camp free from tumult and disorder, he returned to his camp, saying indeed tauntingly, "That even the spirit of the Romans, inherited from Mars, was at length subdued; that they were warred down and had manifestly given up all claim to valour and renown:" but burning inwardly with stifled vexation because he would have to encounter a general by no means like Flaminius and Sempronius; and because the Romans, then at length schooled by their misfortunes, had sought a general a match for Hannibal; and that now he had no longer to fear the headlong violence, but the deliberate prudence of the dictator. Having not yet experienced his constancy, he began to provoke and try his temper, by frequently shifting his camp and laying waste the territories of the allies before his eyes: and one while he withdrew out of sight at quick march, another while he halted suddenly, and concealed himself in some winding of the road, if possible to entrap him on his descending into the plain. Fabius kept marching his troops along the high grounds, at a moderate distance from the enemy, so as neither to let him go altogether nor yet to encounter him. The troops were kept within the camp, except so far as necessary wants compelled them to quit it; and fetched in food and wood not by small nor rambling parties. An outpost of cavalry and light-armed troops, prepared and equipped for acting in cases of sudden alarm, rendered every thing safe to their own soldiers, and dangerous to the scattered plunderers of the enemy. Nor was his whole cause committed to general hazard; while slight contests, of small importance in themselves, commenced on safe ground, with a retreat at hand, accustomed the soldiery, terrified by their former disasters, now at length to think less meanly either of their prowess or good fortune. But he did not find Hannibal a greater enemy to such sound measures than his master of the horse, who was only prevented from plunging the state into ruin by his inferiority in command. Presumptuous and precipitate in his measures, and unbridled in his tongue, first among a few, then openly and publicly, he taunted him with being sluggish instead of patient, spiritless instead of cautious; falsely imputing to him those vices which bordered on his virtues; and raised himself by means of depressing his superiors, which, though a most iniquitous practice, has become more general from the too great successes of many.

Hannibal crosses over from the Hirpini into Samnium; lays waste the territory of Beneventum; takes the town of Telesia; and purposely irritates the dictator, if perchance he could draw him down to a battle on the plain, exasperated by so many indignities and disasters inflicted on his allies. Among the multitude of allies of Italian extraction, who had been captured by Hannibal at the Trasimenus, and dismissed, were three Campanian horsemen, who had even at that time been bribed by many presents and promises from Hannibal to win over the affections of their countrymen to him. These, bringing him word that he would have an opportunity of getting possession of Capua, if he brought his army into the neighbourhood in Campania, induced Hannibal to quit Samnium for Campania; though he hesitated, fluctuating between confidence and distrust, as the affair was of more importance than the authorities. He dismissed them, repeatedly charging them to confirm their promises by acts, and ordering them to return with a greater number, and some of their leading men. Hannibal himself orders his guide to conduct him into the territory of Casinum, being certified by persons acquainted with the country, that if he seized that pass he would deprive the Romans of a passage by which they might get out to the assistance of their allies. But his Punic accent, ill adapted to the pronunciation of Latin names, caused the guide to understand Casilinum, instead of Casinum; and leaving his former course, he descends through the territory of Allifæ, Calatia, and Cales, into the plain of Stella, where, seeing the country enclosed on all sides by mountains and rivers, he calls the guide to him, and asks him where in the world he was? when he replied, that on that day he would lodge at Casilinum: then at length the error was discovered, and that Casinum lay at a great distance in another direction. Having scourged the guide with rods and crucified him, in order to strike terror into all others, he fortified a camp, and sent Maharbal with the cavalry into the Falernian territory to pillage. This depredation reached as far as the waters of Sinuessa; the Numidians caused destruction to a vast extent, but flight and consternation through a still wider space. Yet not even the terror of these things, when all around was consuming in the flames of war, could shake the fidelity of the allies; for this manifest reason, because they lived under a temperate and mild government: nor were they unwilling to submit to those who were superior to them, which is the only bond of fidelity.

But when the enemy's camp was pitched on the Vulturnus, and the most delightful country in Italy was being consumed by fire, and the farm-houses, on all hands, were smoking from the flames, whilst Fabius led his troops along the heights of Mount Massicus, then the strife had nearly been kindled anew, for they had been quiet for a few days, because, as the army had marched quicker than usual, they had supposed that the object of this haste was to save Campania from devastation; but when they arrived at the extreme ridge of Mount Massicus, and the enemy appeared under their eyes, burning the houses of the Falernian territory, and of the settlers of Sinuessa, and no mention made of battle, Minucius exclaims, "Are we come here to see our allies butchered, and their property burned, as a spectacle to be enjoyed? and if we are not moved with shame on account of any others, are we not on account of these citizens, whom our fathers sent as settlers to Sinuessa, that this frontier might be protected from the Samnite foe: which now not the neighbouring Samnite wastes with fire, but a Carthaginian foreigner, who has advanced even thus far from the remotest limits of the world, through our dilatoriness and inactivity? What! are we so degenerate from our ancestors as tamely to see that coast filled with Numidian and Moorish foes, along which our fathers considered it a disgrace to their government that the Carthaginian fleets should cruise? We, who erewhile, indignant at the storming of Saguntum, appealed not to men only, but to treaties and to gods, behold Hannibal scaling the walls of a Roman colony unmoved. The smoke from the flames of our farm-houses and lands comes into our eyes and faces; our ears ring with the cries of our weeping allies, imploring us to assist them oftener than the gods, while we here are leading our troops, like a herd of cattle, through shady forests and lonely paths, enveloped in clouds and woods. If Marcus Furius had resolved to recover the city from the Gauls, by thus traversing the tops of mountains and forests, in the same manner as this modern Camillus goes about to recover Italy from Hannibal, who has been sought out for our dictator in our distress, on account of his unparalleled talents, Rome would be the possession of the Gauls; and I fear lest, if we are thus dilatory, our ancestors will so often have preserved it only for the Carthaginians and Hannibal; but that man and true Roman, on the very day on which intelligence was brought him to Veii, that he was appointed dictator, on the authority of the fathers and the nomination of the people, came down into the plain, though the Janiculum was high enough to admit of his sitting down there, and viewing the enemy at a distance, and on that very day defeated the Gallic legions in the middle of the city, in the place where the Gallic piles are now, and on the following day on the Roman side of Gabii. What many years after this, when we were sent under the yoke at the Caudine forks by the Samnite foe, did Lucius Papirius Cursor take the yoke from the Roman neck and place it upon the proud Samnites, by traversing the heights of Samnium? or was it by pressing and besieging Luceria, and challenging the victorious enemy? A short time ago, what was it that gave victory to Caius Lutatius but expedition? for on the day after he caught sight of the enemy he surprised and overpowered the fleet, loaded with provisions, and encumbered of itself by its own implements and apparatus. It is folly to suppose that the war can be brought to a conclusion by sitting still, or by prayers, the troops must be armed and led down into the plain, that you may engage man to man. The Roman power has grown to its present height by courage and activity, and not by such dilatory measures as these, which the cowardly only designate as cautious." A crowd of Roman tribunes and knights poured round Minucius, while thus, as it were, haranguing, his presumptuous expressions reached the ears of the common soldiers, and had the question been submitted to the votes of the soldiers, they showed evidently that they would have preferred Minucius to Fabius for their general.

Fabius, keeping his attention fixed no less upon his own troops than on the enemy, first shows that his resolution was unconquered by the former. Though he well knew that his procrastination was disapproved, not only in his own camp, but by this time even at Rome, yet, inflexibly adhering to the same line of policy, he delayed through the remainder of the summer, in order that Hannibal, devoid of all hope of a battle, which he so earnestly desired, might now look out for a place for winter quarters, because that district was one of present, but not constant, supply, consisting, as it did, of plantations and vineyards, and all places planted luxurious rather than useful produce. This intelligence was to Fabius by his scouts. When he felt convinced that he would return by the same narrow pass through which he had entered the Falernian territory, he occupied Mount Callicula and Casilinum with a pretty strong guard. Which city, intersected by the river Vulturnus, divides the Falernian and Campanian territories. He himself leads back his troops along the same heights, having sent Lucius Hostilius Mancinus with four hundred of the allied cavalry to reconnoitre; who being one of the crowd of youths who had often heard the master of the horse fiercely haranguing, at first advanced after the manner of a scout, in order that he might observe the enemy in security; and when he saw the Numidians scattered widely throughout the villages, having gotten an opportunity, he also slew a few of them. But from that moment his mind was engrossed with the thoughts of a battle, and the injunctions of the dictator were forgotten, who had charged him, when he had advanced as far as he could with safety, to retreat before he came within the enemy's view. The Numidians, party after party, skirmishing and retreating, drew the general almost to their camp, to the fatigue of his men and horses. Then Karthalo, who had the command of the cavalry, charging at full speed, and having put them to flight before he came within a dart's throw, pursued them for five miles almost in a continuous course. Mancinus, when he saw that the enemy did not desist from the pursuit, and that there was no hope of escape, having encouraged his troops, turned back to the battle though inferior in every kind of force. Accordingly he himself, and the choicest of his cavalry, being surrounded, are cut to pieces. The rest in disorderly retreat fled first to Cales, and thence to the dictator, by ways almost impassable. It happened that on that day Minucius had formed a junction with Fabius, having been sent to secure with a guard the pass above Tarracina, which, contracted into a narrow gorge, overhangs the sea, in order that Hannibal might not be able to get into the Roman territory by the Appian way's being unguarded. The dictator and master of the horse, uniting their forces, lead them down into the road through which Hannibal was about to march his troops. The enemy was two miles from that place.

The following day the Carthaginians filled the whole road between the two camps with his troops in marching order; and though the Romans had taken their stand immediately under their rampart, having a decidedly superior position, yet the Carthaginian came up with his light horse and, with a view to provoke the enemy, carried on a kind of desultory attack, first charging and then retreating. The Roman line remained in its position. The battle was slow and more conformable to the wish of the dictator than of Hannibal. On the part of the Romans there fell two hundred, on the part of the enemy eight hundred. It now began to appear that Hannibal was hemmed in, the road to Casilinum being blockaded; and that while Capua, and Samnium, and so many wealthy allies in the rear of the Romans might supply them with provisions, the Carthaginian, on the other hand, must winter amid the rocks of Formiæ and the sands and hideous swamps of Liternum. Nor did it escape Hannibal that he was assailed by his own arts; wherefore, since he could not escape by way of Casilinum, and since it was necessary to make for the mountains, and pass the summit of Callicula, lest in any place the Romans should attack his troops while enclosed in valleys; having hit upon a stratagem calculated to deceive the sight, and excite terror from its appearance, by means of which he might baffle the enemy, he resolved to come up by stealth to the mountains at the commencement of night. The preparation of his wily stratagem was of this description. Torches, collected from every part of the country, and bundles of rods and dry cuttings, are fastened before the horns of oxen, of which, wild and tame, he had driven away a great number among other plunder of the country: the number of oxen was made up to nearly two thousand. To Hasdrubal was assigned the task of driving to the mountains that herd, after having set fire to their horns, as soon as ever it was dark; particularly, if he could, over the passes beset by the enemy.

As soon as it was dark the camp was moved in silence; the oxen were driven a little in advance of the standards. When they arrived at the foot of the mountains and the narrow passes, the signal is immediately given for setting fire to their horns and driving them violently up the mountains before them. The mere terror excited by the flame, which cast a glare from their heads, and the heat now approaching the quick and the roots of their horns, drove on the oxen as if goaded by madness. By which dispersion, on a sudden all the surrounding shrubs were in a blaze, as if the mountains and woods had been on fire; and the unavailing tossing of their heads quickening the flame, exhibited an appearance as of men running to and fro on every side. Those who had been placed to guard the passage of the wood, when they saw fires on the tops of the mountains, and some over their own heads, concluding that they were surrounded, abandoned their post; making for the tops of the mountains in the direction in which the fewest fires blazed, as being the safest course; however they fell in with some oxen which had strayed from their herds. At first, when they beheld them at a distance, they stood fixed in amazement at the miracle, as it appeared to them, of creatures breathing fire; afterwards, when it showed itself to be a human stratagem, then, forsooth, concluding that there was an ambuscade, as they are hurrying away in flight, with increased alarm, they fall in also with the light-armed troops of the enemy. But the night, when the fear was equally shared, kept them from commencing the battle till morning. Meanwhile Hannibal, having marched his whole army through the pass, and having cut off some of the enemy in the very defile, pitches his camp in the country of Allifæ.

Fabius perceived this tumult, but concluding that it was a snare, and being disinclined for a battle, particularly by night, kept his troops within the works. At break of day a battle took place under the summit of the mountain, in which the Romans, who were considerably superior in numbers, would have easily overpowered the light-armed of the enemy, cut off as they were from their party, had not a cohort of Spaniards, sent back by Hannibal for that very purpose, reached the spot. That body being more accustomed to mountains, and being more adapted, both from the agility of their limbs and also from the character of their arms, to skirmishing amid rocks and crags, easily foiled, by their manner of fighting, an enemy loaded with arms, accustomed to level ground and the steady kind of fighting. Separating from a contest thus by no means equal, they proceeded to their camps; the Spaniards almost all untouched; the Romans having lost a few. Fabius also moved his camp, and passing the defile, took up a position above Allifæ, in a strong and elevated place. Then Hannibal, pretending to march to Rome through Samnium, came back as far as the Peligni, spreading devastation. Fabius led his troops along the heights midway between the army of the enemy and the city of Rome; neither avoiding him altogether, nor coming to an engagement. From the Peligni the Carthaginian turned his course, and going back again to Apulia, reached Geronium, a city deserted by its inhabitants from fear, as a part of its walls had fallen down together in ruins. The dictator formed a completely fortified camp in the territory of Larinum, and being recalled thence to Rome on account of some sacred rites, he not only urged the master of the horse, in virtue of his authority, but with advice and almost with prayers, that he would trust rather to prudence than fortune; and imitate him as a general rather than Sempronius and Flaminius; that he would not suppose that nothing had been achieved by having worn out nearly the whole summer in baffling the enemy; that physicians too sometimes gained more by rest than by motion and action. That it was no small thing to have ceased to be conquered by an enemy so often victorious, and to have taken breath after successive disasters. Having thus unavailingly admonished the master of the horse, he set out for Rome.

In the beginning of the summer in which these events occurred, the war commenced by land and sea in Spain also. To the number of ships which he had received from his brother, equipped and ready for action, Hasdrubal added ten. The fleet of forty ships he delivered to Himilco: and thus setting out from Carthage, kept his ships near the land, while he led his army along the shore, ready to engage with whichever part of his forces the enemy might fall in with. Cneius Scipio, when he heard that the enemy had quitted his winter quarters, at first formed the same plan; but afterwards, not daring to engage him by land, from a great rumour of fresh auxiliaries, he advances to meet him with a fleet of thirty-five ships, having put some chosen soldiers on board. Setting out from Tarraco, on the second day, he reached a convenient station, ten miles from the mouth of the Iberus. Two ships of the Massilians, sent forward from that place reconnoitering, brought word back that the Carthaginian fleet was stationed in the mouth of the river, and that the camp was pitched upon the bank. In order, therefore, to overpower them while off their guard and incautious, by a universal and wide-spread terror, he weighed anchor and advanced. In Spain there are several towers placed in high situations, which they employ both as watch-towers and as places of defence against pirates. From them first, a view of the ships of the enemy having been obtained, the signal was given to Hasdrubal; and a tumult arose in the camp, and on land sooner than on the ships and at sea; the dashing of the oars and other nautical noises not being yet distinctly heard, nor the promontories disclosing the fleet. Upon this, suddenly one horseman after another, sent out by Hasdrubal, orders those who were strolling upon the shore or resting quietly in their tents, expecting any thing rather than the enemy and a battle on that day, immediately to embark and take up arms: that the Roman fleet was now a short distance from the harbour. The horsemen, despatched in every direction, delivered these orders; and presently Hasdrubal himself comes up with the main army. All places resound with noises of various kinds; the soldiers and rowers hurrying together to the ships, rather like men running away from the land than marching to battle. Scarcely had all embarked, when some, unfastening the hawsers, are carried out against the anchors; others cut their cables, that nothing might impede them; and by doing every thing with hurry and precipitation, the duties of mariners were impeded by the preparations of the soldiers, and the soldiers were prevented from taking and preparing for action their arms, by the bustle of the mariners. And now the Roman was not only approaching, but had drawn up his ships for the battle. The Carthaginians, therefore, thrown into disorder, not more by the enemy and the battle than by their own tumult, having rather made an attempt at fighting than commenced a battle, turned their fleet for flight; and as the mouth of the river which was before them could not be entered in so broad a line, and by so many pressing in at the same time, they ran their ships on shore in every part. And being received, some in the shallows, and others on the dry shore, some armed and some unarmed, they escaped to their friends, who were drawn up in battle-array over the shore. Two Carthaginian ships were captured and four sunk on the first encounter.

The Romans, though the enemy was master of the shore, and they saw armed troops lining the whole bank, promptly pursuing the discomfited fleet of the enemy, towed out into the deep all the ships which had not either shattered their prows by the violence with which they struck the shore, or set their keels fast in the shallows. They captured as many as twenty-five out of forty. Nor was that the most splendid result of their victory: but they became masters of the whole sea on that coast by one slight battle; advancing, then, with their fleet to Honosca, and making a descent from the ships upon the coast, when they had taken the city by storm and pillaged it, they afterwards made for Carthage: then devastating the whole surrounding country, they, lastly, set fire also to the buildings contiguous to the wall and gates. Thence the fleet laden with plunder, arrived at Longuntica, where a great quantity of oakum for naval purposes had been collected by Hasdrubal: of this, taking away as much as was sufficient for their necessities, they burnt all the rest. Nor did they only sail by the prominent coasts of the continent, but crossed over into the island Ebusus; where, having with the utmost exertion, but in vain, carried on operations against the city, which is the capital of the island, for two days, when they found that time was wasted to no purpose upon a hopeless task, they turned their efforts to the devastation of the country; and having plundered and fired several villages, and acquired a greater booty than they had obtained on the continent, they retired to their ships, when ambassadors from the Baliares came to Scipio to sue for peace. From this place the fleet sailed back, and returned to the hither parts of the province, whither ambassadors of all the people who dwell on the Iberus, and of many people in the most distant parts of Spain, assembled. But the number of states who really became subject to the authority and dominion of the Romans, and gave hostages, amounted to upwards of one hundred and twenty. The Roman therefore, relying sufficiently on his land forces also, advanced as far as the pass of Castulo. Hasdrubal retired into Lusitania, and nearer the ocean.

After this, it seemed probable that the remainder of the summer would be peaceful; and so it would have been with regard to the Punic enemy: but besides that the tempers of the Spaniards themselves are naturally restless, and eager for innovation, Mandonius, together with Indibilis, who had formerly been petty prince of the Ilergetes, having stirred up their countrymen, came to lay waste the peaceful country of the Roman allies, after the Romans had retired from the pass to the sea-coast. A military tribune with some light-armed auxiliaries being sent against these by Scipio, with a small effort put them all to the rout, as being but a disorderly band: some having been captured and slain, a great portion of them were deprived of their arms. This disturbance, however, brought back Hasdrubal, who was retiring to the ocean, to protect his allies on this side the Iberus. The Carthaginian camp was in the territory of Ilercao, the Roman camp at the New Fleet, when unexpected intelligence turned the war into another quarter. The Celtiberians, who had sent the chief men of their country as ambassadors to the Romans, and had given them hostages, aroused by a message from Scipio, take up arms and invade the province of the Carthaginians with a powerful army; take three towns by storm; and after that, encountering Hasdrubal himself in two battles with, splendid success, slew fifteen thousand and captured four thousand, together with many military standards.

This being the state of affairs in Spain, Publius Scipio came into his province, having been sent thither by the senate, his command being continued to him after his consulate, with thirty long ships, eight thousand soldiers, and a large importation of provisions. That fleet, swelled to an enormous size by a multitude of transports, being descried at a distance, entered safe the port of Tarraco, to the great joy of the citizens and allies. Landing his troops there, Scipio set out and formed a junction with his brother, and thenceforward they prosecuted the war with united courage and counsels. While the Carthaginians, therefore, were occupied with the Celtiberian war, they promptly crossed the Iberus, and not seeing any enemy, pursue their course to Saguntum; for it was reported that the hostages from every part of Spain, having been consigned to custody, were kept in the citadel of that place under a small guard. That pledge alone checked the affections of all the people of Spain, which were inclined towards an alliance with the Romans; lest the guilt of their defection should be expiated with the blood of their children. One man, by a stratagem more subtle than honourable, liberated the Spaniards from this restraint. There was at Saguntum a noble Spaniard, named Abelux, hitherto faithful to the Carthaginians, but now (such are for the most part the dispositions of barbarians) had changed his attachment with fortune; but considering that a deserter going over to enemies without the betraying of something valuable, would be looked upon only as a stigmatized and worthless individual, was solicitous to render as great a service as possible to his new confederates. Having turned over in his mind, then, the various means which, under the favour of fortune, he might employ, in preference to every other, he applied himself to the delivering up of the hostages; concluding that this one thing, above all others, would gain the Romans the friendship of the Spanish chieftains. But since he knew that the guards of the hostages would do nothing without the authority of Bostar, the governor, he addresses himself with craft to Bostar himself. Bostar had his camp without the city, just upon the shore, in order to preclude the approach of the Romans from that quarter. He informs him, taken aside to a secret place, and as if uninformed, in what position affairs were: "That hitherto fear had withheld the minds of the Spaniards to them, because the Romans were at a great distance: that now the Roman camp was on this side the Iberus, a secure fortress and asylum for such as desired a change, that therefore those whom fear could not bind should be attached by kindness and favour." When Bostar, in astonishment, earnestly asked him, what sudden gift of so much importance that could be, he replied, "Send back the hostages to their states: this will be an acceptable boon, privately to their parents, who possess the greatest influence in their respective states, and publicly to the people. Every man wishes to have confidence reposed in him; and confidence reposed generally enforces the fidelity itself. The office of restoring the hostages to their homes, I request for myself; that I may enhance my project by the trouble bestowed, and that I may add as much value as I can to a service in its own intrinsic nature so acceptable." When he had persuaded the man, who was not cunning as compared with Carthaginian minds in general, having gone secretly and by night to the outposts of the enemy, he met with some auxiliary Spaniards; and having been brought by them into the presence of Scipio, he explains what brought him. Pledges of fidelity having been given and received, and the time and place for delivering the hostages having been appointed, he returns to Saguntum. The following day he spent with Bostar, in taking his commands for effecting the business; having so arranged it, that he should go by night, in order that he might escape the observation of the enemy, he was dismissed; and awakening the guards of the youths at the hour agreed upon with them, set out and led them, as if unconsciously, into a snare prepared by his own deceit. They were brought to the Roman camp, and every thing else respecting the restoration of the hostages was transacted as had been agreed upon with Bostar, and in the same course as if the affair had been carried on in the name of the Carthaginians. But the favour of the Romans was somewhat greater than that of the Carthaginians would have been in a similar case; for misfortune and fear might have seemed to have softened them, who had been found oppressive and haughty in prosperity. The Roman, on the contrary, on his first arrival, having been unknown to them before, had begun with an act of clemency and liberality: and Abelux, a man of prudence, did not seem likely to have changed his allies without good cause. Accordingly all began, with great unanimity, to meditate a revolt; and hostilities would immediately have commenced, had not the winter intervened, which compelled the Romans, and the Carthaginians also, to retire to shelter.

Such were the transactions in Spain also during the second summer of the Punic war; while in Italy the prudent delay of Fabius had procured the Romans some intermission from disasters; which conduct, as it kept Hannibal disturbed with no ordinary degree of anxiety, for it proved to him that the Romans had at length selected a general who would carry on the war with prudence, and not in dependence on fortune; so was it treated with contempt by his countrymen, both in the camp and in the city; particularly after that a battle had been fought during his absence from the temerity of the master of the horse, in its issue, as I may justly designate it, rather joyful than successful. Two causes were added to augment the unpopularity of the dictator: one arising out of a stratagem and artful procedure of Hannibal; for the farm of the dictator having been pointed out to him by deserters, he ordered that the fire and sword and every outrage of enemies should be restrained from it alone, while all around were levelled with the ground; in order that it might appear to have been the term of some secret compact: the other from an act of his own, at first perhaps suspicious, because in it he had not waited for the authority of the senate, but in the result turning unequivocally to his highest credit, with relation to the exchange of prisoners: for, as was the case in the first Punic war, an agreement had been made between the Roman and Carthaginian generals, that whichever received more prisoners than he restored, should give two pounds and a half of silver for every man. And when the Roman had received two hundred and forty-seven more than the Carthaginian, and the silver which was due for them, after the matter had been frequently agitated in the senate, was not promptly supplied, because he had not consulted the fathers, he sent his son Quintus to Rome and sold his farm, uninjured by the enemy, and thus redeemed the public credit at his own private expense. Hannibal lay in a fixed camp before the walls of Geronium, which city he had captured and burnt, leaving only a few buildings for the purpose of granaries: thence he was in the habit of sending out two-thirds of his forces to forage; with the third part kept in readiness, he himself remained on guard, both as a protection to his camp, and for the purpose of looking out, if from any quarter an attack should be made upon his foragers.

The Roman army was at that time in the territory of Larinum. Minucius, the master of the horse, had the command of it; the dictator, as was before mentioned, having gone to the city. But the camp, which had been pitched in an elevated and secure situation, was now brought down into the plain; plans of a bolder character, agreeably with the temper of the general, were in agitation; and either an attack was to be made upon the scattered foragers, or upon the camp now left with an inconsiderable guard. Nor did it escape the observation of Hannibal, that the plan of the war had been changed with the general, and that the enemy would act with more boldness than counsel. Hannibal himself too, which one would scarcely credit, though the enemy was near, despatched a third part of his troops to forage, retaining the remaining two-thirds in the camp. After that he advanced his camp itself nearer to the enemy, to a hill within the enemy's view, nearly two miles from Geronium; that they might be aware that he was on the alert to protect his foragers if any attack should be made upon them. Then he discovered an eminence nearer to, and commanding the very camp of the Romans: and because if he marched openly in the day-time to occupy it, the enemy would doubtless anticipate him by a shorter way, the Numidians having been sent privately in the night, took possession of it. These, occupying this position, the Romans, the next day, despising the smallness of their numbers, dislodge, and transfer their camp thither themselves. There was now, therefore, but a very small space between rampart and rampart, and that the Roman line had almost entirely filled; at the same time the cavalry, with the light infantry sent out against the foragers through the opposite part of the camp, effected a slaughter and flight of the scattered enemy far and wide. Nor dared Hannibal hazard a regular battle; because with so few troops, that he would scarcely be able to protect his camp if attacked. And now he carried on the war (for part of his army was away) according to the plans of Fabius, by sitting still and creating delays. He had also withdrawn his troops to their former camp, which was before the walls of Geronium. Some authors affirm that they fought in regular line, and with encountering standards; that in the first encounter the Carthaginian was driven in disorder quite to his camp; but that, a sally thence having been suddenly made all at once, the Romans in their turn became alarmed; that after that the battle was restored by the arrival of Numerius Decimius the Samnite; that this man, the first in family and fortune, not only in Bovianum, whence he came, but in all Samnium, when conducting by command of the dictator to the camp eight thousand infantry and five hundred horse, having shown himself on the rear of Hannibal, seemed to both parties to be a fresh reinforcement coming with Quintus Fabius from Rome; that Hannibal, fearing also some ambuscade, withdrew his troops; and that the Roman, aided by the Samnite, pursuing him, took by storm two forts on that day; that six thousand of the enemy were slain, and about five thousand of the Romans; but that though the loss was so nearly equal, intelligence was conveyed to Rome of a signal victory; and a letter from the master of the horse still more presumptuous.

These things were very frequently discussed, both in the senate and assemblies. When the dictator alone, while joy pervaded the city, attached no credit to the report or letter; and granting that all were true, affirmed that he feared more from success than failure; then Marcus Metilius, a Plebeian tribune, declares that such conduct surely could not be endured. That the dictator, not only when present was an obstacle to the right management of the affair, but also being absent from the camp, opposed it still when achieved; that he studiously dallied in his conduct of the war, that he might continue the longer in office, and that he might have the sole command both at Rome and in the army. Since one of the consuls had fallen in battle, and the other was removed to a distance from Italy, under pretext of pursuing a Carthaginian fleet; and the two prætors were occupied in Sicily and Sardinia, neither of which provinces required a prætor at this time. That Marcus Minucius, the master of the horse, was almost put under a guard, lest he should see the enemy, and carry on any warlike operation. That therefore, by Hercules, not only Samnium, which had now been yielded to the Carthaginians, as if it had been land beyond the Iberus, but the Campanian, Calenian, and Falernian territories had been devastated, while the dictator was sitting down at Casilinum, protecting his own farm with the legions of the Roman people: that the army, eager for battle, as well as the master of the horse, were kept back almost imprisoned within the rampart: that their arms were taken out of their hands, as from captured enemies: at length, as soon as ever the dictator had gone away, having marched out beyond their rampart, that they had routed the enemy and put him to flight. On account of which circumstances, had the Roman commons retained their ancient spirit, that he would have boldly proposed to them to annul the authority of Quintus Fabius; but now he would bring forward a moderate proposition, to make the authority of the master of the horse and the dictator equal; and that even then Quintus Fabius should not be sent to the army, till he had substituted a consul in the room of Caius Flaminius. The dictator kept away from the popular assemblies, in which he did not command a favourable hearing, and even in the senate he was not heard with favourable ears, when his eloquence was employed in praising the enemy, and attributing the disasters of the last two years to the temerity and unskilfulness of the generals; and when he declared that the master of the horse ought to be called to account for having fought contrary to his injunction. That "if the supreme command and administration of affairs were intrusted to him, he would soon take care that men should know, that to a good general fortune was not of great importance; that prudence and conduct governed every thing; that it was more glorious for him to have saved the army at a crisis, and without disgrace, than to have slain many thousands of the enemy."

Speeches of this kind having been made without effect, and Marcus Atilius Regulus created consul, that he might not be present to dispute respecting the right of command, he withdrew to the army on the night preceding the day on which the proposition was to be decided. When there was an assembly of the people at break of day, a secret displeasure towards the dictator, and favour towards the master of the horse, rather possessed their minds, than that men had not sufficient resolution to advise a measure which was agreeable to the public; and though favour carried it, influence was wanting to the bill. One man indeed was found who recommended the law, Caius Terentius Varro, who had been prætor in the former year, sprung not only from humble but mean parentage. They report that his father was a butcher, the retailer of his own meat, and that he employed this very son in the servile offices of that trade.

This young man, when a fortune left him by his father, acquired in such a traffic, had inspired him with the hope of a higher condition, and the gown and forum were the objects of his choice, by declaiming vehemently in behalf of men and causes of the lowest kind, in opposition to the interest and character of the good, first came to the notice of the people, and then to offices of honour. Having passed through the offices of quæstor, plebeian, and curule ædile, and, lastly, that of prætor; when now he raised his mind to the hope of the consulship, he courted the gale of popular favour by maligning the dictator, and received alone the credit of the decree of the people. All men, both at Rome and in the army, both friends and foes, except the dictator himself, considered this measure to have been passed as an insult to him; but the dictator himself bore the wrong which the infuriated people had put upon him, with the same gravity with which he endured the charges against him which his enemies laid before the multitude; and receiving the letter containing a decree of the senate respecting the equalization of the command while on his journey, satisfied that an equal share of military skill was not imparted together with the equal share of command, he returned to the army with a mind unsubdued alike by his fellow-citizens and by the enemy.

But Minucius, who, in consequence of his success and the favour of the populace, was scarcely endurable before now especially, unrestrained by shame or moderation, boasted not more in having conquered Hannibal than Quintus Fabius. "That he, who had been sought out in their distress as the only general, and as a match for Hannibal; that he, an event which no record of history contains, was by the order of the people placed upon an equal footing with himself,—a superior with an inferior officer, a dictator with a master of the horse,—in that very city wherein the masters of the horse are wont to crouch and tremble at the rods and axes of the dictator. With such splendour had his valour and success shone forth. That he therefore would follow up his own good fortune, though the dictator persisted in his delay and sloth; measures condemned alike by the sentence of gods and men." Accordingly, on the first day on which he met Quintus Fabius, he intimated "that the first point to be settled was the manner in which they should employ the command thus equalized. That he was of opinion that the best plan would be for them to be invested with the supreme authority and command either on alternate days, or, if longer intervals were more agreeable, for any determinate periods; in order that the person in command might be a match for the enemy, not only in judgment, but in strength, if any opportunity for action should occur." Fabius by no means approved of this proposition: he said, "that Fortune would have at her disposal all things which the rashness of his colleague had; that his command had been shared with him, and not taken away; that he would never, therefore, willingly withdraw from conducting the war, in whatever post he could with prudence and discretion: nor would he divide the command with him with respect to times or days, but that he would divide the army, and that he would preserve, by his own measures, so much as he could, since it was not allowed him to save the whole." Thus he carried it, that, as was the custom of consuls, they should divide the legions between them: the first and fourth fell to the lot of Minucius, the second and third to Fabius. They likewise divided equally between them the cavalry, the auxiliaries of the allies and of the Latin name. The master of the horse was desirous also that they should have separate camps.

From this Hannibal derived a twofold joy, for nothing which was going on among the enemy escaped him, the deserters revealing many things, and he himself examining by his own scouts. For he considered that he should be able to entrap the unrestrained temerity of Minucius by his usual arts, and that half the force of the sagacity of Fabius had vanished. There was an eminence between the camps of Minucius and the Carthaginians, whoever occupied it would evidently render the position of his enemy less advantageous. Hannibal was not so desirous of gaining it without a contest, though that were worth his while, as to bring on a quarrel with Minucius, who, he well knew, would at all times throw himself in his way to oppose him. All the intervening ground was at first sight unavailable to one who wished to plant an ambuscade, because it not only had not any part that was woody, but none even covered with brambles, but in reality formed by nature to cover an ambush, so much the more, because no such deception could be apprehended in a naked valley and there were in its curvatures hollow rocks, such that some of them were capable of containing two hundred armed men. Within these recesses, five thousand infantry and cavalry are secreted, as many as could conveniently occupy each. Lest, however, in any part, either the motion of any one of them thoughtlessly coming out, or the glittering of their arms, should discover the stratagem in so open a valley, by sending out a few troops at break of day to occupy the before-mentioned eminence, he diverts the attention of the enemy. Immediately, on the first view of them, the smallness of their number was treated with contempt, and each man began to request for himself the task of dislodging the enemy. The general himself, among the most headstrong and absurd, calls to arms to go and seize the place, and inveighs against the enemy with vain presumption and menaces. First, he despatches his light-armed, after that his cavalry, in a close body, lastly, perceiving that succours were also being sent to the enemy, he marches with his legions drawn up in order of battle. Hannibal also, sending band after band, as the contest increased, as aids to his men when distressed, had now completed a regular army, and a battle was fought with the entire strength of both sides. First, the light infantry of the Romans, approaching the eminence, which was preoccupied, from the lower ground, being repulsed and pushed down, spread a terror among the cavalry, which was marching up also and fled back to the standards of the legions: the line of infantry alone stood fearless amidst the panic-struck; and it appeared that they would by no means have been inferior to the enemy, had it been a regular and open battle, so much confidence did the successful battle a few days before inspire. But the troops in ambush created such confusion and alarm, by charging them on both flanks and on their rear, that no one had spirit enough left to fight, or hope enough to try to escape.

Then Fabius, first having heard the shout of the terrified troops, and then having gotten a view of their disordered line, exclaims, "It is so; and no sooner than I feared, has adverse fortune overtaken temerity. Equalled to Fabius in command, he sees that Hannibal is superior to him in courage and in fortune. But another will be the time for reproaches and resentment. Now advance your standards beyond the rampart: let us wrest the victory from the enemy, and a confession of their error from our countrymen." A great part of the troops having been now slain, and the rest looking about for a way to escape; the army of Fabius showed itself on a sudden for their help, as if sent down from heaven. And thus, before he came within a dart's throw or joined battle, he both stayed his friends from a precipitate flight and the enemy from excessive fierceness of fighting. Those who had been scattered up and down, their ranks being broken, fled for refuge from every quarter to the fresh army; those who had fled together in parties, turning upon the enemy, now forming a circle, retreat slowly, now concentrating themselves, stand firm. And now the vanquished and the fresh army had nearly formed one line, and were bearing their standards against the enemy, when the Carthaginians sounded a retreat; Hannibal openly declaring that though he had conquered Minucius, he was himself conquered by Fabius. The greater part of the day having been thus consumed with varying success, Minucius calling together his soldiers, when they had returned to the camp, thus addressed them: "I have often heard, soldiers, that he is the greatest man who himself counsels what is expedient, and that he who listens to the man who gives good advice is the second, but that he who neither himself is capable of counselling, and knows not how to obey another, is of the lowest order of mind. Since the first place of mind and talent has been denied us, let us strive to obtain the second and intermediate kind, and while we are learning to command, let us prevail upon ourselves to submit to a man of prudence. Let us join camps with Fabius, and, carrying our standards to his pavilion, when I have saluted him as my parent, which he deserves on account of the service he has rendered us and of his dignity; you, my soldiers, shall salute those men as patrons, whose arms and right-hands just now protected you: and if this day has conferred nothing else upon us, it hath at least conferred upon us the glory of possessing grateful hearts."

The signal being given, there was a general call to collect the baggage: then setting out, and proceeding in order of march to the dictator's camp, they excited at once the surprise of the dictator himself and all around him. When the standards were planted before the tribunal, the master of the horse, advancing before the rest, having saluted Fabius as father, and the whole body of his troops having, with one voice, saluted the soldiers who surrounded him as patrons, said, "To my parents, dictator, to whom I have just now equalled you, only in name, as far as I could express myself, I am indebted for my life only; to you I owe both my own preservation and that of all these soldiers. That order of the people, therefore, with which I have been oppressed rather than honoured, I first cancel and annul, and (may it be auspicious to me and you, and to these your armies, to the preserved and the preserver,) I return to your authority and auspices, and restore to you these standards and these legions, and I entreat you that, being reconciled, you would order that I may retain the mastership of the horse, and that these soldiers may each of them retain their ranks." After that hands were joined, and when the assembly was dismissed, the soldiers were kindly and hospitably invited by those known to them and unknown: and that day, from having been a little while ago gloomy in the extreme, and almost accursed, was turned into a day of joy. At Rome, the report of the action was conveyed thither, and was afterwards confirmed, not less by letters from the common soldiers of both armies, than from the generals themselves, all men individually extolled Maximus to the skies. His renown was equal with Hannibal, and his enemies the Carthaginians and then at length they began to feel that they were engaged in war with Romans, and in Italy. For the two preceding years they entertained so utter a contempt for the Roman generals and soldiers, that they could scarcely believe that they were waging war with the same nation which their fathers had reported to them as being so formidable.

They relate also, that Hannibal said, as he returned from the field that at length that cloud, which was used to settle on the tops of the mountains, had sent down a shower with a storm.

While these events occur in Italy, Cneius Servilius Geminus, the consul, having sailed round the coast of Sardinia and Corsica with a fleet of one hundred and twenty ships, and received hostages from both places, crossed over into Africa, and before he made a descent upon the continent, having laid waste the island of Meninx, and received from the inhabitants of Cercina ten talents of silver, in order that their fields too might not be burnt and pillaged, he approached the shores of Africa, and landed his troops. Thence the soldiers were led out to plunder, and the crews scattered about just as if they were plundering uninhabited islands and thus, carelessly falling upon an ambuscade, when they were surrounded—the ignorant of the country by those acquainted with it, the straggling by those in close array, they were driven back to then ships in ignominious flight, and with great carnage. As many as one thousand men, together with Sempionius Blæsus, the quæstor, having been lost, the fleet hastily setting sail from the shore, which was crowded with the enemy, proceeded direct for Italy, and was given up at Lilybæum to Titus Otacilius, the prætor, that it might be taken back to Rome by his lieutenant, Publius Sura. The consul himself, proceeding through Sicily on foot, crossed the strait into Italy, summoned, as well as his colleague, Marcus Atilius, by a letter from Quintus Fabius, to receive the armies from him, as the period of his command, which was six months, had nearly expired. Almost all the annalists record that Fabius conducted the war against Hannibal, as dictator Cælius also writes, that he was the first dictator created by the people. But it has escaped Cælius and all the others that Cneius Servilius, the consul, who was then a long way from home in Gaul, which was his province, was the only person who possessed the right of appointing a dictator, and that as the state, terrified by the disasters which had just befallen it, could not abide the delay, it had recourse to the determination that the people should create a prodictator, that his subsequent achievements, his singular renown as a general, and his descendants, who exaggerated the inscription of his statue, easily brought it about that he should be called dictator, instead of prodictator.

The consuls, Atilius and Geminus Servilius, having received, the former the army of Fabius, the latter that of Minucius, and fortified their winter quarters in good time, (it was the close of the autumn,) carried on the war with the most perfect unanimity, according to the plans of Fabius. In many places they fell upon the troops of Hannibal when out on foraging excursions, availing themselves of the opportunity, and both harassing their march and intercepting the stragglers. They did not come to the chance of a general battle, which the enemy tried by every artifice to bring about. And Hannibal was so straitened by the want of provisions, that had he not feared in retiring the appearance of flight, he would have returned to Gaul, no hope being left of being able to subsist an army in those quarters, if the ensuing consuls should carry on the war upon the same plan. The war having been arrested in its progress at Geronium, the winter interrupting it, ambassadors from Naples came to Rome. They carried into the senate-house forty golden goblets, of great weight, and spoke to this effect. "That they knew the treasury of the Romans was exhausted by the war, and since the war was carried on alike in defence of the cities and the lands of the allies, and of the empire and city of Rome, the capital and citadel of Italy, that the Neapolitans thought it but fair that they should assist the Roman people with whatever gold had been left them by their ancestors as well for the decoration of their temples as for the relief of misfortune. If they had thought that there was any resource in themselves, that they would have offered it with the same zeal. That the Roman fathers and people would render an acceptable service to them, if they would consider all the goods of the Neapolitans as their own, and if they would think them deserving, that they should accept a present at their hands, rendered valuable and of consequence rather by the spirit and affection of those who gave it with cheerfulness, than by its intrinsic worth." Thanks were given to the ambassadors for their munificence and attention, and the goblet of least weight was accepted.

During the same days a Carthaginian spy, who had escaped for two years, was apprehended at Rome, and his hands having been cut off, was let go: and twenty-five slaves were crucified for forming a conspiracy in the Campus Martius; his liberty was given to the informer, and twenty thousand *asses* of the heavy standard. Ambassadors were also sent to Philip, king of the Macedonians, to demand Demetrius of Pharia, who, having been vanquished in war had fled to him. Others were sent to the Ligurians, to expostulate with them for having assisted the Carthaginians with their substance and with auxiliaries; and, at the same time, to take a near view of what was going on amongst the Boii and Insubrians. Ambassadors were also sent to the Illyrians to king Pineus, to demand the tribute, the day of payment of which had passed; or if he wished to postpone the day, to receive hostages. Thus, though an arduous war was on their shoulders, no attention to any one concern in any part of the world, however remote, escapes the Romans. It was made a matter of superstitious fear also, that the temple of Concord, which Lucius Manlius, the prætor, had vowed in Gaul two years ago, on occasion of a mutiny, had not been contracted for to that day. Accordingly, Cneius Pupius and Cæso Quinctius Flaminius, created duumviri by Marcus Æmilius, the city prætor, for that purpose, contract for the building a temple in the citadel. By the same prætor a letter was sent to the consuls, agreeably to a decree of the senate, to the effect that, if they thought proper, one of them should come to Rome to elect consuls; and that he would proclaim the election for whatever day they might name. To this it was replied by the consuls, that they could not leave the enemy without detriment to the public; that it would be better, therefore, that the election should be held by an interrex, than that one of the consuls should be called away from the war. It appeared more proper to the fathers, that a dictator should be nominated by a consul, for the purpose of holding the election Lucius Veturius Philo was nominated, who chose Manius Pomponius Matho master of the horse. These having been created with some defect, they were ordered to give up their appointment on the fourteenth day; and the state came to an interregnum.

To the consuls the authority was continued for a year longer. Caius Claudius Centho, son of Appius, and then Publius Cornelius Asina, were appointed interreges by the fathers. During the interregnum of the latter the election was held with a violent contest between the patricians and the people, Caius Terentius Varro, whom, as a man of their own order, commended to their favour by inveighing against the patricians and by other popular arts; who had acquired celebrity by maligning others, by undermining the influence of Fabius, and bringing into contempt the dictatorial authority, the commons strove to raise to the consulship. The patricians opposed him with all their might, lest men, by inveighing against them, should come to be placed on an equality with them. Quintus Bœbius Herennius, a plebeian tribune, and kinsman of Caius Terentius, by criminating not only the senate, but the augurs also, for having prevented the dictator from completing the election, by the odium cast upon them, conciliated favour to his own candidate. He asserted, "that Hannibal had been brought into Italy by the nobility, who had for many years been desirous of a war. That by the fraudulent machinations of the same persons the war had been protracted, whereas it might have been brought to a conclusion. That it had appeared that the war could be maintained with an army consisting of four legions in all, from Marcus Minucius's having fought with success in the absence of Fabius. That two legions had been exposed to be slain by the enemy, and were afterwards rescued from absolute destruction, in order that that man might be saluted as father and patron, who had deprived them of victory before he delivered them from defeat. That subsequently the consuls, pursuing the plans of Fabius, had protracted the war, whereas it was in their power to have put a period to it. That this was an agreement made by the nobility in general; nor would they ever have the war concluded till they had created a consul really plebeian; that is, a new man: for that plebeians who had attained nobility were now initiated into the mysteries, and had begun to look down with contempt upon plebeians, from the moment they ceased to be despised by the patricians. Who was not fully aware that their end and object was, that an interregnum should be formed, in order that the elections might be under the influence of the patricians? That both the consuls had that in view in tarrying with the army: and that afterwards a dictator having been nominated to hold the election contrary to their wishes, they had carried it, as it were, by storm, that the augurs should declare the dictator informally elected. That they therefore had gotten an interregnum; but one consulate was surely in the hands of the Roman people. Thus the people would have that at their own unbiassed disposal, and that they would confer it on that man who would rather conquer in reality than lengthen the term of his command."

When the people had been inflamed by these harangues, though there were three patrician candidates for the consulship, Publius Cornelius Merenda, Lucius Manlius Vulso, and Marcus Æmilius Lepidus, two of plebeian families, who had been ennobled, Caius Atilius Serranus and Quintus Ælius Pætus, one of whom was pontiff, the other an augur, Terentius alone was created consul, that the comitia for choosing his colleague might be in his own management. Then the nobles, finding that the competitors whom they had set up were not strong enough, though he strenuously refused for a long time, prevail upon Æmilius Paulus, who was strongly opposed to the people, to become a candidate. He had been consul before with Marcus Livius, and from the condemnation of his colleague, and almost of himself, had come off scathed. On the next day of the election, all who had opposed Varro withdrawing, he is given to the consul rather as a match to oppose him than as a colleague. Afterwards the assembly for the election of prætors was held, and Manius Pomponius Matho and Publius Furius Philus were chosen. The city lot for the administration of justice at Rome fell to the lot of Pomponius; between Roman citizens and foreigners, to Philus. Two prætors were added, Marcus Claudius Marcellus for Sicily, and Lucius Postumius for Gaul. These were all appointed in their absence; nor was an honour which he had not previously borne committed to any one of them, except the consul Terentius, several brave and able men having been passed over, because, at such a juncture, it did not appear advisable that a new office should be committed to any one.

The forces also were augmented. But how great was the augmentation of infantry and cavalry authors vary so much, that I scarcely dare positively assert. Some state, that ten thousand soldiers were levied as a reinforcement; others, four fresh legions, that there might be eight legions in service. It is said also, that the complement of the legion was increased in respect both to foot and horse, one thousand foot and one hundred horse being added to each, so that each might contain five thousand foot and three hundred horse; and that the allies furnished twice as many cavalry, and an equal number of infantry. Some authorities affirm that there were eighty-seven thousand two hundred soldiers in the Roman camp when the battle of Cannæ was fought. There is no dispute, that the war was prosecuted with greater energy and spirit than during former years, because the dictator had given them a hope that the enemy might be subdued. Before, however, the new-raised legions marched from the city, the decemviri were ordered to have recourse to and inspect the sacred volumes, on account of persons having been generally alarmed by extraordinary prodigies; for intelligence was brought, that it had rained stones on the Aventine at Rome and at Aricia at the same time. That among the Sabines, statues had sweated blood copiously, and at Cære the waters had flowed warm, from a fountain. The latter prodigy excited a greater degree of alarm, because it had frequently occurred. In a street called the Arched Way, near the Campus Martius, several men were struck by lightning and killed. These prodigies were expiated according to the books. Ambassadors from Paestum brought some golden goblets to Rome; they were thanked, as the Neapolitans were, but the gold was not accepted.

During the same time a fleet from Hiero arrived at Ostia with a large cargo of supplies. The Syracusan ambassadors, on being introduced into the senate, delivered this message: "That king Hiero was so much affected at the slaughter announced to him of Caius Flaminius the consul and his troops, that he could not have been more distressed at any disasters which could have befallen himself or his own kingdom; and accordingly, though he was well aware that the greatness of the Roman people was almost more admirable in adversity than prosperity, he had nevertheless sent every thing which good and faithful allies are wont to contribute to assist the operations of war, which he earnestly implored the conscript fathers not to refuse to accept. First of all, for the sake of the omen, they had brought a golden statue of Victory, of three hundred pounds' weight, which they begged them to accept, keep by them, and hold as their own peculiar and lasting possession. That they had also brought three hundred thousand pecks of wheat, and two hundred thousand of barley, that there might be no want of provisions, and that as much more as might be necessary they would convey, as a supply, to whatever place they might appoint. He knew that the Roman people employed no legionary troops or cavalry who were not Romans, or of the Latin confederacy, that he had seen foreign auxiliary as well as native light-armed troops in the Roman camps, he had, therefore, sent one thousand archers and slingers, a suitable force against the Baliares and Moors, and other nations which fought with missile weapons" To these presents they added also advice "That the prætor to whose lot the province of Sicily had fallen, should pass a fleet over to Africa, that the enemy also might have a war in their own country, and that less liberty should be afforded them of sending reinforcements to Hannibal" The senate thus replied to the king. "That Hiero was a good man and an admirable ally, and that from the time he first formed a friendship with the Roman people he had uniformly cultivated a spirit of fidelity, and had munificently assisted the Roman cause at all times and in every place. That this was, as it ought to be, a cause of gratitude to the Roman people. That the Roman people had not accepted gold which had been brought them also from certain states, though they felt gratitude for the act. The Victory and the omen," they said, "they would accept, and would assign and dedicate to that goddess, as her abode, the Capitol, the temple of Jupiter, the best and greatest of gods, hoping that, consecrated in that fortress of the city of Rome, she would continue there firm and immoveable, kind and propitious to the Roman people." The slingers, archers, and corn were handed over to the consuls. To the fleet which Titus Otacilius the proprietor had in Sicily, twenty-five quinqueremes were added, and permission was given him, if he thought it for the interest of the state to pass over into Africa.

The levy completed, the consuls waited a few days, till the allies of the Latin confederacy arrived. At this time the soldiers were bound by an oath, which had never before been the case, dictated by the military tribunes, that they would assemble at the command of the consuls, and not depart without orders; for up to that time the military oath only had been employed; and further, when the soldiers met to divide into decuries or centuries, the cavalry being formed into decuries and the infantry into centuries, all swore together, amongst themselves, of their own accord, that they would not depart or quit their ranks for flight or fear, except for the purpose of taking up or fetching a weapon, and either striking an enemy or saving a countryman. This, from being a voluntary compact among the soldiers themselves, was converted into the legal compulsion of an oath by the tribunes. Before the standards were moved from the city, the harangues of Varro were frequent and furious, protesting that the war had been invited into Italy by the nobles, and that it would continue fixed in the bowels of the state if it employed any more such generals as Fabius; that he would bring the war to conclusion on the very day he got sight of the enemy. His colleague Paulus made but one speech, on the day before they set out from the city, which was more true than gratifying to the people, in which nothing was said severely against Varro, except this only. "That he wondered how any general, before he knew any thing of his own army, or that of the enemy, the situation of the places, or the nature of the country, even now while in the city, and with the gown on, could tell what he must do when in arms, and could even foretell the day on which he would fight standard to standard with the enemy. That, for his own part, he would not, before the time arrived, prematurely anticipate those measures which circumstances imposed on men, rather than men on circumstances. He could only wish that those measures which were taken with due caution and deliberation might turn out prosperously. That temerity, setting aside its folly, had hitherto been also unsuccessful." This obviously appeared, that he would prefer safe to precipitate counsels; but that he might persevere the more constantly in this, Quintus Fabius Maximus is reported to have thus addressed him on his departure.

"If you either had a colleague like yourself, Lucius Æmilius, which is what I should prefer, or you were like your colleague, an address from me would be superfluous. For were you both good consuls, you would do every thing for the good of the state from your own sense of honour, even without my saying a word: and were you both bad consuls, you would neither receive my words into your ears, nor my counsels into your minds. As the case now is, looking at your colleague and yourself, a man of such character, my address will be solely to you; who, I feel convinced, will prove yourself a good man and a worthy citizen in vain, if the state on the other hand should halt. Pernicious counsels will have the same authority and influence as those which are sound. For you are mistaken, Lucius Paulus, if you imagine that you will have a less violent contest with Caius Terentius than with Hannibal. I know not whether the former, your opponent, or the latter, your open enemy, be the more hostile. With the latter you will have to contend in the field only; with the former, at every place and time. Hannibal, moreover, you have to oppose with your own horse and foot; while Varro will head your own soldiers against you. Let Caius Flaminius be absent from your thoughts, even for the omen's sake. Yet he only began to play the madman's consul, in his province, and at the head of the army. This man is raving before he put up for the consulship, afterwards while canvassing for it, and now having obtained it, before he has seen the camp or the enemy. And he who by talking largely of battles and marshalled armies, even now excites such storms among the citizens with their gowns on, what do you think he will effect among the youth in arms, where words are followed forthwith by acts? But be assured, if this man, as he protests he will, shall immediately engage the enemy either I am unacquainted with military affairs, with this kind of war, and the character of the enemy, or another place will become more celebrated than the Trasimenus by our disaster. Neither is this the season for boasting while I am addressing one man; and besides, I have exceeded the bounds of moderation in despising rather than in courting fame. But the case is really this. The only way of conducting the war against Hannibal is that which I adopted: nor does the event only, that instructor of fools, demonstrate it, but that same reasoning which has continued hitherto, and will continue unchangeable so long as circumstances shall remain the same. We are carrying on war in Italy, in our own country, and our own soil. All around us are countrymen and allies in abundance. With arms, men, horses, and provisions, they do and will assist us. Such proofs of their fidelity have they given in our adversity. Time, nay, everyday makes us better, wiser, and firmer. Hannibal, on the contrary, is in a foreign, a hostile land, amidst all hostile and disadvantageous circumstances, far from his home, far from his country; he has peace neither by land nor sea: no cities, no walls receive him: he sees nothing any where which he can call his own: he daily lives by plunder. He has now scarcely a third part of that army which he conveyed across the Iberus. Famine has destroyed more than the sword; nor have the few remaining a sufficient supply of provisions. Do you doubt, therefore, whether by remaining quiet we shall not conquer him who is daily sinking into decrepitude? who has neither provisions nor money? How long before the walls of Geronium, a miserable fortress of Apulia, as if before the walls of Carthage—? But not even in your presence will I boast. See how Cneius Servilius and Atilius, the last consuls, fooled him. This is the only path of safety, Lucius Paulus, which your countrymen will render more difficult and dangerous to you than their enemies will. For your own soldiers will desire the same thing as those of the enemy: Varro, a Roman consul, and Hannibal, a Carthaginian general, will wish the same thing. You alone must resist two generals: and you will resist them sufficiently if you stand firm against the report and the rumours of men; if neither the empty glory of your colleague, and the unfounded calumnies against yourself, shall move you. They say that truth too often suffers, but is never destroyed. He who despises fame will have it genuine. Let them call you coward instead of cautious, dilatory instead of considerate, unwarlike instead of an expert general. I would rather that a sagacious enemy should fear you, than that foolish countrymen should commend you. A man who hazards all things Hannibal will despise, him who does nothing rashly he will fear. And neither do I advise that nothing should be done; but that in what you do, reason should guide you, and not fortune. All things will be within your own power, and your own. Be always ready armed and on the watch, and neither be wanting when a favourable opportunity presents itself, nor give any favourable opportunity to the enemy. All things are clear and sure to the deliberate man. Precipitation is improvident and blind."

The address of the consul in reply was by no means cheerful, admitting that what he said was true, rather than easy to put in practice. He said, "That to him, as dictator, his master of the horse was unbearable: what power or influence could a consul have against a factious and intemperate colleague? That he had in his former consulate escaped a popular conflagration not without being singed: his prayer was, that every thing might happen prosperously; but if, on the contrary, any misfortune should occur, that he would rather expose his life to the weapons of the enemy, than to the votes of his incensed countrymen." Directly after this discourse, it is related that Paulus set out, escorted by the principal senators. The plebeian consul attended his own plebeian party, more distinguished by their numbers than respectability. When they had arrived at the camp, the old and new troops being united, they formed two distinct camps, so that the new and smaller one might be the nearer to Hannibal, and the old one might contain the greater part, and all the choicest of the troops. They then sent to Rome Marcus Atilius, the consul of the former year, who alleged his age in excuse. They appoint Geminus Servilius to the command of a Roman legion, and two thousand of the allied infantry and cavalry in the lesser camp. Hannibal, although he perceived that the forces of the enemy were augmented by one-half, was yet wonderfully rejoiced at the arrival of the consuls; for he had not only nothing remaining of the provisions which he daily acquired by plunder, but there was not even any thing left which he could seize, the corn in all the surrounding country having been collected into fortified cities, when the country was too unsafe; so that, as was afterwards discovered, there scarcely remained corn enough for ten days, and the Spaniards would have passed over to the enemy, through want of food, if the completion of that time had been awaited.

But fortune afforded materials also to the headstrong and precipitate disposition of the consul, for in checking the plundering parties a battle having taken place, of a tumultuary kind, and occasioned rather by a disorderly advance of the soldiers, than by a preconcerted plan, or by the command of the general, the contest was by no means equal with the Carthaginians. As many as one thousand seven hundred of them were slain, but not more than one hundred of the Romans and allies. The consul Paulus, however, who was in command on that day, (for they held the command on alternate days,) apprehending an ambuscade, restrained the victorious troops in their headstrong pursuit; while Varro indignantly vociferated, that the enemy had been allowed to slip out of their hands, and that the war might have been terminated had not the pursuit been stopped. Hannibal was not much grieved at that loss; nay, rather he felt convinced, that the temerity of the more presumptuous consul, and of the soldiers, particularly the fresh ones, would be lured by the bait; and besides, all the circumstances of the enemy were as well known to him as his own: that dissimilar and discordant men were in command; that nearly two-thirds of the army consisted of raw recruits. Accordingly, concluding that he now had both a time and place adapted for an ambuscade, on the following night he led his troops away with nothing but their arms, leaving the camp filled with all their effects, both public and private. His infantry drawn up he conceals on the left, on the opposite side of the adjoining hills; his cavalry on the right; his baggage in an intermediate line he leads over the mountains through a valley, in order that he might surprise the enemy when busy in plundering the camp, deserted, as they would imagine, by its owners, and when encumbered with booty. Numerous fires were left in the camp, to produce a belief that his intention was to keep the consuls in their places by the appearance of a camp, until he could himself escape to a greater distance, in the same manner as he had deceived Fabius the year before.

When it was day, the outpost withdrawn first occasioned surprise, then, on a nearer approach, the unusual stillness. At length, the desertion being manifest, there is a general rush to the pavilions of the consuls, of those who announced the flight of the enemy so precipitate, that they left their camp, with their tents standing; and, that their flight might be the more secret, that numerous fires were left. Then a clamour arose that they should order the standards to be advanced, and lead them in pursuit of the enemy, and to the immediate plunder of the camp. The other consul too was as one of the common soldiers. Paulus again and again urged, that they should see their way before them, and use every precaution. Lastly, when he could no longer withstand the sedition and the leader of the sedition, he sends Marius Statilius, a prefect, with a Lucanian troop, to reconnoitre, who, when he had ridden up to the gates, ordered the rest to stay without the works, and entered the camp himself, attended by two horsemen. Having carefully examined every thing, he brings back word that it was manifestly a snare: that fires were left in that part of the camp which faced the enemy: that the tents were open, and that all their valuables were left exposed: that in some places he had seen silver carelessly thrown about the passages, as if laid there for plunder. This intelligence, which it was hoped would deter their minds from greediness, inflamed them; and the soldiers clamorously declaring, that unless the signal was given they would advance without their leaders, they by no means wanted one, for Varro instantly gave the signal for marching. Paulus, whom, unwilling from his own suggestions to move, the chickens had not encouraged by their auspices, ordered the unlucky omen to be reported to his colleague, when he was now leading the troops out of the gate. And though Varro bore it impatiently, yet the recent fate of Flaminius, and the recorded naval defeat of Claudius, the consul in the first Punic war, struck religious scruples into his mind. The gods themselves (it might almost be said) rather postponed than averted the calamity which hung over the Romans; for it fell out by mere accident, that when the soldiers did not obey the consul who ordered them to return to the camp, two slaves, one belonging to a horseman of Formiæ, the other to one of Sidicinum, who had been cut off by the Numidians among a party of foragers, when Servilius and Atilius were consuls, had escaped on that day to their masters: and being brought into the presence of the consuls, inform them that the whole army of Hannibal was lying in ambush on the other side of the adjoining mountains. The seasonable arrival of these men restored the consuls to their authority, when the ambition of one of them had relaxed his influence with the soldiers, by an undignified compliance.

Hannibal, perceiving that the Romans had been indiscreetly prompted rather than rashly carried to a conclusion, returned to his camp without effecting any thing, as his stratagem was discovered. He could not remain there many days, in consequence of the scarcity of corn; and, moreover, not only among the soldiers, who were mixed up of the off-scouring of various nations, but even with the general himself, day by day new designs arose: for, first, when there had been murmuring of the soldiers, and then an open and clamorous demand of their arrears of pay, and a complaint first of the scarcity of provisions, and lastly of famine; and there being a report that the mercenaries, particularly the Spanish, had formed a plan of passing over to the enemy, it is affirmed that Hannibal himself too sometimes entertained thoughts of flying into Gaul, so that, having left all his infantry, he might hurry away with his cavalry. Such being the plans in agitation, and such the state of feeling in the camp, he resolved to depart thence into the regions of Apulia, which were warmer, and therefore earlier in the harvest. Thinking also, that the farther he retired from the enemy, the more difficult would desertion be to the wavering. He set out by night, having, as before, kindled fires, and leaving a few tents to produce an appearance; that a fear of an ambuscade, similar to the former, might keep the Romans in their places. But when intelligence was brought by the same Lucanian Statilius, who had reconnoitred every place on the other side the mountains, and beyond the camp, that the enemy was seen marching at a distance, then plans began to be deliberated on about pursuing him. The consuls persisted in the same opinions they ever entertained; but nearly all acquiesced with Varro, and none with Paulus except Servilius, the consul of the former year. In compliance with the opinion of the majority, they set out, under the impulse of destiny, to render Cannæ celebrated by a Roman disaster.

Hannibal had pitched his camp near that village, with his back to the wind Vulturnus, which, in those plains which are parched with drought, carries with it clouds of dust. This circumstance was not only very advantageous to the camp, but would be a great protection to them when they formed their line; as they, with the wind blowing only on their backs, would combat with an enemy blinded with the thickly blown dust.

When the consuls, employing sufficient diligence in exploring the road in pursuit of the Carthaginian, had arrived at Cannæ, where they had the enemy in the sight of them, having divided their forces, they fortify two camps with nearly the same interval as before, at Geronium. The river Aufidus, which flowed by both the camps, afforded approach to the watering parties of each, as opportunity served, though not without contest. The Romans in the lesser camp, however, which was on the other side the Aufidus, were more freely furnished with water, because the further bank had no guard of the enemy. Hannibal, entertaining a hope that the consuls would not decline a battle in this tract, which was naturally adapted to a cavalry engagement, in which portion of his forces he was invincible, formed his line, and provoked the enemy by a skirmishing attack with his Numidians. Upon this the Roman camp began again to be embroiled by a mutiny among the soldiers, and the disagreement of the consuls: since Paulus instanced to Varro the temerity of Sempronius and Flaminius; while Varro pointed to Fabius, as a specious example to timid and inactive generals. The latter called both gods and men to witness, "that no part of the blame attached to him that Hannibal had now made Italy his own, as it were, by right of possession; that he was held bound by his colleague; that the swords and arms were taken out of the hands of the indignant soldiers who were eager to fight." The former declared, "that if any disaster should befall the legions thus exposed and betrayed into an ill-advised and imprudent battle, he should be exempt from any blame, though the sharer of all the consequences. That he must take care that their hands were equally energetic in the battle whose tongues were so forward and impetuous."

While time is thus consumed in altercation rather than deliberating, Hannibal, who had kept his troops drawn up in order of battle till late in the day, when he had led the rest of them back into the camp, sends Numidians across the river to attack a watering party of the Romans from the lesser camp. Having routed this disorderly band by shouting and tumult, before they had well reached the opposite bank, they advanced even to an outpost which was before the rampart, and near the, very gates of the camp. It seemed so great an indignity, that now even the camp of the Romans should be terrified by a tumultuary band of auxiliaries, that this cause alone kept back the Romans from crossing the river forthwith, and forming their line, that the chief command was on that day held by Paulus. Accordingly Varro, on the following day, on which it was his turn to hold the command, without consulting his colleague, displayed the signal for battle, and forming his troops, led them across the river. Paulus followed, because he could better disapprove of the proceeding, than withhold his assistance. Having crossed the river, they add to their forces those which they had in the lesser camp; and thus forming their line, place the Roman cavalry in the right wing, which was next the river; and next them the infantry: at the extremity of the left wing the allied cavalry; within them the allied infantry, extending to the centre, and contiguous to the Roman legions. The darters, and the rest of the light-armed auxiliaries, formed the van. The consuls commanded the wings; Terentius the left, Æmilius the right. To Geminus Servilius was committed the charge of maintaining the battle in the centre.

Hannibal, at break of day, having sent before him the Baliares and other light-armed troops, crossed the river, and placed his troops in line of battle, as he had conveyed them across the river. The Gallic and Spanish cavalry he placed in the left wing, opposite the Roman cavalry: the right wing was assigned to the Numidian cavalry, the centre of the line being strongly formed by the infantry, so that both extremities of it were composed of Africans, between which Gauls and Spaniards were placed. One would suppose the Africans were for the most part Romans, they were so equipped with arms captured at the Trebia, and for the greater part at the Trasimenus. The shields of the Gauls and Spaniards were of the same shape; their swords unequal and dissimilar. The Gauls had very long ones, without points. The Spaniards, who were accustomed to stab more than to cut their enemy, had swords convenient from their shortness, and with points. The aspect of these nations in other respects was terrific, both as to the appearance they exhibited and the size of their persons. The Gauls were naked above the navel: the Spaniards stood arrayed in linen vests resplendent with surprising whiteness, and bordered with purple. The whole amount of infantry standing in battle-array was forty thousand, of cavalry ten. The generals who commanded the wings were on the left Hasdrubal, on the right Maharbal: Hannibal himself, with his brother Mago, commanded the centre. The sun very conveniently shone obliquely upon both parties; the Romans facing the south, and the Carthaginians the north; either placed so designedly, or having stood thus by chance. The wind, which the inhabitants of the district call the Vulturnus, blowing violently in front of the Romans, prevented their seeing far by rolling clouds of dust into their faces.

The shout being raised, the auxiliaries charged, and the battle commenced in the first place with the light-armed troops: then the left wing, consisting of the Gallic and Spanish cavalry, engages with the Roman right wing, by no means in the manner of a cavalry battle; for they were obliged to engage front to front; for as on one side the river, on the other the line of infantry hemmed them in, there was no space left at their flanks for evolution, but both parties were compelled to press directly forward. At length the horses standing still, and being crowded together, man grappling with man, dragged him from his horse. The contest now came to be carried on principally on foot. The battle, however, was more violent than lasting; and the Roman cavalry being repulsed, turn their backs. About the conclusion of the contest between the cavalry, the battle between the infantry commenced. At first the Gauls and Spaniards preserved their ranks unbroken, not inferior in strength or courage: but at length the Romans, after long and repeated efforts, drove in with their even front and closely compacted line, that part of the enemy's line in the form of a wedge, which projected beyond the rest, which was too thin, and therefore deficient in strength. These men, thus driven back and hastily retreating, they closely pursued; and as they urged their course without interruption through this terrified band, as it fled with precipitation, were borne first upon the centre line of the enemy; and lastly, no one opposing them, they reached the African reserved troops. These were posted at the two extremities of the line, where it was depressed; while the centre, where the Gauls and Spaniards were placed, projected a little. When the wedge thus formed being driven in, at first rendered the line level, but afterwards, by the pressure, made a curvature in the centre, the Africans, who had now formed wings on each side of them, surrounded the Romans on both sides, who incautiously rushed into the intermediate space; and presently extending their wings, enclosed the enemy on the rear also. After this the Romans, who had in vain finished one battle, leaving the Gauls and Spaniards, whose rear they had slaughtered, in addition commence a fresh encounter with the Africans, not only disadvantageous, because being hemmed in they had to fight against troops who surrounded them, but also because, fatigued, they fought with those who were fresh and vigorous.

Now also in the left wing of the Romans, in which the allied cavalry were opposed to the Numidians, the battle was joined, which was at first languid, commencing with a stratagem on the part of the Carthaginians. About five hundred Numidians, who, besides their usual arms, had swords concealed beneath their coats of mail, quitting their own party, and riding up to the enemy under the semblance of deserters, with their bucklers behind them, suddenly leap down from their horses; and, throwing down their bucklers and javelins at the feet of their enemies, are received into their centre, and being conducted to the rear, ordered to remain there; and there they continued until the battle became general. But afterwards, when the thoughts and attention of all were occupied with the contest, snatching up the shields which lay scattered on all hands among the heaps of slain, they fell upon the rear of the Roman line, and striking their backs and wounding their hams, occasioned vast havoc, and still greater panic and confusion. While in one part terror and flight prevailed, in another the battle was obstinately persisted in, though with little hope. Hasdrubal, who was then commanding in that quarter, withdrawing the Numidians from the centre of the army, as the conflict with their opponents was slight, sends them in pursuit of the scattered fugitives, and joining the Africans, now almost weary with slaying rather than fighting the Spanish and Gallic infantry.

On the other side of the field, Paulus, though severely wounded from a sling in the very commencement of the battle, with a compact body of troops, frequently opposed himself to Hannibal, and in several quarters restored the battle, the Roman cavalry protecting him; who, at length, when the consul had not strength enough even to manage his horse, dismounted from their horses. And when some one brought intelligence that the consul had ordered the cavalry to dismount, it is said that Hannibal observed, "How much rather would I that he delivered them to me in chains." The fight maintained by the dismounted cavalry was such as might be expected, when the victory was undoubtedly on the side of the enemy, the vanquished preferring death in their places to flight; and the conquerors, who were enraged at them for delaying the victory, butchering those whom they could not put to flight. They at length, however, drove the few who remained away, worn out with exertion and wounds. After that they were all dispersed, and such as could, sought to regain their horses for flight. Cneius Lentulus, a military tribune, seeing, as he rode by, the consul sitting upon a stone and covered with blood, said to him: "Lucius Æmilius! the only man whom the gods ought to regard as being guiltless of this day's disaster, take this horse, while you have any strength remaining, and I am with you to raise you up and protect you. Make not this battle more calamitous by the death of a consul. There is sufficient matter for tears and grief without this addition." In reply the consul said: "Do thou indeed go on and prosper, Cneius Servilius, in your career of virtue! But beware lest you waste in bootless commiseration the brief opportunity of escaping from the hands of the enemy. Go and tell the fathers publicly, to fortify the city of Rome, and garrison it strongly before the victorious enemy arrive: and tell Quintus Fabius individually, that Lucius Æmilius lived, and now dies, mindful of his injunctions. Allow me to expire amid these heaps of my slaughtered troops, that I may not a second time be accused after my consulate, or stand forth as the accuser of my colleague, in order to defend my own innocence by criminating another." While finishing these words, first a crowd of their flying countrymen, after that the enemy, came upon them; they overwhelm the consul with their weapons, not knowing who he was: in the confusion his horse rescued Lentulus. After that they fly precipitately. Seven thousand escaped to the lesser camp, ten to the greater, about two thousand to the village itself of Cannæ who were immediately surrounded by Carthalo and the cavalry, no fortifications protecting the village. The other consul, whether by design or by chance, made good his escape to Venusia with about seventy horse, without mingling with any party of the flying troops. Forty thousand foot, two thousand seven hundred horse, there being an equal number of citizens and allies, are said to have been slain. Among both the quæstors of the consuls, Lucius Atilius and Lucius Furius Bibaculus; twenty-one military tribunes; several who had passed the offices of consul, prætor, and ædile; among these they reckon Cneius Servilius Germinus, and Marcus Minucius, who had been master of the horse on a former year, and consul some years before: moreover eighty, either senators, or who had borne those offices by which they might be elected into the senate, and who had voluntarily enrolled themselves in the legions. Three thousand infantry and three hundred cavalry are said to have been captured in that battle.

Such is the battle of Cannæ, equal in celebrity to the defeat at the Allia: but as it was less important in respect to those things which happened after it, because the enemy did not follow up the blow, so was it more important and more horrible with respect to the slaughter of the army; for with respect to the flight at the Allia, as it betrayed the city, so it preserved the army. At Cannæ, scarcely seventy accompanied the flying consul: almost the whole army shared the fate of the other who died. The troops collected in the two camps being a half-armed multitude without leaders, those in the larger send a message to the others, that they should come over to them at night, when the enemy was oppressed with sleep, and wearied with the battle, and then, out of joy, overpowered with feasting: that they would go in one body to Canusium. Some entirely disapproved of that advice. "For why," said they, "did not those who sent for them come themselves, since there would be equal facility of forming a junction? Because, evidently, all the intermediate space was crowded with the enemy, and they would rather expose the persons of others to so great a danger than their own." Others did not so much disapprove, as want courage to fulfil the advice. Publius Sempronius Tuditanus, a military tribune, exclaims, "Would you rather, then, be captured by the most rapacious and cruel enemy, and have a price set upon your heads, and have your value ascertained by men who will ask whether you are Roman citizens or Latin confederates, in order that from your miseries and indignities honour may be sought for another? Not you, at least, if you are the fellow-citizens of Lucius Æmilius, the consul who preferred an honourable death to a life of infamy, and of so many brave men who lie heaped around him. But, before the light overtakes us and more numerous bodies of the enemy beset the way, let us break through those disorderly and irregular troops who are making a noise at our gates. By the sword and courage, a road may be made through enemies, however dense. In a wedge we shall make our way through this loose and disjointed band, as if nothing opposed us. Come along with me therefore, ye who wish the safety of yourselves and the state." Having thus said, he draws his sword, and forming a wedge, goes through the midst of the enemy; and as the Numidians discharged their javelins on their right side, which was exposed, they transferred their shields to the right hand, and thus escaped, to the number of six hundred, to the greater camp; and setting out thence forthwith, another large body having joined them, arrived safe at Canusium. These measures were taken by the vanquished, according to the impulse of their tempers, which his own disposition or which accident gave to each, rather than in consequence of any deliberate plan of their own, or in obedience to the command of any one.

When all others, surrounding the victorious Hannibal, congratulated him, and advised that, having completed so great a battle, he should himself take the remainder of the day and the ensuing night for rest, and grant it to his exhausted troops; Maharbal, prefect of the cavalry, who was of opinion that no time should be lost, said to him, "Nay, rather, that you may know what has been achieved by this battle, five days hence you shall feast in triumph in the Capitol. Follow me: I will go first with the cavalry, that they may know that I am arrived before they know of me as approaching." To Hannibal this project appeared too full of joy, and too great for his mind to embrace it and determine upon it at the instant. Accordingly, he replied to Maharbal, that "he applauded his zeal, but that time was necessary to ponder the proposal." Upon this Maharbal observed, "Of a truth the gods have not bestowed all things upon the same person. You know how to conquer, Hannibal; but you do not know how to make use of your victory." That day's delay is firmly believed to have been the preservation of the city and the empire. On the following day, as soon as it dawned, they set about gathering the spoils and viewing the carnage, which was shocking, even to enemies. So many thousands of Romans were lying, foot and horse promiscuously, according as accident had brought them together, either in the battle or in the flight. Some, whom their wounds, pinched by the morning cold, had roused, as they were rising up, covered with blood, from the midst of the heaps of slain, were overpowered by the enemy. Some too they found lying alive with their thighs and hams cut who, laying bare their necks and throats, bid them drain the blood that remained in them. Some were found with their heads plunged into the earth, which they had excavated; having thus, as it appeared, made pits for themselves, and having suffocated themselves by overwhelming their faces with the earth which they threw over them. A living Numidian, with lacerated nose and ears, stretched beneath a lifeless Roman who lay upon him, principally attracted the attention of all; for when his hands were powerless to grasp his weapon, turning from rage to madness, he had died in the act of tearing his antagonist with his teeth.

The spoils having been gathered for a great part of the day, Hannibal leads his troops to storm the lesser camp, and, first of all, interposing a trench, cuts it off from the river. But as the men were fatigued with toil, watching, and wounds, a surrender was made sooner than he expected. Having agreed to deliver up their arms and horses, on condition that the ransom of every Roman should be three hundred denarii, for an ally two hundred, for a slave one hundred, and that on payment of that ransom they should be allowed to depart with single garments, they received the enemy into the camp, and were all delivered into custody, the citizens and allies being kept separate. While the time is being spent there, all who had strength or spirit enough, to the number of four thousand foot and two hundred horse, quitted the greater camp and arrived at Canusium; some in a body, others widely dispersed through the country, which was no less secure a course: the camp itself was surrendered to the enemy by the wounded and timid troops, on the same terms as the other was. A very great booty was obtained; and with the exception of the men and horses, and what silver there was which was for the most part on the trappings of the horses; for they had but very little in use for eating from, particularly in campaign; all the rest of the booty was given up to be plundered. Then he ordered the bodies of his own troops to be collected for burial. They are said to have been as many as eight thousand of his bravest men. Some authors relate, that the Roman consul also was carefully searched for and buried. Those who escaped to Canusium, being received by the people of that place within their walls and houses only, were assisted with corn, clothes, and provisions for their journey, by an Apulian lady, named Busa, distinguished for her family and riches; in return for which munificence, the senate afterwards, when the war was concluded, conferred honours upon her.

But, though there were four military tribunes there, Fabius Maximus of the first legion, whose father had been dictator the former year; and of the second legion, Lucius Publicius Bibulus and Publius Cornelius Scipio; and of the third legion, Appius Claudius Pulcher, who had been ædile the last year; by the consent of all, the supreme command was vested in Publius Scipio, then a very young man, and Appius Claudius. To these, while deliberating with a few others on the crisis of their affairs, Publius Furius Philus, the son of a man of consular dignity, brings intelligence, "That it was in vain that they cherished hopes which could never be realized: that the state was despaired of, and lamented as lost. That certain noble youths, the chief of whom was Lucius Cæcilius Metellus, turned their attention to the sea and ships, in order that, abandoning Italy, they might escape to some king." When this calamity, which was not only dreadful in itself, but new, and in addition to the numerous disasters they had sustained, had struck them motionless with astonishment and stupor; and while those who were present gave it as their opinion that a council should be called to deliberate upon it, young Scipio, the destined general of this war, asserts, "That it is not a proper subject for deliberation: that courage and action, and not deliberation, were necessary in so great a calamity. That those who wished the safety of the state would attend him forthwith in arms; that in no place was the camp of the enemy more truly, than where such designs were meditated." He immediately proceeds, attended by a few, to the lodging of Metellus; and finding there the council of youths of which he had been apprized, he drew his sword over the heads of them, deliberating, and said, "With sincerity of soul I swear that neither will I myself desert the cause of the Roman republic, nor will I suffer any other citizen of Rome to desert it. If knowingly I violate my oath, then, O Jupiter, supremely great and good, mayest thou visit my house, my family, and my fortune with perdition the most horrible! I require you, Lucius Cæcilius, and the rest of you who are present, to take this oath; and let the man who shall not take it be assured, that this sword is drawn against him." Terrified, as though they were beholding the victorious Hannibal, they all take the oath, and deliver themselves to Scipio to be kept in custody.

During the time in which these things were going on at Canusium, as many as four thousand foot and horse, who had been dispersed through the country in the flight, came to Venusia, to the consul. These the Venusini distributed throughout their families, to be kindly entertained and taken care of; and also gave to each horseman a gown, a tunic, and twenty-five denarii; and to each foot soldier ten denarii, and such arms as they wanted; and every other kind of hospitality showed them, both publicly and privately: emulously striving that the people of Venusia might not be surpassed by a woman of Canusium in kind offices. But the great number of her guests rendered the burden more oppressive to Busa, for they amounted now to ten thousand men. Appius and Scipio, having heard that the other consul was safe, immediately send a messenger to inquire how great a force of infantry and cavalry he had with him, and at the same time to ask, whether it was his pleasure that the army should be brought to Venusia, or remain at Canusium. Varro himself led over his forces to Canusium. And now there was some appearance of a consular army, and they seemed able to defend themselves from the enemy by walls, if not by arms. At Rome intelligence had been received, that not even these relics of their citizens and allies had survived, but that the two consuls, with their armies, were cut to pieces, and all their forces annihilated. Never when the city was in safety was there so great a panic and confusion within the walls of Rome. I shall therefore shrink from the task, and not attempt to relate what in describing I must make less than the reality. The consul and his army having been lost at the Trasimenus the year before, it was not one wound upon another which was announced, but a multiplied disaster, the loss of two consular armies, together with the two consuls: and that now there was neither any Roman camp, nor general nor soldiery: that Apulia and Samnium, and now almost the whole of Italy, were in the possession of Hannibal. No other nation surely would not have been overwhelmed by such an accumulation of misfortune. Shall I compare with it the disaster of the Carthaginians, sustained in a naval battle at the islands Ægates, dispirited by which they gave up Sicily and Sardinia, and thenceforth submitted to become tributary and stipendiary? Or shall I compare with it the defeat in Africa under which this same Hannibal afterwards sunk? In no respect are they comparable, except that they were endured with less fortitude.

Publius Furius Philus and Manius Pomponius, the prætors, assembled the senate in the curia hostilia, that they might deliberate about the guarding of the city; for they doubted not but that the enemy, now their armies were annihilated, would come to assault Rome, the only operation of the war which remained. Unable to form any plan in misfortunes, not only very great, but unknown and undefined, and while the loud lamentations of the women were resounding, and nothing was as yet made known, the living and the dead alike being lamented in almost every house; such being the state of things, Quintus Fabius gave it as his opinion, "That light horsemen should be sent out on the Latin and Appian ways, who, questioning those they met, as some would certainly be dispersed in all directions from the flight, might bring back word what was the fate of the consuls and their armies; and if the gods, pitying the empire, had left any remnant of the Roman name where these forces were; whither Hannibal had repaired after the battle, what he was meditating; what he was doing, or about to do. That these points should be searched out and ascertained by active youths. That it should be the business of the fathers, since there was a deficiency of magistrates, to do away with the tumult and trepidation in the city; to keep the women from coming into public, and compel each to abide within her own threshold; to put a stop to the lamentations of families; to obtain silence in the city; to take care that the bearers of every kind of intelligence should be brought before the prætors; that each person should await at home the bearer of tidings respecting his own fortune: moreover, that they should post guards at the gates, to prevent any person from quitting the city; and oblige men to place their sole hopes of safety in the preservation of the walls and the city. That when the tumult had subsided the fathers should be called again to the senate-house, and deliberate on the defence of the city."

When all had signified their approbation of this opinion, and after the crowd had been removed by the magistrates from the forum, and the senators had proceeded in different directions to allay the tumult; then at length a letter is brought from the consul Terentius, stating, "That Lucius Æmilius, the consul, and his army were slain; that he himself was at Canusium, collecting, as it were after a shipwreck, the remains of this great disaster; that he had nearly ten thousand irregular and unorganized troops. That the Carthaginian was sitting still at Cannæ, bargaining about the price of the captives and the other booty, neither with the spirit of a conqueror nor in the style of a great general." Then also the losses of private families were made known throughout the several houses; and so completely was the whole city filled with grief, that the anniversary sacred rite of Ceres was intermitted, because it was neither allowable to perform it while in mourning, nor was there at that juncture a single matron who was not in mourning. Accordingly, lest the same cause should occasion the neglect of other public and private sacred rites, the mourning was limited to thirty days, by a decree of the senate. Now when the tumult in the city was allayed, an additional letter was brought from Sicily, from Titus Otacilius, the prꜳtor, stating, "that the kingdom of Hiero was being devastated by the Carthaginian fleet: and that, being desirous of affording him the assistance he implored, he received intelligence that another Carthaginian fleet was stationed at the Ægates, equipped and prepared; in order that when the Carthaginians had perceived that he was gone away to protect the coast of Syracuse, they might immediately attack Lilybæum and other parts of the Roman province; that he therefore needed a fleet, if they wished him to protect the king their ally, and Sicily."

The letters of the consul and the prætor having been read, they resolved that Marcus Claudius, who commanded the fleet stationed at Ostia, should be sent to the army to Canusium; and a letter be written to the consul, to the effect that, having delivered the army to the prætor, he should return to Rome the first moment he could, consistently with the interest of the republic. They were terrified also, in addition to these disasters, both with other prodigies, and also because two vestal virgins, Opimia and Floronia, were that year convicted of incontinence; one of whom was, according to custom, buried alive at the Colline gate; the other destroyed herself. Lucius Cantilius, secretary of the pontiff, whom they now call the lesser pontiffs, who had debauched Floronia, was beaten by rods in the comitium, by order of the chief pontiff, so that he expired under the stripes. This impiety being converted into a prodigy, as is usually the case when happening in the midst of so many calamities, the decemviri were desired to consult the sacred books. Quintus Fabius Pictor was also sent to Delphi, to inquire of the oracle by what prayers and offerings they might appease the gods, and what termination there would be to such great distresses. Meanwhile certain extraordinary sacrifices were performed, according to the directions of the books of the fates; among which a Gallic man and woman, and a Greek man and woman, were let down alive in the cattle market, into a place fenced round with stone, which had been already polluted with human victims, a rite by no means Roman. The gods being, as they supposed, sufficiently appeased, Marcus Claudius Marcellus sends from Ostia to Rome, as a garrison for the city, one thousand five hundred soldiers, which he had with him, levied for the fleet. He himself sending before him a marine legion, (it was the third legion,) under the command of the military tribunes, to Teanum Sidicinum, and delivering the fleet to Publius Furius Philus, his colleague, after a few days, proceeded by long marches to Cannsium. Marcus Junius, created dictator on the authority of the senate, and Titus Sempronius, master of the horse, proclaiming a levy, enrol the younger men from the age of seventeen, and some who wore the toga prætexta: of these, four legions and a thousand horse were formed. They send also to the allies and the Latin confederacy, to receive the soldiers according to the terms of the treaty. They order that arms, weapons, and other things should be prepared; and they take down from the temples and porticoes the old spoils taken from the enemy. They adopted also another and a new form of levy, from the scarcity of free persons, and from necessity: they armed eight thousand stout youths from the slaves, purchased at the public expense, first inquiring of each whether he was willing to serve. They preferred this description of troops, though they had the power of redeeming the captives at a less expense.

For Hannibal, after so great a victory at Cannæ, being occupied with the cares of a conqueror, rather than one who had a war to prosecute, the captives having been brought forward and separated, addressed the allies in terms of kindness, as he had done before at the Trebia and the lake Trasimenus, and dismissed them without a ransom; then he addressed the Romans too, who were called to him, in very gentle terms: "That he was not carrying on a war of extermination with the Romans, but was contending for honour and empire. That his ancestors had yielded to the Roman valour; and that he was endeavouring that others might be obliged to yield, in their turn, to his good fortune and valour together. Accordingly, he allowed the captives the liberty of ransoming themselves, and that the price per head should be five hundred denarii for a horseman, three hundred for a foot soldier, and one hundred for a slave." Although some addition was made to that sum for the cavalry, which they stipulated for themselves when they surrendered, yet they joyfully accepted any terms of entering into the compact. They determined that ten persons should be selected, by their own votes, who might go to Rome to the senate; nor was any other guarantee of their fidelity taken than that they should swear that they would return. With these was sent Carthalo, a noble Carthaginian, who might propose terms, if perchance their minds were inclined towards peace. When they had gone out of the camp, one of their body, a man who had very little of the Roman character, under pretence of having forgotten something, returned to the camp, for the purpose of freeing himself from the obligation of his oath, and overtook his companions before night. When it was announced that they had arrived at Rome, a lictor was despatched to meet Carthalo, to tell him, in the words of the dictator, to depart from the Roman territories before night.

An audience of the senate was granted by the dictator to the delegates of the prisoners. The chief of them, Marcus Junius, thus spoke: "There is not one of us, conscript fathers, who is not aware that there never was a nation which held prisoners in greater contempt than our own. But unless our own cause is dearer to us than it should be, never did men fall into the hands of the enemy who less deserved to be disregarded than we do; for we did not surrender our arms in the battle through fear; but having prolonged the battle almost till night-fall, while standing upon heaps of our slaughtered countrymen, we betook ourselves to our camp. For the remainder of the day and during the following night, although exhausted with exertion and wounds, we protected our rampart. On the following day, when, beset by the enemy, we were deprived of water, and there was no hope of breaking through the dense bands of the enemy; and, moreover, not considering it an impiety that any Roman soldier should survive the battle of Cannæ, after fifty thousand of our army had been butchered; then at length we agreed upon terms on which we might be ransomed and let off; and our arms, in which there was no longer any protection, we delivered to the enemy. We had been informed that our ancestors also had redeemed themselves from the Gauls with gold, and that though so rigid as to the terms of peace, had sent ambassadors to Tarentum for the purpose of ransoming the captives. And yet both the fight at the Allia with the Gauls, and at Heraclea with Pyrrhus, was disgraceful, not so much on account of the loss as the panic and flight. Heaps of Roman carcasses cover the plains of Cannæ; nor would any of us have survived the battle, had not the enemy wanted the strength and the sword to slay us. There are, too, some of us, who did not even retreat in the field; but being left to guard the camp, came into the hands of the enemy when it was surrendered. For my part, I envy not the good fortune or condition of any citizen or fellow-soldier, nor would I endeavour to raise myself by depressing another: but not even those men who, for the most part, leaving their arms, fled from the field, and stopped not till they arrived at Venusia or Canusium; not even those men, unless some reward is due to them on account of their swiftness of foot and running, would justly set themselves before us, or boast that there is more protection to the state in them than in us. But you will both find them to be good and brave soldiers, and us still more zealous, because, by your kindness, we have been ransomed and restored to our country. You are levying from every age and condition: I hear that eight thousand slaves are being armed. We are no fewer in number; nor will the expense of redeeming us be greater than that of purchasing these. Should I compare ourselves with them, I should injure the name of Roman. I should think also, conscript fathers, that in deliberating on such a measure, it ought also to be considered, (if you are disposed to be over severe, which you cannot do from any demerit of ours,) to what sort of enemy you would abandon us. Is it to Pyrrhus, for instance, who treated us, when his prisoners, like guests; or to a barbarian and Carthaginian, of whom it is difficult to determine whether his rapacity or cruelty be the greater? If you were to see the chains, the squalid appearance, the loathsomeness of your countrymen, that spectacle would not, I am confident, less affect you, than if, on the other hand, you beheld your legions prostrate on the plains of Cannæ. You may behold the solicitude and the tears of our kinsmen, as they stand in the lobby of your senate-house, and await your answer. When they are in so much suspense and anxiety in behalf of us, and those who are absent, what think you must be our own feelings, whose lives and liberty are at stake? By Hercules! should Hannibal himself, contrary to his nature, be disposed to be lenient towards us, yet we should not consider our lives worth possessing, since we have seemed unworthy of being ransomed by you. Formerly, prisoners dismissed by Pyrrhus, without ransom, returned to Rome; but they returned in company with ambassadors, the chief men of the state, who were sent to ransom them. Would I return to my country, a citizen, and not considered worth three hundred denarii? Every man has his own way of thinking, conscript fathers. I know that my life and person are at stake. But the danger which threatens my reputation affects me most, if we should go away rejected and condemned by you; for men will never suppose that you grudged the price of our redemption."

When he had finished his address, the crowd of persons in the comitium immediately set up a loud lamentation, and stretched out their hands to the senate, imploring them to restore to them their children, their brothers, and their kinsmen. Their fears and affection for their kindred had brought the women also with the crowd of men in the forum. Witnesses being excluded, the matter began to be discussed in the senate. There being a difference of opinion, and some advising that they should be ransomed at the public charge, others, that the state should be put to no expense, but that they should not be prevented redeeming themselves at their own cost; and that those who had not the money at present should receive a loan from the public coffer, and security given to the people by their sureties and properties; Titus Manlius Torquatus, a man of primitive, and, as some considered, over-rigorous severity, being asked his opinion, is reported thus to have spoken: "Had the deputies confined themselves to making a request, in behalf of those who are in the hands of the enemy, that they might be ransomed, I should have briefly given my opinion, without inveighing against any one. For what else would have been necessary but to admonish you, that you ought to adhere to the custom handed down from your ancestors, a precedent indispensable to military discipline. But now, since they have almost boasted of having surrendered themselves to the enemy, and have claimed to be preferred, not only to those who were captured by the enemy in the field, but to those also who came to Venusia and Canusium, and even to the consul Terentius himself; I will not suffer you to remain in ignorance of things which were done there. And I could wish that what I am about to bring before you, were stated at Canusium, before the army itself, the best witness of every man's cowardice or valour; or at least that one person, Publius Sempronius, were here, whom had they followed as their leader, they would this day have been soldiers in the Roman camp, and not prisoners in the power of the enemy. But though the enemy was fatigued with fighting, and engaged in rejoicing for their victory, and had, the greater part of them, retired into their camp, and they had the night at their disposal for making a sally, and as they were seven thousand armed troops, might have forced their way through the troops of the enemy, however closely arrayed; yet they neither of themselves attempted to do this, nor were willing to follow another. Throughout nearly the whole night Sempronius ceased not to admonish and exhort them, while but few of the enemy were about the camp, while there was stillness and quiet, while the night would conceal their design, that they would follow him; that before daybreak they might reach places of security, the cities of their allies. If as Publius Decius, the military tribune in Samnium, said, within the memory of our grandfathers; if he had said, as Calpurnius Flamma, in the first Punic war, when we were youths, said to the three hundred volunteers, when he was leading them to seize upon an eminence situated in the midst of the enemy: LET US DIE, SOLDIERS, AND BY OUR DEATHS RESCUE THE SURROUNDED LEGIONS FROM AMBUSCADE;—if Publius Sempronius had said thus, he would neither have considered you as Romans nor men, had no one stood forward as his companion in so valorous an attempt. He points out to you the road that leads not to glory more than to safety; he restores you to your country, your parents, your wives and children. Do you want courage to effect your preservation? What would you do if you had to die for your country? Fifty thousand of your countrymen and allies on that very day lay around you slain. If so many examples of courage did not move you, nothing ever will. If so great a carnage did not make life less dear, none ever will. While in freedom and safety, show your affection for your country; nay, rather do so while it is your country, and you its citizens. Too late you now endeavour to evince your regard for her when degraded, disfranchised from the rights of citizens, and become the slaves of the Carthaginians. Shall you return by purchase to that degree which you have forfeited by cowardice and neglect? You did not listen to Sempronius, your countryman, when he bid you take arms and follow him; but a little after you listened to Hannibal, when he ordered your arms to be surrendered, and your camp betrayed. But why do I charge those men with cowardice, when I might tax them with villany? They not only refused to follow him who gave them good advice, but endeavoured to oppose and hold him back, had not some men of the greatest bravery, drawing their swords, removed the cowards. Publius Sempronius, I say, was obliged to force his way through a band of his countrymen, before he burst through the enemy's troops. Can our country regret such citizens as these, whom if all the rest resembled, she would not have one citizen of all those who fought at Cannæ? Out of seven thousand armed men, there were six hundred who had courage to force their way, who returned to their country free, and in arms; nor did forty thousand of the enemy successfully oppose them. How safe, think you, would a passage have been for nearly two legions? Then you would have had this day at Canusium, conscript fathers, twenty thousand bold and faithful. But now how can these men be called faithful and good citizens, (for they do not even call themselves brave,) except any man suppose that they showed themselves such when they opposed those who were desirous of forcing their way through the enemy? or, unless any man can suppose, that they do not envy those men their safety and glory acquired by valour, when the must know that their timidity and cowardice were the cause of their ignominious servitude? Skulking in their tents they preferred to wait for the light and the enemy together, when they had an opportunity of sallying forth during the silence of the night. But though they had not courage to sally forth from the camp, had they courage to defend it strenuously? Having endured a siege for several days and nights, did they protect their rampart by their arms, and themselves by their rampart? At length, having dared and suffered every extremity, every support of life being gone, their strength exhausted with famine, and unable to hold their arms, were they subdued by the necessities of nature rather than by arms? At sunrise, the enemy approached the rampart: before the second hour, without hazarding any contest, they delivered up their arms and themselves. Here is their military service for you during two days. When they ought to have stood firm in array and fight on, then they fled back into their camp; when they ought to have fought before their rampart, they delivered up their camp: good for nothing, either in the field or the camp. I redeem you. When you ought to sally from the camp, you linger and hesitate; and when you ought to stay and protect your camp in arms, you surrender the camp, your arms, and yourselves to the enemy. I am of opinion, conscript fathers, that these men should no more be ransomed, than that those should be surrendered to Hannibal, who sallied from the camp through the midst of the enemy, and, with the most distinguished courage, restored themselves to their country."

After Manlius had thus spoken, notwithstanding the captives were related to many even of the senators, besides the practice of the state, which had never shown favour to captives, even from the remotest times, the sum of money also influenced them: for they were neither willing to drain the treasury, a large sum of money having been already issued for buying and arming slaves to serve in the war, nor to enrich Hannibal, who, according to report, was particularly in want of this very thing. The sad reply, that the captives would not be ransomed, being delivered, and fresh grief being added to the former on account of the loss of so many citizens, the people accompanied the deputies to the gate with copious tears and lamentations. One of them went home, because he had evaded his oath by artfully returning to the camp. But when this was known and laid before the senate, they all resolved that he should be apprehended and conveyed to Hannibal by guards, furnished by the state. There is another account respecting the prisoners, that ten came first, and that, the senate hesitating whether they should be admitted into the city or not, they were admitted, on the understanding that they should not have an audience of the senate. That when these staid longer than the expectation of all, three more came, Scribonius, Calpurnius, and Manlius. That then at length a tribune of the people, a relation of Scribonius, laid before the senate the redemption of the captives, and that they resolved that they should not be ransomed. That the three last deputies returned to Hannibal, and the ten former remained, because they had evaded their oath, having returned to Hannibal after having set out, under pretence of learning afresh the names of the captives. That a violent contest took place in the senate, on the question of surrendering them, and that those who thought they ought to be surrendered were beaten by a few votes, but that they were so branded by every kind of stigma and ignominy by the ensuing censors, that some of them immediately put themselves to death, and the rest, for all their life afterwards, not only shunned the forum, but almost the light and publicity. You can more easily wonder that authors differ so much than determine what is the truth. How much greater this disaster was than any preceding, even this is a proof, that such of the allies as had stood firm till that day then began to waver, for no other cause certainly but that they despaired of the empire. The people who revolted to the Carthaginians were these: the Atellani, Calatini, the Hirpini, some of the Apulians, the Samnites, except the Pentrians, all the Bruttians, and the Lucanians. Besides these the Surrentinians, and almost the whole coast possessed by the Greeks, the people of Tarentum, Metapontum, Croton, the Locrians, and all Cisalpine Gaul. Yet not even these losses and defections of their allies so shook the firmness of the Romans, that any mention of peace was made among them, either before the arrival of the consul at

Rome, or after he came thither, and renewed the memory of the calamity they had suffered. At which very juncture, such was the magnanimity of the state, that the consul, as he returned after so severe a defeat, of which he himself was the principal cause, was met in crowds of all ranks of citizens, and thanks bestowed because he had not despaired of the republic, in whose case, had he been a Carthaginian commander, no species of punishment would have been spared.

BOOK XXIII.

The Campanians revolt to Hannibal. Mago is sent to Carthage to announce the victory of Cannæ. Hanno advises the Carthaginian senate to make peace with the Romans, but is overborne by the Barcine faction. Claudius Marcellus the prætor defeats Hannibal at Nola. Hannibal's army is enervated in mind and body by luxurious living at Capua. Casilinum is besieged by the Carthaginians, and the inhabitants reduced to the last extremity of famine. A hundred and ninety-seven senators elected from the equestrian order. Lucius Postumius is, with his army, cut off by the Gauls. Cneius and Publius Scipio defeat Hasdrubal in Spain, and gain possession of that country. The remains of the army, defeated at Cannæ, are sent off to Sicily, there to remain until the termination of the war. An alliance is formed between Philip, king of Macedon, and Hannibal. Sempronius Gracchus defeats the Campanians. Successes of Titus Manlius in Sardinia he takes Hasdrubal the general, Mago, and Hanno prisoners. Claudius Marcellus again defeats the army of Hannibal at Nola, and the hopes of the Romans are revived as to the results of the war.

After the battle of Cannæ, Hannibal, having captured and plundered the Roman camp, had immediately removed from Apulia into Samnium; invited into the territory of the Hirpini by Statius, who promised that he would surrender Compsa. Trebius, a native of Compsa, was conspicuous for rank among his countrymen; but a faction of the Mopsii kept him down—a family of great influence through the favour of the Romans. After intelligence of the battle of Cannæ, and a report of the approach of Hannibal, circulated by the discourse of Trebius, the Mopsian party had retired from the city; which was thus given up to the Carthaginian without opposition, and a garrison received into it. Leaving there all his booty and baggage, and dividing his forces, he orders Mago to receive under his protection the cities of that district which might revolt from the Romans, and to force to defection those which might be disinclined. He himself, passing through the territory of Campania, made for the lower sea, with the intention of assaulting Naples, in order that he might be master of a maritime city. As soon as he entered the confines of the Neapolitan territory, he placed part of his Numidians in ambush, wherever he could find a convenient spot; for there are very many hollow roads and secret windings: others he ordered to drive before them the booty they had collected from the country, and, exhibiting it to the enemy, to ride up to the gates of the city. As they appeared to be few in number and in disorder, a troop of horse sallied out against them, which was cut off, being drawn into an ambuscade by the others, who purposely retreated: nor would one of them have escaped, had not the sea been near, and some vessels, principally such as are used in fishing, observed at a short distance from the shore, afforded an escape for those who could swim. Several noble youths, however, were captured and slain in that affair. Among whom, Hegeas, the commander of the cavalry, fell when pursuing the retreating enemy too eagerly. The sight of the walls, which were not favourable to a besieging force, deterred the Carthaginian from storming the city.

Thence he turned his course to Capua, which was wantoning under a long course of prosperity, and the indulgence of fortune: amid the general corruption, however, the most conspicuous feature was the extravagance of the commons, who exercised their liberty without limit. Pacuvius Calavius had rendered the senate subservient to himself and the commons, at once a noble and popular man, but who had acquired his influence by dishonourable intrigues. Happening to hold the chief magistracy during the year in which the defeat at the Trasimenus occurred, and thinking that the commons, who had long felt the most violent hostility to the senate, would attempt some desperate measure, should an opportunity for effecting a change present itself; and if Hannibal should come into that quarter with his victorious army, would murder the senators and deliver Capua to the Carthaginians; as he desired to rule in a state preserved rather than subverted (for though depraved he was not utterly abandoned), and as he felt convinced that no state could be preserved if bereaved of its public council, he adopted a plan by which he might preserve the senate and render it subject to himself and the commons. Having assembled the senate, he prefaced his remarks by observing, "that nothing would induce him to acquiesce in a plan of defection from the Romans, were it not absolutely necessary; since he had children by the daughter of Appius Claudius, and had a daughter at Rome married to Livius: but that a much more serious and alarming matter threatened them, than any consequences which could result from such a measure. For that the intention of the commons was not to abolish the senate by revolting to the Carthaginians, but to murder the senators, and deliver the state thus destitute to Hannibal and the Carthaginians. That it was in his power to rescue them from this danger, if they would resign themselves to his care, and, forgetting their political dissensions, confide in him." When, overpowered with fear, they all put themselves under his protection, he proceeded: "I will shut you up in the senate-house, and pretending myself to be an accomplice in the meditated crime, I will, by approving measures which I should in vain oppose, find out a way for your safety. For the performance of this take whatever pledge you please." Having given his honour, he went out; and having ordered the house to be closed, placed a guard in the lobby that no one might enter or leave it without his leave.

Then assembling the people, he thus addressed them: "What you have so often wished for, Campanians, the power of punishing an unprincipled and detestable senate, you now have, not at your own imminent peril, by riotously storming the houses of each, which are guarded and garrisoned with slaves and dependants, but free and without danger. Take them all, shut up in the senate-house, alone and unarmed; nor need you do any thing precipitately or blindly. I will give you the opportunity of pronouncing upon the life or death of each, that each may suffer the punishment he has deserved. But, above all, it behoves you so to give way to your resentment, as considering that your own safety and advantage are of greater importance. For I apprehend that you hate these particular senators, and not that you are unwilling to have any senate at all; for you must either have a king, which all abominate, or a senate, which is the only course compatible with a free state. Accordingly you must effect two objects at the same time; you must remove the old senate and elect a new one. I will order the senators to be summoned one by one, and I shall put it to you to decide whether they deserve to live or die: whatever you may determine respecting each shall be done; but before you execute your sentence on the culprit, you shall elect some brave and strenuous man as a fresh senator to supply his place." Upon this he took his seat, and, the names having been thrown together into an urn, he ordered that the name which had the lot to fall out first should be proclaimed, and the person brought forward out of the senate-house. When the name was heard, each man strenuously exclaimed that he was a wicked and unprincipled fellow, and deserved to be punished. Pacuvius then said, "I perceive the sentence which has been passed on this man; now choose a good and upright senator in the room of this wicked and unprincipled one." At first all was silence, from the want of a better man whom they might substitute; afterwards, one of them, laying aside his modesty, nominating some one, in an instant a much greater clamour arose; while some denied all knowledge of him, others objected to him at one time on account of flagitious conduct, at another time on account of his humble birth, his sordid circumstances, and the disgraceful nature of his trade and occupation. The same occurred with increased vehemence with respect to the second and third senators, so that it was evident that they were dissatisfied with the senator himself, but had not any one to substitute for him; for it was of no use that the same persons should be nominated again, to no other purpose than to hear of their vices, and the rest were much more mean and obscure than those who first occurred to their recollection. Thus the assembly separated, affirming that every evil which was most known was easiest to be endured, and ordering the senate to be discharged from custody.

Pacuvius, having thus rendered the senators more subservient to himself than to the commons by the gift of their lives, ruled without the aid of arms, all persons now acquiescing. Henceforward the senators, forgetful of their rank and independence, flattered the commons; saluted them courteously; invited them graciously; entertained them with sumptuous feasts; undertook those causes, always espoused that party, decided as judges in favour of that side, which was most popular, and best adapted to conciliate the favour of the commons. Now, indeed, every thing was transacted in the senate as if it had been an assembly of the people. The Capuans, ever prone to luxurious indulgence not only from natural turpitude, but from the profusion of the means of voluptuous enjoyment which flowed in upon them, and the temptations of all the luxuries of land and sea; at that time especially proceeded to such a pitch of extravagance in consequence of the obsequiousness of the nobles and the unrestrained liberty of the commons, that their lust and prodigality had no bounds. To a disregard for the laws, the magistrates, and the senate, now, after the disaster of Cannæ, was added a contempt for the Roman government also, for which there had been some degree of respect. The only obstacles to immediate revolt were the intermarriages which, from a remote period, had connected many of their distinguished and influential families with the Romans; and, which formed the strongest bond of union, that while several of their countrymen were serving in the Roman armies, particularly three hundred horsemen, the flower of the Campanian nobility, had been selected and sent by the Romans to garrison the cities of Sicily.

The parents and relations of these men with difficulty obtained that ambassadors should be sent to the Roman consul. The consul, who had not yet set out for Canusium, they found at Venusia with a few half-armed troops, an object of entire commiseration to faithful, but of contempt to proud and perfidious allies, like the Campanians. The consul too increased their contempt of himself and his cause, by too much exposing and exhibiting the disastrous state of his affairs; for when the ambassadors had delivered their message, which was, that the senate and people of Capua were distressed that any adverse event should have befallen the Romans, and were promising every assistance in prosecuting the war, he observed, "In bidding us order you to furnish us with all things which are necessary for the war, Campanians, you have rather observed the customary mode of addressing allies, than spoken suitably to the present posture of our affairs; for hath anything been left us at Cannæ, so that, as if we possessed that, we can desire what is wanting to be supplied by our allies? Can we order a supply of infantry, as if we had any cavalry? Can we say we are deficient in money, as if that were the only thing we wanted? Fortune has not even left us anything which we can add to. Our legions, cavalry, arms, standards, horses, men, money, provisions, all perished either in the battle, or in the two camps which were lost the following day. You must, therefore, Campanians, not assist us in the war, but almost take it upon yourselves in our stead. Call to mind how formerly at Saticula we received into our protection and defended your ancestors, when dismayed and driven within their walls; terrified not only by their Samnite but Sidicinian enemies; and how we carried on, with varying success, through a period of almost a century, a war with the Samnites, commenced on your account. Add to this, that when you gave yourselves up to us we granted you an alliance on equal terms, that we allowed you your own laws, and lastly, what before the disaster at Cannæ was surely a privilege of the highest value, we bestowed the freedom of our city on a large portion of you, and held it in common with you. It is your duty, therefore, Campanians, to look upon this disaster which has been suffered as your own, and to consider that our common country must be protected. It is not a Samnite or Tuscan foe we are engaged with, so that the empire taken from us might still continue in Italy. A Carthaginian enemy draws after him from the remotest regions of the world, from the straits of the ocean and the pillars of Hercules, a body of soldiers who are not even natives of Africa, destitute of all laws, and of the condition and almost of the language of men. Savage and ferocious from nature and habit, their general has rendered them still more so, by forming bridges and works with heaps of human bodies; and, what the tongue can scarcely utter, by teaching them to live on human flesh. What man, provided he were born in any part of Italy, would not abominate the idea of seeing and having for his masters these men, nourished with such horrid food, whom even to touch were an impiety; of fetching laws from Africa and Carthage; and of suffering Italy to become a province of the Moors and Numidians? It will be highly honourable, Campanians, that the Roman empire, sinking under this disastrous defeat, should be sustained and restored by your fidelity and your strength. I conceive that thirty thousand foot and four thousand horse may be raised in Campania. You have already abundance of money and corn. If your zeal corresponds with your means, neither will Hannibal feel that he has been victorious, nor the Romans that they have been defeated."

After the consul had thus spoken, the ambassadors were dismissed; and as they were returning home, one of them, named Vibius Virius, observed, "that the time had arrived at which the Campanians might not only recover the territory once injuriously taken away by the Romans, but also possess themselves of the sovereignty of Italy. For they might form a treaty with Hannibal on whatever terms they pleased; and there could be no question but that after Hannibal, having put an end to the war, had himself retired victorious into Africa, and had withdrawn his troops, the sovereignty of Italy would be left to the Campanians." All assenting to Vibius, as he said this, they framed their report of the embassy so that all might conclude that the Roman power was annihilated. Immediately the commons and the major part of the senate turned their attention to revolt. The measure, however, was postponed for a few days at the instigation of the elder citizens. At last, the opinion of the majority prevailed, that the same ambassadors who had gone to the Roman consul should be sent to Hannibal. I find in certain annals, that before this embassy proceeded, and before they had determined on the measure of revolting, ambassadors were sent by the Campanians to Rome, requiring that one of the consuls should be elected from Campania if they wished assistance to the Roman cause.

That from the indignation which arose, they were ordered to be removed from the senate-house, and a lictor despatched to conduct them out of the city and command them to lodge that day without the Roman frontier. But as this request is too much like that which the Latins formerly made, and as Cœlius and other writers had, not without reason, made no mention of it, I have not ventured to vouch for its truth.

The ambassadors came to Hannibal and concluded a treaty of peace with him on the terms, "That no Carthaginian commander should have any authority over a Campanian citizen, nor any Campanian serve in war or perform any office against his will: that Capua should have her own laws and her own magistrates: that the Carthaginian should give to the Campanians three hundred captives selected by themselves, who might be exchanged for the Campanian horse who were serving in Sicily." Such were the stipulations: but in addition to them, the Campanians perpetrated the following atrocities; for the commons ordered that the prefects of the allies and other citizens of Rome should be suddenly seized, while some of them were occupied with military duties, others engaged in private business, and be shut up in the baths, as if for the purpose of keeping them in custody, where, suffocated with heat and vapour, they might expire in a horrid manner. Decius Magius, a man who wanted nothing to complete his influence except a sound mind on the part of his countrymen, had resisted to the uttermost the execution of these measures, and the sending of the embassy to Hannibal, and when he heard that a body of troops was sent by Hannibal, bringing back to their recollection, as examples, the haughty tyranny of Pyrrhus and the miserable slavery of the Tarentines, he at first openly and loudly protested that the troops should not be admitted, then he urged either that they should expel them when received, or, if they had a mind to expiate, by a bold and memorable act, the foul crime they had committed in revolting from their most ancient and intimate allies, that leaving slain the Carthaginian troops they should give themselves back to the Romans. These proceedings, having been reported to Hannibal, for they were not carried on in secret, he at first sent persons to summon Magius into his presence at his camp, then, on his vehemently refusing to come, on the ground that Hannibal had no authority over a Campanian, the Carthaginian, excited with rage, ordered that the man should be seized and dragged to him in chains, but afterwards, fearing lest while force was employed some disturbance might take place, or lest, from excitement of feeling, some undesigned collision might occur, he set out himself from the camp with a small body of troops, having sent a message before him to Marius Blosius, the prætor of Campania, to the effect, that he would be at Capua the next day. Marius calling an assembly, issued an order that they should go out and meet Hannibal in a body, accompanied by their wives and children. This was done by all, not only with obedience, but with zeal, with the full agreement of the common people, and with eagerness to see a general rendered illustrious by so many victories. Decius Magius neither went out to meet him, nor kept himself in private, by which course he might seem to indicate fear from a consciousness of demerit, he promenaded in the forum with perfect composure, attended by his son and a few dependants, while all the citizens were in a bustle to go to see and receive the Carthaginian. Hannibal, on entering the city, immediately demanded an audience of the senate; when the chief men of the Campanians, beseeching him not to transact any serious business on that day, but that he would cheerfully and willingly celebrate a day devoted to festivity in consequence of his own arrival, though naturally extremely prone to anger, yet, that he might not deny them any thing at first, he spent a great part of the day in inspecting the city.

He lodged at the house of the Ninii Celeres, Stenius and Pacuvius, men distinguished by their noble descent and their wealth. Thither Pacuvius Calavius, of whom mention has already been made, who was the head of the party which had drawn over the state to the Carthaginian cause, brought his son, a young man, whom he had forced from the side of Decius Magius, in conjunction with whom he had made a most determined stand for the Roman alliance in opposition to the league with the Carthaginians; nor had the leaning of the state to the other side, or his father's authority, altered his sentiments. For this youth his father procured pardon from Hannibal, more by prayers than by clearing him. Hannibal, overcome by the entreaties and tears of his father, even gave orders that he should be invited with his father to the banquet; to which entertainment he intended to admit no Campanian besides his hosts, and Jubellius Taurea, a man distinguished in war. They began to feast early in the day, and the entertainment was not conformable to the Carthaginian custom, or to military discipline, but as might be expected in a city and in a house both remarkable for luxury, was furnished with all the allurements of voluptuousness. Perolla, the son of Calavius, was the only person who could not be won either by the solicitations of the masters of the house, or those which Hannibal sometimes employed. The youth himself pleaded ill health as an apology, while his father urged as an excuse the disturbed state of his mind, which was not surprising. About sunset, Calavius, who had gone out from the banquet, was followed by his son; and when they had arrived at a retired place, (it was a garden at the back part of the house,) he said, "I have a plan to propose to you, my father, by which we shall not only obtain pardon from the Romans for our crime, in that we revolted from them to the Carthaginian, but shall be held in much higher esteem, than we Campanians ever have been." When the father inquired with surprise what that plan could be, he threw back his gown off his shoulder and exposed to view his side, which was girt with a sword. "Forthwith will I ratify the alliance with Rome with the blood of Hannibal. I was desirous that you should be informed of it first, in case you might prefer to be absent while the deed is performing."

On hearing and seeing which the old man, as though he were actually present at the transactions which were being named to him, wild with fear, exclaimed, "I implore, I beseech you, my son, by all the ties which unite children to parents, that you will not resolve to commit and to suffer every thing that is horrible before the eyes of a father. Did we but a few hours ago, swearing by every deity, and joining right hands, pledge our fidelity to Hannibal, that immediately on separating from the conference we should arm against him the hands which were employed as the sacred pledges of our faith? Do you rise from the hospitable board to which as one of three of the Campanians you have been admitted by Hannibal, that you may ensanguine that very board with the blood of your host. Could I conciliate Hannibal to my son, and not my son to Hannibal? But let nothing be held sacred by you, neither our pledges, nor the sense of religion, nor filial duty; let the most horrid deeds be dared, if with guilt they bring not ruin upon us. Will you singly attack Hannibal? What will that numerous throng of freemen and slaves be doing? What the eyes of all intent on him alone? What those so many right hands? Will they be torpid amidst your madness? Will you be able to bear the look of Hannibal himself, which armed hosts cannot sustain, from which the Roman people shrink with horror? And though other assistance be wanting, will you have the hardihood to strike me when I oppose my body in defence of Hannibal's? But know that through my breast you must strike and transfix him. Suffer yourself to be deterred from your attempt here, rather than to be defeated there. May my entreaties prevail with you, as they did for you this day." Upon this, perceiving the youth in tears, he threw his arms around him, and kissing him affectionately, ceased not his entreaties until he prevailed upon him to lay aside his sword and give his promise that he would do no such thing. The young man then observed, "I will indeed pay to my father the debt of duty which I owe to my country, but I am grieved for you on whom the guilt of having thrice betrayed your country rests; once when you sanctioned the revolt from the Romans; next when you advised the alliance with Hannibal; and thirdly, this day, when you are the delay and impediment of the restoration of Capua to the Romans. Do thou, my country, receive this weapon, armed with which in thy behalf I would fain have defended this citadel, since a father wrests it from me." Having thus said, he threw the sword into the highway over the garden wall, and that the affair might not be suspected, himself returned to the banquet.

The next day an audience of a full senate was given to Hannibal, when the first part of his address was full of graciousness and benignity, in which he thanked the Campanians for having preferred his friendship to an alliance with the Romans, and held out among his other magnificent promises "that Capua should soon become the capital of all Italy, and that the Romans as well as the other states should receive laws from it. That there was, however, one person who had no share in the Carthaginian friendship and the alliance formed with him, Decius Magius, who neither was nor ought to be called a Campanian. Him he requested to be surrendered to him, and that the sense of the senate should be taken respecting his conduct, and a decree passed in his presence." All concurred in this proposition, though a great many considered him as a man undeserving such severe treatment; and that this proceeding was no small infringement of their liberty to begin with. Leaving the senate-house, the magistrate took his seat on the consecrated bench, ordered Decius Magius to be apprehended, and to be placed by himself before his feet to plead his cause. But he, his proud spirit being unsubdued, denied that such a measure could be enforced agreeably to the conditions of the treaty; upon which he was ironed, and ordered to be brought into the camp before a lictor. As long as he was conducted with his head uncovered, he moved along earnestly haranguing and vociferating to the multitude which poured around him on all sides. "You have gotten that liberty, Campanians, which you seek; in the middle of the forum, in the light of day, before your eyes, I, a man second to none of the Campanians, am dragged in chains to suffer death. What greater outrage could have been committed had Capua been captured? Go out to meet Hannibal, decorate your city to the utmost, consecrate the day of his arrival, that you may behold this triumph over a fellow-citizen." As the populace seemed to be excited by him, vociferating these things, his head was covered, and he was ordered to be dragged away more speedily without the gate. Having been thus brought to the camp, he was immediately put on board a ship and sent to Carthage, lest if any commotion should arise at Capua on account of the injustice of the proceeding, the senate also should repent of having given up a leading citizen; and lest if an embassy were sent to request his restoration, he must either offend his new allies by refusing their first petition, or, by granting it, be compelled to retain at Capua a promoter of sedition and disturbance. A tempest drove the vessel to Cyrenæ, which was at that time under the dominion of kings. Here flying for refuge to the statue of king Ptolemy, he was conveyed thence in custody to Alexandria to Ptolemy; and having instructed him that he had been thrown into chains by Hannibal, contrary to the law of treaties, he was liberated and allowed to return to whichever place he pleased, Rome or Capua. But Magius said, that Capua would not be a safe place for him, and that Rome, at a time when there was war between the Romans and Capuans, would be rather the residence of a deserter than a guest. That there was no place that he should rather dwell in, than in the dominions of him whom he esteemed an avenger and the protector of his liberty.

While these things were carrying on, Quintus Fabius Pictor, the ambassador, returned from Delphi to Rome, and read the response of the oracle from a written copy. In it both the gods were mentioned, and in what manner supplication should be made. It then stated, "If you do thus, Romans, your affairs will be more prosperous and less perplexed; your state will proceed more agreeably to your wishes; and the victory in the war will be on the side of the Roman people. After that your state shall have been restored to prosperity and safety, send a present to the Pythian Apollo out of the gains you have earned, and pay honours to him out of the plunder, the booty, and the spoils. Banish licentiousness from among you."

Having read aloud these words, translated from the Greek verse, he added, that immediately on his departure from the oracle, he had paid divine honours to all these deities with wine and frankincense; and that he was ordered by the chief priest of the temple, that, as he had approached the oracle and performed the sacred ceremonies decorated with a laurel crown, so he should embark wearing the crown, and not put it off till he had arrived at Rome. That he had executed all these injunctions with the most scrupulous exactness and diligence, and had deposited the garland on the altar of Apollo at Rome. The senate decreed that the sacred ceremonies and supplications enjoined should be carefully performed with all possible expedition. During these events at Rome and in Italy, Mago, the son of Hamilcar, had arrived at Carthage with the intelligence of the victory at Cannæ. He was not sent direct from the field of battle by his brother, but was detained some days in receiving the submission of such states of the Bruttii as were in revolt. Having obtained an audience of the senate he gave a full statement of his brother's exploits in Italy: "That he had fought pitched battles with six generals, four of whom were consuls, two a dictator and master of the horse, with six consular armies; that he had slain above two hundred thousand of the enemy, and captured above fifty thousand. That out of the four consuls he had slain two; of the two remaining, one was wounded, the other, having lost his whole army, had fled from the field with scarcely fifty men; that the master of the horse, an authority equal to that of consul, had been routed and put to flight; that the dictator, because he had never engaged in a pitched battle, was esteemed a matchless general; that the Bruttii, the Apulians, part of the Samnites and of the Lucanians had revolted to the Carthaginians. That Capua, which was the capital not only of Campania, but after the ruin of the Roman power by the battle of Cannæ, of Italy also, had delivered itself over to Hannibal. That in return for these so many and so great victories, gratitude ought assuredly to be felt and thanks returned to the immortal gods."

Then, in proof of this such joyful news, he ordered the golden rings to be poured out in the vestibule of the senate-house, of which there was such a heap that some have taken upon themselves to say that on being measured they filled three pecks and a half. The statement has obtained and is more like the truth, that there were not more than a peck. He then added, by way of explanation, to prove the greater extent of the slaughter, that none but knights, and of these the principal only, wore that ornament. The main drift of his speech was, "that the nearer the prospect was of bringing the war to a conclusion, the more should Hannibal be aided by every means, for that the seat of war was at a long distance from home and in the heart of the enemy's country. That a great quantity of corn was consumed and money expended; and that so many pitched battles, as they had annihilated the armies of the enemy, had also in some degree diminished the forces of the victor. That a reinforcement therefore ought to be sent; and money for the pay, and corn for the soldiers who had deserved so well of the Carthaginian name." After this speech of

Mago's, all being elated with joy, Himilco, a member of the Barcine faction, conceiving this a good opportunity for inveighing against Hanno, said to him, "What think you now, Hanno? do you now also regret that the war against the Romans was entered upon? Now urge that Hannibal should be given up; yes, forbid the rendering of thanks to the immortal gods amidst such successes; let us hear a Roman senator in the senate-house of the Carthaginians." Upon which Hanno replied, "I should have remained silent this day, conscript fathers, lest, amid the general joy, I should utter any thing which might be too gloomy for you. But now, to a senator, asking whether I still regret the undertaking of the war against the Romans, if I should forbear to speak, I should seem either arrogant or servile, the former of which is the part of a man who is forgetful of the independence of others, the latter of his own. I may answer therefore to Himilco, that I have not ceased to regret the war, nor shall I cease to censure your invincible general until I see the war concluded on some tolerable terms; nor will any thing except a new peace put a period to my regret for the loss of the old one. Accordingly those achievements, which Mago has so boastingly recounted, are a source of present joy to Himilco and the other adherents of Hannibal; to me they may become so; because successes in war, if we have a mind to make the best use of fortune, will afford us a peace on more equitable terms; for if we allow this opportunity to pass by, on which we have it in our power to appear to dictate rather than to receive terms of peace, I fear lest even this our joy should run into excess, and in the end prove groundless. However, let us see of what kind it is even now. I have slain the armies of the enemy, send me soldiers. What else would you ask if you had been conquered? I have captured two of the enemy's camps, full, of course, of booty and provisions; supply me with corn and money. What else would you ask had you been plundered and stripped of your camp? And that I may not be the only person perplexed, I could wish that either Himilco or Mago would answer me, for it is just and fair that I also should put a question, since I have answered Himilco. Since the battle at Cannæ annihilated the Roman power, and it is a fact that all Italy is in a state of revolt; in the first place, has any one people of the Latin confederacy come over to us? In the next place, has any individual of the five and thirty tribes deserted to Hannibal?" When Mago had answered both these questions in the negative, he continued: "there remains then still too large a body of the enemy. But I should be glad to know what degree of spirit and hope that body possesses."

Mago declaring that he did not know; "Nothing," said he, "is easier to be known. Have the Romans sent any ambassadors to Hannibal to treat of peace? Have you, in short, ever heard that any mention has been made of peace at Rome?" On his answering these questions also in the negative: "We have upon our hands then, said he, a war as entire as we had on the day on which Hannibal crossed over into Italy. There are a great many of us alive now who remember how fluctuating the success was in the former Punic war. At no time did our affairs appear in so prosperous a condition as they did before the consulship of Caius Lutatius and Aulus Posthumius. In the consulship of Caius Lutatius and Aulus Posthumius we were completely conquered at the islands Ægates. But if now, as well as then, (oh! may the gods avert the omen!) fortune should take any turn, do you hope to obtain that peace when we shall be vanquished which no one is willing to grant now we are victorious. I have an opinion which I should express if any one should advise with me on the subject of proffering or accepting terms of peace with the enemy; but with respect to the supplies requested by Mago, I do not think there is any necessity to send them to a victorious army; and I give it as my opinion that they should far less be sent to them, if they are deluding us by groundless and empty hopes." But few were influenced by the harangue of Hanno, for both the jealousy which he entertained towards the Barcine family, made him a less weighty authority; and men's minds being taken up with the present exultation, would listen to nothing by which their joy could be made more groundless, but felt convinced, that if they should make a little additional exertion the war might be speedily terminated. Accordingly a decree of the senate was made with very general approbation, that four thousand Numidians should be sent as a reinforcement to Hannibal, with four hundred elephants and many talents of silver. Moreover, the dictator was sent forward into Spain with Mago to hire twenty thousand foot and four thousand horse, to recruit the armies in Italy and Spain.

But these resolutions, as generally happens in the season of prosperity, were executed in a leisurely and slothful manner. The Romans, in addition to their inborn activity of mind, were prevented from delaying by the posture of their affairs. For the consul was not wanting in any business which was to be done by him; and the dictator, Marcus Junius Pera, after the sacred ceremonies were concluded, and after having, as is usual, proposed to the people that he might be allowed to mount his horse; besides the two legions which had been enlisted by the consuls in the beginning of the year, and besides the cohorts collected out of the Picenian and Gallic territories, descended to that last resort of the state when almost despaired of, and when propriety gives place to utility, and made proclamation, that of such persons as had been guilty of capital crimes or were in prison on judgment for debt, those who would serve as soldiers with him, he would order to be released from their liability to punishment and their debts. These six thousand he armed with the Gallic spoils which were carried in the procession at the triumph of Caius Flaminius. Thus he marched from the city at the head of twenty-five thousand men. Hannibal, after gaining Capua, made a second fruitless attempt upon the minds of the Neapolitans, partly by fear and partly by hope: and then marched his troops across into the territory of Nola: not immediately in a hostile attitude, for he did not despair of a voluntary surrender, yet intending to omit nothing which they could suffer or fear, if they delayed the completion of his hopes. The senate, and especially the principal members of it, persevered faithfully in keeping up the alliance with the Romans; the commons, as usual, were all inclined to a change in the government and to espouse the cause of Hannibal, placing before their minds the fear lest their fields should be devastated, and the many hardships and indignities which must be endured in a siege; nor were there wanting persons who advised a revolt. In this state of things, when a fear took possession of the senate, that it would be impossible to resist the excited multitude if they went openly to work, devised a delay of the evil by secret simulation. They pretended that they were agreeable to the revolt to Hannibal; but that it was not settled on what terms they should enter into the new alliance and friendship. Thus having gained time, they promptly sent ambassadors to the Roman prætor, Marcellus Claudius, who was at Casilinum with his army, and informed him what a critical situation Nola was in; that the fields were already in the possession of Hannibal and the Carthaginians, and that the city soon would be, unless succour were sent; that the senate, by conceding to the commons that they would revolt when they pleased, had caused them not to hasten too much to revolt. Marcellus, after bestowing high commendations on the Nolans, urged them to protract the business till his arrival by means of the same pretences; in the mean time, to conceal what had passed between them, as well as all hope of succour from the Romans. He himself marched from Casilinum to Calatia, and thence crossing the Vulturnus, and passing through the territories of Saticula and Trebula, pursuing his course along the mountains above Suessula, he arrived at Nola.

On the approach of the Roman prætor, the Carthaginians retired from the territory of Nola and marched down to the sea close upon Naples, eager to get possession of a maritime town to which there would be a safe course for ships from Africa. But hearing that Naples was held by a Roman prefect, Marcus Junius Silanus, who had been invited thither by the Neapolitans themselves, he left Naples as he had left Nola, and directed his course to Nuceria, which he at length starved into capitulation, after having besieged it for a considerable time, often by open force, and often by soliciting to no purpose sometimes the commons, at other times the nobles; agreeing that they should depart with single garments and without arms. Then, as wishing to appear from the beginning to show lenity to all the inhabitants of Italy except the Romans, he proposed rewards and honours to those who might remain with him, and would be willing to serve with him. He retained none, however, by the hopes he held out; they all dispersed in different directions throughout the cities of Campania, wherever either hospitable connexions or the casual impulse of the mind directed them, but principally to Nola and Naples. About thirty senators, including as it happened all of the first rank, made for Capua; but being shut out thence, because they had closed their gates on Hannibal, they betook themselves to Cumæ. The plunder of Nuceria was, given to the soldiery, the city sacked and burned. Marcellus continued to hold possession of Nola, relying not more from confidence in his own troops than from the favourable disposition of the leading inhabitants. Apprehensions were entertained of the commons, particularly Lucius Bantius, whose having been privy to an attempt at defection, and dread of the Roman prætor, stimulated sometimes to the betrayal of his country, at others, should fortune fail him in that undertaking, to desertion. He was a young man of vigorous mind, and at that time enjoying the greatest renown of almost any of the allied cavalry. Found at Cannæ half dead amid a heap of slain, Hannibal had sent him home, after having had him cured, with the kindest attention, and even with presents. In gratitude for this favour, he had conceived a wish to put Nola under the power and dominion of the Carthaginian; but his anxiety and solicitude for effecting a change did not escape the notice of the prætor. However, as it was necessary that he should be either restrained by penal inflictions or conciliated by favours, he preferred attaching to himself a brave and strenuous ally, to depriving the enemy of him; and summoning him into his presence, in the kindest manner said, "that the fact that he had many among his countrymen who were jealous of him, might be easily collected from the circumstance that not one citizen of Nola had informed him how many were his splendid military exploits. But that it was impossible for the valour of one who served in the Roman camp to remain in obscurity; that many who had served with him had reported to him how brave a man he was, how often and what dangers he had encountered for the safety and honour of the Roman people; and how in the battle of Cannæ he had not given over fighting till, almost bloodless, he was buried under a heap of men, horses, and arms which fell upon him. Go on then," says he, "and prosper in your career of valour, with me you shall receive every honour and every reward, and the oftener you be with me, the more you shall find it will be to your honour and emolument." He presented the young man, delighted with these promises, with a horse of distinguished beauty, ordered the quæstor to give him five hundred denarii, and commanded the lictors to allow him to approach him whenever he might please.

The violent spirit of the youth was so much soothed by the courteous treatment of Marcellus, that thenceforward no one of the allies displayed greater courage or fidelity in aiding the Roman cause. Hannibal being now at the gates, for he had moved his camp back again from Nuceria to Nola, and the commons beginning to turn their attention to revolt afresh, Marcellus, on the approach of the enemy, retired within the walls; not from apprehension for his camp, but lest he should give an opportunity for betraying the city, which too many were anxiously watching for. The troops on both sides then began to be drawn up; the Romans before the walls of Nola, the Carthaginians before their own camp. Hence arose several battles of small account between the city and the camp, with varying success, as the generals were neither willing to check the small parties who inconsiderately challenged the enemy, nor to give the signal for a general engagement. While the two armies continued to be thus stationed day after day, the chief men of the Nolans informed Marcellus, that conferences were held by night between the commons of Nola and the Carthaginians; and that it was fixed, that, when the Roman army had gone out at the gates, they should make plunder of their baggage and packages, then close the gates and post themselves upon the walls, in order that when in possession of the government and the city, they might then receive the Carthaginian instead of the Roman. On receiving this intelligence Marcellus, having bestowed the highest commendations on the senators, resolved to hazard the issue of a battle before any commotion should arise within the city. He drew up his troops in three divisions at the three gates which faced the enemy; he gave orders that the baggage should follow close by, that the servants, suttlers' boys, and invalids should carry palisades; at the centre gate he stationed the choicest of the legionary troops and the Roman cavalry, at the two gates on either side, the recruits, the light-armed, and the allied cavalry. The Nolans were forbidden to approach the walls and gates, and the troops designed for a reserve were set over the baggage, lest while the legions were engaged in the battle an attack should be made upon it. Thus arranged they were standing within the gates. Hannibal, who had waited with his troops drawn up in battle-array, as he had done for several days, till the day was far advanced, at first was amazed that neither the Roman army marched out of the gates, nor any armed man was to be seen on the walls, but afterwards concluding that the conferences had been discovered, and that they were quiet through fear, he sent back a portion of his troops into the camp, with orders to bring into the front line, with speed, every thing requisite for assaulting the city; satisfied that if he urged them vigorously while they were indisposed to action, the populace would excite some commotion in the city. While, in the van, the troops were running up and down in a hurried manner in discharge of their several duties, and the line was advancing up to the gates, suddenly throwing open the gate, Marcellus ordered that the signal should be given, and a shout raised, and that first the infantry and after them the cavalry should burst forth upon the enemy with all possible impetuosity. They had occasioned abundant terror and confusion in the centre of the enemy's line, when, at the two side gates, the lieutenant-generals, Publius Valerius Flaccus and Caius Aurelius, sallied forth upon the wings. The servants, suttlers' boys, and the other multitude appointed to guard the baggage, joined in the shout, so that they suddenly exhibited the appearance of a vast army to the Carthaginians, who despised chiefly their paucity of numbers. For my own part I would not take upon me to assert what some authors have declared, that two thousand eight hundred of the enemy were slain, and that the Romans lost not more than five hundred. Whether the victory was so great or not; it is certain that a very important advantage, and perhaps the greatest during the war, was gained on that day: for not to be vanquished by Hannibal was then a more difficult task to the victorious troops, than to conquer him afterwards.

When Hannibal, all hope of getting possession of Nola being lost, had retired to Acerræ, Marcellus, having closed the gates and posted guards in different quarters to prevent any one from going out, immediately instituted a judicial inquiry in the forum, into the conduct of those who had been secretly in communication with the enemy. He beheaded more than seventy who were convicted of treason, and ordered their foods to be confiscated to the Roman state; and then committing the government to the senate, set out with all his forces, and, pitching a camp, took up a position above Suessula. The Carthaginian, having at first endeavoured to win over the people of Acerræ to a voluntary surrender, but finding them resolved, makes preparations for a siege and assault. But the people of Acerræ had more spirit than power. Despairing therefore, of the defence of the city, when they saw their walls being circumvallated, before the lines of the enemy were completed, they stole off in the dead of night through the opening in the works, and where the watches had been neglected; and pursuing their course through roads and pathless regions, accordingly as design or mistake directed each, made their escape to those towns of Campania which they knew had not renounced their fidelity. After Acerræ was plundered and burnt, Hannibal, having received intelligence that the Roman dictator with the new-raised legions was seen at some distance from Casilinum, and fearing lest, the camp of the enemy being so near, something might occur at Capua, marched his army to Casilinum. At that time Casilinum was occupied by five hundred Prænestines, with a few Romans and Latins, whom the news of the defeat at Cannæ had brought to the same place. These men setting out from home too late, in consequence of the levy at Præneste not being completed at the appointed day, and arriving at Casilinum before the defeat was known there, where they united themselves with other troops, Romans and allies, were proceeding thence in a tolerably large body, but the news of the battle at Cannæ them back to Casilinum. Having spent several days there in evading and concerting plots, in fear themselves and suspected by the Campanians, and having now received certain information that the revolt of Capua and the reception of Hannibal were in agitation, they put the townsmen to the sword by night, and seized upon the part of the town on this side the Vulturnus, for it is divided by that river. Such was the garrison the Romans had at Casilinum; to these was added a cohort of Perusians, in number four hundred and sixty, who had been driven to Casilinum by the same intelligence which had brought the Prænestines a few days before. They formed a sufficient number of armed men for the defence of walls of so limited extent, and protected on one side by the river. The scarcity of corn made them even appear too numerous.

Hannibal having now advanced within a short distance of the place, sent forward a body of Getulians under a commander named Isalca, and orders them in the first place, if an opportunity of parley should be given, to win them over by fair words, to open the gates, and admit a garrison; but, if they persisted in obstinate opposition, to proceed to action, and try if in any part he could force an entrance into the city. When they had approached the walls, because silence prevailed there appeared a solitude; and the barbarian, supposing that they had retired through fear, made preparation for forcing the gates and breaking away the bars, when, the gates being suddenly thrown open, two cohorts, drawn up within for that very purpose, rushed forth with great tumult, and made a slaughter of the enemy. The first party being thus repulsed, Maharbal was sent with a more powerful body of troops; but neither could even he sustain the sally of the cohorts. Lastly, Hannibal, fixing his camp directly before the walls, prepared to assault this paltry city and garrison, with every effort and all his forces, and having completely surrounded the city with a line of troops, lost a considerable number of men, including all the most forward, who were shot from the walls and turrets, while he pressed on and provoked the enemy. Once he was very near cutting them off, by throwing in a line of elephants, when aggressively sallying forth, and drove them in the utmost confusion into the town; a good many, out of so small a number, having been slain. More would have fallen had not night interrupted the battle. On the following day, the minds of all were possessed with an ardent desire to commence the assault, especially after a golden mural crown had been promised, and the general himself had reproached the conquerors of Saguntum with the slowness of their siege of a little fort situated on level ground; reminding them, each and all, of Cannæ, Trasimenus, and Trebia. They then began to apply the vineæ and to spring mines: nor was any measure, whether of open force or stratagem, unemployed against the various attempts of the enemy. These allies of the Romans erected bulwarks against the vineæ, cut off the mines of the enemy by cross-mines, and met their efforts both covertly and openly, till, at last, shame compelled Hannibal to desist from his undertaking; and, fortifying a camp in which he placed a small guard, that the affair might not appear to have been abandoned, he retired into winter quarters to Capua. There he kept, under cover, for the greater part of the winter, that army, which, though fortified by frequent and continued hardships against every human ill, had yet never experienced or been habituated to prosperity. Accordingly, excess of good fortune and unrestrained indulgence were the ruin of men whom no severity of distress had subdued; and so much the more completely, in proportion to the avidity with which they plunged into pleasures to which they were unaccustomed. For sleep, wine, feasting, women, baths, and ease, which custom rendered more seductive day by day, so completely unnerved both mind and body, that from henceforth their past victories rather than their present strength protected them; and in this the general is considered by those who are skilled in the art of war to have committed a greater error than in not having marched his troops to Rome forthwith from the field of Cannæ: for his delay on that occasion might be considered as only to have postponed his victory, but this mistake to have bereaved him of the power of conquering. Accordingly, by Hercules, as though he marched out of Capua with another army, it retained in no respect any of its former discipline; for most of the troops returned in the embrace of harlots; and as soon as they began to live under tents, and the fatigue of marching and other military labours tried them, like raw troops, they failed both in bodily strength and spirit. From that time, during the whole period of the summer campaign, a great number of them slunk away from the standards without furloughs, while Capua was the only retreat of the deserters.

However, when the rigour of winter began to abate, marching his troops out of their winter quarters he returned to Casilinum; where, although there had been an intermission of the assault, the continuance of the siege had reduced the inhabitants and the garrison to the extremity of want. Titus Sempronius commanded the Roman camp, the dictator having gone to Rome to renew the auspices. The swollen state of the Vulturnus and the entreaties of the people of Nola and Acerrae, who feared the Campanians if the Roman troops should leave them, kept Marcellus in his place; although desirous himself also to bring assistance to the besieged. Gracchus, only maintaining his post near Casilinum, because he had been enjoined by the dictator not to take any active steps during his absence, did not stir; although intelligence was brought from Casilinum which might easily overcome every degree of patience. For it appeared that some had precipitated themselves from the walls through famine and that they were standing unarmed upon the walls, exposing their undefended bodies to the blows of the missile weapons. Gracchus, grieved at the intelligence, but not daring to fight contrary to the injunctions of the dictator, and yet aware that he must fight if he openly attempted to convey in provisions, and having no hope of introducing them clandestinely, collected corn from all parts of the surrounding country, and filling several casks sent a message to the magistrate to

Casilinum, directing that they might catch the casks which the river would bring down. The following night, while all were intent upon the river, and the hopes excited by the message from the Romans, the casks sent came floating down the centre of the stream, and the corn was equally distributed among them all. This was repeated the second and third day; they were sent off and arrived during the same night; and hence they escaped the notice of the enemy's guards. But afterwards, the river, rendered more than ordinarily rapid by continual rains, drove the casks by a cross current to the bank which the enemy were guarding; there they were discovered sticking among the osiers which grew along the banks; and, it being reported to Hannibal, from that time the watches were kept more strictly, that nothing sent to the city by the Vulturnus might escape notice. However, nuts poured out at the Roman camp floated down the centre of the river to Casilinum, and were caught with hurdles. At length they were reduced to such a degree of want, that they endeavoured to chew the thongs and skins which they tore from their shields, after softening them in warm water; nor did they abstain from mice or any other kind of animals. They even dug up every kind of herb and root from the lowest mounds of their wall; and when the enemy had ploughed over all the ground producing herbage which was without the wall, they threw in turnip seed, so that Hannibal exclaimed, Must I sit here at Casilinum even till these spring up? and he, who up to that time had not lent an ear to any terms, then at length allowed himself to be treated with respecting the ransom of the free persons. Seven ounces of gold for each person were agreed upon as the price; and then, under a promise of protection, they surrendered themselves. They were kept in chains till the whole of the gold was paid, after which they were sent back to Cumæ, in fulfilment of the promise. This account is more credible than that they were slain by a body of cavalry, which was sent to attack them as they were going away. They were for the most part Prænestines. Out of the five hundred and seventy who formed the garrison, almost one half were destroyed by sword or famine; the rest returned safe to Præneste with their prætor Manicius, who had formerly been a scribe. His statue placed in the forum at Præneste, clad in a coat of mail, with a gown on, and with the head covered, formed an evidence of this account; as did also three images with this legend inscribed on a brazen plate, "Manicius vowed these in behalf of the soldiers who were in the garrison at Casilinum." The same legend was inscribed under three images placed in the temple of Fortune.

The town of Casilinum was restored to the Campanians, strengthened by a garrison of seven hundred soldiers from the army of Hannibal, lest on the departure of the Carthaginian from it, the Romans should assault it. To the Prænestine soldiers the Roman senate voted double pay and exemption from military service for five years. On being offered the freedom of the state, in consideration of their valor, they would not make the exchange. The account of the fate of the Perusians is less clear, as no light is thrown upon it by any monument of their own, or any decree of the Romans. At the same time the Petelini, the only Bruttian state which had continued in the Roman alliance, were attacked not only by the Carthaginians, who were in possession of the surrounding country, but also by the rest of the Bruttian states, on account of their having adopted a separate policy. The Petelini, unable to bear up against these distresses, sent ambassadors to Rome to solicit aid, whose prayers and entreaties (for on being told that they must themselves take measures for their own safety, they gave themselves up to piteous lamentations in the vestibule of the senate-house) excited the deepest commiseration in the fathers and the people. On the question being proposed a second time to the fathers by Manius Pomponius, the prætor, after examining all the resources of the empire, they were compelled to confess that they had no longer any protection for their distant allies, and bid them return home, and having done every thing which could be expected from faithful allies, as to what remained to take measures for their own security in the present state of fortune. On the result of this embassy being reported to the Petelini, their senate was suddenly seized with such violent grief and dismay, that some advised that they should run away wherever each man could find an asylum, and abandon the city. Some advised, that as they were deserted by their ancient allies, they should unite themselves with the rest of the Bruttian states, and through them surrender themselves to Hannibal. The opinion however which prevailed was that of those who thought that nothing should be done in haste and rashly, and that they should take the whole matter into their consideration again. The next day, when they had cooled upon it, and their trepidation had somewhat subsided, the principal men carried their point that they should collect all their property out of the fields, and fortify the city and the walls.

Much about the same time letters were brought from Sicily and Sardinia. That of Titus Otacilius the propraetor was first read in the senate. It stated that Lucius Furius the praetor had arrived at Lilybaeum from Africa with his fleet. That he himself, having been severely wounded, was in imminent danger of his life; that neither pay nor corn was punctually furnished to the soldiers or the marines; nor were there any resources from which they could be furnished. That he earnestly advised that such supplies should be sent with all possible expedition; and that, if it was thought proper, they should send one of the new praetors to succeed him.

Nearly the same intelligence respecting corn and pay was conveyed in a letter from Aulus Cornelius Mammula, the propraetor, from Sardinia. The answer to both was, that there were no resources from whence they could be supplied, and orders were given to them that they should themselves provide for their fleets and armies. Titus Otacilius having sent ambassadors to Hiero, the only source of assistance the Romans had, received as much money as was wanting to pay the troops and a supply of corn for six months. In Sardinia, the allied states contributed liberally to Cornelius. The scarcity of money at Rome also was so great, that on the proposal of Marcus Minucius, plebeian tribune, a financial triumvirate was appointed, consisting of Lucius Æmilius Papus, who had been consul and censor, Marcus Atilius Regulus, who had been twice consul, and Lucius Scribonius Libo, who was then plebeian tribune. Marcus and Caius Atilius were also created a duumvirate for dedicating the temple of Concord, which Lucius Manlius had vowed when praetor. Three pontiffs were also created, Quintus Caecilius Metellus, Quintus Fabius Maximus, and Quintus Fulvius Flaccus, in the room of Publius Scantinius deceased, and of Lucius Æmilius Paulus the consul, and of Quintus Ælius Paetus, who had fallen in the battle of Cannae.

The fathers having repaired, as far as human counsels could effect it, the other losses from a continued series of unfortunate events, at length turned their attention on themselves, on the emptiness of the senate-house, and the paucity of those who assembled for public deliberation. For the senate-roll had not been reviewed since the censorship of Lucius Æmilius and C. Flaminius, though unfortunate battles, during a period of five years, as well as the private casualties of each, had carried off so many senators. Manius Pomponius, the praetor, as the dictator was now gone to the army after the loss of Casilinum, at the earnest request of all, brought in a bill upon the subject. When Spurius Carvilius, after having lamented in a long speech not only the scantiness of the senate, but the fewness of citizens who were eligible into that body, with the design of making up the numbers of the senate and uniting more closely the Romans and the Latin confederacy, declared that he strongly advised that the freedom of the state should be conferred upon two senators from each of the Latin states, if the Roman fathers thought proper, who might be chosen into the senate to supply the places of the deceased senators. This proposition the fathers listened to with no more equanimity than formerly to the request when made by the Latins themselves. A loud and violent expression of disapprobation ran through the whole senate-house. In particular, Manlius reminded them that there was still existing a man of that stock, from which that consul was descended who formerly threatened in the Capitol that he would with his own hand put to death any Latin senator he saw in that house. Upon which Quintus Fabius Maximus said, "that never was any subject introduced into the senate at a juncture more unseasonable than the present, when a question had been touched upon which would still further irritate the minds of the allies, who were already hesitating and wavering in their allegiance. That that rash suggestion of one individual ought to be annihilated by the silence of the whole body; and that if there ever was a declaration in that house which ought to be buried in profound and inviolable silence, surely that above all others was one which deserved to be covered and consigned to darkness and oblivion, and looked upon as if it had never been made." This put a stop to the mention of the subject. They determined that a dictator should be created for the purpose of reviewing the senate, and that he should be one who had been a censor, and was the oldest living of those who had held that office. They likewise gave orders that Caius Terentius, the consul, should be called home to nominate a dictator; who, leaving his troops in Apulia, returned to Rome with great expedition; and, according to custom, on the following night nominated Marcus Fabius Buteo dictator, for six months, without a master of the horse, in pursuance of the decree of the senate.

He having mounted the rostrum attended by the lictors, declared, that he neither approved of there being two dictators at one time, which had never been done before, nor of his being appointed dictator without a master of the horse; nor of the censorian authority being committed to one person, and to the same person a second time; nor that command should be given to a dictator for six months, unless he was created for active operations. That he would himself restrain within proper bounds those irregularities which chance, the exigencies of the times, and necessity had occasioned. For he would not remove any of those whom the censors Flaminius and Æmilius had elected into the senate; but would merely order that their names should be transcribed and read over, that one man might not exercise the power of deciding and determining on the character and morals of a senator; and would so elect in place of deceased members, that one rank should appear to be preferred to another, and not man to man. The old senate-roll having been read, he chose as successors to the deceased, first those who had filled a curule office since the censorship of Flaminius and Æmilius, but had not yet been elected into the senate, as each had been earliest created. He next chose those who had been ædiles, plebeian tribunes, or quæstors; then of those who had never filled the office of magistrate, he selected such as had spoils taken from an enemy fixed up at their homes, or had received a civic crown. Having thus elected one hundred and seventy-seven senators, with the entire approbation of his countrymen, he instantly abdicated his office, and, bidding the lictors depart, he descended from the rostrum as a private citizen, and mingled with the crowd of persons who were engaged in their private affairs, designedly wearing away this time, lest he should draw off the people from the forum for the purpose of escorting him home. Their zeal, however, did not subside by the delay, for they escorted him to his house in great numbers. The consul returned to the army the ensuing night, without acquainting the senate, lest he should be detained in the city on account of the elections.

The next day, on the proposition of Manius Pomponius the prætor, the senate decreed that a letter should be written to the dictator, to the effect, that if he thought it for the interest of the state, he should come, together with the master of the horse and the prætor, Marcus Marcellus, to hold the election for the succeeding consuls, in order that the fathers might learn from them in person in what condition the state was, and take measures according to circumstances. All who were summoned came, leaving lieutenant-generals to hold command of the legions. The dictator, speaking briefly and modestly of himself, attributed much of the glory Of the campaign to the master of the horse, Tiberius Sempronius Gracchus. He then gave out the day for the comitia, at which the consuls created were Lucius Posthumius in his absence, being then employed in the government of the province of Gaul, for the third time, and Tiberius Sempronius Gracchus, who was then master of the horse and curule ædile. Marcus Valerius Lævinus, Appius Claudius Pulcher, Quintus Fulvius Flaccus, and Quintus Mucius Scævola, were then created prætors. After the election of the magistrates, the dictator returned to his army, which was in winter quarters at Teanum, leaving his master of the horse at Rome, to take the sense of the fathers relative to the armies to be enlisted and embodied for the service of the year, as he was about to enter upon the magistracy after a few days. While busily occupied with these matters, intelligence arrived of a fresh disaster—fortune crowding into this year one calamity after another—that Lucius Posthumius, consul elect, himself with all his army was destroyed in Gaul. He was to march his troops through a vast wood, which the Gauls called Litana. On the right and left of his route, the natives had sawed the trees in such a manner that they continued standing upright, but would fall when impelled by a slight force. Posthumius had with him two Roman legions, and besides had levied so great a number of allies along the Adriatic Sea, that he led into the enemy's country twenty-five thousand men. As soon as this army entered the wood, the Gauls, who were posted around its extreme skirts, pushed down the outermost of the sawn trees, which falling on those next them, and these again on others which of themselves stood tottering and scarcely maintained their position, crushed arms, men, and horses in an indiscriminate manner, so that scarcely ten men escaped. For, most of them being killed by the trunks and broken boughs of trees, the Gauls, who beset the wood on all sides in arms killed the rest, panic-struck by so unexpected a disaster. A very small number, who attempted to escape by a bridge, were taken prisoners, being intercepted by the enemy who had taken possession of it before them. Here Posthumius fell, fighting with all his might to prevent his being taken. The Boii having cut off his head, carried it and the spoils they stole off his body, in triumph into the most sacred temple they had. Afterwards they cleansed the head according to their custom, and having covered the skull with chased gold, used it as a cup for libations in their solemn festivals, and a drinking cup for their high priests and other ministers of the temple. The spoils taken by the Gauls were not less than the victory. For though great numbers of the beasts were crushed by the falling trees, yet as nothing was scattered by flight, every thing else was found strewed along the whole line of the prostrate band.

The news of this disaster arriving, when the state had been in so great a panic for many days, that the shops were shut up as if the solitude of night reigned through the city; the senate gave it in charge to the ædiles to go round the city, cause the shops to be opened, and this appearance of public affliction to be removed. Then Titus Sempronius, having assembled the senate, consoled and encouraged the fathers, requesting, "that they who had sustained the defeat at Cannæ with so much magnanimity would not now be cast down with less calamities. That if their arms should prosper, as he hoped they would, against Hannibal and the Carthaginians, the war with the Gauls might be suspended and deferred without hazard. The gods and the Roman people would have it in their power to revenge the treachery of the Gauls another time. That they should now deliberate about the Carthaginian foe, and the forces with which the war was to be prosecuted." He first laid before them the number of foot and horse, as well citizens as allies, that were in the dictator's army. Then Marcellus gave an account of the amount in his. Those who knew were asked what troops were in Apulia with Caius Terentius Varro the consul. But no practicable plan could be devised for raising consular armies sufficient to support so important a war. For this reason, notwithstanding a just resentment irritated them, they determined that Gaul should be passed over for that year. The dictator's army was assigned to the consul; and they ordered such of the troops of Marcellus's army as had fled from Cannæ, to be transported into Sicily, to serve there as long as the war continued in Italy. Thither, likewise, were ordered to be sent as unfit to serve with him, the weakest of the dictator's troops, no time of service being appointed, but the legal number of campaigns. The two legions in the city were voted to the other consul who should be elected in the room of Posthumius; and they resolved that he should be elected as soon as the auspices would permit. Besides, two legions were immediately to be recalled from Sicily, out of which the consul, to whom the city legions fell, might take what number of men he should have occasion for. The consul Caius Terentius Varro was continued in his command for one year, without lessening the army he had for the defence of Apulia.

During these transactions and preparations in Italy, the war in Spain was prosecuted with no less vigour; but hitherto more favourably to the Romans. The two generals had divided their troops, so that Cneius acted by land, and Publius by sea. Hasdrubal, general of the Carthaginians, sufficiently trusting to neither branch of his forces, kept himself at a distance from the enemy, secured by the intervening space and the strength of his fortifications, until, after much solicitation, four thousand foot and five hundred horse were sent him out of Africa as a reinforcement. At length, inspired with fresh hopes, he moved nearer the enemy; and himself also ordered a fleet to be equipped and prepared for the protection of the islands and sea-coasts. In the very onset of renewing the war, he was greatly embarrassed by the desertion of the captains of his ships, who had ceased to entertain a sincere attachment towards the general and the Carthaginian cause, ever since they were severely reprimanded for abandoning the fleet in a cowardly manner at the Iberus. These deserters had raised an insurrection among the Tartessians, and at their instigation some cities had revolted; they had even taken one by force. The war was now turned from the Romans into that country, which he entered in a hostile manner, and resolved to attack Galbus, a distinguished general of the Tartessians, who with a powerful army kept close within his camp, before the walls of a city which had been captured but a few days before. Accordingly, he sent his light-armed troops in advance to provoke the enemy to battle, and part of his infantry to ravage the country throughout in every direction, and to cut off stragglers. There was a skirmish before the camp, at the same time that many were killed and put to flight in the fields. But having by different routes returned to their camp, they so quickly shook off all fear, that they had courage not only to defend their lines, but challenge the enemy to fight. They sallied out, therefore, in a body from the camp, dancing according to their custom. Their sudden boldness terrified the enemy, who a little before had been the assailants. Hasdrubal therefore drew off his troops to a tolerably steep eminence, and secured further by having a river between it and the enemy. Here the parties of light-armed troops which had been sent in advance, and the horse which had been dispersed about, he called in to join him. But not thinking himself sufficiently secured by the eminence or the river, he fortified his camp completely with a rampart. While thus fearing and feared alternately, several skirmishes occurred, in which the Numidian cavalry were not so good as the Spanish, nor the Moorish darters so good as the Spanish targetteers, who equalled them in swiftness, but were superior to them in strength and courage.

The enemy seeing they could not, by coming up to Hasdrubal's camp, draw him out to a battle, nor assault it without great difficulty, stormed Asena, whither Hasdrubal, on entering their territories, had laid up his corn and other stores. By this they became masters of all the surrounding country. But now they became quite ungovernable, both when on march and within their camp.

Hasdrubal, therefore, perceiving their negligence, which, as usual, was the consequence of success, after having exhorted his troops to attack them while they were straggling and without their standards, came down the hill, and advanced to their camp in order of battle. On his approach being announced in a tumultuous manner, by men who fled from the watchposts and advanced guards, they shouted to arms; and as each could get his arms, they rushed precipitately to battle, without waiting for the word, without standards, without order, and without ranks. The foremost of them were already engaged, while some were running up in parties, and others had not got out of their camp. However, at first, the very boldness of their attack terrified the enemy. But when they charged their close ranks with their own which were thin, and were not able to defend themselves for want of numbers, each began to look out for others to support him; and being repulsed in all quarters they collected themselves in form of a circle, where being so closely crowded together, body to body, armour to armour, that they had not room to wield their arms, they were surrounded by the enemy, who continued to slaughter them till late in the day. A small number, having forced a passage, made for the woods and hills. With like consternation, their camp was abandoned, and next day the whole nation submitted. But they did not continue long quiet, for immediately upon this, Hasdrubal received orders from Carthage to march into Italy with all expedition. The report of which, spreading over Spain, made almost all the states declare for the Romans. Accordingly he wrote immediately to Carthage, to inform them how much mischief the report of his march had produced. "That if he really did leave Spain, the Romans would be masters of it all before he could pass the Iberus. For, besides that he had neither an army nor a general whom he could leave to supply his place, so great were the abilities of the Roman generals who commanded there, that they could scarcely be opposed with equal forces. If, therefore, they had any concern for preserving Spain, they ought to send a general with a powerful army to succeed him. To whom, however prosperous all things might prove, yet the province would not be a position of ease."

Though this letter made at first a great impression on the senate, yet, as their interest in Italy was first and most important, they did not at all alter their resolution in relation to Hasdrubal and his troops. However, they despatched Himilco with a complete army, and an augmented fleet, to preserve and defend Spain both by sea and land. When he had conveyed over his land and naval forces, he fortified a camp; and having drawn his ships upon dry land, and surrounded them with a rampart, he marched with a chosen body of cavalry, with all possible expedition; using the same caution when passing through people who were wavering, and those who were actually enemies; and came up with Hasdrubal. As soon as he had informed him of the resolutions and orders of the senate, and in his turn been thoroughly instructed in what manner to prosecute the war in Spain, he returned to his camp; his expedition more than any thing else saving him, for he quitted every place before the people could conspire. Before Hasdrubal quitted his position he laid all the states in subjection to him under contribution. He knew well that Hannibal purchased a passage through some nations; that he had no Gallic auxiliaries but such as were hired; and that if he had undertaken so arduous a march without money, he would scarcely have penetrated so far as the Alps. For this reason, having exacted the contributions with great haste, he marched down to the Iberus. As soon as the Roman generals got notice of the Carthaginian senate's resolution, and Hasdrubal's march, they gave up every other concern, and uniting their forces, determined to meet him and oppose his attempt. They reflected, that when it was already so difficult to make head against Hannibal alone in Italy, there would be an end of the Roman empire in Spain, should Hasdrubal join him with a Spanish army. Full of anxiety and care on these accounts, they assembled their forces at the Iberus, and crossed the river; and after deliberating for some time whether they should encamp opposite to the enemy, or be satisfied with impeding his intended march by attacking the allies of the Carthaginians, they made preparations for besieging a city called Ibera, from its contiguity to the river, which was at that time the wealthiest in that quarter. When Hasdrubal perceived this, instead of carrying assistance to his allies, he proceeded himself to besiege a city which had lately placed itself under the protection of the Romans; and thus the siege which was now commenced was given up by them, and the operations of the war turned against Hasdrubal himself.

For a few days they remained encamped at a distance of five miles from each other, not without skirmishes, but without going out to a regular engagement. At length the signal for battle was given out on both sides on one and the same day, as though by concert, and they marched down into the plain with all their forces. The Roman army stood in triple line; a part of the light troops were stationed among the first line, the other half were received behind the standards, the cavalry covering the wings. Hasdrubal formed his centre strong with Spaniards, and placed the Carthaginians in the right wing, the Africans and hired auxiliaries in the left. His cavalry he placed before the wings, attaching the Numidians to the Carthaginian infantry, and the rest to the Africans. Nor were all the Numidians placed in the right wing, but such as taking two horses each into the field are accustomed frequently to leap full armed, when the battle is at the hottest, from a tired horse upon a fresh one, after the manner of vaulters: such was their own agility, and so docile their breed of horses. While they stood thus drawn up, the hopes entertained by the generals on both sides were pretty much upon an equality; for neither possessed any great superiority, either in point of the number or quality of the troops. The feelings of the soldiers were widely different. Their generals had, without difficulty, induced the Romans to believe, that although they fought at a distance from their country, it was Italy and the city of Rome that they were defending. Accordingly, they had brought their minds to a settled resolution to conquer or die; as if their return to their country had hinged upon the issue of that battle. The other army consisted of less determined men; for they were principally Spaniards, who would rather be vanquished in Spain, than be victorious to be dragged into Italy. On the first onset, therefore, ere their javelins had scarcely been thrown, their centre gave ground, and the Romans pressing on with great impetuosity, turned their backs. In the wings the battle proceeded with no less activity; on one side the Carthaginians, on the other the Africans, charged vigorously, while the Romans, in a manner surrounded, were exposed to a twofold attack. But when the whole of the Roman troops had united in the centre, they possessed sufficient strength to compel the wings of the enemy to retire in different directions; and thus there were two separate battles, in both of which the Romans were decidedly superior, as after the defeat of the enemy's centre they had the advantage both in the number and strength of their troops. Vast numbers were slain on this occasion; and had not the Spaniards fled precipitately from the field ere the battle had scarce begun, very few out of the whole army would have survived. There was very little fighting of the cavalry, for as soon as the Moors and Numidians perceived that the centre gave way, they fled immediately with the utmost precipitation, leaving the wings uncovered, and also driving the elephants before them. Hasdrubal, after waiting the issue of the battle to the very last, fled from the midst of the carnage with a few attendants. The Romans took and plundered the camp. This victory united with the Romans whatever states of Spain were wavering, and left Hasdrubal no hope, not only of leading an army over into Italy, but even of remaining very safely in Spain. When these events were made generally known at Rome by letters from the Scipios, the greatest joy was felt, not so much for the victory, as for the stop which was put to the passage of Hasdrubal into Italy.

While these transactions were going on in Spain, Petilia, in Bruttium, was taken by Himilco, an officer of Hannibal's, several months after the siege of it began. This victory cost the Carthaginians much blood and many wounds, nor did any power more subdue the besieged than that of famine; for after having consumed their means of subsistence, derived from fruits and the flesh of every kind of quadrupeds, they were at last compelled to live upon skins found in shoemakers' shops, on herbs and roots, the tender barks of trees, and berries gathered from brambles: nor were they subdued until they wanted strength to stand upon the walls and support their arms. After gaining Petilia, the Carthaginian marched his forces to Consentia, which being less obstinately defended, he compelled to surrender within a few days. Nearly about the same time, an army of Bruttians invested Croton, a Greek city, formerly powerful in men and arms, but at the present time reduced so low by many and great misfortunes, that less than twenty thousand inhabitants of all ages remained. The enemy, therefore, easily got possession of a city destitute of defenders: of the citadel alone possession was retained, into which some of the inhabitants fled from the midst of the carnage during the confusion created by the capture of the city. The Locrians too revolted to the Bruttians and Carthaginians, the populace having been betrayed by the nobles. The Rhegians were the only people in that quarter who continued to the last in faithful attachment to the Romans, and in the enjoyment of their independence. The same alteration of feeing extended itself into Sicily also; and not even the family of Hiero altogether abstained from defection; for Gelo, his oldest son, conceiving a contempt for his father's old age, and, after the defeat of Cannæ, for the alliance with Rome, went over to the Carthaginians; and he would have created a disturbance in Sicily, had he not been carried off, when engaged as arming the people and soliciting the allies, by a death so seasonable that it threw some degree of suspicion even upon his father. Such, with various result, were the transactions in Italy, Africa, Sicily, and Spain during this year. At the close of the year, Quintus Fabius Maximus requested of the senate, that he might be allowed to dedicate the temple of Venus Erycina, which he had vowed when dictator. The senate decreed, that Tiberius Sempronius, the consul elect, as soon as ever he had entered upon his office, should propose to the people, that they should create Quintus Fabius duumvir, for the purpose of dedicating the temple. Also, in honour of Marcus Æmilius Lepidus, who had been consul twice and augur, his three sons, Lucius, Marcus, and Quintus exhibited funeral games and twenty-two pairs of gladiators for three days in the forum. The curule ædiles, Caius Lætorius, and Tiberius

Sempronius Gracchus consul elect, who during his ædileship had been master of the horse, celebrated the Roman games, which were repeated for three days. The plebeian games of the ædiles, Marcus Aurelius Cotta and Marcus Claudius Marcellus, were thrice repeated. At the conclusion of the third year of the Punic war, Tiberius Sempronius Gracchus the consul entered upon his office on the ides of March. Of the prætors, Quintus Fulvius Flaccus, who had before been consul and censor, had by lot the city jurisdiction; Marcus Valerius Lævinus, the foreign. Sicily fell to the lot of Appius Claudius Pulcher; Sardinia to Quintus Mucius Scævola. The people ordered that Marcus Marcellus should be in command as proconsul, because he was the only Roman general who had been successful in his operations in Italy since the defeat at Cannæ.

The senate decreed, the first day they deliberated in the Capitol, that double taxes should be imposed for that year, one moiety of which should be immediately levied, as a fund from which pay might be given forthwith to all the soldiers, except those who had been at Cannæ. With regard to the armies they decreed, that Tiberius Sempronius the consul should appoint a day for the two city legions to meet at Cales, whence these legions should be conveyed into the Claudian camp above Suenula. That the legions which were there, and they consisted principally of the troops which had fought at Cannæ, Appius Claudius Pulcher, the prætor, should transport into Sicily; and that those in Sicily should be removed to Rome. Marcus Claudius Marcellus was sent to the army, which had been ordered to meet at Cales on a certain day, with orders to march the city legions thence to the Claudian camp. Titus Metilius Croto, lieutenant-general, was sent by Appius Claudius Pulcher to receive the old army and remove it into Sicily. People at first had expected in silence that the consul would hold an assembly for the election of a colleague, but afterwards perceiving that Marcus Marcellus, whom they wished above all others to be consul this year, on account of his brilliant success during his prætorship, was removed to a distant quarter, as it were on purpose, a murmuring arose in the senate-house, which the consul perceiving, said "Conscript fathers, it was conducive to the interest of the state, both that Marcus Marcellus should go into Campania to make the exchange of the armies, and that the assembly should not be proclaimed before he had returned thence after completing the business with which he was charged, in order that you might have him as consul whom the situation of the republic required and yourselves prefer." Thus nothing was said about the assembly till Marcellus returned. Meanwhile Quintus Fabius Maximus and Titus Otacilius Crassus were created duumvirs for dedicating temples, Otacilius to Mens, Fabius to Venus Erycina. Both are situated in the Capitol, and separated by one channel. It was afterwards proposed to the people, to make Roman citizens of the three hundred Campanian horsemen who had returned to Rome after having faithfully served their period, and also that they should be considered to have been citizens of Cumæ from the day before that on which the Campanians had revolted from the Roman people. It had been a principal inducement to this proposition, that they themselves said they knew not to what people they belonged, having left their former country, and being not yet admitted into that to which they had returned. After Marcellus returned from the army, an assembly was proclaimed for electing one consul in the room of Lucius Posthumius. Marcellus was elected with the greatest unanimity, and was immediately to enter upon his office, but as it thundered while he entered upon it, the augurs were summoned, who pronounced that they considered the creation formal, and the fathers spread a report that the gods were displeased, because on that occasion, for the first time, two plebeians had been elected consuls. Upon Marcellus's abdicating his office, Fabius Maximus, for the third time, was elected in his room. This year the sea appeared on fire; at Sinuessa a cow brought forth a horse foal; the statues in the temple of Juno Sospita Lanuvium flowed down with blood; and a shower of stones fell in the neighbourhood of that temple: on account of which shower the nine days' sacred rite was celebrated, as is usual on such occasions, and the other prodigies were carefully expiated.

The consuls divided the armies between them. The army which Marcus Junius the dictator had commanded fell to the lot of Fabius. To that of Sempronius fell the volunteer slaves, with twenty-five thousand of the allies. To Marcus Valerius the prætor were assigned the legions which had returned from Sicily. Marcus Claudius, proconsul, was sent to that army which lay above Suessula for the protection of Nola. The prætors set out for Sicily and Sardinia. The consuls issued a proclamation, that as often as they summoned a senate, the senators and those who had a right to give their opinion in the senate, should assemble at the Capuan gate. The prætors who were charged with the administration of justice, fixed their tribunals in the public fish market; there they ordered sureties to be entered into, and here justice was administered this year. Meanwhile news was brought to Carthage, from which place Mago, Hannibal's brother, was on the point of carrying over into Italy twelve thousand foot, fifteen hundred horse, twenty elephants, and a thousand talents of silver, under a convoy of sixty men of war, that the operations of the war had not succeeded in Spain, and that almost all the people in that province had gone over to the Romans. There were some who were for sending Mago with that fleet and those forces into Spain, neglecting Italy, when an unexpected prospect of regaining Sardinia broke upon them. They were informed, that "the Roman army there was small, that Aulus Cornelius, who had been prætor there, and was well acquainted with the province, was quitting it, and that a new one was expected. Moreover, that the minds of the Sardinians were now wearied with the long continuance of rule; and that during the last year it had been exercised with severity and rapacity. That the people were weighed down with heavy taxes, and an oppressive contribution of corn: that there was nothing wanting but a leader to whom they might revolt." This secret embassy had been sent by the nobles, Hampsicora being the chief contriver of the measure, who at that time was first by far in wealth and influence. Disconcerted and elated almost at the same time by these accounts, they sent Mago with his fleet and forces into Spain, and selecting Hasdrubal as general for Sardinia, assigned to him about as large a force as to Mago. At Rome, the consuls, after transacting what was necessary to be done in the city now prepared themselves for the war. Tiberius Sempronius appointed a day for his soldiers to assemble at Sinuessa; and Quintus Fabius also, having first consulted the senate, issued a proclamation, that all persons should convey corn from the fields into fortified towns, before the calends of June next ensuing: if any neglected to do so he would lay waste his lands, sell his slaves by auction, and burn his farm-houses. Not even the prætors, who were created for the purpose of administering justice, were allowed an exemption from military employments. It was resolved that Valerius the prætor should go into Apulia, to receive the army from Terentius, and that, when the legions from Sicily had arrived, he should employ them principally for the protection of that quarter. That the army of Terentius should be sent into Sicily, with some one of the lieutenant-generals. Twenty-five ships were given to Marcus Valerius, to protect the sea-coast between Brundusium and Tarentum. An equal number was given to Quintus Fulvius, the city prætor, to protect the coasts in the neighbourhood of the city. To Caius Terentius, the proconsul, it was given in charge to press soldiers in the Picenian territory, and to protect that part of the country; and Titus Otacilius Crassus, after he had dedicated the temple of Mens in the Capitol, was invested with command, and sent into Sicily to take the conduct of the fleet.

On this contest, between the two most powerful people in the world, all kings and nations had fixed their attention. Among them Philip, king of the Macedonians, regarded it with greater anxiety, in proportion as he was nearer to Italy, and because he was separated from it only by the Ionian Sea. When he first heard that Hannibal had crossed the Alps, as he was rejoiced that a war had arisen between the Romans and the Carthaginians, so while their strength was yet undetermined, he felt doubtful which he should rather wish to be victorious. But after the third battle had been fought and the third victory had been on the side of the Carthaginians, he inclined to fortune, and sent ambassadors to Hannibal. These, avoiding the harbours of Brundusium and Tarentum, because they were occupied by guards of Roman ships, landed at the temple of Juno Lacinia. Thence passing through Apulia, on their way to Capua, they fell in with the Roman troops stationed to protect the country, and were conveyed to Marcus Valerius Lævinus, the prætor, who lay encamped in the neighbourhood of Luceria. Here Xenophanes, who was at the head of the embassy, fearlessly stated, that he was sent by King Philip to conclude a treaty of alliance and friendship with the Roman people, and that he had commissions to the Roman consuls, senate, and people. The prætor, highly delighted with this new alliance with a distinguished potentate, amidst the desertions of her old allies, courteously entertained these enemies as guests, and furnished them with persons to accompany them carefully to point out the roads, and inform them what places, and what passes, the Romans or the enemy occupied. Xenophanes passing through the Roman troops came into Campania, whence, by the shortest way, he entered the camp of Hannibal, and concluded a treaty of alliance and friendship with him on the following terms: That "King Philip, with as large a fleet as he could, (and it was thought he could make one of two hundred ships,) should pass over into Italy, and lay waste the sea-coast, that he should carry on the war by land and sea with all his might; when the war was concluded, that all Italy, with the city of Rome itself, should be the property of the Carthaginians and Hannibal, and that all the booty should be given up to Hannibal. That when Italy was completely subdued they should sail into Greece, and carry on war with such nations as the king pleased. That the cities on the continent and the islands which border on Macedonia, should belong to Philip, and his dominions."

A treaty was concluded between the Carthaginian general and the ambassadors, upon nearly these terms; and Gisgo, Bostar, and Mago were sent as ambassadors with them to receive the ratification of the king in person. They arrived at the same place, near the temple of Juno Lacinia, where the vessel lay concealed in a creek. Setting out thence, when they had got into the open sea, they were descried by the Roman fleet, which was guarding the coasts of Calabria. Publius Valerius Flaccus having sent fly-boats to pursue and bring back the ship, the king's party at first attempted to fly; but afterwards, finding that they were overmatched in swiftness, they delivered themselves up to the Romans, and were brought to the commander of the fleet. Upon being asked by him who they were, whence they came, and whither they were going, Xenophanes, having once been pretty successful, made up a fictitious story and said, "that he was sent from Philip to the Romans; that he had succeeded in reaching Marcus Valerius, to whom alone he had safe access; that he was unable to make his way through Campania, which was beset with the troops of the enemy." But afterwards the Carthaginian dress and manners excited suspicions of the messengers of Hannibal, and when interrogated, their speech betrayed them; then on their companions being removed to separate places, and intimidated by threats, even a letter from Hannibal to Philip was discovered, and the agreement made between the king of the Macedonians and the Carthaginian. These points having been ascertained, the best course appeared to be, to convey the prisoners and their companions as soon as possible to the senate at Rome, or to the consuls, wheresoever they might be; for this service five of the fastest sailing vessels were selected, and Lucius Valerius Antias sent in command of them, with orders to distribute the ambassadors through all the ships separately, and take particular care that they should hold no conversation or consultation with each other. About the same time Aulus Cornelius Mammula, on his return from the province of Sardinia, made a report of the state of affairs in the island; that every body contemplated war and revolt; that Quintus Mucius who succeeded him, being on his arrival affected by the unwholesomeness of the air and water, had fallen into a disorder rather lingering than dangerous, and would for a long time be incapable of sustaining the violent exertion of the war; that the army there, though strong enough for the protection of a province in a state of tranquillity, was, nevertheless, not adequate to the maintenance of the war which seemed to be about to break out. Upon which the fathers decreed, that Quintus Fulvius Flaccus should enlist five thousand foot and four hundred horse, and take care that the legion thus formed should be transported as soon as possible into Sardinia, and send invested with command whomsoever he thought fit to conduct the business of the war until Mucius had recovered. For this service Titus Manlius Torquatus was sent; he had been twice consul and censor, and had subdued the Sardinians during his consulate. Nearly about the same time a fleet sent from Carthage to Sardinia under the conduct of Hasdrubal, surnamed the Bald, having suffered from a violent tempest, was driven upon the Balearian islands, where a good deal of time was lost in refitting the ships, which were hauled on shore, so much were they damaged, not only in their rigging but also in their hulls.

As the war was carried on in Italy with less vigour since the battle of Cannæ, the strength of one party having been broken, and the energy of the other relaxed, the Campanians of themselves made an attempt to subjugate Cumæ, at first by soliciting them to revolt from the Romans, and when that plan did not succeed, they contrived an artifice by which to entrap them. All the Campanians had a stated sacrifice at Hamæ. They informed the Cumans that the Campanian senate would come there, and requested that the Cuman senate should also be present to deliberate in concert, in order that both people might have the same allies and the same enemies; they said that they would have an armed force there for their protection, that there might be no danger from the Romans or Carthaginians. The Cumans, although they suspected treachery, made no objection, concluding that thus the deception they meditated might be concealed. Meanwhile Tiberius Sempronius, the Roman consul, having purified his army at Sinuessa, where he had appointed a day for their meeting, crossed the Vulturnus, and pitched his camp in the neighbourhood of Liternum. As his troops were stationed here without any employment, he compelled them frequently to go through their exercise, that the recruits, which consisted principally of volunteer slaves, might accustom themselves to follow the standards, and know their own centuries in battle While thus engaged, the general was particularly anxious for concord, and therefore enjoined the lieutenant-generals and the tribunes that "no disunion should be engendered among the different orders, by casting reproaches on any one on account of his former condition. That the veteran soldier should be content be placed on an equal footing with the tiro, the free-man with the volunteer slave; that all should consider those men sufficiently respectable in point of character and birth, to whom the Roman people had intrusted their arms and standards; that the measures which circumstances made it necessary to adopt, the same circumstances also made it necessary to support when adopted." This was not more carefully prescribed by the generals than observed by the soldiers; and in a short time the minds of all were united in such perfect harmony, that the condition from which each became a soldier was almost forgotten. While Gracchus was thus employed, ambassadors from Cumæ brought him information of the embassy which had come to them from the Campanians, a few days before, and the answer they had given them; that the festival would take place in three days from that time; that not only the whole body of their senate, but that the camp and the army of the Campanians would be there. Gracchus having directed the Cumans to convey every thing out of their fields into the town, and to remain within their walls, marched himself to Cumæ, on the day before that on which the Campanians were to attend the sacrifice. Hamæ was three miles distant from his position. The Campanians had by this time assembled there in great numbers according to the plan concerted; and not far off Marius Alfius, Medixtuticus, which is the name of the chief magistrate of the Campanians, lay encamped in a retired spot with fourteen thousand armed men, considerably more occupied in making preparation for the sacrifice and in concerting the stratagem to be executed during it, than in fortifying his camp or any other military work. The sacrifice at Hamæ lasted for three days. It was a nocturnal rite, so arranged as to be completed before midnight. Gracchus, thinking this the proper time for executing his plot, placed guards at the gates to prevent any one from carrying out intelligence of his intentions; and having compelled his men to employ the time from the tenth hour in taking refreshment and sleep, in order that they might be able to assemble on a signal given as soon as it was dark. He ordered the standards to be raised about the first watch, and marching in silence, reached Hamæ at midnight; where, finding the Campanian camp in a neglected state, as might be expected during a festival, he assaulted it at every gate at once; some he butchered while stretched on the ground asleep, others as they were returning unarmed after finishing the sacrifice. In the tumultuous action of this night more than two thousand men were slain, together with the general himself, Marius Alfius, and thirty-four military standards were captured.

Gracchus, having made himself master of the enemy's camp with the loss of less than a hundred men, hastily returned to Cumæ, fearful of an attack from Hannibal, who lay encamped above Capua on Tifata; nor did his provident anticipation of the future deceive him; for as soon as intelligence was brought to Capua of this loss, Hannibal, concluding that he should find at Hamæ this army, which consisted for the most part of recruits and slaves, extravagantly elated with its success, despoiling the vanquished and collecting booty, marched by Capua at a rapid pace, ordering those Campanians whom he met in their flight to be conducted to Capua under an escort, and the wounded to be conveyed in carriages. He found at Hamæ the camp abandoned by the enemy, where there was nothing to be seen but the traces of the recent carnage, and the bodies of his allies strewed in every part. Some advised him to lead his troops immediately thence to Cumæ, and assault the town. Though Hannibal desired, in no ordinary degree, to get possession of Cumæ at least, as a maritime town, since he could not gain Neapolis; yet as his soldiers had brought out with them nothing besides their arms on their hasty march, he retired to his camp on Tifata. But, wearied with the entreaties of the Campanians, he returned thence to Cumæ the following day, with every thing requisite for besieging the town; and having thoroughly wasted the lands of Cumæ, pitched, his camp a mile from the town, in which Gracchus had stayed more because he was ashamed to abandon, in such an emergency, allies who implored his protection and that of the Roman people, than because he felt confidence in his army. Nor dared the other consul, Fabius, who was encamped at Cales, lead his troops across the Vulturnus, being employed at first in taking new auspices, and afterwards with the prodigies which were reported one after another; and while expiating these, the aruspices answered that they were not easily atoned.

While these causes detained Fabius, Sempronius was besieged, and now works were employed in the attack. Against a very large wooden tower which was brought up to the town, the Roman consul raised up another considerably higher from the wall itself; for he had made use of the wall, which was pretty high of itself, as a platform, placing strong piles as supports. From this the besieged at first defended their walls and city, with stones, javelins, and other missiles; but lastly, when they perceived the tower advanced into contact with the wall they threw upon it a large quantity of fire, making use of blazing fire-brands; and while the armed men were throwing themselves down from the tower in great numbers, in consequence of the flames thus occasioned, the troops sallying out of the town at two gates at once, routed the enemy, and drove them back to their camp; so that the Carthaginians that day were more like persons besieged than besiegers. As many as one thousand three hundred of the Carthaginians were slain, and fifty-nine made prisoners, having been unexpectedly overpowered, while standing careless and unconcerned near the walls and on the outposts, fearing any thing rather than a sally. Gracchus sounded a retreat, and withdrew his men within the walls, before the enemy could recover themselves from the effects of this sudden terror. The next day Hannibal, supposing that the consul, elated with his success, would engage him in a regular battle, drew up his troops in battle-array between the camp and the city; but finding that not a man was removed from the customary guard of the town, and that nothing was hazarded upon rash hopes, he returned to Tifata without accomplishing any thing. At the same time that Cumæ was relieved from siege, Tiberius Sempronius, surnamed Longus, fought successfully with the Carthaginian general, Hanno, at Grumentum in Lucania. He slew above two thousand of the enemy, losing two hundred and eighty of his own men. He took as many as forty-one military standards. Hanno, driven out of the Lucanian territory, drew back among the Bruttii. Three towns belonging to the Hirpinians, which had revolted from the Romans, were regained by force by the prætor, Marcus Valerius, Vercellius and Sicilius, the authors of the revolt, were beheaded; above a thousand prisoners sold by auction; and the rest of the booty having been given up to the soldiery, the army was marched back to Luceria.

While these things were taking place in Lucania and Hirpinia, the five ships, which were conveying to Rome the captured ambassadors of the Macedonians and Carthaginians, after passing round the whole coast of Italy from the upper to the lower sea, were sailing by Cumæ, when, it not being known whether they belonged to enemies or allies, Gracchus despatched some ships from his fleet to meet them. When it was ascertained, in the course of their mutual inquiries that the consul was at Cumæ, the ships put in there, the captives were brought before the consul, and their letters placed in his hands. The consul, after he had read the letters of Philip and Hannibal, sent them all, sealed up, to the senate by land, ordering that the ambassadors should be conveyed thither by sea. The ambassadors and the letters arriving at Rome nearly on the same day, and on examination the answers of the ambassadors corresponding with the contents of the letters, at first intense anxiety oppressed the fathers, on seeing what a formidable war with Macedonia threatened them, when with difficulty bearing up against the Punic war; yet so far were they from sinking under their calamities, that they immediately began to consider how they might divert the enemy from Italy, by commencing hostilities themselves. After ordering the prisoners to be confined in chains, and selling their attendants by public auction, they decreed, that twenty more ships should be got ready, in addition to the twenty-five ships which Publius Valerius Flaccus had been appointed to command. These being provided and launched, and augmented by the five ships which had conveyed the captive ambassadors to Rome, a fleet of fifty ships set sail from Ostia to Tarentum. Publius Valerius was ordered to put on board the soldiers of Varro, which Lucius Apustius, lieutenant-general, commanded at Tarentum; and, with this fleet of fifty ships, not only to protect the coast of Italy, but also to make inquiry respecting the Macedonian war. If the plans of Philip corresponded with his letter, and the discoveries made by his ambassadors, he was directed to acquaint the prætor, Marcus Valerius, with it, who, leaving Lucius Apustius, lieutenant-general, in command of the army, and going to Tarentum to the fleet, was to cross over to Macedonia with all speed, and endeavour to detain Philip in his own dominions. The money which had been sent into Sicily to Appius Claudius, to be repaid to Hiero, was assigned for the support of the fleet and the maintenance of the Macedonian war. This money was conveyed to Tarentum, by Lucius Apustius, lieutenant-general, and with it Hiero sent two hundred thousand pecks of wheat, and a hundred thousand of barley.

While the Romans were engaged in these preparations and transactions, the captured ship, which formed one of those which had been sent to Rome, made its escape on the voyage and returned to Philip; from which source it became known that the ambassadors with their letters had been made prisoners. Not knowing, therefore, what had been agreed upon between Hannibal and his ambassadors, or what proposals they were to have brought back to him, he sent another embassy with the same instructions. The ambassadors sent to Hannibal were Heraclitus, surnamed Scotinus, Crito of Beræa, and Sositheus of Magnesia; these successfully took and brought back their commissions, but the summer had passed before the king could take any step or make any attempt. Such an influence had the capture of one vessel, together with the ambassadors, in deferring a war which threatened the Romans. Fabius crossed the Vulturnus, after having at length expiated the prodigies, and both the consuls prosecuted the war in the neighbourhood of Capua. Fabius regained by force the towns Compulteria, Trebula, and Saticula, which had revolted to the Carthaginians; and in them were captured the garrisons of Hannibal and a great number of Campanians. At Nola, as had been the case the preceding year, the senate sided with the Romans, the commons with Hannibal; and deliberations were held clandestinely on the subject of massacring the nobles and betraying the city; but to prevent their succeeding in their designs, Fabius marched his army between Capua and the camp of Hannibal on Tifata, and sat down in the Claudian camp above Suessula, whence he sent Marcus Marcellus, the proconsul, with those forces which he had under him, to Nola for its protection.

In Sardinia also the operations of the war, which had been intermitted from the time that Quintus Mucius, the prætor, had been seized with a serious illness, began to be conducted by Titus Manlius, the prætor. Having hauled the ships of war on shore at Carale, and armed his mariners, in order that he might prosecute the war by land, and received the army from the prætor, he made up the number of twenty-two thousand foot and twelve hundred horse. Setting out for the territory of the enemy with these forces of foot and horse, he pitched his camp not far from the camp of Hampsicora. It happened that Hampsicora was then gone among the Sardinians, called Pelliti, in order to arm their youth, whereby he might augment his forces. His son, named Hiostus, had the command of the camp, who coming to an engagement, with the presumption of youth, was routed and put to flight. In that battle as many as three thousand of the Sardinians were slain, and about eight hundred taken alive. The rest of the army at first wandered in their flight through the fields and woods, but afterwards all fled to a city named Cornus, the capital of that district, whither there was a report that their general had fled; and the war in Sardinia would have been brought to a termination by that battle, had not the Carthaginian fleet under the command of Hasdrubal, which had been driven by a storm upon the Balearian islands, come in seasonably for inspiring a hope of renewing the war. Manlius, after hearing of the arrival of the Punic fleet, returned to Carale, which afforded Hampsicora an opportunity of forming a junction with the Carthaginian. Hasdrubal, having landed his forces and sent back his fleet to Carthage, set out under the guidance of Hampsicora, to lay waste the lands of the allies of the Romans; and he would have proceeded to Carale, had not Manlius, meeting him with his army, restrained him from this wide-spread depredation. At first their camps were pitched opposite to each other, at a small distance; afterwards skirmishes and slight encounters took place with varying success; lastly, they came down into the field and fought a regular pitched battle for four hours. The Carthaginians caused the battle to continue long doubtful, for the Sardinians were accustomed to yield easily; but at last, when the Sardinians fell and fled on all sides around them, the Carthaginians themselves were routed. But as they were turning their backs, the Roman general, wheeling round that wing with which he had driven back the Sardinians, intercepted them, after which it was rather a carnage than a battle. Two thousand of the enemy, Sardinians and Carthaginians together, were slain, about three thousand seven hundred captured, with twenty-seven military standards.

Above all, the general, Hasdrubal, and two other noble Carthaginians having been made prisoners, rendered the battle glorious and memorable; Mago, who was of the Barcine family, and nearly related to Hannibal, and Hanno, the author of the revolt of the Sardinians, and without doubt the instigator of this war. Nor less did the Sardinian generals render that battle distinguished by their disasters; for not only was Hiostus, son of Hampsicora, slain in the battle, but Hampsicora himself flying with a few horse, having heard of the death of his son in addition to his unfortunate state, committed suicide by night, lest the interference of any person should prevent the accomplishment of his design. To the other fugitives the city of Cornus afforded a refuge, as it had done before; but Manlius, having assaulted it with his victorious troops, regained it in a few days. Then other cities also which had gone over to Hampsicora and the Carthaginians, surrendered themselves and gave hostages, on which having imposed a contribution of money and corn, proportioned to the means and delinquency of each, he led back his troops to Carale. There launching his ships of war, and putting the soldiers he had brought with him on board, he sailed to Rome, reported to the fathers the total subjugation of Sardinia, and handed over the contribution of money to the quæstors, of corn to the ædiles, and the prisoners to the prætor Fulvius. During the same time, as Titus Otacilius the prætor, who had sailed over with a fleet of fifty ships from Lilybæum to Africa, and laid waste the Carthaginian territory, was returning thence to Sardinia, to which place it was reported that Hasdrubal had recently crossed over from the Baleares, he fell in with his fleet on its return to Africa; and after a slight engagement in the open sea, captured seven ships with their crews. Fear dispersed the rest far and wide, not less effectually than a storm. It happened also, at the same time, that Bomilcar arrived at Locri with soldiers sent from Carthage as a reinforcement, bringing with him also elephants and provisions. In order to surprise and overpower him, Appius Claudius, having hastily led his troops to Messana, under pretext of making the circuit of the province, crossed over to Locri, the tide being favourable. Bomilcar had by this time left the place, having set out for Bruttium to join Hanno. The Locrians closed their gates against the Romans, and

Appius Claudius returned to Rome without achieving any thing, by his strenuous efforts. The same summer Marcellus made frequent excursions from Nola, which he was occupying with a garrison, into the lands of the Hirpini and Caudine Samnites, and so destroyed all before him with fire and sword, that he renewed in Samnium the memory of her ancient disasters.

Ambassadors were therefore despatched from both nations at the same time to Hannibal, who thus addressed the Carthaginian: "Hannibal, we carried on hostilities with the Roman people, by ourselves and from our own resources, as long as our own arms and our own strength could protect us. Our confidence in these failing, we attached ourselves to king Pyrrhus. Abandoned by him, we accepted of a peace, dictated by necessity, which we continued to observe up to the period when you arrived in Italy, through a period of almost fifty years. Your valour and good fortune, not more than your unexampled humanity and kindness displayed towards our countrymen, whom, when made prisoners, you restored to us, so attached us to you, that while you our friend were in health and safety, we not only feared not the Romans, but not even the anger of the gods, if it were lawful so to express ourselves. And yet, by Hercules, you not only being in safety and victorious, but on the spot, (when you could almost hear the shrieks of our wives and children, and see our buildings in flames,) we have suffered, during this summer, such repeated devastations, that Marcellus, and not Hannibal, would appear to have been the conqueror at Cannæ; while the Romans boast that you had strength only to inflict a single blow; and having as it were left your sting, now lie torpid. For near a century we waged war with the Romans, unaided by any foreign general or army; except that for two years Pyrrhus rather augmented his own strength by the addition of our troops, than defended us by his. I will not boast of our successes, that two consuls and two consular armies were sent under the yoke by us, nor of any other joyful and glorious events which have happened to us. We can tell of the difficulties and distresses we then experienced, with less indignation than those which are now occurring. Dictators, those officers of high authority, with their masters of horse, two consuls with two consular armies, entered our borders, and, after having reconnoitred and posted reserves, led on their troops in regular array to devastate our country. Now we are the prey of a single proprætor, and of one little garrison, for the defence of Nola. Now they do not even confine themselves to plundering in companies, but, like marauders, range through our country from one end to the other, more unconcernedly than if they were rambling through the Roman territory. And the reason is this, you do not protect us yourself, and the whole of our youth, which, if at home, would keep us in safety, is serving under your banners. We know nothing either of you or your army, but we know that it would be easy for the man who has routed and dispersed so many Roman armies, to put down these rambling freebooters of ours, who roam about in disorder to whatsoever quarter the hope of booty, however groundless, attracts them. They indeed will be the prey of a few Numidians, and a garrison sent to us will also dislodge that at Nola, provided you do not think those men undeserving that you should protect them as allies, whom you have esteemed worthy of your alliance."

To this Hannibal replied, "that the Hirpini and Samnites did every thing at once: that they both represented their sufferings, solicited succours, and complained that they were undefended and neglected. Whereas, they ought first to have represented their sufferings, then to have solicited succours; and lastly, if those succours were not obtained, then, at length, to make complaint that assistance had been implored without effect. That he would lead his troops not into the fields of the Hirpini and Samnites, lest he too should be a burthen to them, but into the parts immediately contiguous, and belonging to the allies of the Roman people, by plundering which, he would enrich his own soldiers, and cause the enemy to retire from them through fear. With regard to the Roman war, if the battle of Trasimenus was more glorious than that at Trebia, and the battle of Cannæ than that of Trasimenus, that he would eclipse the fame of the battle of Cannæ by a greater and more brilliant victory." With this answer, and with munificent presents, he dismissed the ambassadors. Having left a pretty large garrison in Tifata, he set out with the rest of his troops to go to Nola. Thither came Hanno from the Bruttii with recruits and elephants brought from Carthage. Having encamped not far from the place, every thing, upon examination, was found to be widely different from what he had heard from the ambassadors of the allies. For Marcellus was doing nothing, in such a way that he could be said to have committed himself rashly either to fortune or to the enemy. He had gone out on plundering expeditions, having previously reconnoitred, planted strong guards, and secured a retreat; the same caution was observed and the same provisions made, as if Hannibal were present. At this time, when he perceived the enemy on the approach, he kept his forces within the walls, ordered the senators of Nola to patrol the walls, and explore on all hands what was doing among the enemy. Of these Herennius Bassus and Herius Petrius, having been invited by Hanno, who had come up to the wall, to a conference, and gone out with the permission of Marcellus, were thus addressed by him, through an interpreter. After extolling the valour and good fortune of Hannibal, and vilifying the majesty of the Roman people, which he represented as sinking into decrepitude with their strength; he said, "but though they were on an equality in these respects, as once perhaps they were, yet they who had experienced how oppressive the government of Rome was towards its allies, and how great the clemency of Hannibal, even towards all his prisoners of the Italian name, were bound to prefer the friendship and alliance of the Carthaginians to those of the Romans." If both the consuls with their armies were at Nola, still they would no more be a match for Hannibal than they had been at Cannæ, much less would one prætor with a few raw soldiers be able to defend it. It was a question which concerned themselves more than Hannibal whether he should take possession of Nola as captured or surrendered, for that he would certainly make himself master of it, as he had done with regard to Capua and Nuceria, and what difference there was between the fate of Capua and Nuceria, the Nolans themselves, situated as they were nearly midway between them, were well aware. He said he was unwilling to presage the evils which would result to the city if taken by force, but would in preference pledge himself that if they would deliver up Nola, together with Marcellus and his garrison, no other person than themselves should dictate the conditions on which they should come into the friendship and alliance of Hannibal.

To this Herennius Bassus replied, that, "a friendship had subsisted now for many years between the Romans and the Nolans, which neither party up to that day regretted; and even had they been disposed to change their friends upon a change of fortune, it was now too late to change; had they intended to surrender themselves to Hannibal, they should not have called a Roman garrison to their aid: that all fortunes both were now and should to the last be shared with those who had come to their protection." This conference deprived Hannibal of the hope of gaining Nola by treachery; he therefore completely invested the city, in order that he might attack the walls in every part at once. Marcellus, when he perceived that he had come near to the walls, having drawn up his troops within the gate, sallied forth with great impetuosity; several were knocked down and slain on the first charge: afterwards the troops running up to those who were engaged, and their forces being thus placed on an equality? the battle began to be fierce; nor would there have been many actions equally memorable, had not the combatants been separated by a shower of rain attended with a tremendous storm. On that day, after having engaged in a slight contest, and with inflamed minds, they retired, the Romans to the city, the Carthaginians to their camp. Of the Carthaginians, however, there fell from the shock of the first sally not more than thirty, of the Romans not one. The rain continued without intermission through the whole night, until the third hour of the following day, and therefore, though both parties were eager for the contest, they nevertheless kept themselves within their works for that day. On the third day Hannibal sent a portion of his troops into the lands of the Nolans to plunder. Marcellus perceiving this, immediately led out his troops and formed for battle, nor did Hannibal decline fighting. The interval between the city and the camp was about a mile. In that space, and all the country round Nola consists of level ground, the armies met. The shout which was raised on both sides, called back to the battle, which had now commenced, the nearest of those cohorts which had gone out into the fields to plunder. The Nolans too joined the Roman line. Marcellus having highly commended them, desired them to station themselves in reserve, and to carry the wounded out of the field but not take part in the battle, unless they should receive a signal from him.

It was a doubtful battle; the generals exerting themselves to the utmost in exhorting, and the soldiers in fighting Marcellus urged his troops to press vigorously on men who had been vanquished but three days before, who had been put to flight at Cumæ only a few days ago, and who had been driven from Nola the preceding year by himself, as general, though with different troops. He said, "that all the forces of the enemy were not in the field; that they were rambling about the country in plundering parties, and that even those who were engaged, were enfeebled with Campanian luxury, and worn out with drunkenness, lust, and every kind of debauchery, which they had been indulging in through the whole winter. That the energy and vigour had left them, that the strength of mind and body had vanished, by which the Pyrenees and the tops of the Alps had been passed. That those now engaged were the remains of those men, with scarcely strength to support their arms and limbs. That Capua had been a Cannæ to Hannibal; that there his courage in battle, his military discipline, the fame he had already acquired, and his hopes of future glory, were extinguished." While Marcellus was raising the spirits of his troops by thus inveighing against the enemy, Hannibal assailed them with still heavier reproaches. He said, "he recognised the arms and standards which he had seen and employed at Trebia and Trasimenus, and lastly at Cannæ; but that he had indeed led one sort of troops into winter quarters at Capua, and brought another out. Do you, whom two consular armies could never withstand, with difficulty maintain your ground against a Roman lieutenant-general, and a single legion with a body of auxiliaries? Does Marcellus now a second time with impunity assail us with a band of raw recruits and Nolan auxiliaries? Where is that soldier of mine, who took off the head of Caius Flaminius, the consul, after dragging him from his horse? Where is the man who slew Lucius Paulus at Cannæ? Is it that the steel hath lost its edge? or that your right hands are benumbed? or what other miracle is it? You who, when few, have been accustomed to conquer numbers, now scarce maintain your ground, the many against the few. Brave in speech only, you were wont to boast that you would take Rome by storm if you could find a general to lead you. Lo! here is a task of less difficulty. I would have you try your strength and courage here. Take Nola, a town situated on a plain, protected neither by river nor sea; after that, when you have enriched yourselves with the plunder and spoils of that wealthy town, I will either lead or follow you whithersoever you have a mind."

Neither praises nor reproaches had any effect in confirming their courage. Driven from their ground in every quarter, while the Romans derived fresh spirits, not only from the exhortations of their general, but from the Nolans, who, by their acclamations in token of their good wishes, fed the flame of battle, the Carthaginians turned their backs, and were driven to their camp, which the Roman soldiers were eager to attack; but Marcellus led them back to Nola, amidst the great joy and congratulations even from the commons, who hitherto had been more favourable to the Carthaginians. Of the enemy more than five thousand were slain on that day, six hundred made prisoners, with nineteen military standards and two elephants. Four elephants were killed in the battle. Of the Romans less than a thousand were killed. The next day was employed by both parties in burying their dead, under a tacit truce. Marcellus burnt the spoils of the enemy, in fulfilment of a vow to Vulcan. On the third day after, on account of some pique, I suppose, or in the hope of more advantageous service, one thousand two hundred and seventy-two horsemen, Numidians and Spaniards, deserted to Marcellus. The Romans had frequently availed themselves of their brave and faithful service in that war. After the conclusion of the war, portions of land were given to the Spaniards in Spain, to the Numidians in Africa, in consideration of their valour. Having sent Hanno back from Nola to the Bruttians with the troops with which he had come, Hannibal went himself into winter quarters in Apulia, and took up a position in the neighbourhood of Arpi. Quintus Fabius, as soon as he heard that Hannibal was set out into Apulia, conveyed corn, collected from Nola and Naples, into the camp above Suessula; and having strengthened the fortifications and left a garrison sufficient for the protection of the place during the winter, moved his camp nearer to Capua, and laid waste the Campanian lands with fire and sword; so that at length the Campanians, though not very confident in their strength, were obliged to go out of their gates and fortify a camp in the open space before the city. They had six thousand armed men, the infantry, unfit for action. In their cavalry they had more strength. They therefore harassed the enemy by attacking them with these. Among the many distinguished persons who served in the Campanian cavalry was one Cerrinus Jubellius, surnamed Taurea. Though of that extraction, he was a Roman citizen, and by far the bravest horseman of all the Campanians, insomuch that when he served under the Roman banners, there was but one man, Claudius Asellus, a Roman, who rivalled him in his reputation as a horseman. Taurea having for a long time diligently sought for this man, riding up to the squadrons of the enemy, at length having obtained silence, inquired where Claudius Asellus was, and asked why, since he had been accustomed to dispute about their merit in words, he would not decide the matter with the sword, and if vanquished give him *spolia opima*, or if victorious take them.

Asellus, who was in the camp, having been informed of this, waited only to ask the consul leave to depart from the ordinary course and fight an enemy who had challenged him. By his permission, he immediately put on his arms, and riding out beyond the advanced guards called on Taurea by name, and bid him come to the encounter when he pleased. By this time the Romans had gone out in large bodies to witness the contest, and the Campanians had crowded not only the rampart of the camp, but the walls of the city to get a view of it. After a flourish of expressions of mutual defiance, they spurred on their horses with their spears pointed. Then evading each other's attacks, for they had free space to move in, they protracted the battle without a wound. Upon this the Campanian observed to the Roman, "This will be only a trial of skill between our horses and not between horsemen, unless we ride them down from the plain into this hollow way. There, as there will be no room for retiring, we shall come to close quarters." Almost quicker than the word, Claudius leaped into the hollow way. Taurea, bold in words more than in reality, said, "Never be the ass in the ditch;" an expression which from this circumstance became a common proverb among rustics. Claudius having rode up and down the way to a considerable distance, and again come up into the plain without meeting his antagonist, after reflecting in reproachful terms on the cowardice of the enemy, returned in triumph to the camp, amidst great rejoicing and congratulation. To the account of this equestrian contest, some histories add a circumstance which is certainly astonishing, how true it is, is an open matter of opinion that Claudius, when in pursuit of Taurea, who fled back to the city, rode in at one of the gates of the enemy which stood open and made his escape unhurt through another, the enemy being thunderstruck at the strangeness of the circumstance.

The camps were then undisturbed, the consul even moved his camp back, that the Campanians might complete their sowing, nor did he do any injury to the lands till the blades in the corn-fields were grown sufficiently high to be useful for forage. This he conveyed into the Claudian camp above Suessula, and there erected winter quarters. He ordered Marcus Claudius, the proconsul, to retain at Nola a sufficient force for the protection of the place, and send the rest to Rome, that they might not be a burthen to their allies nor an expense to the republic. Tiberius Gracchus also, having led his legions from Cumæ to Luceria in Apulia, sent Marcus Valerius, the prætor, thence to Brundusium with the troops which he had commanded at Luceria, with orders to protect the coast of the Sallentine territory, and make provisions with regard to Philip and the Macedonian war. At the close of the summer, the events of which I have described, letters arrived from Publius and Cneius Scipio, stating the magnitude and success of their operations in Spain, but that the army was in want of money, clothing, and corn, and that then crews were in want of every thing. With regard to the pay, they said, that if the treasury was low, they would adopt some plan by which they might procure it from the Spaniards, but that the other supplies must certainly be sent from Rome, for otherwise neither the army could be kept together nor the province preserved. When the letters were read, all to a man admitted that the statement was correct, and the request reasonable, but it occurred to their minds, what great forces they were maintaining by land and sea, and how large a fleet must soon be equipped if a war with Macedon should break out, that Sicily and Sardinia, which before the war had wielded a revenue, were scarcely able to maintain the troops which protected those provinces, that the expenses were supplied by a tax, that both the number of the persons who contributed this tax was diminished by the great havoc made in their armies at the Trasimenus and Cannæ, and the few who survived, if they were oppressed with multiplied impositions, would perish by a calamity of a different kind. That, therefore, if the republic could not subsist by credit, it could not stand by its own resources. It was resolved, therefore, that Fulvius, the prætor, should present himself to the public assembly of the people, point out the necessities of the state, and exhort those persons who had increased their patrimonies by farming the public revenues, to furnish temporary loans for the service of that state, from which they had derived their wealth, and contract to supply what was necessary for the army in Spain, on the condition of being paid the first when there was money in the treasury. These things the prætor laid before the assembly, and fixed a day on which he would let on contract the furnishing the army in Spain with clothes and corn, and with such other things as were necessary for the crews.

When the day arrived, three companies, of nineteen persons, came forward to enter into the contract; but they made two requests: one was, that they should be exempt from military service while employed in that revenue business; the second was, that the state should bear all losses of the goods they shipped, which might arise either from the attacks of the enemy or from storms. Having obtained both their requests, they entered into the contract, and the affairs of the state were conducted by private funds. This character and love of country uniformly pervaded all ranks. As all the engagements were entered into with magnanimity, so were they fulfilled with the strictest fidelity; and the supplies were furnished in the same manner as formerly, from an abundant treasury. At the time when these supplies arrived, the town of Illiturgi was being besieged by Hasdrubal, Mago, and Hamilcar the son of Bomilcar, on account of its having gone over to the Romans. Between these three camps of the enemy, the Scipios effected an entrance into the town of their allies, after a violent contest and great slaughter of their opponents, and introduced some corn, of which there was a scarcity; and after exhorting the townsmen to defend their walls with the same spirit which they had seen displayed by the Roman army fighting in their behalf, led on their troops to attack the largest of the camps, in which Hasdrubal had the command. To this camp the two other generals of the Carthaginians with their armies came, seeing that the great business was to be done there. They therefore sallied from the camp and fought. Of the enemy engaged there were sixty thousand; of the Romans about sixteen; the victory, however, was so decisive, that the Romans slew more than their own number of the enemy, and captured more than three thousand, with nearly a thousand horses and fifty-nine military standards, five elephants having been slain in the battle. They made themselves masters of the three camps on that day. The siege of Illiturgi having been raised, the Carthaginian armies were led away to the siege of Intibili; the forces having been recruited out of that province, which was, above all others, fond of war, provided there was any plunder or pay to be obtained, and at that time had an abundance of young men. A second regular engagement took place, attended with the same fortune to both parties; in which above three thousand of the enemy were slain, more than two thousand captured, together with forty-two standards and nine elephants. Then, indeed, almost all the people of Spain came over to the Romans, and the achievements in Spain during that summer were much more important than those in Italy.

BOOK XXIV.

Hieronymus, king of Syracuse, whose grandfather Hiero had been a faithful ally of Rome, revolts to the Carthaginians, and for his tyranny is put to death by his subjects. Tiberius Sempronius Gracchus, the proconsul, defeats the Carthaginians under Hanno at Beneventum chiefly by the services of the slaves in his army, whom he subsequently liberated. Claudius Marcellus, the consul, besieges Syracuse. War is declared against Philip, king of Macedon, he is routed by night at Apollonia and retreats into Macedonia. This war is intrusted to Valerius the prætor. Operations of the Scipios against the Carthaginians in Spain. Syphax, king of the Numidians, is received into alliance by the Romans, and is defeated by Masinissa, king of the Massillians, who fought on the side of the Carthaginians. The Celtiberians joined the Romans, and their troops having been taken into pay, mercenary soldiers for the first time served in a Roman camp.

On his return from Campania into Bruttium, Hanno, with the assistance and under the guidance of the Bruttians, made an attempt upon the Greek cities; which were the more disposed to continue in alliance with the Romans, because they perceived that the Bruttians, whom they feared and hated, had taken part with the Carthaginians. The first place attempted was Rhegium, where several days were spent without effect. Meanwhile the Locrians hastily conveyed from the country into the city, corn, wood, and other things necessary for their use, as also that no booty might be left for the enemy. The number of persons which poured out of every gate increased daily, till at length those only were left in the city whose duty it was to repair the walls and gates, and to collect weapons in the fortresses. Against this mixed multitude, composed of persons of all ages and ranks, while rambling through the country, and for the most part unarmed, Hamilcar, the Carthaginian, sent out his cavalry, who, having been forbidden to hurt any one, only interposed their squadrons, so as to cut them off from the city when dispersed in flight. The general himself, having posted himself upon an eminence which commanded a view of the country and the city, ordered a cohort of Bruttians to approach the walls, call out the leaders of the Locrians to a conference, and promising them the friendship of Hannibal, exhort them to deliver up the city. At first the Bruttians were not believed in any thing they stated in the conference, but afterwards, when the Carthaginian appeared on the hills, and a few who had fled back to the city brought intelligence that all the rest of the multitude were in the power of the enemy, overcome with fear, they said they would consult the people. An assembly of the people was immediately called, when, as all the most fickle of the inhabitants were desirous of a change of measures and a new alliance, and those whose friends were cut off by the enemy without the city, had their minds bound as if they had given hostages, while a few rather silently approved of a constant fidelity than ventured to support the opinion they approved, the city was surrendered to the Carthaginians, with an appearance of perfect unanimity. Lucius Atilius, the captain of the garrison, together with the Roman soldiers who were with him, having been privately led down to the port, and put on board a ship, that they might be conveyed to Rhegium, Hamilcar and the Carthaginians were received into the city on condition that an alliance should be formed on equal terms; which condition, when they had surrendered, the Carthaginian had very nearly not performed, as he accused them of having sent away the Roman fraudulently, while the Locrians alleged that he had spontaneously fled. A body of cavalry went in pursuit of the fugitives, in case the tide might happen to detain them in the strait, or might carry the ships to land. The persons whom they were in pursuit of they did not overtake, but they descried some ships passing over the strait from Messana to Rhegium. These contained Roman troops sent by the prætor, Claudius, to occupy the city with a garrison. The enemy therefore immediately retired from Rhegium. At the command of Hannibal, peace was concluded with the Locrians on these terms: that "they should live free under their own laws; that the city should be open to the Carthaginians, the harbour in the power of the Locrians. That their alliance should rest on the principle, that the Carthaginian should help the Locrian and the Locrian the Carthaginian in peace and war."

Thus the Carthaginian troops were led back from the strait, while the Bruttians loudly complained that Locri and Rhegium, cities which they had fixed in their minds that they should have the plundering of, they had left untouched. Having therefore levied and armed fifteen thousand of their own youth, they set out by themselves to lay siege to Croto, which was also a Greek city, and on the coast, believing that they would obtain a great accession to their power, if they could get possession of a city upon the sea-coast, which had a port and was strongly defended by walls. This consideration annoyed them, that they neither could venture on the business without calling in the Carthaginians to their assistance, lest they should appear to have done any thing in a manner unbecoming allies, and on the other hand, lest, if the Carthaginian general should again show himself to have been rather an umpire of peace than an auxiliary in war, they should fight in vain against the liberty of Croto, as before in the affair of the Locrians. The most advisable course, therefore, appeared to be, that ambassadors should be sent to Hannibal, and that a stipulation should be obtained from him that Croto, when reduced, should be in possession of the Bruttians. Hannibal replied, that it was a question which should be determined by persons on the spot, and referred them to Hanno, from whom they could obtain no decisive answer. For they were unwilling that so celebrated and opulent a city should be plundered, and were in hopes that if the Bruttians should attack it, while the Carthaginians did not ostensibly approve or assist in the attack, the inhabitants would the more readily come over to them. The Crotonians were not united either in their measures or wishes. All the states of Italy were infected with one disease, as it were, the commons dissented from the nobles, the senate favouring the Romans, while the commons endeavoured to draw the states over to the Carthaginians. A deserter announced to the Bruttii that such a dissension prevailed in the city, that Aristomachus was the leader of the commons, and the adviser of the surrender of the city, that the city was of wide extent and thinly inhabited, that the walls in every part were in ruins, that it was only here and there that the guards and watches were kept by senators, and that wherever the commons kept guard, there an entrance lay open. Under the direction and guidance of the deserter, the Bruttians completely invested the city, and being received into it by the commons, got possession of every part, except the citadel, on the first assault. The nobles held the citadel, which they had taken care beforehand to have ready as a refuge against such an event. In the same place Aristomachus took refuge, as though he had advised the surrender of the city to the Carthaginians, and not to the Bruttians.

The wall of the city of Croto in circuit extended through a space of twelve miles, before the arrival of Pyrrhus in Italy. After the devastation occasioned by that war, scarcely half the city was inhabited. The river which had flowed through the middle of the town, now ran on the outside of the parts which were occupied by buildings, and the citadel was at a distance from the inhabited parts. Six miles from this celebrated city stood the temple of Juno Lacinia, more celebrated even than the city itself, and venerated by all the surrounding states. Here was a grove fenced with a dense wood and tall fir trees, with rich pastures in its centre, in which cattle of every kind, sacred to the goddess, fed without any keeper; the flocks of every kind going out separately and returning to their folds, never being injured, either from the lying in wait of wild beasts, or the dishonesty of men. These flocks were, therefore, a source of great revenue, from which a column of solid gold was formed and consecrated; and the temple became distinguished for its wealth also, and not only for its sanctity. Some miracles are attributed to it, as is generally the case with regard to such remarkable places. Rumour says that there is an altar in the vestibule of the temple, the ashes of which are never moved by any wind. But the citadel of Croto, overhanging the sea on one side, on the other, which looks towards the land, was protected formerly by its natural situation only, but was afterwards surrounded by a wall. It was in this part that Dionysius, the tyrant of Sicily, took it by stratagem, approaching by way of some rocks which faced from it. This citadel, which was considered sufficiently secure, was now occupied by the nobles of Croto, the Bruttians, in conjunction even with their own commons, besieging them. The Bruttians, however, perceiving at length that it was impossible to take the citadel by their own efforts, compelled by necessity, implored the aid of Hanno. He endeavoured to bring the

Crotonians to surrender, under an agreement that they should allow a colony of Bruttians to settle there; so that their city, desolate and depopulated by wars, might recover its former populousness: but not a man besides Aristomachus did he move; they affirmed, that "they would die sooner than, mixing with Bruttians, be turned to the rites, manners, and laws, and soon the language also of others." Aristomachus alone, since he was neither able to persuade them to surrender, nor could obtain an opportunity for betraying the citadel as he had betrayed the city, deserted to Hanno. A short time afterwards ambassadors of Locri, entering the citadel with the permission of Hanno, persuaded them to allow themselves to be removed to Locri, and not resolve to hazard extremities. They had already obtained leave from Hannibal to do this, by ambassadors sent for this purpose. Accordingly, Croto was evacuated, and the inhabitants were conducted to the sea, where they embarked; and the whole multitude removed to Locri. In Apulia, Hannibal and the Romans did not rest even during the winter. The consul Sempronius wintered at Luceria, Hannibal not far from Arpi. Slight engagements took place between them, accordingly as either side had an opportunity or advantage; by which the Roman soldiery were improved, and became daily more guarded and more secure against stratagems.

In Sicily, the death of Hiero, and the transfer of the government to his grandson, Hieronymus, had completely altered all things with regard to the Romans. Hieronymus was but a boy, as yet scarcely able to bear liberty, still less sovereign power. His guardians and friends gladly observed in him a disposition which might be easily plunged into every kind of vice; which Hiero foreseeing, is said to have formed an intention, in the latter part of his long life, of leaving Syracuse free, lest the sovereignty which had been acquired and established by honourable means, should be made a sport of and fall into ruin, under the administration of a boy. This plan of his his daughters strenuously opposed, who anticipated that the boy would enjoy the name of royalty, but that the administration of all affairs would be conducted by themselves and their husbands, Andranodorus and Zoippus, for these were left the principal of his guardians. It was not an easy task for a man in his ninetieth year, beset night and day by the winning artifices of women, to disenthral his judgment, and to consult only the good of the state in his domestic affairs. Accordingly, all he did was to leave fifteen guardians over his son, whom he entreated, on his death-bed, to preserve inviolate that alliance with the Romans, which he had himself cultivated for fifty years, and to take care that the young king should, above all things, tread in the steps of his father, and in that course of conduct in which he had been educated. Such were his injunctions. On the death of the king, the will was brought forward by the guardians, and the young king, who was now about fifteen, introduced into the public assembly, where a few persons, who had been placed in different parts on purpose to raise acclamations, expressed their approbation of the will; while all the rest were overwhelmed with apprehensions, in the destitute condition of the state, which had lost as it were its parent. The funeral of the king was then performed, which was honoured more by the love and affection of his citizens than the attentions of his kindred. Andranodorus next effected the removal of the other guardians, giving out that Hieronymus had now attained the years of manhood, and was competent to assume the government; and thus, by voluntarily resigning the guardianship which he shared with several others, united the powers of all in himself.

It would scarcely have been easy even for any good and moderate king, succeeding one so deeply rooted in their affections as Hiero was, to obtain the favour of the Syracusans. But Hieronymus, forsooth, as if he was desirous of exciting regret for the loss of his grandfather by his own vices, showed, immediately on his first appearance, how completely every thing was changed. For those who for so many years had seen Hiero and his son Gelon differing from the rest of the citizens neither in the fashion of their dress nor any other mark of distinction, now beheld the purple, the diadem, and armed guards, and their king sometimes proceeding from his palace in a chariot drawn by four white horses, according to the custom of the tyrant Dionysius. This costliness in equipage and appearance was accompanied by corresponding contempt of everybody, capricious airs, insulting expressions, difficulty of access, not to strangers only, but even to his guardians also, unheard of lusts, inhuman cruelty. Terror so great took possession of every body therefore, that some of his guardians, either by a voluntary death, or by exile, anticipated the tenor of his inflictions. Three of those persons to whom alone belonged a more familiar access to the palace, Andranodorus and Zoippus, sons-in-law of Hiero, and one Thraso, were not much attended to upon other subjects, but the two former exerting themselves in favour of the Carthaginians, while Thraso argued for the Roman alliance, they sometimes engaged the attention of the young king by their zeal and earnestness. It was at this time that a conspiracy formed against the life of the tyrant was discovered by a certain servant, of the same age as Hieronymus, who from his very childhood had associated with him on entirely familiar terms. The informer was able to name one of the conspirators, Theodotus, by whom he himself had been solicited. He was immediately seized, and delivered to Andranodorus to be subjected to torture, when, without hesitation, he confessed as to himself, but concealed his accomplices. At last, when racked with every species of torture, beyond the power of humanity to bear, pretending to be overcome by his sufferings, he turned his accusation from the guilty to the innocent, and feigned that Thraso was the originator of the plot, without whose able guidance, he said, they never would have been bold enough to attempt so daring a deed, he threw the guilt upon such innocent men, near the king's person, as appeared to him to be the most worthless, while fabricating his story amid groans and agonies. The naming of Thraso gave the highest degree of credibility to the story in the mind of the tyrant. Accordingly he was immediately given up to punishment, and others were added who were equally innocent. Not one of the conspirators, though their associate in the plot was for a long time subjected to torture, either concealed himself or fled, so great was their confidence in the fortitude and fidelity of Theodotus, and so great was his firmness in concealing their secret.

Thus on the removal of Thraso, who formed the only bond which held together the alliance with the Romans, immediately affairs clearly indicated defection. Ambassadors were sent to Hannibal, who sent back in company with a young man of noble birth named Hannibal, Hippocrates and Epicydes, natives of Carthage, and of Carthaginian extraction on their mother's side, but whose grandfather was an exile from Syracuse. Through their means an alliance was formed between Hannibal and the tyrant of Syracuse; and, with the consent of Hannibal, they remained with the tyrant. As soon as Appius Claudius, the prætor, whose province Sicily was, had received information of these events, he sent ambassadors to Hieronymus; who, upon stating that the object of their mission was to renew the alliance which had subsisted between the Romans and his grandfather, were heard and dismissed in an insulting manner, Hieronymus asking them sneeringly, "how they had fared at the battle of Cannæ? for that the ambassadors of Hannibal stated what could hardly be credited." He said, "he wished to know the truth, in order that before he made up his mind, he might determine which he should espouse as offering the better prospect." The Romans replied, that they would return to him when he had learned to receive embassies with seriousness; and, after having cautioned, rather than requested him, not rashly to change his alliance, they withdrew. Hieronymus sent ambassadors to Carthage, to conclude a league in conformity with the alliance with Hannibal. It was settled in the compact, that after they had expelled the Romans from Sicily, (which would speedily be effected if the Carthaginians sent ships and troops,) the river Himera, which divides the island in nearly equal portions, should be the limit of the Carthaginian and Syracusan dominions. Afterwards, puffed up by the flattery of those persons who bid him be mindful, not of Hiero only, but of king Pyrrhus, his maternal grandfather, he sent another embassy, in which he expressed his opinion that equity required that the whole of Sicily should be conceded to him, and that the dominion of Italy should be acquired as the peculiar possession of the Carthaginians. This levity and inconstancy of purpose in a hot-headed youth, did not excite their surprise, nor did they reprove it, anxious only to detach him from the Romans.

But every thing conspired to hurry him into perdition. For having sent before him Hippocrates and Epicydes with two thousand armed men, to make an attempt upon those cities which were occupied by Roman garrisons, he himself also proceeded to Leontium with all the remaining troops, which amounted to fifteen thousand foot and horse, when the conspirators (who all happened to be in the army) took possession of an uninhabited house, which commanded a narrow way, by which the king was accustomed to go to the forum. The rest stood here prepared and armed, waiting for the king to pass by. One of them, by name Dinomenes, as he was one of the body-guards, had the task assigned him of keeping back the crowd behind in the narrow way, upon some pretext, when the king approached the door. All was done according to the arrangement. Dinomenes having delayed the crowd, by pretending to lift up his foot and loosen a knot which was too tight, occasioned such an interval, that an attack being made upon the king, as he passed by unattended by his guards, he was pierced with several wounds before any assistance could be brought. When the shout and tumult was heard, some weapons were discharged on Dinomenes, who now openly opposed them; he escaped from them, however, with only two wounds. The body-guard, as soon as they saw the king prostrate, betook themselves to flight. Of the assassins, some proceeded to the forum to the populace, who were rejoiced at the recovery of their liberty; others to Syracuse to anticipate the measures of Andranodorus and the rest of the royal party. Affairs being in this uncertain state, Appius Claudius perceiving a war commencing in his neighbourhood, informed the senate by letter, that Sicily had become reconciled to the Carthaginians and Hannibal. For his own part, in order to frustrate the designs of the Syracusans, he collected all his forces on the boundary of the province and the kingdom. At the close of this year, Quintus Fabius, by the authority of the senate, fortified and garrisoned Puteoli, which, during the war, had begun to be frequented as an emporium. Coming thence to Rome to hold the election, he appointed the first day for it which could be employed for that purpose, and, while on his march, passed by the city and descended into the Campus Martius. On that day, the right of voting first having fallen by lot on the junior century of the Anien tribe, they appointed Titus Otacilius and Marcus Æmilius Regillus, consuls, when Quintus Fabius, having obtained silence, delivered the following speech:

"If we had either peace in Italy, or had war with such an enemy that the necessity to be careful was less urgent than it is, I should consider that man as wanting in respect for your liberty, who would at all impede that zealous desire which you bring with you into the Campus Martius, of conferring honours on whom you please. But since during the present war, and with the enemy we have now to encounter, none of our generals have ever committed an error which has not been attended with most disastrous consequences to us, it behoves you to use the same circumspection in giving your suffrages for the creation of consuls, which you would exert were you going armed into the field of battle. Every man ought thus to say to himself I am nominating a consul who is to cope with the general Hannibal. In the present year, at Capua, when Jubellius Taurea, the most expert horseman of the Campanians, gave a challenge, Claudius Asellus, the most expert among the Roman horsemen, was pitted against him. Against the Gaul who at a former period gave a challenge on the bridge of the Anio, our ancestors sent Titus Manlius, a man of resolute courage and great strength. It was for the same reason, I cannot deny it, that confidence was placed in Marcus Valerius, not many years ago, when he took arms against a Gaul who challenged him to combat in a similar manner. In the same manner as we wish to have our foot and horse more powerful, but if that is impracticable, equal in strength to the enemy, so let us find out a commander who is a match for the general of the enemy. Though we should select the man as general whose abilities are greater than those of any other in the nation, yet still he is chosen at a moment's warning, his office is only annual; whereas he will have to cope with a veteran general who has continued in command without interruption, unfettered by any restrictions either of duration or of authority, which might prevent him from executing or planning every thing according as the exigencies of the war shall require. But with us the year is gone merely in making preparations, and when we are only commencing our operations. Having said enough as to what sort of persons you ought to elect as consuls, it remains that I should briefly express my opinion of those on whom the choice of the prerogative century has fallen. Marcus Æmilius Regillus is flamen of Quirinus, whom we can neither send abroad nor retain at home without neglecting the gods or the war. Otacilius is married to my sister's daughter, and has children by her, but the favours you have conferred upon me and my ancestors, are not such as that I should prefer private relationship to the public weal. Any sailor or passenger can steer the vessel in a calm sea, but when a furious storm has arisen, and the vessel is hurried by the tempest along the troubled deep, then there is need of a man and pilot We are not sailing on a tranquil sea, but have already well nigh sunk with repeated storms, you must therefore employ the utmost caution and foresight in determining who shall sit at the helm Of you, Titus Otacilius, we have had experience in a business of less magnitude, and, certainly you have not given us any proof that we ought to confide to you affairs of greater moment The fleet which you commanded this year we fitted out for three objects: to lay waste the coast of Africa, to protect the shores of Italy, but, above all, to prevent the conveyance of reinforcements with pay and provisions from Carthage to Hannibal. Now if Titus Otacilius has performed for the state, I say not all, but any one of these services, make him consul But if, while you had the command of the fleet supplies of whatever sort were conveyed safe and untouched to Hannibal, even as though he had no enemy on the sea, if the coast of Italy has been more infested this year than that of Africa, what can you have to urge why you should be preferred before all others as the antagonist of Hannibal? Were you consul, we should give it as our opinion that a dictator should be appointed in obedience to the example of our ancestors Nor could you feel offended that some one in the Roman nation was deemed superior to you in war It concerns yourself more than any one else, Titus Otacilius, that there be not laid upon your shoulders a burthen under which you would fall I earnestly exhort you, that with the same feelings which would influence you if standing armed for battle, you were called upon suddenly to elect two generals, under whose conduct and auspices you were to fight, you would this day elect your consuls, to whom your children are to swear allegiance, at whose command they are to assemble, and under whose protection and care they are to serve. The Trasimene Lake and Cannæ are melancholy precedents to look back upon, but form useful warnings to guard against similar disasters Crier, call back the younger century of the Amen tribe to give their votes again"

Titus Otacilius, vociferating in the most furious manner, that his object was to continue in the consulship, the consul ordered the lictors to go to him, and as he had not entered the city, but had proceeded directly without halting from his march to the Campus Martius, admonished him that the axes were in the fasces which were carried before him. The prerogative century proceeded to vote a second time, when Quintus Fabius Maximus for the fourth time, and Marcus Marcellus for the third time, were created consuls. The other centuries voted for the same persons without any variation. One prætor, likewise, Quintus Fulvius Flaccus, was re-elected; the other new ones who were chosen, were Titus Otacilius Crassus a second time, Quintus Fabius, son of the consul, who was at that time curule ædile, and Publius Cornelius Lentulus. The election of the prætors completed, a decree of the senate was passed, that Quintus Fulvius should have the city department out of the ordinary course, and that he in preference to any other should command in the city while the consuls were absent in the war. Great floods happened twice during this year, and the Tiber overflowed the fields, with great demolition of houses and destruction of men and cattle. In the fifth year of the second Punic war Quintus Fabius Maximus for the fourth time, and Marcus Claudius Marcellus for the third time, entering upon their office, drew the attention of the state upon them in a more than ordinary degree, for there had not been two such consuls now for many years. The old men observed, that thus Maximus Rullus and Publius Decius were declared consuls for conducting the Gallic war; that thus afterwards Papirius and Carvilius were appointed to that office against the Samnites, the Bruttians, and the Lucanian with the Tarentine people. Marcellus, who was with the army, was created consul in his absence; to Fabius, who was present and held the election himself, the office was continued. The critical state of affairs, the exigencies of the war, and the danger which threatened the state, prevented any one from looking narrowly into the precedent, or suspecting that the consul was actuated by an excessive love of command; on the contrary, they applauded his magnanimity in that when he knew the state was in want of a general of the greatest ability, and that he was himself confessedly such an one, he thought less of the personal odium which might arise out of the transaction, than of the good of the state.

On the day on which the consuls entered on their office, the senate was assembled in the Capitol, and in the first place a decree was passed to the effect that the consuls should draw lots, and settle between themselves which should hold the election for the creation of censors, before they proceeded to join the army. Next, all those who had the command of armies were continued in their offices, and ordered to remain in their provinces; Tiberius Gracchus at Luceria, where he was with an army of volunteer slaves; Caius Terentius Varro in the Picenian, and Manius Pomponius in the Gallic territory. Of the prætors of the former year, it was settled that Quintus Mucius should have the government of Sardinia as proprætor, Marcus Valerius the command of the sea-coast near Brundusium, watchful against all the movements of Philip, king of the Macedonians. To Publius Cornelius Lentulus, the prætor, the province of Sicily was assigned. Titus Otacilius received the same fleet which he had employed the year before against the Carthaginians. Many prodigies were reported to have happened this year, which increased in proportion as they were believed by the credulous and superstitious. That crows had built a nest within the temple of Juno Sospita at Lanuvium; that a green palm-tree had taken fire in Apulia; that a pool at Mantua, formed by the overflowing of the river Mincius, had assumed the appearance of blood; that it had rained chalk at Cales, and blood at Rome in the cattle market; that a fountain under ground in the Istrian street had discharged so violent a stream of water, that rolling along with the impetuosity of a torrent, it carried away the butts and casks which were near it; that the public court in the Capitol had been struck by lightning; also the temple of Vulcan in the Campus Martius, a nut-tree in the Sabine territory, a wall and gate at Gabii. Now other miracles were published: that the spear of Mars at Præneste moved forward of its own accord; that in Sicily an ox had spoken; that a child in the womb of its mother cried out Io Triumphe! in the country of the Marrucinians; at Spoletum, that a woman was transformed into a man; at Hadria, that an altar, with appearances as of men surrounding it in white clothing, was seen in the heavens. Nay, even in the city of Rome itself, after a swarm of bees had been seen in the forum, some persons roused the citizens to arms, affirming that they saw armed legions on the Janiculum; but those who were on the Janiculum at the time, declared that they had seen no person there besides the usual cultivators of the hill. These prodigies were expiated by victims of the larger kind, according to the response of the aruspices; and a supplication was ordered to all the deities who had shrines at Rome.

The ceremonies which were intended to propitiate the gods being completed, the consuls took the sense of the senate on the state of the nation, the conduct of the war, what troops should be employed, and where they were severally to act. It was resolved that eighteen legions should be engaged in the war; that the consuls should take two each; that two should be employed in each of the provinces of Gaul, Sicily, and Sardinia; that Quintus Fabius, the prætor, should have the command of two in Apulia, and Tiberius Gracchus of two legions of volunteer slaves in the neighbourhood of Luceria; that one each should be left for Caius Terentius, the proconsul, for Picenum, and to Marcus Valerius for the fleet off Brundusium, and two for the protection of the city. To complete this number of legions six fresh ones were to be enlisted, which the consuls were ordered to raise as soon as possible; and also to prepare the fleet, so that, together with the ships which were stationed off the coasts of Calabria, it might amount that year to one hundred and fifty men of war. The levy completed, and the hundred new ships launched, Quintus Fabius held the election for the creation of censors, when Marcus Atilius Regulus and Publius Furius Philus were chosen. A rumour prevailing that war had broken out in Sicily, Titus Otacilius was ordered to proceed thither with his fleet; but as there was a deficiency of sailors, the consuls, in conformity with a decree of the senate, published an order that those persons who themselves or whose fathers had been rated in the censorship of Lucius Æmilius and Caius Flaminius, at from fifty to one hundred thousand *asses*, or whose property had since reached that amount, should furnish one sailor and six months' pay; from one to three hundred thousand, three sailors with a year's pay; from three hundred thousand to a million, five sailors; above one million, seven sailors; that senators should furnish eight sailors with a year's pay. The sailors furnished according to this proclamation being armed and equipped by their masters, embarked with cooked provisions for thirty days. Then first it happened that the Roman fleet was manned at the expense of individuals.

These unusually great preparations alarmed the Campanians particularly, lest the Romans should commence the year's campaign with the siege of Capua. They therefore sent ambassadors to Hannibal, to implore him to bring his army to Capua, and tell him that new armies were levying at Rome for the purpose of besieging it; and that there was not any city the defection of which had excited more hostile feelings. As they announced this with so much fear, Hannibal concluded he must make haste lest the Romans should get there before him; and setting out from Arpi, took up his position in his old camp at Tifata, above Capua. Leaving his Numidians and Spaniards for the protection both of the camp and Capua, he went down thence with the rest of his troops to the lake Avernus on the pretence of performing sacrifice, but in reality to make an attempt upon Puteoli and the garrison in it. Maximus, on receiving intelligence that Hannibal had set out from Arpi, and was returning to Campania, went back to his army, pursuing his journey without intermission by night or by day. He also ordered Tiberius Gracchus to bring up his troops from Luceria to Beneventum, and Quintus Fabius the prætor, the son of the consul, to go to Luceria in the room of Gracchus. At the same time the two prætors set out for Sicily, Publius Cornelius to join his army, Otacilius to take the command of the sea-coast and the fleet; the rest also proceeded to their respective provinces, and those who were continued in command remained in the same countries as in the former year.

While Hannibal was at the lake Avernus, five noble youths came to him from Tarentum. They had been made prisoners partly at the lake Trasimenus, and partly at Cannæ, and had been sent home by the Carthaginian with the same civility which he had shown towards all the Roman allies. They stated to him that, impressed with gratitude for his favours, they had succeeded in inducing a large portion of the Tarentine youth to prefer his alliance and friendship to that of the Romans; and that they were sent by their countrymen as ambassadors to request Hannibal to bring his forces nearer to Tarentum; that if his standards and camp were within sight of Tarentum, that city would be delivered into his hands without delay; that the commons were under the influence of the youth, and the state of Tarentum in the hands of the commons. Hannibal after bestowing the highest commendations upon them, and loading them with immense promises, bid them return home to mature their plans, saying that he would be there in due time. With these hopes, the Tarentines were dismissed. Hannibal had himself conceived the strongest desire of getting possession of Tarentum. He saw that it was a city opulent and celebrated, on the coast, and lying conveniently over against Macedonia. And that as the Romans were in possession of Brundusium, king Philip would make for this port if he crossed over into Italy. Having completed the sacrifice for which he came, and during his stay there laid waste the territory of Cumæ as far as the promontory of Misenum, he suddenly marched his troops thence to Puteoli to surprise the Roman garrison there. It consisted of six thousand men, and the place was secured not only by its natural situation, but by works also. The Carthaginian having waited there three days, and attempted the garrison in every quarter, without any success, proceeded thence to devastate the territory of Naples, influenced by resentment more than the hope of getting possession of the place. The commons of Nola, who had been long disaffected to the Romans and at enmity with their own senate, moved into the neighbouring fields on his approach; and in conformity with this movement ambassadors came to invite Hannibal to join them, bringing with them a positive assurance that the city would be surrendered to him. The consul, Marcellus, who had been called in by the nobles, anticipated their attempt. In one day he had reached Suessula from Cales, though the river Vulturnus had delayed him crossing; and from thence the ensuing night introduced into Nola for the protection of the senate, six thousand foot and three hundred horse. The dilatoriness of Hannibal was in proportion to the expedition which the consul used in every thing he did in order to preoccupy Nola. Having twice already made the attempt unsuccessfully, he was slower to place confidence in the Nolans.

During the same time, the consul, Fabius, came to attempt Casilinum, which was occupied by a Carthaginian garrison; and, as if by concert, Hanno approached Beneventum on one side from the Bruttians, with a large body of foot and horse, while on the other side Gracchus approached it from Luceria. The latter entered the town first. Then, hearing that Hanno had pitched his camp three miles from the city, at the river Calor, and from thence was laying waste the country, he himself marched without the walls, and pitching his camp about a mile from the enemy, harangued his soldiers. The legions he had consisted for the most part of volunteer slaves, who chose rather to earn their liberty silently by another year's service, than demand it openly. The general, however, on quitting his winter quarters, had perceived that the troops murmured, asking when the time would arrive that they should serve as free citizens. He had written to the senate, stating not so much what they wanted as what they had deserved; he said they had served him with fidelity and courage up to that day, and that they wanted nothing but liberty, to bring them up to the model of complete soldiers. Permission was given him to act in the business as he thought for the interest of the state, and, accordingly, before he engaged with the enemy, he declared that the time was now arrived for obtaining that liberty which they had so long hoped for; that on the following day he should fight a pitched battle on a level and open plain, in which the contest would be decided by valour only, without any fear of ambuscade. The man who should bring back the head of an enemy, he would instantly order to be set free; but that he would punish, in a manner suited to a slave, the man who should quit his post; that every man's fortune was in his own hands; that not he himself alone would authorize their enfranchisement, but the consul, Marcus Marcellus, and the whole body of the fathers, who, on being consulted by him on the subject, had left the matter to his disposal. He then read the letter of the consul and the decree of the senate, on which they raised a general shout of approbation, demanded to be led to battle, and vehemently urged him to give the signal forthwith. Gracchus broke up the assembly, after proclaiming the battle for the following day. The soldiers, highly delighted, particularly those whose enfranchisement was to be the reward of one day's prowess, employed the remaining time in getting ready their arms.

The next day, as soon as the trumpets began to sound, they were the first to assemble at the general's tent, armed and ready for action. When the sun had risen, Gracchus led out his troops to the field of battle; nor did the enemy delay to engage him. His troops consisted of seventeen thousand infantry, principally Bruttians and Lucanians, with twelve hundred horse, among which were very few Italians, almost all the rest being Numidians and Moors. The contest was fierce and protracted. For four hours neither side had the advantage, nor did any other circumstance more impede the Romans, than that the heads of their enemies were made the price of their liberty. For when each man had gallantly slain his enemy, first, he lost time in cutting off his head, which was done with difficulty amid the crowd and confusion, and secondly, all the bravest troops ceased to be engaged in fight, as their right hands were employed in holding the heads; and thus the battle was left to be sustained by the inactive and cowardly. But when the military tribunes reported to Gracchus that the soldiers were employed not in wounding any of the enemy who were standing, but in mangling those who were prostrate, their right hands being occupied in holding the heads of men instead of their swords, he promptly ordered a signal to be given that they should throw down the heads and charge the enemy; that they had given evident and signal proofs of valour, and that the liberty of such brave men was certain. Then the fight was revived, and the cavalry also were sent out against the enemy. The Numidians engaging them with great bravery, and the contest between the cavalry being carried on with no less spirit than that between the infantry, the victory again became doubtful; when, the generals on both sides vilifying their opponents, the Roman saying, that their enemies were Bruttians and Lucanians, who had been so often vanquished and subjugated by their ancestors; the Carthaginian, that the troops opposed to them were Roman slaves, soldiers taken out of a workhouse; at last Gracchus exclaimed, that his men had no ground to hope for liberty unless the enemy were routed and put to flight that day.

These words at length kindled their courage so effectually, and renewing the shout, as if suddenly changed into other men, they bore down upon the enemy with such impetuosity that they could not longer be withstood. First, of the Carthaginians who stood before the standards; then the standards were thrown into disorder; and lastly the whole line was compelled to give way. They then turned their backs downright, and fled precipitately to their camp with such terror and consternation, that not a man made stand in the gates or on the rampart; while the Romans, who pursued them so close as to form almost a part of their body commenced the battle anew, enclosed within the rampart of the enemy. Here the battle was more bloody as the combatants had less room to move, from the narrowness of the place in which they fought. The prisoners too assisted; for snatching up swords in the confusion, and forming themselves into a body, they slew the Carthaginians in the rear and prevented their flight. Thus less than two thousand men out of so large an army, and those principally cavalry, effected their escape with their commander, all the rest were slain or taken prisoners. Thirty-eight standards were taken. Of the victors about two thousand fell. All the booty except that of the prisoners was given up to the soldiery. Such cattle also as the owners should identify within thirty days was excepted. When they returned to their camp loaded with spoil, about four thousand of the volunteer slaves who had fought with less spirit, and had not joined in breaking into the enemy's camp, through fear of punishment, took possession of a hill not far from the camp. Being brought down thence the next day by a military tribune, it happened that they arrived during an assembly of the soldiers which Gracchus had called. At this assembly the proconsul, having first rewarded the veteran soldiers with military presents, according to the valour displayed, and the service rendered by each man in the engagement, then observed, with respect to the volunteer slaves, that he would rather that all should be praised by him whether deserving it or not, than that any one should be chastised on that day. I bid you, said he, all be free, and may the event be attended with advantage, happiness, and prosperity to the state and to yourselves. These words were followed by the most cordial acclamations, the soldiers sometimes embracing and congratulating one another, at other times lifting up their hands to heaven, and praying that every blessing might attend the Roman people, and Gracchus in particular; when Gracchus addressed them thus: "Before I had placed you all on an equal footing with respect to the enjoyment of liberty, I was unwilling to affix any marks by which the brave and dastardly soldier might be distinguished. But now the pledge given by the state being redeemed, lest all distinction between courage and cowardice should disappear, I shall order that the names of those persons be laid before me, who, conscious of their dastardly conduct in the battle, have lately seceded. I shall have them cited before me, when I shall bind them by an oath, that none of them, except such as shall have the plea of sickness, will, so long as they serve, take either meat or drink in any other posture than standing. This penalty you will bear with patience when you reflect that it is impossible your cowardice could be marked with a slighter stigma." He then gave the signal for packing up the baggage; and the soldiers, sporting and jesting as they drove and carried their booty, returned to Beneventum in so playful a mood, that they appeared to be returning, not from the field of battle, but from a feast celebrated on some remarkable holiday. All the Beneventans pouring out in crowds to meet them at the gate, embraced, congratulated, and invited the troops to entertainments. They had all prepared banquets in the courts of their houses, to which they invited the soldiers, and of which they entreated Gracchus to allow them to partake. Gracchus gave permission, with the proviso that they should feast in the public street. Each person brought every thing out before his door. The volunteers feasted with caps of liberty on their heads, or filletted with white wool; some reclining at the tables, others standing, who at once partook of the repast, and waited upon the rest. It even seemed a fitting occasion that Gracchus, on his return to Rome, should order a picture representing the festivities of that day to be executed in the temple of Liberty, which his father caused to be built on the Aventine out of money arising from fines, and which his father also dedicated.

While these events occurred at Beneventum, Hannibal having laid waste the territory of Naples, moved his camp to Nola. The consul, as soon as he was aware of his approach, sent for Pomponius the proprætor, with the troops he had in the camp above Suessula; and then prepared to meet the enemy and to make no delay in fighting. He sent out Caius Claudius Nero in the dead of night with the main strength of the cavalry, through the gate which was farthest removed from the enemy, with orders to make a circuit so as not to be observed, and then slowly to follow the enemy as they moved along, and as soon as he perceived the battle begun, to charge them on the rear. Whether Nero was prevented from executing these orders by mistaking the route, or from the shortness of the time, is doubtful. Though he was absent when the battle was fought, the Romans had unquestionably the advantage; but as the cavalry did not come up in time, the plan of the battle which had been agreed upon was disconcerted and Marcellus, not daring to follow the retiring enemy, gave the signal for retreat when his soldiers were conquering More than two thousand of the enemy are said, however, to have fallen on that day; of the Romans, less than four hundred. Nero, after having fruitlessly wearied both men and horses, through the day and night, without even having seen the enemy, returned about sunset; when the consul went so far in reprimanding him as to assert, that he had been the only obstacle to their retorting on the enemy the disaster sustained at Cannæ. The following day the Roman came into the field, but the Carthaginian, beaten even by his own tacit confession, kept within his camp. Giving up all hope of getting possession of Nola, a thing never attempted without loss, during the silence of the night of the third day he set out for Tarentum, which he had better hopes of having betrayed to him.

Nor were the Roman affairs administered with less spirit at home than in the field. The censors being freed from the care of letting out the erection of public works, from the low state of the treasury, turned their attention to the regulation of men's morals, and the chastisement of vices which sprung up during the war, in the same manner as constitutions broken down by protracted disease, generate other maladies. In the first place, they cited those persons who, after the battle of Cannæ, were said to have formed a design of abandoning the commonwealth, and leaving Italy. The chief of these was Lucius Cæcilius Metellus, who happened to be then quæstor. In the next place, as neither he nor the other persons concerned were able to exculpate themselves on being ordered to make their defence, they pronounced them guilty of having used words and discourse prejudicial to the state, that a conspiracy might be formed for the abandonment of Italy. After them were cited those persons who showed too much ingenuity in inventing a method of discharging the obligation of their oath, namely, such of the prisoners as concluded that the oath which they had sworn to return, would be fulfilled by their going back privately to Hannibal's camp, after setting out on their journey. Such of these and of the above-mentioned as had horses at the public expense were deprived of them, and all were degraded from their tribes and disfranchised. Nor was the attention of the censors confined to the regulation of the senate and the equestrian order. They erased from the lists of the junior centuries the names of all who had not served during the last four years, unless they were regularly exempted, or were prevented by sickness. Those too, amounting to more than two thousand names, were numbered among the disfranchised, and were all degraded. To this more gentle stigma affixed by the censors, a severe decree of the senate was added, to the effect that all those whom the censor had stigmatized, should serve on foot, and be sent into Sicily to join the remains of the army of Cannæ, a class of soldiers whose time of service was not to terminate till the enemy was driven out of Italy. The censors, in consequence of the poverty of the treasury, having abstained from receiving contracts for the repairs of the sacred edifices, the furnishing of curule horses, and similar matters, the persons who had been accustomed to attend auctions of this description, came to the censors in great numbers, and exhorted them to "transact all their business and let out the contracts in the same manner as if there were money in the treasury. That none of them would ask for money out of the treasury before the war was concluded." Afterwards the owners of those slaves whom Tiberius Sempronius had manumitted at Beneventum, came to them, stating that they were sent for by the public bankers, to receive the price of their slaves, but that they would not accept of it till the war was concluded. This disposition on the part of the commons to sustain the impoverished treasury having manifested itself, the property of minors first, and then the portions of widows, began to be brought in; the persons who brought them being persuaded, that their deposit would no where be more secure and inviolable than under the public faith. If any thing was bought or laid in for the widows and minors, an order upon the quæstor was given for it. This liberality in individuals flowed from the city into the camp also, insomuch that no horseman or centurion would accept of his pay, and those who would accept it were reproached with the appellation of mercenary men.

Quintus Fabius, the consul, was encamped before Casilinum, which was occupied by a garrison of two thousand Campanians and seven hundred of the soldiers of Hannibal. The commander was Statius Metius, who was sent there by Cneius Magius Atellanus, who was that year Medixtuticus and was arming the slaves and people without distinction, in order to assault the Roman camp, while the consul was intently occupied in the siege of Casilinum. None of these things escaped Fabius. He therefore sent to his colleague at Nola, "That another army was requisite, which might be opposed to the Campanians, while the siege of Casilinum was going on; that either he should come himself, leaving a force sufficient for the protection of Nola, or if the state of Nola required him to stay there, in consequence of its not being yet secure against the attempts of Hannibal, that he should summon Tiberius Gracchus, the proconsul, from Beneventum." On this message, Marcellus, leaving two thousand troops in garrison at Nola, came to Casilinum with the rest of his forces; and at his arrival the Campanians, who were already in motion, desisted from their operations. Thus the siege of Casilinum was commenced by the two consuls. But as the Roman soldiers received many wounds as they rashly approached the walls, and as they did not succeed satisfactorily in their attempts. Fabius gave it as his opinion that this, which was a small matter, though as difficult as more important ones, should be abandoned, and that they should retire from the place, as affairs of greater moment were pressing. Marcellus, however, succeeded in persuading him that they should not go away with their object unaccomplished, observing that as there were many objects which great generals should not attempt, so when once attempted they should not be abandoned, because the mere report in either case would have important consequences. Upon this the vineæ and all kinds of military works and engines were applied; in consequence of which, the Campanians entreated Fabius to allow them to retire to Capua in safety; when a few of them having come out of the town, Marcellus took possession of the gate through which they passed, and first slew all indiscriminately who were near the gate, and then rushing in, the slaughter commenced in the town also. About fifty of the Campanians, who at first came out of the city, having fled for refuge to Fabius, arrived safe at Capua under his protection. Thus Casilinum was captured on an accidental opportunity which occurred during the conferences and delay of those who were soliciting protection. The prisoners, both those who were Campanians and those who were Hannibal's soldiers, were sent to Rome, where they were shut up in a prison. The crowd of townsmen was distributed among the neighbouring people to be kept in custody.

At the same time that the consuls retired from Casilinum, their object having been accomplished, Gracchus, who was in Lucania, sent, under a prefect of the allies, some cohorts which he had levied in that country to ravage the lands of the enemy. These, as they were straggling in a careless manner, Hanno surprising, retorted upon his enemy a defeat not much less disastrous than he had himself received at Beneventum, and then hastily retired to the territory of the Bruttians, lest Gracchus should overtake him. Of the consuls, Marcellus returned to Nola, whence he had come, Fabius proceeded to Samnium to waste the lands, and recover by force the cities which had revolted. The Samnites of Caudium suffered the severest devastation; their fields were laid waste by fire for a wide extent, and both men and cattle were conveyed away as booty. The towns of Compulteria, Telesia, Compsa, Melæ, Fulfulæ, and Orbitanium, were taken by storm. Blandæ, belonging to the Lucanians, and Æcæ to the Apulians, were taken after a siege. Twenty-five thousand of the enemy were captured or slain in these towns, and three hundred and seventy deserters recovered; who, being sent to Rome by the consul, were all of them beaten with rods in the comitium, and thrown down from the rock. Such were the achievements of Fabius within the space of a few days. Ill health detained Marcellus from active operations at Nola. The town of Accua also was taken by storm, during the same period, by the prætor Quintus Fabius, whose province was the neighbourhood of Luceria; he also fortified a stationary camp at Ardonea. While the Romans were thus employed in different quarters, Hannibal had reached Tarentum, utterly destroying every thing whichsoever way he went. In the territory of Tarentum, the troops at length began to march in a peaceable manner. There nothing was violated, nor did they ever go out of the road; it was evident that this was done not from the moderation of the soldiery, or their general, but to conciliate the affections of the Tarentines. However, on advancing almost close to the walls without perceiving any movement, which he expected would occur on the sight of his vanguard, he pitched his camp about a mile off the city. Three days before the arrival of Hannibal, Marcus Livius, who had been sent by Marcus Valerius, the proprætor, commanding the fleet at Brundusium, had enlisted the young nobility of Tarentum, and stationing guards at every gate, and round the walls, wherever circumstances made it necessary, had kept such a strict watch both by day and night, as to give no opportunity for making any attempt either to the enemy or doubtful allies. On this account several days were consumed there to no purpose, when Hannibal, as none of those who had come to him at the lake Avernus, either came themselves or sent any letter or message, perceiving that he had carelessly followed delusive promises, moved his camp thence. Even after this he did not offer any violence to the Tarentine territory, not quitting the hope of shaking their allegiance to the Romans, though his simulated lenity had hitherto been of no advantage to him; but as soon as he came to Salapia he collected stores of corn there from the Metapontine and Heraclean lands; for midsummer was now past, and the situation pleased him as a place for winter quarters. From hence the Moors and Numidians were detached to plunder the territory of Sallentum, and the neighbouring woods of Apulia, from which not much booty of any other sort was obtained, but principally droves of horses, four thousand of which were distributed among his horsemen to be broken.

The Romans, since a war by no means to be despised was springing up in Sicily, and the death of the tyrant had furnished the Syracusans with more enterprising leaders, rather than changed their attachment to the Carthaginian cause, or the state of their minds, decreed that province to Marcus Marcellus, one of their consuls. After the assassination of Hieronymus, at first a tumult had taken place among the soldiery in the territory of the Leontines. They exclaimed furiously that the manes of the king should be appeased with the blood of the conspirators. Afterwards the frequent repetition of the word liberty, which was restored to them, a word so delightful to the ear, the hopes they had conceived of largesses from the royal treasury, and of serving in future under better generals, the relation of the horrid crimes and more horrid lusts of the tyrant, effected such an alteration in their sentiments, that they suffered to lie unburied the corpse of the king, whom a little before they regretted. As the rest of the conspirators remained behind, in order to keep the army on their side, Theodotus and Sosis, mounted on the king's horses, rode off to Syracuse with all possible speed, that they might surprise the king's party, while unacquainted with all that had occurred. But they were anticipated not only by report, than which nothing is swifter in such affairs, but also by a messenger who was one of the royal servants. In consequence, Andranodorus had occupied with strong garrisons the Insula and the citadel, and every other convenient part which he could. After sunset, when it was now growing dark, Theodotus and Sosis rode in by the Hexapylum, and displayed the royal vest stained with blood, and the ornament of the king's head; then passing through the Tycha, and calling the people at once to liberty and arms, bid them assemble in the Achradina. Some of the multitude ran out into the streets, some stood in the porches of their houses, while others looked out from the roofs and windows, and inquired what was the matter. Every part of the city was filled with lights and noises of various kinds. Assemblies of armed men were formed in the open spaces. Those who had no arms tore down from the temple of the Olympian Jupiter the spoils of the Gauls and Illyrians, which had been presented to Hiero by the Roman people, and hung up there by him; at the same time offering up prayers to Jupiter, that he would willingly, and without feeling offence, lend those consecrated weapons to those who were arming themselves in defence of their country, of the temples of their gods, and their liberty. This multitude was also joined by the watches which were stationed through the principal quarters of the city. In the island, Andranodorus, among other places, secured the public granaries by a garrison. This place, which was enclosed by a wall of stones hewn square, and built up on high, after the manner of a citadel, was occupied by a body of youth, who had been appointed to garrison it, and these sent messengers to the Achradina, to give information that the granaries and the corn were in the power of the senate.

At break of day the whole populace, armed and unarmed, assembled at the senate-house in the Achradina: where from the altar of Concord, which stood there, one of the nobles, named Polyænus, delivered a liberal and temperate address. He said, that "men who had experienced servitude and contumely, were enraged against an evil which was well known, but that the Syracusans had rather heard from their fathers than seen with their own eyes the disasters which civil discord introduces." He said, "he commended them for the alacrity with which they had taken arms; but that he should commend them more if they should abstain from using them unless compelled by extreme necessity. At present he advised that ambassadors should be sent to Andranodorus, to charge him to submit to the direction of the senate and the people, to throw open the gates of the island, and withdraw the garrison. If he resolved to usurp the sovereignty of which he had been appointed guardian, that he would recommend that their liberty be recovered more energetically from Andranodorus than it had been from Hieronymus." From this assembly ambassadors were despatched. The senate began now to meet, which though during the reign of Hiero it had continued to be the public council of the state, from the time of his death up to the present had never been assembled or consulted upon any subject. When the ambassadors came to Andranodorus, he was himself moved by the unanimous opinion of his countrymen, by their having possession of other parts of the city, and by the fact that the strongest part of the island was betrayed and placed in the hands of others; but his wife, Demarata, the daughter of Hiero, still swelling with the pride of royalty and female presumption, called him out from the presence of the ambassadors, and reminded him of the expression so often repeated by the tyrant Dionysius, "that a man ought only to relinquish sovereign power when dragged by the feet, and not while sitting on horseback. That it was an easy thing, at any moment one pleased, to give up possession of grandeur, but that to create and obtain them was difficult and arduous. That he should obtain from the ambassadors a little time to deliberate, and to employ it in fetching the soldiers from the Leontines; to whom, if he promised the royal treasure, every thing would be at his disposal." This advice, suggested by a woman, Andranodorus neither entirely rejected nor immediately adopted, considering it the safer way to the attainment of power to temporize for the present. Accordingly he told the ambassadors to carry word back, that he should act subserviently to the senate and the people. The next day, as soon as it was light, he threw open the gates of the island, and came into the forum of the Achradina; then mounting the altar of Concord, from which Polyænus had delivered his harangue the day before, he commenced a speech by soliciting pardon for his delay. "He had kept the gates closed," he said, "not as separating his own from the public interest, but from fear as to where the carnage would stop when once the sword was drawn; whether they would be satisfied with the blood of the tyrant, which was sufficient for their liberty, or whether all who were connected with the court, by consanguinity, affinity, or any offices, would, as implicated in another's guilt, be butchered. After he perceived that those who had liberated their country were desirous of preserving it when liberated, and that the counsels of all were directed towards the public good, he had not hesitated to restore to his country his own person and every thing else which had been committed to his honour and guardianship, since the person who had intrusted him with them had fallen a victim to his own madness." Then turning to the persons who had killed the tyrant, and calling on Theodotus and Sosis by name, he said, "You have performed a memorable deed, but believe me, your glory is only beginning, not yet perfected; and there still remains great danger lest the enfranchised state should be destroyed, if you do not provide for its tranquillity and harmony."

At the conclusion of this speech, he laid the keys of the gates and of the royal treasure at their feet; and on that day, retiring from the assembly in the highest spirits, they made supplication with their wives and children at all the temples of the gods. On the following day an assembly was held for the election of prætors. Andranodorus was created among the first; the rest consisted for the most part of the destroyers of the tyrant; two of these, Sopater and Dinomenes, they appointed in their absence. These, on hearing of what had passed at Syracuse, conveyed thither the royal treasure which was at Leontini, and put it into the hands of quæstors appointed for that purpose. The treasure also in the island and the Achradina was delivered to them, and that part of the wall which formed too strong a separation between the island and the other parts of the city, was demolished by general consent. Every thing else which was done was in conformity with this inclination of their minds to liberty. Hippocrates and Epicydes, on hearing of the death of the tyrant, which Hippocrates had wished to conceal even by putting the messenger to death, being deserted by the soldiery, returned to Syracuse, as that appeared the safest course under present circumstances; but lest if they appeared there in common they should become objects of suspicion, and looked upon as persons who were seeking an opportunity of effecting some change, they in the first place addressed themselves to the prætors and then through them to the senate. They declared, that "they were sent by Hannibal to Hieronymus, as to a friend and ally; that they had obeyed the orders of that man whom their general wished them to obey; that they desired to return to Hannibal; but as the journey would not be safe, as armed Romans were ranging at large through the whole of Sicily, that they requested to be furnished with some escort which might convey them in safety to Locri in Italy; and that thus they would confer a great obligation upon Hannibal, with little trouble." The request was easily obtained, for they were desirous of getting rid of these generals of the king, who were skilled in war, and at once necessitous and enterprising. But they did not exert themselves so as to effect what they desired with the requisite speed. Meanwhile these young men, who were of a military turn and accustomed to the soldiers, employed themselves in circulating charges against the senate and nobles, sometimes in the minds of the soldiers themselves, sometimes of the deserters, of which the greater part were Roman sailors, at other times of men belonging to the lowest order of the populace, insinuating, that "what they were secretly labouring and contriving to effect, was to place Syracuse under the dominion of the Romans with the pretence of a renewed alliance, and then that faction and the few promoters of the alliance would be supreme."

The crowds of persons disposed to hear and credit these insinuations which flowed into Syracuse from every quarter increased daily, and afforded hopes, not only to Epicydes but to Andranodorus also, of effecting a revolution. The latter, wearied at length by the importunities of his wife, who warned him, "that now was the favourable time for seizing the government, while every thing was in confusion in consequence of liberty being recent and not yet regularly established; while a soldiery supported by the royal pay was to be met with, and while generals sent by Hannibal and accustomed to the soldiery might forward the attempt;" he communicated his design with Themistus, who had married the daughter of Gelon, and a few days afterwards incautiously disclosed it to a certain tragic actor, named Ariston, to whom he was in the habit of committing other secrets. He was a man of reputable birth and fortune, nor did his profession disgrace them, for among the Greeks no pursuit of that kind was considered dishonourable. He therefore discovered the plot to the prætors, from a conviction that his country had a superior claim upon his fidelity. These having satisfied themselves that his statement was not false by indubitable proofs, took the advice of the elder senators, and with their sanction, having placed a guard at the doors, slew Themistus and Andranodorus as soon as they had entered the senate-house. A disturbance arising in consequence of this act, which, as none but the prætors knew the cause of it, wore an appearance of atrocity, the prætors, having at length procured silence, introduced the informer into the senate-house; and after he had in a regular manner detailed to the senate every particular, showing that the conspiracy owed its origin to the marriage of Harmonia, the daughter of Gelon, with Themistus; that the African and Spanish auxiliaries had been prepared to murder the prætors and others of the nobility; that it had been given out that their goods were to be the booty of the assassins; that already a band of mercenaries accustomed to obey the command of Andranodorus had been procured for the reoccupation of the island; and having then distinctly represented to them the several parts which the persons implicated in the transaction were performing, and having brought under their view the entire plot prepared for execution with men and arms; it seemed to the senate that they had fallen as justly as Hieronymus had. A shout was raised before the senate-house by a crowd of people variously disposed and uncertain of the facts; but as they were conducting themselves in a furious and menacing manner, the bodies of the conspirators in the vestibule of the senate-house restrained them with such alarm, that they silently followed the more discreet part of the commons to an assembly. Sopater was the person commissioned by the senate and his colleague to explain the affair.

Treating them as if they stood upon their trial, he began with their past lives; and insisted that Andranodorus and Themistus were the authors of every act of iniquity and impiety which had been perpetrated since the death of Hiero. "For what," said he, "did the boy Hieronymus ever do of his own accord? What could he do who had scarce as yet arrived at puberty? His tutors and guardians had ruled, while the odium rested on another. Therefore they ought to have been put to death either before Hieronymus or with him. Nevertheless those men, deservedly marked out for death, had attempted fresh crimes after the decease of the tyrant; first openly, when, closing the gates of the island, Andranodorus declared himself heir to the throne, and kept that as proprietor which he had held only in the capacity of guardian; afterwards, when betrayed by those who were in the island and blockaded by the whole body of the citizens who held the Achradina, he endeavoured to obtain, by secret and artful means, that sovereignty which he had in vain attempted openly; whom not even benefits and honorary distinction could move, for even this conspirator against the liberty of his country was created prætor among her liberators. But that wives of royal blood had infected them with this thirst for royalty, one having married the daughter of Hiero, the other the daughter of Gelon." On hearing these words, a shout arose from every part of the assembly, that "none of these women ought to live, and that not one of the royal family should be left alive." Such is the nature of the populace; they are either cringing slaves or haughty tyrants. They know not how with moderation to spurn or to enjoy that liberty which holds the middle place; nor are there generally wanting ministers, the panders to their resentment, who incite their eager and intemperate minds to blood and carnage. Thus, on the present occasion, the prætors instantly proposed the passing of a decree, which was consented to almost before it was proposed, that all the royal family should be put to death; and persons despatched for the purpose by the prætors, put to death Demarata, the daughter of Hiero, and Harmonia, the daughter of Gelon, the wives of Andranodorus and Themistus.

There was a daughter of Hiero, named Heraclea, the wife of Zoippus, who, having been sent by Hieronymus as ambassador to king Ptolemy, had become a voluntary exile.

As soon as she was apprized that they were coming to her also, she fled for refuge into the chapel to the household gods, accompanied by her two virgin daughters, with dishevelled hair, and other marks of wretchedness. In addition to this, she had recourse to prayers also; she implored them "by the memory of her father, Hiero, and her brother, Gelon, that they would not suffer her, a guiltless person, to be consumed by their hatred of Hieronymus. That all that she had derived from his reign was the exile of her husband. That neither did she enjoy the same advantages as her sister while Hieronymus was alive, nor was her cause the same as hers now he was dead. What? Though her sister would have shared the throne with Andranodorus, had he succeeded in his designs, she must have been in servitude with the rest. Can any one doubt, that if information should be conveyed to Zoippus that Hieronymus had been put to death, and that Syracuse was free, he would instantly embark and return to his native land. But how are all human hopes deceived! His wife and children are struggling for their lives in his native land, now blessed with liberty! In what manner standing in the way of liberty or the laws? What danger could arise to any one from them, from a solitary, and in a manner, widowed woman and girls living in a state of orphanage? But perhaps it will be granted that no danger is to be apprehended from them, but alleged that the whole royal family is detested. If this were the case, she entreated that they would banish them far from Syracuse and Sicily, and order them to be conveyed to Alexandria, the wife to her husband, the daughters to their father." Seeing that their ears and minds were unimpressed, and that certain of them were drawing their swords to prevent a fruitless consumption of time, she gave over entreating for herself, and began to implore them to "spare, at least, her daughters, at an age which even exasperated enemies spared." She entreated them "that they would not, in their revenge on tyrants, themselves imitate the crimes which were odious to them." While thus employed, they dragged her from the sanctuary and murdered her; and after that they fell upon the virgins, who were sprinkled with the blood of their mother; who, distracted alike by fear and grief, and as if seized with madness, rushed out of the chapel with such rapidity, that had there been an opening by which they might have escaped into the street, they would have filled the city with confusion. As it was, they several times made their escape through the midst of so many armed men with their persons uninjured in the contracted space which the house afforded, and extricated themselves from their grasp, though they had to disengage themselves from so many and such strong hands; but at length enfeebled by wounds, and after covering every place with blood, they fell down lifeless. This murder, piteous as it was in itself, was rendered still more so by its happening that a short time after it a message arrived that they should not be killed, as the minds of the people were now turned to compassion. This compassion then gave rise to a feeling of anger, because so much haste had been shown in carrying the punishment into effect, and because no opportunity was left for relenting or retracing the steps of their passion. The multitude therefore gave vent to their indignation, and demanded an election to supply the places of Andranodorus and Themistus, for both of them had been prætors; an election by no means likely to be agreeable to the prætors.

The day was fixed for the election, when, to the surprise of all, one person from the extremity of the crowd nominated Epicydes, and then another from the same quarter nominated Hippocrates. Afterwards the voices in favour of these persons increased with the manifest approbation of the multitude. The assembly was one of a heterogeneous character, consisting not only of the commons, but a crowd of soldiers, with a large admixture even of deserters, who were desirous of innovation in every thing. The prætors, at first, concealed their feelings, and were for protracting the business; but at length, overcome by the general opinion, and apprehensive of a sedition, they declared them the prætors. These did not, however, immediately openly avow their sentiments, though they were chagrined that ambassadors had been sent to Appius Claudius to negotiate a ten days' truce, and that on obtaining this, others were sent to treat for the renewal of the old alliance. The Romans, with a fleet of a hundred ships, were then stationed at Murgantia, waiting the issue of the commotion raised at Syracuse by the death of the tyrants, and to what their recent acquisition of liberty would impel the people. Meanwhile, the Syracusan ambassadors were sent by Appius Claudius to Marcellus on his coming into Sicily, and Marcellus having heard the conditions of peace, and being of opinion that matters might be brought to a settlement, himself also sent ambassadors to Syracuse to treat with the prætors in person on the renewal of the alliance. But now by no means the same state of quiet and tranquillity existed there. Hippocrates and Epicydes, their fears being removed, after that intelligence had arrived that a Carthaginian fleet had put in at Pachynum, complained sometimes to the mercenary soldiers, at other times to the deserters, that Syracuse was being betrayed to the Romans. And when Appius began to station his ships at the mouth of the port, in order to inspire the other party with courage, their false insinuations appeared to receive great corroboration; and on the first impulse, the populace had even run down in a disorderly manner to prevent them from disembarking.

While affairs were in this unsettled state, it was resolved to call an assembly; in which, when some leaned to one side and some to the other, and an insurrection being on the point of breaking out, Apollonides, one of the nobles, delivered a speech fraught with salutary advice, considering the critical state of affairs: "Never," he said, "had a state a nearer prospect of safety and annihilation. For if they would all unanimously espouse the cause either of the Romans or the Carthaginians, there could be no state whose condition would be more prosperous and happy; but if they pulled different ways, the war between the Romans and Carthaginians would not be more bloody than that which would take place between the Syracusans themselves, in which both the contending parties would have their forces, their troops, and their generals, within the same walls. Every exertion ought therefore to be made that all might think alike. Which alliance would be productive of the greater advantages, was a question of quite a secondary nature, and of less moment; though the authority of Hiero ought to be followed in preference to that of Hieronymus in the selection of allies, and a friendship of which they had had a happy experience through a space of fifty years, ought to be chosen rather than one now untried and formerly unfaithful. That it ought also to have some weight in their deliberations, that peace with the Carthaginians might be refused in such a manner as not immediately, at least, to have a war with them, while with the Romans they must forthwith have either peace or war." The less of party spirit and warmth appeared in this speech the greater weight it had. A military council also was united with the prætors and a chosen body of senators; the commanders of companies also, and the præfects of the allies, were ordered to consult conjointly. After the question had been agitated with great warmth, at length, as there appeared to be no means of carrying on a war with the Romans, it was resolved that a treaty of peace should be formed, and that ambassadors should be sent with those from Rome to ratify the same.

Not many days intervened before ambassadors came from the Leontines, requesting troops to protect their frontiers; an embassy which appeared to afford a very favourable opportunity for disencumbering the city of a turbulent and disorderly rabble, and for removing their leaders to a distance. The prætor, Hippocrates, was ordered to lead the deserters thither. Many of the mercenary auxiliaries accompanying them made them number four thousand armed men. This expedition gave great delight both to those who were sent and those who sent them, for to the former an opportunity was afforded of change which they had long desired, while the latter were rejoiced because they considered that a kind of sink of the city had been drained off. But they had, as it were, only relieved a sick body for a time, that it might afterwards fall into a more aggravated disease. For Hippocrates began to ravage the adjoining parts of the Roman province, at first by stealthy excursions, but afterwards, when Appius had sent a body of troops to protect the lands of the allies, he made an attack with all his forces upon the guard posted over against him, and slew many. Marcellus, when informed of this, immediately sent ambassadors to Syracuse, who said that the faith of the treaty had been broken, and that there would never be wanting a cause for hostilities, unless Hippocrates and Epicydes were removed not only from Syracuse, but far from all Sicily. Epicydes, lest by being present he should be arraigned for the offence committed by his absent brother, or should be wanting on his own part in stirring up a war, proceeded himself also to the Leontines; and seeing that they were already sufficiently exasperated against the Romans, he endeavoured to detach them from the Syracusans also. His argument was, that the terms on which they had formed a treaty of peace with the Romans were, that whatever people had been subject to their kings should be placed under their dominion; and that now they were not satisfied with liberty unless they could also exercise kingly power and dominion over others. The answer, therefore, he said, which they ought to send back was, that the Leontines also considered themselves entitled to liberty, either on the ground that the tyrant fell in the streets of their city, or that there the shout was first raised for liberty; and that they were the persons who, abandoning the king's generals, flocked to Syracuse. That, therefore, either that article must be expunged from the treaty, or that that term of it would not be admitted. They easily persuaded the multitude; and when the ambassadors of Syracuse complained of the slaughter of the Roman guard, and ordered that Hippocrates and Epicydes should depart either to Locri or any other place they pleased, provided they quitted Sicily, a reply was made to them in a haughty manner, "that they had neither placed themselves at the disposal of the Syracusans to make a peace for them with the Romans, nor were they bound by the treaties of other people." This answer the Syracusans laid before the Romans, declaring at the same time that "the Leontines were not under their control, and that, therefore, the Romans might make war on them without violating the treaty subsisting between them; that they would also not be wanting in the war, provided that when brought again under subjection, they should form a part of their dominion, agreeably to the conditions of the peace."

Marcellus marched with his entire forces against Leontini, having sent for Appius also, in order that he might attack it in another quarter; when, such was the ardour of the troops in consequence of the indignation they felt at the Roman guards being put to the sword during the negotiations for a peace, that they took the town by storm on the first assault. Hippocrates and Epicydes, perceiving that the enemy were getting possession of the walls and breaking open the gates, retired with a few others into the citadel, from which they fled unobserved during the night to Herbessus. The Syracusans, who had marched from home with eight thousand troops, were met at the river Myla by a messenger, who informed them that the city was taken. The rest which he stated was a mixture of truth and falsehood; he said that there had been an indiscriminate massacre of the soldiers and the townsmen, and that he did not think that one person who had arrived at puberty had survived; that the town had been pillaged, and the property of the rich men given to the troops. On receiving such direful news the army halted; and while all were under violent excitement, the generals, Sosis and Dinomenes, consulted together as to the course to be taken. The scourging and beheading of two thousand deserters had given to this false statement a plausibility which excited alarm; but no violence was offered to any of the Leontine or other soldiers after the city was taken; and every man's property was restored to him, with the exception only of such as was destroyed in the first confusion which attended the capture of the city. The troops, who complained of their fellow-soldiers having been betrayed and butchered, could neither be induced to proceed to Leontini, nor wait where they were for more certain intelligence. The prætors, perceiving their minds disposed to mutiny, but concluding that their violence would not be of long continuance, if those who had led them on to such folly were removed, led the troops to Megara, whence they themselves with a few horsemen proceeded to Herbessus, under the expectation of having the city betrayed to them in the general consternation; but being disappointed in this attempt, they resolved to resort to force, and moved their camp from Megara on the following day, in order to attack Herbessus with all their forces. Hippocrates and Epicydes having formed the design of putting themselves into the hands of the soldiers, who were for the most part accustomed to them, and were now incensed at the report of the massacre of their comrades, not so much as a safe measure on the first view of it as that it was their only course, now that all hope was cut off, went out to meet the army. It happened that the troops which marched in the van were six hundred Cretans, who had been engaged in the service of Hieronymus under their command, and were under obligation to Hannibal, having been captured at the Trasimenus among the Roman auxiliaries, and dismissed by him. Hippocrates and Epicydes, recognising them by their standards and the fashion of their armour, held out olive branches, and the fillets usually worn by suppliants, and implored them to receive them into their ranks, protect them when received, and not betray them to the Syracusans, by whom they themselves would soon be delivered up to the Romans to be butchered.

But the Cretans with one accord called out to them to be of good courage; that they would share every fortune with them. During this conversation, the vanguard had halted, and the march was delayed; nor had the cause of the delay as yet reached the generals. After the report had spread that Hippocrates and Epicydes were there, and a voice was heard through the whole army, which showed evidently that the troops were pleased at their arrival, the prætors immediately gallopped to the front, and earnestly asked "what was the meaning of that violation of discipline, which the Cretans had committed in holding conference with the enemy, and allowing them to mingle with their ranks without the authority of the prætors." They ordered Hippocrates to be seized and thrown into chains. On hearing which such a clamour was raised, first by the Cretans and then by the rest, that it was quite evident if they proceeded farther that they would have cause to fear. In this state of anxiety and perplexity, they gave orders to march back to Megara, whence they had set out, and sent messengers to Syracuse, to give information of their present condition. Hippocrates added a deception, seeing that the minds of the troops were disposed to entertain every suspicion. Having sent some Cretans to lie in wait in the roads, he read a letter he pretended had been intercepted, but which he had written himself. The address was: "The prætors of Syracuse to the consul Marcellus." After the customary wishing of health, it stated "that he had acted duly and properly in sparing none of the Leontines, but that the cause of all the mercenary troops was the same, and that Syracuse would never be tranquil while there were any foreign auxiliaries in the city or in the army. That it was therefore necessary that he should endeavour to get into his power those who were encamped at Megara, with their prætors, and by punishing them, at length restore Syracuse to liberty." After this letter had been read, they ran to seize their arms in every direction, with so great a clamour, that the prætors, in the utmost consternation, rode away to Syracuse during the confusion. The mutiny, however, was not quelled even by their flight, but an attack was made upon the Syracusan soldiers; nor would any one have escaped their violence, had not Hippocrates and Epicydes opposed the resentment of the multitude, not from pity or any humane motive, but lest they should cut off all hope of effecting their return; and that they might have the soldiers, both as faithful supporters of their cause, and as hostages, and conciliate to themselves their relatives and friends, in the first place by so great an obligation, and in the next by reason of the pledge. Having also experienced that the populace could be excited by any cause, however groundless or trifling, they procured a soldier of the number of those who were besieged at Leontini, whom they suborned to carry a report to Syracuse, corresponding with that which had been falsely told at the Myla; and by vouching for what he stated, and relating as matters which he had seen, those things of which doubts were entertained, to kindle the resentment of the people.

This man not only obtained credit with the commons, but being introduced into the senate-house, produced an impression upon the senate also. Some men of no small authority openly declared, that it was very fortunate that the rapacity and cruelty of the Romans had been made apparent in the case of the Leontines; that if they had entered Syracuse, they would have committed the same or even more horrible acts, as there the temptations to rapacity would have been greater. All, therefore, advised that the gates should be closed and the city guarded, but not the same persons were objects of fear or hatred to all alike. Among the soldiers of every kind, and a great part of the people, the Roman name was hated. The prætors, and a few of the nobles, though enraged by the fictitious intelligence, rather directed their cautions against a nearer and more immediate evil. Hippocrates and Epicycles were now at the Hexapylum; and conversations were taking place, fomented by the relatives of the native soldiers who were in the army, touching the opening of the gates, and the allowing their common country to be defended from the violence of the Romans. One of the doors of the Hexapylum was now thrown open, and the troops began to be taken in at it, when the prætors interposed; and first by commands and menaces, then by advice, they endeavoured to deter them from their purpose, and last of all, every other means proving ineffectual, forgetful of their dignity, they tried to move them by prayers, imploring them not to betray their country to men heretofore the satellites of the tyrant, and now the corrupters of the army. But the ears of the excited multitude were deaf to all these arguments, and the exertions made from within to break open the gates, were not less than those without; the gates were all broken open, and the whole army received into the Hexapylum. The prætors, with the youth of the city, fled into the Achradina; the mercenary soldiers and deserters, with all the soldiers of the late king who were at Syracuse, joined the forces of the enemy. The Achradina also was therefore taken on the first assault, and all the prætors, except such as escaped in the confusion, were put to the sword. Night put an end to the carnage. On the following day the slaves were invited to liberty, and those bound in prison were released; after which this mixed rabble created Hippocrates and Epicydes their prætors, and thus Syracuse, when for a brief period the light of liberty had shone on it, relapsed into her former state of servitude.

The Romans, on receiving information of these events, immediately moved their camp from Leontini to Syracuse. It happened at this time that ambassadors were sent by Appius in a quinquereme, to make their way through the harbour. A quadrireme was sent in advance, which was captured as soon as it entered the mouth of the harbour, and the ambassadors with difficulty made their escape. And now not only the laws of peace but of war also were not regarded, when the Roman army pitched their camp at Olympium, a temple of Jupiter, a mile and a half from the city. From which place also it was thought proper that ambassadors should be sent forward; these were met by Hippocrates and Epicydes with their friends without the gate, to prevent their entering the city. The Roman, who was appointed to speak, said that "he did not bring war, but aid and assistance to the Syracusans, not only to such as, escaping from the midst of the carnage, fled to the Romans for protection, but to those also, who, overpowered by fear, were submitting to a servitude more shocking, not only than exile, but than death. Nor would the Romans suffer the horrid murder of their friends to go unavenged. If, therefore, those who had taken refuge with them were allowed to return to their country with safety, the authors of the massacre delivered up, and the Syracusans reinstated in the enjoyment of their liberty and laws, there would be no necessity for arms; but if these things were not done, they would direct their arms unceasingly against those who delayed them, whoever they might be." Epicydes replied, that "if they had been commissioned with any message for them, they would have given them an answer; and when the government of Syracuse was in the hands of those persons to whom they were come, they might visit Syracuse again. If they should commence hostilities, they would learn by actual experience that it was by no means the same thing to besiege Syracuse and Leontini." With this he left the ambassadors and closed the gate. The siege of Syracuse then commenced by sea and land at the same time; by land on the side of the Hexapylum; by sea on the side of the Achradina, the wall of which is washed by its waves; and as the Romans felt a confidence that as they had taken Leontini by the terror they occasioned on the first assault, they should be able in some quarter to effect an entrance into a city so desert, and diffused over so large an extent of ground, they brought up to the walls every kind of engine for besieging cities.

And an attempt made with so much energy would have succeeded, had it not been for one person then at Syracuse. That person was Archimedes, a man of unrivalled skill in observing the heavens and the stars, but more deserving of admiration as the inventor and constructor of warlike engines and works, by means of which, with a very slight effort, he turned to ridicule what the enemy effected with great difficulty. The wall which ran along unequal eminences, most of which were high and difficult of access, some low and open to approach along level vales, he furnished with every kind of warlike engine, as seemed suitable to each particular place. Marcellus attacked from the quinqueremes the wall of the Achradina, which, as before stated, was washed by the sea. From the other ships the archers and slingers and light infantry, whose weapon is difficult to be thrown back by the unskilful, allowed scarce any person to remain upon the wall unwounded. These, as they required room for the discharge of their missiles, kept their ships at a distance from the wall. Eight more quinqueremes joined together in pairs, the oars on their inner sides being removed, so that side might be placed to side, and which forming as it were ships, were worked by means of the oars on the outer sides, carried turrets built up in stories, and other engines employed in battering walls. Against this naval armament, Archimedes placed on different parts of the walls engines of various dimensions. Against the ships which were at a distance he discharged stones of immense weight. Those which were nearer he assailed with lighter, and therefore more numerous missiles. Lastly, in order that his own men might heap their weapons upon the enemy, without receiving any wounds themselves, he perforated the wall from the top to the bottom with a great number of loop-holes, about a cubit in diameter, through which some with arrows, others with scorpions of moderate size, assailed the enemy without being seen. Certain ships which came nearer to the walls in order to get within the range of the engines, he placed upon their sterns, raising up their prows by throwing upon them an iron grapple, attached to a strong chain, by means of a tolleno which projected from the wall, and overhung them, having a heavy counterpoise of lead which forced back the lever to the ground; then the grapple being suddenly disengaged, the ship falling as it were from the wall, was, by these means, to the utter consternation of the mariners, dashed in such a manner against the water, that even if it fell back in an erect position it took in a great quantity of water. Thus the attack by sea was foiled, and their whole efforts were directed to an attack by land with all their forces. But on this side also the place was furnished with a similar array of engines of every kind, procured at the expense of Hiero, who had given his attention to this object through a course of many years, and constructed by the unrivalled abilities of Archimedes. The nature of the place also assisted them; for the rock which formed the foundation of the wall was for the most part so steep, that not only materials discharged from engines, but such as were rolled down by their own gravity, fell upon the enemy with great force; the same cause rendered the approach to the city difficult, and the footing unsteady. Wherefore, a council being held, it was resolved, since every attempt was frustrated, to abstain from assaulting the place, and keeping up a blockade, only to cut off the provisions of the enemy by sea and land.

Meanwhile, Marcellus, who had set out with about a third part of the army, to recover the towns which, during the commotion, had gone over to the Carthaginians, regained Helorus and Herbessus by voluntary surrender. Megara, which he took by storm, he demolished and plundered, in order to terrify the rest, but particularly the Syracusans. Much about the same time, Himilco, who had kept his fleet for a long time at the promontory of Pachynus, landed twenty-five thousand infantry, three thousand horse, and twelve elephants, at Heraclea, which they call Minoa. This force was much greater than that which he had before on board his fleet at Pachynus. But after Syracuse was seized by Hippocrates, he proceeded to Carthage, where, being aided by ambassadors from Hippocrates, and a letter from Hannibal, who said that now was the time to recover Sicily with the highest honour, while his own advice given in person had no small influence, he had prevailed upon the Carthaginians to transport into Sicily as large a force as possible, both of foot and horse. Immediately on his arrival he retook Heraclea, and within a few days after Agrigentum; and in the other states which sided with the Carthaginians, such confident hopes were kindled of driving the Romans out of Sicily, that at last even those who were besieged at Syracuse took courage; and thinking that half their forces would be sufficient for the defence of the city, they divided the business of the war between them in such a manner, that Epicydes superintended the defence of the city, while Hippocrates, in conjunction with Himilco, prosecuted the war against the Roman consul. The latter, having passed by night through the intervals between the posts, with ten thousand foot and five hundred horse, was pitching a camp near the city Acrillæ, when Marcellus came upon them, while engaged in raising the fortifications, on his return from Agrigentum, which was already occupied by the enemy, having failed in his attempt to get there before the enemy by expeditious marching, Marcellus calculated upon any thing rather than meeting with a Syracusan army at that time and place; but still through fear of Himilco and the Carthaginians, for whom he was by no means a match with the forces he had with him, he was marching with all possible circumspection, and with his troops so arranged, as to be prepared for any thing which might occur.

It happened that the caution he had observed with intent to guard him against the Carthaginians, proved useful against the Sicilians. Having caught them in disorder and dispersed, employed in forming their camp, and for the most part unarmed, he cut off all their infantry. Their cavalry, having commenced a slight engagement, fled to Acræ with Hippocrates. This battle having checked the Sicilians in their purpose of revolting from the Romans, Marcellus returned to Syracuse, and a few days after Himilco, being joined by Hippocrates, encamped on the river Anapus, about eight miles distant from that place. Nearly about the same time, fifty-five ships of war of the Carthaginians, with Bomilcar as commander of the fleet, put into the great harbour of Syracuse from the sea, and a Roman fleet of thirty quinqueremes landed the first legion at Panormus; and so intent were both the contending powers upon Sicily, that the seat of war might seem to have been removed from Italy. Himilco, who thought that the Roman legion which had been landed at Panormus, would doubtless fall a prey to him on its way to Syracuse, was mistaken in his road; for the Carthaginian marched through the inland parts of the country, while the legion, keeping along the coast, and attended by the fleet, came up with Appius Claudius, who had advanced to Pachynum with a part of his forces to meet it. Nor did the Carthaginians delay longer at Syracuse. Bomilcar, who at the same time that he did not feel sufficient confidence in his naval strength, as the Romans had a fleet more than double his number, was aware that delay which could be attended with no good effect, would only increase the scarcity of provisions among the allies by the presence of his troops, sailed out into the deep, and crossed over into Africa. Himilco, who had in vain followed Marcellus to Syracuse, to see if he could get any opportunity of engaging him before he was joined by larger forces, failing in this object, and seeing that the enemy were secured at Syracuse, both by their fortifications and the strength of their forces, to avoid wasting time in sitting by as an idle spectator of the siege of his allies, without being able to do any good, marched his troops away, in order to bring them up wherever the prospect of revolt from the Romans might invite him, and wherever by his presence he might inspire additional courage in those who espoused his interest. He first got possession of Murgantia, the Roman garrison having been betrayed by the inhabitants themselves. Here a great quantity of corn and provisions of every kind had been laid up by the Romans.

To this revolt the minds of other states also were stimulated; and the Roman garrisons were now either driven out of the citadels, or treacherously given up and overpowered. Enna, which stood on an eminence lofty and of difficult ascent on all sides, was impregnable on account of its situation, and had besides in its citadel a strong garrison commanded by one who was very unlikely to be overreached by treachery, Lucius Pinarius, a man of vigorous mind, who relied more on the measures he took to prevent treachery, than on the fidelity of the Sicilians; and at that time particularly the intelligence he had received of so many cities being betrayed, and revolting, and of the massacre of the garrisons, had made him solicitous to use every precaution. Accordingly, by day and night equally, every thing was kept in readiness, and every place furnished with guards and watches, the soldiery being continually under arms and at their posts. But when the principal men in Enna, who had already entered into a covenant with Himilco to betray the garrison, found that they could get no opportunity of circumventing the Roman, they resolved to act openly. They urged, that "the city and the citadel ought to be under their control, as they had formed an alliance with the Romans on the understanding that they were to be free, and had not been delivered into their custody as slaves. That they therefore thought it just that the keys of the gates should be restored to them. That their honour formed the strongest tie upon good allies, and that the people and senate of Rome would entertain feelings of gratitude towards them if they continued in friendship with them of their own free will, and not by compulsion." The Roman replied, that "he was placed there by his general to protect the place; that from him he had received the keys of the gates and the custody of the citadel, trusts which he held not subject to his own will, nor that of the inhabitants of Enna, but to his who committed them to him. That among the Romans, for a man to quit his post was a capital offence, and that parents had sanctioned that law by the death even of their own children. That the consul Marcellus was not far off; that they might send ambassadors to him, who possessed the right and liberty of deciding." But they said, they would certainly not send to him, and solemnly declared, that as they could not obtain their object by argument, they would seek some means of asserting their liberty. Pinarius upon this observed, "that if they thought it too much to send to the consul, still they would, at least, grant him an assembly of the people, that it might be ascertained whether these denunciations came from a few, or from the whole state." An assembly of the people was proclaimed for the next day, with the general consent.

After this conference, he returned into the citadel, and assembling his soldiers, thus addressed them: "Soldiers, I suppose you have heard in what manner the Roman garrisons have been betrayed and cut off by the Sicilians of late. You have escaped the same treachery, first by the kindness of the gods, and secondly by your own good conduct, in unremittingly standing and watching under arms. I wish the rest of our time may be passed without suffering or committing dreadful things. This caution, which we have hitherto employed, has been directed against covert treachery, but not succeeding in this as they wished, they now publicly and openly demand back the keys of the gates; but as soon as we shall have delivered them up, Enna will be instantly in the hands of the Carthaginians, and we shall be butchered under circumstances more horrid than those with which the garrison of Murgantia were massacred. I have with difficulty procured a delay of one night for deliberation, that I might employ it in acquainting you with the danger which threatens you. At daybreak they intend holding a general assembly for the purpose of criminating me, and stirring up the people against you; to-morrow, therefore, Enna will be inundated either with your blood, or that of its own inhabitants. If they are beforehand with you, you will have no hope left, but if you anticipate their proceedings, you will have no danger. Victory will belong to that side which shall have drawn the sword first. You shall all, therefore, full armed, attentively wait the signal. I shall be in the assembly, and by talking and disputing will spin out the time till every thing shall be ready. When I shall have given the signal with my gown, then, mind me raising a shout on all sides rush upon the multitude, and fell all before you with the sword, taking care that no one survive from whom either force or fraud can be apprehended. You, mother Ceres and Proserpine, I entreat, and all ye other gods, celestial and infernal, who frequent this city and these consecrated lakes and groves, that you would lend us your friendly and propitious aid, as we adopt this measure not for the purpose of inflicting, but averting injury. I should exhort you at greater length my soldiers, if you were about to fight with armed men, men unarmed and off their guard, you will slay to satiety. The consul's camp too is near, so that nothing can be apprehended from Himilco and the Carthaginians'."

Being allowed to retire immediately after this exhortation, they employed themselves in taking refreshment. The next day they stationed themselves some in one place and others in another, to block up the streets, and shut up the ways by which the townsmen might escape, the greater part of them stationing themselves upon and round the theatre, as they had been accustomed before also to be spectators of the assemblies. When the Roman præfect, having been brought into the presence of the people by the magistrates, said, that the power and authority of deciding the question appertained to the consul, and not to him, repeating for the most part what he had urged the day before, first of all a small number, and then more, desired him to give up the keys, but afterwards all with one consent demanded it, and when he hesitated and delayed, threatened him furiously, and seemed as though they would not further delay violent extremities then the præfect gave the signal agreed upon with his gown and the soldiers, who had been long anxiously waiting the signal, and in readiness, raising a shout, ran down, some of them from the higher ground, upon the rear of the assembly while others blocked up the passages leading out of the crowded theatre. The people of Enna thus shut up in the pit were put to the sword, being heaped one upon another not only in consequence of the slaughter, but also from their own efforts to escape, for some scrambling over the heads of others, and those that were unhurt falling upon the wounded, and the living upon the dead, they were accumulated together. Thence they ran in every direction throughout the city, when nothing was any where to be seen but flight and bloodshed, as though the city had been captured, for the rage of the soldiery was not less excited in putting to the sword an unarmed rabble, than it would have been had the heat of battle and an equality of danger stimulated it. Thus possession of Enna was retained, by an act which was either atrocious or unavoidable. Marcellus did not disapprove of the deed, and gave up the plunder of the place to the soldiery, concluding that the Sicilians, deterred by this example, would refrain from betraying their garrisons. As this city was situated in the heart of Sicily, and was distinguished both on account of the remarkable strength of its natural situation, and because every part of it was rendered sacred by the traces it contained of the rape of Proserpine of old, the news of its disaster spread though the whole of Sicily in nearly one day, and as people considered that by this horrid massacre violence had been done not only to the habitations of men, but even of the gods, then indeed those who even before this event were in doubt which side they should take, revolted to the Carthaginians Hippocrates and Himilco, who had in vain brought up their troops to Enna at the invitation of the traitors, retired thence, the former to Murgantia, the latter to Agrigentum. Marcellus retrograded into the territory of Leontium, and after collecting a quantity of corn and other provisions in his camp there, left a small body of troops to protect it, and then went to carry on the siege of Syracuse. Appius Claudius having been allowed to go from thence to Rome to put up for the consulship, he appointed Titus Quintus Crispinus to command the fleet and the old camp in his room. He himself fortified his camp, and built huts for his troops at a distance of five miles from Hexapylum, at a place called Leon. These were the transactions in Sicily up to the beginning of the winter.

The same summer the war with king Philip, as had been before suspected, broke out. Ambassadors from Oricum came to Marcus Valerius, the prætor, who was directing his fleet around Brundusium and the neighbouring coasts of Calabria, with intelligence, that Philip had first made an attempt upon Apollonia, having approached it by sailing up the river with a hundred and twenty barks with two banks of oars; after that, not succeeding so speedily as he had hoped, that he had brought up his army secretly to Oricum by night; which city, as it was situated on a plain, and was not secured either by fortifications or by men and arms, was overpowered at the first assault. At the same time that they delivered this intelligence, they entreated him to bring them succour, and repel that decided enemy of the Romans by land or by a naval force, since they were attacked for no other cause than that they lay over against Italy. Marcus Valerius, leaving Publius Valerius lieutenant-general charged with the protection of that quarter, set sail with his fleet equipped and prepared, having put on board of ships of burthen such soldiers as there was not room for in the men of war, and reached Oricum on the second day; and as that city was occupied by a slight garrison, which Philip had left on his departure thence, he retook it without much opposition. Here ambassadors came to him from Apollonia, stating that they were subjected to a siege because they were unwilling to revolt from the Romans, and that they would not be able any longer to resist the power of the Macedonians, unless a Roman force were sent for their protection. Having undertaken to perform what they wished, he sent two thousand chosen armed men in ships of war to the mouth of the river, under the command of Quintus Nævius Crista, præfect of the allies, a man of enterprise, and experienced in military affairs. Having landed his troops, and sent back the ships to join the rest of the fleet at Oricum, whence he had come, he marched his troops at a distance from the river, by a way not guarded at all by the king's party, and entered the city by night, so that none of the enemy perceived him. During the following day they remained quiet, to afford time for the præfect to inspect the youth of Apollonia, together with the arms and resources of the city. Having derived considerable confidence from a review and inspection of these, and at the same time discovering from scouts the supineness and negligence which prevailed among the enemy, he marched out of the city during the dead of night without any noise, and entered the camp of the enemy, which was in such a neglected and exposed state, that it was quite clear that a thousand men had passed the rampart before any one perceived them, and that had they abstained from putting them to the sword, they might have penetrated to the royal pavilion. The killing of those who were nearest the gate aroused the enemy; and in consequence, they were all seized with such alarm and dismay, that not only none of the rest attempted to take arms or endeavour to expel the enemy from the camp, but even the king himself, betaking himself to flight, in a manner half naked and just as he was when roused from his sleep, hurried away to the river and his ships in a garb scarcely decent for a private soldier, much less for a king. Thither also the rest of the multitude fled with the utmost precipitation. Little less than three thousand men were slain or made prisoners in the camp; considerably more, however, were captured than slain. The camp having been plundered, the Apollonians removed into their city the catapults, ballistas, and other engines which had been got together for the purpose of assaulting their city, for the protection of their walls, in case at any time a similar conjuncture should arise; all the rest of the plunder which the camp afforded was given up to the Romans. Intelligence of these events having been carried to Oricum, Marcus Valerius immediately brought his fleet to the mouth of the river, that the king might not attempt to make his escape by ship. Thus Philip, having lost all hope of being able to cope with his enemies by land or sea, and having either hauled on shore or burnt his ships, made for Macedonia by land, his troops being for the most part unarmed and despoiled of their baggage. The Roman fleet, with Marcus Valerius, wintered at Oricum.

The same year the war was prosecuted in Spain with various success; for before the Romans crossed the Iberus, Mago and Hasdrubal had routed an immense army of Spaniards; and the farther Spain would have revolted from the Romans, had not Publius Cornelius, hastily crossing the Iberus with his army, given a seasonable stimulus to the wavering resolutions of his allies by his arrival among them. The Romans first encamped at a place called the High Camp, which is remarkable for the death of the great Hamilcar.

It was a fortress strongly defended by works, and thither they had previously conveyed corn; but as the whole circumjacent country was full of enemy's troops, and the Roman army on its march had been charged by the cavalry of the enemy without being able to take revenge upon them, two thousand men, who either loitered behind or had strayed through the fields, having been slain, the Romans quitted this place to get nearer to a friendly country, and fortified a camp at the mount of Victory. To this place came Cneius Scipio with all his forces, and Hasdrubal, son of Gisgo, and a third Carthaginian general, with a complete army, all of whom took up a position opposite the Roman camp and on the other side the river. Publius Scipio, going out with some light troops to take a view of the surrounding country, was observed by the enemy; and he would have been overpowered in the open plain, had he not seized an eminence near him. Here too he was closely invested, but was rescued from the troops which environed him by the arrival of his brother. Castulo, a city of Spain, so strong and celebrated, and so closely connected with the Carthaginians, that Hannibal had taken a wife from it, revolted to the Romans. The Carthaginians commenced the siege of Illiturgi, because there was a Roman garrison in it; and it seemed that they would carry the place, chiefly in consequence of a lack of provisions. Cneius Scipio, setting out with a legion lightly equipped, in order to bring succour to his allies and the garrison, entered the city, passing between the two camps of the enemy, and slaying a great number of them. The next day also he sallied out and fought with equal success. Above twelve thousand were slain in the two battles, more than a thousand made prisoners, and thirty-six military standards captured. In consequence of this they retired from Illiturgi. After this the siege of Bigerra, a city which was also in alliance with the Romans, was commenced by the Carthaginians; but Scipio coming up, raised the siege without experiencing any opposition.

The Carthaginians then removed their camp to Munda, whither the Romans speedily followed them. Here a pitched battle was fought, which lasted almost four hours; and while the Romans were carrying all before them in the most glorious manner, the signal for retreat was sounded, because the thigh of Cneius Scipio had been transfixed with a javelin. The soldiers round about him were thrown into a state of great alarm, lest the wound should be mortal. However, there was no doubt but that if they had not been prevented by the intervention of this accident, they might have taken the Carthaginian camp that day. By this time, not only the men, but the elephants, were driven quite up to the rampart; and even upon the top of it nine and thirty elephants were pierced with spears. In this battle, too, as many as twelve thousand are said to have been slain, nearly three thousand captured, with fifty-seven military standards. The Carthaginians retired thence to the city Auringis, whither the Romans followed them, in order to take advantage of their terror. Here Scipio again fought them, having been carried into the field in a small litter; the victory was decisive; but not half so many of the enemy were slain as before, because fewer survived to fight. But this family, which possessed a natural talent at renewing war and restoring its effects, in a short time recruited their army, Mago having been sent by his brother to press soldiers, and assumed courage to try the issue of a fresh struggle. Though the soldiers were for the most part different, yet as they fought in a cause which had so often been unsuccessful within the space of a few days, they carried into the field the same state of mind as those which had been engaged before, and the issue of the battle was similar. More than eight thousand were slain, not much less than a thousand captured, with fifty-eight military standards. The greater part of the spoils had belonged to the Gauls, consisting of golden chains and bracelets in great numbers. Also two distinguished Gallic petty princes, whose names were Mœnicaptus and Civismarus, fell in this battle. Eight elephants were captured and three slain. When affairs went on so prosperously in Spain, the Romans began to feel ashamed that Saguntum, on account of which the war had originated, should continue for now the eighth year in the power of the enemy. Accordingly, having expelled by force the Carthaginian garrison, they retook that town, and restored it to such of the ancient inhabitants as had survived the fury of the war. The Turditanians also, who had been the cause of the war between that people and the Carthaginians, they reduced under their power, sold them as slaves, and razed their city.

Such were the achievements in Spain during the consulate of Quintus Fabius and Marcus Claudius. At Rome, as soon as the new plebeian tribunes entered upon their office, Lucius Metellus, a plebeian tribune, immediately appointed a day for impleading the censors, Publius Furius and Marcus Atilius, before the people. In the preceding year, when he was quæstor, they had deprived him of his horse, removed him from his tribe, and disfranchised him, on account of the conspiracy entered into at Cannæ to abandon Italy. But being aided by the other nine tribunes, they were forbidden to answer while in office, and were discharged. The death of Publius Furius prevented their completing the lustrum. Marcus Atilius abdicated his office. An assembly for the election of consuls was held by Quintus Fabius Maximus. The consuls elected were Quintus Fabius Maximus, son of the consul, and Tiberius Sempronius Gracchus a second time, both being absent. The prætors appointed were Marcus Atilius, and the two curule ædiles, Publius Sempronius Tuditanus and Cneius Fulvius Centumalus, together with Marcus Æmilius Lepidus. It is recorded, that the scenic games were this year, for the first time, celebrated for four days by the curule ædiles. The ædile Tuditanus was the man who made his way through the midst of the enemy at Cannæ when all the rest were paralysed with fear, in consequence of that dreadful calamity. As soon as the elections were completed, the consuls elect having been summoned to Rome, at the instance of Quintus Fabius, the consul, entered upon their office, and took the sense of the senate respecting the war, their own provinces as well as those of the prætors, and also respecting the armies to be employed, and which each of them was to command.

The provinces and armies were thus distributed: the prosecution of the war with Hannibal was given to the consuls, and of the armies, one which Sempronius himself had commanded, and another which the consul Fabius had commanded, each consisting of two legions. Marcus Æmilius, the prætor, who had the foreign jurisdiction, was to have Luceria as his province, with the two legions which Quintus Fabius, then consul, had commanded as prætor, his colleague, Marcus Atilius, the city prætor, undertaking the duties of his office. The province of Ariminum fell to the lot of Publius Sempronius, that of Suessula to Cneius Fulvius, with two legions each likewise; Fulvius taking with him the city legions; Tuditanus receiving his from Manius Pomponius. The following generals were continued in command, and their provinces assigned to them thus: to Marcus Claudius, so much of Sicily as lay within the limits of the kingdom of Hiero; to Lentulus, the proprætor, the old province in that island; to Titus Otacilius, the fleet; no additional troops were assigned to them. Marcus Valerius had Greece and Macedonia, with the legion and the fleet which he had there; Quintus Mucius had Sardinia, with his old army, consisting of two legions; Caius Terentius, Picenum, with one legion which he then commanded. Besides, orders were given to enlist two legions for the city, and twenty thousand men from the allies. With these leaders and these forces did they fortify the Roman empire against the many wars which had either actually broken out, or were suspected at one and the same time. After enlisting the city legions and raising troops to make up the numbers of the others, the consuls, before they quitted the city, expiated the prodigies which were reported. A wall and a gate had been struck by lightning; and at Aricia even the temple of Jupiter had been struck by lightning. Other illusions of the eyes and ears were credited as realities. An appearance as of ships had been seen in the river at Tarracina, when there were none there. A clashing of arms was heard in the temple of Jupiter Vicilinus, in the territory of Compsa; and a river at Amiternum had flowed bloody. These prodigies having been expiated according to a decree of the pontiffs, the consuls set out, Sempronius for Lucania, Fabius for Apulia. The father of the latter came into the camp at Suessula, as his lieutenant-general; and when the son advanced to meet him, the lictors, out of respect for his dignity, went on in silence. The old man rode past eleven of the fasces, when the consul ordered the lictor nearest to him to take care and he called to him to dismount; then at length dismounting, he exclaimed, "I wished to try, my son, whether you were duly sensible that you are a consul."

To this camp came Dasias Altinius of Arpi privately and by night, attended by three slaves, with a promise that if he should receive a reward for it, he would engage to betray Arpi to them. Fabius having laid the matter before a council, some were of opinion that "he ought to be scourged and put to death as a deserter, as a man of unstable mind, and a common enemy to both sides; who, after the defeat at Cannæ, had gone over to Hannibal and drawn Arpi into revolt, as if it were right that a man's fidelity should vary according to the fluctuations of fortune; and who now, when the Roman cause, contrary to his hopes and wishes, was as it were rising up again, would seem to aggravate his baseness by recompensing those whom he had formerly betrayed, by fresh betrayal. That a man whose custom it was to espouse one side, while his heart was on another, was unworthy of confidence as an ally, and contemptible as an enemy; that he ought to be made a third example to deserters, in addition to the betrayers of Falerii and Pyrrhus." On the other hand, Fabius, the father of the consul, observed, that, "forgetful of circumstances, men were apt to exercise a free judgment on every question in the heat of war, as in time of peace; for though in the present instance that which ought rather to form the object of their endeavours and to occupy their thoughts, is by what means it may be brought about that none of the allies may revolt from the Roman people, yet that they never think of; but, on the contrary, they urge that an example ought to be made of any who might repent and look back upon their former alliance. But if it is allowable to forsake the Romans, and not allowable to return to them, who can doubt but that in a short time the Romans, deserted by their allies, will see every state in Italy united in leagues with the Carthaginians. Not, however, that he was of opinion that any confidence was to be reposed in Altinius, but he would invent some middle course of proceeding. Treating him neither as an enemy nor as a friend for the present, his wish was, that he should be kept during the war in some city whose fidelity could be relied on, at a short distance from the camp, in a state of easy restraint; and that when the war was concluded, they should then deliberate whether he more deserved to be punished for his former defection, or pardoned for his present return." The opinion of Fabius was approved of. Altinius was bound in chains and given into custody, together with his companions, and a large quantity of gold which he brought with him was ordered to be kept for him. He was kept at Cales, where, during the day, he was unconfined, but attended by guards who locked him up at night. He was first missed and inquired for at his house at Arpi. but afterwards, when the report of his absence had spread through the city, a violent sensation was excited, as if they had lost their leader, and, from the apprehension of some attempt to alter the present state of things, messengers were immediately despatched to Hannibal. With this the Carthaginian was far from being displeased, both because he had long regarded the man himself with suspicion, as one of doubtful fidelity, and because he had now been lucky enough to get a pretext for possessing himself of the property of so wealthy a person. But that the world might suppose that he had yielded to resentment more than to avarice, he added cruelty to rapacity; for he summoned his wife and children to the camp, and after having made inquiry, first, respecting the flight of Altinius, and then, touching the quantity of gold and silver which was left at his house, and informed himself on all these points, he burned them alive.

Fabius, setting out from Suessula, first set about the siege of Arpi; and having pitched his camp about half a mile from it, he took a near view of the site and walls of the city, and resolved to attack it, in preference, in that quarter where it was most secured by works, and where the least care was taken in guarding it. After getting all things together which could be of use in besieging a city, he selected the most efficient of the centurions out of the whole army, placing them under the command of tribunes of approved valour, and giving them six hundred soldiers, a number which was thought sufficient for the purpose. These he ordered to bring the scaling ladders to the place which he had marked out, as soon as the signal of the fourth watch had sounded. In this part there was a low and narrow gate, opening into a street which was little frequented, and which led through a deserted part of the city. He ordered them, after scaling the wall, to proceed to this gate, and break down the bars on the inside by force, and when they were in possession of that part of the city, to give a signal with a cornet, that the rest of the troops might be brought up, observing that he would have every thing prepared and ready. These orders were executed promptly, and that which seemed likely to impede their operations, served more than any thing to conceal them. A shower of rain, which came on suddenly at midnight, compelled the guards and watches to slip away from their posts and take shelter in the houses; and the noise of the shower, which was somewhat copious, at first prevented their hearing that which was made by the men in breaking open the gate. Afterwards, when it fell upon the ear more gently and uniformly, it lulled a great number of the men to sleep. After they had secured possession of the gate, they placed cornet-players in the street at equal distances, and desired them to sound, in order to call the consul. This being done according to the plan previously agreed upon, the consul ordered the troops to march, and a little before daylight entered the city through the broken gate.

Then at length the enemy were roused, the shower was now subsiding, and daylight coming on. Hannibal had a garrison of about five thousand armed men in the city, and the inhabitants themselves had three thousand men in arms; these the Carthaginians placed in front against the enemy, to guard against any treachery on their rear. The fight was carried on at first in the dark, and in the narrow streets, the Romans having seized not only the streets, but the houses also nearest the gate, that they might not be struck or wounded by any thing discharged at them from above. Some of the Arpinians and Romans recognised each other, which led to conversations, in which the Romans asked them, what it was they meant? for what offence on the part of the Romans, or what service on that of the Carthaginians, they, who were Italians, made war in favour of foreigners and barbarians, against their ancient allies the Romans, and endeavoured to render Italy tributary and stipendiary to Africa? The Arpinians urged in excuse of themselves, that in ignorance of all the circumstances, they had been sold to the Carthaginians by their nobility, and that they were kept in a state of thraldom and oppression by the few. A beginning having been made, greater numbers on both sides entered into conversation; and at length the prætor of Arpi was brought by his countrymen before the consul, and after exchanging assurances in the midst of the standards and the troops, the Arpinians suddenly turned their arms against the Carthaginians, in favour of the Romans. Some Spaniards also, little less than a thousand in number, after only stipulating with the consul that the Carthaginian garrison might be allowed to march out unhurt, passed over to the consul. The gates were therefore thrown open for the Carthaginians; and being allowed to go out unmolested, in conformity with the stipulation, they joined Hannibal in Salapia. Thus was Arpi restored to the Romans, without the loss of a life, except that of one man, who was formerly a traitor, and recently a deserter. The Spaniards were ordered to receive a double allowance of provisions, and on very many occasions the republic availed itself of their brave and faithful services. While one of the consuls was in Apulia, and the other in Lucania, a hundred and twelve Campanian noblemen, having gone out of Capua, with the permission of the magistrates, under pretence of collecting booty from the enemy's lands, came into the Roman camp, which lay above Suessula. They told the soldiers, forming the vanguard, that they wished to speak with the prætor. Cneius Fulvius commanded the camp; who, on being informed of the circumstance, ordered ten of them to be brought into his presence unarmed; and after hearing their request, (and all they asked was, that when the Romans should recover Capua, their property might be restored to them,) they were all received under his protection. The other prætor, Sempronius Tuditanus, took by force the town of Aternum; more than seven thousand were captured, with a considerable quantity of coined brass and silver. A dreadful fire happened at Rome, which continued for two nights and a day; every thing was burnt to the ground between the Salinæ and the Carmental gate, with the Æquimælium and the Jugarian street. In the temples of Fortune, Mater Matuta, and Hope, which latter stood without the gate, the fire, spreading to a wide extent, consumed much both sacred and profane.

The same year, the two Cornelii, Publius and Cneius, as affairs were now in a prosperous state in Spain, and they had recovered many ancient allies, and attached fresh ones to them, extended their views even to Africa. Syphax was a king of the Numidians, who had suddenly become hostile to the Carthaginians; to him they sent three centurions as ambassadors, to form a treaty of friendship and alliance with him; and to promise, that, if he persevered in pressing the war against the Carthaginians, he would render an acceptable service to the senate and people of Rome, and they would endeavour to requite the favour with large additions, and at a seasonable time. This embassy was gratifying to the barbarian; and when conversing with the ambassadors on the art of war he heard the observations of those experienced soldiers, by comparing his own practice with so regular a system of discipline, he became sensible of how many things he himself was ignorant. Then he entreated them to give the first proof of their being good and faithful allies, "by letting two of them carry back the result of their embassy to their generals, while one remained with him as his instructor in military science, observing that the Numidian nation were unacquainted with the method of carrying on war with foot forces, being useful only as mounted soldiers. That it was in this manner that their ancestors had carried on war even from the first origin of their nation, and to this they were habituated from their childhood. But that they had to contend with an enemy who relied upon the prowess of their infantry; with whom, if they wished to be placed upon an equality in respect of efficient strength, they must also furnish themselves with infantry. That his dominions abounded with a large quantity of men fit for the purpose, but that he was unacquainted with the art of arming, equipping, and marshalling them; that all his infantry were unwieldy and unmanageable, like a rabble collected together by chance."

The ambassadors answered, that they would comply with his request for the present, on his engaging to send him back immediately, if their generals did not approve of what they had done. The name of the person who staid behind with the king was Quintus Statorius. With the two other Romans, the Numidian sent ambassadors into Spain, to receive the ratification of the alliance from the Roman generals. He gave it in charge to the same persons, forthwith to induce the Numidians, who were serving as auxiliaries among the Carthaginian troops, to go over to the other side. Statorius raised a body of infantry for the king out of the large number of young men which he found; and having formed them into companies, in close imitation of the Roman method, taught them to follow their standards and keep their ranks when being marshalled, and when performing their evolutions; and he so habituated them to military works and other military duties, that in a short time the king relied not more on his cavalry than on his infantry; and in a regular and pitched battle, fought on a level plain, he overcame his enemies, the Carthaginians. In Spain also the arrival of the king's ambassadors was of the greatest advantage to the Romans, for at the news thereof the Numidians began rapidly to pass over. Thus the Romans and Syphax were united in friendship, which the Carthaginians hearing of, immediately sent ambassadors to Gala, who reigned in another part of Numidia, over a nation called Massylians.

Gala had a son named Masinissa, seventeen years of age, but a youth of such talents, that even at that time it was evident that he would render the kingdom more extensive and powerful than when he received it. The ambassadors represented that, "since Syphax had united himself with the Romans, that by their alliance he might strengthen his hands against the kings and nations of Africa, it would be better for Gala also to unite with the Carthaginians as soon as possible, before Syphax crossed over into Spain, or the Romans into Africa; that Syphax might be overpowered, while as yet he derived nothing from his league with the Romans but the name of it." Gala, his son claiming to be intrusted with the conduct of the war, was easily prevailed upon to send an army, which, joined by the legions of the Carthaginians, totally defeated Syphax in a great battle. In this thirty thousand men are said to have been slain. Syphax, with a few horsemen, fled from the field, and took refuge among the Maurusian Numidians, a nation dwelling at the extremity of Africa, near the ocean, and over against Gades. But the barbarians flocking to his standard from all sides, in consequence of his great renown, he speedily armed a very large force. Before he passed over with these forces into Spain, which was separated only by a narrow strait, Masinissa came up with his victorious army; and here he acquired great glory in the prosecution of the war with Syphax, in which he acted alone and unsupported by any aid from the Carthaginians. In Spain nothing worth mentioning was performed, except that the Romans drew over to their side the Celtiberian youth, by giving them the same pay which they had stipulated with the Carthaginians to pay them. They also sent above three hundred Spaniards of the greatest distinction into Italy, to bring over their countrymen, who served among the auxiliary troops of Hannibal. The only memorable circumstance of this year in Spain was, that the Romans then, for the first time, employed mercenary troops in their camp, namely, the Celtiberians.

BOOK XXV.

Publius Cornelius Scipio, afterwards called Africanus, elected œdile before he had attained the age required by the law. The citadel of Tarentum, in which the Roman garrison had taken refuge, betrayed to Hannibal. Games instituted in honour of Apollo, called Apollinarian. Quintus Fulvius and Appius Claudius, consuls, defeat Hanno the Carthaginian general. Tiberius Sempronius Gracchus betrayed by a Lucanian to Mago, and slain. Centenius Penula, who had been a centurion, asks the senate for the command of an army, promising to engage and vanquish Hannibal, is cut off with eight thousand men. Cneius Fulvius engages Hannibal, and is beaten, with the loss of sixteen thousand men slain, he himself escapes with only two hundred horsemen. Quintus Fulvius and Appius Claudius, consuls, lay siege to Capua. Syracuse taken by Claudius Marcellus after a siege of three years. In the tumult occasioned by taking the city, Archimedes is killed while intently occupied on some figures which he had drawn in the sand. Publius and Cornelius Scipio, after having performed many eminent services in Spain, are slain, together with nearly the whole of their armies, eight years after their arrival in that country; and the possession of that province would have been entirely lost, but for the valour and activity of Lucius Marcius, a Roman knight, who, collecting the scattered remains of the vanquished armies, utterly defeats the enemy, storming their two camps, killing thirty-seven thousand of them, and taking eighteen hundred together with an immense booty.

Hannibal passed the summer during which these events occurred in Africa and Italy, in the Tarentine territory, with the hope of having the city of the Tarentines betrayed to him. Meanwhile some inconsiderable towns belonging to them, and to the Sallentines, revolted to him. At the same time, of the twelve states of the Bruttians, which had in a former year gone over to the Carthaginians, the Consentians and Thurians returned to the protection of the Roman people. And more would have done the same, had not Titus Pomponius Veientanus, præfect of the allies, having acquired the appearance of a regular general, in consequence of several successful predatory expeditions in the Bruttian territory, got together a tumultuary band, and fought a battle with Hanno. In that battle, a great number of men, consisting, however, of a disorderly rabble of slaves and rustics, were slain or captured. The least part of the loss was, that the præfect himself was taken prisoner; for he was not only in the present instance guilty of having rashly engaged the enemy, but previously, in the capacity of farmer of the revenue, by iniquitous practices of every description, had shown himself faithless and injurious to the state, as well as the companies. Among the Lucanians, the consul, Sempronius, fought several small battles, but none worthy of being recorded, he also took several inconsiderable towns. In proportion as the war was protracted, and the sentiments no less than the circumstances of men fluctuated accordingly as events flowed prosperously or otherwise, the citizens were seized with such a passion for superstitious observances, and those for the most part introduced from foreign countries, that either the people or the gods appeared to have undergone a sudden change. And now the Roman rites were growing into disuse, not only in private, and within doors, but in public also; in the forum and Capitol there were crowds of women sacrificing, and offering up prayers to the gods, in modes unusual in that country. A low order of sacrificers and soothsayers had enslaved men's understandings, and the numbers of these were increased by the country people, whom want and terror had driven into the city, from the fields which were lain uncultivated during a protracted war, and had suffered from the incursions of the enemy, and by the profitable cheating in the ignorance of others which they carried on like an allowed and customary trade. At first, good men gave protest in private to the indignation they felt at these proceedings, but afterwards the thing came before the fathers, and formed a matter of public complaint. The ædiles and triumviri, appointed for the execution of criminals, were severely reprimanded by the senate for not preventing these irregularities, but when they attempted to remove the crowd of persons thus employed from the forum, and to overthrow the preparations for their sacred rites, they narrowly escaped personal injury. It being now evident, that the evil was too powerful to be checked by inferior magistrates, the senate commissioned Marcus Atilius, the city prætor, to rid the people of these superstitions. He called an assembly, in which he read the decree of the senate, and gave notice, that all persons who had any books of divination, or forms of prayer, or any written system of sacrificing, should lay all the aforesaid books and writings before him before the calends of April; and that no person should sacrifice in any public or consecrated place according to new or foreign rites.

Several of the public priests too died this year: Lucius Cornelius Lentulus, chief pontiff, Caius Papirius Maso, son of Caius, a pontiff, Publius Furius Philo, an augur, and Caius Papirius Maso, son of Lucius, a decemvir for the superintendence of sacred rites. In lieu of Lentulus, Marcus Cornelius Cethegus, in lieu of Papirius Cnæius, Servilius Cæpio, were created pontiffs. Lucius Quinctius Flaminius was created augur, and Lucius Cornelius Lentulus decemvir for the superintendence of sacred rites. The time for the election of consuls was now approaching; but as it was not thought proper to call the consuls away from the war with which they were intently occupied, Tiberius Sempronius, the consul, nominated Caius Claudius Centho as dictator to hold the election. He appointed Quintus Fulvius Flaccus as his master of the horse. On the first day on which the election could be held, the dictator appointed as consuls, Quintus Fulvius Flaccus, his master of the horse, and Appius Claudius Pulcher, who had held the government of Sicily as prætor. The prætors created were Cneius Fulvius Flaccus, Caius Claudius Nero, Marcus Junius Silanus, Publius Cornelius Sulla. The election completed, the dictator retired from his office. This year, Publius Cornelius Scipio, afterwards surnamed Africanus, held the office of curule ædile, with Marcus Cornelius Cethegus; and when the tribunes of the people opposed his pretensions to the ædileship, alleging, that no notice ought to be taken of him, because he had not attained the legal age for candidateship, he observed, "if the citizens in general are desirous of appointing me ædile, I am old enough." Upon this the people ran to their respective tribes to give their votes, with feelings so strongly disposed in his favour, that the tribunes on a sudden abandoned their attempt. The largesses bestowed by the ædiles were the following: the Roman games were sumptuously exhibited, considering the present state of their resources; they were repeated during one day, and a gallon of oil was given to each street. Lucius Villius Tapulus, and Marcus Fundanius Fundulus, the plebeian ædiles, accused some matrons of misconduct before the people, and some of them they convicted and sent into exile. The plebeian games were repeated during two days, and a feast in honour of Jupiter was celebrated on occasion of the games.

Quintus Fulvius Flaccus, for the third time, and Appius Claudius entered upon the office of consuls. The prætors determined their provinces by lot. Publius Cornelius Sulla received both the city and the foreign jurisdiction, formerly allotted to two persons, Cneius Fulvius Flaccus, Apulia, Caius Claudius Nero, Suessula, and Marcus Junius

Silanus, Tuscany. To the consuls the conduct of the war with Hannibal was decreed with two legions each, one taking the troops of Quintus Fabius, the consul of the former year, the other those of Fulvius Centumalus. Of the prætors, Fulvius Flaccus was to have the legions which were in Luceria under Æmilius the prætor, Nero Claudius those in Picenum under Caius Terentius, each raising recruits for himself to fill up the number of his troops. To Marcus Junius the city legions of the former year were assigned, to be employed against the Tuscans. Tiberius Sempronius Gracchus and Publius Sempronius Tuditanus were continued in command in their provinces of Lucania and Gaul with the armies they had, as was also Publius Lentulus in that part of Sicily which formed the ancient Roman province. Marcus Marcellus had Syracuse, and that which was the kingdom of Hiero. Titus Otacilius was continued in the command of the fleet, Marcus Valerius in that of Greece, Quintus Mucius Scævola in that of Sardinia. The Cornelii, Publius and Cneius, were continued in the command of Spain. In addition to the armies already existing, two legions for the service of the city were levied by the consuls, and a total of twenty-three legions was made up this year. The levy of the consuls was impeded by the conduct of Marcus Posthumius Pyrgensis, almost accompanied with a serious disturbance. Posthumius was a farmer of the revenue, who, for knavery and rapacity, practised through a course of many years, had no equal except Titus Pomponius Veientanus, who had been taken prisoner the former year by the Carthaginians under the conduct of Hanno, while carelessly ravaging the lands in Lucania. As the state had taken upon itself the risk of any loss which might arise from storms to the commodities conveyed to the armies, not only had these two men fabricated false accounts of shipwrecks, but even those which had really occurred were occasioned by their own knavery, and not by accident. Their plan was to put a few goods of little value into old and shattered vessels, which they sank in the deep, taking up the sailors in boats prepared for the purpose, and then returning falsely the cargo as many times more valuable than it was. This fraudulent practice had been pointed out to Marcus Atilius, the prætor in a former year, who had communicated it to the senate; no decree, however, had been passed censuring it, because the fathers were unwilling that any offence should be given to the order of revenue farmers while affairs were in such a state. The people were severer avengers of the fraud; and at length two tribunes of the people, Spurius and Lucius Carvilius, being moved to take some active measure, as they saw that this conduct excited universal disgust, and had become notorious, proposed that a fine of two hundred thousand asses should be imposed on Marcus Posthumius. When the day arrived for arguing the question, the people assembled in such numbers, that the area of the Capitol could scarcely contain them; and the cause having been gone through, the only hope of safety which presented itself was, that Caius Servilius Casca, a tribune of the people, a connexion and relation of Posthumius, should interpose his protest before the tribes were called to give their votes. The witnesses having been produced, the tribunes caused the people to withdraw, and the urn was brought, in order that the tribes should draw lots which should give the vote first. Meanwhile, the farmers of the revenue urged Casca to stop the proceedings for that day. The people, however, loudly opposed it; and Casca happened to be sitting on the most prominent part of the rostrum, whose mind fear and shame were jointly agitating. Seeing that no dependence was to be placed in him for protection, the farmers of the revenue, forming themselves into a wedge, rushed into the void space occasioned by the removal of the people for the purpose of causing disturbance, wrangling at the same time with the people and the tribunes. The affair had now almost proceeded to violence, when Fulvius Flaccus, the consul, addressing the tribunes, said, "Do you not see that you are degraded to the common rank, and that an insurrection will be the result, unless you speedily dismiss the assembly of the commons."

The commons being dismissed, the senate was assembled, when the consuls proposed the consideration of the interruption experienced by the assembly of the commons, in consequence of the violence and audacity of the farmers of the revenue. They said, that "Marcus Furius Camillus, whose banishment was followed by the downfall of the city, had suffered himself to be condemned by his exasperated countrymen. That before him, the decemviri, according to whose laws they lived up to the present day, and afterwards many men of the first rank in the state, had submitted to have sentence passed upon them by the people. But Posthumius Pyrgensis had wrested from the Roman people their right of suffrage, had dissolved the assembly of the commons, had set at nought the authority of the tribunes, had drawn up a body of men in battle-array against the Roman people; and seized upon a post, in order to cut off the tribunes from the commons, and prevent the tribes being called to give their votes. That the only thing which had restrained the people from bloodshed and violence, was the forbearance of the magistrates in giving way for the moment to the fury and audacity of a few individuals, and suffering themselves and the Roman people to be overcome; and that no opportunity might be afforded those who were seeking an occasion of violence, in dissolving, agreeably to the wish of the defendant himself, that assembly which he was about to interrupt by force of arms." Observations of this kind having been urged with a warmth proportioned to the atrocity of the conduct which called them forth, by all the most respectable persons, and the senate having passed a decree to the effect that the violence offered was prejudicial to the state, and a precedent of pernicious tendency, immediately the Carvilii, tribunes of the people, giving up the action for a fine, appointed a day on which Posthumius should be tried capitally, and ordered, that unless he gave bail, he should be apprehended by the beadle, and carried to prison. Posthumius gave bail, but did not appear. The tribunes then proposed to the commons, and the commons resolved, that if Marcus Posthumius did not appear before the calends of May, and if on being cited on that day he did not answer, and sufficient cause were not shown why he did not, he would be adjudged an exile, his goods would be sold, and himself interdicted from water and fire. They then proceeded to indict capitally, and demand bail of each of the persons who had been the promoters of the disorder and riot. At first they threw into prison those who did not give bail, and afterwards even such as could; upon which the greater part of them went into exile, to avoid the danger to which this proceeding exposed them.

The knavery of the revenue farmers, and their subsequent audacious conduct to screen themselves from its effects, thus terminated. An assembly was then held for the creation of a chief pontiff. The new pontiff, Marcus Cornelius Cethegus, presided. The election was contested with the greatest obstinacy by three candidates, Quintus Fulvius Flaccus, the consul, who had been twice consul before and censor, Titus Manlius Torquatus, who had himself also been distinguished by two consulships and the censorship, and Publius Licinius Crassus, who was about to stand for the office of curule ædile. In this contest, the last-mentioned candidate, though a young man, beat the others, who were his superiors in years, and had filled offices of honour. Before him there had not been a man for a hundred and twenty years, except Publius Cornelius Calussa, who had been created chief pontiff without having sat in the curule chair. Though the consuls found great difficulty in completing the levy, for in consequence of the scarcity of young men, it was not easy to procure enough for the two purposes of forming the new city legions, and recruiting the old ones, the senate forbade them to desist from the attempt, and ordered two triumvirates to be appointed, one of which within, the other without the fiftieth mile from the city, might ascertain the utmost number of free-born men which were to be found in the villages, and market towns, and hamlets, and enlist whom they thought strong enough to bear arms, though they had not attained the military age. That the tribunes of the people, if they thought proper, should propose to the people, that such as should take the military oath being under seventeen years, should be allowed to reckon their period of service in the same manner as if they had enlisted at seventeen or older. The two triumvirates, created agreeably to this decree of the senate, enlisted free-born men throughout the country. At the same time a letter from Marcellus from Sicily, respecting the petition of the troops who served with Publius Lentulus, was read in the senate. These troops were the relics of the disaster at Cannæ, and had been sent out of the way into Sicily, as has been mentioned before, on an understanding that they should not be brought home before the conclusion of the Carthaginian war.

With the permission of Lentulus, these men sent the most distinguished of the cavalry and centurions, and a select body of the legionary infantry, as ambassadors to Marcellus, to his winter quarters. Having obtained leave to speak, one of them thus addressed him: "We should have approached you, Marcus Marcellus, when consul in Italy, as soon as that decree of the senate was passed respecting us, which, though not unjust, was certainly severe, had we not hoped, that being sent into a province which was in a state of disorder in consequence of the death of its kings, to carry on an arduous war against the Sicilians and Carthaginians together, we should make atonement to the state by our blood and wounds, in the same manner as, within the memory of our fathers, those who were taken prisoners by Pyrrhus at Heraclea, made atonement by fighting against the same Pyrrhus. And yet, for what fault of ours, conscript fathers, did you then, or do you now, feel displeasure towards us; for when I look upon you, Marcus Marcellus, I seem to behold both the consuls and the whole body of the senate; and had you been our consul at Cannæ, a better fate would have attended the state as well as ourselves. Permit me, I entreat you, before I complain of the hardship of our situation, to clear ourselves of the guilt with which we are charged. If it was neither by the anger of the gods, nor by fate, according to whose laws the course of human affairs is unalterably fixed, but by misconduct that we were undone at Cannæ; but whose was that misconduct; the soldiers', or that of their generals? For my own part, I, as a soldier, will never say a word of my commander, particularly when I know that he received the thanks of the senate for not having despaired of the state; and who has been continued in command through every year since his flight from Cannæ. We have heard that others also who survived that disaster, who were military tribunes, solicit and fill offices of honour, and have the command of provinces. Do you then, conscript fathers, pardon yourselves and your children, while you exercise severity towards such insignificant persons as we are? It was no disgrace to a consul and other leading persons in the state, to fly when no other hope remained; and did you send your soldiers into the field as persons who must of necessity die there? At the Allia nearly the whole army fled; at the Caudine Forks the troops delivered up their arms to the enemy, without even making an effort; not to mention other disgraceful defeats of our armies. Yet, so far from any mark of infamy being sought for, which might be fixed upon these troops, the city of Rome was recovered by means of those very troops who had fled to Veii from the Allia; and the Caudine legions, which had returned to Rome without their arms, being sent back armed to Samnium, brought under the yoke that very enemy who had exulted in the disgrace which, in this instance, attached to them. But is there a man who can bring a charge of cowardice or running away against the army which fought at Cannæ, where more than fifty thousand men fell; from whence the consul fled with only seventy horsemen; where not a man survived, except perchance those whom the enemy left, being wearied with killing? When the proposal to ransom the prisoners was negatived, we were the objects of general commendation, because we reserved ourselves for the service of the state; because we returned to the consul to Venusia, and exhibited an appearance of a regular army. Now we are in a worse condition than those who were taken prisoners in the time of our fathers; for they only had their arms, the nature of their service, and the place where they might pitch their tents in the camp altered; all which, however, they got restored by one service rendered to the state, and by one successful battle. Not one of them was sent away into banishment; not one was deprived of the hope of completing the period of his service; in short, an enemy was assigned to them, fighting with whom they might at once terminate their life or their disgrace. We, to whom nothing can be objected, except that it is owing to us that any Roman soldier has survived the battle of Cannæ, are removed far away, not only from our country and Italy, but even from an enemy; where we may grow old in exile, where we can have no hope or opportunity of obliterating our disgrace, of appeasing the indignation of our countrymen, or, in short, of obtaining an honourable death. We seek neither to have our ignominy terminated, nor our virtue rewarded, we only ask to be allowed to make trial of our courage, and to exercise our virtue. We seek for labour and danger that we may discharge the duty of men and soldiers. A war is carrying on in Sicily, now for the second year, with the utmost vigour on both sides. The Carthaginians are storming some cities, the Romans others, armies of infantry and horse are engaging in battle, at Syracuse the war is prosecuted by sea and by land. We hear distinctly the shout of the combatants, and the din of arms, while we ourselves lie inactive and unemployed, as if we had neither hands nor arms. The consul, Sempronius has now fought many pitched battles with the enemy with legions of slaves. They receive as the fruits of their exertion their liberty, and the rights of citizens. Let us at least be employed by you as slaves purchased for the service of this war, let us be allowed to combat with the enemy and acquire our freedom by fighting. Do you wish to make trial of our valour by sea, by land, in a pitched battle, or in the assault of towns? We ask as our portion all those enterprises which present the greatest difficulty and danger, that what ought to have been done at Cannæ may be done as soon as possible, for the whole of our subsequent lives has been doomed to ignominy."

At the conclusion of this speech they prostrated themselves at the knees of Marcellus. Marcellus replied, that the question was neither within his authority nor his power, that he would, however, write to the senate, and be guided in every thing he did by the judgment of the fathers. This letter was brought to the new consuls, and by them read in the senate, and, on the question being put relative to this letter, they decreed, "that the senate saw no reason why the interests of the republic should be intrusted to the hands of soldiers who had deserted then comrades, in battle, at Cannæ. If Marcus Marcellus, the proconsul, thought otherwise, that he should act as he deemed consistent with the good of the republic and his own honour, with this proviso, however, that none of these men should be exempt from service, nor be presented with any military reward in consideration of valour, or be conveyed back to Italy, while the enemy was in that country." After this, agreeably to the decree of the senate, and the order of the people, an election was held by the city prætor, at which five commissioners were created for the purpose of repairing the walls and turrets, and two sets of triumviri, one to search for the property belonging to the temples, and to register the offerings, the other for repairing the temples of Fortune and Mother Matuta within the Carmental gate, and also that of Hope without the gate, which had been destroyed by fire the year before. Dreadful storms occurred at this time. It rained stones for two days without intermission in the Alban mount. Many places were struck by lightning; two buildings in the Capitol, the rampart in the camp above Suessula in many places, and two of the men on guard were killed. A wall and certain towers at Cannæ were not only struck with lightning, but demolished. At Reate, a vast rock was seen to fly about; the sun appeared unusually red and blood-like. On account of these prodigies there was a supplication for one day, and the consuls employed themselves for several days in sacred rites; at the same time there was a sacred rite performed through nine days. An accidental circumstance which occurred at a distance, hastened the revolt of Tarentum, which had now for a long time been the object of the hopes of Hannibal and of the suspicion of the Romans. Phileas, a native of Tarentum, who had been a long time at Rome under the pretence of an embassy, being a man of a restless mind, and ill brooking that inactive state in which he considered that his powers had been for too long a time sinking into imbecility, discovered for himself a means of access to the Tarentine hostages. They were kept in the court of the temple of Liberty, and guarded with less care, because it was neither the interest of themselves nor of their state to escape from the Romans. By corrupting two of the keepers of the temple, he was enabled to hold frequent conferences with them, at which he solicited them to come into this design; and having brought them out of their place of confinement as soon as it was dark, he became the companion of their clandestine flight, and got clear away. As soon as day dawned, the news of their escape spread through the city, and a party sent in pursuit, having seized them all at Tarracina, brought them back. They were led into the Comitium, and after being scourged with rods, with the approbation of the people, were thrown down from the rock.

The severity of this punishment exasperated the inhabitants of two of the most distinguished Greek states in Italy, not only publicly as communities, but privately as individuals, according as each was connected, either by relationship or friendship, with those who had been so disgracefully put to death. Of these about thirteen noble Tarentine youths formed a conspiracy, the chief of whom were Nico and Philemenus. Concluding that it would be right to confer with Hannibal before they took any step, they went to him, having been allowed to go out of the city by night on pretence of hunting. When they were now not far from the camp, all the rest hid themselves in a wood by the road side; but Nico and Philemenus, proceeding to the advanced guard, were seized, and at their own request brought before Hannibal. Having laid before him the motives of their plan, and the object they had in view, they received the highest commendation, and were loaded with promises; and that their countrymen might believe that they had gone out of the city to obtain plunder, they were desired to drive to the city some cattle of the Carthaginians which had been sent out to graze. A promise was given them that they might do this without danger or interruption. The booty of the young men attracted notice, and less astonishment was therefore felt that they should frequently repeat the attempt. At a second meeting with Hannibal they entered into a solemn engagement, that the Tarentines should be free, enjoying their own laws, and all their rights uninterfered with; that they should neither pay any tribute to the Carthaginians, nor receive a garrison against their will; that their present garrison should be delivered up to the Carthaginians. These points being agreed upon, Philemenus then began to repeat more frequently his customary practice of going out and returning to the city followed by his dogs, and furnished with the other requisites for hunting; for he was remarkable for his fondness of hunting; and generally bringing home something which he had captured or taken away from the enemy, who had purposely placed it in his way he presented it to the commander or the guards of the gates. They supposed that he preferred going and returning by night through fear of the enemy. After this practice had become so familiar, that at whatever time of the night he gave a signal, by whistling, the gate was opened, Hannibal thought that it was now time to put the plan in execution. He was at the distance of three days' journey, and to diminish the wonder which would be felt at his keeping his camp fixed in one and the same place so long, he feigned himself ill. Even to the Romans who formed the garrison of Tarentum, his protracted inactivity had ceased to be an object of suspicion.

But after he determined to proceed to Tarentum, selecting from his infantry and cavalry ten thousand men, whom, from activity of body, and lightness of arms, he judged best adapted for the expedition, he began his march in the fourth watch of the night; and sending in advance about eighty Numidian horsemen, ordered them to scour the country on each side of the road, and narrowly examine every place, lest any of the rustics who might have observed his army at a distance should escape; to bring back those who were got before, and kill those whom they met, that they might appear to the neighbouring inhabitants to be a plundering party, rather than a regular army. Hannibal himself, marching at a rapid pace, pitched his camp about fifteen miles from Tarentum; and without telling his soldiers even there, what was their destination, he only called them together and admonished them to march all of them in the road, and not to suffer any one to turn aside or deviate from the line; and above all, that they would be on the watch, so as to catch the word of command, and not do any thing without the order of their leaders; that in due time he would issue his commands as to what he wished to be done. About the same hour a rumour reached Tarentum, that a few Numidian horsemen were devastating the fields, and had terrified the rustics through a wide extent of country; at which intelligence the Roman præfect took no further step than to order a division of his cavalry to go out the following day at sunrise to check the depredations of the enemy; and so far was he from directing his attention to any thing else on this account, that on the contrary, this excursion of the Numidians was a proof to him that Hannibal and his army had not moved from his camp. Early in the night Hannibal put his troops in motion, and Philemenus, with his customary burden of prey taken in hunting, was his guide. The rest of the conspirators waited the accomplishment of what had been concerted; and the agreement was, that Philemenus, while bringing in his prey through the small gate by which he was accustomed to pass, should introduce some armed men, while Hannibal in another quarter approached the gate called Temenis, which faced the east, in that quarter which was towards the continent, near the tombs which were within the walls. When he drew near to the gate, Hannibal raised a fire according to agreement, which made a blaze; the same signal was returned by Nico, and the fires were extinguished on both sides. Hannibal led his troops on in silence to the gate. Nico suddenly fell upon the guards while asleep, slew them in their beds, and opened the gate. Hannibal then entered with his infantry, ordering his cavalry to stay behind, that they might be able to bring their assistance wherever it was required without obstruction. Philemenus also in another quarter approached the small gate by which he was accustomed to pass and re-pass. His voice, which was well known, for he said he could scarcely bear the weight of the huge beast he had gotten, and his signal, which had now become familiar, having roused the guard, the small gate was opened. Two youths carrying in a boar, Philemenus himself followed, with a huntsman, unencumbered, and while the attention of the guard was incautiously turned upon those who carried the boar, in consequence of its astonishing size, he transfixed him with a hunting spear. About thirty armed men then entering, slew the rest of the guards, and broke open the adjoining gate, when a body of troops, in regular array, instantly rushed in. Being conducted hence in silence to the forum, they joined Hannibal. The Carthaginian then sent the Tarentines, with two thousand Gauls formed into three divisions, in different directions through the city, with orders to occupy the most frequented streets. A confusion arising, the Romans were put to the sword on all hands. The townsmen were spared; but in order to insure this, he instructed the Tarentine youths, when they saw any of their friends at a distance, to bid them be quiet and silent, and be of good courage.

The tumult and clamour was now such as usually takes place in a captured city, but no man knew for certain what was the occasion. The Tarentines supposed that the Romans had suddenly risen to plunder the city. To the Romans it appeared, that some commotion had been set on foot by the townsmen with a treacherous design. The præfect, who was awakened at the first alarm, escaped to the port, whence getting into a boat he was conveyed round to the citadel. The sound of a trumpet also from the theatre excited alarm; for it was a Roman trumpet, prepared by the conspirators for this very purpose; and as it was blown unskilfully by a Grecian, it could not be ascertained who gave the signal, or to whom it was given. At dawn of the day, the Romans recognised the Carthaginian and Gallic arms, which removed all doubt; and the Greeks, seeing the bodies of slain Romans spread about in all directions, perceived that the city had been taken by Hannibal. When the light had increased, so that they could discriminate with greater certainty, and the Romans who survived the carnage had taken refuge in the citadel, the tumult now beginning to subside a little, Hannibal gave orders to assemble the Tarentines without their arms. All of them attended the assembly, except those who had accompanied the Romans in their retreat to the citadel, to share every fortune with them. Here Hannibal having addressed the Tarentines in terms of kindness, and appealed to the services he had rendered to those of their countrymen whom he had captured at the Trasimenus and at Cannæ, and having at the same time inveighed against the haughty domination of the Romans, desired that they would every one of them retire to their respective houses, and inscribe their names upon their doors; declaring, that he should give orders that those houses which had not the names written upon them should be plundered. That if any man should write his name upon the house of a Roman, (and the Romans occupied houses by themselves,) he should treat him as an enemy. Having dismissed the assembly, and the names inscribed upon the doors having made it easy to distinguish the house of an enemy from that of a friend, on a signal given, the troops ran in every direction to plunder the lodgings of the Romans, and a considerable booty was found.

The next day he led his troops to assault the citadel; but seeing that it was protected by very high rocks towards the sea, which washed the greater part of it, and formed it into a sort of peninsula, and towards the city by a wall and ditch, and consequently that it could not be taken by assault or by works; lest the design to protect the Tarentines should detain him from the prosecution of more important objects, and lest the Romans should have the power of sallying from the citadel whenever they pleased against the Tarentines, if left without a strong protecting force, he resolved to cut off the communication between the citadel and city by a rampart; not without a hope that he might have an opportunity of fighting with the Romans, when attempting to obstruct the work; and if they should sally forth too eagerly, that by killing many of them the strength of the garrison would be so far reduced, that the Tarentines alone would be easily able to defend themselves from them. After they had begun, the Romans, suddenly throwing open the gate, rushed in upon the workmen. The guard stationed before the works allowed itself to be driven back, in order that their boldness might be increased by success, and that they might pursue them when driven back, in greater numbers, and to a greater distance. Then on a signal given, the Carthaginians, whom Hannibal kept in readiness for this purpose, sprang up on all sides; nor could the Romans sustain the attack, but were prevented from precipitate flight by the narrowness of the ground, by impediments occasioned in some places by the works already commenced, in others by the preparations for the work. Most of them were driven headlong into the ditch, and more were killed in the flight than in the battle. After this the work was commenced without any attempt to obstruct it. A large ditch was formed, within which a rampart was thrown up. He prepared also to add a wall at a small distance, and on the same side, that they might defend themselves from the Romans even without a garrison. He, however, left them a small force, at once for their protection and to assist in building the wall. The general himself, setting out with the rest of his forces, pitched his camp at the river Galæsus, five miles from the city. Returning from this position to inspect the work, which had gone on somewhat faster than he had anticipated, he conceived a hope that the citadel might even be taken by storm; for it was not protected by an elevated situation as the other parts were, but placed upon a plain, and separated from the city only by a wall and ditch. While subjected to an attack from every kind of military engine and work, a reinforcement sent from Metapontum inspired the Romans with courage to assault the works of the enemy, by a sudden attack, under cover of the night. Some of them they threw down, others they destroyed by fire, and thus there was an end to Hannibal's attempts against the citadel in that quarter. His only remaining hope was in a siege; nor did that afford a good prospect of success, because, occupying a citadel which was placed on a peninsula and commanded the entrance of the harbour, they had the sea open to them, while the city, on the contrary, was deprived of any supplies by sea: and thus the besiegers were in greater danger of want than the besieged. Hannibal assembled the chief men of the Tarentines, and laid before them all the present difficulties. He said, "That he could neither discover any method by which a citadel so well fortified could be taken, nor could he hope for any favourable result from a siege, while the enemy was master of the sea; but that if ships could be obtained, by which the introduction of supplies might be prevented, the enemy would either immediately evacuate it, or surrender themselves." The Tarentines agreed with him; but were of opinion, that "he who gave the advice ought also to assist in carrying it into execution; for if the Carthaginian ships were brought there from Sicily, they would be able to effect it; but by what means could their own ships, shut up as they were in a confined harbour, the mouth of which was in the command of the enemy, be brought out into the open sea." "They shall be brought out," said Hannibal. "Many things which are difficult in themselves, are easily effected by contrivance. You have a city situated upon a plain; you have level and sufficiently wide roads extending in every direction. By the road which runs through the midst of the city from the harbour to the sea I will convey your ships in waggons without any great difficulty, and the sea will be ours which the enemy now commands. We will invest the citadel on one side by sea, on the other by land; nay, rather, in a short time, we will take it either abandoned by the enemy, or with the enemy in it." This speech not only inspired hopes of accomplishing the object, but excited the greatest admiration of the general. Waggons were immediately collected from every quarter and joined together; machines were employed to haul the ships on shore, and the road was prepared, in order that the waggons might run more easily, and thus the difficulty of passing be diminished. Beasts of burden and men were next collected, and the work was actively commenced. After the lapse of a few days, the fleet, equipped and ready for action, sailed round the citadel, and cast anchor just before the mouth of the harbour. Such was the state of things at Tarentum, when Hannibal left it and returned to his winter quarters. Authors, however, are divided as to whether the defection of the Tarentines took place in the present or former year. The greater number, and those who, from their age, were more able to recollect these events, represent it to have occurred in the present year.

The Latin holidays detained the consuls and prætors at Rome till the fifth of the calends of May; on which day, having completed the solemnities on the mount, they proceeded to their respective provinces. Afterwards a new difficulty respecting religious matters arose out of the prophetic verses of Marcius, who had been a distinguished soothsayer; and on a search being made the year before, for books of this description, agreeably to a decree of the senate, these verses had fallen into the hands of Marcus Atilius, the city prætor, who had the management of that business, and he had immediately handed them over to the new prætor, Sulla. The importance attached to one of the two predictions of Marcius, which was brought to light after the event to which it related had occurred, and the truth of which was confirmed by the event, attached credence to the other, the time of whose fulfilment had not yet arrived. In the former prophecy, the disaster at Cannæ was predicted in nearly these words: "Roman of Trojan descent, fly the river Canna, lest foreigners should compel thee to fight in the plain of Diomede. But thou wilt not believe me until thou shalt have filled the plain with blood, and the river carries into the great sea, from the fruitful land, many thousands of your slain countrymen, and thy flesh becomes a prey for fishes, birds, and beasts inhabiting the earth. For thus hath Jupiter declared to me." Those who had served in that quarter recognised the correspondence with respect to the plains of the Argive Diomede and the river Canna, as well as the defeat itself. The other prophecy was then read, which was more obscure, not only because future events are more uncertain than past, but also from being more perplexed in its style of composition. "Romans, if you wish to expel the enemy and the ulcer which has come from afar, I advise, that games should be vowed, which may be performed in a cheerful manner annually to Apollo; when the people shall have given a portion of money from the public coffers, that private individuals then contribute, each according to his ability. That the prætor shall preside in the celebration of these games, who holds the supreme administration of justice to the people and commons. Let the decemviri perform sacrifice with victims after the Grecian fashion. If you do these things properly you will ever rejoice, and your affairs will be more prosperous, for that deity will destroy your enemies who now, composedly, feed upon your plains." They took one day to explain this prophecy. The next day a decree of the senate was passed, that the decemviri should inspect the books relating to the celebration of games and sacred rites in honour of Apollo. After they had been consulted, and a report made to the senate, the fathers voted, that "games should be vowed to Apollo and celebrated; and that when the games were concluded, twelve thousand *asses* should be given to the prætor to defray the expense of sacred ceremonies, and also two victims of the larger sort." A second decree was passed, that "the decemviri should perform sacrifice in the Grecian mode, and with the following victims: to Apollo, with a gilded ox, and two white goats gilded; to Latona, with a gilded heifer." When the prætor was about to celebrate the games in the Circus Maximus, he issued an order, that during the celebration of the games, the people should pay a contribution, as large as was convenient, for the service of Apollo. This is the origin of the Apollinarian games, which were vowed and celebrated in order to victory, and not restoration to health, as is commonly supposed. The people viewed the spectacle in garlands; the matrons made supplications; the people in general feasted in the courts of their houses, throwing the doors open; and the day was distinguished by every description of ceremony.

While Hannibal was in the neighbourhood of Tarentum, and both the consuls in Samnium, though they seemed as if they were about to besiege Capua, the Campanians were experiencing famine, that calamity which is the usual attendant of a protracted siege. It was occasioned by the Roman armies' having prevented the sowing of the lands. They therefore sent ambassadors to Hannibal, imploring him to give orders that corn should be conveyed to Capua from the neighbouring places, before both the consuls led their legions into their fields, and all the roads were blocked up by the troops of the enemy. Hannibal ordered Hanno to pass with his army from Bruttium into Campania, and to take care that the Campanians were supplied with corn. Hanno, setting out from Bruttium with his army, and carefully avoiding the camp of the enemy and the consuls who were in Samnium, when he drew near to Beneventum, pitched his camp on an eminence three miles from the city. He next ordered that the corn which had been collected during the summer, should be brought from the neighbouring people in alliance with him, into his camp, assigning a guard to escort those supplies. He then sent a messenger to the Capuans, fixing a day when they should attend at his camp to receive the corn, bringing with them vehicles and beasts of every description, collected from every part of their country. The Campanians executed this business with their usual indolence and carelessness. Somewhat more than four hundred vehicles, with a few beasts of burden besides, were sent. After receiving a reproof from Hanno for this conduct, who told them, that not even hunger, which excited dumb animals to exertion, could stimulate them to diligence, another day was named when they were to fetch the corn after better preparation. All these transactions being reported to the Beneventans, just as they occurred, they lost no time in sending ten ambassadors to the Roman consuls, who were encamped in the neighbourhood of Bovianum. The consuls, hearing what was going on at Capua, arranged it so that one of them should lead an army into Campania; and Fulvius, to whose lot that province had fallen, setting out by night, entered the walls of Beneventum. Being now near the enemy, he obtained information that Hanno had gone out to forage with a portion of his troops; that the Campanians were supplied with corn by a quæstor; that two thousand waggons had arrived together with an undisciplined and unarmed rabble; that every thing was done in a disorderly and hurried manner; and that the form of a camp, and all military subordination, were destroyed by the intermixture of rustics out of the neighbourhood. This intelligence being sufficiently authenticated, the consul ordered his soldiers to get ready only their standards and arms against the next night, as he must attack the Carthaginian camp. They set out at the fourth watch of the night, leaving all their packages and baggage of every description at Beneventum; and arriving a little before daylight at the camp, they occasioned such a panic, that, had the camp been situated on level ground, it might doubtlessly have been taken on the first assault. The height of its situation and the works defended it; for they could not be approached on any side except by a steep and difficult ascent. At break of day a hot engagement commenced, when the Carthaginians not only defended their rampart, but having more even ground, threw down the enemy as they attempted to ascend the steep.

Persevering courage, however, at length prevailed over every impediment, and they made their way up to the ditch and rampart in several parts at the same time, but with many wounds and much loss of soldiers. The consul, therefore assembling the military tribunes, said they must desist from this inconsiderate enterprise; and that it appeared to him to be the safer course, that the troops should be led back to Beneventum for that day, and then on the following day to pitch his camp close to that of the enemy, so that the Campanians could not quit it, nor Hanno return to it; and in order that that object might be attained with the greater ease, that he should send for his colleague and his army; and that they would direct their whole force on that point. This plan of the general was disconcerted, after the signal began to sound for a retreat, by the clamours of the soldiery, who despised so pusillanimous an order. Nearest to the gate of the enemy's camp was a Pelignian cohort, whose commander, Vibius Accuæus, seizing the standard, threw it over the rampart. Then pronouncing a curse upon himself and his cohort, if the enemy got possession of that standard, he rushed forward before the rest, and crossing the ditch and rampart, burst into the camp of the enemy. The Pelignians were now fighting within the rampart, when in another quarter Valerius Flaccus, a military tribune of the third legion, taunting the Romans with cowardice for conceding to allies the honour of taking the camp. Titus Pedanius, first centurion of the first century, snatched the standard out of the hands of the standard-bearer, and cried out, "Soon shall this standard, and this centurion, be within the rampart of the enemy; let those follow who would prevent the standard's being captured by the enemy." Crossing the ditch, he was followed first by the men of his own maniple, and then by the whole legion. By this time the consul also, changing his plan on seeing them crossing the rampart, began to incite and encourage his soldiers, instead of calling them off; representing to them, how critical and perilous was the situation of the bravest cohort of their allies and a legion of their countrymen. All, therefore, severally exerting themselves to the utmost, regardless whether the ground were even or uneven, while showers of weapons were thrown against them from all sides, the enemy opposing their arms and their persons to obstruct them, made their way and burst in. Many who were wounded, even those whose blood and strength failed them, pressed forward, that they might fall within the rampart of the enemy. The camp, therefore, was taken in an instant, as if it had been situated upon level ground, and not completely fortified. What followed was a carnage rather than a battle. The troops of both sides being huddled together within the rampart, above six thousand of the enemy were slain; above seven thousand, together with the Campanians who fetched the corn, and the whole collection of waggons and beasts of burden, were captured. There was also a great booty, which Hanno in his predatory excursions, which he had been careful to make in every quarter, had drawn together from the lands of the allies of the Romans. After throwing down the camp of the enemy, they returned thence to Beneventum; and there both the consuls (for Appius Claudius came thither a few days after) sold the booty and distributed it, making presents to those by whose exertions the camp of the enemy had been captured; above all, to Accuæus the Pelignian, and Titus Pedanius, first centurion of the third legion. Hanno, setting off from Cominium in the territory of Cere, whither intelligence of the loss of the camp had reached him, with a small party of foragers, whom he happened to have with him, returned to Bruttium, more after the manner of a flight than a march.

The Campanians, when informed of the disaster which had befallen themselves and their allies, sent ambassadors to Hannibal to inform him, that "the two consuls were at Beneventum, which was a day's march from Capua; that the war was all but at their gates and their walls; and that if he did not hasten to their assistance, Capua would fall into the power of the enemy sooner than Arpi had; that not even Tarentum itself, much less its citadel, ought to be considered of so much consequence as to induce him to deliver up to the Roman people, abandoned and undefended, Capua, which he used to place on an equal footing with Carthage." Hannibal, promising that he would not neglect the interest of the Campanians, sent, for the present, two thousand horse, with the ambassadors, aided by which, they might secure their lands from devastation. The Romans, meanwhile, among the other things which engaged their attention, had an eye to the citadel of Tarentum, and the garrison besieged therein. Caius Servilius, lieutenant-general, having been sent, according to the advice of the fathers, by Publius Cornelius, the prætor, to purchase corn in Etruria, made his way into the harbour of Tarentum, through the guard-ships of the enemy, with some ships of burden. At his arrival, those who before, having very slight hopes of holding out, were frequently invited by the enemy, in conferences, to pass over to them, now, on the contrary, were the persons to invite and solicit the enemy to come over to them; and now, as the soldiers who were at Metapontum had been brought to assist in guarding the citadel of Tarentum, the garrison was sufficiently powerful. In consequence of this measure, the Metapontines, being freed from the fears which had influenced them, immediately revolted to Hannibal. The people of Thurium, situated on the same coast, did the same. They were influenced not more by the defection of the Metapontines and Tarentines, with whom they were connected, being sprung from the same country, Achaia, than by resentment towards the Romans, in consequence of the recent execution of the hostages. The friends and relations of these hostages sent a letter and a message to Hanno and Mago, who were not far off among the Bruttii, to the effect, that if they brought their troops up to the walls, they would deliver the city into their hands. Marcus Atinius was in command at Thurium, with a small garrison, who they thought might easily be induced to engage rashly in a battle, not from any confidence which he reposed in his troops, of which he had very few, but in the youth of Thurium, whom he had purposely formed into centuries, and armed against emergencies of this kind. The generals, after dividing their forces between them, entered the territory of Thurium; and Hanno, with a body of infantry, proceeded towards the city in hostile array. Hanno staid behind with the cavalry, under the cover of some hills, conveniently placed for the concealment of an ambush. Atinius, having by his scouts discovered only the body of infantry, led his troops into the field, ignorant both of the domestic treachery and of the stratagem of the enemy. The engagement with the infantry was particularly dull, a few Romans in the first rank engaging while the Thurians rather waited than helped on the issue. The Carthaginian line retreated, on purpose that they might draw the incautious enemy to the back of the hill, where their cavalry were lying in ambush; and when they had come there, the cavalry rising up on a sudden with a shout, immediately put to flight the almost undisciplined rabble of the Thurians, not firmly attached to the side on which they fought. The Romans, notwithstanding they were surrounded and hard pressed on one side by the infantry, on the other by the cavalry, yet prolonged the battle for a considerable time; but at length even they were compelled to turn their backs, and fled towards the city. There the conspirators, forming themselves into a dense body, received the multitude of their countrymen with open gates; but when they perceived that the routed Romans were hurrying towards the city, they exclaimed that the Carthaginian was close at hand, and that the enemy would enter the city mingled with them, unless they speedily closed the gates. Thus they shut out the Romans, and left them to be cut up by the enemy. Atinius, however, and a few others were taken in. After this for a short time there was a division between them, some being of opinion that they ought to defend the city, others that they ought, after all that had happened, to yield to fortune, and deliver up the city to the conquerors; but, as it generally happens, fortune and evil counsels prevailed. Having conveyed Atinius and his party to the sea and the ships, more because they wished that care should be taken of him, in consequence of the mildness and justice of his command, than from regard to the Romans, they received the Carthaginians into the city. The consuls led their legions from Beneventum into the Campanian territory, with the intention not only of destroying the corn, which was in the blade, but of laying siege to Capua; considering that they would render their consulate illustrious by the destruction of so opulent a city, and that they would wipe away the foul disgrace of the empire, from the defection of a city so near remaining unpunished for three years. Lest, however, Beneventum should be left without protection, and that in case of any sudden emergency, if Hannibal should come to Capua, in order to bring assistance to his friends, which they doubted not he would do, the cavalry might be able to sustain his attack, they ordered Tiberius Gracchus to come from Lucania to Beneventum with his cavalry and light-armed troops and to appoint some person to take the command of the legions and stationary camp, for the defence of Lucania.

An unlucky prodigy occurred to Gracchus, while sacrificing, previous to his departure from Lucania. Two snakes gliding from a secret place to the entrails, after the sacrifice was completed, ate the liver; and after having been observed, suddenly vanished out of sight. The sacrifice having been repeated according to the admonition of the aruspices, and the vessel containing the entrails being watched with increased attention, it is reported that the snakes came a second, and a third time, and, after tasting the liver, went away untouched. Though the aruspices forewarned him that the portent had reference to the general, and that he ought to be on his guard against secret enemies and machinations, yet no foresight could avert the destiny which awaited him. There was a Lucanian, named Flavius, the leader of that party which adhered to the Romans when the others went over to Hannibal; he was this year in the magistracy, having been created prætor by the same party. Suddenly changing his mind, and seeking to ingratiate himself with the Carthaginians, he did not think it enough that he himself should pass over to them, or that he should induce the Lucanians to revolt with him, unless he ratified his league with the enemy with the head and blood of the general, betrayed to them, though his guest. He entered into a secret conference with Mago, who had the command in Bruttium, and receiving a solemn promise from him, that he would take the Lucanians into his friendship, without interfering with their laws, if he should betray the Roman general to the Carthaginians, he conducted Mago to a place to which he was about to bring Gracchus with a few attendants. He then directed Mago to arm his infantry and cavalry, and to occupy the retired places there, in which he might conceal a very large number of troops. After thoroughly inspecting and exploring the place on all sides, a day was agreed upon for the execution of the affair. Flavius came to the Roman general, and said, that "he had begun a business of great importance, for the completion of which, it was necessary to have the assistance of Gracchus himself. That he had persuaded the prætors of all the states which had revolted to the Carthaginians in the general defection of Italy, to return into the friendship of the Romans, since now the Roman power too, which had almost come to ruin by the disaster at Cannæ was daily improving and increasing, while the strength of Hannibal was sinking into decay, and was almost reduced to nothing. He had told them that the Romans would be disposed to accept an atonement for their former offence; that there never was any state more easy to be entreated, or more ready to grant pardon; how often, he had observed to them, had they forgiven rebellion even in their own ancestors! These considerations," he said, "he had himself urged, but that they would rather hear the same from Gracchus himself in person, and touching his right hand, carry with them that pledge of faith. That he had agreed upon a place with those who were privy to the transaction, out of the way of observation, and at no great distance from the Roman camp; that there the business might be settled in few words, so that all the Lucanian states might be in the alliance and friendship of the Romans." Gracchus, not suspecting any treachery either from his words or the nature of the proposal, and being caught by the probability of the thing, set out from the camp with his lictors and a troop of horse, under the guidance of his host, and fell headlong into the snare. The enemy suddenly arose from their lurking-place, and Flavius joined them; which made the treachery obvious. A shower of weapons was poured from all sides on Gracchus and his troop. He immediately leaped from his horse, and ordering the rest to do the same, exhorted them, that "as fortune had left them only one course, they would render it glorious by their valour. And what is there left," said he, "to a handful of men, surrounded by a multitude, in a valley hemmed in by a wood and mountains, except death? The only question was, whether, tamely exposing themselves to be butchered like cattle, they should die unavenged; or whether, drawing the mind off from the idea of suffering and anticipation of the event, and giving full scope to fury and resentment, they should fall while doing and daring, covered with hostile blood, amid heaps of arms and bodies of their expiring foes." He desired that "all would aim at the Lucanian traitor and deserter;" adding, that "the man who should send that victim to the shades before him, would acquire the most distinguished glory, and furnish the highest consolation for his own death." While thus speaking, he wound his cloak round his left arm, for they had not even brought their shields out with them, and then rushed upon the enemy. The exertion made in the fight was greater than could be expected from the smallness of the number. The bodies of the Romans were most exposed to the javelins, with which, as they were thrown on all sides from higher ground into a deep valley, they were transfixed. The Carthaginians seeing Gracchus now bereft of support, endeavoured to take him alive; but he having descried his Lucanian host among the enemy, rushed with such fury into their dense body that it became impossible to save his life without a great loss. Mago immediately sent his corpse to Hannibal, ordering it to be placed, with the fasces which were taken at the same time, before the tribunal of the general. This is the true account; Gracchus fell in Lucania, near the place called the Old Plains.

There are some who have put forth an account, stating, that when in the territory of Beneventum, near the river Calor, having gone out from his camp with his lictors and three servants, for the purpose of bathing, he was slain while naked and unarmed, and endeavouring to defend himself with the stones which the river brought down, by a party of the enemy which happened to be concealed among the osiers which grew upon the banks. Others state, that having gone out five hundred paces from the camp, at the instance of the aruspices, in order to expiate the prodigies before mentioned on unpolluted ground, he was cut off by two troops of Numidians who happened to be lying in ambush there. So different are the accounts respecting the place and manner of the death of so illustrious and distinguished a man. Various also are the accounts of the funeral of Gracchus. Some say that he was buried by his own friends in the Roman camp; others relate, and this is the more generally received account, that a funeral pile was erected by Hannibal, in the entrance of the Carthaginian camp; that the troops under arms performed evolutions, with the dances of the Spaniards, and motions of the arms and body, which were customary with the several nations; while Hannibal himself celebrated his obsequies with every mark of respect, both in word and deed. Such is the account of those who assert that the affair occurred in Lucania. If you are disposed to credit the statement of those who relate that he was slain at the river Calor, the enemy got possession only of the head of Gracchus; which being brought to Hannibal, he immediately despatched Carthalo to convey it into the Roman camp to Cneius Cornelius, the quæstor, who buried the general in the camp, the Beneventans joining the army in the celebration.

The consuls having entered the Campanian territory, while devastating the country on all sides, were alarmed, and thrown into confusion, by an eruption of the townsmen and Mago with his cavalry. They called in their troops to their standards from the several quarters to which they were dispersed, but having been routed when they had scarcely formed their line, they lost above fifteen hundred men. The confidence of the Campanians, who were naturally presumptuous, became excessive in consequence of this event, and in many battles they challenged the Romans; but this one battle, which they had been incautiously and imprudently drawn into, had increased the vigilance of the consuls. Their spirits were restored, while the presumption of the other party was diminished, by one trifling occurrence; but in war nothing is so inconsiderable as not to be capable, sometimes, of producing important consequences. Titus Quinctius Crispinus was a guest of Badius, a Campanian, united with him by the greatest intimacy. Their acquaintance had increased from the circumstance of Badius having received the most liberal and kind attentions at the house of Crispinus, in a fit of illness, at Rome, before the Campanian revolt. On the present occasion, Badius, advancing in front of the guards, which were stationed before the gate, desired Crispinus to be called; and Crispinus, on being informed of this, thinking that a friendly and familiar interview was requested, and the memory of their private connexion remaining even amidst the disruption of public ties, advanced a little from the rest. When they had come within view of each other, Badius exclaimed, "I challenge you to combat, Crispinus; let us mount our horses, and making the rest withdraw, let us try which is the better soldier." In reply, Crispinus said, that "neither of them were in want of enemies to display their valour upon; for his own part, even if he should meet him in the field he would turn aside, lest he should pollute his right-hand with the blood of a guest;" and then turning round, was going away. But the Campanian, with increased presumption, began to charge him with cowardice and effeminacy, and cast upon him reproaches which he deserved himself, calling him "an enemy who sheltered himself under the title of host, and one who pretended to spare him for whom he knew himself not to be a match. If he considered; that when public treaties were broken, the ties of private connexion were not severed with them, then Badius the Campanian openly, and in the hearing of both armies, renounced his connexion of hospitality with Titus Quinctius Crispinus the Roman. He said, that there could exist no fellowship or alliance with him and an enemy whose country and tutelary gods, both public and private, he had come to fight against. If he was a man, he would meet him." Crispinus hesitated for a long time; but the men of his troop at length prevailed upon him not to allow the Campanian to insult him with impunity. Waiting, therefore, only to ask his generals whether they would allow him to fight, contrary to rule, with an enemy who had challenged him; having obtained their permission, he mounted his horse, and addressing Badius by name, called him out to the combat. The Campanian made no delay. They engaged with their horses excited to hostility. Crispinus transfixed Badius with his spear in the left shoulder, over his shield. He fell from his horse in consequence of the wound; and Crispinus leaped down to despatch him as he lay, on foot. But Badius, before his enemy was upon him, ran off to his friends, leaving his horse and buckler. Crispinus, decorated with the spoils, and displaying the horse and arms which he had seized together with the bloody spear, was conducted amid the loud plaudits and congratulations of the soldiery into the presence of the consuls, where he was highly commended, and was presented with gifts.

Hannibal, having moved his camp from the territory of Beneventum to Capua, drew out his troops in order of battle the third day after his arrival; not entertaining the least doubt but that, as the Campanians had fought successfully a few days ago when he was absent, the Romans would be still less able to withstand him and his army, which had been so often victorious. After the battle had commenced, the Roman line was distressed chiefly from the attack of the cavalry, being overwhelmed with their darts, till the signal was given to the Roman cavalry to direct their horses against the enemy; thus it was a battle of the cavalry. But at this time the Sempronian army, commanded by Cneius Cornelius the quæstor, being descried at a distance, excited alarm in both parties equally, lest those who were approaching should be fresh enemies. As if by concert, therefore, both sounded a retreat; and the troops were withdrawn from the field to their camps, in an equal condition; a greater number, however, of the Romans fell in the first charge of the cavalry. The consuls, to divert the attention of Hannibal from Capua, departed thence on the following night in different directions, Fulvius into the territory of Cuma, Claudius into Lucania. The next day Hannibal, having received intelligence that the camp of the Romans was deserted, and that they had gone off in different directions in two divisions, doubtful at first which he should follow, commenced the pursuit of Appius; who, after leading him about whichever way he pleased, returned by another route to Capua. Hannibal, while in this quarter, had another opportunity of gaining an advantage. Marcus Centenius, surnamed Penula, was distinguished among the centurions of the first rank by the size of his person, and his courage. Having gone through his period of service, he was introduced to the senate by Publius Cornelius Sulla, when he requested of the fathers that five thousand men might be placed at his disposal. He said, that "as he was acquainted with the character of the enemy, and the nature of the country, he should speedily perform some service; and that he would employ those arts by which our generals and armies had been hitherto ensnared against the inventor of them." This was not promised more foolishly than it was believed; as if the qualifications of a soldier and a general were the same. Instead of five, eight thousand men were given him, half Romans, half allies. He himself also got together a considerable number of volunteers, in the country, on his march; and having almost doubled his force, arrived in Lucania, where Hannibal had halted after having in vain pursued Claudius. No doubt could be entertained of the issue of a contest which was to take place between Hannibal, as general on one side, and a centurion on the other; between armies, one of which had grown old in victory, the other entirely inexperienced, and for the most part even tumultuary and half-armed. As soon as the troops came within sight of each other, and neither of them declined an engagement, the lines were formed. The battle, notwithstanding the utter disparity of the contending parties, lasted more than two hours, the Roman troops acting with the greatest spirit as long as their general survived. But after that he had fallen, for he continually exposed himself to the weapons of the enemy, not only from regard to his former character, but through fear of the disgrace which would attach to him if he survived a disaster occasioned by his own temerity, the Roman line was immediately routed. But so completely were they prevented from flying, every way being beset by the cavalry, that scarcely a thousand men escaped out of so large an army; the rest were destroyed on all hands, in one way or other.

The siege of Capua was now resumed by the consuls with the utmost energy. Every thing requisite for the business was conveyed thither and got in readiness. A store of corn was collected at Casilinum; at the mouth of the Vulturnus, where a town now stands, a strong post was fortified; and a garrison was stationed in Puteoli, which Fabius had formerly fortified, in order to have the command of the neighbouring sea and the river. Into these two maritime forts, the corn recently sent from Sicily, with that which Marcus Junius, the prætor, had bought up in Etruria, was conveyed from Ostia, to supply the army during the winter. But, in addition to the disaster sustained in Lucania, the army also of volunteer slaves, who had served during the life of Gracchus with the greatest fidelity, as if discharged from service by the death of their general, left their standards. Hannibal was not willing that Capua should be neglected, or his allies deserted, at so critical a juncture; but, having obtained such success from the temerity of one Roman general, his attention was fixed on the opportunity which presented itself of crushing the other general and his army. Ambassadors from Apulia reported that Cneius Fulvius, the prætor, had at first conducted his measures with caution, while engaged in besieging certain towns of Apulia, which had revolted to Hannibal; but that afterwards, in consequence of extraordinary success, both himself and his soldiers, being glutted with booty, had so given themselves up to licentiousness and indolence, that all military discipline was disregarded. Having frequently on other occasions, as well as but a few days ago, experienced what an army was good for, when conducted by an unskilful commander, he moved his camp into Apulia.

The Roman legions, and the prætor, Fulvius, were in the neighbourhood of Herdonia, where, receiving intelligence of the approach of the enemy, they had nearly torn up the standards and gone out to battle without the prætor's orders; nor did any thing tend more to prevent it than the assured hope they entertained that they could do so whenever they pleased, consulting only their own will. The following night, Hannibal having obtained information that the camp was in a state of tumult, and that most of the troops were in a disorderly manner urging the general to give the signal, and calling out to arms, and therefore feeling convinced that an opportunity presented itself for a successful battle, distributed three thousand light troops in the houses in the neighbourhood, and among the thorns and woods. These, on a signal being given, were to rise up from their lurking-place with one accord; and Mago, with about two thousand horse, was ordered to occupy all the roads in the direction in which he supposed their flight would be directed. Having made these preparations during the night, he led his troops into the field at break of day. Nor did Fulvius decline the challenge; not so much from any hope of success entertained by himself, as drawn by the blind impetuosity of his soldiers. Accordingly, the line itself was formed with the same want of caution with which they entered the field, agreeably to the whim of the soldiers, who came up as chance directed, and took their stations just where they pleased; which they afterwards abandoned, as fear or caprice suggested. The first legion and the left wing of the allied troops were drawn up in front. The line was extended to a great length, the tribunes remonstrating, that there was no strength in it, and that wherever the enemy made the charge they would break through it: but no salutary advice reached their minds, nor even their ears. Hannibal was now come up, a general of a totally different character, with an army neither similar in its nature, nor similarly marshalled. The consequence was, that the Romans did not so much as sustain their shout and first attack. Their general, equal to Centenius in folly and temerity, but by no means to be compared with him in courage, when he saw things going against him, and his troops in confusion, hastily mounting his horse, fled from the field with about two hundred horsemen. The rest of the troops, beaten in front, and surrounded on the flank and rear, were slaughtered to such a degree, that out of eighteen thousand men, not more than two thousand escaped. The enemy got possession of the camp.

When these disastrous defeats, happening one upon another, were reported at Rome, great grief and consternation seized the city. But still, as the consuls had been hitherto successful when it was most important, they were the less affected by these disasters. Caius Lætorius and Marcus Metilius were sent as ambassadors to the consuls, with directions carefully to collect the remains of the two armies, and use every endeavour to prevent their surrendering themselves to the enemy, through fear or despair, (which was the case after the battle of Cannæ,) and to search for the deserters from the army of volunteer slaves. Publius Cornelius was charged with the same business; to him also the levy was intrusted. He caused an order to be issued throughout the market and smaller towns, that search should be made for the volunteer slaves, and that they should be brought back to their standards. All these things were executed with the most vigilant care. The consul, Appius Claudius, having placed Decius Junius in command at the mouth of the Vulturnus, and Marcus Aurelius Cotta at Puteoli, with directions to send off the corn immediately to the camp, as each of the ships from Etruria and Sardinia arrived with it, returned himself to Capua, and found his colleague Quintus Fulvius at Casilinum, conveying every requisite thence, and making every preparation for the siege of Capua. Both of them then joined in besieging the city, summoning Claudius Nero, the prætor, from the Claudian camp at Suessula; who, leaving a small garrison there, marched down to Capua with all the rest of his forces. Thus there were three generals' tents erected round Capua; and three armies, applying themselves to the work in different parts, proceeded to surround the city with a ditch and rampart, erecting forts at moderate intervals. The Campanians attempting to obstruct the work, a battle was fought in several places at once; the consequence of which was, that at length the Campanians confined themselves within their gates and walls. Before, however, these works were carried quite round, ambassadors were sent to Hannibal to complain that Capua was abandoned, and almost given up to the Romans, and to implore him, that he would now, at least, bring them assistance, when they were not only besieged, but surrounded by a rampart. A letter was sent to the consuls from Publius Cornelius, the prætor, directing that before they completely enclosed Capua with their works, they should grant permission to such of the Campanians as chose to quit Capua, and take their property with them. That those should retain their liberty, and all their possessions, who quitted it before the ides of March, but that those who quitted it after that day, as well as those who continued there, would be considered as enemies. Proclamation was made to the Campanians to this effect, but it was received with such scorn, that they spontaneously used insulting language and menaces. Hannibal had marched his legions from Herdonea to Tarentum, with the hope of getting possession of the citadel of that place, by force or stratagem. But not succeeding there, he turned his course to Brundusium, thinking that town would be betrayed to him, but, while fruitlessly spending time there also, the Campanian ambassadors came to him with complaints and entreaties. Hannibal answered them in a proud manner, that he had before raised the siege of Capua, and that now the consuls would not sustain his approach. The ambassadors, dismissed with these hopes, with difficulty effected their return to Capua, which was by this time surrounded by a double trench and rampart.

At the time when the circumvallation of Capua was carrying on with the greatest activity, the siege of Syracuse, which had been forwarded by intestine treachery, in addition to the efforts and bravery of the general and his army, was brought to a conclusion. For in the beginning of spring, Marcellus being in doubt whether he should direct the operations of the war against Himilco and Hippocrates at Agrigentum, or press the siege of Syracuse, though he saw that it was impossible to take the city by force, which, from its situation, both with respect to sea and land, was impregnable, nor by famine, as it was supported by an uninterrupted supply of provisions from Carthage, yet that he might leave no course untried, directed the Syracusan deserters (and there were in the Roman camp some men in this situation of the highest rank, who had been driven out of the city during the defection from the Romans, because they were averse to a change of measures) to sound the feelings of those who were of the same party in conferences, and to promise them, that if Syracuse was delivered up, they should have their liberty, and be governed by their own laws. There was no opportunity however, of having a conference; for as many were suspected of disaffection, the attention and observation of all were exerted, lest any thing of the kind should occur unknown to them. One of the exiles, who was a servant, having been allowed to enter the city in the character of a deserter, assembled a few persons, and opened a conversation upon the subject. After this, certain persons, covering themselves with nets in a fishing smack, were in this way conveyed round to the Roman camp, and conferred with the fugitives. The same was frequently repeated by different parties, one after another; and at last they amounted to eighty. But after every thing had been concerted for betraying the city, the plot was reported to Epicydes, by one Attalus, who felt hurt that he had not been intrusted with the secret; and they were all put to death with torture. This attempt having miscarried, another hope was immediately raised. One Damippus, a Lacedæmonian, who had been sent from Syracuse to king Philip, had been taken prisoner by the Roman fleet. Epicydes was particularly anxious to ransom this man above any other; nor was Marcellus disinclined to grant it; the Romans, even at this time, being desirous of gaining the friendship of the Ætolians, with whom the Lacedæmonians were in alliance. Some persons having been sent to treat respecting his ransom, the most central and convenient place to both parties for this purpose appeared to be at the Trogilian port, near the tower called Galeagra. As they went there several times, one of the Romans, having a near view of the wall, and having determined its height, as nearly as it could be done by conjecture, from counting the stones, and by forming an estimate, in his own mind, what was the height of each stone in the face of the work; and having come to the conclusion that it was considerably lower than he himself and all the rest had supposed it, and that it was capable of being scaled with ladders of moderate size, laid the matter before Marcellus. It appeared a thing not to be neglected; but as the spot could not be approached, being on this very account guarded with extraordinary care, a favourable opportunity of doing it was sought for. This a deserter suggested, who brought intelligence that the Syracusans were celebrating the festival of Diana; that it was to last three days, and that as there was a deficiency of other things during the siege, the feasts would be more profusely celebrated with wine, which was furnished by Epicydes to the people in general, and distributed through the tribes by persons of distinction. When Marcellus had received this intelligence, he communicated it to a few of the military tribunes; then having selected, through their means, such centurions and soldiers as had courage and energy enough for so important an enterprise, and having privately gotten together a number of scaling-ladders, he directed that a signal should be given to the rest of the troops to take their refreshment, and go to rest early, for they were to go upon an expedition that night. Then the time, as it was supposed, having arrived, when, after having feasted from the middle of the day, they would have had their fill of wine, and have begun to sleep, he ordered the soldiers of one company to proceed with the ladders, while about a thousand armed men were in silence marched to the spot in a slender column. The foremost having mounted the wall, without noise or confusion, the others followed in order; the boldness of the former inspiring even the irresolute with courage.

The thousand armed men had now taken a part of the city, when the rest, applying a greater number of ladders, mounted the wall on a signal given from the Hexapylos. To this place the former party had arrived in entire solitude; as the greater part of them, having feasted in the towers, were either asleep from the effects of wine, or else, half asleep, were still drinking. A few of them, however, they surprised in their beds, and put to the sword. They began then to break open a postern gate near the Hexapylos, which required great force; and a signal was given from the wall by sounding a trumpet, as had been agreed upon. After this, the attack was carried on in every quarter, not secretly, but by open force; for they had now reached Epipolæ, a place protected by numerous guards, where the business was to terrify the enemy, and not to escape their notice. In effect they were terrified; for as soon as the sound of the trumpets was heard, and the shouts of the men who had got possession of the walls and a part of the city, the guards concluded that every part was taken, and some of them fled along the wall, others leaped down from it, or were thrown down headlong by a crowd of the terrified townsmen. A great part of the inhabitants, however, were ignorant of this disastrous event, all of them being overpowered with wine and sleep; and because, in a city of so wide extent, what was perceived in one quarter was not readily made known through the whole city. A little before day, Marcellus having entered the city with all his forces, through the Hexapylos, which was forced open roused all the townsmen; who ran to arms, in order, if possible, by their efforts, to afford succour to the city, which was now almost taken. Epicydes advanced with a body of troops at a rapid pace from the Insula, which the Syracusans themselves call Nasos, not doubting but that he should be able to drive out what he supposed a small party, which had got over the wall through the negligence of the guards. He earnestly represented to the terrified inhabitants who met him, that they were increasing the confusion, and that in their accounts they made things greater and more important than they really were. But when he perceived that every place around Epipolæ was filled with armed men, after just teasing the enemy with the discharge of a few missiles, he marched back to the Achradina, not so much through fear of the number and strength of the enemy, as that some intestine treachery might show itself, taking advantage of the opportunity, and he might find the gates of the Achradina and island closed upon him in the confusion. When Marcellus, having entered the walls, beheld this city as it lay subjected to his view from the high ground on which he stood, a city the most beautiful, perhaps, of any at that time, he is said to have shed tears over it; partly from the inward satisfaction he felt at having accomplished so important an enterprise, and partly in consideration of its ancient renown. The fleets of the Athenians sunk there, and two vast armies destroyed, with two generals of the highest reputation, as well as the many wars waged with the Carthaginians with so much peril arose before his mind; the many and powerful tyrants and kings; but above all Hiero, a king who was not only fresh in his memory, but who was distinguished for the signal services he had rendered the

Roman people, and more than all by the endowments which his own virtues and good fortune had conferred. All these considerations presenting themselves at once to his recollection, and reflecting, that in an instant every thing before him would be in flames, and reduced to ashes; before he marched his troops to the Achradina, he sent before him some Syracusans, who, as was before observed, were among the Roman troops, to induce the enemy, by a persuasive address, to surrender the city.

The gates and walls of the Achradina were occupied principally by deserters, who had no hopes of pardon in case of capitulation. These men would neither suffer those who were sent to approach the walls, nor to address them. Marcellus, therefore, on the failure of this attempt, gave orders to retire to the Euryalus, which is an eminence at the extremity of the city, at the farthest point from the sea, and commanding the road leading into the fields and the interior of the island, and is conveniently situated for the introduction of supplies. This fort was commanded by Philodemus, an Argive, who was placed in this situation by Epicydes. Marcellus sent Sosis, one of the regicides, to him. After a long conversation, being put off for the purpose of frustrating him, he brought back word to Marcellus, that Philodemus had taken time to deliberate. This man postponing his answer day after day, till Hippocrates and Himilco should quit their present position, and come up with their legions; not doubting but that if he should receive them into the fort, the Roman army, shut up as it was within the walls, might be annihilated, Marcellus, who saw that the Euryalus would neither be delivered up to him, nor could be taken by force, pitched his camp between Neapolis and Tycha, which are names of divisions of the city, and are in themselves like cities; fearful lest if he entered populous parts of the city, he should not be able to restrain his soldiers, greedy of plunder, from running up and down after it. When three ambassadors came to him from Tycha and Neapolis with fillets and other badges of supplicants, imploring him to abstain from fire and slaughter, Marcellus, having held a council respecting these entreaties, for so they were, rather than demands, ordered his soldiers, according to the unanimous opinion of the council, not to offer violence to any free person, but told them that every thing else might be their booty. The walls of the houses forming a protection for his camp, he posted guards and parties of troops at the gates, which were exposed, as they faced the streets, lest any attack should be made upon his camp while the soldiers were dispersed in pursuit of plunder. After these arrangements, on a signal given, the soldiers dispersed for that purpose; and though they broke open doors and every place resounded in consequence of the alarm and confusion created, they nevertheless refrained from blood. They did not desist from plunder till they had gutted the houses of all the property which had been accumulated during a long period of prosperity. Meanwhile, Philodemus also, who despaired of obtaining assistance, having received a pledge that he might return to Epicydes in safety, withdrew the garrison, and delivered up the fortress to the Romans. While the attention of all was engaged by the tumult occasioned in that part of the city which was captured, Bomilcar, taking advantage of the night, when, from the violence of the weather the Roman fleet was unable to ride at anchor in the deep, set out from the bay of Syracuse, with thirty-five ships, and sailed away into the main without interruption; leaving fifty-five ships for Epicydes and the Syracusans; and having informed the Carthaginians in what a critical situation Syracuse was placed, returned, after a few days, with a hundred ships; having, as report says, received many presents from Epicydes out of the treasure of Hiero.

Marcellus, by gaining possession of the Euryalus, and placing a garrison in it, was freed from one cause of anxiety; which was, lest any hostile force received into that fortress on his rear might annoy his troops, shut up and confined as they were within the walls. He next invested the Achradina, erecting three camps in convenient situations, with the hope of reducing those enclosed within it to the want of every necessary. The outposts of both sides had remained inactive for several days, when the arrival of Hippocrates and Himilco suddenly caused the Romans to be attacked aggressively on all sides; for Hippocrates, having fortified a camp at the great harbour, and given a signal to those who occupied the Achradina, attacked the old camp of the Romans, in which Crispinus had the command; and Epicydes sallied out against the outposts of Marcellus, the Carthaginian fleet coming up to that part of the shore which lay between the city and the Roman camp, so that no succour could be sent by Marcellus to Crispinus. The enemy, however, produced more tumult than conflict; for Crispinus not only drove back Hippocrates from his works, but pursued him as he fled with precipitation, while Marcellus drove Epicydes into the city; and it was considered that enough was now done even to prevent any danger arising in future from their sudden sallies. They were visited too by a plague; a calamity extending to both sides, and one which might well divert their attention from schemes of war. For as the season of the year was autumn, and the situation naturally unwholesome, though this was much more the case without than within the city, the intolerable intensity of the heat had an effect upon the constitution of almost every man in both the camps. At first they sickened and died from the unhealthiness of the season and climate; but afterwards the disease was spread merely by attending upon, and coming in contact with, those affected; so that those who were seized with it either perished neglected and deserted, or else drew with them those who sat by them and attended them, by infecting them with the same violence of disease. Daily funerals and death were before the eye; and lamentations were heard from all sides, day and night. At last, their feelings had become so completely brutalized by being habituated to these miseries, that they not only did not follow their dead with tears and decent lamentations, but they did not even carry them out and bury them; so that the bodies of the dead lay strewed about, exposed to the view of those who were awaiting a similar fate; and thus the dead were the means of destroying the sick, and the sick those who were in health, both by fear and by the filthy state and the noisome stench of their bodies. Some preferring to die by the sword, even rushed alone upon the outposts of the enemy. The violence of the plague, however, was much greater in the Carthaginian than the Roman army; for the latter, from having been a long time before Syracuse, had become more habituated to the climate and the water. Of the army of the enemy, the Sicilians, as soon as they perceived that diseases had become very common from the unwholesomeness of the situation, dispersed to their respective cities in the neighbourhood; but the Carthaginians, who had no place to retire to, perished, together with their generals, Hippocrates and Himilco, to a man. Marcellus, on seeing the violence with which the disease was raging, had removed his troops into the city, where their debilitated frames were recruited in houses and shade. Many however, of the Roman army were cut off by this pestilence.

The land forces of the Carthaginians being thus destroyed, the Sicilians, who had served under Hippocrates retired to two towns of no great size, but well secured by natural situation and fortifications; one was three miles, the other fifteen, from Syracuse. Here they collected a store of provisions from their own states, and sent for reinforcements. Meanwhile, Bomilcar, who had gone a second time to Carthage, by so stating the condition of their allies as to inspire a hope that they might not only render them effectual aid, but also that the Romans might in a manner be made prisoners in the city which they had captured, induced the Carthaginians to send with him as many ships of burden as possible, laden with every kind of provisions, and to augment the number of his ships. Setting sail, therefore, from Carthage with a hundred and thirty men of war and seven hundred transports, he had tolerably fair winds for crossing over to Sicily, but was prevented by the same wind from doubling Cape Pachynum. The news of the approach of Bomilcar, and afterwards his unexpected delay, excited alternate fear and joy in the Romans and Syracusans. Epicydes, apprehensive lest if the same wind which now detained him should continue to blow from the east for several days, the Carthaginian fleet would return to Africa, put the Achradina in the hands of the generals of the mercenary troops, and sailed to Bomilcar; whom he at length prevailed upon to try the issue of a naval battle, though he found him with his fleet stationed in the direction of Africa, and afraid of fighting, not so much because he was unequal in the strength or the number of his ships, for he had more than the Romans, as because the wind was more favourable to the Roman fleet than to his own. Marcellus also seeing that an army of Sicilians was assembling from every part of the island, and that the Carthaginian fleet was approaching with a great want of supplies, though inferior in the number of his ships, resolved to prevent Bomilcar from coming to Syracuse, lest, blocked up in the city of his enemies, he should be pressed both by sea and land. The two hostile fleets were stationed near the promontory of Pachynum, ready to engage as soon as the sea should become calm enough to admit of their sailing out into the deep. Accordingly, the east wind, which had blown violently for several days, now subsiding, Bomilcar got under sail first, his van seeming to make for the main sea, in order to double the promontory with greater ease; but seeing the Roman ships bearing down upon him, terrified by some unexpected occurrence, it is not known what, he sailed away into the main sea; and sending messengers to Heraclea, to order the transports to return to Africa, he passed along the coast of Sicily and made for Tarentum. Epicydes, thus suddenly disappointed in such great expectations, to avoid returning to endeavour to raise the siege of a city, a great part of which was already in the hands of the enemy, sailed to Agrigentum, intending to wait the issue of the contest, rather than take any new measures when there.

Intelligence of these events having been carried into the camp of the Sicilians, that Epicydes had departed from Syracuse, that the island was deserted by the Carthaginians, and almost again delivered up to the Romans; after sounding the inclinations of the besieged in conferences, they sent ambassadors to Marcellus, to treat about terms of capitulation. They had not much difficulty in coming to an agreement, that all the parts of the island which had been under the dominion of their kings should be ceded to the Romans; that the rest, with their liberty and their own laws, should be preserved to the Sicilians. They then invited to a conference the persons who had been intrusted with the management of affairs by Epicydes; to whom they said, that they were sent from the army of the Sicilians, at once to Marcellus and to them, that both those who were besieged and those who were not might share the same fortune; and that neither of them might stipulate any thing for themselves separately. They were then allowed to enter, in order to converse with their relations and friends; when, laying before them the terms which they had made with Marcellus, and holding out to them a hope of safety, they induced them to join with them in an attack upon the prefects of Epicydes, Polyclitus, Philistion, and Epicydes, surnamed Sindon. Having put them to death, they summoned the multitude to an assembly; and after complaining of the famine, at which they had been accustomed to express their dissatisfaction to each other in secret, they said, that "although they were pressed by so many calamities, they had no right to accuse Fortune, because it was at their own option how long they should continue to suffer them. That the motive which the Romans had in besieging Syracuse was affection for the Syracusans, and not hatred; for when they heard that the government was usurped by Hippocrates and Epicydes, the creatures first of Hannibal and then of Hieronymus, they took arms and began to besiege the city, in order to reduce not the city itself, but its cruel tyrants. But now that Hippocrates is slain, Epicydes shut out of Syracuse, his præfects put to death, and the Carthaginians driven from the entire possession of Sicily by sea and land, what reason can the Romans have left why they should not desire the preservation of Syracuse, in the same manner as they would if Hiero were still lining, who cultivated the friendship of Rome with unequalled fidelity? That, therefore, neither the city nor its inhabitants were in any danger, except from themselves, if they neglected an opportunity of restoring themselves to the favour of the Romans; and that no so favourable a one would ever occur as that which presented itself at the present instant, immediately upon its appearing that they were delivered from their insolent tyrants."

This speech was received with the most unqualified approbation of all present. It was resolved, however, that prætors should be elected before the nomination of deputies; which being done, some of the prætors themselves were sent as deputies to Marcellus, the chief of whom thus addressed him: "Neither in the first instance did we Syracusans revolt from you, but Hieronymus, whose impiety towards you was by no means so great as towards us; nor afterwards was it any Syracusan who disturbed the peace established by the death of the tyrant, but Hippocrates and Epicydes, creatures of the tyrant; while we were overpowered, on the one hand by fear, and on the other by treachery. Nor can any one say that there ever was a time when we were in possession of our liberty, when we were not also at peace with you. In the present instance, manifestly, as soon as ever we became our own masters, by the death of those persons who held Syracuse in subjection, we lost no time in coming to deliver up our arms, to surrender ourselves, our city, and our walls, and to refuse no conditions which you shall impose upon us. To you, Marcellus, the gods have given the glory of having captured the most renowned and beautiful of the Grecian cities. Every memorable exploit which we have at any time achieved by land or sea accrues to the splendour of your triumph. Would you wish that it should be known only by fame, how great a city has been captured by you, rather than that she should stand as a monument even to posterity; so that to every one who visits her by sea or land, she may point out at one time our trophies gained from the Athenians and Carthaginians, at another time those which you have gained from us; and that you should transmit Syracuse unimpaired to your family, to be kept under the protection and patronage of the race of the Marcelli? Let not the memory of Hieronymus have greater weight with you than that of Hiero. The latter was your friend for a much longer period than the former was your enemy. From the latter you have realized even benefits, while the frenzy of Hieronymus only brought ruin upon himself." At the hands of the Romans all things were obtainable and secure. There was a greater disposition to war, and more danger to be apprehended among themselves; for the deserters, thinking that they were delivered up to the Romans, induced the mercenary auxiliaries to entertain the same apprehension; and hastily seizing their arms, they first put the prætors to death, and then ran through the city to massacre the Syracusans. In their rage they slew all whom chance threw in their way, and plundered every thing which presented itself; and then, lest they should have no leaders, they elected six prætors, so that three might have the command in the Achradina, and three in the island. At length, the tumult having subsided, and the mercenary troops having ascertained, by inquiry, what had been negotiated with the Romans, it began to appear, as was really the case, that their cause and that of the deserters were different.

The ambassadors returned from Marcellus very opportunely. They informed them that they had been influenced by groundless suspicions, and that the Romans saw no reason why they should inflict punishment upon them. Of the three præfects of the Achradina one was a Spaniard, named Mericus. To him one of the Spanish auxiliaries was designedly sent, among those who accompanied the ambassadors. Having obtained an interview with Mericus in the absence of witnesses, he first explained to him the state in which he had left Spain, from which he had lately returned: "That there every thing was in subjection to the Roman arms; that it was in his power, by doing the Romans a service, to become the first man among his countrymen, whether he might be inclined to serve with the Romans, or to return to his country. On the other hand, if he persisted in preferring to hold out against the siege, what hope could he have, shut up as he was by sea and land?" Mericus was moved by these suggestions, and when it was resolved upon to send ambassadors to Marcellus, he sent his brother among them; who, being brought into the presence of Marcellus, apart from the rest, by means of the same Spaniard, after receiving an assurance of protection, arranged the method of carrying their object into effect, and then returned to the Achradina. Mericus then, in order to prevent any one from conceiving a suspicion of treachery, declared, that he did not like that deputies should be passing to and fro; he thought that they should neither admit nor send any; and in order that the guards might be kept more strictly, that such parts as were most exposed should be distributed among the prefects, each being made responsible for the safety of his own quarter. All approved of the distribution of the posts. The district which fell to the lot of Mericus himself extended from the fountain Arethusa to the mouth of the large harbour, of which he caused the Romans to be informed. Accordingly, Marcellus ordered a transport with armed men to be towed by a quadrireme to the Achradina during the night, and the soldiers to be landed in the vicinity of that gate which is near the fountain of Arethusa. This order having been executed at the fourth watch, and Mericus having received the soldiers when landed at the gate, according to the agreement, Marcellus assaulted the walls of the Achradina with all his forces at break of day, so that he not only engaged the attention of those who occupied the Achradina, but also bands of armed men, quitting their own posts ran to the spot from the island, in order to repel the furious attack of the Romans. During this confusion, some light ships which had been prepared beforehand, and had sailed round, landed a body of armed men at the island; these suddenly attacking the half-manned stations and the opened door of the gate at which the troops had a little before run out, got possession of the island without much opposition, abandoned as it was, in consequence of the flight and trepidation of its guards. Nor were there any who rendered less service, or showed less firmness in maintaining their posts, than the deserters; for as they did not repose much confidence even in those of their own party, they fled in the middle of the contest. When Marcellus learnt that the island was taken, one quarter of the Achradina in the hands of his troops, and that Mericus, with the men under his command, had joined them, he sounded a retreat, lest the royal treasure, the fame of which was greater than the reality, should be plundered.

The impetuosity of the soldiers having been checked, time and opportunity to escape were given to the deserters in the Achradina; and the Syracusans, at length delivered from their fears, threw open the gates of the Achradina, and sent deputies to Marcellus, requesting only safety for themselves and children. Having summoned a council, to which the Syracusans were invited who were among the Roman troops, having been driven from home during the disturbances, Marcellus replied, "that the services rendered by Hiero through a period of fifty years, were not more in number than the injuries committed against the Roman people in these few years by those who had had possession of Syracuse; but that most of these injuries had justly recoiled upon their authors, and that they had inflicted much more severe punishment upon themselves for the violation of treaties, than the Roman people desired. That he was indeed now besieging Syracuse for the third year, but not that the Romans might hold that state in a condition of slavery, but that the ringleaders of the deserters might not keep it in a state of thraldom and oppression. What the Syracusans could do was exemplified, either by the conduct of those Syracusans who were among the Roman troops, or that of the Spanish general, Mericus, who had delivered up the post which he was appointed to command, or, lastly, by the late but bold measure adopted by the Syracusans themselves. That the greatest possible recompence for all the evils and dangers which he had for so long a time undergone, both by sea and land, around the walls of Syracuse, was the reflection, that he had been able to take that city." The quæstor was then sent with a guard to the island, to receive and protect the royal treasure. The city was given up to be plundered by the soldiery, after guards had been placed at each of the houses of those who had been with the Roman troops. While many acts exhibited horrid examples of rage and rapacity, it is recorded that Archimedes, while intent on some figures which he had described in the dust, although the confusion was as great as could possibly exist in a captured city, in which soldiers were running up and down in search of plunder, was put to death by a soldier, who did not know who he was; that Marcellus was grieved at this event, and that pains were taken about his funeral, while his relations also for whom diligent inquiry was made, derived honour and protection from his name and memory. Such, for the most part, was the manner in which Syracuse was captured. The quantity of booty was so great, that had Carthage itself, which was carrying on a contest on equal terms, been captured, it would scarcely have afforded so much. A few days before the taking of Syracuse, Titus Otacilius passed over from Lilybæum to Utica with eighty quinqueremes, and entering the harbour before it was light, took some transports laden with corn; then landing, he laid waste a considerable portion of the country around Utica, and brought back to his ships booty of every description. He returned to Lilybæum, the third day after he set out, with a hundred and thirty transports laden with corn and booty. The corn he sent immediately to Syracuse; and had it not been for the very seasonable arrival of this supply, a destructive famine threatened alike the victors and the vanquished.

Nothing very memorable had been done in Spain for about two years, the operations of the war consisting more in laying plans than in fighting; but during the same summer in which the events above recorded took place, the Roman generals, quitting their winter quarters, united their forces; then a council was summoned; and the opinions of all accorded, that since their only object hitherto had been to prevent Hasdrubal from pursuing his march into Italy, it was now time that an effort should be made to bring the war in Spain to a termination; and they thought that the twenty thousand Celtiberians, who had been induced to take arms that winter, formed a sufficient accession to their strength. There were three armies of the enemy. Hasdrubal, son of Gisgo, and Mago, who had united their forces, were about a five days' journey from the Romans. Hasdrubal, son of Hamilcar, who was the old commander in Spain, was nearer to them: he was with his army near the city Anitorgis. The Roman generals were desirous that he should be overpowered first; and they hoped that they had enough and more than enough strength for the purpose. Their only source of anxiety was, lest the other Hasdrubal and Mago, terrified at his discomfiture, should protract the war by withdrawing into trackless forests and mountains. Thinking it, therefore, the wisest course to divide their forces and embrace the whole Spanish war, they arranged it so that Publius Cornelius should lead two-thirds of the Roman and allied troops against Mago and Hasdrubal, and that Cneius Cornelius, with the remaining third of the original army, and with the Celtiberians added to them, should carry on the war with the Barcine Hasdrubal. The two generals and their armies, setting out together, preceded by the Celtiberians, pitched their camp near the city Anitorgis, within sight of the enemy, the river only separating them. Here Cneius Scipio, with the forces above mentioned, halted, but Publius Scipio proceeded to the portion of the war assigned to him.

Hasdrubal perceiving that there were but few Roman troops in the camp, and that their whole dependence was on the Celtiberian auxiliaries; and having had experience of the perfidy of the barbarian nations in general, and particularly of all those nations among which he had served for so many years; as there was every facility of intercourse, for both camps were full of Spaniards, by secret conferences with the chiefs of the Celtiberians, he agreed with them, for a large consideration, to take their forces away. Nor did they conceive it to be any great crime; for the object was not that they should turn their arms against the Romans, while the reward which they were to receive to abstain from the war was large enough to remunerate them for their service in it. At the same time the mere rest from labour, the return to their homes, with the pleasure of seeing their friends and property, were pleasing to the generality. Accordingly, the multitude were prevailed upon as easily as their leaders. They had, moreover, nothing to fear from the Romans, in consequence of the smallness of their numbers, should they endeavour to detain them by force. It will indeed be the duty of all Roman generals to take care, and the instances here recorded should be considered as strong arguments, never to place so much confidence in foreign auxiliaries, as not to retain in their camps a preponderance of their own strength and of that force which is properly their own. The Celtiberians, suddenly taking up their standards, marched away, replying only to the Romans, who asked the cause of their departure and entreated them to stay, that they were called away by a war at home. Scipio seeing that his allies could be detained neither by prayers nor force, and that he was neither a match for his enemy without them, nor could again effect a junction with his brother, no other course which promised safety offering itself, resolved to retire as far as possible, carefully using every caution not to encounter the enemy any where on level ground. On his departing, the enemy, crossing the river, pursued him almost in his footsteps.

During the same period an equal terror and a greater danger pressed upon Publius Scipio. Masinissa was a young man at that time an ally of the Carthaginians, whom afterwards the friendship of the Romans rendered illustrious and powerful. He not only opposed himself with his Numidian cavalry to Scipio on his approach, but afterwards harassed him incessantly day and night, so as both to cut off his stragglers, who had gone out to a distance from the camp in search of wood and forage, and riding up to the very gates of his camp, and charging into the midst of his advanced guards, to fill every quarter with the utmost confusion. By night also alarm was frequently occasioned in the gates and rampart by his sudden attacks. Nor was there any time or place at which the Romans were exempt from fear and anxiety; and driven within their rampart, and deprived of every necessary, they suffered in a manner a regular siege; and it appeared that it would have been still straiter, if Indibilis, who it was reported was approaching with seven thousand five hundred Suessetani, should form a junction with the Carthaginians. Scipio, though a wary and provident general, overpowered by difficulties, adopted the rash measure of going to meet Indibilis by night, with the intention of fighting him wherever he should meet him. Leaving, therefore, a small force in his camp, under the command of Titus Fonteius, lieutenant-general, he set out at midnight, and meeting with the enemy, came to battle with him. The troops fought in the order of march rather than of battle. The Romans, however, had the advantage, though in an irregular fight; but the Numidian cavalry, whose observation the general supposed that he had escaped, suddenly spreading themselves round his flanks, occasioned great terror. After a new contest had been entered into with the Numidians, a third enemy came up in addition to the rest, the Carthaginian generals having come up with their rear when they were now engaged in fighting. Thus the Romans were surrounded on every side by enemies; nor could they make up their minds which they should attack first, or in what part, forming themselves into a close body, they should force their way through. The general, while fighting and encouraging his men, exposing himself wherever the strife was the hottest, was run through the right side with a lance; and when the party of the enemy, which, formed into a wedge, had charged the troops collected round the general, perceived Scipio falling lifeless from his horse, elated with joy, they ran shouting through the whole line with the news that the Roman general had fallen. These words spreading in every direction, caused the enemy to be considered as victors, and the Romans as vanquished. On the loss of the general the troops immediately began to fly from the field; but though it was not difficult to force their way through the Numidians and the other light-armed auxiliaries, yet it was scarcely possible for them to escape so large a body of cavalry, and infantry equal to horses in speed. Almost more were slain in the flight than in the battle; nor would a man have survived, had not night put a stop to the carnage, the day by this time rapidly drawing to a close.

After this, the Carthaginian generals, who were not slow in following up their victory, immediately after the battle, scarcely giving their soldiers necessary rest, hurry their army to Hasdrubal, son of Hamilcar; confidently hoping, that after uniting their forces with his, the war might be brought to a conclusion. On their arrival, the warmest congratulations passed between the troops and their generals, who were delighted with their recent victory; for they had not only destroyed one distinguished general and all his men, but looked forward to another victory of equal magnitude as a matter of certainty. The intelligence of this great disaster had not yet reached the Romans; but there prevailed a kind of melancholy silence and mute foreboding, such as is usually found in minds which have a presentiment of impending calamity. The general himself, besides feeling that he was deserted by his allies, and that the forces of the enemy were so much augmented, was disposed from conjecture and reasoning rather to a suspicion that some defeat had been sustained, than to any favourable hopes. "For how could Hasdrubal and Mago bring up their troops without opposition, unless they had terminated their part of the war? How was it that his brother had not opposed his progress or followed on his rear? in order that if he could not prevent the armies and generals of the enemy from forming a junction, he might himself join his forces with his brother's." Disturbed with these cares, he believed that the only safe policy for the present was to retire as far as possible; and, accordingly, he marched a considerable distance thence in one night, the enemy not being aware of it, and on that account continuing quiet. At dawn, perceiving that their enemy had decamped, they sent the Numidians in advance, and began to pursue them as rapidly as possible. The Numidians overtook them before night, and charged; sometimes their rear, at other times their flanks. They then began to halt and defend themselves as well as they could; but Scipio exhorted them at once to fight so as not to expose themselves, and march at the same time, lest the infantry should overtake them.

But having made but little progress for a long time, in consequence of his making his troops sometimes advance and at others halt, and night now drawing on, Scipio recalled his troops from the battle, and collecting them, withdrew to a certain eminence, not very safe, indeed, particularly for dispirited troops, but higher than any of the surrounding places. There, at first, his infantry, drawn up around his baggage and cavalry, which were placed in their centre, had no difficulty in repelling the attacks of the charging Numidians; but afterwards, when three generals with three regular armies marched up in one entire body, and it was evident that his men would not be able to do much by arms in defending the position without fortifications, the general began to look about, and consider whether he could by any means throw a rampart around; but the hill was so bare, and the soil so rough, that neither could a bush be found for cutting a palisade, nor earth for making a mound, nor the requisites for making a trench or any other work; nor was the place naturally steep or abrupt enough to render the approach and ascent difficult to the enemy, as it rose on every side with a gentle acclivity. However, that they might raise up against them some semblance of a rampart, they placed around them the panniers tied to the burdens, building them up as it were to the usual height, and when there was a deficiency of panniers for raising it, they presented against the enemy a heap of baggage of every kind. The Carthaginian armies coming up, very easily marched up the eminence, but were stopped by the novel appearance of the fortification, as by something miraculous, when their leaders called out from all sides, asking "what they stopped at? and why they did not tear down and demolish that mockery, which was scarcely strong enough to impede the progress of women and children; that the enemy, who were skulking behind their baggage, were, in fact, captured and in their hands." Such were the contemptuous reproofs of their leaders. But it was not an easy task either to leap over or remove the burdens raised up against them, or to cut through the panniers, closely packed together and covered completely with baggage. When the removal of the burdens had opened a way to the troops, who were detained by them for a long time, and the same had been done in several quarters, the camp was now captured on all sides; the Romans were cut to pieces on all hands, the few by the many, the dispirited by the victorious. A great number of the men, however, having fled for refuge into the neighbouring woods, effected their escape to the camp of Publius Scipio, which Titus Fonteius commanded. Some authors relate that Cneius Scipio was slain on the eminence on the first assault of the enemy; others that he escaped with a few attendants to a castle near the camp; this, they say, was surrounded with fire, by which means the doors which they could not force were consumed; that it was thus taken, and all within, together with the general himself, put to death. Cneius Scipio was slain in the eighth year after his arrival in Spain, and on the twenty-ninth day after the death of his brother. At Rome the grief occasioned by their death was not more intense than that which was felt throughout Spain. The sorrow of the citizens, however, was partly distracted by the loss of the armies, the alienation of the province, and the public disaster, while in Spain they mourned and regretted the generals themselves, Cneius, however, the more, because he had been longer in command of them, had first engaged their affections, and first exhibited a specimen of Roman justice and forbearance.

When it seemed that the Roman armies were annihilated, and Spain lost, one man recovered this desperate state of affairs. There was in the army one Lucius Marcius, the son of Septimus, a Roman knight, an enterprising youth, and possessing a mind and genius far superior to the condition in which he had been born. To his high talents had been added the discipline of Cneius Scipio, under which he had been thoroughly instructed during a course of so many years in all the qualifications of a soldier. This man, having collected the troops which had been dispersed in the flight, and drafted some from the garrisons, had formed an army not to be despised, and united it with Titus Fonteius, the lieutenant-general of Publius Scipio. But so transcendent was the Roman knight in authority and honour among the troops, that when, after fortifying a camp on this side of the Iberus, it had been resolved that a general of the two armies should be elected in an assembly of the soldiers, relieving each other in the guard of the rampart, and in keeping the outposts until every one had given his vote, they unanimously conferred the supreme command upon Lucius Marcius. All the intervening time, which was but short, was occupied in fortifying their camp and collecting provisions, and the soldiers executed every order not only with vigour, but with feelings by no means depressed. But when intelligence was brought them that Hasdrubal, son of Gisgo, who was coming to put the finishing stroke to the war, had crossed the Iberus and was drawing near, and when they saw the signal for battle displayed by a new commander, then calling to mind whom they had had for their leaders a little while ago, relying on what leaders and what forces they used to go out to fight, they all suddenly burst into tears and beat their heads, some raising their hands to heaven and arraigning the gods, others prostrating themselves upon the ground and invoking by name each his own former commander. Nor could their lamentations be restrained, though the centurions endeavoured to animate their companies, and though Marcius himself soothed and remonstrated with them, asking them "why they had given themselves up to womanish and unavailing lamentations rather than summon up all their courage to protect themselves and the commonwealth together, and not suffer their generals to lie unavenged?" But suddenly a shout and the sound of trumpets were heard; for by this time the enemy were near the rampart. Upon this, their grief being suddenly converted into rage, they hastily ran to arms, and, as it were, burning with fury, rushed to the gates and charged the enemy, while advancing in a careless and disorderly manner. This unexpected event instantly struck terror into the Carthaginians, who wondering whence so many enemies could have sprung up so suddenly, as the army had been almost annihilated; what could have inspired men who had been vanquished and routed with such boldness and confidence in themselves; what general could have arisen now that the two Scipios were slain; who could command the camp, and who had given the signal for battle; in consequence of these so many and so unexpected circumstances, at first, being in a state of complete uncertainty and amazement, they gave ground; but afterwards, discomfited by the violence of the charge, they turned their backs; and either there would have been a dreadful slaughter of the flying enemy, or a rash and dangerous effort on the part of the pursuers, had not Marcius promptly given the signal for retreat, and by throwing himself in the way of the front rank, and even holding some back with his own hands, repressed the infuriated troops. He then led them back to the camp, still eager for blood and slaughter. When the Carthaginians, who were at first compelled to fly with precipitation from the rampart of their enemy, saw that no one pursued them, concluding that they had stopped from fear, now on the other hand went away to their camp at an easy pace, with feelings of contempt for the enemy. There was a corresponding want of care in guarding their camp; for though the enemy were near, yet it seemed that they were but the remains of the two armies which had been cut to pieces a few days before. As in consequence of this all things were neglected in the enemy's camp, Marcius having ascertained this, addressed his mind to a measure which on the first view of it might appear rather rash than bold: it was, aggressively to assault the enemy's camp, concluding that the camp of Hasdrubal, while alone, might be carried with less difficulty than his own could be defended, if the three armies and as many generals should again unite; taking into consideration also that either if he succeeded he would retrieve their prostrate fortune, or if repulsed, still, by making the attack himself, he would rescue himself from contempt.

Lest, however, the suddenness of the affair, and the fear of night, should frustrate a measure which was in itself ill adapted to his condition, he thought it right that his soldiers should be addressed and exhorted; and having called an assembly, he discoursed as follows: "Soldiers, either my veneration for our late commanders, both living and dead, or our present situation, may impress on every one the belief that this command, as it is highly honourable to me, conferred by your suffrages, so is it in its nature a heavy and anxious charge. For at a time when I should be scarcely so far master of myself as to be able to find any solace for my afflicted mind, did not fear deaden the sense of sorrow, I am compelled to take upon myself alone the task of consulting for the good of you all; a task of the greatest difficulty when under the influence of grief. And not even at that critical moment, when I ought to be considering in what manner I may be enabled to keep together for my country these remains of two armies, can I divert my mind from the affliction which incessantly preys upon me. For bitter recollection is ever present, and the Scipios ever disturb me with anxious cares by day and dreams by night, frequently rousing me from my sleep, and imploring me not to suffer themselves nor their soldiers, your companions in war, who had been victorious in this country for eight years, nor the commonwealth to remain unrevenged; enjoining me also to follow their discipline and their plans; and desiring that as there was no one more obedient to their commands while they were alive than I, so after their death I would consider that conduct as best, which I might have the strongest reason for believing they would have adopted in each case. I could wish also that you, my soldiers, should not show your respect for them by lamentations and tears, as if they were dead; (for they still live and flourish in the fame of their achievements;) but that whenever the memory of those men shall occur to you, you would go into battle as though you saw them encouraging you and giving you the signal. Nor certainly could anything else than their image presenting itself yesterday to your eyes and minds, have enabled you to fight that memorable battle, in which you proved to the enemy that the Roman name had not become extinct with the Scipios; and that the energy and valour of that people, which had not been overwhelmed by the disaster at Cannæ, would, doubtlessly, emerge from the severest storms of fortune. Now since you have dared so much of your own accord, I have a mind to try how much you will dare when authorized by your general: for yesterday, when I gave the signal for retreat while you were pursuing the routed enemy with precipitation, I did not wish to break your spirit, but to reserve it for greater glory and more advantageous opportunities; that you might afterwards, when prepared and armed, seize an occasion of attacking your enemy while off their guard, unarmed, and even buried in sleep. Nor do I entertain the hope of gaining an opportunity of this kind rashly, but from the actual state of things. Doubtless, if any one should ask even himself, by what means, though few in number and disheartened by defeat, you defended your camp against troops superior in number and victorious, you would give no other answer than that, as this was the very thing you were afraid of, you had kept every place secured by works and yourselves ready and equipped. And so it generally happens: men are least secure against that which fortune causes not to be feared; because you leave unguarded and exposed what you think is not necessary to be cared about. There is nothing whatever which the enemy fear less at the present time, than lest we, who were a little while ago besieged and assaulted, should aggressively assault their camp ourselves. Let us dare, then, to do that which it is incredible we should have the courage to attempt; it will be most easy from the very fact of its appearing most difficult. At the third watch of the night I will lead you thither in silence. I have ascertained by means of scouts that they have no regular succession of watches, no proper outposts. Our shout at their gates, when heard, and the first assault, will carry their camp. Then let that carnage be made among men, torpid with sleep, terrified at the unexpected tumult, and overpowered while lying defenceless in their beds, from which you were so grieved to be recalled yesterday. I know that the measure appears to you a daring one; but in difficult and almost desperate circumstances the boldest counsels are always the safest. For if when the critical moment has arrived, the opportunity of seizing which is of a fleeting nature, you delay ever so little, in vain do you seek for it afterwards when it has been neglected. One army is near us; two more are not far off. We have some hopes if we make an attack now; and you have already made trial of your own and their strength. If we postpone the time and cease to be despised in consequence of the fame of yesterday's irruption, there is danger lest all the generals and all the forces should unite. Shall we be able then to withstand three generals and three armies, whom Cneius Scipio with his army unimpaired could not withstand? As our generals have perished by dividing their forces, so the enemy may be overpowered while separated and divided. There is no other mode of maintaining the war; let us, therefore, wait for nothing but the opportunity of the ensuing night. Now depart, with the favour of the gods, and refresh yourselves, that, unfatigued and vigorous, you may burst into the enemy's camp with the same spirit with which you have defended your own." This new enterprise, proposed by their new general, they received with joy; and the more daring it was the more it pleased them. The remainder of the day was spent in getting their arms in readiness and recruiting their strength, the greater part of the night was given to rest, and at the fourth watch they were in motion.

At a distance of six miles beyond their nearest camp lay other forces of the Carthaginians. A deep valley, thickly planted with trees, intervened. Near about the middle of this wood a Roman cohort and some cavalry were placed in concealment with Punic craft. The communication between the two armies being thus cut off, the rest of the forces were marched in silence to the nearest body of the enemy; and as there were no outposts before the gates, and no guards on the rampart, they entered quite into the camp, as though it had been their own, no one any where opposing them. The signals were then sounded and a shout raised. Some put the enemy to the sword when half asleep; others threw fire upon the huts, which were covered in with dry straw; others blocked up the gates to intercept their escape. The enemy, who were assailed at once with fire, shouting, and the sword, were in a manner bereaved of their senses, and could neither hear each other, nor take any measures for their security. Unarmed, they fell into the midst of troops of armed men: some hastened to the gates; others, as the passes were flocked up, leaped over the rampart, and as each escaped they fled directly towards the other camp, where they were cut off by the cohort and cavalry rushing forward from their concealment, and were all slain to a man. And even had any escaped from that carnage, the Romans, after taking the nearer camp, ran over to the other with such rapidity, that no one could have arrived before them with news of the disaster. In this camp, as they were far distant from the enemy, and as some had gone off just before daylight for forage, wood, and plunder, they found every thing in a still more neglected and careless state. Their arms only were placed at the outposts, the men being unarmed, and either sitting and reclining upon the ground, or else walking up and down before the rampart and the gates. On these men, thus at their ease and unguarded, the Romans, still hot from the recent battle, and flushed with victory, commenced an attack; no effectual opposition therefore could be made to them in the gates. Within the gates, the troops having rushed together from every part of the camp at the first shout and alarm, a furious conflict arose; which would have continued for a long time, had not the bloody appearance of the Roman shields discovered to the Carthaginians the defeat of the other forces, and consequently struck them with dismay. This alarm produced a general flight; and all except those who were overtaken with the sword, rushing out precipitately wherever they could find a passage, abandoned their camp. Thus, in a night and a day, two camps of the enemy were carried, under the conduct of Lucius Marcius. Claudius, who translated the annals of Acilius out of Greek into Latin, states that as many as thirty-seven thousand men were slain, one thousand eight hundred and thirty made prisoners, and a great booty obtained; among which was a silver shield of a hundred and thirty-eight pounds' weight, with an image upon it of the Barcine Hasdrubal. Valerius Antias states, that the camp Of Mago only was captured, and seven thousand of the enemy slain; and that in the other battle, when the Romans sallied out and fought with Hasdrubal, ten thousand were slain, and four thousand three hundred captured. Piso writes, that five thousand were slain in an ambuscade when Mago incautiously pursued our troops who retired. With all, the name of the general, Marcius, is mentioned with great honour, and to his real glory they add even miracles. They say, that while he was haranguing his men a stream of fire poured from his head without his perceiving it, to the great terror of the surrounding soldiers; and that a shield, called the Marcian, with an image of Hasdrubal upon it, remained in the temple up to the time of the burning of the Capitol, a monument of his victory over the Carthaginians. After this, affairs continued for a considerable time in a tranquil state in Spain, as both parties, after giving and receiving such important defeats, hesitated to run the hazard of a general battle.

During these transactions in Spain, Marcellus, after the capture of Syracuse, having settled the other affairs in Sicily with so much honour and integrity as not only to add to his own renown, but also to the majesty of the Roman people, conveyed to Rome the ornaments of the city, together with the statues and pictures with which Syracuse abounded. These were certainly spoils taken from enemies, and acquired according to the laws of war; but hence was the origin of the admiration of the products of Grecian art, and to that freedom with which at present all places, both sacred and profane, are despoiled; which at last recoiled upon the Roman gods, and first upon that very temple which was so choicely adorned by Marcellus. For foreigners were in the habit of visiting the temples dedicated by Marcellus near the Capuan gate, on account of their splendid ornaments of this description, of which a very small portion can be found. Embassies from almost all the states of Sicily came to him. As their cases were different, so were also the terms granted to them. Those who had either not revolted or had returned to the alliance before the capture of Syracuse, were received and honoured as faithful allies. Those who had been induced to submit through fear after the capture of Syracuse, as vanquished, received laws from the conqueror. The Romans, however, had still remaining a war of no small magnitude at Agrigentum, headed by Epicydes and Hanno, generals in the late war, and a third new one sent by Hannibal in the room of Hippocrates, a Libyphœnician by nation, and a native of Hippo, called by his countrymen Mutines; an energetic man, and thoroughly instructed in all the arts of war under the tuition of

Hannibal. To this man the Numidian auxiliaries were assigned by Epicydes and Hanno. With these he so thoroughly overran the lands of his enemies, and visited his allies with such activity, in order to retain them in their allegiance, and for the purpose of bringing them seasonable aid as each required it, that in a short time he filled all Sicily with his fame, nor was greater confidence placed in any one else by those who favoured the Carthaginian interest. Accordingly the Carthaginian and Syracusan generals, who had been hitherto compelled to keep within the walls of Agrigentum, not more at the advice of Mutines than from the confidence they reposed in him, had the courage to go out from the walls, and pitched a camp near the river Himera. When this was announced to Marcellus, he immediately advanced and sat down at a distance of about four miles from the enemy, with the intention of waiting to see what steps they took, and what they meditated. But Mutines allowed no room or time for delay or deliberation, but crossed the river, and, charging the outposts of his enemy, created the greatest terror and confusion. The next day, in an engagement which might almost be called regular, he compelled his enemy to retire within their works. Being called away by a mutiny of the Numidians, which had broken out in the camp, and in which about three hundred of them had retired to Heraclea Minoa, he set out to appease them and bring them back; and is said to have earnestly warned the generals not to engage with the enemy during his absence. Both the generals were indignant at this conduct, but particularly Hanno, who was before disturbed at his reputation. "Is it to be borne," said he, "that a mongrel African should impose restraints upon me, a Carthaginian general, commissioned by the senate and people?" Epicydes, who wished to wait, was prevailed upon by him to agree to their crossing the river and offering battle; for, said he, if they should wait for Mutines, and the battle should terminate successfully, Mutines would certainly have the credit of it.

But Marcellus, highly indignant that he who had repulsed Hannibal from Nola, when rendered confident by his victory at Cannæ, should succumb to enemies whom he had vanquished by sea and land, ordered his soldiers immediately to take arms and raise the standards. While marshalling his army, ten Numidians rode up rapidly from the enemy's line with information that their countrymen, first induced by the same causes which brought on the mutiny, in which three hundred of their number retired to Heraclea, and secondly, because they saw their commander, just on the approach of a battle, sent out of the way by generals who wished to detract from his glory, would not take any part in the battle. This deceitful nation made good their promise in this instance. Accordingly the spirits of the Romans were increased by the intelligence, which was speedily conveyed through the lines, that the enemy were abandoned by the cavalry, which the Romans principally feared; while at the same time the enemy were dispirited, not only because they were deprived of the principal part of their strength, but further, because they were afraid lest they should themselves be attacked by their own cavalry. Accordingly, there was no great resistance made: the first shout and onset determined the business. The Numidians who stood quiet in the wings during the action, when they saw their party turning their backs, accompanied them in their flight only for a short time; but when they perceived that they were all making for Agrigentum with the most violent haste, they turned off to the neighbouring towns round about, through fear of a siege. Many thousand men were slain and captured, together with eight elephants. This was the last battle which Marcellus fought in Sicily, after which he returned victorious to Syracuse. The year was now about closing; the senate therefore decreed that Publius Cornelius, the prætor, should send a letter to Capua to the consuls, with directions that while Hannibal was at a distance, and nothing of any great importance was going on at Capua, one of them, if they thought fit, should come to Rome to elect new magistrates. On the receipt of the letter, the consuls arranged it between themselves, that Claudius should hold the election, and Fulvius remain at Capua. The consuls created by Claudius were Cneius Fulvius Centumalus, and Publius Sulpicius Galba, the son of Servius, who had never exercised any curule magistracy. After this Lucius Cornelius Lentulus, Marcus Cornelius Cethegus, Caius Sulpicius, and Caius Calpurnius Piso, were created prætors. Piso had the city jurisdiction; Sulpicius, Sicily; Cethegus, Apulia; Lentulus, Sardinia. The consuls were continued in command for a year longer.

BOOK XXVI.

Hannibal encamps on the banks of the Anio, within three miles of Rome. Attended by two thousand horsemen, he advances close to the Colline gate to take a view of the walls and situation of the city. On two successive days the hostile armies are hindered from engaging by the severity of the weather. Capua taken by Quintus Fulvius and Appius Claudius, the chief nobles die, voluntarily, by poison. Quintus Fulvius having condemned the principal senators to death, at the moment they are actually tied to the stakes, receives despatches from Rome, commanding him to spare their lives, which he postpones reading until the sentence is executed. Publius Scipio, offering himself for the service, is sent to command in Spain, takes New Carthage in one day. Successes in Sicily. Treaty of friendship with the Ætolians. War with Philip, king of Macedonia, and the Acarnanians.

The consuls, Cneius Fulvius Centumalus and Publius Sulpicius Galba, having entered on their office on the ides of March, assembled the senate in the Capitol, and took the opinion of the fathers on the state of the republic, the manner of conducting the war, and on what related to the provinces and the armies. Quintus Fulvius and Appius Claudius, the consuls of the former year, were continued in command; and the armies which they before had were assigned to them, it being added that they should not withdraw from Capua, which they were besieging, till they had taken it. The Romans were now solicitously intent upon this object, not from resentment so much, which was never juster against any city, as from the consideration that as this city, so celebrated and powerful, had by its defection drawn away several states, so when reduced it would bring back their minds to respect for the former supreme government. Two prætors also of the former year, Marcus Junius and Publius Sempronius, were each continued in command of the two legions which they had under them, the former in Etruria, the latter in Gaul. Marcus Marcellus also was continued in command, that he might, as proconsul, finish the war in Sicily with the army he had there. If he wanted recruits he was to take them from the legions which Publius Cornelius, the proprætor, commanded in Sicily, provided he did not choose any soldier who was of the number of those whom the senate had refused to allow to be discharged, or to return home till the war was put an end to. To Caius Sulpicius, to whose lot Sicily had fallen, the two legions which Publius Cornelius had commanded were assigned, to be recruited from the army of Cneius Fulvius, which had been shamefully beaten, and had experienced a dreadful loss the year before in Apulia. To soldiers of this description the senate had assigned the same period of service as to those who fought at Cannæ; and as an additional mark of ignominy upon both, they were not allowed to winter in towns, or to build huts for wintering within the distance of ten miles from any town. To Lucius Cornelius, in Sardinia, the two legions which Quintus

Mucius had commanded were assigned; if recruits were wanted, the consuls were ordered to enlist them. To Titus Otacilius and Marcus Valerius was allotted the protection of the coasts of Sicily and Greece, with the legions and fleets which they had commanded. The Greek coast had fifty ships with one legion; the Sicilian, a hundred ships with two legions. Twenty-three legions were employed by the Romans in carrying on the war this year by land and sea.

In the beginning of the year, on a letter from Lucius Marcius being laid before the senate, they considered his achievements as most glorious; but the title of honour which he assumed (for though he was neither invested with the command by the order of the people, nor by the direction of the fathers, his letter ran in this form, "The proprætor to the senate") gave offence to a great many. It was considered as an injurious precedent for generals to be chosen by the armies, and for the solemn ceremony of elections, held under auspices, to be transferred to camps and provinces, and (far from the control of the laws and magistrates) to military thoughtlessness. And though some gave it as their opinion, that the sense of the senate should be taken on the matter, yet it was thought more advisable that the discussion should be postponed till after the departure of the horsemen who brought the letter from Marcius. It was resolved, that an answer should be returned respecting the corn and clothing of the army, stating, that the senate would direct its attention to both those matters; but that the letter should not be addressed to Lucius Marcius, proprætor, lest he should consider that as already determined which was the very point they reserved for discussion. After the horsemen were dismissed, it was the first thing the consuls brought before the senate; and the opinions of all to a man coincided, that the plebeian tribunes should be instructed to consult the commons with all possible speed, as to whom they might resolve to send into Spain to take the command of that army which had been under the conduct of Cneius Scipio. The plebeian tribunes were instructed accordingly, and the question was published. But another contest had pre-engaged the minds of the people: Caius Sempronius Blæsus, having brought Cneius Fulvius to trial for the loss of the army in Apulia, harassed him with invectives in the public assemblies: "Many generals," he reiterated, "had by indiscretion and ignorance brought their armies into most perilous situations, but none, save Cneius Fulvius, had corrupted his legions by every species of excess before he betrayed them to the enemy; it might therefore with truth be said, that they were lost before they saw the enemy, and that they were defeated, not by Hannibal, but by their own general. No man, when he gave his vote, took sufficient pains in ascertaining who it was to whom he was intrusting an army. What a difference was there between this man and Tiberius Sempronius! The latter having been intrusted with an army of slaves, had in a short time brought it to pass, by discipline and authority, that not one of them in the field of battle remembered his condition and birth, but they became a protection to our allies and a terror to our enemies. They had snatched, as it were, from the very jaws of Hannibal, and restored to the Roman people, Cumæ, Beneventum, and other towns. But Cneius Fulvius had infected with the vices peculiar to slaves, an army of Roman citizens, of honourable parentage and liberal education; and had thus made them insolent and turbulent among their allies, inefficient and dastardly among their enemies, unable to sustain, not only the charge, but the shout of the Carthaginians. But, by Hercules, it was no wonder that the troops did not stand their ground in the battle, when their general was the first to fly; with him, the greater wonder was that any had fallen at their posts, and that they were not all the companions of Cneius Fulvius in his consternation and his flight. Caius Flaminius, Lucius Paullus, Lucius Posthumius, Cneius and Publius Scipio, had preferred falling in the battle to abandoning their armies when in the power of the enemy. But Cneius Fulvius was almost the only man who returned to Rome to report the annihilation of his army. It was a shameful crime that the army of Cannæ should be transported into Sicily, because they fled from the field of battle, and not be allowed to return till the enemy has quitted Italy; that the same decree should have been lately passed with respect to the legions of Cneius Fulvius; while Cneius Fulvius himself has no punishment inflicted upon him for running away, in a battle brought about by his own indiscretion; that he himself should be permitted to pass his old age in stews and brothels, where he passed his youth, while his troops, whose only crime was that they resembled their general, should be sent away in a manner into banishment, and suffer an ignominious service. So unequally," he said, "was liberty shared at Rome by the rich and the poor, by the ennobled and the common people."

The accused shifted the blame from himself to his soldiers; he said, "that in consequence of their having in the most turbulent manner demanded battle, they were led into the field, not on the day they desired, for it was then evening, but on the following; that they were drawn up at a suitable time and on favourable ground; but either the reputation or the strength of the enemy was such, that they were unable to stand their ground. When they all fled precipitately, he himself also was carried away with the crowd, as had happened to Varro at the battle of Cannæ, and to many other generals. How could he, by his sole resistance, benefit the republic, unless his death would remedy the public disasters? that he was not defeated in consequence of a failure in his provisions; that he had not, from want of caution, been drawn into a disadvantageous position; that he had not been cut off by an ambuscade in consequence of not having explored his route, but had been vanquished by open force, and by arms, in a regular engagement. He had not in his power the minds of his own troops, or those of the enemy. Courage and cowardice were the result of each man's natural constitution." He was twice accused, and the penalty was laid at a fine. On the third accusation, at which witnesses were produced, he was not only overwhelmed with an infinity of disgraceful charges, but a great many asserted on oath, that the flight and panic commenced with the prætor, that the troops being deserted by him, and concluding that the fears of their general were not unfounded, turned their backs; when so strong a feeling of indignation was excited, that the assembly clamorously rejoined that he ought to be tried capitally. This gave rise to a new controversy; for when the tribune, who had twice prosecuted him as for a finable offence, now, on the third occasion, declared that he prosecuted him capitally; the tribunes of the commons being appealed to, said, "they would not prevent their colleague from proceeding, as he was permitted according to the custom of their ancestors, in the manner he himself preferred, whether according to the laws or to custom, until he had obtained judgment against a private individual, convicting him either of a capital or finable offence." Upon this, Sempronius said, that he charged Cneius Fulvius with the crime of treason; and requested Caius Calpurnius, the city prætor, to appoint a day for the comitia. Another ground of hope was then tried by the accused, viz. if his brother, Quintus Fulvius, could be present at his trial, who was at that time flourishing in the fame of his past achievements and in the near expectation of taking Capua. Fulvius wrote to the senate, requesting the favour in terms calculated to excite compassion, in order to save the life of his brother; but the fathers replied, that the interest of the state would not admit of his leaving Capua. Cneius Fulvius, therefore, before the day appointed for the comitia arrived, went into exile to Tarquinii, and the commons resolved that it was a legal exile.

Meanwhile all the strength of the war was directed against Capua. It was, however, more strictly blockaded than besieged. The slaves and populace could neither endure the famine, nor send messengers to Hannibal through guards so closely stationed. A Numidian was at length found, who, on undertaking to make his way with it, was charged with a letter; and going out by night, through the midst of the Roman camp, in order to fulfil his promise, he inspired the Campanians with confidence to try the effect of a sally from every quarter, while they had any strength remaining. In the many encounters which followed, their cavalry were generally successful, but their infantry were beaten: however, it was by no means so joyful to conquer, as it was miserable to be worsted in any respect by a besieged and almost subdued enemy. A plan was at length adopted, by which their deficiency in strength might be compensated by stratagem. Young men were selected from all the legions, who, from the vigour and activity of their bodies, excelled in swiftness; these were supplied with bucklers shorter than those worn by horsemen, and seven javelins each, four feet in length, and pointed with steel in the same manner as the spears used by light-armed troops. The cavalry taking one of these each upon their horses, accustomed them to ride behind them, and to leap down nimbly when the signal was given. When, by daily practice, they appeared to be able to do this in an orderly manner, they advanced into the plain between the camp and the walls, against the cavalry of the Campanians, who stood there prepared for action. As soon as they came within a dart's cast, on a signal given, the light troops leaped down, when a line of infantry formed out of the body of horse suddenly rushed upon the cavalry of the enemy, and discharged their javelins one after another with great rapidity; which being thrown in great numbers upon men and horses indiscriminately, wounded a great many. The sudden and unsuspected nature of the attack, however, occasioned still greater terror; and the cavalry charging them, thus panic-struck, chased them with great slaughter as far as their gates. From that time the Roman cavalry had the superiority; and it was established that there should be velites in the legions. It is said that Quintus Navius was the person who advised the mixing of infantry with cavalry, and that he received honour from the general on that account.

While affairs were in this state at Capua, Hannibal was perplexed between two objects, the gaining possession of the citadel of Tarentum, and the retaining of Capua. His concern for Capua, however, prevailed, on which he saw that the attention of every body, allies and enemies, was fixed; and whose fate would be regarded as a proof of the consequences resulting from defection from the Romans. Leaving therefore, a great part of his baggage among the Bruttians, and all his heavier armed troops, he took with him a body of infantry and cavalry, the best he could select for marching expeditiously, and bent his course into Campania. Rapidly as he marched he was followed by thirty-three elephants. He took up his position in a retired valley behind Mount Tifata, which overhung Capua. Having at his coming taken possession of fort Galatia, the garrison of which he dislodged by force, he then directed his efforts against those who were besieging Capua. Having sent forward messengers to Capua stating the time at which he would attack the Roman camp, in order that they also, having gotten themselves in readiness for a sally, might at the same time pour forth from all their gates, he occasioned the greatest possible terror; for on one side he himself attacked them suddenly, and on the other side all the Campanians sallied forth, both foot and horse, joined by the Carthaginian garrison under the command of Bostar and Hanno. The Romans, lest in so perilous an affair they should leave any part unprotected, by running together to any one place, thus divided their forces: Appius Claudius was opposed to the Campanians; Fulvius to Hannibal; Caius Nero, the proprætor, with the cavalry of the sixth legion, placed himself in the road leading to Suessula; and Caius Fulvius Flaccus, the lieutenant-general, with the allied cavalry, on the side opposite the river Vulturnus. The battle commenced not only with the usual clamour and tumult, but in addition to the din of men, horses, and arms, a multitude of Campanians, unable to bear arms, being distributed along the walls, raised such a shout together with the clangour of brazen vessels, similar to that which is usually made in the dead of night when the moon is eclipsed, that it diverted the attention even of the combatants. Appius easily repulsed the Campanians from the rampart. On the other side Hannibal and the Carthaginians, forming a larger force, pressed hard on Fulvius. There the sixth legion gave way; being repulsed, a cohort of Spaniards with three elephants made their way up to the rampart. They had broken through the centre of the Roman line, and were in a state of anxious and perilous suspense, whether to force their way into the camp, or be cut off from their own army. When Fulvius saw the disorder of the legion, and the danger the camp was in, he exhorted Quintus Navius, and the other principal centurions, to charge the cohort of the enemy which was fighting under the rampart; he said, "that the state of things was most critical; that either they must retire before them, in which case they would burst into the camp with less difficulty than they had experienced in breaking through a dense line of troops, or they must cut them to pieces under the rampart: nor would it require a great effort; for they were few, and cut off from their own troops, and if the line which appeared broken, now while the Romans were dispirited, should turn upon the enemy on both sides, they would become enclosed in the midst, and exposed to a twofold attack." Navius, on hearing these words of the general, snatched the standard of the second company of spearmen from the standard-bearer, and advanced with it against the enemy, threatening that he would throw it into the midst of them unless the soldiers promptly followed him and took part in the fight. He was of gigantic stature, and his arms set him off; the standard also, raised aloft, attracted the gaze both of his countrymen and the enemy. When, however, he had reached the standards of the Spaniards, javelins were poured upon him from all sides, and almost the whole line was turned against him; but neither the number of his enemies nor the force of the weapons could repel the onset of this hero.

Marcus Atilius, the lieutenant-general, also caused the standard of the first company of principes of the same legion to be borne against a cohort of the Spaniards. Lucius Portius Licinus and Titus Popilius, the lieutenant-generals, who had the command of the camp, fought valiantly in defence of the rampart, and slew the elephants while in the very act of crossing it. The carcasses of these filling up the ditch, afforded a passage for the enemy as effectually as if earth had been thrown in, or a bridge erected over it; and a horrid carnage took place amid the carcasses of the elephants which lay prostrate. On the other side of the camp, the Campanians, with the Carthaginian garrison, had by this time been repulsed, and the battle was carried on immediately under the gate of Capua leading to Vulturnus. Nor did the armed men contribute so much in resisting the Romans, who endeavoured to force their way in, as the gate itself, which, being furnished with ballistas and scorpions, kept the enemy at bay by the missiles discharged from it. The ardour of the Romans was also clamped by the general, Appius Claudius, receiving a wound; he was struck by a javelin in the upper part of his breast, beneath the left shoulder, while encouraging his men before the front line. A great number, however, of the enemy were slain before the gate, and the rest were driven in disorder into the city. When Hannibal saw the destruction of the cohort of Spaniards, and that the camp of the enemy was defended with the utmost vigour, giving up the assault, he began to withdraw his standards, making his infantry face about, but throwing out his cavalry in the rear lest the enemy should pursue them closely. The ardour of the legions to pursue the enemy was excessive, but Flaccus ordered a retreat to be sounded, considering that enough had been achieved to convince the Campanians, and Hannibal himself, how unable he was to afford them protection. Some who have undertaken to give accounts of this battle, record that eight thousand of the army of Hannibal, and three thousand Campanians, were slain; that fifteen military standards were taken from the Carthaginians, and eighteen from the Campanians. In other authors I find the battle to have been by no means so important, and that there was more of panic than fighting; that a party of Numidians and Spaniards suddenly bursting into the Roman camp with some elephants, the elephants, as they made their way through the midst of the camp, threw down their tents with a great noise, and caused the beasts of burden to break their halters and run away. That in addition to the confusion occasioned, a stratagem was employed; Hannibal having sent in some persons acquainted with the Latin language, for he had some such with him, who might command the soldiers, in the name of the consuls, to escape every one as fast as he could to the neighbouring mountains, since the camp was lost; but that the imposture was soon discovered, and frustrated with a great slaughter of the enemy; that the elephants were driven out of the camp by fire. However commenced, and however terminated, this was the last battle which was fought before the surrender of Capua. Seppius Lesius was Medixtuticus, or chief magistrate of Capua, that year, a man of obscure origin and slender fortune. It is reported that his mother, when formerly expiating a prodigy which had occurred in the family in behalf of this boy, who was an orphan, received an answer from the aruspex, stating, that "the highest office would come to him;" and that not recognising, at Capua, any ground for such a hope, exclaimed, "the state of the Campanians must be desperate indeed, when the highest office shall come to my son." But even this expression, in which the response was turned into ridicule, turned to be true, for those persons whose birth allowed them to aspire to high offices, refusing to accept them when the city was oppressed by sword and famine, and when all hope was lost, Lesius, who complained that Capua was deserted and betrayed by its nobles, accepted the office of chief magistrate, being the last Campanian who held it.

But Hannibal, when he saw that the enemy could not be drawn into another engagement, nor a passage be forced through their camp into Capua, resolved to remove his camp from that place and leave the attempt unaccomplished, fearful lest the new consuls might cut off his supplies of provision. While anxiously deliberating on the point to which he should next direct his course, an impulse suddenly entered his mind to make an attack on Rome, the very source of the war. That the opportunity of accomplishing this ever coveted object, which occurred after the battle of Cannæ, had been neglected, and was generally censured by others, he himself did not deny. He thought that there was some hope that he might be able to get possession of some part of the city, in consequence of the panic and confusion which his unexpected approach would occasion, and that if Rome were in danger, either both the Roman generals, or at least one of them, would immediately leave Capua; and if they divided their forces, both generals being thus rendered weaker, would afford a favourable opportunity either to himself or the Campanians of gaining some advantage. One consideration only disquieted him, and that was, lest on his departure the Campanians should immediately surrender. By means of presents he induced a Numidian, who was ready to attempt any thing, however daring, to take charge of a letter; and, entering the Roman camp under the disguise of a deserter, to pass out privately on the other side and go to Capua. As to the letter, it was full of encouragement. It stated, that "his departure, which would be beneficial to them, would have the effect of drawing off the Roman generals and armies from the siege of Capua to the defence of Rome. That they must not allow their spirits to sink; that by a few days' patience they would rid themselves entirely of the siege." He then ordered the ships on the Vulturnus to be seized, and rowed up to the fort which he had before erected for his protection. And when he was informed that there were as many as were necessary to convey his army across in one night, after providing a stock of provisions for ten days, he led his legions down to the river by night, and passed them over before daylight.

Fulvius Flaccus, who had discovered from deserters that this would happen, before it took place, having written to Rome to the senate to apprize them of it, men's minds were variously affected by it according to the disposition of each. As might be expected in so alarming an emergency, the senate was immediately assembled, when Publius Cornelius, surnamed Asina, was for recalling all the generals and armies from every part of Italy to protect the city, disregarding Capua and every other concern. Fabius Maximus thought that it would be highly disgraceful to retire from Capua, and allow themselves to be terrified and driven about at the nod and menaces of Hannibal. "Was it probable that he, who, though victorious at Cannæ, nevertheless dared not approach the city, now, after having been repulsed from Capua, had conceived hopes of making himself master of Rome? It was not to besiege Rome, but to raise the siege of Capua that he was coming. Jupiter, the witness of treaties violated by Hannibal, and the other deities, would defend the city of Rome with that army which is now at the city." To these opposite opinions, that of Publius Valerius Flaccus, which recommended a middle course, was preferred. Regardful of both objects, he thought that a letter should be written to the generals at Capua, informing them of the force they had at the city for its protection, and stating, that as to the number of forces which Hannibal was bringing with him, or how large an army was necessary to carry on the siege of Capua, they themselves knew. If one of the generals and a part of the army could be sent to Rome, and at the same time Capua could be efficiently besieged by the remaining general and army, that then Claudius and Fulvius should settle between themselves which should continue the siege of Capua, and which should come to Rome to protect their capital from being besieged. This decree of the senate having been conveyed to Capua, Quintus Fulvius, the proconsul, who was to go to Rome, as his colleague was ill from his wound, crossed the Vulturnus with a body of troops, to the number of fifteen thousand infantry and a thousand horse, selected from the three armies. Then having ascertained that Hannibal intended to proceed along the Latin road, he sent persons before him to the towns on and near the Appian way, Setia, Cora, and Lanuvium, with directions that they should not only have provisions ready in their towns, but should bring them down to the road from the fields which lay out of the way, and that they should draw together into their towns troops for their defence, in order that each state might be under its own protection.

On the day he crossed the Vulturnus, Hannibal pitched his camp at a small distance from the river. The next day, passing by Cales, he reached the Sidicinian territory, and having spent a day there in devastating the country, he led his troops along the Latin way through the territory of Suessa, Allifæ, and Casinum. Under the walls of Casinum he remained encamped for two days, ravaging the country all around; thence passing by Interamna and Aquinum, he came into the Fregellan territory, to the river Liris, where he found the bridge broken down by the Fregellans in order to impede his progress. Fulvius also was detained at the Vulturnus, in consequence of Hannibal's having burnt the ships, and the difficulty he had in procuring rafts to convey his troops across that river from the great scarcity of materials. The army having been conveyed across by rafts, the remainder of the march of Fulvius was uninterrupted, a liberal supply of provisions having been prepared for him, not only in all the towns, but also on the sides of the road; while his men, who were all activity, exhorted each other to quicken their pace, remembering that they were going to defend their country. A messenger from Fregella, who had travelled a day and a night without intermission, arriving at Rome, caused the greatest consternation; and the whole city was thrown into a state of alarm by the running up and down of persons who made vague additions to what they heard, and thus increased the confusion which the original intelligence created. The lamentations of women were not only heard from private houses, but the matrons from every quarter, rushing into the public streets, ran up and down around the shrines of the gods, sweeping the altars with their dishevelled hair, throwing themselves upon their knees and stretching their uplifted hands to heaven and the gods, imploring them to rescue the city of Rome out of the hands of their enemies, and preserve the Roman mothers and their children from harm. The senate sat in the forum near the magistrates, in case they should wish to consult them. Some were receiving orders and departing to their own department of duty; others were offering themselves wherever there might be occasion for their aid. Troops were posted in the citadel, in the Capitol, upon the walls around the city, and also on the Alban mount, and the fort of Æsula. During this confusion, intelligence was brought that Quintus Fulvius, the proconsul, had set out from Capua with an army; when the senate decreed that Quintus Fulvius should have equal authority with the consuls, lest on entering the city his power should cease. Hannibal, having most destructively ravaged the Fregellan territory, on account of the bridge having been broken down, came into the territory of the Lavici, passing through those of Frusino, Ferentinum, and Anagnia; thence passing through Algidum he directed his course to Tusculum; but not being received within the walls, he went down to the right below Tusculum to Gabii; and marching his army down thence into the territory of the Pupinian tribe, he pitched his camp eight miles from the city. The nearer the enemy came, the greater was the number of fugitives slain by the Numidians who preceded him, and the greater the number of prisoners made of every rank and age.

During this confusion, Fulvius Flaccus entered the city with his troops through the Capuan gate, passed through the midst of the city, and through Carinæ, to Esquiliæ; and going out thence, pitched his camp between the Esquiline and Colline gates. The plebeian ædiles brought a supply of provisions there. The consuls and the senate came to the camp, and a consultation was held on the state of the republic. It was resolved that the consuls should encamp in the neighbourhood of the Colline and Esquiline gates; that Caius Calpurnius, the city prætor, should have the command of the Capitol and the citadel; and that a full senate should be continually assembled in the forum, in case it should be necessary to consult them amidst such sudden emergencies. Meanwhile, Hannibal advanced his camp to the Anio, three miles from the city, and fixing his position there, he advanced with two thousand horse from the Colline gate as far as the temple of Hercules, and riding up, took as near a view as he could of the walls and site of the city. Flaccus, indignant that he should do this so freely, and so much at his ease, sent out a party of cavalry, with orders to displace and drive back to their camp the cavalry of the enemy. After the fight had begun, the consuls ordered the Numidian deserters who were on the Aventine, to the number of twelve hundred, to march through the midst of the city to the Esquiliæ, judging that no troops were better calculated to fight among the hollows, the garden walls, and tombs, or in the enclosed roads which were on all sides. But some persons, seeing them from the citadel and Capitol as they filed off on horseback down the Publician hill, cried out that the Aventine was taken. This circumstance occasioned such confusion and terror, that if the Carthaginian camp had not been without the city, the whole multitude, such was their alarm, would have rushed out. They then fled for refuge into their houses and upon the roofs, where they threw stones and weapons on their own soldiers as they passed along the streets, taking them for enemies. Nor could the tumult be repressed, or the mistake explained, as the streets were thronged with crowds of rustics and cattle, which the sudden alarm had driven into the city. The battle between the cavalry was successful, and the enemy were driven away; and as it was necessary to repress the tumults which were arising in several quarters without any cause, it was resolved that all who had been dictators, consuls, or censors, should be invested with authority till such time as the enemy had retired from the walls. During the remainder of the day and the following night, several tumults arose without any foundation, and were repressed.

The next day Hannibal, crossing the Anio, drew out all his forces in order of battle; nor did Flaccus and the consuls decline to fight. When the troops on both sides were drawn up to try the issue of a battle, in which Rome was to be the prize of the victors, a violent shower of rain mingled with hail created such disorder in both the lines, that the troops, scarcely able to hold their arms, retired to their camps, less through fear of the enemy than of any thing else. On the following day, likewise, a similar tempest separated the armies marshalled on the same ground; but after they had retired to their camps the weather became wonderfully serene and tranquil. The Carthaginians considered this circumstance as a Divine interposition, and it is reported that Hannibal was heard to say, "That sometimes he wanted the will to make himself master of Rome, at other times the opportunity." Two other circumstances also, one inconsiderable, the other important, diminished his hopes. The important one was, that while he lay with his armed troops near the walls of the city, he was informed that troops had marched out of it with colours flying, as a reinforcement for Spain; that of less importance was, that he was informed by one of his prisoners, that the very ground on which his camp stood was sold at this very time, without any diminution in its price. Indeed, so great an insult and indignity did it appear to him that a purchaser should be found at Rome for the very soil which he held and possessed by right of conquest, that he immediately called a crier, and ordered that the silversmiths' shops, which at that time stood around the Roman forum, should be put up for sale. Induced by these circumstances he retired to the river Tutia, six miles from the city, whence he proceeded to the grove of Feronia, where was a temple at that time celebrated for its riches. The Capenatians and other states in the neighbourhood, by bringing here their first-fruits and other offerings according to their abilities, kept it decorated with abundance of gold and silver. Of all these offerings the temple was now despoiled. After the departure of Hannibal, vast heaps of brass were found there, as the soldiers, from a religious feeling, had thrown in pieces of uncoined brass. The spoliation of this temple is undoubted by historians; but Cælius asserts, that Hannibal, in his progress to Rome, turned out of his way to it from Eretum. According to him his route commenced with Amiternum, Cætilii, and Reate. He came from Campania into Samnium, and thence into Pelignia; then passing the town Sulmio, he entered the territory of the Marrucini; thence through the Alban territory he came to that of the Marsi, from which he came to Amiternum and the village of Foruli. Nor is this diversity of opinion a proof that the traces of so great an army could be confounded in the lapse of so brief a period. That he went that way is evident. The only question is, whether he took this route to the city, or returned by it from the city into Campania?

With regard to Capua, Hannibal did not evince such obstinate perseverance in raising the siege of it as the Romans did in pressing it; for quitting Lucania, he came into the Bruttian territory, and marched to the strait and Rhegium with such rapidity, that he was very near taking the place by surprise, in consequence of the suddenness of his arrival. Though the siege had been urged with undiminished vigour during his absence, yet Capua felt the return of Flaccus; and astonishment was excited that Hannibal had not returned with him. Afterwards they learnt, by conversations, that they were abandoned and deserted, and that the Carthaginians had given up all hopes of retaining Capua. In addition to this a proclamation was made by the proconsul, agreeably to a decree of the senate, and published among the enemy, that any Campanian citizen who came over before a stated day should be indemnified. No one, however, came over, as they were held together by fear more than fidelity; for the crimes they had committed during their revolt were too great to admit of pardon. As none of them passed over to the enemy, consulting their own individual interest, so no measure of safety was taken with regard to the general body. The nobility had deserted the state, nor could they be induced to meet in the senate, while the office of chief magistrate was filled by a man who had not derived honour to himself from his office, but stripped the office of its influence and authority by his own unworthiness. Now none of the nobles made their appearance even in the forum, or any public place, but shut themselves up in their houses, in daily expectation of the downfall of their city, and their own destruction together. The chief responsibility in every thing devolved upon Bostar and Hanno, the præfects of the Punic garrison, who were anxious on account of their own danger, and not that of their allies. They addressed a letter to Hannibal, in terms, not only of freedom, but severity, charging him with "delivering, not only Capua into the hands of the enemy, but with treacherously abandoning themselves also, and their troops, to every species of torture;" they told him "he had gone off to the Bruttians, in order to get out of the way, as it were, lest Capua should be taken before his eyes; while, by Hercules, the Romans, on the contrary, could not be drawn off from the siege of Capua, even by an attack upon their city. So much more constant were the Romans in their enmity than the Carthaginians in their friendship. If he would return to Capua and direct the whole operations of the war to that point, that both themselves and the Campanians would be prepared for a sally. That they had crossed the Alps not to carry on a war with the people of Rhegium nor Tarentum. That where the Roman legions were, there the armies of the Carthaginians ought to be. Thus it was that victories had been gained at Cannæ and Trasimenus; by uniting, by pitching their camp close to that of the enemy, by trying their fortune." A letter to this effect was given to some Numidians who had already engaged to render their services for a stated reward. These men came into the camp to Flaccus under pretence of being deserters, with the intention of quitting it by seizing an opportunity, and the famine, which had so long existed at Capua, afforded a pretext for desertion which no one could suspect. But a Campanian woman, the paramour of one of the deserters, unexpectedly entered the camp, and informed the Roman general that the Numidians had come over according to a preconcerted plan of treachery, and were the bearers of letters to Hannibal; that she was prepared to convict one of the party of that fact, as he had discovered it to her. On being brought forward, he at first pretended, with considerable pertinacity, that he did not know the woman; but afterwards, gradually succumbing to the force of truth, when he saw the instruments of torture called for and preparing, he confessed that it was so. The letters were produced, and a discovery was made of an additional fact, before concealed, that other Numidians were strolling about in the Roman camp, under pretence of being deserters. Above seventy of these were arrested, and, with the late deserters, scourged with rods; and after their hands had been cut off, were driven back to Capua. The sight of so severe a punishment broke the spirit of the Campanians.

The people, rushing in crowds to the senate-house, compelled Lesius to assemble a senate, and openly threatened the nobles, who had now for a long time absented themselves from the public deliberations, that unless they attended the meeting of the senate, they would go round to their houses and drag them all before the public by force. The fear of this procured the magistrate a full senate. Here, while the rest contended for sending ambassadors to the Roman generals, Vibius Virrius, who had been the instigator of the revolt from the Romans, on being asked his opinion, observed, that "those persons who spoke of sending ambassadors, and of peace, and a surrender, did not bear in mind either what they would do if they had the Romans in their power, or what they themselves must expect to suffer. What! do you think," says he, "that your surrender will be like that in which formerly we placed ourselves and every thing belonging to us at the disposal of the Romans, in order that we might obtain assistance from them against the Samnites? Have you already forgotten at what a juncture we revolted from the Romans, and what were their circumstances? Have you forgotten how at the time of the revolt we put to death, with torture and indignity, their garrison, which might have been sent out? How often, and with determined hostility, we have sallied out against them when besieging us, and assaulted their camp? How we invited Hannibal to come and cut them off? And how most recently we sent him hence to lay siege to Rome? But come, retrace on the other hand what they have done in hostility towards us, that you may learn therefrom what you have to hope for. When a foreign enemy was in Italy, and that enemy Hannibal; when the flame of war was kindled in every quarter; disregarding every other object, disregarding even Hannibal himself, they sent two consuls with two consular armies to lay siege to Capua. This is the second year, that, surrounded with lines and shut up within our walls, they consume us by famine, having suffered in like manner with ourselves the extremest dangers and the severest hardships, having frequently had their troops slain near their rampart and trenches, and at last having been almost deprived of their camp. But I pass over these matters. It has been usual, even from of old, to suffer dangers and hardships in besieging an enemy's city. The following is a proof of their animosity and bitter hatred. Hannibal assaulted their camp with an immense force of horse and foot, and took a part of it. By so great a danger they were not in the least diverted from the siege. Crossing the Vulturnus, he laid waste the territory of Cales with fire. Such calamities inflicted upon their allies had no effect in calling them off. He ordered his troops to march in hostile array to the very city of Rome. They despised the tempest which threatened them in this case also. Crossing the Anio, he pitched his camp three miles from the city, and lastly, came up to the very walls and gates. He gave them to understand that he would take their city from them, unless they gave up Capua. But they did not give it up. Wild beasts, impelled by headlong fury and rage, you may divert from their object to bring assistance to those belonging to them, if you attempt to approach their dens and their young. The Romans could not be diverted from Capua by the blockade of Rome, by their wives and children, whose lamentations could almost be heard from this place, by their altars, their hearths, the temples of their gods, and the sepulchres of their ancestors profaned and violated. So great was their avidity to bring us to punishment, so insatiable their thirst for drinking our blood. Nor, perhaps, without reason. We too would have done the same had the opportunity been afforded us. Since, however, the gods have thought proper to determine it otherwise, though I ought not to shrink from death, while I am free, while I am master of myself, I have it in my power, by a death not only honourable but mild, to escape the tortures and indignities which the enemy hope to inflict upon me. I will not see Appius Claudius and Quintus Fulvius in the pride and insolence of victory, nor will I be dragged in chains through Rome as a spectacle in a triumph, that afterwards in a dungeon, or tied to a stake, after my back has been lacerated with stripes, I may place my neck under a Roman axe. I will neither see my native city demolished and burnt, nor the matrons, virgins, and free-born youths of Campania dragged to constupration. Alba, from which they themselves derived their origin, they demolished from her foundations, that there might remain no trace of their rise and extraction, much less can I believe they will spare Capua, towards which they bear a more rancorous hatred than towards Carthage. For such of you, therefore, as have a mind to yield to fate, before they behold such horrors, a banquet is furnished and prepared at my house. When satiated with wine and food, the same cup which shall have been given to me shall be handed round to them. That potion will rescue our bodies from torture, our minds from insult, our eyes and ears from seeing and hearing all those cruelties and indignities which await the vanquished. There will be persons in readiness who will throw our lifeless bodies upon a large pile kindled in the court-yard of the house. This is the only free and honourable way to death. Our very enemies will admire our courage, and Hannibal will learn that those whom he deserted and betrayed were brave allies."

More of those who heard this speech of Virrius approved of the proposal contained in it, than had strength of mind to execute what they approved. The greater part of the senate being not without hopes that the Romans, whose clemency they had frequently had proof of in many wars, would be exorable by them also, decreed and sent ambassadors to surrender Capua to the Romans. About twenty-seven senators, following Vibius Virrius to his home, partook of the banquet with him; and after having, as far as they could, withdrawn their minds, by means of wine, from the perception of the impending evil, all took the poison. They then rose from the banquet, after giving each other their right hands, and taking a last embrace, mingling their tears for their own and their country's fate; some of them remained, that they might be burned upon the same pile, and the rest retired to their homes. Their veins being filled in consequence of what they had eaten, and the wine they drank, rendered the poison less efficacious in expediting death; and accordingly, though the greater part of them languished the whole of that night and part of the following day, all of them, however, breathed their last before the gates were opened to the enemy. The following day the gate of Jupiter, which faced the Roman camp, was opened by order of the proconsul, when one legion and two squadrons of allies marched in at it, under the command of Caius Fulvius, lieutenant-general. When he had taken care that all the arms and weapons to be found in Capua should be brought to him; having placed guards at all the gates to prevent any one's going or being sent out, he seized the Carthaginian garrison, and ordered the Campanian senators to go into the camp to the Roman generals. On their arrival they were all immediately thrown into chains, and ordered to lay before the quæstor an account of all the gold and silver they had. There were seventy pounds of gold, and three thousand two hundred of silver. Twenty-five of the senators were sent to Cales, to be kept in custody, and twenty-eight to Teanum; these being the persons by whose advice principally it appeared that the revolt from the Romans had taken place.

Fulvius and Claudius were far from being agreed as to the punishment of the Campanian senators. Claudius was disposed to grant their prayer for pardon, but Fulvius was more inclined to severity. Appius, therefore, was for referring the entire disposal of the question to the Roman senate. He thought it right also, that the fathers should have the opportunity of asking them whether any of the Latin confederates, or of the municipal towns, had taken part in these designs, and whether they had derived any assistance from them in the war. Fulvius, on the contrary, urged that they ought by no means to run the hazard of having the minds of faithful allies harassed by doubtful accusations, and subjected to informers who never cared at all what they did or what they said. For this reason he said that he should prevent and put a stop to any such inquiry. After this conversation they separated; Appius not doubting but that his colleague, though he expressed himself so warmly, would, nevertheless, wait for a letter from Rome, in an affair of such magnitude. But Fulvius, fearing that his designs would be frustrated by that very means, dismissed his council, and commanded the military tribunes and the præfects of the allies to give notice to two thousand chosen horsemen to be in readiness at the third trumpet. Setting out for Teanum with this body of cavalry, he entered the gate at break of day, and proceeded direct to the forum; and a number of people having flocked together at the first entrance of the horsemen, he ordered the Sidicinian magistrate to be summoned; when he desired him to bring forth the Campanians whom he had in custody. These were all accordingly brought forth, scourged, and beheaded. He then proceeded at full speed to Cales; where, when he had taken his seat on the tribunal, and while the Campanians, who had been brought forth, were being bound to the stake, an express arrived from Rome, and delivered to him a letter from Caius Calpurnius, the prætor, and a decree of the senate. A murmur immediately pervaded the whole assembly, beginning at the tribunal, that the entire question respecting the Campanians was referred to the decision of the fathers, and Fulvius, suspecting this to be the case, took the letter, and without opening it put it into his bosom, and then commanded the crier to order the lictor to do his duty. Thus punishment was inflicted on those also who were at Cales. The letter was then read, together with the decree of the senate, when it was too late to prevent the business which was already executed, and which had been accelerated by every means to prevent its being obstructed. When Fulvius was now rising from his seat, Jubellius Taurea, a Campanian making his way through the middle of the city and the crowd, called upon him by name, and when Flaccus, who wondered greatly what he could want, had resumed his seat, he said, "Order me also to be put to death, that you may be able to boast, that a much braver man than yourself has been put to death by you." Fulvius at first said, that the man could not certainly be in his senses, then, that he was restrained by a decree of the senate, even though he might wish it, when Jubellius exclaimed "Since, after the capture of my country, and the loss of my relations and friends, after having killed, with my own hand, my wife and children to prevent their suffering any indignity, I am not allowed even to die in the same manner as these my countrymen, let a rescue be sought in courage from this hated existence." So saying, he thrust a sword, which he had concealed under his garment, right through his breast, and fell lifeless at the general's feet.

Because not only what related to the punishment of the Campanians, but most of the other particulars of this affair, were transacted according to the judgment of Flaccus alone, some authors affirm that Appius Claudius died about the time of the surrender of Capua, and that this same Taurea neither came to Cales voluntarily nor died by his own hand, but that while he was being tied to the stake among the rest, Flaccus, who could not distinctly hear what he vociferated from the noise which was made, ordered silence, when Taurea said the things which have been before related "that he, a man of the greatest courage, was being put to death by one who was by no means his equal in respect to valour." That immediately on his saying this, the herald, by command of the proconsul, pronounced this order. "Lictor, apply the rods to this man of courage, and execute the law upon him first." Some authors also relate, that he read the decree of the senate before he beheaded them, but that as there was a clause in it, to the effect, that if he thought proper he should refer the entire question to the senate, he construed it that the decision as to what was most for the interest of the state was left to himself. He returned from Cales to Capua. Atella and Calatia surrendered themselves, and were received. Here also the principal promoters of the revolt were punished. Thus eighty principal members of the senate were put to death, and about three hundred of the Campanian nobles thrown into prison. The rest were distributed through the several cities of the Latin confederacy, to be kept in custody, where they perished in various ways. The rest of the Campanian citizens were sold. The remaining subject of deliberation related to the city and its territory. Some were of opinion that a city so eminently powerful, so near, and so hostile, ought to be demolished. But immediate utility prevailed, for on account of the land, which was evidently superior to any in Italy from the variety and exuberance of its produce, the city was preserved that it might become a settlement of husbandmen. For the purpose of peopling the city, a number of sojourners, freed-men, dealers, and artificers, were retained, but all the land and buildings were made the property of the Roman state. It was resolved, however, that Capua should only be inhabited and peopled as a city, that there should be no body-politic, nor assembly of the senate or people, nor magistrates. For it was thought that a multitude not possessing any public council, without a ruling power, and unconnected by the participation of any common rights, would be incapable of combination. They resolved to send a præfect annually from Rome to administer justice. Thus were matters adjusted at Capua, upon a plan in every respect worthy of commendation. Punishment was inflicted upon the most guilty with rigour and despatch, the populace dispersed beyond all hope of return, no rage vented in fire and ruins upon the unoffending houses and walls. Together also with advantage, a reputation for clemency was obtained among the allies, by the preservation of a city of the greatest celebrity and opulence, the demolition of which, all Campania, and all the people dwelling in the neighbourhood of Campania, would have bewailed, while their enemies were compelled to admit the ability of the Romans to punish their faithless allies, and how little assistance could be derived from Hannibal towards the defence of those whom he had taken under his protection.

The Roman senate having gone through every thing which required their attention relative to Capua, decreed to Caius Nero six thousand foot and three hundred horse, whichever he should himself choose out of those two legions which he had commanded at Capua, with an equal number of infantry, and eight hundred horse of the Latin confederacy. This army Nero embarked at Puteoli, and conveyed over into Spain. Having arrived at Tarraco with his ships, landed his troops, hauled his ships ashore, and armed his mariners to augment his numbers, he proceeded to the river Iberus, and received the army from Titus Fonteius and Lucius Marcius. He then marched towards the enemy. Hasdrubal, son of Hamilcar, was encamped at the black stones in Ausetania, a place situated between the towns Illiturgi and Mentissa. The entrance of this defile Nero seized, and Hasdrubal, to prevent his being shut up in it, sent a herald to engage that, if he were allowed to depart thence, he would convey the whole of his army out of Spain. The Roman general having received this proposition gladly, Hasdrubal requested the next day for a conference, when the Romans might draw up conditions relative to the surrender of the citadels of the towns, and the appointment of a day on which the garrisons might be withdrawn, and the Carthaginians might remove every thing belonging to them without imposition. Having obtained his point in this respect, Hasdrubal gave orders that as soon as it was dark, and during the whole of the night afterwards, the heaviest part of his force should get out of the defile by whatever way they could. The strictest care was taken that many should not go out that night, that the very fewness of their numbers might both be more adapted to elude the notice of the enemy from their silence, and to an escape through confined and rugged paths. Next day they met for the conference; but that day having been spent, on purpose, in speaking and writing about a variety of subjects, which were not to this point, the conference was put off to the next day. The addition of the following night gave him time to send still more out; nor was the business concluded the next day. Thus several days were spent in openly discussing conditions, and as many nights in privately sending the Carthaginian troops out of their camp; and after the greater part of the army had been sent out, he did not even keep to those terms which he had himself proposed; and his sincerity decreasing with his fears, they became less and less agreed. By this time nearly all the infantry had cleared the defile, when at daybreak a dense mist enveloped the whole defile and the neighbouring plains; which Hasdrubal perceiving, sent to Nero to put off the conference to the following day, as the Carthaginians held that day sacred from the transaction of any serious business. Not even then was the cheat suspected. Hasdrubal having gained the indulgence he sought for that day also, immediately quitted his camp with his cavalry and elephants, and without creating any alarm escaped to a place of safety. About the fourth hour the mist, being dispelled by the sun, left the atmosphere clear, when the Romans saw that the camp of the enemy was deserted. Then at length Claudius, recognising the Carthaginian perfidy, and perceiving that he had been caught by trickery, immediately began to pursue the enemy as they moved off, prepared to give battle; but they declined fighting. Some skirmishes, however, took place between the rear of the Carthaginians and the advanced guard of the Romans.

During the time in which these events occurred, neither did those states of Spain which had revolted after the defeat that was sustained, return to the Romans, nor did any others desert them. At Rome, the attention of the senate and people, after the recovery of Capua, was not fixed in a greater degree upon Italy than upon Spain. They resolved that the army there should be augmented and a general sent. They were not, however, so clear as to the person whom they should send, as that, where two generals had fallen within the space of thirty days, he who was to supply the place of them should be selected with unusual care. Some naming one person, and others another, they at length came to the resolution that the people should assemble for the purpose of electing a proconsul for Spain, and the consuls fixed a day for the election. At first they waited in expectation that those persons who might think themselves qualified for so momentous a command would give in their names, but this expectation being disappointed, their grief was renewed for the calamity they had suffered, and then regret for the generals they had lost. The people thus afflicted, and almost at their wits' end, came down, however, to the Campus Martius on the day of the election, where, turning towards the magistrates, they looked round at the countenances of their most eminent men, who were earnestly gazing at each other, and murmured bitterly, that their affairs were in so ruinous a state, and the condition of the commonwealth so desperate, that no one dared undertake the command in Spain. When suddenly Publius Cornelius, son of Publius who had fallen in Spain, who was about twenty-four years of age, declaring himself a candidate, took his station on an eminence from which he could be seen by all. The eyes of the whole assembly were directed towards him, and by acclamations and expressions of approbation, a prosperous and happy command were at once augured to him. Orders were then given that they should proceed to vote, when not only every century, but every individual to a man, decided that Publius Scipio should be invested with the command in Spain. But after the business had been concluded, and the ardour and impetuosity of their zeal had subsided, a sudden silence ensued, and a secret reflection on what they had done, whether their partiality had not got the better of their judgment? They chiefly regretted his youth, but some were terrified at the fortune which attended his house and his name, for while the two families to which he belonged were in mourning, he was going into a province where he must carry on his operations between the tombs of his father and his uncle.

Perceiving the solicitude and anxiety which people felt, after performing the business with so much ardour, he summoned an assembly, in which he discoursed in so noble and high minded a manner, on his years, the command intrusted to him, and the war which he had to carry on, as to rekindle and renew the ardour which had subsided, and inspire the people with more confident hopes than the reliance placed on human professions, or reasoning on the promising appearance of affairs, usually engenders. For Scipio was not only deserving of admiration for his real virtues, but also for his peculiar address in displaying them, to which he had been formed from his earliest years;—effecting many things with the multitude, either by feigning nocturnal visions or as with a mind divinely inspired; whether it was that he was himself, too, endued with a superstitious turn of mind, or that they might execute his commands and adopt his plans without hesitation, as if they proceeded from the responses of an oracle. With the intention of preparing men's minds for this from the beginning, he never at any time from his first assumption of the manly gown transacted any business, public or private, without first going to the Capitol, entering the temple, and taking his seat there; where he generally passed a considerable time in secret and alone. This practice, which was adhered to through the whole of his life, occasioned in some persons a belief in a notion which generally prevailed, whether designedly or undesignedly propagated, that he was a man of divine extraction; and revived a report equally absurd and fabulous with that formerly spread respecting Alexander the Great, that he was begotten by a huge serpent, whose monstrous form was frequently observed in the bedchamber of his mother, but which, on any one's coming in, suddenly unfolding his coils, glided out of sight. The belief in these miraculous accounts was never ridiculed by him, but rather increased by his address; neither positively denying any such thing nor openly affirming it. There were also many other things, some real and others counterfeit, which exceeded in the case of this young man the usual measure of human admiration, in reliance on which the state intrusted him with an affair of so much difficulty, and with so important a command, at an age by no means ripe for it. To the forces in Spain, consisting of the remains of the old army, and those which had been conveyed over from Puteoli by Claudius Nero, ten thousand infantry and a thousand horse were added; and Marcus Junius Silanus, the proprætor, was sent to assist in the management of affairs. Thus with a fleet of thirty ships, all of which were quinqueremes, he set sail from the mouth of the Tiber, and coasting along the shore of the Tuscan Sea, the Alps, and the Gallic Gulf, and then doubling the promontory of the Pyrenees, landed his troops at Emporiæ, a Greek city, which also derived its origin from Phocaea. Ordering his ships to attend him, he marched by land to Tarraco; where he held a congress of deputies from all the allies; for embassies had poured forth from every province on the news of his arrival. Here he ordered his ships to be hauled on shore, having sent back the four triremes of the Massilians which had, in compliment to him, attended him from their home. After that, he began to give answers to the embassies of the several states, which had been in suspense on account of the many vicissitudes of the war; and this with so great dignity, arising from the great confidence he had in his own talents, that no presumptuous expression ever escaped him; and in every thing he said there appeared at once the greatest majesty and sincerity.

Setting out from Tarraco, he visited the states of his allies and the winter quarters of his army; and bestowed the highest commendations upon the soldiers, because, though they had received two such disastrous blows in succession, they had retained possession of the province, and not allowing the enemy to reap any advantage from their successes, had excluded them entirely from the territory on this side of the Iberus, and honourably protected their allies. Marcius he kept with him, and treated him with such respect, that it was perfectly evident there was nothing he feared less than lest any one should stand in the way of his own glory. Silanus then took the place of Nero, and the fresh troops were led into winter quarters. Scipio having in good time visited every place where his presence was necessary, and completed every thing which was to be done, returned to Tarraco. The reputation of Scipio among his enemies was not inferior to that which he enjoyed among his allies and countrymen. They felt also a kind of presentiment of what was to come, which occasioned the greater apprehension, the less they could account for their fears, which had arisen without any cause. They had retired to their winter quarters in different directions. Hasdrubal, son of Gisgo, had gone quite to the ocean and Gades; Mago into the midland parts chiefly above the forest of Castulo; Hasdrubal, son of Hamilcar, wintered in the neighbourhood of Saguntum, close upon the Iberus. At the close of the summer in which Capua was recovered and Scipio entered Spain, a Carthaginian fleet, which had been fetched from Sicily to Tarentum, to cut off the supplies of the Roman garrison in the citadel of that place, had blocked up all the approaches to the citadel from the sea; but by lying there too long, they caused a greater scarcity of provisions to their friends than to their enemies. For so much corn could not be brought in for the townsmen, along the coasts which were friendly to them, and through the ports which were kept open through the protection afforded by the Carthaginian fleet, as the fleet itself consumed, which had on board a crowd made up of every description of persons. So that the garrison of the citadel, which was small in number, could be supported from the stock they had previously laid in without importing any, while that which they imported was not sufficient for the supply of the Tarentines and the fleet. At length the fleet was sent away with greater satisfaction than it was received. The scarcity of provisions, however, was not much relieved by it; because when the protection by sea was removed corn could not be brought in.

At the close of the same summer, Marcus Marcellus arriving at the city from his province of Sicily, an audience of the senate was given him by Caius Calpurnius, the prætor, in the temple of Bellona. Here, after discoursing on the services he had performed, and complaining in gentle terms, not on his own account more than that of his soldiers, that after having completely reduced the province, he had not been allowed to bring home his army, he requested that he might be allowed to enter the city in triumph; this he did not obtain. A long debate took place on the question, whether it was less consistent to deny a triumph on his return to him, in whose name, when absent, a supplication had been decreed and honours paid to the immortal gods, for successes obtained under his conduct; or, when they had ordered him to deliver over his army to a successor, which would not have been decreed unless there were still war in the province, to allow him to triumph, as if the war had been terminated, when the army, the evidence of the triumph being deserved or undeserved, were absent. As a middle course between the two opinions, it was resolved that he should enter the city in ovation. The plebeian tribunes, by direction of the senate, proposed to the people, that Marcus Marcellus should be invested with command during the day on which he should enter the city in ovation. The day before he entered the city he triumphed on the Alban mount; after which he entered the city in ovation, having a great quantity of spoils carried before him, together with a model of the capture of Syracuse. The catapultas and ballistas, and every other instrument of war were carried; likewise the rich ornaments laid up by its kings during a long continuance of peace; a quantity of wrought silver and brass, and other articles, with precious garments, and a number of celebrated statues, with which Syracuse had been adorned in such a manner as to rank among the chief Grecian cities in that respect. Eight elephants were also led as an emblem of victory over the Carthaginians. Sosis, the Syracusan, and Mericus, the Spaniard, who preceded him with golden crowns, formed not the least interesting part of the spectacle; under the guidance of one of whom the Romans had entered Syracuse by night, while the other had betrayed to them the island and the garrison in it. To both of them the freedom of the city was given, and five hundred acres of land each. Sosis was to have his portion in the Syracusan territory, out of the lands which had belonged either to the kings or the enemies of the Roman people, together with a house at Syracuse, which had belonged to any one of those persons who had been punished according to the laws of war. Mericus and the Spaniards who had come over with him were ordered to have a city and lands assigned to them in Sicily, which had belonged to some of those who had revolted from the Romans. It was given in charge to Marcus Cornelius to assign them the city and lands wherever he thought proper. In the same country, four hundred acres of land were decreed to Belligenes, by whose means Mericus had been persuaded to come over. After the departure of Marcellus from Sicily, a Carthaginian fleet landed eight thousand infantry and three thousand Numidian cavalry. To these the Murgantian territories revolted; Hybla, Macella, and certain other towns of less note followed their defection. The Numidians also, headed by Mutines, ranging without restraint through the whole of Sicily, ravaged with fire the lands of the allies of the Romans. In addition to these unfortunate circumstances, the Roman soldiers, incensed partly because they had not been taken from the province with their general, and partly because they had been forbidden to winter in towns, discharged their duties negligently, and wanted a a leader more than inclination for a mutiny. Amid these difficulties Marcus Cornelius, the prætor, sometimes by soothing, at other times by reproving them, pacified the minds of the soldiers; and reduced to obedience all the states which had revolted; out of which he gave Murgantia to those Spaniards who were entitled to a city and land, in conformity with the decree of the senate.

As both the consuls had Apulia for their province, and as there was now less to be apprehended from Hannibal and the Carthaginians, they were directed to draw lots for the provinces of Apulia and Macedonia. Macedonia fell to the lot of Sulpicius, who succeeded Lævinus. Fulvius having been called to Rome on account of the election, held an assembly to elect new consuls; when the junior Veturian century, which had the right of voting first, named Titus Manlius Torquatus and Titus Otacilius. A crowd collecting round Manlius, who was present, to congratulate him, and it being certain that the people would concur in his election, he went, surrounded as he was with a multitude of persons, to the tribunal of the consul, and requested that he would listen to a few words from him; and that he would order the century which had voted to be recalled. While all present were waiting impatiently to hear what it was he was going to ask, he alleged as an excuse the weakness of his eyes; observing, that "a pilot or a general might fairly be charged with presumption who should request that the lives and fortunes of others might be intrusted to him, when in every thing which was to be done he must make use of other people's eyes. Therefore he requested, that, if it seemed good to him, he would order the junior Veturian century to come and vote again; and to recollect, while electing consuls, the war which they had in Italy, and the present exigencies of the state. That their ears had scarcely yet ceased to ring with the noise and tumult raised by the enemy, when but a few months ago they nearly scaled the walls of Rome." This speech was followed by the century's shouting out, one and all, that "they would not in the least alter their vote, but would name the same persons for consuls;" when Torquatus replied, "neither shall I as consul be able to put up with your conduct, nor will you be satisfied with my government. Go back and vote again, and consider that you have a Punic war in Italy, and that the leader of your enemies is Hannibal." Upon this the century, moved by the authority of the man and the shouts of admirers around, besought the consul to summon the elder Veturian century; for they were desirous of conferring with persons older than themselves, and to name the consuls in accordance with their advice. The elder Veturian century having been summoned, time was allowed them to confer with the others by themselves in the *ovile*. The elders said that there were three persons whom they ought to deliberate about electing, two of them having already served all the offices of honour, namely, Quintus Fabius and Marcus Marcellus; and if they wished so particularly to elect some fresh person as consul to act against the Carthaginians, that Marcus Valerius Lævinus had carried on operations against king Philip by sea and land with signal success. Thus, three persons having been proposed to them to deliberate about, the seniors were dismissed, and the juniors proceeded to vote. They named as consuls, Marcus Claudius Marcellus, then glorious with the conquest of Sicily, and Marcus Valerius, both in their absence. All the centuries followed the recommendation of that which voted first. Let men now ridicule the admirers of antiquity. Even if there existed a republic of wise men, which the learned rather imagine than know of; for my own part I cannot persuade myself that there could possibly be a nobility of sounder judgment, and more moderate in their desire of power, or a people better moralled. Indeed that a century of juniors should have been willing to consult their elders, as to the persons to whom they should intrust a command by their vote, is rendered scarcely probable by the contempt and levity with which the parental authority is treated by children in the present age.

The assembly for the election of prætors was then held, at which Publius Manlius Vulso, Lucius Manlius Acidinus, Caius Lætorius, and Lucius Cincius Alimentus were elected. It happened that just as the elections were concluded, news was brought that Titus Otacilius, whom it seemed the people would have made consul in his absence, with Titus Manlius, had not the course of the elections been interrupted, had died in Sicily. The games in honour of Apollo had been performed the preceding year, and on the motion of Calpurnius, the prætor, that they should be performed this year also, the senate decreed that they should be vowed every year for the time to come. The same year several prodigies were seen and reported. At the temple of Concord, a statue of Victory, which stood on the roof, having been struck by lightning and thrown down, stuck among the figures of Victory, which were among the ornaments under the eaves, and did not fall to the ground from thence. Both from Anagnia and Fregellæ it was reported that a wall and some gates had been struck by lightning. That in the forum of Sudertum streams of blood had continued flowing through a whole day; at Eretum, that there had been a shower of stones; and at Reate, that a mule had brought forth. These prodigies were expiated with victims of the larger sort, the people were commanded to offer up prayers for one day, and perform the nine days' sacred rite. Several of the public priests died off this year, and fresh ones were appointed. In the room of Manius Æmilius Numida, decemvir for sacred rites, Marcus Æmilius Lepidus was appointed; in the room of Manius Pomponius Matho, the pontiff, Caius Livius; in the room of Spurius Carvilius Maximus, the augur, Marcus Servilius. As Titus Otacilius Crassus, a pontiff, died after the year was concluded, no person was nominated to succeed him. Caius Claudius, flamen of Jupiter, retired from his office, because he had distributed the entrails improperly.

During the same time Marcus Valerius Lævinus, having first sounded the intentions of the leading men by means of secret conferences, came with some light ships to a council of the Ætolians, which had been previously appointed to meet for this very purpose. Here having proudly pointed to the capture of Syracuse and Capua, as proofs of the success of the Roman arms in Sicily and Italy, he added, that "it was a custom with the Romans, handed down to them from their ancestors, to respect their allies; some of whom they had received into their state, and had admitted to the same privileges they enjoyed themselves, while others they treated so favourably that they chose rather to be allies than citizens. That the Ætolians would be honoured by them so much the more, because they were the first of the nations across the sea which had entered into friendship with them. That Philip and the Macedonians were troublesome neighbours to them, but that he had broken their strength and spirits already, and would still further reduce them to that degree, that they should not only evacuate the cities which they had violently taken from the Ætolians, but have Macedonia itself disturbed with war. And that as to the Acarnanians, whose separation from their body was a source of grief to the Ætolians, he would place them again under their ancient system of jurisdiction and dominion." These assertions and promises of the Roman general, Scopas, who was at that time prætor of the nation, and Dorymachus, a leading man among the Ætolians, confirmed on their own authority, extolling the power and greatness of the Roman people with less reserve, and with greater force of conviction. However, the hope of recovering Acarnania principally moved them. The terms, therefore, were reduced to writing, on which they should enter into alliance and friendship with the Roman people, and it was added, that "if it were agreeable to them and they wished it, the Eleans and Lacedæmonians, with Attalus, Pleuratus, and Scerdilædas, should be included on the same conditions." Attalus was king of Asia; the latter, kings of the Thracians and Illyrians. The conditions were, that "the Ætolians should immediately make war on Philip by land, in which the Romans should assist, with not less than twenty quinqueremes. That the site and buildings, together with the walls and lands, of all the cities as far as Corcyra, should become the property of the Ætolians, every other kind of booty, of the Romans. That the Romans should endeavour to put the Ætolians in possession of Acarnania. If the Ætolians should make peace with Philip, they should insert a stipulation that the peace should stand good only on condition that they abstained from hostilities against the Romans, their allies, and the states subject to them. In like manner, if the Romans should form an alliance with the king, that they should provide that he should not have liberty to make war upon the Ætolians and their allies." Such were the terms agreed upon; and copies of them having been made, they were laid up two years afterwards by the Ætolians at Olympia, and by the Romans in the Capitol, that they might be attested by these consecrated records. The delay had been occasioned by the Ætolian ambassadors' having been detained at Rome. This, however, did not form an impediment to the war's proceeding. Both the Ætolians immediately commenced war against Philip, and Lævinus taking, all but the citadel, Zacynthus, a small island near to Aetolia, and having one city of the same name with the island; and also taking Æniadæ and Nasus from the Acarnanians, annexed them to the Ætolians; and also considering that Philip was sufficiently engaged in war with his neighbours to prevent his thinking of Italy, the Carthaginians, and his compact with Hannibal, he retired to Corcyra.

To Philip intelligence of the defection of the Ætolians was brought while in winter quarters at Pella. As he was about to march an army into Greece at the beginning of the spring, he undertook a sudden expedition into the territories of Oricum and Apollonia, in order that Macedonia might not be molested by the Illyrians, and the cities bordering upon them, in consequence of the terror he would thus strike them with in turn. The Apollonians came out to oppose him, but he drove them, terrified and dismayed, within their walls. After devastating the adjacent parts of Illyricum he turned his course into Pelagonia, with the same expedition. He then took Sintia, a town of the Dardanians, which would have afforded them a passage into Macedonia. Having with the greatest despatch performed these achievements, not forgetting the war made upon him by the Ætolians and Romans in conjunction, he marched down into Thessaly through Pelagonia, Lyncus, and Bottiæa. He trusted that people might be induced to take part with him in the war against the Ætolians, and, therefore, leaving Perseus with four thousand armed men at the gorge, which formed the entrance into Thessaly, to prevent the Ætolians from passing it, before he should be occupied with more important business, he marched his army into Macedonia, and thence into Thrace and Mædica. This nation had been accustomed to make incursions into Macedonia when they perceived the king engaged in a foreign war, and the kingdom left unprotected. Accordingly, he began to devastate the lands in the neighbourhood of Phragandæ, and to lay siege to the city Jamphorina, the capital and chief fortress of Mædica. Scopas, on hearing that the king had gone into Thrace, and was engaged in a war there, armed all the Ætolian youths, and prepared to invade Acarnania. The Acarnanian nation, unequal to their enemy in point of strength, and seeing that they had lost Æniadæ and Nasus, and moreover that the Roman arms were threatening them, prepare the war rather with rage than prudence. Having sent their wives, children, and those who were above sixty years old into the neighbouring parts of Epirus, all who were between the ages of fifteen and sixty, bound each other by an oath not to return unless victorious. That no one might receive into his city or house, or admit to his table or hearth, such as should retire from the field vanquished, they drew up a form of direful execration against their countrymen who should do so; and the most solemn entreaty they could devise, to friendly states. At the same time they entreated the Epirotes to bury in one tomb such of their men as should fall in the encounter, adding this inscription over their remains: HERE LIE THE ACARNANIANS, WHO DIED WHILE FIGHTING IN DEFENCE OF THEIR COUNTRY, AGAINST THE VIOLENCE AND INJUSTICE OF THE ÆTOLIANS. Having worked up their courage to the highest pitch by these means, they fixed their camp at the extreme borders of their country in the way of the enemy; and sending messengers to Philip to inform him of the critical situation in which they stood, they obliged him to suspend the war in which he was engaged, though he had gained possession of Jamphorina by surrender, and had succeeded in other respects. The ardour of the Ætolians was damped, in the first instance, by the news of the combination formed by the Acarnanians; but afterwards the intelligence of Philip's approach compelled them even to retreat into the interior of the country. Nor did Philip proceed farther than Dium, though he had marched with great expedition to prevent the Acarnanians being overpowered; and when he had received information that the Ætolians had returned out of Acarnania, he also returned to Pella.

Lævinus set sail from Corcyra in the beginning of the spring, and doubling the promontory Leucate, arrived at Naupactus; when he gave notice that he should go thence to Anticyra, in order that Scopas and the Ætolians might be ready there to join him. Anticyra is situated in Locris, on the left hand as you enter the Corinthian Gulf. The distance between Naupactus and this place is short both by sea and land. In about three days after, the attack upon this place commenced on both elements. The attack from the sea produced the greatest effect, because there were on board the ships engines and machines of every description, and because the Romans besieged from that quarter. In a few days, therefore, the town surrendered, and was delivered over to the Ætolians, the booty, according to compact, was given up to the Romans. Lævinus then received a letter informing him, that he had been elected consul in his absence, and that Publius Sulpicius was coming as his successor. He arrived at Rome later than he was generally expected, being detained by a lingering illness. Marcus Marcellus, having entered upon the consulship on the ides of March, assembled the senate on that day merely for form's sake He declared, that "in the absence of his colleague he would not enter into any question relative to the state or the provinces." He said, "he well knew there were crowds of Sicilians in the neighbourhood of the city at the country-houses of those who maligned him, whom he was so far from wishing to prevent from openly publishing, at Rome, the charges which had been circulated and got up against him by his enemies, that did they not pretend that they entertained some fear of speaking of a consul in the absence of his colleague, he would forthwith have given them a hearing of the senate. That when his colleague had arrived, he would not allow any business to be transacted before the Sicilians were brought before the senate. That Marcus Cornelius had in a manner held a levy throughout all Sicily, in order that as many as possible might come to Rome to prefer complaints against him, that the same person had filled the city with letters containing false representations that there was still war in Sicily, in order to detract from his merit." The consul, having acquired on that day the reputation of having a well-regulated mind, dismissed the senate, and it appeared that there would be almost a total suspension of every kind of business till the other consul returned to the city. The want of employment, as usual, produced expressions of discontent among the people. They complained of the length of the war, that the lands around the city were devastated wherever Hannibal had marched his hostile troops; that Italy was exhausted by levies, and that almost every year their armies were cut to pieces, that the consuls elected were both of them fond of war, men over-enterprising and impetuous, who would probably stir up war in a time of profound peace, and therefore were the less likely to allow the state to breathe in time of war.

A fire which broke out in several places at once in the neighbourhood of the forum, on the night before the festival of Minerva, interrupted these discourses. Seven shops, where five were afterwards erected, and the banks, which are now called the new banks, were all on fire at once. Afterwards the private dwellings caught, for there were no public halls there then, the prisons called the Quarry, the fish-market, and the royal palace. The temple of Vesta was with difficulty saved, principally by the exertions of thirteen slaves, who were redeemed at the public expense and manumitted. The fire continued for a day and a night. It was evident to every body that it was caused by human contrivance, because the flames burst forth in several places at once, and those at a distance from each other. The consul, therefore, on the recommendation of the senate, publicly notified, that whoever should make known by whose act the conflagration was kindled, should rewarded, if a free-man, with money, if a slave, with liberty. Induced by this reward, a slave of the Campanian family, the Calavii, named Mannus, gave information that "his masters, with five noble Campanian youths, whose parents had been executed by Fulvius, were the authors of the fire, and that they would commit various other acts of the same kind if they were not seized." Upon this they were seized, as well as their slaves. At first, the informer and his evidence were disparaged, for that "he had run away from his masters the day before in consequence of a whipping, and that from an event which had happened by mere chance, he had fabricated this charge, from resentment and wantonness." But when they were charged by their accusers face to face, and the ministers of their villanies begin to be examined in the middle of the forum, they all confessed, and punishment was inflicted upon the masters and their accessory slaves. The informer received his liberty and twenty thousand *asses*. The consul Lævinus, while passing by Capua, was surrounded by a multitude of Campanians, who besought him, with tears, that they might be permitted to go to Rome to the senate, so that if they could at length be in any degree moved by compassion, they might not carry their resentment so far as to destroy them utterly, nor suffer the very name of the Campanian nation to be obliterated by Quintus Flaccus. Flaccus declared, that "he had individually no quarrel with the Campanians, but that he did entertain an enmity towards them on public grounds and because they were foes, and should continue to do so as long as he felt assured that they had the same feelings towards the Roman people; for that there was no nation or people on earth more inveterate against the Roman name. That his reason for keeping them shut up within their walls was, that if any of these got out any where they roamed through the country like wild beasts, tearing and massacring whatever fell in their way. That some of them had deserted to Hannibal, others had gone and set fire to Rome; that the consul would find the traces of the villany of the Campanians in the half-burnt forum. That the temple of Vesta, the eternal fire, and the fatal pledge for the continuance of the Roman empire deposited in the shrine, had been the objects of their attack. That in his opinion it was extremely unsafe for any Campanians to be allowed to enter the walls of Rome." Lævinus ordered the Campanians to follow him to Rome, after Flaccus had bound them by an oath to return to Capua on the fifth day after receiving an answer from the senate. Surrounded by this crowd, and followed also by the Sicilians and Aeolians, who came out to meet him, he went to Rome; taking with him into the city as accusers of two men who had acquired the greatest celebrity by the overthrow of two most renowned cities, those whom they had vanquished in war. Both the consuls, however, first proposed to the senate the consideration of the state of the commonwealth, and the arrangements respecting the provinces.

On this occasion Lævinus reported the state of Macedonia and Greece, of the Ætolians, Acarnanians, and Locrians, and the services he had himself performed there on sea and land. That "Philip, who was bringing an army against the Ætolians, had been driven back by him into Macedonia, and compelled to retire into the heart of his kingdom. That the legion might therefore be withdrawn from that quarter, and that the fleet was sufficient to keep the king out of Italy." Thus much he said respecting himself and the province where he had commanded. The consuls jointly proposed the consideration of the provinces, when the senate decreed, that, "Italy and the war with Hannibal should form the province of one of the consuls; that the other should have the command of the fleet which Titus Otacilius had commanded, and the province of Sicily, in conjunction with Lucius Cincius, the prætor." The two armies decreed to them were those in Etruria and Gaul, consisting of four legions. That the two city legions of the former year should be sent into Etruria and the two which Sulpicius, the consul, had commanded, into Gaul; that he should have the command of Gaul, and the legions there whom the consul, who had the province of Italy, should appoint. Caius Calpurnius, having his command continued to him for a year after the expiration of his prætorship, was sent into Etruria. To Quintus Fulvius also the province of Capua was decreed, with his command continued for a year. The army of citizens and allies was ordered to be reduced, so that, out of two, one legion should be formed consisting of five thousand foot and three hundred horse, those being discharged who had served the greatest number of campaigns. That of the allies there should be left seven thousand infantry and three hundred horse, the same rule being observed with regard to the periods of their service in discharging the old soldiers. With Cneius Fulvius, the consul of the former year, no change was made touching his province of Apulia nor his army; only he was continued in command for a year. Publius Sulpicius, his colleague, was ordered to discharge the whole of his army excepting the marines. It was ordered also, that the army which Marcus Cornelius had commanded, should be sent out of Sicily as soon as the consul arrived in his province. The soldiers which had fought at Cannæ, amounting to two legions, were assigned to Lucius Cincius, the prætor, for the occupation of Sicily. As many legions were assigned to Publius Manlius Vulso, the prætor, for Sardinia, being those which Lucius Cornelius had commanded in that province the former year. The consuls were directed so to raise legions for the service of the city, as not to enlist any one who had served in the armies of Marcus Claudius, Marcus Valerius, or Quintus Fulvius, so that the Roman legions might not exceed twenty-one that year.

After the senate had passed these decrees, the consuls drew lots for their provinces. Sicily and the fleet fell to the lot of Marcellus; Italy, with the war against Hannibal, to Lævinus. This result so terrified the Sicilians, who were standing in sight of the consuls waiting the determination of the lots, that their bitter lamentations and mournful cries both drew upon them the eyes of all at the time, and afterwards furnished matter for conversation. For they went round to the several senators in mourning garments, affirming, that "they would not only abandon, each of them, his native country, but all Sicily, if Marcellus should again go thither with command. That he had formerly been implacable toward them for no demerit of theirs, what would he do now, when exasperated that they had come to Rome to complain of him? That it would be better for that island to be overwhelmed with the fires of Aetna, or sunk in the sea, than to be delivered up, as it were, for execution to an enemy." These complaints of the Sicilians, having been carried round to the houses of the nobility, and frequently canvassed in conversations, which were prompted partly by compassion for the Sicilians and partly by dislike for Marcellus, at length reached the senate also. The consuls were requested to take the sense of the senate on an exchange of provinces. Marcellus said, that "if the Sicilians had already had an audience of the senate, his opinion perhaps might have been different, but as the case now stood, lest any one should be able to say that they were prevented by fear from freely venting their complaints respecting him, to whose power they were presently about to be subject, he was willing, if it made no difference to his colleague, to exchange provinces with him. That he deprecated a premature decision on the part of the senate, for since it would be unjust that his colleague should have the power of selecting his province without drawing lots, how much greater injustice would it be, nay, rather indignity, for his lot to be transferred to him." Accordingly the senate, having rather shown than decreed what they wished, adjourned. An exchange of provinces was made by the consuls of themselves, fate hurrying on Marcellus to encounter Hannibal, that he might be the last of the Roman generals, who, by his fall, when the affairs of the war were most prosperous, might add to the glory of that man, from whom he derived the reputation of having been the first Roman general who defeated him.

After the provinces had been exchanged, the Sicilians, on being introduced into the senate, discoursed largely on the constant fidelity of king Hiero to the Roman people, converting it into a public merit. They said, "that the tyrants, Hieronymus, and, after him, Hippocrates and Epicydes, had been objects of detestation to them, both on other accounts and especially on account of then deserting the Romans to take part with Hannibal. For this cause Hieronymus was put to death by the principal young men among them, almost with the public concurrence, and a conspiracy was formed to murder Epicydes and Hippocrates, by seventy of the most distinguished of their youth; but being left without support in consequence of the delay of Marcellus, who neglected to bring up his troops to Syracuse at the time agreed upon, they were all, on an indictment that was made, put to death by the tyrants. That Marcellus, by the cruelty exercised in the sacking of Leontini, had given occasion to the tyranny of Hippocrates and Epicydes. From that time the leading men among the Syracusans never ceased going over to Marcellus, and promising him that they would deliver the city to him whenever he pleased; but that he, in the first instance, was disposed rather to take it by force, and afterwards, finding it impossible to effect his object by sea or land, after trying every means, he preferred having Syracuse delivered to him by Sosis, a brazier, and Mericus, a Spaniard, to receiving it from the principal men of Syracuse, who had so often offered it to him voluntarily to no purpose; doubtless in order that he might with a fairer pretext butcher and plunder the most ancient allies of the Roman people. If it had not been Hieronymus who revolted to Hannibal, but the people and senate of Syracuse; if the body of the Syracusan people, and not their tyrants, Hippocrates and Epicydes, who held them in thraldom, had closed the gates against Marcellus; if they had carried on war with the Roman people with the animosity of Carthaginians, what more could Marcellus have done in hostility than he did, without levelling Syracuse with the ground? Nothing indeed was left at Syracuse except the walls and gutted houses of her city, the temples of her gods broken open and plundered; her very gods and their ornaments having been carried away. From many their possessions also were taken away, so that they were unable to support themselves and their families, even from the naked soil, the only remains of their plundered property. They entreated the conscript fathers, that they would order, if not all, at least such of their property as could be found and identified, to be restored to the owners." After they had made these complaints, Lævinus ordered them to withdraw from the senate-house, that the senate might deliberate on their requests, when Marcellus exclaimed, "Nay, rather let them stay here, that I may reply to their charges in their presence, since we conduct your wars for you, conscript fathers, on the condition of having as our accusers those whom we have conquered with our arms. Of the two cities which have been captured this year, let Capua arraign Fulvius, and Syracuse Marcellus."

The deputies having been brought back into the senate-house, the consul said: "I am not so unmindful of the dignity of the Roman people and of the office I fill as consul, conscript fathers, as to make a defence against charges brought by Greeks, had the inquiry related only to my own delinquency. But it is not so much what I have done, as what they deserved to suffer, which comes into dispute. For if they were not our enemies, there was no difference between sacking Syracuse then, and when Hiero was alive. But if, on the other hand, they have renounced their connexion with us, attacked our ambassadors sword in hand, shut us out of their city and walls, and defended themselves against us with an army of Carthaginians, who can feel indignant that they should suffer the hostilities they have offered? I turned away from the leading men of the Syracusans, when they were desirous of delivering up the city to me, and esteemed Sosis and Mericus as more proper persons for so important an affair. Now you are not the meanest of the Syracusans, who reproach others with the meanness of their condition. But who is there among you, who has promised that he would open the gates to me, and receive my armed troops within the city? You hate and execrate those who did so; and not even here can you abstain from speaking with insult of them; so far is it from being the case that you would yourselves have done any thing of the kind. The very meanness of the condition of those persons, conscript fathers, with which these men reproach them, forms the strongest proof that I did not turn away from any man who was willing to render a service to our state. Before I began the siege of Syracuse I attempted a peace, at one time by sending ambassadors, at another time by going to confer with them; and after that they refrained not from laying violent hands on my ambassadors, nor would give me an answer when I held an interview with their chief men at their gates, then, at length, after suffering many hardships by sea and land, I took Syracuse by force of arms. Of what befell them after their city was captured they would complain with more justice to Hannibal, the Carthaginians, and those who were vanquished with them, than to the senate of the victorious people. If, conscript fathers, I had intended to conceal the fact that I had despoiled Syracuse, I should never have decorated the city of Rome with her spoils. As to what things I either took from individuals or bestowed upon them, as conqueror, I feel assured that I have acted agreeably to the laws of war, and the deserts of each. That you should confirm what I have done, conscript fathers, certainly concerns the commonwealth more than myself, since I have discharged my duty faithfully; but it is the duty of the state to take care, lest, by rescinding my acts, they should render other commanders for the time to come less zealous. And since, conscript fathers, you have heard both what the Sicilians and I had to say, in the presence of each other, we will go out of the senate-house together, in order that in my absence the senate may deliberate more freely." Accordingly, the Sicilians having been dismissed, he himself also went away to the Capitol to levy soldiers.

The other consul then proposed to the fathers the consideration of the requests of the Sicilians, when a long debate took place. A great part of the senate acquiesced in an opinion which originated with Titus Manlius Torquatus, "that the war ought to have been carried on against the tyrants, the enemies both of the Syracusans and the Roman people; that the city ought to have been recovered, not captured; and, when recovered, should have been firmly established under its ancient laws and liberty, and not distressed by war, when worn out with a wretched state of bondage. That in the contest between the tyrants and the Roman general, that most beautiful and celebrated city, formerly the granary and treasury of the Roman people, which was held up as the reward of the victor, had been destroyed; a city by whose munificence and bounty the commonwealth had been assisted and adorned on many occasions, and lastly, during this very Punic war. Should king Hiero, that most faithful friend of the Roman empire, rise from the shades, with what face could either Syracuse or Rome be shown to him, when, after beholding his half-demolished and plundered native city, he should see, on entering Rome, the spoils of his country in the vestibule, as it were, of the city, and almost in the very gates?" Although these and other similar things were said, to throw odium upon the consul and excite compassion for the Sicilians, yet the fathers, out of regard for Marcellus, passed a milder decree, to the effect, "that what Marcellus had done while prosecuting the war, and when victorious, should be confirmed. That for the time to come, the senate would look to the affairs of Syracuse, and would give it in charge to the consul Lævinus, to consult the interest of that state, so far as it could be done without detriment to the commonwealth." Two senators having been sent to the Capitol to request the consul to return to the senate-house, and the Sicilians having been called in, the decree of the senate was read. The deputies were addressed in terms of kindness, and dismissed, when they threw themselves at the knees of the consul, Marcellus, beseeching him to pardon them for what they had said for the purpose of exciting compassion, and procuring relief from their calamities, and to receive themselves and the city of Syracuse under his protection and patronage; after which, the consul addressed them kindly and dismissed them.

An audience of the senate was then granted to the Campanians. Their speech was more calculated to excite compassion, but their case less favourable, for neither could they deny that they deserved the punishment they had suffered, nor were there any tyrants to whom they could transfer their guilt. But they trusted that sufficient atonement had been made by the death of so many of their senators by poison and the hands of the executioner. They said, "that a few only of their nobles remained, being such as were not induced by the consciousness of their demerit to adopt any desperate measure respecting themselves, and had not been condemned to death through the resentment of their conquerors. That these implored the restoration of their liberty, and some portion of their goods for themselves and families, being citizens of Rome, and most of them connected with the Romans by affinity and now too near relationship, in consequence of intermarriages which had taken place for a long period." After this they were removed from the senate-house, when for a short time doubts were entertained whether it would be right or not to send for Quintus Fulvius from Capua, (for Claudius, the proconsul, died after the capture of that place,) that the question might be canvassed in the presence of the general who had been concerned, as was done in the affair between Marcellus and the Sicilians. But afterwards, when they saw in the senate Marcus Atilius, and Caius Fulvius, the brother of Flaccus, his lieutenant-generals, and Quintus Minucius, and Lucius Veturius Philo, who were also his lieutenant-generals, who had been present at every transaction; and being unwilling that Fulvius should be recalled from Capua, or the Campanians put off, Marcus Atilius Regulus, who possessed the greatest weight of any of those present who had been at Capua, being asked his opinion, thus spoke: "I believe I assisted at the council held by the consuls after the capture of Capua, when inquiry was made whether any of the Campanians had deserved well of our state; and it was found that two women had done so; Vestia Oppia, a native of Atella and an inhabitant of Capua, and Faucula Cluvia, formerly a common woman. The former had daily offered sacrifice for the safety and success of the Roman people, and the latter had clandestinely supplied the starving prisoners with food. The sentiments of all the rest of the Campanians towards us had been the same," he said, "as those of the Carthaginians; and those who had been decapitated by Fulvius, were the most conspicuous in rank, but not in guilt. I do not see," said he, "how the senate can decide respecting the Campanians who are Roman citizens, without an order of the people. And the course adopted by our ancestors, in the case of the Satricani when they had revolted, was, that Marcus Antistius, the plebeian tribune, should first propose and the commons make an order, that the senate should have the power of pronouncing judgment upon the Satricani. I therefore give it as my opinion, that application should be made to the plebeian tribunes, that one or more of them should propose to the people a bill, by which we may be empowered to determine in the case of the Campanians." Lucius Atilius, plebeian tribune, proposed to the people, on the recommendation of the senate, a bill to the following effect: "Concerning all the Campanians, Atellanians, Calatinians, and Sabatinians, who have surrendered themselves to the proconsul Fulvius, and have placed themselves under the authority and dominion of the Roman people; also concerning what things they have surrendered, together with their persons, both lands and city, divine or human, together with their utensils and whatsoever else they have surrendered; concerning these things, Roman citizens, I ask you what it is your pleasure should be done." The commons thus ordered: "Whatsoever the senate on oath, or the majority of those present, may determine, that we will and order."

The senate having taken the matter into their consideration in conformity with this order of the people, first restored to Oppia and Cluvia their goods and liberty; directing, that if they wished to solicit any other rewards from the senate, they should come to Rome. Separate decrees were passed respecting each of the Campanian families, all of which it is not worth while to enumerate. The goods of some were to be confiscated; themselves, their children, and their wives were to be sold, excepting such of their daughters as had married before they came into the power of the Roman people. Others were ordered to be thrown into chains, and their cases to be considered at a future time. They made the amount of income the ground on which they decided, whether the goods of the rest of the Campanians should be confiscated or not. They voted, that all the cattle taken except the horses, all the slaves except adult males, and every thing which did not belong to the soil, should be restored to the owners. They ordered that all the Campanians, Atellanians, Calatinians, and Sabatinians, except such as were themselves, or whose parents were, among the enemy, should be free, with a proviso, that none of them should become a Roman citizen or a Latin confederate; and that none of those who had been at Capua while the gates were shut should remain in the city or territory of Capua after a certain day. That a place should be assigned to them to inhabit beyond the Tiber, but not contiguous to it. That those who had neither been in Capua nor in any Campanian city which had revolted from the Romans during the war, should inhabit a place on this side the river Liris towards Rome; and that those who had come over to the Romans before Hannibal arrived at Capua, should be removed to a place on this side the Vulturnus, with a proviso, that none of them should have either land or house within fifteen miles of the sea. That such of them as were removed to a place beyond the Tiber, should neither themselves nor their posterity acquire or possess any property any where, except in the Veientian, Sutrian, or Nepetian territories; and, except on condition, that no one should possess a greater extent of land than fifty acres. That the goods of all the senators, and such as had been magistrates at Capua, Calatia, and Atella, should be sold at Capua; but that the free persons who were decreed to be exposed to sale, should be sent to Rome and sold there. As to the images and brazen statues, which were said to have been taken from the enemy, whether sacred or profane, they referred them to the college of pontiffs. They sent the Campanians away, considerably more grieved than they were when they came, in consequence of these decrees; and now they no longer complained of the severity of Quintus Fulvius towards them, but of the malignity of the gods and their own accursed fortune.

After the Sicilians and Campanians were dismissed, a levy was made; and after the troops had been enlisted for the army, they then began to consider about making up the number of rowers; but as there was neither a sufficient supply of men for that purpose, nor any money at that time in the treasury by which they might be purchased or paid, the consuls issued an edict, that private persons should furnish rowers in proportion to their income and rank, as had been done before, with pay and provisions for thirty days. So great was the murmuring and indignation of the people, on account of this edict, that a leader, rather than matter, was wanting for an insurrection. It was said, that "the consuls, after having ruined the Sicilians and Campanians, had undertaken to destroy and lacerate the Roman commons; that, drained as they had been for so many years by taxes, they had nothing left but wasted and naked lands. That the enemy had burned their houses, and the state had taken away their slaves, who were the cultivators of their lands, at one time by purchasing them at a low rate for soldiers, at another by commanding a supply of rowers. If any one had any silver or brass it was taken away from him, for the payment of rowers or for annual taxes. That no force could compel and no command oblige them to give what they had not got. That they might sell their goods and then vent their cruelty on their persons, which were all that remained to them. That they had nothing even left from which they could be redeemed." These complaints were uttered not in secret, but publicly in the forum, and before the eyes of the consuls themselves, by an immense crowd which surrounded them; nor could the consuls appease them now by coercing nor by soothing them. Upon this they said that three days should be allowed them to consider of the matter; which interval the consuls employed in examining and planning. The following day they assembled the senate to consider of raising a supply of rowers; and after arguing at great length that the people's refusal was fair, they brought their discourse to this point, that whether it were just or unjust, this burden must be borne by private individuals. For from what source could they procure rowers, when there was no money in the treasury? and how, without fleets, could Sicily be kept in subjection, or Philip be prevented from entering Italy, or the shores of Italy be protected?

In this perplexing state of affairs, when all deliberation was at a stand, and a kind of torpor had seized on men's minds, Lævinus, the consul, observed, that "as the magistrates were more honoured than the senators, and the senators than the people, so also ought they to be the first in taking upon themselves every thing that was burdensome and arduous. If you would enjoin any duty on an inferior, and would first submit yourself and those belonging to you to the obligation, you will find everybody else more ready to obey; nor is an expense thought heavy, when the people see every one of their principal men taking upon himself more than his proportion of it. Are we then desirous that the Roman people should have and equip a fleet? that private individuals should without repugnance furnish rowers? Let us first execute the command ourselves. Let us, senators, bring into the treasury to-morrow all our gold, silver, and coined brass, each reserving rings for himself, his wife, and children, and a bulla for his son; and he who has a wife or daughters, an ounce weight of gold for each. Let those who have sat in a curule chair have the ornaments of a horse, and a pound weight of silver, that they may have a salt-cellar and a dish for the service of the gods. Let the rest of us, senators, reserve for each father of a family, a pound weight only of silver and five thousand coined *asses*. All the rest of our gold, silver, and coined brass, let us immediately carry to the triumviri for banking affairs, no decree of the senate having been previously made; that our voluntary contributions, and our emulation in assisting the state, may excite the minds, first, of the equestrian order to emulate us, and after them of the rest of the community. This is the only course which we, your consuls, after much conversation on the subject, have been able to discover. Adopt it, then, and may the gods prosper the measure. If the state is preserved, she can easily secure the property of her individual members, but by betraying the public interests you would in vain preserve your own." This proposition was received with such entire approbation, that thanks were spontaneously returned to the consuls. The senate was then adjourned, when every one of the members brought his gold, silver, and brass into the treasury, with such emulation excited, that they were desirous that their names should appear among the first on the public tables; so that neither the triumviri were sufficient for receiving nor the notaries for entering them. The unanimity displayed by the senate was imitated by the equestrian order, and that of the equestrian order by the commons. Thus, without any edict, or coercion of the magistrates, the state neither wanted rowers to make up the numbers, nor money to pay them; and after every thing had been got in readiness for the war, the consuls set out for their provinces.

Nor was there ever any period of the war, when both the Carthaginians and the Romans, plunged alike in vicissitudes, were in a state of more anxious suspense between hope and fear. For on the side of the Romans, with respect to their provinces, their failure in Spain on the one hand, and their successes in Sicily on the other, had blended joy and sorrow; and in Italy, the loss of Tarentum was an injury and a source of grief to them, while the unexpected preservation of the citadel with the garrison was matter of joy to them. The sudden terror and panic occasioned by the siege and attack of Rome, was turned into joy by the capture of Capua, a few days after. Their affairs beyond sea also were equalized by a kind of compensation. Philip had become their enemy at a juncture somewhat unseasonable; but then the Ætolians, and Attalus, king of Asia, were added to their allies; fortune now, in a manner, promising to the Romans the empire of the east. The Carthaginians also set the loss of Capua against the capture of Tarentum; and as they considered it as glorious to them to have reached the walls of Rome without opposition, so they were chagrined at the failure of their attempt, and they felt ashamed that they had been held in such contempt, that while they lay under the walls of Rome, a Roman army was marched out for Spain at an opposite gate. With regard also to Spain itself, the greater the reason was to hope that the war there was terminated, and that the Romans were driven from the country, after the destruction of two such renowned generals and their armies, so much the greater was the indignation felt, that the victory had been rendered void and fruitless by Lucius Marcius, a general irregularly appointed. Thus fortune balancing events against each other, all was suspense and uncertainty on both sides, their hopes and their fears being as strong as though they were now first commencing the war.

What grieved Hannibal more than any thing was the fact, that Capua having been more perseveringly besieged by the Romans than defended by him, had turned from him the regard of many of the states of Italy, and it was not only impossible for him to retain possession of all these by means of garrisons, unless he could make up his mind to tear his army into a number of small portions, which at that time was most inexpedient, but he could not, by withdrawing the garrisons, leave the fidelity of his allies open to the influence of hope, or subject to that of fear. His disposition, which was strongly inclined to avarice and cruelty, induced him to plunder the places he could not keep possession of, that they might be left for the enemy in a state of desolation. This resolution was equally horrid in principle and in its issue, for not only were the affections of those who suffered such harsh treatment alienated from him, but also of the other states, for the warning affected a greater number than did the calamity. Nor did the Roman consul fail to sound the inclinations of the cities, whenever any prospect of success presented itself. Dasius and Blasius were the principal men in Salapia, Dasius was the friend of Hannibal, Blasius, as far as he could do it with safety, promoted the Roman interest, and, by means of secret messengers, had given Marcellus hopes of having the place betrayed to him, but the business could not be accomplished without the assistance of Dasius. After much and long hesitation and even then more for the want of a better plan than from any hope of success, he addressed himself to Dasius; but he, being both adverse to the measure and also hostile to his rival in the government, discovered the affair to Hannibal. Both parties were summoned, and while Hannibal was transacting some business on his tribunal, intending presently to take cognizance of the case of Blasius, and the accuser and the accused were standing apart from the crowd, which was put back, Blasius solicited Dasius on the subject of surrendering the city; when he exclaimed, as if the case were now clearly proved, that he was being treated with about the betrayal of the city, even before the eyes of Hannibal. The more audacious the proceeding was, the less probable did it appear to Hannibal and those who were present. They considered that the charge was undoubtedly a matter of rivalry and animosity, and that it had been brought because it was of such a nature that, not admitting of being proved by witnesses, it could the more easily be fabricated. Accordingly the parties were dismissed. But Blasius, notwithstanding, desisted not from his bold undertaking, till by continually harping upon the same subject, and proving how conducive such a measure would be to themselves and their country, he carried his point that the Punic garrison, consisting of five hundred Numidians, and Salapia, should be delivered up to Marcellus. Nor could it be betrayed without much bloodshed, consisting of the bravest of the cavalry in the whole Punic army. Accordingly, though the event was unexpected, and their horses were of no use to them in the city, yet hastily taking arms, during the confusion, they endeavoured to force their way out; and not being able to escape, they fell fighting to the last, not more than fifty of them falling into the hands of the enemy alive. The loss of this body of cavalry was considerably more detrimental to Hannibal than that of Salapia, for the Carthaginian was never afterwards superior in cavalry, in which he had before been most effective.

During this time the scarcity of provisions in the citadel of Tarentum was almost intolerable; the Roman garrison there, and Marcus Livius, the præfect of the garrison and the citadel, placing all their dependence in the supplies sent from Sicily; that these might safely pass along the coast of Italy, a fleet of about twenty ships was stationed at Rhegium. Decius Quinctius, a man of obscure birth, but who had acquired great renown as a soldier, on account of many acts of bravery, had charge of the fleet and the convoys. At first he had five ships, the largest of which were two triremes, given to him by Marcellus, but afterwards, in consequence of his spirited conduct on many occasions, three quinqueremes were added to his number, at last, by exacting from the allied states of Rhegium, Velia, and Paestum, the ships they were bound to furnish according to treaty, he made up a fleet of twenty ships, as was before stated. This fleet setting out from Rhegium, was met at Sacriportus, about fifteen miles from the city by Democrates, with an equal number of Tarentine ships. It happened that the Roman was then coming with his sails up, not expecting an approaching contest, but in the neighbourhood of Croto and Sybaris, he had supplied his ships with rowers, and had his fleet excellently equipped and armed for the size of his vessels, and it also happened, that just at the time when the enemy were in sight, the wind completely fell, so that there was sufficient time to furl their sails, and get their rowers and soldiers in readiness for the approaching action. Rarely elsewhere have regular fleets engaged with so much spirit, for they fought for what was of greater importance than the fleets themselves. The Tarentines, in order that, having recovered their city from the Romans after the lapse of almost a century, they might also rescue their citadel, hoping also to cut off the supplies of their enemy, if by a naval battle they could deprive them of the dominion of the sea. The Romans, that, by keeping possession of the citadel, they might prove that Tarentum was lost not by the strength and valour of their enemies, but by treachery and stealth. Accordingly, the signal having been given on both sides, they charged each other with the beaks of their ships, and neither did they draw back their own, nor allow the ships of the enemy with which they were engaged to separate from them, having thrown then grappling irons, and thus the battle was carried on in such close quarters, that they fought not only with missile weapons, but in a manner foot to foot even with their swords. The prows joined together remained stationary, while the sterns were moved round by the force of their adversaries' oars. The ships were crowded together in so small a compass, that scarcely one weapon fell into the sea without taking effect. They pressed front against front like lines of troops engaging on land, and the combatants could pass from one ship to another. But the contest between two ships which had engaged each other in the van, was remarkable above the rest. In the Roman ship was Quinctius himself, in the Tarentine, Nico, surnamed Perco, who hated, and was hated by, the Romans, not only on public grounds, but also personally, for he belonged to that faction which had betrayed Tarentum to Hannibal. This man transfixed Quinctius with a spear while off his guard, and engaged at once in fighting and encouraging his men, and he immediately fell headlong with his arms over the prow. The victorious Tarentine promptly boarded the ship, which was all in confusion from the loss of the commander, and when he had driven the enemy back, and the Tarentines had got possession of the prow, the Romans, who had formed themselves into a compact body, with difficulty defending the stern, suddenly another trireme of the enemy appeared at the stern. Thus the Roman ship, enclosed between the two, was captured. Upon this a panic spread among the rest, seeing the commander's ship captured, and flying in every direction, some were sunk in the deep and some rowed hastily to land, where, shortly after, they became a prey to the Thurians and Metapontines. Of the storeships which followed, laden with provisions, a very few fell into the hands of the enemy; the rest, shifting their sails from one side to another with the changing winds, escaped into the open sea. An affair took place at Tarentum at this time, which was attended with widely different success; for a party of four thousand men had gone out to forage, and while they were dispersed, and roaming through the country, Livius, the commander of the citadel and the Roman garrison, who was anxious to seize every opportunity of striking a blow, sent out of the citadel Caius Persius, an active officer, with two thousand soldiers, who attacked them suddenly when widely dispersed and straggling about the fields; and after slaying them for a long time on all hands, drove the few that remained of so many into the city, to which they fled in alarm and confusion, and where they rushed in at the doors of the gates, which were half-opened that the city might not be taken in the same attack. In this manner affairs were equally balanced at Tarentum, the Romans being victorious by land, and the Tarentines by sea. Both parties were equally disappointed in their hope of receiving provisions after they were within sight.

While these events were occurring, the consul, Lævinus, after a great part of the year had elapsed, having arrived in Sicily, where he had been expected by both the old and new allies, considered it his first and principal duty to adjust the affairs of Syracuse, which were still in a state of disorder, the peace being but recent. He then marched his legions to Agrigentum, the seat of the remaining part of the war, which was occupied by a strong garrison of Carthaginians; and here fortune favoured his attempt. Hanno was commander-in-chief of the Carthaginians, but their whole reliance was placed upon

Mutines and the Numidians. Mutines, scouring the whole of Sicily, employed himself in carrying off spoil from the allies of the Romans; nor could he by force or stratagem be cut off from Agrigentum, or prevented from sallying from it whenever he pleased. The renown which he gained by this conduct, as it began now to eclipse the fame of the commander-in-chief, was at last converted into a source of jealousy; so that even now his successes were not as acceptable as they ought to have been, on account of the person who gained them. For these reasons Hanno at last gave his commission to his own son, concluding that by taking away his command he should also deprive him of the influence he possessed with the Numidians. But the result was very different; for their former attachment to him was increased by the envy incurred by him. Nor did he brook the affront put upon him by this injurious treatment, but immediately sent secret messengers to Lævinus, to treat about delivering up Agrigentum. After an agreement had been entered into by means of these persons, and the mode of carrying it into execution concerted, the Numidians seized on a gate which leads towards the sea, having driven the guards from it, or put them to the sword, and then received into the city a party of Romans sent for that purpose; and when these troops were now marching into the heart of the city and the forum with a great noise, Hanno, concluding that it was nothing more than a disturbance and secession of the Numidians, such as had happened before, advanced to quell the mutiny; but observing at a distance that the numbers were greater than those of the Numidians, and hearing the Roman shout, which was far from being new to him, he betook himself to flight before he came within reach of their weapons. Passing out of the town at a gate in the opposite quarter, and taking Epicydes to accompany him, he reached the sea with a few attendants; and having very seasonably met with a small vessel, they abandoned to the enemy Sicily, for which they had contended for so many years, and crossed over into Africa. The remaining multitude of Carthaginians and Sicilians fled with headlong haste, but as every passage by which they could escape was blockaded up, they were cut to pieces near the gates. On gaining possession of the town, Lævinus scourged and beheaded those who took the lead in the affairs of Agrigentum. The rest, together with the booty, he sold. All the money he sent to Rome. Accounts of the sufferings of the Agrigentines spreading through all Sicily, all the states suddenly turned to the Romans. In a short time twenty towns were betrayed to them, and six taken by storm. As many as forty put themselves under their protection, by voluntary surrender. The consul having rewarded and punished the leading men of these states, according to their several deserts, and compelled the Sicilians, now that they had at length laid aside arms, to turn their attention to the cultivation of their lands, in order that the island might by its produce not only maintain its inhabitants, but, as it had frequently done on many former occasions, add to the supplies of Rome and Italy, he returned into Italy, taking with him a disorderly multitude from Agathyrna. These were as many as four thousand men, made up of a mixed assemblage of every description of persons, exiles, bankrupts, the greater part of them felons, who had supported themselves by rapine and robbery, both when they lived in their native towns, under the restraint of the laws, and also after that a coincidence in their fortunes, brought about by causes different in each case, had congregated them at Agathyrna. These men Lævinus thought it hardly safe to leave in the island, when an unwonted tranquillity was growing up, as the materials of fresh disturbances; and besides, they were likely to be useful to the Rhegians, who were in want of a band of men habituated to robbery, for the purpose of committing depredations upon the Bruttian territory. Thus, so far as related to Sicily, the war was this year terminated.

In Spain, in the beginning of spring, Publius Scipio, having launched his ships, and summoned the auxiliary troops of his allies to Tarraco by an edict, ordered his fleet and transports to proceed thence to the mouth of the Iberus. He also ordered his legions to quit their winter quarters, and meet at the same place; and then set out from Tarraco, with five thousand of the allies, to join the army. On his arrival at the camp he considered it right to harangue his soldiers, particularly the old ones who had survived such dreadful disasters; and therefore, calling an assembly, he thus addressed them: "Never was there a new commander before myself who could, with justice and good reason, give thanks to his soldiers before he had availed himself of their services. Fortune laid me under obligations to you before I set eyes on my province or your camp; first, on account of the respect you have shown to my father and uncle, both in their lifetime and since their death; and secondly, because by your valour you have recovered and preserved entire, for the Roman people, and me their successor, the possession of the province which had been lost in consequence of so dreadful a calamity. But since, now, by the favour of the gods, our purpose and endeavour is not that we may remain in Spain ourselves, but that the Carthaginians may not; and not to stand on the bank of the Iberus, and hinder the enemy from crossing that river, but cross it first ourselves, and carry the war to the other side, I fear lest to some among you the enterprise should appear too important and daring, considering your late misfortunes, which are fresh in your recollection, and my years. There is no person from whose mind the memory of the defeats sustained in Spain could be obliterated with more difficulty than from mine; inasmuch as there my father and uncle were both slain within the space of thirty days, so that one death after another was accumulated on my family. But as the orphanhood and desolation of my own family depresses my mind, so both the good fortune and valour of our nation forbid me to despair of the safety of the state. It has happened to us by a kind of fatality, that in all important wars we have been victorious, after having been defeated. I pass over those wars of ancient date with Porsena, the Gauls, and Samnites. I will begin with the Punic wars. How many fleets, generals, and armies were lost in the former war? Why should I mention what has occurred in this present war? I have either been myself present at all the defeats sustained, or have felt more than any other those from which I was absent. What else are the Trebia, the Trasimenus, and Cannæ, but monuments of Roman armies and consuls slain? Add to these the defection of Italy, of the greater part of Sicily and Sardinia, and the last terror and panic, the Carthaginian camp pitched between the Anio and the walls of Rome, and the victorious Hannibal seen almost in our gates. Amid this general ruin, the courage of the Roman people alone stood unabated and unshaken. When every thing lay prostrate on the ground, it was this that raised and supported the state. You, first of all, my soldiers, under the conduct and auspices of my father, opposed Hasdrubal on his way to the Alps and Italy, after the defeat of Cannæ, who, had he formed a junction with his brother, the Roman name would now have been extinct. These successes formed a counterpoise to those defeats. Now, by the favour of the gods, every thing in Italy and Sicily is going on prosperously and successfully, every day affording matter of fresh joy, and presenting things in a better light. In Sicily, Syracuse and Agrigentum have been captured, the enemy entirely expelled the island, and the province placed again under the dominion of the Romans. In Italy, Arpi has been recovered and Capua taken. Hannibal has been driven into the remotest corner of Bruttium, having fled thither all the way from Rome, in the utmost confusion; and now he asks the gods no greater boon than that he might be allowed to retire in safety, and quit the territory of his enemy. What then, my soldiers, could be more preposterous than that you, who here supported the tottering fortune of the Roman people, together with my parents, (for they may be equally associated in the honour of that epithet,) when calamities crowded one upon another in quick succession, and even the gods themselves, in a manner, took part with Hannibal, should now sink in spirits when every thing is going on happily and prosperously? Even with regard to the events which have recently occurred, I could wish that they had passed with as little grief to me as to you. At the present time the immortal gods who preside over the destinies of the Roman empire, who inspired all the centuries to order the command to be given to me, those same gods, I say, by auguries and auspices, and even by nightly visions, portend entire success and joy. My own mind also, which has hitherto been to me the truest prophet, presages that Spain will be ours; that the whole Carthaginian name will in a short time be banished from this land, and will fill both sea and land with ignominious flight. What my mind presages spontaneously, is also supported by sound reasoning. Their allies, annoyed by them, are by ambassadors imploring our protection; their three generals, having differed so far as almost to have abandoned each other, have divided their army into three parts, which they have drawn off into regions as remote as possible from each other. The same fortune now threatens them which lately afflicted us; for they are both deserted by their allies, as formerly we were by the Celtiberians, and they have divided their forces, which occasioned the ruin of my father and uncle. Neither will their intestine differences allow them to unite, nor will they be able to cope with us singly. Only do you, my soldiers, favour the name of the Scipios, favour the offspring of your generals, a scion springing up from the trunks which have been cut down. Come then, veterans, lead your new commander and your new army across the Iberus, lead us across into a country which you have often traversed, with many a deed of valour. I will soon bring it to pass that, as you now trace in me a likeness to my father and uncle in my features, countenance, and figure, I will so restore a copy of their genius, honour, and courage, to you, that every man of you shall say that his commander, Scipio, has either returned to life, or has been born again."

Having animated his troops with this harangue, and leaving Marcus Silanus with three thousand infantry and three hundred horse, for the protection of that district, he crossed the Iberus with all the rest of his troops, consisting of twenty-five thousand infantry and two thousand five hundred horse. Though certain persons there endeavoured to persuade him that, as the Carthaginian armies had retired from each other into three such distant quarters, he should attack the nearest of them; yet concluding that if he did so there was danger lest he should cause them to concentrate all their forces, and he alone should not be a match for so many, he determined for the present to make an attack upon New Carthage, a city not only possessing great wealth of its own, but also full of every kind of military store belonging to the enemy; there were their arms, their money, and the hostages from every part of Spain. It was, besides, conveniently situated, not only for a passage into Africa, but also near a port sufficiently capacious for a fleet of any magnitude, and, for aught I know, the only one on the coast of Spain which is washed by our sea. No one but Caius Lælius knew whither he was going. He was sent round with the fleet, and ordered so to regulate the sailing of his ships, that the army might come in view and the fleet enter the harbour at the same time. Both the fleet and army arrived at the same time at New Carthage, on the seventh day after leaving the Iberus. The camp was pitched over against that part of the city which looks to the north. A rampart was thrown up as a defence on the rear of it, for the front was secured by the nature of the ground. Now the situation of New Carthage is as follows: at about the middle of the coast of Spain is a bay facing for the most part the south-west, about two thousand five hundred paces in depth, and a little more in breadth. In the mouth of this bay is a small island forming a barrier towards the sea, and protecting the harbour from every wind except the south-west. From the bottom of the bay there runs out a peninsula, which forms the eminence on which the city is built; which is washed in the east and south by the sea, and on the west is enclosed by a lake which extends a little way also towards the north, of variable depth according as the sea overflows or ebbs. An isthmus of about two hundred paces broad connects the city with the continent, on which, though it would have been a work of so little labour, the Roman general did not raise a rampart; whether his object was to make a display of his confidence to the enemy from motives of pride, or that he might have free regress when frequently advancing to the walls of the city.

Having completed the other requisite works, he drew up his ships in the harbour, that he might exhibit to the enemy the appearance of a blockade by sea also; he then went round the fleet, and having warned the commanders of the ships to be particularly careful in keeping the night-watches, because an enemy, when besieged, usually tried every effort and in every quarter at first, he returned into his camp; and in order to explain to his soldiers the reason why he had adopted the plan of commencing the war with the siege of a city, in preference to any other, and also by exhortations to inspire them with hopes of making themselves masters of it, he summoned them to an assembly, and thus addressed them: "Soldiers, if any one among you suppose that you have been brought here to attack a single city, that man takes a more exact account of your present labour than of its profitable result from it. For you will in truth attack the walls of a single city, but in that single city you will have made yourselves masters of all Spain. Here are the hostages of all her most distinguished kings and states; and as soon as you shall have gained possession of these, they will immediately deliver into your hands every thing which is now subject to the Carthaginians. Here is the whole of the enemy's treasure, without which they cannot carry on the war, as they are keeping mercenary troops, and which will be most serviceable to us in conciliating the affections of the barbarians. Here are their engines, their arms, their tackle, and every requisite in war; which will at once supply you, and leave the enemy destitute. Besides, we shall gain possession of a city, not only of the greatest beauty and wealth, but also most convenient as having an excellent harbour, by means of which we may be supplied with every requisite for carrying on the war both by sea and land. Great as are the advantages we shall thus gain, we shall deprive our enemies of much greater. This is their citadel, their granary, their treasury, their magazine, their receptacle for every thing. Hence there is a direct passage into Africa; this is the only station for a fleet between the Pyrenees and Gades; this gives to Africa the command of all Spain. But as I perceive you are arrayed and marshalled, let us pass on to the assault of New Carthage, with our whole strength, and with undaunted courage." Upon this, they all with, one accord cried out that it should be done; and he led them to Carthage, and ordered that the assault should be made both by sea and land.

On the other side, Mago, the Carthaginian general, perceiving that a siege was being prepared for both by sea and land, himself also disposed his forces thus: he placed two thousand of the townsmen to oppose the enemy, on the side facing the Roman camp; he occupied the citadel with five hundred soldiers, and stationed five hundred on a rising ground, facing the east; the rest of his troops he ordered, intent on every thing that occurred, to hasten with assistance wherever the shout, or any sudden emergency, might call them. Then, throwing open the gate, he sent out those he had drawn up in the street leading to the camp of the enemy. The Romans, according to the direction of their general, retired a little, in order that they might be nearer to the reserved troops which were to be sent to their assistance during the engagement. At first they stood with pretty equal force, but afterwards the reserved troops, sent from time to time from the camp, not only obliged the enemy to turn their backs, but followed them up so close when flying in disorder, that had not a retreat been sounded, they seemed as though they would have rushed into the city together with the fugitives. The consternation in the field was not greater than in every part of the city; many of the outposts were abandoned in panic and flight; and the walls were deserted, as they leaped down each in the part nearest him. Scipio, who had gone out to an eminence called Mercury's hill, perceiving that the walls were abandoned by their defenders in many parts, ordered all his men to be called out of his camp and advance to take the city, and orders them to bring the scaling-ladders. The general himself, covered by the shields of three stout young men, (for now an immense number of missiles of every description were let fly from the walls,) came up to the city, cheered them on, and gave the requisite orders; and, what was of the utmost importance in exciting the courage of his men, he appeared among them a witness and spectator of the valour or cowardice of each. Accordingly, they rushed forward, amidst wounds and weapons; nor could the walls, or the armed troops which stood upon them, repel them from eagerly mounting them. At the same time an attack was commenced by the fleet upon that part of the city which was washed by the sea. But here the alarm occasioned was greater than the force which could be employed; for while they were bringing the boats to shore, and hastily landing the ladders and the men, each man pressing forward to gain the land the shortest way, they hindered one another by their very haste and eagerness.

In the mean time, the Carthaginians had now filled the walls again with armed men, who were supplied with a great quantity of missiles from the immense stores which they had laid up. But neither men nor missiles, nor any thing else, so effectually defended them as the walls themselves, for very few of the ladders were equal to the height of them, and all those which were longer than the rest were proportionably weaker. Accordingly, those who were highest being unable to mount from them, and being followed, nevertheless, by others, they broke from the mere weight upon them. Some, though the ladders stood, a dizziness having come over their eyes in consequence of the height, fell to the ground. And as men and ladders were every where tumbling down, while the boldness and alacrity of the enemy were increased by the mere success, the signal for retreat was sounded, which afforded hopes to the besieged, not only of present rest after such a laborious contest, but also for the future, as it appeared their city could not be taken by scalade and siege. To raise works they considered would be attended with difficulty, and would give time to their generals to bring them assistance. Scarcely had the first tumult subsided, when Scipio ordered other fresh and unfatigued troops to take the ladders from those who were tired and wounded and assault the city with increased vigour. Having received intelligence that the tide was ebbing, and having before been informed by some fishermen of Tarraco who used to pass through the lake, sometimes in light boats, and, when these ran aground, by wading, that it afforded an easy passage to the wall for footmen, he led some armed men thither in person. It was about mid-day, and besides that the water was being drawn off naturally, in consequence of the tide receding, a brisk north wind rising impelled the water in the lake, which was already in motion, in the same direction as the tide, and rendered it so shallow, that in some parts the water reached only to the navel, while in others it scarcely rose above the knees. Scipio, referring this discovery, which he had made by his own diligence and penetration, to the gods and to miracle, which had turned the course of the sea, withdrawn it from the lake, and opened ways never before trodden by human feet to afford a passage to the Romans, ordered them to follow Neptune as their guide, and passing through the middle of the lake, make good their way to the walls.

Those who renewed the assault by land experienced great difficulty; for they were baffled not only by the height of the walls, but also because they exposed the Romans, as they approached them, to the missiles of the enemy from different quarters, so that their sides were endangered more than the fronts of their bodies. But in the other quarter five hundred passed without difficulty through the lake, and then mounted the wall, for neither was it defended by any fortifications, because there they thought the city was sufficiently protected by the nature of the place and the lake, nor were there any outposts or guards stationed there, because all were engaged in bringing succour to that quarter in which the danger appeared. Having entered the city without opposition, they proceeded direct, with all possible speed, to that gate near which the contest was concentrated; and so intently occupied with this were not only the minds, but the eyes and ears of all, both of those who were engaged in fighting, and of those who were looking on and encouraging the combatants, that no one perceived that the city had been captured in their rear till the weapons fell upon their backs, and they had an enemy on both sides of them. Then, the defenders having been thrown into confusion through fear, both the walls were captured, and the gate began to be broken open both from within and from without; and presently, the doors having been broken to pieces by blows, in order that the way might not be obstructed, the troops rushed in. A great number had also got over the walls, but these employed themselves in putting the townsmen to the sword; those which entered by the gate, forming a regular body, with officers and in ranks, advanced through the midst of the city into the forum. Scipio then perceiving that the enemy fled in two different directions, some to the eminence which lay eastward, which was occupied by a garrison of five hundred men, others to the citadel, into which Mago himself also had fled for refuge, together with almost all the troops which had been driven from the walls, sent part of his forces to storm the hill, and part he led in person against the citadel. Not only was the hill captured at the first assault, but Mago also, after making an effort to defend it, when he saw every place filled with the enemy, and that there was no hope, surrendered himself and the citadel, with the garrison. Until the citadel was surrendered, the massacre was continued in every quarter throughout the city; nor did they spare any one they met who had arrived at puberty: but after that, on a signal given, a stop was put to the carnage, and the victors turned their attention to the plunder, of which there was an immense quantity of every description.

Of males of free condition, as many as ten thousand were captured. Of these he allowed to depart such as were citizens of New Carthage; and restored to them their city, and all their property which the war had left them. The artisans amounted to two thousand, whom he assigned to the Roman people as their property; holding out to them a hope of speedy emancipation, provided they should address themselves strenuously to the service of the war. Of the rest of the mass of inhabitants, the young men and able-bodied slaves he assigned for the service of the fleet, to fill up the numbers of the rowers. He had also augmented his fleet with five ships which he had captured. Besides this multitude, there remained the Spanish hostages, to whom as much attention was paid as if they had been children of allies. An immense quantity of military stores was also taken; one hundred and twenty catapultæ of the larger size, two hundred and eighty-one of the smaller; twenty-three ballistæ of the larger size, fifty-two of the smaller; an immense number of scorpions of the larger and smaller size, and also of arms and missile weapons;

and seventy-four military standards. Of gold and silver, an immense quantity was brought to the general; there were two hundred and seventy-six golden bowls, almost all of them weighing a pound; of silver, wrought and coined, eighteen thousand three hundred pounds' weight; and of silver vessels an immense number. All these were weighed and reckoned to the quæstor, Caius Flaminius. There were twenty thousand pecks of wheat, and two hundred and seventy of barley. One hundred and thirteen ships of burden were boarded and captured in the harbour, some of them with their cargoes, consisting of corn and arms, besides brass, iron, sails, spartum, and other naval materials, of use in equipping a fleet; so that amid such large military stores which were captured, Carthage itself was of the least consideration.

Having ordered Caius Lælius with the marines to guard the city, Scipio led back his legions to the camp the same day in person; and as his soldiers were tired, as they had in one day gone through every kind of military labour; for they had engaged the enemy in the field, and had undergone very great fatigue and danger in taking the city; and after they had taken it had fought, and that on disadvantageous ground, with those who had fled to the citadel, he ordered them to attend to themselves. The next day, having assembled the land and naval forces, he, in the first place, ascribed praise and thanks to the immortal gods, who had not only in one day made him master of the wealthiest city in Spain, but had previously collected in it the riches of almost all Africa and Spain; so that while his enemy had nothing left, he and his army had a superabundance of every thing. He then commended in the highest terms the valour of his soldiers, because that neither the sally of the enemy, nor the height of the walls, nor the unexplored fords of the lake, nor the fort standing upon a high hill, nor the citadel, though most strongly fortified, had deterred them from surmounting and breaking through every thing. Therefore, though all credit was due to them all, he said that the man who first mounted the wall ought to be distinguished above the rest, by being honoured with a mural crown; and he desired that he who thought himself worthy of that reward would claim it. Two persons laid claim to it, Quintus Trebellius, a centurion of the fourth legion, and Sextus Digitius, a marine. Nor did these contest so fiercely as each excited the zeal of his own body of men. Caius Lælius, admiral of the fleet, patronized the marines, and Marcus Sempronius Tuditanus, the legionary troops. As this contest began almost to assume the character of a mutiny, Scipio having notified that he should appoint three delegates, who, after making themselves acquainted with the case, and examining the witnesses, might decide which had been the first to scale the wall and enter the town, added Publius Cornelius Caudinus, a middle party, to Lælius and Sempronius, the advocates of the two parties, and ordered these three delegates to sit and determine the cause. But as the contest was now carried on with increased warmth, because those high characters, who had acted more as moderators of the zeal of both than as advocates of any particular party, were withdrawn, Caius Lælius, leaving the council, went up to the tribunal of Scipio and informed him, "that the contest was proceeding without bounds or moderation, and that they had almost come to blows. But still, though no violence should take place, that the proceedings formed a most hateful precedent, for that the honours due to valour were being sought by fraud and perjury. That on one side stood the legionary troops, on the other the marines, ready to swear by all the gods what they wished, rather than what they knew, to be true, and to involve in the guilt of perjury not only themselves and their own persons, but the military standards, the eagles, and their solemn oath of allegiance. That he laid these matters before him, in accordance with the opinion of Publius Cornelius and Marcus Sempronius." Scipio, after highly praising Lælius, summoned an assembly, and then declared, "that he had ascertained satisfactorily that Quintus Trebellius and Sextus Digitius had mounted the wall at the same time, and that he presented them both with mural crowns in consideration of their valour." He then gave presents to the rest, according to the merit and valour of each. Above all he honoured Caius Lælius, the admiral of the fleet, by the placing him upon an equality with himself, and bestowing upon him every kind of commendation, and also by presenting him with a golden crown and thirty oxen.

He then ordered the Spanish hostages to be summoned. What the number of these was I feel reluctant to state, because in some authors I find that it was about three hundred, in others seven hundred and twenty-five. There is the same difference between authors with regard to the other particulars. One writes that the Punic garrison consisted of ten thousand, another of seven, a third of not more than two thousand. In some you may find that ten thousand persons were captured, in others above twenty-five thousand. I should have stated the number of scorpions captured, both of the greater and smaller size, at sixty, if I had followed the Greek author, Silenus, if Valerius Antius, of the larger at six thousand, of the smaller at thirteen, so great is the extent of falsehood. Nor are they agreed even respecting the commanders, most say that Lælius commanded the fleet, but some say Marcus Junius Silanus. Valerius Antius says, that Arines commanded the Punic garrison, and was given up to the Romans; other writers say it was Mago. They are not agreed respecting the number of the ships taken, respecting the weight of gold and silver, and of the money brought into the public treasury. If we must assent to some of their statements, the medium is nearest to the truth. However, Scipio having summoned the hostages, first bid them all keep up their spirits observing, "that they had fallen into the hands of the Roman people, who chose to bind men to them by benefits rather than by fear, and keep foreign nations attached to them by honour and friendship, rather than subject them to a gloomy servitude." Then receiving the names of the states to which they belonged, he took an account of the captives, distinguishing the number belonging to each people, and sent messengers to their homes, to desire that they would come and take back their respective friends. If ambassadors from any of the states happened to be present, he delivered their countrymen to them in person, and assigned to them the quæstor, Caius Flaminius, the charge of kindly taking care of the rest. Meanwhile, there advanced from the midst of the crowd of hostages a woman in years, the wife of Mandonius, who was the brother of Indibilis, the chieftain of the Illergetians; she threw herself weeping at the general's feet, and began to implore him to give particularly strict injunctions to their guardians with respect to the care and treatment of females. Scipio replied, that nothing certainly should be wanting; when the woman rejoined: "We do not much value such things, for what is not good enough for such a condition? A care of a different kind disquiets me, when beholding the age of these females; for I am myself no longer exposed to the danger peculiar to females." Around her stood the daughters of Indibilis, in the bloom of youth and beauty, with others of equal rank, all of whom looked up to her as a parent. Scipio then said: "Out of regard for that discipline which I myself and the Roman nation maintain, I should take care that nothing, which is any where held sacred, should be violated among us. In the present case, your virtue and your rank cause me to observe it more strictly; for not even in the midst of misfortunes have you forgotten the delicacy becoming matrons." He then delivered them over to a man of tried virtue, ordering him to treat them with no less respect and modesty than the wives and mothers of guests.

The soldiers then brought to him a female captive, a grown-up virgin, of such exquisite beauty, that whichever way she walked she attracted the eyes of every body. Scipio, on making inquiries as to her country and parentage, heard, among other particulars, that she was betrothed to a young prince of the Celtiberians, named Allucius. He immediately, therefore, summoned from their abode her parents and lover, and having heard in the mean time that the latter was desperately enamoured of her, as soon as he arrived he addressed him in a more studied manner than her parents. "A young man myself," said he, "I address myself to a young man, and therefore there need be the less reserve in this conversation. As soon as your intended bride, having been captured by my soldiers, was brought into my presence, and I was informed that she was endeared to you, which her beauty rendered probable, considering that I should myself wish that my affection for my intended bride, though excessive, should meet with indulgence, could I enjoy the pleasures suited to my age, (particularly in an honourable and lawful love,) and were not my mind engrossed by public affairs, I indulge as far as I can your passion. Your mistress, while under my protection, has received as much respect as under the roof of her own parents, your father-in-law and mother-in-law. She has been kept in perfect safety for you, that she might be presented to you pure, a gift worthy of me and of you. This only reward I bargain for in return for the service I have rendered you, that you would be a friend to the Roman people, and if you believe that I am a true man, as these nations knew my father and uncle to have been heretofore, that you would feel assured that in the Roman state there are many like us, and that no nation in the world at the present time can be mentioned, with which you ought to be less disposed that you, or those belonging to you, should be at enmity, or with which you would rather be in friendship." The young man, overcome at once with joy and modesty, clung to Scipio's right hand, and invoked all the gods to recompense him in his behalf, since he himself was far from possessing means proportioned either to his own wishes or Scipio's deserts. He then addressed himself to the parents and relatives of the damsel, who, on receiving her back without any reward, whom they had brought a very large weight of gold to redeem, entreated Scipio to accept it from them as a present to himself; affirming, that if he would do so, they should feel as grateful for it as they did for the restoration of their daughter inviolate. As they were so earnest in their entreaties, Scipio promised to accept it, and ordered it to be laid at his feet. Then calling Allucius to him, he said: "To the dowry which you are about to receive from your father-in-law, let these marriage presents also from me be added;" bidding him take away the gold and keep it for himself. Delighted with these presents and honours, he was dismissed to his home, where he inspired his countrymen with the deserved praises of Scipio, observing, "that a most godlike youth had come among them, who conquered every thing, not only by arms, but by kindness and generosity." Accordingly, making a levy among his dependants, he returned to Scipio after a few days, with fourteen hundred chosen horsemen.

Scipio kept Lælius with him until he had disposed of the captives, hostages, and booty, in accordance with his advice; but when all these matters were satisfactorily arranged, he gave him a quinquereme; and selecting from the captives Mago, and about fifteen senators who had been made prisoners at the same time with him, put them on board, and sent him to Rome with the news of his victory. He himself employed the few days he had resolved to stay at Carthage, in exercising his naval and land forces. On the first day the legions under arms performed evolutions through a space of four miles; on the second day he ordered them to repair and clean their arms before their tents; on the third day they engaged in imitation of a regular battle with wooden swords, throwing javelins with the points covered with balls; on the fourth day they rested; on the fifth they again performed evolutions under arms. This succession of exercise and rest they kept up as long as they staid at Carthage. The rowers and mariners, pushing out to sea when the weather was calm, made trial of the manageableness of their ships by mock sea-fights. Such exercises, both by sea and land, without the city prepared their minds and bodies for war. The city itself was all bustle with warlike preparations, artificers of every description being collected together in a public workshop. The general went round to all the works with equal attention. At one time he was employed in the dock-yard with his fleet, at another he exercised with the legions; sometimes he would devote his time to the inspection of the works, which were every day carried on with the greatest eagerness by a multitude of artificers both in the workshops, and in the armoury and docks. Having put these preparations in a train, repaired the walls in a part where they had been shattered, and placed bodies of troops to guard the city, he set out for Tarraco; and on his way thither was visited by a number of embassies, some of which he dismissed, having given them answers on his journey, others he postponed till his arrival at Tarraco; at which place he had appointed a meeting of all his new and old allies. Here ambassadors from almost all the people dwelling on this side the Iberus, and from many dwelling in the further Spain, met. The Carthaginian generals at first industriously suppressed the rumour of the capture of Carthage; but afterwards, when it became too notorious to be concealed or dissembled, they disparaged its importance by their language. They said, that "by an unexpected attack, and in a manner by stealth, in one day, one city of Spain had been snatched out of their hands; that a presumptuous youth, elated with the acquisition of this, so inconsiderable an advantage, had, by the extravagance of his joy, given it the air of an important victory; but that as soon as he should hear that three generals and three victorious armies of his enemies were approaching, the deaths which had taken place in his family would occur to his recollection." Such was the tone in which they spoke of this affair to the people, though they were, at the same time, far from ignorant how much their strength had been diminished, in every respect, by the loss of Carthage.

END OF VOLUME II

ENDNOTES

[1] In the original, *lati clavi*. The latus clavus was a tunic, or vest, ornamented with a broad stripe of purple on the fore part, worn by the senators; the knights wore a similar one, only ornamented with a narrower stripe. Gold rings were also used as badges of distinction, the common people wore iron ones.

[2] The duration of Alexander's military career.

[3] The *comitia curiata*, or assemblies of the curiae, alone had the power of conferring military command; no magistrate, therefore, could assume the command without the previous order of their assembly. In time, this came to be a mere matter of form; yet the practice always continued to be observed.

[4] 5*s*. 3¼*d*.

[5] £1.

[6] £1614. 11*s* 8*d*.

[7] When the auspices were to be taken from the chickens, the keeper threw some of them food upon the ground, in their sight, and opened the door of then coop. If they did not come out; if they came out slowly; if they refused to feed, or ate in a careless manner, the omen was considered as bad. On the contrary, if they rushed out hastily and ate greedily, so that some of the food fell from their mouths on the ground, this was considered as an omen of the best import; it was called *tripudium solistinum*, originally, *terripavium*, from *terra*, and *pavire*, to strike.

[8] These marks of honour were bestowed for having saved the lives of citizens, or for having been the first to mount walls or ramparts.

[9] £4940 13*s*.

[10] £322 18*s*. 4*d*.

[11] £1259 7*s*. 6*d*.

[12] Thucydides seems to be specially referred to.

[13] The Barcine faction derived its name from Hamilcar, who was surnamed Barca. Hanno appears to have been at the head of the opposite party.

[14] A.U.C. 526, thirteen years after the conclusion of the first Punic war, being the sixth treaty between the Carthaginians and Romans. The first was a commercial agreement made during the first consulate, in the year that the Tarquins were expelled from Rome; but is not mentioned by Livy. The second is noted by him, lib. vii. 27, and the third, lib. ix. 43. The fourth was concluded during the war with Pyrrhus and the Tarentines, Polyb. V. iii. 25] and the fifth was the memorable treaty at the close of the first war.

[15] Alluding to the first treaty made in the year that the kings were expelled from Rome.

[16] The Carpetani have already been mentioned, chap. v. The Oretani, then neighbours, occupied the country lying between the sources of the Bætis and the Anas, or what are now called the Guadalquiver and Guadiana. In a part of Orospeda they deduced their name from a city called Oretum, the site of which has been brought to light in a paltry village to which the name of Oreto still remains.—*D'Anville*.

[17] from Pænus, Carthaginian.

[18] Because Spain was his proper province as consul.

[19] The ancient name of Portugal.

[20] Calpe, a mountain or rather rock in Spain, and Abyla in Africa, fabled to have been placed by Hercules as marks of his most distant voyage, are now well known as

Gibraltar and Ceuta.

THE END

Lightning Source UK Ltd.
Milton Keynes UK
UKHW040801150419
341045UK00001B/263/P

9 781420 933857